COMPUTER SCIENCE with PYTHON

for CBSE Class XI

Reema Thareja
Assistant Professor
Department of Computer Science
Shyama Prasad Mukherji College
University of Delhi

All rights reserved. No part of this book may be modified, reproduced or utilised in any form, or by any means, electronic or mechanical, including photocopying, recording or by any information storage and retrieval system, in any form of binding or cover other than in which it is published, without permission in writing from the publisher.

COMPUTER SCIENCE WITH PYTHON FOR CBSE CLASS XI

UNIVERSITIES PRESS (INDIA) PRIVATE LIMITED

Registered office
3-6-747/1/A & 3-6-754/1, Himayatnagar, Hyderabad 500 029, Telangana, India
info@universitiespress.com; www.universitiespress.com

Distributed by
Orient Blackswan Private Limited

Registered office
3-6-752 Himayatnagar, Hyderabad 500 029, Telangana, India

Other offices
Bengaluru, Chennai, Guwahati, Hyderabad, Kolkata,
Mumbai, New Delhi, Noida, Patna, Visakhapatnam

© Universities Press (India) Private Ltd 2022

ISBN: 978-93-89211-90-0

Cover and book design
© Universities Press (India) Private Ltd 2022

Typeset in Adobe Garamond Pro 10.5 *by*
SRS Publishing Services, Puducherry

Printed in India by
Yash Printographics, Greater Noida 201 310

Published by
Universities Press (India) Private Limited
3-6-747/1/A & 3-6-754/1, Himayatnagar, Hyderabad 500 029, Telangana, India

Disclaimer
Care has been taken to confirm the accuracy of information printed in this book. The author and the publisher, however, cannot accept any responsibility for errors or omissions or for consequences from the application of the information in this book and make no warranty, express or implied, with respect to its contents. This textbook does not constitute a standard, specification or regulation. The trademarks or manufacturers' names appear/are used in this book only because they are considered essential to the object of subject discussion and do not necessarily constitute endorsement of the product/standard by the author or publisher. All products and company names are trademarks[TM] or registered[®] trademarks of their respective holders. Use of them does not imply any affiliation with or endorsement by them.

*I dedicate this book to my family and my uncle Mr B L Theraja,
who is a well-known author himself.*

Contents

Preface — *xvii*
About the Author — *xix*

Chapter 1: Computer Systems and Organization — 1

- 1.1 Basic Computer Organization — 1
  - 1.1.1 Central Processing Unit (CPU) — 2
- 1.2 Input Devices — 3
  - 1.2.1 Keyboard — 3
  - 1.2.2 Mouse — 4
  - 1.2.3 Touchpad — 4
  - 1.2.4 Joystick — 4
  - 1.2.5 Touchscreen — 5
  - 1.2.6 Image Scanner — 5
  - 1.2.7 Stylus — 6
  - 1.2.8 Barcode Reader — 6
  - 1.2.9 Optical Mark Recognition (OMR) — 6
  - 1.2.10 Magnetic Ink Character Reader (MICR) — 7
  - 1.2.11 Digital Camera — 7
- 1.3 Output Devices — 7
  - 1.3.1 Monitor or VDU (Visual Display Unit) — 7
  - 1.3.2 Speakers — 8
  - 1.3.3 Printer — 9
  - 1.3.4 Projector — 9
  - 1.3.5 Plotters — 10
- 1.4 Organization of Computer's Memory — 10
- 1.5 Types of Computer Memory — 10
  - 1.5.1 Cache Memory — 10
  - 1.5.2 Primary Memory — 11
  - 1.5.3 Secondary Memory — 13
- 1.6 Ports on the Computer — 14
- 1.7 The System Bus — 17
- 1.8 Computer Hardware and Software — 17
- 1.9 General-purpose Application Software — 19

	1.10	Classification of Software	19
	1.11	Customized Software	21
	1.12	Utility Software	21
	1.13	Mobile System Organization	22
		1.13.1 Mobile Central Processing Unit	23
		1.13.2 Mobile System Memory	23
		1.13.3 Storage	24
		1.13.4 Power Management	24

Key Terms | Chapter Highlights | Review Questions | Fill in the Blanks | State True or False | Multiple Choice Questions | Answers

Chapter 2: Information Representation — 29

2.1	The Binary Language	29
2.2	Decimal Number System	30
2.3	Binary Number System	30
	2.3.1 Converting Binary Number into Decimal	31
	2.3.2 Converting Decimal Number to Binary	31
2.4	Octal Number System	32
	2.4.1 Converting Octal Number into Decimal	32
	2.4.2 Converting Decimal Number to Octal	32
	2.4.3 Converting an Octal Number into Binary Equivalent	33
	2.4.4 Converting a Binary Number into Octal Form	33
2.5	Hexadecimal Number System	34
	2.5.1 Converting Hexadecimal Number into Decimal	34
	2.5.2 Converting Decimal Number into Hexadecimal	35
	2.5.3 Converting a Hexadecimal Number into Binary Equivalent	35
	2.5.4 Converting a Binary Number into Hexadecimal	35
2.6	Working with Fractions	36
2.7	Signed Number Representation in Binary Form	37
2.8	Binary Addition	39
2.9	ASCII Code	39
2.10	Unicode	39
2.11	Indian Script Code for Information Interchange (ISCII)	41

Key Terms | Chapter Highlights | Review Questions | Fill in the Blanks | State True or False | Multiple Choice Questions | Answers

Chapter 3: Boolean Algebra — 45

3.1	Boolean Algebra	46
3.2	Venn Diagrams	47
3.3	Truth Tables	47
3.4	Basic Laws of Boolean Algebra	48

Contents   **vii**

		3.4.1	Identity Law	48
		3.4.2	Idempotency Theorem	49
		3.4.3	Complement Law	49
		3.4.4	Involution Theorem	49
		3.4.5	Commutative Law	49
		3.4.6	Associative Law	49
		3.4.7	Distributive Law	50
		3.4.8	Absorption Law	51
		3.4.9	Consensus Law	51
		3.4.10	De Morgan's Laws	52
		3.4.11	Duality Principle	53
	3.5	Precedence of Boolean Operators		53
	3.6	Logic Diagrams and Boolean Expressions		53
		3.6.1	Logic Gate	53
	3.7	Formulating Boolean Expression from Logic Gates		55
	3.8	Universal Gates		56
		3.8.1	NAND Universal Gate	56
		3.8.2	NOR Universal Gate	57

Key Terms | Chapter Highlights | Review Questions | Fill in the Blanks | State True or False | Multiple Choice Questions | Answers

Chapter 4: System Software and Computing Techniques   65

	4.1	Operating System – The Manager of Computer's Resources		65
		4.1.1	Allocating Memory	66
		4.1.2	Processes Scheduling for CPU	68
	4.2	Commonly Used Operating Systems		69
	4.3	Types of Operating System		70
		4.3.1	Batch Processing Systems	70
		4.3.2	Single-user, Single-task Operating System	70
		4.3.3	Multi-programming Systems	71
		4.3.4	Time-sharing Systems or Multi-tasking Operating System	71
		4.3.5	Multiprocessor Systems	71
		4.3.6	Distributed Operating Systems	71
		4.3.7	Real-time Operating System	72
		4.3.8	Mobile Operating Sytem	72
		4.3.9	Embedded Operating System	73
	4.4	Types of Operating System Based on User Interface		73
		4.4.1	Command Line Interface (CLI) or Character User Interface (CUI)	73
		4.4.2	Graphical User Interface (GUI)	74
	4.5	Device Driver		75

4.6		Booting the Computer	75
4.7		What is BIOS?	75
4.8		Program Translators	76
4.9		Linker and Loader	77
4.10		Device Management by the Operating System	78
4.11		Cloud Computing	79
	4.11.1	Types of Cloud Computing	79
	4.11.2	Uses of Cloud Computing	80
	4.11.3	Advantages	80
4.12		Blockchain Technology	81
	4.12.1	Key Terminology	81
	4.12.2	Applications of Blockchain	82
	4.12.3	Pillars of Blockchain	82
	4.12.4	Hashing in Blockchain	83

Key Terms | Chapter Highlights | Review Questions | Fill in the Blanks | State True or False | Multiple Choice Questions | Answers

Chapter 5: Algorithms and Pseudocodes — 89

5.1		Algorithm	89
5.2		Some More Algorithms	91
5.3		Flowchart	91
	5.3.1	Significance of a Flowchart	95
	5.3.2	Advantages of Flowchart	95
	5.3.3	Limitations of using Flowcharts	95
5.4		Pseudocodes	95
	5.4.1	Keywords Used while Writing Pseudocodes	95
	5.4.2	Advantages	98
	5.4.3	Disadvantages	98
	5.4.4	Guiding Principles	98
5.5		Decomposition	99
5.6		Problem-solving in Real Life	99
	5.6.1	Problem Decomposition	99
	5.6.2	Top-down vs. Bottom-up Approach	99

Key Terms | Chapter Highlights | Review Questions | Fill in the Blanks | State True or False | Multiple Choice Questions | Answers

Chapter 6: Basics of Computational Thinking — 105

6.1		Computational Skills	105
6.2		Programming Language Python	105
	6.2.1	Limitations of Python	106
	6.2.2	History of Python	107

	6.2.3	Applications of Python	107
	6.2.4	The Future of Python	108
6.3	Writing and Executing the First Python Program		108
6.4	Interactive Python		109
6.5	Writing Python Programs Using the Idle Editor		110
6.6	Python Character Set		111
6.7	Python Tokens		111
6.8	Literal Constants		111
	6.8.1	Numbers	111
	6.8.2	Strings	113
6.9	Type Conversion		117

Key Terms | Chapter Highlights | Review Questions | Fill in the Blanks | State True or False | Multiple Choice Questions | Give the Output | Answers

Chapter 7: Python – Building Blocks — 125

7.1	Variables and Indentifiers		125
	7.1.1	Creating Variables	126
	7.1.2	Data Types of Identifiers	126
	7.1.3	Assigning or Initializing Values to Variables	127
7.2	Multiple Assignments		128
	7.2.1	Data Type Boolean	128
7.3	Input Operation		129
7.4	Comments		129
	7.4.1	Multi-line Comments	130
7.5	Reserved Words		130
7.6	Indentation		130
7.7	Operators and Expressions		131
	7.7.1	Arithmetic Operators	131
	7.7.2	Comparison Operators	132
	7.7.3	Assignment and In-place or Shortcut Operators	132
	7.7.4	Unary Operators	132
	7.7.5	Bitwise Operators	133
	7.7.6	Shift Operators	133
	7.7.7	Logical Operators	134
	7.7.8	Membership Operators	134
	7.7.9	Identity Operators	134
	7.7.10	Operators Precedence and Associativity	135
7.8	Expressions in Python		136

Programmer's Zone — *136*

Key Terms | Chapter Highlights | Review Questions | Programming Exercises | Fill in the Blanks | State True or False | Multiple Choice Questions | Give the Output | Find the Error | Answers

Chapter 8:	**Decision Control Statements**		**153**
8.1	Selection/conditional Branching Statements		153
8.2	`if` Statement		154
	8.2.1	Implementing `if` statement in Python	154
8.3	`if-else` Statement		155
8.4	Nested `if` Statements		156
8.5	`if-elif-else` Statement		156

Programmer's Zone — *158*
Key Terms | Chapter Highlights | Review Questions |
Programming Exercises | Fill in the Blanks | State True or False |
Multiple Choice Questions | Give the Output | Answers

Chapter 9:	**Basic Loop Structures/Iterative Statements**	**169**
9.1	`while` Loop	169
9.2	`for` Loop	170
9.3	The `range()` Function	171
9.4	Selecting an Appropriate Loop	172
9.5	Nested Loops	172
9.6	The `break` Statement	173
9.7	The `continue` Statement	173
9.8	The `pass` Statement	174
9.9	The `else` Statement Used with Loops	174

Programmer's Zone — *175*
Key Terms | Chapter Highlights | Review Questions |
Programming Exercises | Fill in the Blanks | State True or False |
Multiple Choice Questions | Give the Output | Find the Error | Answers

Chapter 10:	**Functions and Modules**		**193**
10.1	Function		193
	10.1.1	Need for Functions	194
	10.1.2	Calling a Function	194
10.2	Modules		195
	10.2.1	Module Loading and Execution	195
	10.2.2	The `from...import` Statement	195
	10.2.3	Name of Module	196
10.3	The `dir()` Function		197
10.4	Packages in Python		197
10.5	Python – Math Module		197
10.6	Built-in Functions		199
10.7	Composition		200
10.8	Function Declaration and Definition		200
10.9	Function Definition		201

10.10	Variable Scope and Lifetime	203
	10.10.1 Local and Global Variables	203
	10.10.2 Resolution of Names	204
10.11	The `return` Statement	205
10.12	The `random` Module in Python	206

Programmer's Zone   *208*
Key Terms | Chapter Highlights | Review Questions |
Programming Exercises | Fill in the Blanks | State True or False |
Multiple Choice Questions | Give the Output | Find the Error | Answers

Chapter 11: Strings   217

11.1	String Indexing	217
11.2	Finding the Number of Characters in a String	217
11.3	Traversing a String	218
11.4	Concatenating, Appending and Multiplying Strings	219
11.5	The `str()` Function	220
11.6	Strings are Immutable	220
11.7	String Formatting Operator	221
11.8	The `format()` Function	222
11.9	Built-in String Methods and Functions	222
11.10	Comparing Strings	226
11.11	`ord()` and `chr()` Functions	226
11.12	`in` and `not in` operators	226

Programmer's Zone   *227*
Key Terms | Chapter Highlights | Review Questions |
Programming Exercises | Fill in the Blanks | State True or False |
Multiple Choice Questions | Give the Output | Find the Error | Answers

Chapter 12: Lists   241

12.1	Accessing Values in Lists	241
12.2	The `eval()` Function	242
12.3	Updating Values in Lists	242
12.4	Relational Operations on Lists	243
12.5	Nested Lists	244
12.6	List Aliasing and Cloning	244
12.7	Deleting Elements	245
12.8	Deep Copies and Shallow Copies in Python	245
12.9	Basic List Operations	246
12.10	List Methods	247

Programmer's Zone   *250*
Key Terms | Chapter Highlights | Review Questions |
Programming Exercises | Fill in the Blanks | State True or False |
Multiple Choice Questions | Give the Output | Find the Error | Answers

Chapter 13: Tuple — 265

13.1	Creating a Tuple	265
13.2	Utility of Tuples	266
13.3	Accessing Values in a Tuple	267
13.4	Updating Tuple	267
13.5	Deleting Elements in Tuple	268
13.6	Joining Tuples	268
13.7	Unpacking Tuples	269
13.8	Basic Tuple Operations	269
13.9	Tuple Assignment	270
13.10	Accessing Using Index	271
13.11	Tuples for Returning Multiple Values	271
13.12	Nested Tuples	271
13.13	The count() Method	272
13.14	The zip() Function	272
13.15	Advantages of Tuple Over List	274

Programmer's Zone — *274*
Key Terms | Chapter Highlights | Review Questions |
Programming Exercises | Fill in the Blanks | State True or False |
Multiple Choice Questions | Give the Output | Find the Error | Answers

Chapter 14: Dictionaries — 285

14.1	Creating a Dictionary	285
	14.1.1 Creating a Dictionary Using dict() Method	286
14.2	Accessing Values in a Dictionary	286
14.3	Adding an Item in a Dictionary	287
14.4	Modifying an Item in a Dictionary	287
14.5	Deleting Items	287
	14.5.1 The pop() Method	287
14.6	Traversing a Dictionary	289
14.7	Nested Dictionaries	290
14.8	The copy() Method	290
14.9	Built-in Dictionary Functions and Methods	290
14.10	Difference Between a List and a Dictionary	291

Programer's Zone — *292*
Key Terms | Chapter Highlights | Review Questions |
Programming Exercises | Fill in the Blanks | State True or False |
Multiple Choice Questions | Give the Output | Find the Error | Answers

Chapter 15: Sorting — 305

- 15.1 Bubble Sort — 305
  - 15.1.1 Bubble Sort Example — 305
  - 15.1.2 Algorithm for Bubble Sort — 307
  - 15.1.3 Complexity of Bubble Sort — 308
  - 15.1.4 Applications of Bubble Sort — 309
- 15.2 Insertion Sort — 309
  - 15.2.1 The Insertion Sort Technique — 309
  - 15.2.2 Example of Insertion Sort — 310
  - 15.2.3 Algorithm for Insertion Sort — 311
  - 15.2.4 Advantages of Insertion Sort — 311
  - 15.2.5 Applications — 312
  - 15.2.6 Complexity of Insertion Sort Algorithm — 312

Key Terms | Chapter Highlights | Review Questions | Programming Exercises | Fill in the Blanks | State True or False | Multiple Choice Questions | Answers

Chapter 16: Society, Law and Ethics - I — 317

- 16.1 The Internet – Ocean of Information and Opportunities — 317
  - 16.1.1 Advantages — 318
- 16.2 Netiquette — 319
- 16.3 Ethics in Computing — 320
- 16.4 Issues in Cyber Safety — 320
  - 16.4.1 Plagiarism — 320
  - 16.4.2 Hacking — 321
  - 16.4.3 Disrespecting Values and Traditions — 322
  - 16.4.4 Spreading Rumor and Cyber Bullying — 322
  - 16.4.5 Phishing — 323
  - 16.4.6 Spamming — 324
  - 16.4.7 Spoofing — 325
  - 16.4.8 Eavesdropping — 325
  - 16.4.9 Digital Footprint — 326
  - 16.4.10 Social Networking Sites and Specific Usage Rules — 326
- 16.5 Malware — 327
  - 16.5.1 VIRUS (Vital Information Resources Under Seige) — 327
  - 16.5.2 Worms — 329
  - 16.5.3 Trojan Horse — 330
  - 16.5.4 Adware — 330

	16.5.5	Spyware	331
	16.5.6	Keyloggers	331
	16.5.7	Ransomware	331
	16.5.8	Sweeper Attacks	331
16.6	Safely Accessing Websites and Communicating Data		332
	16.6.1	Firewall	332
	16.6.2	Antivirus – Definition and Examples	333
	16.6.3	Cyber Safety	334

Key Terms | Chapter Highlights | Review Questions | Fill in the Blanks | State True or False | Tick the Right Answer | Multiple Choice Questions | Answers

Chapter 17: Society, Law and Ethics - II — 341

17.1	Individual Right to Privacy		341
	17.1.1	Elements of Right to Privacy	341
17.2	Intellectual Property Rights (IPR)		342
	17.2.1	Copyright	342
	17.2.2	Trademarks	342
	17.2.3	Design Rights	342
	17.2.4	Patents	342
	17.2.5	Right of Publicity	343
	17.2.6	Trade Secrets	343
17.3	Plagiarism		344
17.4	Digital Rights Management (DRM)		345
	17.4.1	How Digital Rights Management Works	345
	17.4.2	Challenges of Digital Rights Management	346
17.5	Software Licensing		346
	17.5.1	Types of Software Licenses	347
	17.5.2	GPL or General Public License	348
	17.5.3	Apache Software License (ASL)	348
17.6	Open Source		348
	17.6.1	Difference between Open-source Software and Other Types of Software	348
	17.6.2	Benefits of Open-source Software	349
17.7	Creative Common License		349
17.8	Privacy		351
	17.8.1	Key Information Privacy Principles	351
17.9	Computer Fraud		352
17.10	Illegal Downloading		353
17.11	Internet Frauds and Scams		353
17.12	Information Technology Act 2000		354
	17.12.1	Salient Features of IT Act	354
17.13	Child Pornography		355

17.14	Cyber Forensics	355
17.15	Technology and Society	356
	17.15.1 Positive Impacts	356
	17.15.2 Negative Impacts	357
17.16	E-waste Management	358
	17.16.1 Development of Waste Recycling Technologies	359
	17.16.2 Formal vs. Informal Recycling	359
	17.16.3 Alternative Solutions of Disposal	360
17.17	Identity Theft	361
	17.17.1 Avoiding Identity Thefts	361
	17.17.2 Steps to Protect One's Data	362
	17.17.3 Spotting Identity Theft and Dealing with It	363
17.18	Unique ID and Biometrics	363
	17.18.1 Processing Biometric Data	363
	17.18.2 How Biometrics Work	364
	17.18.3 Downsides of Biometrics	364
	17.18.4 How to Protect Your Biometric Data	365
17.19	Gender Issues While Teaching and Using Computers	365
	17.19.1 Reasons for Gender Gap	366
	17.19.2 Advantages of Gender Diversity	366
	17.19.3 Results of Gender Gap	366
	17.19.4 Steps to Promote Women	367
17.20	Disability Issues While Teaching and Using Computers	367
	17.20.1 Types of Disabilities	367
	17.20.2 Using Computers and Technology to Address Disability Issues	368

Key Terms | Chapter Highlights | Review Questions | Fill in the Blanks | State True or False | Multiple Choice Questions | Answers

Preface

We all know that Information Technology (IT) is the buzzword of the 21st century. We use computers to store, retrieve, transmit and manipulate data. Today, computers are used to perform every other task such as publishing a newspaper, designing a building, coaching sports players and training pilots in flight simulators. Computers have become so widespread that almost every electrical and electronic device (like washing machines, air conditioners, etc.) has a small embedded computer within it. Even the mobile phones that we use are smart phones (phones with computing technology) that are connected to the Internet. Information technology has revolutionized our lifestyle. Thus in today's scenario, learning about computers is mandatory not only for students pursuing a career in engineering and technology but also for those in other professions like journalism, nursing, archaeology, construction and management, to name a few.

Computing skills always help one to be more productive and self-sufficient. Therefore, a basic knowledge of computers and their underlying technology will pay rich dividends in the future. In this context, Python is an open-source, excellent, easy, high-level, interpreted, interactive, object-oriented and a reliable language that uses English-like words. It is also a versatile language that supports development of a wide range of applications ranging from simple text processing to WWW browsers to games. Moreover, programmers can embed Python within their C, C++, COM, ActiveX, CORBA, and Java programs to give 'scripting' capabilities for users.

Python has a huge user base that is constantly growing. The strength of Python can be understood from the fact that this programming language is the most preferred language of companies like Nokia, Google, YouTube and even NASA for its easy syntax. The support for multiple programming paradigms, including object-oriented programming, functional Python programming, and parallel programming models makes it an ideal choice for the programmers.

However, no student can learn to program just by reading a book; rather, it is a skill that must be developed by practice. So, after learning the rudiments of program writing, students will find in this book, a number of examples and exercises that would help them learn to design efficient programs. The book presents various programming examples that have already been implemented and tested using Python 3.8.3.

KEY FEATURES

This book is aimed at serving as a textbook for students enrolled in Class XI of CBSE. Divided into two main sections – Introduction to IT and Python Programming, it introduces the concepts of Information Technology and Python programming language so that the students can use the key ideas learnt to solve real-world problems. The book aims to acquaint the reader with the basics of computer science before introducing the Python Programming language as a multifaceted tool with diverse functions. To this end it includes several student-friendly features:

Comprehensive Coverage: The book provides comprehensive coverage of all important topics from the examination point-of-view.

Easy to Understand: The book uses very simple language to explain the concepts and breaks down technical jargons to simpler terms for the student's benefit.

Pictorial Approach: Numerous well-labelled diagrams are provided throughout the text for clear understanding of the concepts.

Practical Orientation: Replete with solved examples and chapter-end exercises in the form of objective type questions and review questions, the book's well-defined pedagogy enables students to check their understanding of the concepts.

Glossary: A list of key terms is provided at the end of each chapter to facilitate easy revision.

Informative Textboxes: Important concepts are highlighted throughout the text for a quick recap.

Programmer's Zone examples are used in context to help the students understand the technique of programming.

Complementary App for CUCET: Students can download the free mobile app Jruma from Google Play Store or Apple Store for additional learning resources. The app would help them to recapitulate and test their understanding of the concepts learnt in Classes XI and XII. The app will also be useful for the students to hone their Computer Science (CS) and Logical Reasoning (LR) skills. CS and LR is a mandatory section in the CUCET and all other entrance exams the students may take throughout their professional career.

ACKNOWLEDGMENTS

The writing of this text book was a mammoth task for which a lot of help was required from many people. Fortunately, I have had the fine support of my family, friends and fellow members of the teaching staff at the Shyama Prasad Mukherji College.

My special thanks would always go to my father Late Sh. Janak Raj Thareja, my mother Smt. Usha Thareja, my brother Pallav and sisters Kimi and Rashi who were a source of abiding inspiration and are a divine blessing for me. I am especially indebted to my son Goransh, who has been very patient and cooperative in letting me realize my dreams. I am obliged to my uncle Mr B L Theraja for his inspiration and guidance in writing this book.

Last but not the least, my acknowledgements will always be incomplete if I do not thank the editorial team at Universities Press (India) Private Limited that gave me this brilliant opportunity to utilize my writing skills.

Reema Thareja
reema_thareja@yahoo.com

About the Author

Reema Thareja is Assistant Professor at Shyama Prasad Mukherji College, University of Delhi. She has over 15 years of experience, teaching computer science for various courses including BA, BSc, MSc, BBA, MBA, BCA and MCA. She has authored several books, including those on Computer Fundamentals, C Programming, OOPS with C++, Data Structures, Data Warehousing and Python Programming, which are well-accepted across the globe. She has also written books on Data Science and Machine Learning in R for the current academic session.

Dr Thareja has published 17 research papers in journals of national and international repute. In addition, she has got the acceptance for four more papers. A recipient of 64 Google Scholar Citations, she has launched a Computer Science Learning and Quizzing mobile app, Jruma, for both Android and iOS devices.

A recipient of the Nobel Laureate Maria Goeppert–Mayer Inspiring Woman of the Year 2021 Award in the field of Computer Science by International Multi-disciplinary Research Foundation (IMRF), Dr Thareja was also among "India's Top 50 Women Leaders in the Education Industry" recognized by uLektz Wall of Fame for the year 2020. She has conducted several faculty development programs, student workshops and webinars in India and the US, and participated in the International Dialogue on Empowered Future – Women's Role on the eve of International Women's Day 2021.

A member of the Computer Society of India and Editorial Board and Keynote Speaker of the IMRF Conference Board, Dr Thareja is a skilled motivator who helps students utilize their untapped skills and reinvent themselves. She was recently conferred with the Knowledge Mobilization Award at the Seventh Annual Research Awards event organized by Shri Param Hans Education and Research Trust and has been invited as a speaker for the Global Virtual Summit to be held in New York this summer.

Computer Systems and Organization

Chapter Objectives

The first chapter of the book gives an introduction about the computer, its components, organization, related hardware and software. It includes a detailed discussion on the following topics:

- Basic organization and components of a computer including ALU, CU, CPU and devices for input, output and storage
- Input devices like keyboard, mouse, touch screen, touch pad, scanner, stylus, bar code reader, OMR, MICR and digital camera
- Output devices including printer, plotter, monitor, speaker and projector
- Classification of computer's memory as cache memory, primary or secondary memory
- Understanding their features to differentiate between them
- Ports on the computer that allow users to connect a variety of devices through them
- System bus that transfers data to and from computer's memory and devices connected to the computer
- Software and their classification based on the technique adopted to acquire them
- Utility software and customized software

We all have seen computers being used in our homes, schools, offices, and in fact every other place we visit. The smartphones that we have in our hands is also an example of a small computer. Today, it is just impossible to think of our lives without this machine.

A computer is an electronic machine that takes data and instructions as input and performs computations on data based on the specified instructions.

1.1 BASIC COMPUTER ORGANIZATION

A computer performs five major operations which include:

1. accepting data or instructions (input)
2. storing data
3. processing data
4. displaying results (output) and
5. controlling and co-ordinating all operations inside a computer.

To perform these functions, the different parts of a computer interact with each other as shown in the Fig. 1.1.

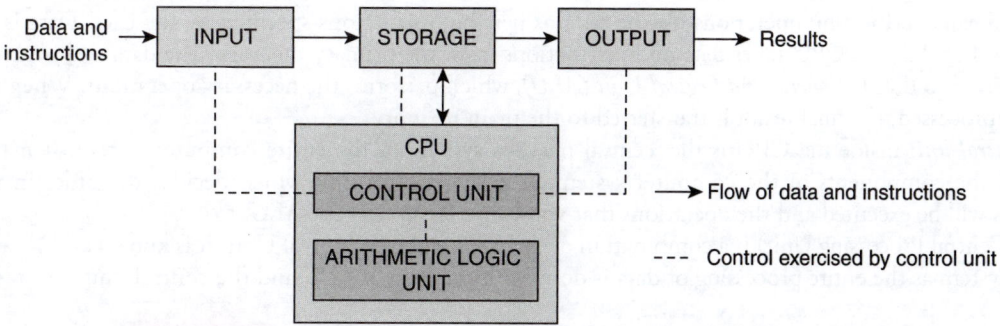

Figure 1.1 Interaction between different parts of a computer system

Input: The process of entering data and instructions into the computer system is known as input. Users can provide input to the computer using different input devices like keyboard, mouse, scanner, trackball, etc.

Storage: Storage is the process of saving data, instructions and results of processing permanently in the computer's memory. Once our work is stored in computer, we can use it at any time. A computer has two types of storage areas:

> Computers understand binary language which consists of only two symbols (0s and 1s); so it is the responsibility of the input devices to convert the input data into binary codes.

Primary Storage: Primary storage or the main memory is that storage area of the computer which is directly accessible by the CPU at a very fast speed. It can be used to store data, instructions and recently generated results of processing. However, the primary storage is very expensive and therefore limited in capacity. Another drawback of main memory is that it is volatile in nature, that is, as soon as the computer is switched off, the information stored in it gets erased. Hence, it cannot be used as a permanent storage of useful data and programs (a program is a set of or collection of instructions) for future use. Example, RAM (Random Access Memory)

Secondary Storage: Also known as the secondary memory or auxiliary memory, it is just the opposite of primary memory. It is cheaper and therefore available in large capacity. Secondary memory is non-volatile. This means that it can be used to permanently store all our data and instructions irrespective of whether or not they are currently being used by the CPU. For example, hard disk (you store your files in C drive, D drive), pen drive, etc., for future use.

Table 1.1 highlights the key differences between primary and secondary memory.

Table 1.1 Difference between primary and secondary memory

Primary Memory	Secondary Memory
• It is more expensive	• It is cheaper
• It is faster to access	• It is slower to access
• It is more efficient than secondary memory	• It is less efficient than primary memory
• Directly accessed by the CPU	• Cannot be accessed directly by the CPU
• It is volatile in nature	• It is non-volatile in nature
• Storage capacity is limited	• Large storage capacity
• Consumes less power	• Consumes more power
• Stores data temporarily	• Stores data permanently
• Holds instructions and data when a program is executing.	• The secondary memory holds data and programs that not currently being executed by the CPU.

Output: Output is the reverse of input. It is the process of giving the result of data processing to the outside world (external to the computer system). The results are given through output devices like monitor, printer, etc. Now that the computer accepts data only in binary form and the result of processing is also in the binary form, the result cannot be directly given to the user. *The output devices therefore convert the results available in binary codes into a human readable language before displaying it to the user.*

1.1.1 Central Processing Unit (CPU)

Processing means performing operations on the data as per the instructions specified by the user. Data is processed in the CPU. For this, the CPU takes data and instructions from the primary memory. The data and instructions are then transferred to the *Arithmetic and Logical Unit (ALU)*, which performs the necessary operations. When the data is completely processed, the final result is transferred to the main memory.

The *control unit* inside the CPU is the 'central nervous system' of the entire computer system. It manages and controls all the components of the computer system. It is the control unit which decides the order in which the instructions will be executed and the operations that will be performed by the ALU.

CPU (Central Processing Unit) is a combination of the ALU and the Control Unit. It is known as the 'brain' of the computer system as the entire processing of data is done with the help of ALU and the control unit.

1.2 INPUT DEVICES

We have read that data and instructions that we enter into the computer are called *input.* And devices that help us to give input to the computer are called *input devices.*

Some commonly used input devices are keyboard, mouse, microphone, web camera, scanner, joystick, etc.

1.2.1 Keyboard

A keyboard is the main input device for computers. Computer keyboards look very similar to the keyboards of typewriters, with some additional keys, as shown in Fig. 1.2. Using a keyboard, a user can type a document, use keystroke shortcuts, access menus, play games, and perform numerous other tasks. Most keyboards have between 80 and 110 keys, which include the following:

Alphabetic keys include the letters of the English alphabet. The layout of the keyboard is known as QWERTY for its first six letters. The QWERTY pattern has been a standard right from the time computer keyboards were introduced.

Numeric keys include Arabic numerals (0–9), arranged in the same configuration found on calculators to speed up data entry of numbers. When the Num Lock key is set to ON, the user can type numbers, dot, or input the symbols /, *, –, and +. When the Num Lock key is set to OFF, the numeric keys can be used to move the cursor on the screen. A set of numeric keys are also present at the top of alphabet keys.

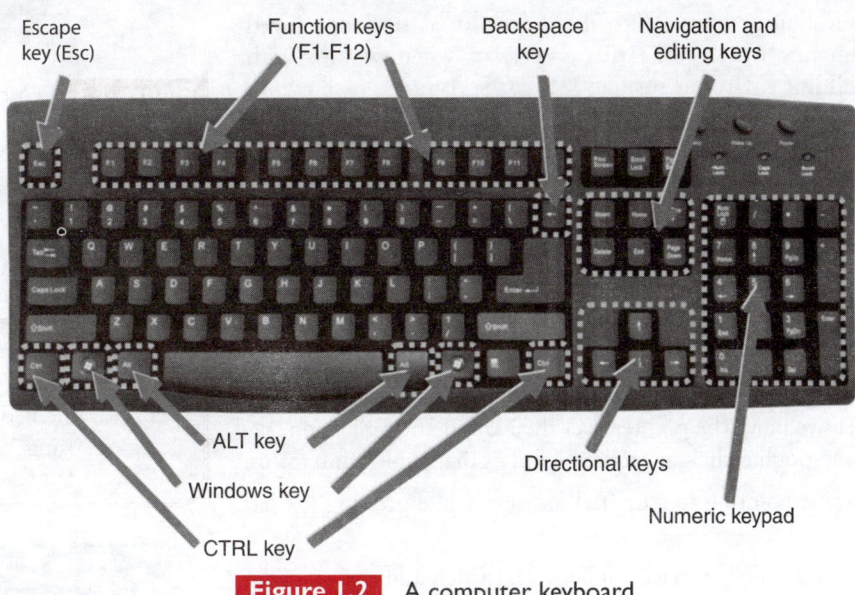

Figure 1.2 A computer keyboard

Function keys are used by applications and operating systems to input specific commands. They are often placed on the top of the keyboard in a single row. Function keys can be programmed so that their functionality varies from one program to another. For example, the F5 key can be used to execute a Python script.

Arrow keys arranged in an inverted *T*-type fashion between the alphabetic and the numeric keys, and are used to move the cursor on the screen in small increments.

Home and End keys are used to move the cursor to the beginning and end of the current line, respectively.

PageUp and PageDown move the cursor up and down by one screen at a time, respectively. **Insert key** is used to enter a character between two existing characters.

> Keys such as Shift, Ctrl, and Alt are called *modifier keys* because they are used to modify the normal function of a key. For example, Shift + character (lower case) makes the computer display the character in upper case.

Delete key deletes a character at the cursor position.

Shortcut key is used to access the options available by pressing the right mouse button.

Esc key cancels the selected option.

Pause key suspends a command/process in progress.

Print Screen key captures everything on the screen as an image. The image can be pasted into any document.

Wireless Keyboard can be operated without connecting it to the computer. It is powered by a battery and allows users to work up to 10 feet from its receiver. This is especially desirable when we want to keep our desk uncluttered without wires. However, on the downside, greater the distance between the wireless keyboard and the receiver monitor, more is the delay in receiving the keystrokes.

> Many a time, a few keystrokes get dropped.

Bluetooth Wireless Keyboard Bluetooth is one of the most popular methods of syncing a wireless keyboard with a computer. Such a keyboard is well-suited for offices as it creates a reliable connection without cluttering the desk.

1.2.2 Mouse

Mouse is an input device that was invented by Douglas Engelbart in 1963. It is the key input device used in a graphical user interface (GUI). Mouse can be used to handle the pointer on the screen to perform various functions such as opening an application or a file. With the mouse, users no longer need to memorize commands, which was earlier a necessity when working with text-based command line environments like MS-DOS. A mouse is shown in Fig. 1.3.

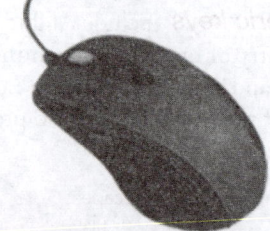

Figure 1.3 A computer mouse

A mouse has two buttons and a scroll wheel. It can be held in the hand and easily moved, without lifting, along a hard, flat surface to move the cursor to the desired location—up, down, left, or right. Once the mouse is placed at an appropriate position, a user may perform the following operations:

Point Placing the pointer over a word or an object on the screen by moving the mouse on the desk is termed as pointing.

Click Pressing either the left or the right button of the mouse is known as clicking. Clicking a mouse button initiates some action; for example, when we click the right button by pointing the mouse on a word, a menu pops up on the screen. When we move the pointer over the icon of an application, say Internet Explorer, and double-click on it, then it opens that application for us.

> A cordless or wireless mouse is not connected to a computer. The movement of the mouse is detected using radio waves or infrared light waves.

Drag Dragging means pointing to a desired location while pressing the left button.

Scroll The scroll wheel, which is placed in between the left and right buttons of the mouse, is used to vertically scroll through long documents.

1.2.3 Touchpad

Touchpad or a trackpad, as shown in Fig. 1.4, is a small, flat, rectangular stationary pointing device with a sensitive surface of 1.5–2 square inches. A user has to slide his or her fingertips across the surface of the pad to point to a specific object on the screen. The surface translates the motion and position of the user's fingers to a relative position on the screen.

Figure 1.4 A laptop touchpad

1.2.4 Joystick

Joystick is a cursor control device widely used in computer games and computer-aided design (CAD)/computer-aided manufacturing (CAM) applications. It consists of a handheld lever that pivots on one end and transmits its coordinates to a computer (shown in Fig. 1.5).

The joystick has one or more push buttons, called switches, whose position can be read by the computer. The lever of a joystick moves in all directions to control the movement of the pointer on the computer screen and its function is similar to that of a mouse. With the mouse, the cursor stops moving as soon as we stop moving the mouse. However, in the case of the joystick, the pointer continues moving in the direction to which the joystick is pointing. To stop the pointer, the user must return the joystick to its upright position.

Figure 1.5 Joystick on a gaming console

1.2.5 Touchscreen

Touchscreen (shown in Fig. 1.6) is a display screen that can identify the occurrence and position of a touch inside the display region. A user can touch the screen by using either a finger or a stylus. Such touchscreen displays are available on computers, laptops, Personal Digital Assistants (PDAs), and mobile phones.

Touchscreen monitors are an easy way of entering information into computers (or mobile phones). They have become more and more commonplace as their price has steadily dropped over the past decade. These days, touchscreen monitors are widely used in different applications including point-of-sale (POS) cash registers, automated teller machines (ATMs), car navigation screens, mobile phones, gaming consoles, and any other types of appliance that require users to input and receive information instantly.

Figure 1.6 Tablet touchscreen monitor

1.2.6 Image Scanner

Image Scanner (shown in Fig. 1.7) is a device that captures images, printed text, and handwritten text, from different sources such as photographic prints, posters, and magazines and converts them into digital images for editing and display on computers.

Some scanners have graphics software such as Adobe Photoshop to help users resize or modify captured images.

Figure 1.7 Image scanner

The scanners that we see in our colleges or offices are flatbed scanners. In this type, the document to be scanned is placed on a glass pane and an opaque cover is lowered over it. A sensor and light move along the pane, reflecting off the image placed on the glass. The reflected image is scanned onto a computer for further processing.

Advantages
- Any printed or handwritten document can be scanned and stored in a computer for further processing.
- The scanned and stored document will never deteriorate in quality with time. The document can be displayed and printed whenever required.
- There is no fear of loss of documents. Users can scan important documents and store them permanently in the computer.

Disadvantages
- Scanners are usually costlier than other input devices.
- The documents that are scanned and stored as images are bigger in size as compared to other equivalent text files.

Text documents are scanned and stored as images. Therefore, they occupy more space and are also un-editable because computers cannot interpret individual characters in images. To make these documents occupy lesser space, the scanned document can be passed through optical character recognition (OCR) software (see Fig. 1.8) where the images of individual characters are recognised and stored as a doc file. However, this method cannot be used for documents where illustrations or mathematical equations are present.

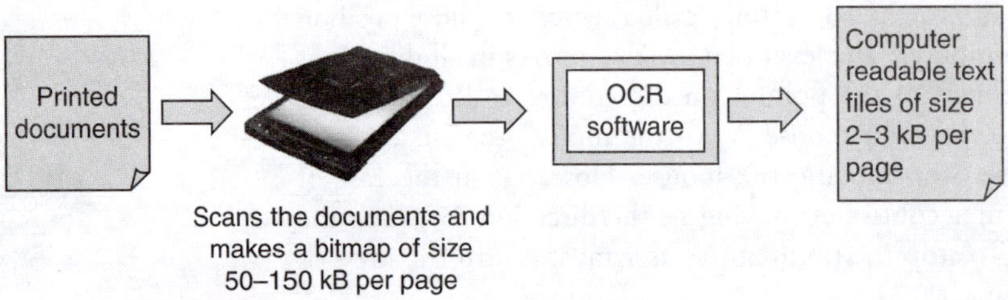

Printed documents → Scans the documents and makes a bitmap of size 50–150 kB per page → OCR software → Computer readable text files of size 2–3 kB per page

Figure 1.8 Conversion of printed documents to text file

1.2.7 Stylus

Stylus is a pen-shaped input device used to enter information or write on the touchscreen of a hand-held device (see Fig. 1.9). It is a small stick that can also be used to draw lines on a surface as input into a device, choose an option from a menu, move the cursor to another location on the screen, take notes, and create short messages. The stylus usually slides into a slot built into the device for that purpose.

Figure 1.9 Stylus

1.2.8 Barcode Reader

Barcode Reader (also price scanner or POS scanner) as shown in Fig. 1.10, is a handheld input device that is used to capture and read information stored in a barcode. It consists of a scanner, a decoder, and a cable used to connect the reader to a computer. The function of the barcode reader is to capture and translate the barcode into numerals and/or alphabets. It is connected to a computer for further processing of the captured information.

A barcode reader works by directing a beam of light across the barcode and measuring the amount of light reflected back.

The scanner converts this light energy into electrical energy. The decoder then converts these signals into data and sends it to the computer for processing. These days, barcode readers are widely used in following areas:

- Supermarkets and retail stores as POS devices
- To take inventory in retail stores
- To check out books from a library
- To track manufacturing and shipping movement
- To keep track of employee login
- To identify hospital patients
- To tabulate the results of direct mail marketing returns
- To tag honeybees used in research

Advantages
- Barcode readers are cheap.
- They are portable.
- They are handy and easy to use.

Disadvantages
- Barcode readers must be handled with care. If they develop a scratch, the user may not be able to read the code.
- They can interpret information using a limited series of thin and wide bars. To interpret other unique identifiers, the bar display area must be widened.

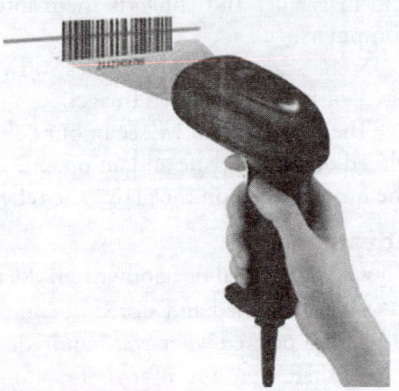

Figure 1.10 Barcode reader

1.2.9 Optical Mark Recognition (OMR)

Optical Mark Recognition (OMR) is the process of electronically extracting data from marked fields, such as checkboxes and fill-in fields, on printed forms. The optical mark reader, as shown in Fig. 1.11, is fed

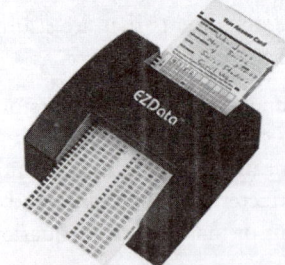

Figure 1.11 Optical mark recognition

with an OMR sheet that has pen or pencil marks in pre-defined positions to indicate each selected response (such as answers for multiple-choice questions in an entrance examination).

The OMR sheet is scanned by the reader to detect the presence of a mark by measuring the reflected light levels. The dark or the marked areas reflect less light than the unmarked ones. The OM reader interprets these pattern marks and spaces, and stores the interpreted data in a computer for storage, analysis, and reporting. The error rate for OMR technology is less than 1%. For this reason, OMR is widely used for applications in which large numbers of hand-filled forms have to be quickly processed with great accuracy, such as surveys, reply cards, questionnaires, ballots, or sheets for multiple-choice questions.

Advantage

Optical mark readers work at very high speeds. They can read up to 9,000 forms per hour.

Disadvantages
- It is difficult to gather large amounts of information using an OMR.
- Some data may be missing in the scanned document.
- It is a sensitive device that rejects the OMR sheet if it is folded, torn, or crushed.

1.2.10 Magnetic Ink Character Reader (MICR)

Magnetic Ink Character Reader (MICR) is used to verify the legitimacy of paper documents, especially bank cheques (Fig. 1.12). It is a high-speed magnetic recognition device that can recognize magnetic ink printed characters (refer Fig. 1.13). The printed characters provide important information (such as cheque number, bank IFSC Code, customer account number, and, in some cases, the amount on the cheque) for processing to the receiving party.

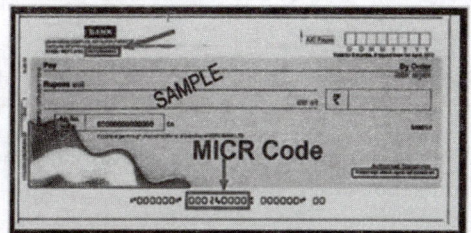

Figure 1.12 Magnetic ink character reader

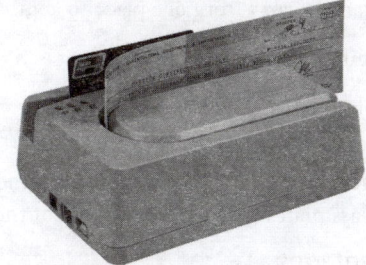

Figure 1.13 Magnetic ink printer

1.2.11 Digital Camera

Digital Camera is used to click photographs and record videos (See Fig. 1.14). These pictures and videos are stored in a small memory chip placed inside the camera. To transfer all the pictures and videos in the computer, you simply need to connect the digital camera with the computer.

Figure 1.14 Digital camera

1.3 OUTPUT DEVICES

Devices that gives the output are called *output devices.* Some commonly used output devices are monitor, printer, speakers, headphone, etc.

1.3.1 Monitor or VDU (Visual Display Unit)

The computer monitor looks like a TV screen. Whatever we type on the keyboard can be seen on the monitor as output. Monitors are available in different sizes like 15, 17, 21 inches. You must use a bigger size monitor as it causes less strain to your eyes. There are three types of monitors – Cathode Ray Tube (CRT) monitor, Liquid Crystal Display (LCD) and Plasma monitor (Figs. 1.15 a, b and c).

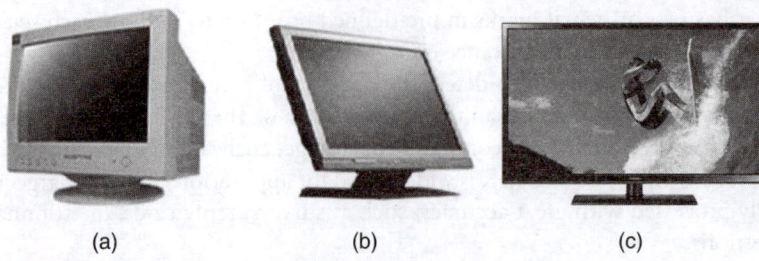

Figure 1.15 (a) Cathode ray tube, (b) Liquid crystal display and (c) Plasma monitors

The output seen on the monitor is called *soft copy* output because we can see it for the time when the computer is switched on.

CRT monitors are the traditional type of monitors used in computers and televisions. These are the first type of monitors that were used in the early days of computers are now being gradually phased out in favour of the more efficient and less power consuming LCD monitors. However, CRT monitors are still used by graphics professionals because of their accurate rendering of colours. The difference between CRT and LCD monitors are presented in Table 1.2.

Table 1.2 Comparison of CRT and LCD monitors

Cathode Ray Tube (CRT) Monitor	Liquid Crystal Display (LCD) Monitor
Very big in size	Light weight
Difficult to carry from one place to another	Easy to carry from one place to another
Consumes more electricity	Consumes less electricity
Very big in size	Light weight

Plasma Monitors are thin and flat monitors widely used in televisions and computers. The plasma display contains two glass plates that have hundreds of thousands of tiny cells filled with xenon and neon gases.

Advantages
- The technology used in plasma monitors allows producing a very wide screen using extremely thin materials.
- Very bright images are formed which look good from almost every angle.
- These monitors are not heavy and are thus easily portable.

Disadvantages
- These monitors are very expensive.
- They have a high-power consumption.
- Since the images are phosphor-based, at times, they may suffer from flicker.

1.3.2 Speakers

Speakers help us to listen to music. Other sounds from the computer can also be heard from speakers (Fig. 1.16(a)). For example, when you switch on your computer a welcome sound is heard. Usually two speakers are attached to a computer.

Headphone: It is used to listen to music from computer. We can also use headphone while chatting with our friends through computer. With speakers, users can enjoy music, movie, or a game, and the voice will be spread across the entire room (Fig. 1.16(b)). With good quality speakers, the voice will also be audible even to people sitting in another room or even to neighbours!

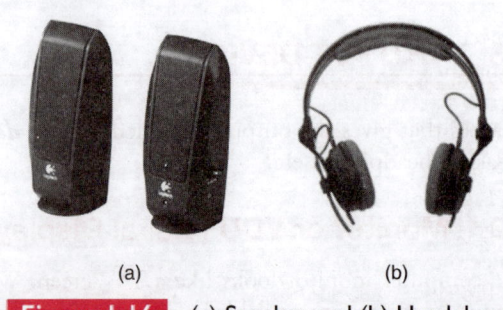

Figure 1.16 (a) Speaker and (b) Headphone

These days, monitors also have a speaker fitted inside them.

However, in case the user wants to enjoy loud music without disturbing the people nearby, a *headphone* can be used. Headphones are small devices that fit in or on the ear, and give about the same quality and power of the sound as the speakers, only to the listener. Most of today's headphones feature some noise-cancelling technologies, so that the listener may listen to only the sound from the speakers and not anything else from the surrounding environment.

Users often use headphones to chat with people over the Internet. With headphones, they are assured that the conversation is heard only by them. However, in addition to the headphones, they are also required to use a separate microphone to talk to the other person. Hence, another device called the *headset* was developed to allow users to talk and listen at the same time, using the same device. Headsets are widely used in call centres and other telephone-intensive jobs, and for personal use on the computer to facilitate comfortable simultaneous conversation and typing.

1.3.3 Printer

A printer is a device that takes the text and graphics information from a computer and prints it on to a paper (Fig. 1.17). Printers are available in the market in various sizes, speeds, sophistication, and costs. Usually, more expensive printers are used for higher-resolution colour printing. The qualities of printers that are of interest to users include:

Figure 1.17 Printer

Colour printouts are needed for presentations, maps, and other pages where colour is part of the information. Colour printers can also be set to print only in monochrome. These printers are more expensive, so if the users do not have a specific need for colour or usually take lot of printouts, they will find a black-and-white printer cheaper to operate.

Resolution of a printer means the sharpness of text and images rendered on paper. It is usually expressed in dots per inch (dpi). Even the least expensive printer provides sufficient resolution for most purposes at 600 dpi.

Speed means number of pages that are printed in one minute. The speed of a printer is an important factor for users who have a large number of pages to print. While high-speed printers are quite expensive, the inexpensive printers, on the other hand, can print only about 3–6 sheets per minute. Colour printing is even slower.

Memory Most printers have a small amount of memory (for example, 1 MB), which can be expanded by the user. Having more memory enhances the speed of printing.

Plotters A plotter is a printing device that is usually used to print vector graphics with high print quality. They are widely used to draw maps, in scientific applications, and in CAD, CAM, and computer aided engineering (CAE).

Architects use plotters to draw blueprints of the structures they are working on. A plotter is basically a printer that interprets commands from a computer to make line drawings on paper with one or more automated pens. Since plotters are much more expensive than printers, they are used only for specialized applications.

Hewlett–Packard is the leading vendor of plotters worldwide.

1.3.4 Projector

A projector (Fig. 1.18) is a device that takes an image from a video source and projects it onto a screen or another surface. These days, projectors are used for a wide range of applications, varying from home theatre systems for projecting movies and television programs onto a screen much larger than even the biggest available television, to organizations for projecting information and presentations onto screens large enough for rooms filled with many people.

Figure 1.18 Projector

Projectors also allow users to change/adjust some features of the image such as brightness, sharpness, and colour settings, similar to the features available in a standard television. Projectors are now available in a variety of different shapes and sizes, and are produced by many different companies.

Projectors can be broadly classified into two categories depending on the technology they use.

LCD Projector These projectors make use of their own light to display the image on the screen/wall. They are based on LCD technology. To use these projectors, the room must be first darkened, else the image formed will be blurred.

Digital Light Processing (DLP) Projector uses a number of mirrors to reflect the light. When using the DLP projector, the room may or may not be darkened because it displays a clear image in both situations.

1.3.5 Plotters

A plotter (Fig. 1.19) is a printing device that is usually used to print vector graphics with high print quality. They are widely used to draw maps, in scientific applications, and in CAD, CAM, and computer aided engineering (CAE).

Architects use plotters to draw blueprints of the structures they are working on. A plotter is basically a printer that interprets commands from a computer to make line drawings on paper with one or more automated pens. Since plotters are much more expensive than printers, they are used only for specialized applications.

Hewlett–Packard is the leading vendor of plotters worldwide.

Figure 1.19 Plotter

1.4   ORGANIZATION OF COMPUTER'S MEMORY

Computers are electronic machines that can be either on or off. In computer, ON means 1 and OFF means 0. Like any other machine, computer understands only these two digits. So, every data and instruction that we give to the computer are converted into a series of 1s and 0s.

Memory of the computer is divided into a large number of cells where each cell can store one digit, either 0 or 1. More the number of cells, more data can be stored and therefore higher will be the storage capacity of memory. The storage capacity of a computer's memory is measured in units like Bytes, Kilo Bytes, Giga Bytes, Tera Bytes, etc. as shown in Table 1.3.

Table 1.3   Units for measurement of computer memory

Smaller Unit	Larger Unit	Symbol
8 Bits	1 Byte	B
1024 Bytes	1 Kilo Byte	KB
1024 Kilo Bytes	1 Mega Byte	MB
1024 Mega Bytes	1 Giga Byte	GB
1024 Giga Bytes	1 Tera Byte	TB
1024 Tera Bytes	1 Peta Byte	PB
1024 Peta Bytes	1 Exa Byte	EB
1024 Exa Bytes	1 Zeta Byte	ZB
1024 Zeta Bytes	1 Yotta Byte	YB

1.5   TYPES OF COMPUTER MEMORY

We have read that a computer's memory is used to store data and instructions, either temporarily or permanently. It can be broadly divided into three groups: cache memory, primary (main) memory and secondary memory (See Fig. 1.20).

1.5.1 Cache Memory

Cache memory is a volatile, small-sized and high-speed memory which is used to speed up the work of CPU (Fig. 1.21). The cache memory stores those parts of data and instructions that are being repeatedly used by the CPU. Since cache memory is a high-speed memory, it is very expensive and therefore used in small quantity.

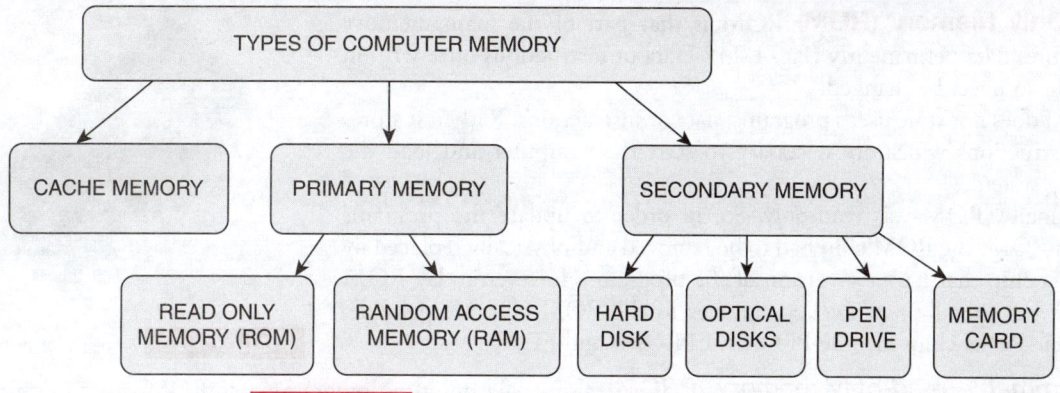

Figure 1.20 Classification of computer memory

Cache memory is used to store instructions and data that are repeatedly required to execute programs thereby improving the overall system speed and increase the performance of the computer. Keeping frequently accessed data and instructions in the cache avoids the need for accessing the slower primary memory.

1.5.2 Primary Memory

There are two types of primary memory: RAM and ROM.

Random Access Memory (RAM) RAM is a volatile (stores data only when the power is on) storage area within the computer (Fig. 1.22). It stores data temporarily so that it can be accessed by the CPU. The information stored in RAM is loaded from the computer's hard disk or any other secondary memory (like optical drive, pen drive, magnetic tape). These days, computers have 8GB to 16GB of RAM. *More the RAM, more is the number of programs/ applications that can be run and shorter is the time taken to execute an instruction.* There are two types of RAM—SRAM and DRAM.

Figure 1.21 Cache memory

SRAM (Static RAM) This type of RAM holds data without an external refresh as long as it is powered. This is in striking contrast with the DRAM which must be refreshed multiple times in a second to hold its data contents.

However, SRAM is faster and more reliable than DRAM. SRAM is often used as cache memory. Static RAM chips are used in cars, household appliances, and handheld electronic devices.

Figure 1.22 Random access memory

DRAM (Dynamic RAM) SRAM and DRAM are both types of RAM and stores data as long as power is supplied to its circuits. DRAM is the most common type of memory used in personal computers, workstations, and servers today. Table 1.4 illustrates the difference between SRAM and DRAM.

Table 1.4 Comparison of SRAM and DRAM

SRAM	DRAM
• Design based on transistor technology	• Design based on capacitor technology
• More expensive	• Cheaper than SRAM
• Consumes more power	• Consumes less power
• Limited storage capacity	• Storage capacity is more than SRAM
• Fast	• Slower than SRAM
• Requires more space	• Requires less space

Read Only Memory (ROM) ROM is that part of the main memory which stores data permanently (Fig. 1.23). Data or instructions once written in ROM can never be changed.

ROM does not store user's programs, data or instructions. Rather, it stores those instructions which are necessary to start the computer and load the operating system.

Originally, ROM was read-only. So, in order to update the programs stored in ROM, the ROM chip had to be removed and physically replaced by the ROM chip that has new version of the program. However, today ROM chips are not literally *read-only*, as updates to the ROM chip are possible. Rewritable ROM chips include PROMs, EPROMs and EEPROMs.

Figure 1.23 Read only memory

Programmable read-only memory (PROM) also called one-time programmable ROM can be written to or programmed using a special device called a PROM programmer.

Erasable programmable read-only memory (EPROM) is a type of ROM that can be erased and re-programmed. The EPROM can be erased by exposing the chip to strong ultraviolet light typically for 10 minutes or longer and then rewritten.

Electrically erasable programmable read-only memory (EEPROM) allows its entire or selected contents to be electrically erased, then rewritten electrically. The process of writing an EEPROM is also known as flashing.

The difference between RAM and ROM is given in Table 1.5.

Table 1.5 Difference between RAM and ROM

RAM	ROM
• Data can be read as well as written	• Data can only be read
• Stores data temporarily	• Stores data permanently
• Stores the data of user while computer is being used	• Data is stored during the time of fabrication
• It is required while computer is being used to run applications	• It is required for starting the computer and storing important programs

How It All Works Together: Cache memory is faster than the main memory. So, if CPU gets data and instructions at a faster speed, it can process that data faster. So, let us see how it works.

- *Step 1:* CPU needs data and instructions, so it requests for these inputs from the cache memory.
- *Step 2:* If cache memory has the required data and instruction, it gives them to CPU.
  If cache memory does not have that data and instruction, it then asks for them from the RAM.
- *Step 3:* If the RAM has the data and instruction, it sends them to cache. The cache memory gives them to CPU. The cache memory also stores a copy of this data and instruction in itself so that in future if CPU asks for it again, it does not have to ask from the RAM.

If RAM also does not have the data and instruction, it takes the information from the secondary memory that stores all data and instructions permanently. After getting the data and instructions, it gives the information to the cache memory and also stores a copy of it.

The interaction between the CPU and the different types of memories is shown in Fig. 1.24.

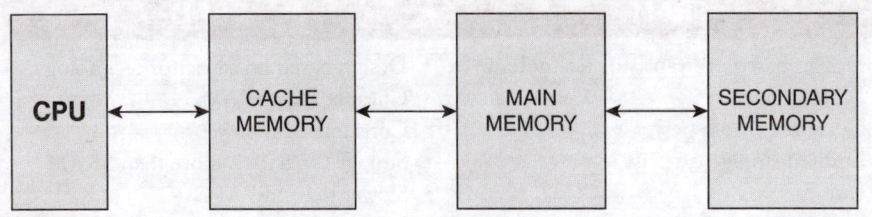

Figure 1.24 Interaction between CPU and cache, main, primary and secondary memories

1.5.3 Secondary Memory

The secondary memory or the external memory is non-volatile memory that stores user's data, instructions and programs permanently. It is slower than the main memory. CPU cannot directly access the secondary memory. So, whenever we open a program or file stored on secondary memory, it is copied from there to the main memory.

Hard Disk: Every computer has a hard disk installed in it (Fig. 1.25). Hard disk is the main storage device of any computer. It has the highest storage capacity. The hard disk is placed inside the CPU box. As compared to other secondary storage devices, hard disk is the fastest device. It is more expensive and heavier than other storage devices.

All the programs that we use on computer like MS Paint, WordPad, MS Word, Games, Calculator, etc. are stored on the hard disk. Apart from these, operating system files and other system software are also stored on the hard disk. Moreover, all the files that we create or download are stored in the hard disk.

The C: drive (and D:, E: drives on some computers) that we see in the File Explorer actually refers to the hard disk of the computer. These days, hard disks can store several Tera Bytes (TB) of data and every year with improved technology the storage capacity of hard disk increases many times.

Figure 1.25 Hard disk

> Anything you save to your computer, such as a picture, file, program or video, is sent to your hard drive for storage.

Optical Storage Discs: Optical storage discs use light to store data. They are very light, weighing around 15–20 grams and thus portable. Because of their portability, they are widely used to transfer data from one computer to another.

The only limitation of these devices is that they are fragile (delicate) and prone to scratches. Scratches can affect the readability of data.

CD (Compact Disc): CDs are small circular plastic discs on which music, games, movies and computer programs are stored (Fig. 1.26(a)). A CDs can store up to 700 MB of data. This means that an audio CD can store 80 minutes of audio.

(a)   (b)

Figure 1.26 (a) Compact disc and (b) Digital versatile disc

> A CD Player can read a CD. But a DVD Player can read both CD and DVD.

There are two types of CDs- CD-R and CD-RW. CD-R stands for CD – Read only. Data, once written, can only be read. You cannot write on the CD again. CD-RW are those CDs that can be read as well as written.

DVD (Digital Versatile Disc): DVD is also a circular plastic disc which looks exactly like a CD. A DVD can store data either on one side or on both sides (Fig. 1.26(b)). DVD that can store data only one side can store 4.7 GB data and the one that can store data on both sides can store 9.4 GB data.

Like CDs there are two types of DVDs - DVD-R and DVD-RW. DVD-R stands for DVD – Read only. Data, once written, can only be read. You cannot write on the DVD again, you just read it multiple times. DVD-RW are those DVDs that can be read as well as written.

Blu-ray Disc (BD): A Blu-ray Disc (Fig. 1.27) looks exactly similar to a DVD but it can store five times more data than a DVD can store. Moreover, the quality of video, audio and pictures stored on a Blu-ray disc is much better than that stored on a CD or a DVD. Therefore, these days Blu-ray discs are replacing the use of CDs and DVDs for storing music, games, movies and computer programs.

Figure 1.27 Blu-ray disc

A single-sided Blu-ray disc can hold up to 25 GB of data. Blu-ray player can read Blu-ray discs, DVDs, and CDs. But a DVD Player or a CD Player cannot read a Blu-ray Disc.

Pen Drive: A pen drive is a light weight key chain like storage device that is used to transfer files from one computer to another (Fig. 1.28(a)). A pen drive can store much more data than a CD, DVD or a Blu Ray Disc. These days, Pen drives with storage capacity 1 TB are available in the market.

> Do you know that if you have a USB port in your car, then you can enjoy your favorite music by storing your favorite songs in a pen drive and plugging the pen drive into the USB port.

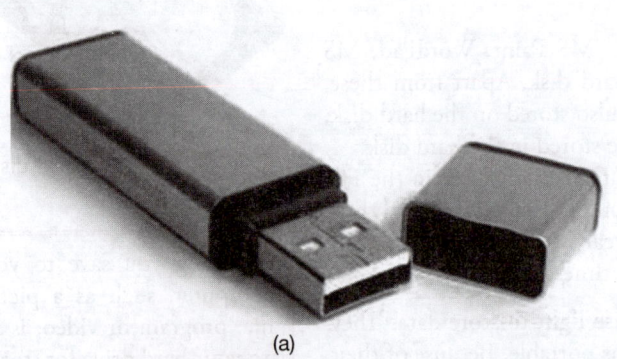

Figure 1.28 (a) Pen drive and (b) Pen drive plugged into USB port of a laptop

Though pen drives are little expensive than CDs and floppy disks (which were used till 2005), they have still succeeded in replacing them because of their capability of storing more data and transferring it at a faster speed. A pen drive is also called a USB Drive because it is plugged into the USB port of the computer (Fig. 1.28(b)).

The main advantage of pen drive is that unlike a CD, DVD or Blu Ray disc, it is not affected by scratches.

Memory Card: Memory card, also known as a flash card or multimedia card, is a storage device that is used to store pictures, files, videos, programs and games (Fig. 1.29). It is used to transfer these data and files between two computers, smartphones, tablets or digital cameras. For example, we can plug in the memory card in our phone to store our pictures and videos. To transfer these files to a computer, we can use a card reader and connect it to the USB port of the computer. This will help us to transfer files just in the same way we transfer files between computer and pen drive.

> We insert SD card in our smart phones to increase its storage capacity. These SD cards are nothing but memory cards.

Figure 1.29 Memory card

1.6 PORTS ON THE COMPUTER

At the back end of the desktop case, there are a number of ports. These ports allow most of the computer's external hardware devices (like monitor, keyboard, printer, speakers, mouse, etc) to be connected to the computer. Some commonly used ports are discussed below.

USB: **USB (Universal Serial Bus) Port** is a plug-and-play port that allows a computer to communicate with a wide range of devices including keyboards, mouse, digital cameras, pen drives, music players, etc. in smart phones and tablet computers. The USB port is used both for charging as well as for data transfer (Fig. 1.30). Have you ever seen your parents copying pictures from their smart phone in to the computer?

Figure 1.30 USB port

Ethernet Port: This allows a computer to be connected to a network using a wire or cable (Fig. 1.31).

FireWire Port: This port was invented by Apple is used to transfer large amount of data at very fast speed. The latest version of FireWire port can transfer data at the speed of 800 Mbps and this is further expected to jump to an unbelievable speed of 3.2 Gbps (Fig. 1.32). Up to 63 devices can be connected to a FireWire bus. Windows operating systems (98 and later) and Mac OS (8.6 and later) both support this type of port for data transfer between computer and devices (like scanner, digital camera, etc.).

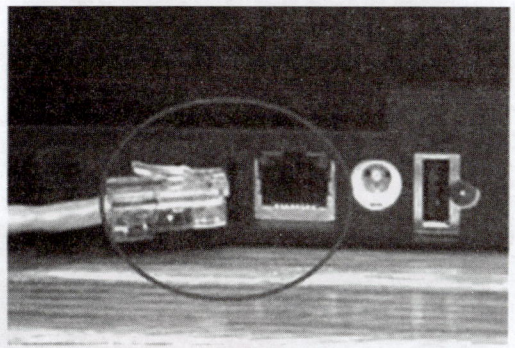
Figure 1.31 Ethernet port

Figure 1.32 FireWire port

VGA Port: VGA stands for Video Graphics Array. The VGA port connects monitor to a computer's video card. It has 15 holes. Figures 1.33 (a) and (b) show the VGA cable and VGA connector respectively.

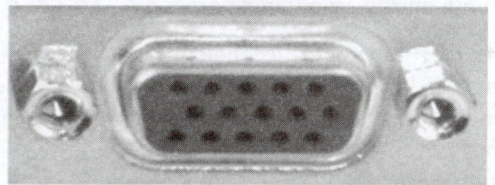
Figure 1.33 (a) VGA cable (b) VGA connector

Modem Port is used to connect a PC's modem to the telephone network.

Serial Port: This is the port to which a device that sends data one bit at a time is connected. Serial port can be used to connect devices like mouse, modem, a computer (to make a network to transfer files) and printer (Fig. 1.34).

> Newer devices however prefer USB port over a serial port.

Serial ports are also known as communication ports (or COM ports). Since a serial port uses only one wire to transmit the data, one bit at a time, it transfers data slower than other ports.

Parallel port: These ports, found at the back of the computer, can send 8 bits (1 byte) at a time simultaneously (in parallel). Hence, data transmission is faster through these ports as compared to serial ports (Fig. 1.35). Parallel ports are used to connect printers, scanners, CD writers etc.

PS/2 Port: PS/2 ports are round in shape and consist of 6 pins (Fig. 1.36). They were used to connect keyboards and mouse in the past. They were introduced in 1987 but today they have been *completely* replaced by the much faster, and more flexible, USB port.

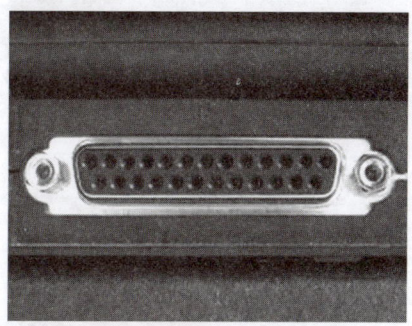
Figure 1.34 Serial port

> With the introduction of USB, FireWire, and other faster ports, parallel ports are seldom used these days. In fact, many new computers and laptops do not even have a parallel port.

Figure 1.35 Parallel port

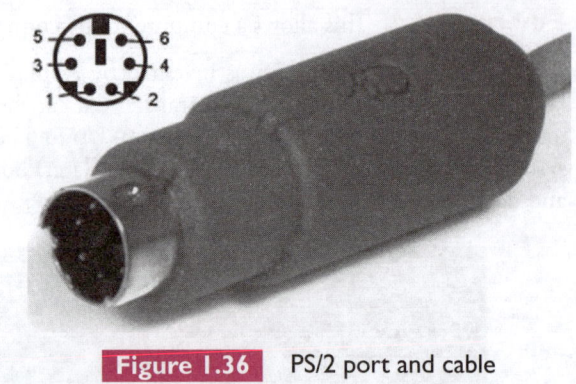

Figure 1.36 PS/2 port and cable

Infrared Port: The infrared port allows devices to exchange data without using cables (Fig. 1.37). The remote control of our TV sets uses this technology. Devices like adapters, dongles, notebooks, PDAs, cell phones, handhelds, pagers, scanners, digital cameras, printers, fax machines, bar code scanners, set top boxes, toys, wrist watches, etc. can be connected to the computer using this port.

As the name suggests, the infrared port is used to exchange data using infrared waves. But for such exchange, the device and the computer both must have infrared ports.

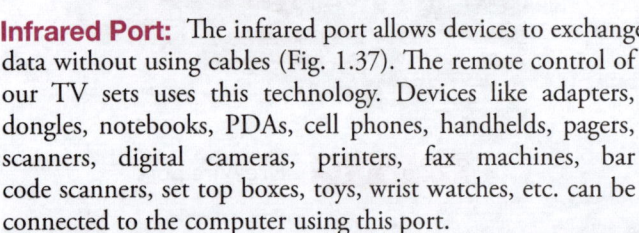

Figure 1.37 Infrared port

Bluetooth Port: The Bluetooth technology is cheap, consumes low energy, and is widely used to connect audio devices, PDAs and mobile phones. Bluetooth uses short-range radio frequencies to transmit information effectively within a range of 32 feet, or 10 metres at a rate of about 2 megabits per second.

The common ports seen behind the case of a typical desktop is shown in Fig. 1.38

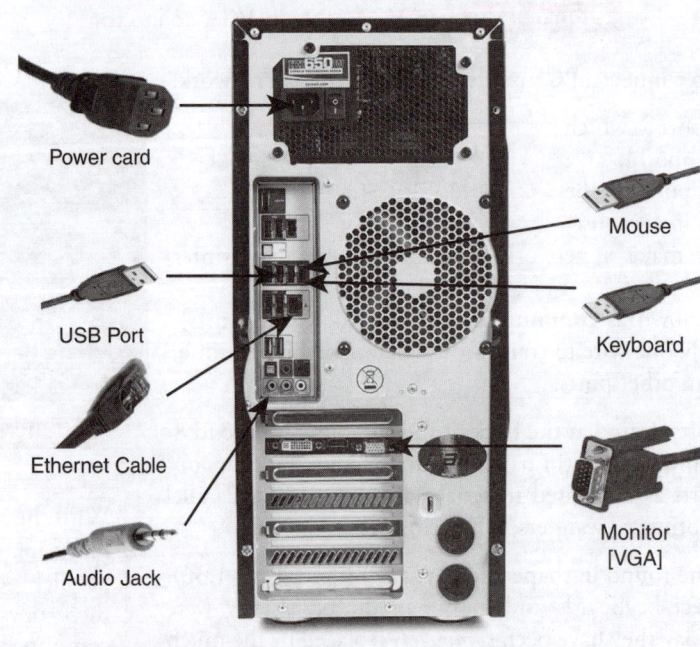

Figure 1.38 Common ports on a desktop CPU

1.7 THE SYSTEM BUS

The inside of a computer has many wires, also known as buses, which help the different components of the computer system to communicate with each other. The bus acts as a **common pathway** through which information flows from one component to another (Fig. 1.39). There are three main types of buses in the computer.

Data Bus: The data bus transfers data between the CPU and other devices.

Address Bus: The address bus carries address of data to be transferred. (Note that data is itself transferred using data bus).

Control Bus: The control bus carries the control instructions. It specifies what work has to be performed and by whom. For example, Read or Write operation and whether memory will do it or any input/output device.

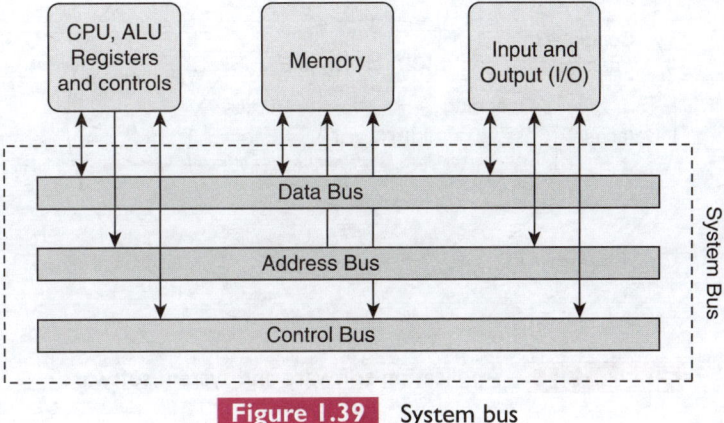

Figure 1.39 System bus

1.8 COMPUTER HARDWARE AND SOFTWARE

The TV sets that we have at home is just a dumb box if it is unable to show any program. Similarly, a computer is just a dumb box if it does not allow users to work with any applications. Thus, the TV and the programs that run on TV are two separate things. Similarly, the computer and the applications that run on computer are distinct from each other. The easiest way to distinguish between them is that one that can be touched (like the TV set and the computer) is the hardware and the other which cannot be touched (like program and applications) is the software.

Hardware: All the physical parts that can be touched are called hardware (refer Fig. 1.40). For example, all input, output and memory devices form the computer hardware.

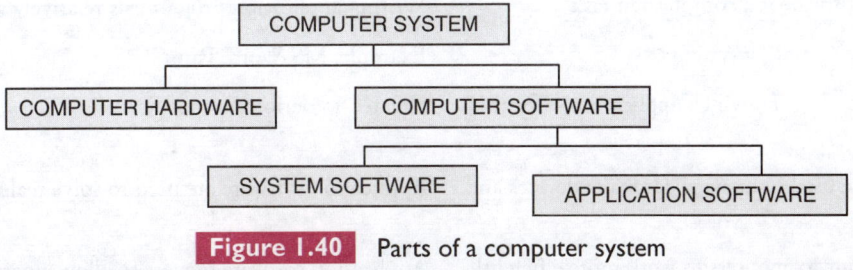

Figure 1.40 Parts of a computer system

Software: It is the computer's hardware part that performs all the work (input, output, storage, processing, etc). But, the hardware works only when the software commands it to work and provides instructions on how to carry out the work.

The computer hardware cannot think and make decisions on its own. So, it needs a software to instruct what has to be done.

> A program is a set of instructions. And a software is a collection of programs that performs a specific task.

Computer software can be broadly classified into two groups: system software and application software.

Application Software: Application software is designed to solve a particular problem for users. Examples of application software include MS Word, MS PowerPoint, MS Excel, games, web browser, etc.

System Software: System software represents programs that enables the hardware to run properly. It acts as an interface between the hardware of the computer and the application software. System software provides an environment in which users can create and/or run their applications. Figure 1.41 illustrates the relationship between application software and system software. Table 1.6 illustrates the difference between application and system software

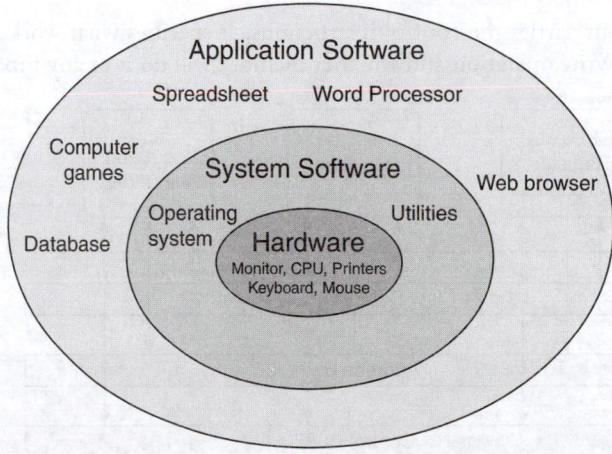

Figure 1.41 Application software and system software

Table 1.6 Difference between application and system software

System Software	Application Software
It is a collection of programs that enables the users to interact with hardware components efficiently	It is a collection of programs written for a specific application.
It controls and manages the hardware	It uses the services provided by the system software to interact with hardware components
System software is machine dependent	It is machine independent
The programmer must understand the architecture of the machine and hardware details to write a system software	The programmer ignores the architecture of the machine and hardware details to write an application software
Writing a system software is a complicated task	Writing application programs is relatively very easy
Example: compiler, operating system	Example: MS-Word, Paint
Created to provide a base on which application software is used	Created to perform a specific task
System software are used to manage hardware devices and other software	Application software are used to solve real world problems
System software allow computers to work more efficiently	Application software focuses to allow a particular task work efficiently
System software directly interacts with the hardware	Application software cannot directly interact with the hardware

1.9 GENERAL-PURPOSE APPLICATION SOFTWARE

While using smartphones, your parents must have used the term app frequently. Basically, an app, or the short form of application, is a type of software that allows you to perform a particular task.

An app or application for desktop or laptop computers is known as desktop application. Correspondingly, an app or application for a smartphone is known as mobile app. When you open an app, it runs using the operating system until you close it.

Some general-purpose application software that we frequently use are given below.

Word Processor: It is the most commonly used software. A word processor is used to type documents, letters, memos, etc. On Windows, MS Word is the most popularly used word processor.

 Presentation Software: A presentation software is used to display information in the form of a slide show. For example, in a PowerPoint slide you can easily insert, edit and format text or images. The slides can be presented one after the other and animation effects can be added while displaying the information. You can also add audio and videos in your slides.

Spreadsheet Software: A spreadsheet is a software that arranges data using rows and columns. It is used to make report cards, record expenses, salaries, balance sheets, etc. On Windows, MS Excel the most popularly used spreadsheet software.

 **Database Software:** It is used to create and manage records. For example, in a school, a database of all the students is created that stores the details about each student such as class, address, phone number, fees submitted, etc. On Windows, MS Access is the most popularly used database software.

Desktop Publishing Software (DTP): It allows users to design books, newspapers, magazines to give them a professional look. These days, Photoshop, GIMP, Corel Draw are popularly used DTP software.

 Entertainment Software: This software allows users to play audio and video files on the computer. Windows Media Player, VLC Media Player, Real Player, are some examples of entertainment software.

Multimedia and Animation Software: This software is used to combine text, pictures and sounds to make an animated video. Example, of such a software is Adobe Flash.

 Communication Software: The communication software allows users to connect their computer to the Internet. Once connected, you can search for information, send emails, chat with your friends, download apps and shop online. Examples of communication software include Google Chrome, Opera, Safari, Internet Explorer, etc.

1.10 CLASSIFICATION OF SOFTWARE

Software can also be categorized based on the cost to acquire (or get) it. The different categories based on this classification are as given below:

Shareware A shareware software is usually distributed on a free or trial basis for few days. After that period, the user has to buy it to use it further.

Liteware It is a type of shareware software with limited functions. This means that in a liteware software, some functionalities can be used only when the full version is purchased (Fig. 1.42).

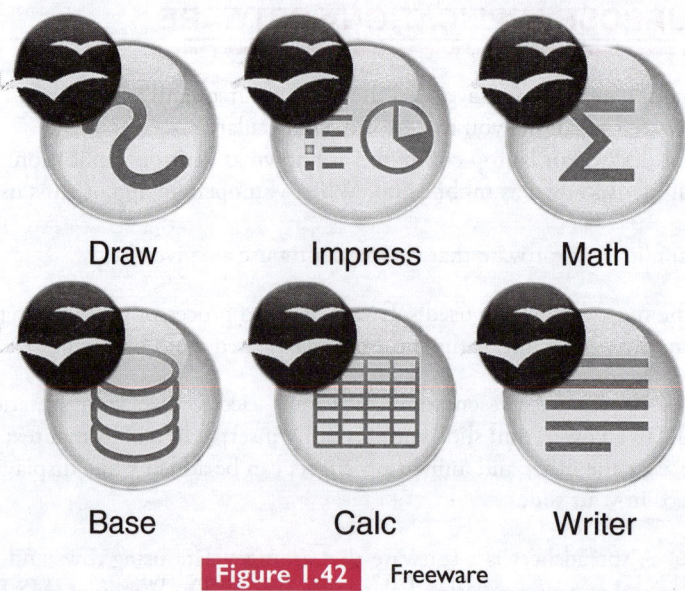

Figure 1.42   Freeware

Freeware A freeware software can be downloaded for free but with some restrictions. Also, users are not allowed to make any changes in the software.

Public Domain Software Public Domain software can be downloaded for free and does not have any without restriction.

Open-source Software A type of software which can be freely downloaded and even distributed to others. Also, its source code (or set of instructions) is also available for free so that anybody in the world can see how the software was created and also make changes in it to improve it further.

Proprietary Software Software that has to be purchased before use. For example, Microsoft Office that includes Microsoft Word, Microsoft Excel, Microsoft PowerPoint, etc is a proprietary software created by Microsoft Company. We have to first pay a fee to use this software (Fig. 1.43).

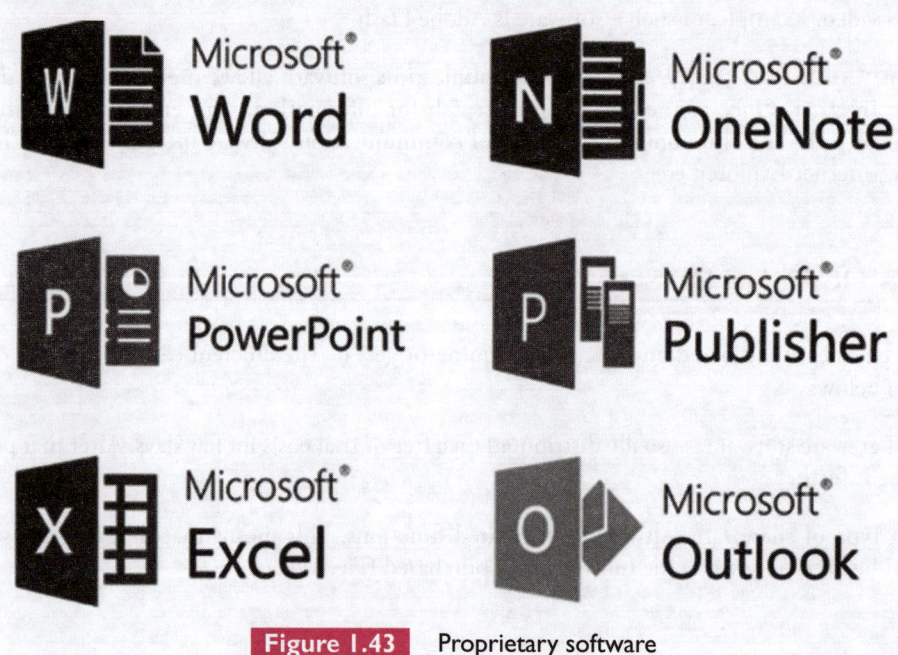

Figure 1.43   Proprietary software

Table 1.7 lists the differences between open source and proprietary software.

Table 1.7 Comparison of open-source and proprietary software

Feature	Open-source Software	Proprietray Software
Ownership	No owner as software is developed and tested through open collaboration.	Software owned by the individual or company that had developed it.
Right to use	Anyone can use the code	Only the individual or the company who has paid a license fee to the owner can use it
Right to modify	Anyone having a good understanding of the code can modify the software	Only the individual or the company who owns the software can modify it
Availability of source code	Yes	No
Maintenance and Support	Community support and Commercial support (if available)	Commercial support
Bug/Error Fixing	Can be done anyone having a good understanding of the code	Can be done only by the company who owns that software
Flexibility	Due to less restrictions more people can join, collaborate and innovate	More restrictions limit the scope of innovation
Example	GIMP, GAMBAS, Open Office, Python	MacOS, MS Office Suite, Java, Adobe Photoshop

1.11 CUSTOMIZED SOFTWARE

Have you ever gone to a tailor? Why do you go to him? The answer is either to get a dress stitched exactly according to your measurements or to get the dress altered to make it fit as per your measurements. So, we can say that we go to a tailor get a customized dress (according to us, the customer). Similarly, we have a customized software, that is, a software that is customized exactly according to the user's needs.

A company opts for a customized software when the pre-written software (already written software) available does not meet its requirements. In such cases, the company can get the customized software made in two ways,

- First, create the customized software *in-house* (if the organization has an IT team)
- Second, *outsource* it to another company.

Continuing with our example, you can customize the dress either by anyone in your family if someone knows stitching; otherwise you can give your dress to a tailor. In the same way, a company can get it done in their own company if they have a team of IT professionals or get it done by another company.

1.12 UTILITY SOFTWARE

Utility software is used to analyze, configure, optimize and maintain the computer system. Utility programs may be requested by application programs during their execution. for multiple purposes. Some of them are listed below.

Disk defragmenters can be used to detect computer files whose contents are broken across several locations on the hard disk, and move the fragments to one location in order to increase efficiency.

Disk checkers scan the contents of a hard disk to find files or areas that are corrupted in some way. This helps the hard drive to operate more efficiently.

Disk cleaners can be used to locate files that are either not required for computer operation, or take up considerable amounts of space. Disk cleaner helps the user to decide what to delete when their hard disk is full.

Disk space analyzers is used for visualizing the disk space usage by getting the size for each folder (including sub folders) and files in folder or drive.

Disk partitions are used to divide an individual drive into multiple logical drives, each with its own file system. Each partition is then treated as an individual drive.

Backup utilities can be used to make a copy of all information stored on a disk. In case a disk failure occurs, backup utilities can be used to restore the entire disk. Even if a file gets deleted accidentally, the backup utility can be used to restore the deleted file.

Disk compression is used to enhance the capacity of the disk by compressing/uncompressing the contents of a disk.

File managers allow users to conveniently perform tasks like deleting, renaming, cataloging, moving, copying, merging, generating and modifying files.

System profilers provides detailed information about the software installed and hardware attached to the computer.

Antivirus utilities are used to scan for computer viruses and other malware (software with malicious intentions).

Data compression utilities are used to reduce the size of a file.

Cryptographic utilities encrypt and decrypt files to prevent unauthorized users from reading them.

Launcher applications can be used as a convenient access point for application software.

Registry cleaners can be used to clean and optimize the Windows registry by deleting the old registry keys that are no longer in use.

Network utilities can be used to analyze the computer's network connectivity, configure network settings, check data transfer or log events.

1.13 MOBILE SYSTEM ORGANIZATION

We all have seen and used smartphones, but do you know that they are small computers with comparatively less memory and computing power. Parts of a mobile system are given in Fig. 1.44.

Computer Systems and Organization

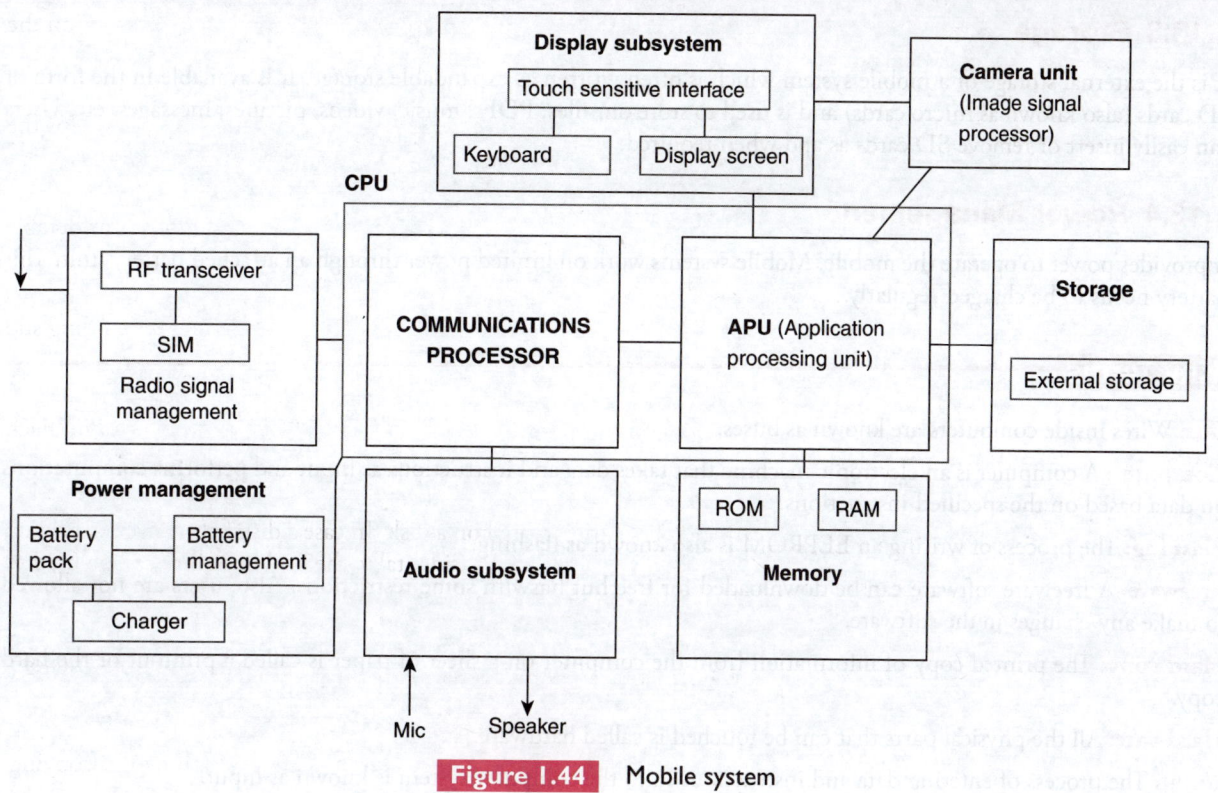

Figure 1.44 Mobile system

1.13.1 Mobile Central Processing Unit

As the name suggests, Mobile CPU is the brain of the computer that performs all processing functions (like calculations, playing audio/video files, controlling all other components, etc). The Mobile CPU has two types of processors – Communications Processing Unit and Applications Processing Unit.

Communications Processing Unit: It is the mobile system's input–output unit that helps to make and receive phone calls. For this, it takes the services from Radio Frequency Transceiver and the mobile's Audio Sub-system (comprising of microphone and speaker). The Radio Frequency Transceiver connects SIM card (that acts as a modem) with the cellular network's base station through radio signals to allow users access 3G, 4G, LTE and 5G services.

Applications Processing Unit: It is used to control the execution of all mobile apps installed in the mobile system.

Display Subsystem: It provides display facilities and touch-sensitive interface for receiving input and displaying output.

Camera Subsystem: It supports improved image processing and video experience.

1.13.2 Mobile System Memory

Like the computer system, the mobile system supports two types of memories – **RAM and ROM**. All the installed apps are first loaded in RAM for execution. More the RAM, higher is the number of applications that can be run simultaneously and faster is the performance of the mobile system.

RAM is a volatile memory, so any data in RAM is lost as soon as the mobile is switched off. However, ROM is that part of mobile's memory that is not accessible for users to write into it. All operating system files and pre-installed apps are stored in ROM. You must have noticed that you never get access to the entire memory as mentioned in phone's details. This is because some of the space is already occupied by system files and other important apps.

1.13.3 Storage

It is the external storage of a mobile system which is often written as expandable storage. It is available in the form of SD cards (also known as micro cards) and is used to store our files, PDFs, music, videos, pictures, messages, etc. Users can easily insert or remove SD cards as and when required.

1.13.4 Power Management

It provides power to operate the mobile. Mobile systems work on limited power through an attached battery unit. This battery needs to be charged regularly.

Key Terms

Bus: Wires inside computers are known as buses.

Computer: A computer is an electronic machine that takes data and instructions as input and performs computations on data based on the specified instructions.

Flashing: The process of writing an EEPROM is also known as flashing.

Freeware: A freeware software can be downloaded for free but haswith some restrictions. Also, users are not allowed to make any changes in the software.

Hard copy: The printed copy of information from the computer on a sheet of paper is called a printout or the hard copy.

Hardware: All the physical parts that can be touched is called hardware.

Input: The process of entering data and instructions in to the computer system is known as input.

Liteware: It is a type of shareware software with limited functions. This means that in a liteware software, some functionalities can be used only when the full version is purchased.

Open source software: A type of software which can be freely downloaded and even distributed to others.

Output: Output is the process of giving the result of data processing to the outside world.

Primary storage: Storage area of the computer which is directly accessible by the CPU at a very fast speed.

Processing: Performing operations on the data as per the instructions specified by the user.

Program: A set of instructions which direct hardware devices what work to perform.

Public domain software: Public domain software can be downloaded for free and does not have any restriction.

Secondary storage: Storage area of the computer which permanently stores user's files.

Shareware: A shareware software is usually distributed on a free or trial basis for few days. After that period, user has to buy it to use it further.

Soft copy: The output seen on the monitor is called soft copy output.

Software: A collection of programs that performs a specific task.

Storage: Storage is the process of saving data, instructions and results of processing permanently in the computer's memory.

Chapter Highlights

- The control unit inside the CPU manages and controls all the components of the computer system.
- In computer, ON means 1 and OFF means 0. Like any other machine, computers understand only these two digits.
- Memory of the computer is divided into a large number of cells where each cell can store one digit – either 0 or 1.

- The cache memory stores those parts of data and instructions that are repeatedly used by the CPU.
- SRAM holds data without an external refresh as long as it is powered. This is in striking contrast with the DRAM which must be refreshed multiple times per second to hold its data contents.
- ROM is that part of the main memory which stores data permanently. Data or instructions, once written in ROM, can never be changed.
- The secondary memory or the external memory is non-volatile memory that stores user's data, instructions and programs permanently. It is slower than the main memory.
- Ports allow most of the computer's external hardware devices to be connected to the computer.
- Application software is designed to solve a particular problem for users.
- System software represents programs that enable the hardware to run properly.
- A company opts for a customized software when the pre-written software available do not meet its requirements.
- Utility software is used to analyze, configure, optimize and maintain the computer system.

Review Questions

1. Define computer and explain its basic organization.
2. Differentiate between primary and secondary storage.
3. Explain the different parts of CPU.
4. Write a short note input devices.
5. Briefly explain any three output devices.
6. Differentiate between CRT and LCD.
7. Explain the different types of computer's memory.
8. Differentiate between SRAM and DRAM.
9. What are the different types of ROM?
10. Differentiate between RAM and ROM.
11. Write a short note on secondary storage devices of the computer.
12. Compare different optical discs.
13. Define ports and explain any three of them.
14. Define buses. What are the three type of buses?
15. Differentiate between computer hardware and software.
16. Differentiate between system software and application software.
17. Differentiate between proprietary and open source software.
18. Write a short note on utility software.
19. In what two ways can software be customized?
20. With the help of a diagram, explain the organization of a mobile system.

Fill in the Blanks

1. _____ storage area of the computer is directly accessible by the CPU at a very fast speed.
2. Data is processed based on _____ given.
3. Data processing is done by _____ of the _____.

4. _____ decides the order in which the instructions will be executed and the operations that will be performed by the ALU.
5. _____ is used instead of a mouse on the laptop computers.
6. The output seen on the monitor is called _____.
7. Speed of a printer is measured in _____.
8. Memory of the computer is divided into a large number of _____.
9. _____ is a type of primary memory that stores data permanently.
10. Optical storage discs use _____ to store data.
11. To transfer files to a computer, memory card reader is connected to the _____ port of the computer.
12. External hardware devices are connected to a computer using _____.
13. _____ bus transfers data between the CPU and other devices.
14. A _____ software that arranges data using rows and columns.
15. A _____ software is usually distributed on a free or trial basis for few days.
16. A company opts for a _____ software when the pre-written software (already written software) available do not meet its requirements.
17. _____ scan the contents of a hard disk to find files or areas that are corrupted in some way.
18. _____ provides detailed information about the software installed and hardware attached to the computer.
19. _____ is the brain of the computer that performs all processing.
20. The _____ connects SIM card with cellular network's base station.

State True or False

1. The process of entering data and instructions in to the computer system is known as output.
2. RAM is an example of secondary memory.
3. Touch screen is an input as well as output device.
4. ON means 0 and OFF means 1.
5. SRAM must be refreshed multiple times in a second to hold its data contents.
6. PROM can be erased by exposing the chip to strong ultraviolet light typically for 10 minutes or longer.
7. CPU cannot directly access the secondary memory.
8. A single sided CD can hold up to 25 GB of data.
9. Latest pen drives can store more data than a BD.
10. Serial ports are faster than parallel ports.
11. The infrared port allows devices to exchange data through cables.
12. In liteware software, some functionalities can be used only when the full version is purchased.
13. Disk defragmenters are used to detect computer files whose contents are broken across several locations on the hard disk, and move the fragments to one location in order to increase efficiency.
14. Data compression utilities are used to increase the size of a file.
15. Disk partitions are used to make a single drive in the hard disk.
16. Communication Processing Unit is used to control the execution of all mobile apps installed in the mobile system.
17. SD cards are used as Read Only Memory in mobile systems.

Multiple Choice Questions

1. A computer takes _____ as input.
   a. data b. instructions c. Both of these. d. None of these.
2. Storage involves storing _____ .
   a. data b. instructions c. results of processing d. All of these.
3. Which of the following is not a feature of main memory?
   a. Limited b. Expensive c. Volatile d. Slow
4. Monitor, printer, speakers and headphone are examples of _____ devices.
   a. Input b. Output c. Processing d. Memory
5. Which of the following devices can be used to hear sound from the computer?
   a. Speaker b. headphone c. headset d. All of these.
6. 1024 MB = 1 ____.
   a. KB b. TB c. GB d. ZB
7. Which type of memory is used to store those parts of data and instructions that are being repeatedly used by the CPU?
   a. Main memory b. Cache memory c. Secondary memory d. All of these
8. Which of the following is used for cache memory?
   a. SRAM b. DRAM c. PROM d. EEPROM
9. Instructions which are necessary to start the computer and load the operating system are stored in _____.
   a. RAM b. ROM c. Cache memory d. Secondary memory
10. The fastest of the given memories is _____.
    a. Cache b. RAM c. ROM d. Hard Disk
11. Which of the following memory has the highest storage capacity?
    a. Cache b. RAM c. ROM d. Hard Disk
12. Instructions to read or write data are carried by _____ bus.
    a. data b. address c. control d. All of these.
13. MS Access is an example of _____ software.
    a. Word Processor b. Spreadsheet c. Database d. DTP
14. _____ is a software which can be freely downloaded and even distributed to others.
    a. Open Source Software b. Liteware
    c. Shareware d. Freeware
15. Which software is used to analyze, configure, optimize and maintain the computer system?
    a. Application b. Open Source c. Utility d. Shareware
16. Which utility software is used to locate files that are either not required for computer operation, or take up considerable amounts of space?
    a. Disk cleaner b. Disk checker c. Disk space analyser d. Backup
17. Cryptographic utilities are used to _____ files to prevent unauthorized users?
    a. encrypt b. decrypt c. Both of these. d. None of these.

Answers

Fill in the Blanks
1. Primary
2. instructions
3. ALU, CPU
4. Control unit
5. Touchpad
6. soft copy output
7. Pages Per Minute (PPM)
8. cells
9. ROM

10. light
11. USB
12. ports
13. Data
14. spreadsheet
15. shareware
16. customized
17. Disk checkers
18. System profilers
19. Mobile CPU
20. Radio Frequency Transceiver

State True or False
1. False
2. False
3. True
4. False
5. False
6. False
7. True
8. False
9. True
10. False
11. False
12. True
13. True
14. False
15. False
16. False
17. False

Multiple Choice Questions
1. c
2. d
3. d
4. b
5. d
6. c
7. b
8. a
9. b
10. a
11. d
12. c
13. b
14. a
15. c
16. a
17. c

Information Representation

2

Chapter Objectives

In this chapter, we shall study the representation of data in computer's memory using the language of 0s and 1s. It elaborates on the following concepts:

- Machine language
- Binary number system
- Octal number system
- Hexadecimal number system
- Conversions from one number system to another
- Storing negative values and fractional numbers
- Addition, subtraction, multiplication and division of binary values

Just as human beings need language to communicate, computers also need a language to communicate with users and other components attached to it. While we can understand multiple languages, computers just understand one language – the binary language which is also known as machine language.

2.1 THE BINARY LANGUAGE

Our language consists of many symbols. For example, the English language has 26 alphabets and Hindi has a different set of characters. However, the binary language has only two symbols – 0 or 1. Since binary means two, the machine language is better known as the binary language.

In binary language, a single digit is called a *bit*, a group of 8 bits is known as *byte*, 1024 bytes form 1 *kilobyte*, so on and so forth (Fig. 2.1).

Why the Computer Understands Only Binary Language
The computer is an electronic machine. Like all machines, it understands just two states – ON or OFF. Therefore, computers use these two states to read and write data. A switch ON is represented by 1 and switch OFF corresponds to 0.

Every data, be it text, audio, video or image is represented using a long string of 1s and 0s.

Advantages of Machine Language
- Programs written in machine language are directly understood and executed by the computers. Hence, no translation is required.
- Program execution is fast and efficient.

Disadvantages of Machine Language
- For each type of CPU, a different machine language is required. Hence, machine language programs are machine dependent.
- This is the hardest of all computer languages.
- Writing, understanding and modifying programs written in machine language is very complex and time consuming.
- There is high possibility of making errors (Fig. 2.2) while writing machine language programs.
- Only scientists and researchers are able to write programs using machine language.

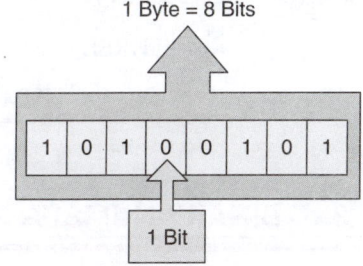

1 byte	= 8 bits
1 kilobyte	= 1024 bytes
1 megabyte	= 1024 kilobyte
1 gigabyte	= 1024 megabyte
1 terabyte	= 1024 gigabyte

Figure 2.1 Computer memory units

Figure 2.2 Machine language is error-prone

- Locating and correcting errors is difficult in machine language programs.
- The whole process of writing and updating codes in machine language is very time consuming as it requires a lot of calculations to write just a single instruction.

2.2 DECIMAL NUMBER SYSTEM

In Mathematics, we follow the decimal number system. But computers follow a different number system which is known as the Binary Number System. However, before going into this new number system, let us first revise our concepts of the decimal number system (Table 2.1).

> All number systems have digits starting from 0 to $n-1$ where n is the base of the number system.

The decimal number system has base 10.

- It has digits 0–9.
- It is a positional number system where each digit is a power of 10 (the base). For example, if we have the number 123, then we read this number as One Hundred Twenty Three. The number is formed by the following calculations.

Table 2.1 Decimal number system

Position	Positional Value	Digit	Place Value
ONE	$10^0 = 1$	3	$1 \times 3 = 3$
TWO	$10^1 = 10$	2	$10 \times 2 = 20$
THREE	$10^2 = 10 \times 10 = 100$	1	$100 \times 1 = 100$
NUMBER FORMED BY DIGITS =			$100 + 20 + 3 = 123$

2.3 BINARY NUMBER SYSTEM

The *binary number system* is a Base-2 number system that follows the same set of rules that are followed by the decimal number system. It has digits 0 and 1 since here $n = 2$ and every number system has digits from 0 to n – 1, i.e., 0 – 1.

Every bit (or **B**inary Dig**it**) is specified using powers of two. When we write a binary number, each binary digit is multiplied by an appropriate power of 2 which is based on the position in the number. This means that each binary digit has a positional value just the double of its previous bit as $2^0 = 1$, $2^1 = 2$, $2^2 = 4$, $2^3 = 8$, $2^4 = 16$, $2^5 = 32$, so on and so forth (exactly the double of the previous value). If we have a binary value 011, then its decimal equivalent value can be given as shown in Table 2.2.

> Any number raised to the power 0 is equal to 1.

Table 2.2 Binary number system

Position	Positional Value	Digit	Place Value
ONE	$2^0 = 1$	1	$1 \times 1 = 1$
TWO	$2^1 = 2$	1	$2 \times 1 = 2$
THREE	$2^2 = 2 \times 2 = 4$	0	$4 \times 0 = 0$
NUMBER FORMED BY DIGITS =			$1 + 2 + 0 = 3$

2.3.1 Converting Binary Number into Decimal

To convert a binary number into decimal, multiply the value of each digit (i.e., 1 or 0) by its positional value in the number. Then, add the results together.

Example 2.1 Convert the following binary numbers into their decimal equivalent.

a. $(110)_2$ b. $(1101)_2$ c. $(11001)_2$ d. $(101010)_2$ e. $(1011011)_2$

a. $(110)_2$
$= 1 \times 2^2 + 1 \times 2^1 + 0 \times 2^0$
$= 1 \times 4 + 1 \times 2 + 0 \times 1$
$= 4 + 2 + 0$
$= 6$

b. $(1101)_2$
$= 1 \times 2^3 + 1 \times 2^2 + 0 \times 2^1 + 1 \times 2^0$
$= 1 \times 8 + 1 \times 4 + 0 \times 2 + 1 \times 1$
$= 8 + 4 + 0 + 1$
$= 13$

c. $(11001)_2$
$= 1 \times 2^4 + 1 \times 2^3 + 0 \times 2^2 + 0 \times 2^1 + 1 \times 2^0$
$= 1 \times 16 + 1 \times 8 + 0 \times 4 + 0 \times 2 + 1 \times 1$
$= 16 + 8 + 0 + 0 + 1$
$= 25$

d. $(101010)_2$
$= 1 \times 2^5 + 0 \times 2^4 + 1 \times 2^3 + 0 \times 2^2 + 1 \times 2^1 + 0 \times 2^0$
$= 1 \times 32 + 0 \times 16 + 1 \times 8 + 0 \times 4 + 1 \times 2 + 0 \times 1$
$= 32 + 0 + 8 + 0 + 2 + 0$
$= 42$

e. $(1011011)_2$
$= 1 \times 2^6 + 0 \times 2^5 + 1 \times 2^4 + 1 \times 2^3 + 0 \times 2^2 + 1 \times 2^1 + 1 \times 2^0$
$= 1 \times 64 + 0 \times 32 + 1 \times 16 + 1 \times 8 + 0 \times 4 + 1 \times 2 + 1 \times 1$
$= 64 + 0 + 16 + 8 + 0 + 2 + 1$
$= 91$

2.3.2 Converting Decimal Number to Binary

To convert a decimal number into binary, keep dividing the number by 2 until the quotient becomes zero and keep a record of remainders obtained at each step. When the quotient becomes zero, write all the remainders in the reverse order (staring from the last remainder to the first). For example, to convert decimal number 42 into binary, we repeatedly divide the number by 2 and write the remainders obtained.

Start writing remainders from the bottom so that the last remainder obtained is written first. Therefore, $(42)_{10} = (101010)_2$

2	42	R
2	21	0
2	10	1
2	5	0
2	2	1
2	1	0
	0	1

Example 2.2 Convert the following decimal numbers into their binary equivalent.

a. $(8)_{10}$ b. $(13)_{10}$ c. $(27)_{10}$ d. $(45)_{10}$ e. $(81)_{10}$

$(8)_{10}$

2	8	R
2	4	0
2	2	0
	1	0
	0	1

$(8)_{10} = (1000)_2$

$(13)_{10}$

2	13	R
2	6	1
2	3	0
2	1	1
	0	1

$(13)_{10} = (1101)_2$

$(27)_{10}$

2	27	R
2	13	1
2	6	1
2	3	0
2	1	1
	0	1

$(27)_{10} = (11011)_2$

$(45)_{10}$

2	45	R
2	22	1
2	11	0
2	5	1
2	2	1
2	1	0
	0	1

$(45)_{10} = (101101)_2$

$(81)_{10}$

2	81	R
2	40	1
2	40	1
2	20	0
2	10	0
2	5	0
2	2	1
2	1	0
	0	1

$(81)_{10} = (1010001)_2$

2.4 OCTAL NUMBER SYSTEM

The *octal number system* is a Base-8 number system that follows the same set of rules that are followed by the decimal and binary number systems. It has digits 0 to 7, since here the base, $n = 8$ and every number system has digits from 0 to $n - 1$, i.e., $0 - 7$.

Every octal digit is specified using powers of eight. When we write an octal number, each octal digit is multiplied by an appropriate power of 8 which is based on the position in the number. This means that each octal digit has a positional value eight times its previous digit. Hence, the positional value of each digit in an octal number can be given as $8^0 = 1$, $8^1 = 8$, $8^2 = 64$, $8^3 = 512$, $8^4 = 4096$, and so forth. If we have an octal number 361, then its decimal equivalent value can be given as shown in Table 2.3.

Table 2.3 Octal number system

Position	Positional Value	Digit	Place Value
ONE	$8^0 = 1$	1	$1 \times 1 = 1$
TWO	$8^1 = 8$	6	$8 \times 6 = 48$
THREE	$8^2 = 8 \times 8 = 64$	3	$64 \times 3 = 192$
NUMBER FORMED BY DIGITS =			$1 + 48 + 192 = 241$

2.4.1 Converting Octal Number into Decimal

To convert an octal number into decimal, multiply the value of each digit by its positional value in the number. Then, add the results together.

Example 2.3 Convert the following octal numbers into decimal equivalent.

a. $(125)_8$ b. $(1023)_8$ c. $(11001)_8$ d. $(101010)_8$ e. $(11234)_8$

a. $(125)_8$
$= 1 \times 8^2 + 2 \times 8^1 + 5 \times 8^0$
$= 1 \times 64 + 1 \times 8 + 0 \times 1$
$= 64 + 8 + 0$
$= 72$

b. $(1023)_8$
$= 1 \times 8^3 + 0 \times 8^2 + 2 \times 8^1 + 3 \times 8^0$
$= 1 \times 512 + 0 \times 64 + 2 \times 8 + 3 \times 1$
$= 512 + 0 + 16 + 3$
$= 531$

c. $(11001)_8$
$= 1 \times 2^4 + 1 \times 2^3 + 0 \times 2^2 + 0 \times 2^1 + 1 \times 2^0$
$= 1 \times 16 + 1 \times 8 + 0 \times 4 + 0 \times 2 + 1 \times 1$
$= 16 + 8 + 0 + 0 + 1$
$= 25$

d. $(101010)_8$
$= 1 \times 8^5 + 0 \times 8^4 + 1 \times 8^3 + 0 \times 8^2 + 1 \times 8^1 + 0 \times 8^0$
$= 1 \times 32768 + 0 \times 4096 + 1 \times 512 + 0 \times 64 + 1 \times 8 + 0 \times 1$
$= 32768 + 0 + 512 + 0 + 8 + 0$
$= 33288$

e. $(11234)_8$
$= 1 \times 8^4 + 1 \times 8^3 + 2 \times 8^2 + 3 \times 8^1 + 4 \times 8^0$
$= 1 \times 4096 + 1 \times 512 + 2 \times 64 + 3 \times 8 + 4 \times 1$
$= 4096 + 512 + 128 + 24 + 4$
$= 4764$

2.4.2 Converting Decimal Number to Octal

To convert a decimal number into octal, keep dividing the number by 8 until the quotient becomes zero and keep a record of remainders obtained at each step. When the quotient becomes zero, write all the remainders in the reverse order (staring from the last remainder to the first). For example, to convert decimal number 420 into octal, we repeatedly divide the number by 8 and write the remainders obtained.

8	420	R
8	52	4
8	6	4
	0	6

$(420)_{10} = (644)_8$

Example 2.4 Convert the following decimal numbers into octal equivalent.

a. $(71)_{10}$ b. $(136)_{10}$ c. $(275)_{10}$ d. $(1234)_{10}$ e. $(11111)_{10}$

$(71)_{10}$ 　　　$(136)_{10}$ 　　　$(27)_{10}$ 　　　$(45)_{10}$ 　　　$(81)_{10}$

8	71	R
8	8	7
8	1	0
	0	1

8	136	R
8	17	0
8	2	1
	0	2

8	275	R
8	34	3
8	4	2
8	0	4

8	1234	R
8	154	1
8	19	0
8	2	1
8	0	1

8	11111	R
8	1388	7
8	173	4
8	21	5
8	2	5
8	0	2

$(71)_{10} = (107)_8$　　$(136)_{10} = (210)_8$　　$(275)_{10} = (423)_8$

$(1234)_{10} = (2322)_8$

$(11111)_{10} = (25547)_8$

2.4.3 Converting an Octal Number into Binary Equivalent

To convert an octal number into its binary equivalent, replace each octal digit with its binary equivalent. The binary and octal values for decimal numbers 0 to 7 are given in Table 2.4.

Table 2.4 Binary and octal equivalent of Digits 0–7

Dec	0	1	2	3	4	5	6	7
Bin	000	001	010	011	100	101	110	111
Oct	0	1	2	3	4	5	6	7

For example, $(54)_8$ can be converted into its binary equivalent using the following steps:

Step 1: Write the binary equivalent of 5, which is equal to 101.
Step 2: Write the binary equivalent of 4, which is equal to 100.
Step 3: Merge the two values. Therefore, $(54)_8 = (101100)_2$.

Let us take another example and convert $(263)_8$ into its binary form.

Step 1: Write the binary equivalent of 2, which is equal to 010.
Step 2: Write the binary equivalent of 6, which is equal to 110.
Step 3: Write the binary equivalent of 3, which is equal to 011.
Step 4: Merge the values. Therefore, $(263)_8 = (010110011)_2$.

2.4.4 Converting a Binary Number into Octal Form

To convert a binary number into its octal equivalent, divide the binary number into groups of bits, where each group consists of exactly 3 bits (except the last bit or the most significant bit (MSB)). Convert each group into its equivalent octal number. Combine these individual octal numbers to get the final result.

For example, the steps to convert $(101100)_2$ into octal form are as follows:

Step 1: Divide the number into groups of 3 bits each, starting from the Least Significant Bit or LSB (from one's place). Therefore, 101 100

Step 2: Convert each group of binary bits into its equivalent octal number. Thus, we have 5 4.

Step 3: Merge the octal values to get the final result. Hence, $(101100)_2 = (54)_8$.

Let us take another example and convert $(11010101)_2$ into its octal equivalent.

Step 1: Divide the number into groups of 3 bits each. Therefore, 11 010 101 or 011 010 101. If the number of bits is not a multiple of 3 then add 0s to the left.
Step 2: Convert each group of binary bits into its equivalent octal number. Thus, we have 3 2 5.
Step 3: Merge the octal values to get the final result. Hence, $(11010101)_2 = (325)_8$.

2.5 HEXADECIMAL NUMBER SYSTEM

The *hexadecimal number system* is a Base-16 number system that follows the same set of rules that are followed by the decimal, binary and octal number system. It has digits 0 to 9 and characters from A – F or a – f to represent values from 10 – 15. Since here the base, $n = 16$ and every number system has digits from 0 to n – 1; there are 15 different symbols: 0 – 9 and A – F.

Every hexadecimal digit is specified using powers of sixteen. When we write a hexadecimal number, each hexadecimal digit is multiplied by an appropriate power of 16 which is based on the position in the number. This means that each hexadecimal digit has a positional value that is sixteen times its previous digit. Hence, the positional value of each digit in a hexadecimal number can be given as $16^0 = 1$, $16^1 = 16$, $16^2 = 256$, $16^3 = 4096$, $16^4 = 65536$, and so on. If we have a hexadecimal number 219, then its decimal equivalent value can be given as shown in Table 2.5.

Table 2.5 Hexadecimal number system

Position	Positional Value	Digit	Place Value
ONE	$16^0 = 1$	9	$1 \times 9 = 9$
TWO	$16^1 = 16$	1	$16 \times 1 = 16$
THREE	$16^2 = 16 \times 16 = 256$	2	$256 \times 2 = 512$
NUMBER FORMED BY DIGITS =			$9 + 16 + 512 = 537$

2.5.1 Converting Hexadecimal Number into Decimal

To convert a hexadecimal number into decimal, multiply the value of each digit by its positional value in the number. Then, add the results together.

Example 2.5 Convert the following octal numbers into decimal equivalent.

a. $(25)_{16}$ b. $(123)_{16}$ c. $(10AD)_{16}$ d. $(201F3)_{16}$ e. $(ABCD)_{16}$

a. $(25)_{16}$
= $2 \times 16^1 + 5 \times 16^0$
= $2 \times 16 + 5 \times 1$
= $32 + 5$
= 37

b. $(123)_{16}$
= $1 \times 16^2 + 2 \times 16^1 + 3 \times 16^0$
= $1 \times 256 + 2 \times 16 + 3 \times 1$
= $256 + 32 + 3$
= 291

c. $(10AD)_{16}$
= $1 \times 16^3 + 0 \times 16^2 + A \times 16^1 + D \times 16^0$
= $1 \times 4096 + 0 \times 256 + 10 \times 16 + 13 \times 1$
         (because, A = 10 and D = 13)
= $4096 + 0 + 160 + 13$
= 4269

d. $(201F3)_{16}$
= $2 \times 16^4 + 0 \times 16^3 + 1 \times 16^2 + F \times 16^1 + 3 \times 16^0$
= $2 \times 65536 + 0 \times 4096 + 1 \times 256 + 15 \times 16 + 3 \times 1$ (because F = 15)
= $131072 + 0 + 256 + 240 + 3$
= 131571

e. $(ABCD)_{16}$
= $A \times 16^3 + B \times 16^2 + C \times 16^1 + D \times 16^0$
= $10 \times 4096 + 11 \times 256 + 12 \times 16 + 13 \times 1$
         (because, A = 10, B = 11, C = 12, D = 13)
= $40960 + 2816 + 192 + 13$
= 43981

2.5.2 Converting Decimal Number into Hexadecimal

To convert a decimal number into hexadecimal, keep dividing the number by 16 until the quotient becomes zero and keep a record of remainders obtained at each step. When the quotient becomes zero, write all the remainders in the reverse order (staring from the last remainder to the first). For example, to convert decimal number 872 into hexadecimal, we repeatedly divide the number by 16 and write the remainders obtained.

16	872	R
16	54	8
16	3	6
	0	3

Example 2.6 Convert the following decimal numbers into hexadecimal equivalent.

a. $(65)_{10}$ b. $(652)_{10}$ c. $(1234)_{10}$ d. $(987)_{10}$ e. $(10945)_{10}$

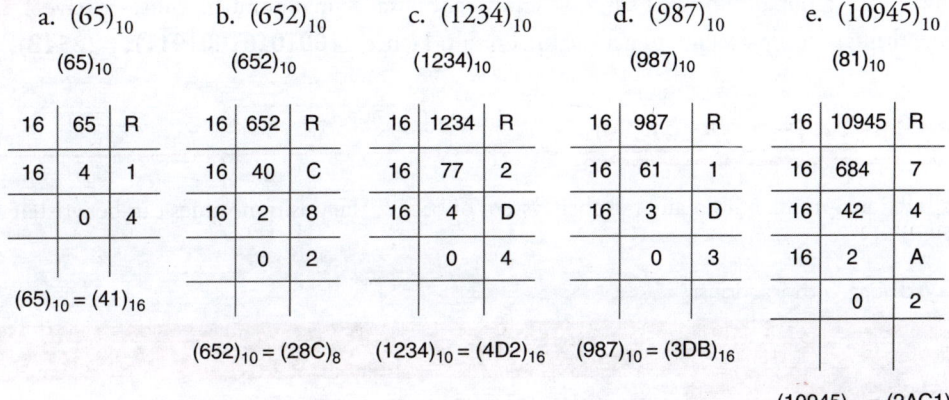

$(65)_{10} = (41)_{16}$

$(652)_{10} = (28C)_8$

$(1234)_{10} = (4D2)_{16}$

$(987)_{10} = (3DB)_{16}$

$(10945)_{10} = (2AC1)_{16}$

2.5.3 Converting a Hexadecimal Number into Binary Equivalent

To convert a hexadecimal number into its binary equivalent, replace each hexadecimal digit with its binary equivalent using Table 2.6.

Table 2.6 Binary and hexadecimal equivalent of decimal numbers 0–15

Dec	0	1	2	3	4	5	6	7	8	9	10	11	12	13	14	15
Bin	0000	0001	0010	0011	0100	0101	0110	0111	1000	1001	1010	1011	1100	1101	1110	1111
Hex	0	1	2	3	4	5	6	7	8	9	A	B	C	D	E	F

For example, $(5A4)_{16}$ can be converted into its binary equivalent using the following steps:

Step 1: Write the binary equivalent of 5, which is equal to 0101.
Step 2: Write the binary equivalent of A, which is equal to 1010.
Step 3: Write the binary equivalent of 4, which is equal to 0100.
Step 4: Merge the two values. Therefore, $(5A4)_{16} = (010110100100)_2$.

Let us take another example and convert $(2D3F)_{16}$ into its binary form.

Step 1: Write the binary equivalent of 2, which is equal to 0010.
Step 2: Write the binary equivalent of D, which is equal to 1101.
Step 3: Write the binary equivalent of 3, which is equal to 0011.
Step 4: Write the binary equivalent of F, which is equal to 1111.
Step 5: Merge the values. Therefore, $(2D3F)_{16} = (0010110100111111)_2$.

2.5.4 Converting a Binary Number into Hexadecimal

To convert a binary number into its hexadecimal equivalent, divide the binary number into groups of bits, where each group consists of exactly 4 bits (except the last). Convert each group into its equivalent hexadecimal number. Combine these individual hexadecimal numbers to get the final result.

For example, the steps to convert $(10101001)_2$ into hexadecimal form are as follows:

Step 1: Divide the number into groups of 4 bits each, starting from the LSB (from one's place). Therefore, 1010 1001
Step 2: Convert each group of binary bits into its equivalent hexadecimal number. Thus, we have A 9.
Step 3: Merge the hexadecimal values to get the final result. Hence, $(10101001)_2 = (A9)_{16}$.

Let us take another example and convert $(10010101001011)_2$ into its hexadecimal equivalent.

Step 1: Divide the number into groups of 4 bits each. Therefore, 0010 0101 0100 1011. If the number of bits is not a multiple of 4, then add 0s to the right.

Step 2: Convert each group of binary bits into its equivalent hexadecimal number. Thus, we have 2 5 4 B.

Step 3: Merge the hexadecimal values to get the final result. Hence, $(10010101001011)_2 = (254B)_{16}$.

2.6 WORKING WITH FRACTIONS

Generally, for a fractional number a, in any number system of base b, the position values can be written as illustrated in Table 2.7.

Table 2.7 Working with fractions

Position	5	4	3	2	1	0	.	-1	-2	-3	-4	-5
Position value in decimal	10^5	10^4	10^3	10^2	10^1	10^0		10^{-1}	10^{-2}	10^{-3}	10^{-4}	10^{-5}
Position value in binary	2^5	2^4	2^3	2^2	2^1	2^0		2^{-1}	2^{-2}	2^{-3}	2^{-4}	2^{-5}
Position value in octal	8^5	8^4	8^3	8^2	8^1	8^0		8^{-1}	8^{-2}	8^{-3}	8^{-4}	8^{-5}
Position value in hexadecimal	16^5	16^4	16^3	16^2	16^1	16^0		16^{-1}	16^{-2}	16^{-3}	16^{-4}	16^{-5}

1. **Convert $(11010.1010)_2$ into decimal:**

   $(11010.1010)_2 = 1 \times 2^4 + 1 \times 2^3 + 0 \times 2^2 + 1 \times 2^1 + 0 \times 2^0 + 1 \times 2^{-1} + 0 \times 2^{-2} + 1 \times 2^{-3} + 0 \times 2^{-4}$
   $= 1 \times 16 + 1 \times 8 + 0 \times 4 + 1 \times 2 + 0 \times 1 + 1 \times 1/2 + 0 \times 1/4 + 1 \times 1/8 + 0 \times 1/16$
   $= 16 + 8 + 0 + 2 + 0 + 0.5 + 0 + 0.125 + 0$
   $= 26.625$

2. **Convert $(123.45)_8$ into decimal:**

   $(123.45)_8 = 1 \times 8^2 + 2 \times 8^1 + 7 \times 8^0 + 3 \times 8^{-1} + 5 \times 8^{-2}$
   $= 1 \times 64 + 2 \times 8 + 3 \times 1 + 4 \times 1/8 + 5 \times 1/64$
   $= 64 + 16 + 3 + 0.5 + 0.078125$
   $= 83.578125$

3. **Convert $(789.AB)_{16}$ into decimal:**

   $(789.AB)_{16} = 7 \times 16^2 + 8 \times 16^1 + 9 \times 16^0 + A \times 16^{-1} + B \times 16^{-2}$
   $= 7 \times 256 + 8 \times 16 + 9 \times 1 + A \times 1/16 + B \times 1/256$
   $= 1792 + 128 + 9 + 0.625 + 0.04296875$
   $= 1929.66796875$

We will now discuss the procedure to **convert a fractional binary/octal/hexadecimal number into its decimal equivalent.** For this, break the number into two parts. The first part consists of digits before the decimal point, and the second part contains digits after the point. A separate procedure is applied to convert these individual parts of the decimal number into binary. While the whole number part (before the decimal) is converted using repeated division by 2, 8 or 16 and considering the remainders, the fractional part, on the other hand, is converted by repeated multiplication with 2, 8 or 16 and considering only the whole number part of the result. (Only digits after decimal point are multiplied each time with 2, 8 or 16 depending on the target number system).

Information Representation

$(123)_{10}$

2	123	R
2	61	1
2	30	1
2	15	0
2	7	1
2	3	1
2	1	1
2	0	1

$(123)_{10} = (1111011)_2$

$(0.25)_{10}$

0.25
× 2
―――
0.50
× 2
―――
1.00
× 2
―――
0.00

$(0.25)_{10} = (010)_2$

Note the digit before the decimal point obtained from the first multiplication to the last.

$(123.25)_{10} = (1111011.010)_2$

$(365)_{10}$

8	365	R
8	45	5
8	5	5
8	0	5

$(365)_{10} = (555)_8$

$(0.98)_{10}$

0.98
× 8
―――
7.84
× 8
―――
6.72
× 8
―――
5.76

$(0.25)_{10} = (765)_8$

Note the digit before the decimal point obtained from the first multiplication to the last.

$(365.98)_{10} = (555.765)_8$

$(1234)_{10}$

16	1234	R
16	77	2
16	4	D
16	0	4

$(365)_{10} = (555)_8$

$(0.567)_{10}$

0.567
× 16
―――
9.072
× 16
―――
8.52
× 8
―――
8.32

$(0.567)_{10} = (9B8)_8$

Note the digit before the decimal point obtained from the first multiplication to the last.

$(1234.567)_{10} = (4D2.9B8)_{16}$

2.7 SIGNED NUMBER REPRESENTATION IN BINARY FORM

Signed number representation is required to represent negative numbers in the binary number system. We usually represent negative numbers by preceding it with a – sign (minus sign). But in binary language, there are only two symbols: 0 and 1. Hence, we need a different technique to encode the minus sign in terms of 0s and 1s. The three widely used ways of writing negative numbers in binary format are:

Sign-and-magnitude
It is the simplest technique in which the most significant bit (MSB) or the rightmost bit (having highest positional value) is set to 0 for a positive number, and set to 1 for a negative number. The other bits denote the value of the number.

38 Computer Science with Python for CBSE Class XI

Hence, a byte having eight bits can use only seven bits to specify its value and one bit is used to denote the sign of the number. Using 7 bits, 2^7 numbers that is from –127 to +127 can be represented. Table 2.8 illustrates how signed numbers are represented using sign-and-magnitude method.

Table 2.8 Representing signed numbers

Decimal	8th bit or Sign bit	7th bit	6th bit	5th bit	4th bit	3rd bit	2nd bit	1st bit
+18	0	0	0	1	0	0	1	0
–72	1	1	0	0	1	0	0	0
+54	0	0	1	1	0	1	1	0
–108	1	1	1	0	1	1	0	0

One's Complement

The one's complement representation of a negative number is obtained by performing the following steps:

Step 1: Write the binary representation of the number's positive part.

Step 2: Invert each bit in the binary representation of the positive number (obtained in Step 1). Inverting means writing a 1 when it is 0 and vice versa.

Example 2.7 Represent –39 and –61 using one's complement form.

– 39

Step 1: The binary representation of + 39 = 0010 0111
Step 2: Invert each bit. So, 0010 0111 becomes 1101 1000.
Hence, –39 in binary form using one's complement is **1101 1000**.

– 61

Step 1: The binary representation of + 61 = 0011 1101
Step 2: Invert each bit. So, 0011 1101 becomes 1100 0010.
Hence, –61 in binary form using one's complement is **1100 0010**.

Two's Complement

In one's complement method, +0 is represented as 00000000 and –0 is represented as 11111111. In sign-and-magnitude method, –0 is represented as 10000000. These different representations sometimes become problematic. Therefore, to avoid such a situation, the two's complement representation is generally used. This representation is obtained in the following two steps:

Step 1: Write the binary representation of the number's positive counterpart.

Step 2: Invert each bit in the binary representation of the positive number (obtained in Step 1). Inverting means writing a 1 when it is 0 and vice versa.

Step 3: Add 1 to the result obtained in Step 2:

Example 2.8 Represent –86 and –100 using two's complement form.

– 86

Step 1: The binary representation of + 86 = 0101 0110
Step 2: Invert each bit. So, 0101 0110 becomes 1010 1001.
Step 3: Add 1 to the result obtained in Step 2. So, we get 1010 1010.
Hence, –86 in binary form using one's complement is **1010 1010**.

−100

Step 1: The binary representation of + 100 = 0110 0100.
Step 2: Invert each bit. So, 0110 0100 becomes 1001 1011.
Step 3: Add 1 to the result obtained in Step 2. So, we get 1001 1100.
Hence, −100 in binary form using one's complement is **1001 1100**.

The main advantage of using two's complement is that there is only one zero (0000 0000). For example, when converting −0 in two's complement form, complementing the bits gives 11111111 and adding 1 gives 0000 0000 and a carry bit of 1. When we add numbers in two's complement, we discard the carry from the last bit. Hence, the result is only 0000 0000.

> Out of the three ways, the two's complement method is the most popular for representing signed numbers in the binary number system.

2.8 BINARY ADDITION

To add two binary numbers, just remember four rules.

$$0 + 0 = 0$$
$$0 + 1 = 1$$
$$1 + 0 = 1$$
$$1 + 1 = 0 \text{ and a carry } 1$$

In decimal number system, while adding 3 + 9, the result is 12. We write 2 below and pass 1 as carry to the next digit. In the same way, when working with binary numbers, 1 + 1 = 0 and carry 1 to the next digit. This is because 1 + 1 = 2. In binary 2 means 10; hence the result. Let us now use these rules to practise addition of binary numbers.

```
   11011        11000       100010110
  +00100       +00011      +000101001
  ------       ------      ---------
   11111        11011       100111111


    11 1         11 1
   01101        01110       100010110
  +01001       +10011      +011111011
  ------       ------      ---------
   10110       100001       1000010001
```

2.9 ASCII CODE

ASCII stands for American Standard Code for Information Interchange. It is a 7-bit character code (refer Figure 4.7) that was introduced by the American National Standards Institute (ANSI) and is used by personal and workstation computers. Values in ASCII codes are represented as their 4-bit binary equivalents stored in the lower nibble, while the upper nibble contains 011 and has no bearing on the value of the represented number.

ASCII is the most common format for text files in computers and on the Internet. It can define 128 different characters because it is a 7-bit code, and can support 27 combinations. The various ASCII characters are listed in Table 2.9.

2.10 UNICODE

ASCII, which is the most widely used encoding scheme, is a 7-bit code that can support only 128 character definitions. These 128 characters can be used easily for English characters, numbers, and punctuation symbols but there is negligible or no support for the characters in other languages of the world. Therefore, organizations started creating their own encoding schemes for other languages' characters, thereby defeating the concept of a universal or standard code for information exchange. Moreover, each new scheme was of different length, and programs were supposed to determine which encoding scheme they would be using.

Table 2.9 ASCII Codes

Dec	Hx	Oct	Chr	Dec	Hx	Oct	Html	Chr	Dec	Hx	Oct	Html	Chr	Dec	Hx	Oct	Html	Chr
0	0	000	NUL (null)	32	20	040	&#32;	Space	64	40	100	&#64;	@	96	60	140	&#96;	`
1	1	001	SOH (start of heading)	33	21	041	&#33;	!	65	41	101	&#65;	A	97	61	141	&#97;	a
2	2	002	STX (start of text)	34	22	042	"	"	66	42	102	&#66;	B	98	62	142	&#98;	b
3	3	003	ETX (end of text)	35	23	043	&#35;	#	67	43	103	&#67;	C	99	63	143	&#99;	c
4	4	004	EOT (end of transmission)	36	24	044	&#36;	$	68	44	104	&#68;	D	100	64	144	&#100	d
5	5	005	ENQ (enquiry)	37	25	045	&#37;	%	69	45	105	&#69;	E	101	65	145	&#101	e
6	6	006	ACK (acknowledge)	38	26	046	&	&	70	46	106	&#70;	F	102	66	146	&#102	f
7	7	007	BEL (bell)	39	27	047	'	'	71	47	107	&#71;	G	103	67	147	&#103	g
8	8	010	BS (backspace)	40	28	050	&#40;	(	72	48	110	&#72;	H	104	68	150	&#104	h
9	9	0il	TAB (horizontal tab)	41	29	051	&#41;	)	73	49	111	&#73;	I	105	69	151	&#105	i
10	A	012	LF (NL line feed, new line)	42	2A	052	&#42;	*	74	4A	112	&#74;	J	106	6A	152	&#106	j
11	B	013	VT (vertical tab)	43	2B	053	&#43;	+	75	4B	113	&#75;	K	107	6B	153	&#107	k
12	C	014	FF (NP form feed, new page)	44	2C	054	&#44;	,	76	4C	114	&#76;	L	108	6C	154	&#108	l
13	D	015	CR (carriage return)	45	2D	055	&#45;	-	77	4D	115	&#77;	M	109	6D	155	&#109	m
14	E	016	SO (shift out)	46	2E	056	&#46;	.	78	4E	116	&#78;	N	110	6E	156	&#110	n
15	F	017	SI (shift in)	47	2F	057	&#47;	.	79	4F	117	&#79;	O	111	6F	157	&#111	o
16	10	020	DLE (data link escape)	48	30	060	&#48;	/	80	50	120	&#80;	P	112	70	160	&#112	p
17	11	021	DC1 (device control 1)	49	31	061	&#49;	1	81	51	121	&#81;	Q	113	71	161	&#113	q
18	12	022	DC2 (device control 2)	50	32	062	&#50;	2	82	52	122	&#82;	R	114	72	162	&#114	r
19	13	023	DC3 (device control 3)	51	33	063	&#51;	3	83	53	123	&#83;	S	115	73	163	&#115	s
20	14	024	DC4 (device control 4)	52	34	064	&#52;	4	84	54	124	&#84;	T	116	74	164	&#116	t
21	15	025	NAK (negative acknowledge)	53	35	065	&#53;	5	85	55	125	&#85;	U	117	75	165	&#117	u
22	16	026	SYN (synchronous idle)	54	36	066	&#54;	6	86	56	126	&#86;	V	118	76	166	&#118	v
23	17	027	ETB (end of trans. block)	55	37	067	&#55;	7	87	57	127	&#87;	W	119	77	167	&#119	w
24	18	030	CAN (cancel)	56	38	070	&#56;	8	88	58	130	&#88;	X	120	78	170	&#120	x
25	19	031	EH (end of medium)	57	39	071	&#57;	9	89	59	131	&#89;	Y	121	79	171	&#121	y
26	1A	032	SUB (substitute)	58	3A	072	&#58;	:	90	5A	132	&#90;	Z	122	7A	172	&#122	z
27	1B	033	ESC (escape)	59	3B	073	&#59;	;	91	5B	133	&#91;	[	123	7B	173	&#123	{
28	1C	034	FS (file separator)	60	3C	074	&#60;	<	92	5C	134	&#92;	\	124	7C	174	&#124	|
29	1D	035	GS (group separator)	61	3D	075	&#61;	=	93	5D	135	&#93;	]	125	7D	175	&#125	}
30	1E	036	RS (record separator)	62	3E	076	&#62;	>	94	5E	136	&#94;	^	126	7E	176	&#126	~
31	1F	037	US (unit separator)	63	3F	077	&#63;	?	95	5F	137	&#95;	_	127	7F	177	&#127	DEL

The only solution to this problem was to have a new encoding scheme that could unify all the different encoding schemes to minimize confusion between the different schemes. This led to the development of Unicode, which can represent characters (including punctuation marks, diacritics, mathematical symbols, technical symbols and arrows) as integers. It has several character encoding forms including:

- **UTF-8:** This uses only 8 bits to encode English characters. This format is widely used in email and on the Internet.
- **UTF-16:** This uses 16 bits to encode the most commonly used characters. A 16-bit Unicode can represent more than 65,000 characters. Moreover, any Unicode character represented in the UTF-16 form can be converted to the UTF-8 form and vice versa without losing information.
- **UTF-32:** This uses 32 bits to encode the characters. A 32-bit Unicode can represent more than 100,000 characters.

> UTF stands for Unicode Transformation Unit.

Besides representing the characters of different languages, UTF also reserves some codes for private use, which hardware and software vendors can assign internally for their own characters and symbols.

Nowadays, Unicode is widely used to represent text for computer processing, as it provides a consistent way of encoding multilingual characters. This makes it convenient to exchange text files internationally. The growing popularity of Unicode suggests that it will eventually supplant ASCII as the standard coding scheme.

2.11 INDIAN SCRIPT CODE FOR INFORMATION INTERCHANGE (ISCII)

To facilitate the use of Indian languages on computers and make data interchange possible, it was important to have a common standard for coding Indian scripts. Therefore, in 1991, the Bureau of Indian Standards adopted the Indian Standard Code for Information Interchange (ISCII) which is pronounced as "is -kii".

ISCII is an 8-bit standard in which the lower 128 characters (0-127) conform to ASCII standard and the higher 128 characters (128–255) encode characters are used to form Indian scripts. Even the Unicode preserves the ISCII encoding strategy in their encoding. Unicode is based on the ISCII-1988 revision and is a superset of the ISCII-1991 character encoding. Thus, texts encoded in ISCII-1991 are automatically converted to Unicode values and back to their original encoding without loss of information.

In ISCII, some examples of mnemonics used for Indian scripts include – DEV: Devanagari, PNJ: Punjabi, GJR: Gujarati, ORI: Oriya, BNG: Bengali, ASM: Assamese, TLG: Telugu, KND: Kannada, MLM: Malayalam, TML: Tamil, RMN: Roman. For example, ISCII-91 DEV is character encoding for characters from Devanagari which is used to write Hindi. Similarly, ISCII-91 ORI is the character encoding for Oriya.

Some salient aspects of the ISCII representation are:

- It represents all the Indian scripts.
- Supports ASCII as well as aksharas of the Indian languages.
- ISCII also assigns codes for the Matras of Indian languages.
- Special characters have also been used to specify how a consonant in a syllable should be rendered.
- A special character is used to identify the script to be used for rendering the text.

Key Terms

Bit: A single digit in binary language is called a bit.

Byte: A group of 8 bits is known as a byte.

One's complement: A technique of representing negative numbers in binary language by inverting each bit in the number.

Two's complement: A technique of representing negative numbers in binary language by adding 1 to the one's complement of the number.

ASCII: A 7-bit character code that stores 4-bit binary equivalent of the character (or any other value) in the lower nibble and 011 in the upper nibble.

Unicode: A code that can represent characters including punctuation marks, diacritics, mathematical symbols, technical symbols and arrows as integers.

ISCII: A code that facilitates the use of Indian languages on computers and provides a common standard for coding Indian scripts.

Chapter Highlights

- The binary language has only two symbols – 0 or 1.
- Every data – be it text, audio, video or image is represented using bits.
- A number system with base n has digits from 0 to $n - 1$.
- When we write a binary number, each binary digit is multiplied by an appropriate power of 2, which is based on the position in the number.

- To convert a binary/octal/hexadecimal number into decimal, multiply the value of each digit by its positional value in the number.
- To convert a decimal number into binary/octal/hexadecimal, keep dividing the number by 2 until the quotient becomes zero
- The *octal* number system is a Base-8 number system that has digits 0 to 7.
- To convert a decimal number into octal, keep dividing the number by 8 until the quotient becomes zero.
- To convert an octal number into its binary equivalent, replace each octal digit with its binary equivalent.
- To convert a binary number into its octal equivalent, divide the binary number into groups of bits, where each group consists of exactly 3 bits (except the last or the MSB). Convert each group into its equivalent octal number. Combine these individual octal numbers to get the final result.
- The *hexadecimal* number system is a Base-16 number system that has digits 0 to 9 and characters from A – F or a – f to represent values from 10 – 15.
- To convert a hexadecimal number into its binary equivalent, replace each hexadecimal digit with its binary equivalent.
- To convert a binary number into its hexadecimal equivalent, divide the binary number into groups of 4 bits and then convert each group into its equivalent hexadecimal number. Combine these individual hexadecimal numbers to get the final result.
- Signed number representation is required to represent negative numbers in the binary number system.
- ASCII can be used easily for English characters, numbers and punctuation symbols. However, there is negligible or no support for the characters in other languages of the world.

Review Questions

1. Why is computer language known as the binary language?
2. Why does computer understand only binary language?
3. List two advantages of machine language.
4. Write any three disadvantages of writing programs in machine language.
5. How are negative numbers stored in binary language?
6. Why is two's complement preferred over one's complement technique of representing negative numbers in binary?
7. Write a short note on ASCII code.
8. Give a major drawback of ASCII code.
9. What is Unicode?
10. How is ISCII different from ASCII and Unicode?
11. Convert the following binary numbers to decimal.
    a. $(010101)_2$ b. $(1110001)_2$ c. $(1001011)_2$ d. $(01110.101)_2$
12. Convert the following decimal numbers into binary.
    a. $(9)_{10}$ b. $(159)_{10}$ c. $(2107)_{10}$ d. $(12036)_{10}$
13. Convert the following octal numbers into decimal.
    a. $(71)_8$ b. $(765)_8$ c. $(6324)_8$ d. $(10005.765)_8$
14. Convert the following octal numbers into binary
    a. $(71)_8$ b. $(765)_8$ c. $(6324)_8$ d. $(10005)_8$
15. Convert the following binary numbers to octal.
    a. $(010101)_2$ b. $(1110001)_2$ c. $(1001011)_2$ d. $(0111010)_2$

16. Convert the following hexadecimal numbers into decimal.
    a. $(1A)_{16}$ b. $(2B3)_{16}$ c. $(1049)_{16}$ d. $(125F.DE)_{16}$
17. Convert the following decimal numbers into hexadecimal
    a. $(71)_{16}$ b. $(765)_{16}$ c. $(6324)_8$ d. $(10005)_8$
18. Convert the following hexadecimal numbers into binary
    a. $(1A)_{16}$ b. $(2B3)_{16}$ c. $(1049)_{16}$ d. $(125F)_{16}$
19. Convert the following binary numbers to hexadecimal.
    a. $(010101)_2$ b. $(1110001)_2$ c. $(1001011)_2$ d. $(0111010)_2$
20. Represent the following numbers in binary using sign-and-magnitude technique.
    a. 29 b. –35 c. 17 d. –101
21. Represent the following negative numbers in binary using 1's complement technique.
    a. –19 b. –35 c. –57 d. –101
22. Represent the following negative numbers in binary using 2's complement technique.
    a. –90 b. –39 c. –46 d. –234
23. Add the following binary numbers:
    a. 1100010 and 1011100
    b. 11110000 and 010101010
    c. 100011101 and 011110
    d. 10101010101 and 1001111111

Fill in the Blanks

1. Binary language understands only _____ symbols.
2. _____ bytes form 1 kilobyte.
3. The _____ number system is a Base-8 number system.
4. To convert a binary number into its octal equivalent, divide the binary number into groups of _____ bits.
5. The hexadecimal number system is a Base-_____ number system.
6. In sign-and-magnitude technique, the rightmost bit is set to 0 for a _____ number.
7. ASCII stands for _____.
8. _____ can represent characters including punctuation marks, diacritics, mathematical symbols, technical symbols and arrows as integers.
9. UTF stands for _____.
10. _____ is used to represent text for encoding multilingual characters.
11. ISCII stands for _____.

State True or False

1. A single digit in binary language is called a byte.
2. Programs written in machine language is first translated and then executed by the computers.
3. To convert a decimal number into binary, keep dividing the number by 2 until the quotient becomes one.
4. When converting a decimal number into binary, remainders are written in reverse order.
5. Octal number system has digits from 0 to 9.
6. In hexadecimal number system, digits 10–15 can be represented either by a–f or by A–F.
7. Signed number representation is required to represent positive numbers in the binary number system.

8. A negative number has 1 in its MSB when stored using sign-and-magnitude technique.
9. Two's complement is obtained by inverting each bit in the number.
10. Unicode is a 7-bit character code that stores 4-bit binary equivalent of the character (or any other value) in the lower nibble and 011 in the upper nibble.
11. Any Unicode character represented in the UTF-16 form can be converted to the UTF-8 form and vice versa without losing information.
12. Unicode can be used to exchange text files internationally.
13. ISCII is compatible with ASCII.

Multiple Choice Questions

1. A group of how many bits is known as a byte?
   a. 2   b. 4   c. 8   d. 16
2. A number system with base n has digits from 0 to _____.
   a. 1   b. n c. $n-1$ d. 9
3. To convert a binary number into its hexadecimal equivalent, divide the binary number into groups of how many bits?
   a. 1   b. 2   c. 4   d. 8
4. ASCII is a ____ - bit code that is widely used on the internet.
   a. 1   b. 3   c. 5   d. 7
5. ISCII can be used to encode _____ characters.
   a. 128   b. 255   c. 127   d. 256

Answers

Fill in the Blanks
1. two
2. 1024
3. octal
4. 3
5. 16
6. positive
7. American Standard Code for Information Interchange
8. Unicode
9. Unicode Transformation Unit
10. Unicode
11. Indian Script Code for Information Interchange

State True or False
1. False
2. False
3. False
4. True
5. False
6. True
7. False
8. True
9. False
10. False
11. True
12. True
13. True

Multiple Choice Questions
1. 8 bytes
2. $n-1$
3. 4
4. 7
5. 256

Boolean Algebra

3

Chapter Objectives

Having discussed binary number system in the previous chapter, we now go a step ahead and unravel the working of digital components using binary values. In this chapter, we will therefore learn the following concepts.

- Boolean operators and their precedence
- Fundamentals of Boolean Algebra
- Concept of truth tables
- Laws governing Boolean Algebra
- Implementing Boolean expressions using logic gates

We already know that computers understand only two digits, 0 and 1. These binary computers work on propositional logic wherein a proposition may be TRUE or FALSE. These propositions may also be stated as functions of other propositions that are connected by three basic logical connectives – AND, OR and NOT. For example,

> Proposition is a statement or assertion that expresses a judgement or opinion.

"I will go for shopping if I get good marks in Exams or a merit certificate in Sports."

The above statement connects the proposition – I will go for shopping – functionally to two propositions: if I get good marks in Exams or a merit certificate in Sports. This scenario can be represented as shown in the Fig. 3.1.

Figure 3.1 Simple proposition

From the above discussion we can conclude that the meaning of the OR connective is that the corresponding output is TRUE if either one of the inputs or both are true; otherwise it is false.

We can make this proposition a little more complex by saying I will go for shopping if I my friend does not come to my home and if I get good marks in Exams or a merit certificate in Sports. The proposition can be represented diagrammatically as shown in Fig. 3.2. Thus, we see that a complex proposition can be easily stated in terms of binary variables (two variables) and binary operators (OR, AND, NOT). For this purpose, the mathematician George Boole developed **Boolean algebra** in 1854. However, before starting with Boolean Algebra, let us first go through Boolean operators in technical terms.

Figure 3.2 Complex proposition

Logical AND (&&): Logical AND operator is used to simultaneously evaluate two conditions or expressions with relational operators. If expressions on both the sides (left and right side) of the logical operator are true then the whole expression is true. The truth table of logical AND operator is given in Table 3.1.

Example,

```
(a < b) && (b > c)
```

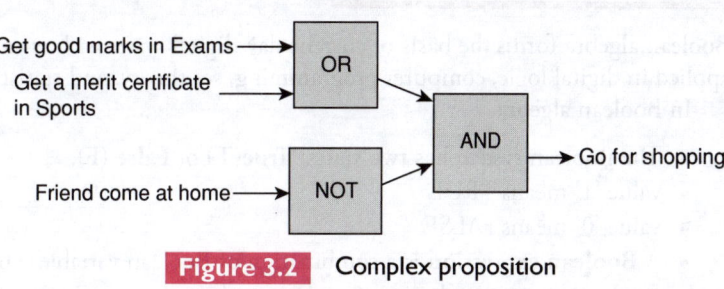

Table 3.1 Truth table of Logical AND

A	B	A &&B
0	0	0
0	1	0
1	0	0
1	1	1

The expression to the left is `a < b` and that on the right is `b > c`. The whole expression is true only if both expressions are true i.e., if `b` is greater than `a` and `c`.

Logical OR (||): Logical OR operator is used to simultaneously evaluate two conditions or expressions with relational operators. If one or both the expressions on the left side and right side of the logical operator is true then the whole expression is true. The truth table of logical OR operator is given in Table 3.2.

Example,

$$(a < b)\ ||\ (b > c)$$

Table 3.2 Truth table of Logical OR

A	B	A || B
0	0	0
0	1	1
1	0	1
1	1	1

The expression to the left is `a < b` and that on the right is `b > c`. The whole expression is true if either `b` is greater than `a` or `b` is greater than `c`.

Logical NOT (!): The logical NOT operator takes a single expression and negates the value of the expression. That is, Logical NOT produces a zero if the expression evaluates to a non-zero value and produces a 1 if the expression produces a zero. In other words, it just reverses the value of the expression. The truth table of logical NOT operator is given in Table 3.3.

Table 3.3 Truth table of Logical NOT

A	!A
0	1
1	0

Note: Logical expressions operate in a short cut fashion and stop the evaluation when it knows for sure what the final outcome would be. For example, in a logical expression involving logical AND, if the first operand is false, then the second operand is not evaluated as it is for sure that the result will be false. Similarly, for a logical expression involving logical OR, if the first operand is true, then the second operand is not evaluated as it is for sure that the result will be true.

But this approach has a side-effect. For example, consider the following expression:

$$(x > 9)\ \&\&\ (y{++} > 0) \quad OR \quad (x > 9)\ ||\ (y{++} > 0)$$

In the above logical AND expression if the first operand is false then the entire expression will not be evaluated and thus the value of `y` will never be incremented. Same is the case with the logical OR expression. If the first expression is true then the second will never be evaluated and value of `y` will never be incremented.

3.1 BOOLEAN ALGEBRA

Boolean algebra forms the basis of current-day digital systems. It is extensively used to design digital circuits that are applied in digital logic, computer programming, set theory, and statistics.

In Boolean algebra,

- The Boolean system has two states: **True**(T) or **False** (F).
- value '1' means TRUE
- value '0' means FALSE
- A **Boolean expression** is a combination of Boolean variables and Boolean operators.
- Boolean operators take certain inputs and produce an output based on a predetermined table of results (also known as the ***truth table***).
- Boolean operator AND (conjunction) is shown as a '.' and in some texts as '∩'. For example, A.B or A ∩ B means A and B. AND operator takes two (or more) inputs and returns a '1' only when both inputs are '1'.
- Boolean operator OR (disjunction) is shown as a '+' and in some texts as '∪'. For example, A + B or A ∪ B means A or B. OR operator takes two (or more) inputs and returns a '1' when any (or all) of the inputs are '1'.
- Boolean NOT (negation) is shown as ''' and in some texts as '¬'. It simply negates the value of the operand. For example, A′ means NOT A. If the input is 1, the output will be 0 and vice versa.

3.2 VENN DIAGRAMS

A Venn diagram can be used to represent Boolean operations using shaded overlapping regions. In the Venn diagrams (Fig. 3.3) that are presented in this section, there is one circular region for each variable. The interior and exterior of a region of a particular variable corresponds to the values 1 (true) and 0 (false) respectively. The Venn diagrams corresponding to AND, OR and NOT operations are shown below. In the diagrams, the shaded area indicates value '1' of the operation and the non-shaded area denotes the value '0'.

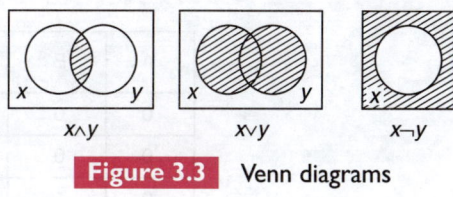

Figure 3.3 Venn diagrams

- **For AND operation**, the region common to both circles is shaded to indicate that $x \wedge y$ is 1 when both variables are 1. The non-shaded area indicates that $x \wedge y$ is 0 for the other three combinations of variables x and y.
- **For the OR operation**, the Venn diagram has a shaded area in the regions that lie inside either or both circles.
- **For the NOT operation**, the Venn diagram represents complement x' by shading the region *not* inside the circle.

Venn diagrams are useful to understand and visualize the laws of Boolean algebra. Let us see examples to justify the use of Venn diagrams to understand laws.

Example 3.1 **Absorption Law:** $x \cap (x \cup y) = x$.

Shade the portion for $x \cup y$. Next shade the portion for x. Then shade the area that is common in both the Venn diagrams. The resultant shaded area will be the whole of the x circle.

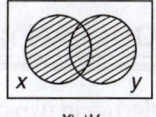 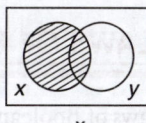 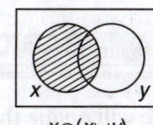

Example 3.2 **Double Negation Law:** $(x')' = x$

Shade the x circle. Then shade the area not in x. this will give the region for x'. Next shade the area that is not in x', which will be the whole circle of x.

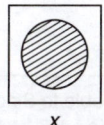  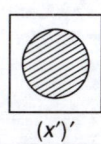

Example 3.3 **De Morgan's Law:** $x' \cap y' = (x \cup y)'$

To visualize De Morgan's law, shade the area that is neither in x nor in y. Then for the RHS, start with shading the area corresponding to $x \cup y$ which is the area either in one or in both the circles. Finally, shade the area that is not in the region of $x \cup y$. See the diagram it is the same area that we had shaded for the LHS.

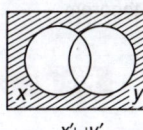 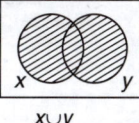 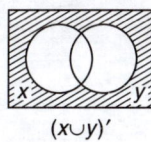

3.3 TRUTH TABLES

A truth table is used to describe a Boolean function of n input variables. A truth table lists all possible values of input combinations of the function and the output that will be produced based on these input combinations. Such a table provides a useful visual tool for defining the input–output relationship of binary variables in a Boolean function.

A Boolean function of n variables has 2^n rows of possible input combinations. Each row specifies the output of the Boolean function for a different combination. The truth tables for Boolean operators AND, OR and NOT are shown in the Fig. 3.4.

A	B	Z = A · B
0	0	0
0	1	0
1	0	0
1	1	1

A	B	Z = A + B
0	0	0
0	1	1
1	0	1
1	1	1

A	Z = A'
0	1
1	0

Figure 3.4 Truth tables

A truth table can be used to represent one or more Boolean functions. For example, the truth Boolean function: $Z = A \cup (B \cap C)$ is given in Fig. 3.5.

A	B	C	B ∩ C	Z = A ∪ (B ∩ C)
0	0	0	0	0
0	0	1	0	0
0	1	0	0	0
0	1	1	1	1
1	0	0	0	1
1	0	1	0	1
1	1	0	0	1
1	1	1	1	1

Figure 3.5 Truth table for $Z = A \cup (B \cap C)$

3.4 BASIC LAWS OF BOOLEAN ALGEBRA

We will divide the laws of Boolean algebra in two categories – laws applicable for a single variable and laws for multiple variables as shown in Fig. 3.6.

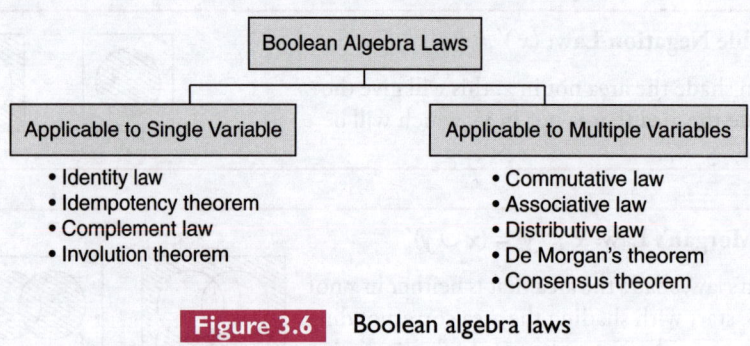

Figure 3.6 Boolean algebra laws

3.4.1 Identity Law

The identity law states that a term OR'ed with a 0 or AND'ed with a 1 will always equal that term. Similarly, a term OR'ed with a 1 is always 1 and a term AND'ed with a 0 will always become result in 0.

1. **A + 0 = A**
   Let us take example, if A = 0, then 0 + 0 = 0 which is equal to A.
   If A = 1, then 1 + 0 = 1, which is again equal to A.
2. **A + 1 = 1**
   Let us take example, if A = 0, then 0 + 1 = 1.
   If A = 1, then 1 + 1 = 1.
3. **A · 0 = 0**
   Let us take example, if A = 0, then 0 · 0 = 0.
   If A = 1, then 1 · 0 = 0.
4. **A · 1 = A**
   Let us take example, if A = 0, then 0 · 1 = 0, which is equal to A.
   If A = 1, then 1 · 1 = 1, which is again equal to A.

3.4.2 Idempotency Theorem

The idempotency law states that a term AND'ed with itself or OR'ed with itself is equal to that term.

1. **A + A = A**
   Let us take example, if A = 0, then 0 + 0 = 0, which is equal to A.
   If A = 1, then 1 + 1 = 1, which is again equal to A (here, A + B means a true value that is a non-zero value).
2. **A · A = A**
   Let us take example, if A = 0, then 0 · 0 = 0, which is equal to A.
   If A = 1, then 1 · 1 = 1, which is again equal to A.

3.4.3 Complement Law

The complement law states that a term AND'ed with its complement always results in 0 and a term OR'ed with its complement gives a result 1.

1. **A + A' = 1**
   Let us take example, if A = 0, then 0 + 1 = 1.
   If A = 1, then 1 + 0 = 1.
2. **A · A' = 0**
   Let us take example, if A = 0, then 0 · 0 = 0, which is equal to A.
   If A = 1, then 1 · 1 = 1, which is again equal to A.

3.4.4 Involution Theorem

The involution theorem, also known as double negation law, states that a term that is inverted twice is equal to the original term.

$$(A')' = A$$

Let us take an example. If A = 0, then (0')' can be solved as 1' = 0, which is equal to A.
If A = 1, then (1')' can be solved as 0' = 1, which is equal to A.

3.4.5 Commutative Law

The commutative law states that the order of application of two separate terms is not important.

1. **A + B = B + A**
2. **A · B = B · A**

Let us prove this law using a truth table (Fig. 3.7) of the Boolean functions.

A	B	A + B	B + A	A	B	A · B	B · A
0	0	0	0	0	0	0	0
0	1	1	1	0	1	0	0
1	0	1	1	1	0	0	0
1	1	1	1	1	1	1	1

Figure 3.7 Truth table for A · B = B · A

3.4.6 Associative Law

The associative law allows the removal of brackets from an expression and regrouping of the variables.

1. **A + (B + C) = (A + B) + C**
2. **A · (B · C) = (A · B) · C**

Let us prove this law using a truth table (Fig. 3.8) of the Boolean functions.

A	B	C	A + (B + C)	(A + B) + C
0	0	0	0	0
0	0	1	1	1
0	1	0	1	1
0	1	1	1	1
1	0	0	1	1
1	0	1	1	1
1	1	0	1	1
1	1	1	1	1

A	B	C	A · (B · C)	(A · B) · C
0	0	0	0	0
0	0	1	0	0
0	1	0	0	0
0	1	1	0	0
1	0	0	0	0
1	0	1	0	0
1	1	0	0	0
1	1	1	1	1

Figure 3.8 Truth table for associative law

3.4.7 Distributive Law

The distributive law enables multiplication or factoring out of an expression.

1. $A(B + C) = A \cdot B + A \cdot C$

   Let us prove this law using a truth table (Fig. 3.9) of the Boolean functions.

A	B	C	B + C	A · (B + C)	A · B	A · C	A · B + A · C
0	0	0	0	0	0	0	0
0	0	1	1	0	0	0	0
0	1	0	1	0	0	0	0
0	1	1	1	0	0	0	0
1	0	0	0	0	0	0	0
1	0	1	1	1	0	1	1
1	1	0	1	1	1	0	1
1	1	1	1	1	1	1	1

Figure 3.9 Truth table for distributive law

2. $A + B \cdot C = (A + B)(A + C)$

   R.H.S $= (A + B) \cdot (A + C)$
   $= A \cdot A + A \cdot B + A \cdot C + B \cdot C$ (opening the brackets and multiplying)
   $= A + A \cdot B + A \cdot C + B \cdot C$ (Since, A.A = A)
   $= A \cdot (1 + B) + A \cdot C + B \cdot C$ (Take A common from first two terms)
   $= A + A \cdot C + B \cdot C$ (Since 1 + B = 1 and A.1 = A)
   $= A (1 + C) + B \cdot C$ (Since 1 + c = 1 and A.1 = A)
   $= A + B \cdot C =$ L.H.S

   Let us prove this law using the truth table (Fig. 3.10).

A	B	C	B·C	A+B·C	A+B	A+C	(A+B)·(A+C)
0	0	0	0	0	0	0	0
0	0	1	0	0	0	1	0
0	1	0	0	0	1	0	0
0	1	1	1	1	1	1	1
1	0	0	0	1	1	1	1
1	0	1	0	1	1	1	1
1	1	0	0	1	1	1	1
1	1	1	1	1	1	1	1

Figure 3.10 Truth table for distributive law

3.4.8 Absorption Law

The absorption law permits reduction of a complicated expression in to a simpler one by absorbing like terms.

1. $A + A \cdot B = A$
   L.H.S. $= A + A.B$
   $= A \cdot 1 + A \cdot B$ (Since $A.1 = A$)
   $= A(1 + B)$ (Since $1 + B = 1$)
   $= A \cdot 1$
   $= A$

2. $A \cdot (A + B) = A$
   L.H.S $= A \cdot (A + B)$
   $= A \cdot A + A \cdot B$
   $= A + A \cdot B$ (Since $A \cdot A = 1$)
   $= A \cdot 1 + A \cdot B$ (Since $A \cdot 1 = A$)
   $= A \cdot (1 + B)$
   $= A \cdot 1$ (Since $1 + B = 1$)
   $= A$ (Since $A \cdot 1 = A$)

3. $A + A' \cdot B = A + B$
   L.H.S. $= A + A'.B$
   $= (A + A') \cdot (A + B)$ (Apply distributive law in which $A + BC = (A+B).(A+C)$)
   $= 1 \cdot (A + B)$ (Since $A + A' = 1$)
   $= A + B$

4. $A.(A' + B) = A.B$
   L.H.S. $= A.(A' + B)$
   $= A \cdot A' + A \cdot B$
   $= 0 + A \cdot B$ (Since $A \cdot A' = 0$)
   $= A.B$ (Since $A + 0 = A$)

3.4.9 Consensus Law

Consensus law is the conjunction of all the unique literals of the terms, excluding the literal which is not negated in one term but negated in the other.

1. $A \cdot B + A' \cdot C + B \cdot C = A \cdot B + A' \cdot C$

   L.H.S. $= A \cdot B + A' \cdot C + B \cdot C$

   $= A \cdot B + A' \cdot C + B \cdot C \cdot 1$ (Since $A \cdot 1 = A$)

   $= A \cdot B + A' \cdot C + B \cdot C \cdot (A + A')$

   $= A \cdot B + A' \cdot C + A \cdot B \cdot C + A' \cdot B \cdot C$

   $= A \cdot B + A \cdot B \cdot C + A' \cdot C + A' \cdot B \cdot C$

   $= A \cdot B (1 + C) + A' \cdot C (1 + B)$

   $= A \cdot B + A'C$ (Since $1 + C = 1$ and $1 + B = 1$)

2. $(A + B)(\bar{A} + C)(B + C) = (A+B)(\bar{A}+C)$

   L.H.S $= (A + B)(A' + C)(B + C)$

   $= (A \cdot A' + A' \cdot B + A \cdot C + B \cdot C)(B + C)$ (opening the brackets)

   $= (A' \cdot B + A \cdot C + B \cdot C)(B + C)$ ($A.A' = 0$)

   $= A' \cdot B \cdot B + A \cdot B \cdot C + B \cdot B \cdot C + A' \cdot B \cdot C + A \cdot C \cdot C + B \cdot C \cdot C$

       (opening the brackets)

   $= A' \cdot B + A \cdot B \cdot C + B \cdot C + A' \cdot B \cdot C + A \cdot C + B \cdot C$ ($A.A = A$)

   $= A' \cdot B + B \cdot C (A + A') + B \cdot C + A \cdot C$ ($A + A = A$)

   $= A' \cdot B + B \cdot C + A \cdot C$ ($A + A' = 1$)

   R.H.S $= (A + B)(A' + C)$

   $= A \cdot A' + A' \cdot B + A \cdot C + B \cdot C$

   $= A' \cdot B + A \cdot C + B \cdot C$

Therefore, L.H.S. = R.H.S

3.4.10 De Morgan's Laws

There are two laws of De Morgan that can be given as below:

1. **$(A + B)' = A' \cdot B'$**

   The first De Morgan law states that two separate terms NAND'ed together gives the same result when these two terms are complemented and then AND'ed together.

   Let us prove this law using the truth table as shown in Figs. 3.11(a) and 3.11(b).

A	B	A + B	(A + B)'	A'	B'	A' · B'
0	0	0	1	1	1	1
0	1	1	0	1	0	0
1	0	1	0	0	1	0
1	1	1	0	0	0	0

Figure 3.11(a)   Truth table for De Morgan's law

2. **$(A \cdot B)' = A' + B'$**

   The second De Morgan law states that two separate terms NOR'ed together gives the same result when these two terms are complemented and then OR'ed together.

   Let us prove this law using the truth table.

A	B	A + B	(A · B)'	A'	B'	A' + B'
0	0	0	1	1	1	0
0	1	0	1	1	0	1
1	0	0	1	0	1	1
1	1	1	0	0	0	1

Figure 3.11(b)   Truth table for De Morgan's law

3.4.11 Duality Principle

The duality property states that all binary expressions remain valid when following two steps are performed:

Step 1: Swap OR and AND operators.
Step 2: Replace all 1's by 0's and 0's by 1's.

For example, consider the expression $0 \cdot 1 = 0$. The dual of this expression is $1 + 0 = 1$
Similarly, the dual of expression $1 \cdot 1 = 1$ is $0 + 0 = 0$

Example 3.4 **Convert the expression A · (B + C) to its dual.**

A.B + A.C
Dual expression = (A + B) · (A + C)

3.5 PRECEDENCE OF BOOLEAN OPERATORS

Boolean expressions include Boolean operators. Like arithmetic expressions, Boolean expressions have an order of precedence and parentheses can be used to group operands to change the order of evaluation. If there are several operators in an expression with the same precedence, then they are evaluated left to right. The precedence of Boolean operators is given in Fig. 3.12.

For example, in the expression, A || B && C first B && C will be evaluated and then A be OR'ed with the result. Let us learn this concept through more examples.

Operator	Precedence
!	High
&&	Medium
||	Low

Figure 3.12 Boolean operators

In expression **A && B || C && D,** first A && B will be performed followed by C && D followed by OR between the two results.
In expression **A && B && C || D,** first A && B will be evaluated followed by && with C followed by || with D.
In expression **!A && B || C,** first !A will be performed followed by && followed by ||.

3.6 LOGIC DIAGRAMS AND BOOLEAN EXPRESSIONS

A logic diagram is a pictorial representation of a combination of logic gates to specify a Boolean expression. Therefore, we can directly obtain the Boolean expression by analyzing the circuit diagram or vice versa.

3.6.1 Logic Gate

Logic gates are the basic building blocks of any digital system. All digital systems are constructed using logic gates. Basically, a logic gate is an electronic circuit having one or more than one binary input and only one binary output. Some important logic gates that we will be reading in this section are AND gate, OR gate, NOT gate, NAND gate, EXOR gate, EXNOR gate and NOR gate.

AND gate

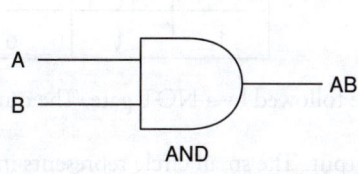

2 Input AND gate		
A	B	A.B
0	0	0
0	1	0
1	0	0
1	1	1

The AND gate is an electronic circuit that gives a **high** output (1) only if **all** its inputs are high.

OR gate

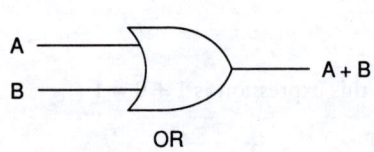

2 Input OR gate		
A	B	A + B
0	0	0
0	1	1
1	0	1
1	1	1

The OR gate is an electronic circuit that gives a high output (1) if **one or more** of its inputs are high.

NOT gate

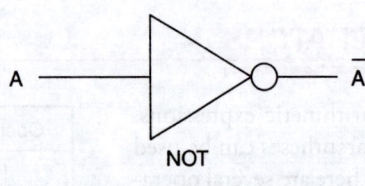

NOT gate	
A	$\bar{A}$
0	1
1	0

The NOT gate, also known as an inverter, is an electronic circuit that produces an inverted version of the input at its output. If the input variable is A, the inverted output is known as NOT A.

NAND gate

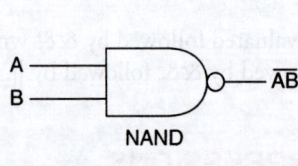

2 Input NAND gate		
A	B	$\overline{A.B}$
0	0	1
0	1	1
1	0	1
1	1	0

A NAND gate or a NOT-AND gate is equal to an AND gate followed by a NOT gate. The outputs of all NAND gates are high if **any** of the inputs are low. The symbol is an AND gate with a small circle on the output. The small circle represents inversion.

NOR gate

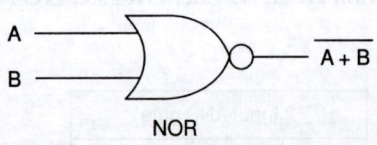

2 Input NOR gate		
A	B	$\overline{A + B}$
0	0	1
0	1	0
1	0	0
1	1	0

The NOR gate or the NOT-OR gate is equal to an OR gate followed by a NOT gate. The outputs of NOR gate is low if **any** of the inputs are high.

The symbol is an OR gate with a small circle on the output. The small circle represents inversion.

Boolean Algebra

EXOR gate

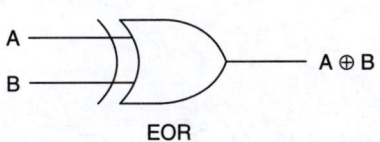

2 Input EXOR gate		
A	B	A ⊕ B
0	0	0
0	1	1
1	0	1
1	1	0

The **Exclusive-OR** gate gives a high output if **either, but not both**, of its two inputs are high. An encircled plus sign (⊕) is used to show the EXOR operation.

EXNOR gate

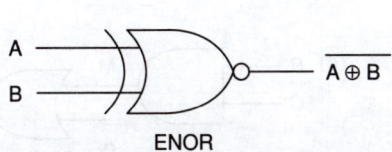

2 Input EXNOR gate		
A	B	$\overline{A \oplus B}$
0	0	1
0	1	0
1	0	0
1	1	1

The **Exclusive-NOR** gate circuit does the opposite to the EXOR gate. It will give a low output if either, but not both, of its two inputs are high. The symbol is an EXOR gate with a small circle on the output. The small circle represents inversion.

Using combinations of logic gates, complex operations can be performed. Theoretically, there is no limit to the number of gates that can be used in a single digital system. But practically, only a limited number of gates can be packed into a single digital system.

> A number of logic gates are combined to form an IC (Integrated Circuit). As IC technology advances, the physical volume for each individual logic gate decreases. Digital devices of the same or smaller size can perform ever-more-complicated operations at a higher speed.

3.7 FORMULATING BOOLEAN EXPRESSION FROM LOGIC GATES

Let us convert a logic circuit diagram to a Boolean expression. For this, first list the inputs at the correct place and then process the inputs through the gates by considering one gate at a time. Write the output of each gate. This will give you the resulting Boolean expression of each of the gates.

For example, consider the logic circuit diagram given in Fig. 3.13 and obtain its corresponding Boolean expression.

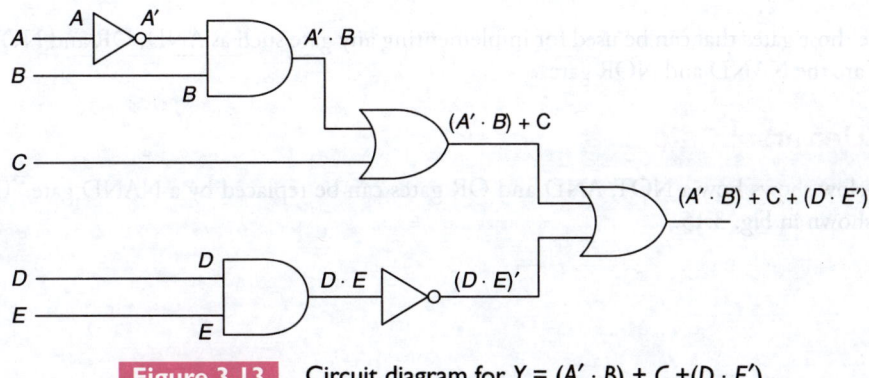

Figure 3.13 Circuit diagram for Y = (A' · B) + C +(D · E')

Converting a Boolean expression into its equivalent logic diagram is a little tricky as it requires a good understanding of order of operation given below.

1. Parentheses
2. NOT
3. AND
4. OR

Now, let us draw the circuit diagram for the Boolean expression: Y = (A + B · C) + (B′ + C)

First see the parentheses, (A + B.C). Within these parentheses, we will first perform the AND operation followed by the OR operation.

Now consider the second parentheses, (B′ + C). Within these parentheses, we will first perform the NOT operation followed by the OR operation.

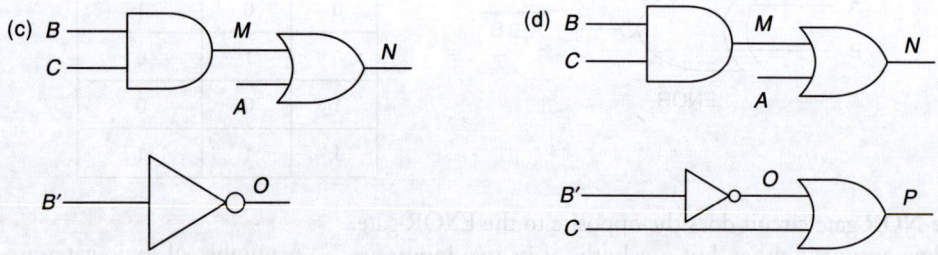

Finally, the OR operation between the two parentheses is performed in Fig. e. Note that in Fig. f, the same figure has been re-drawn with single inputs of input variables.

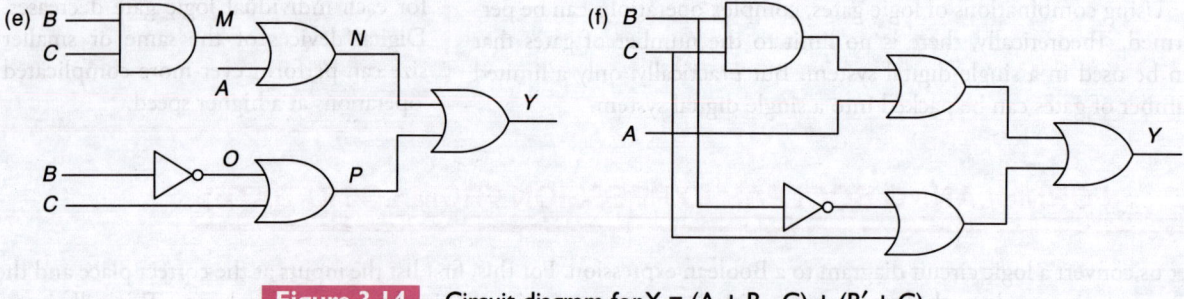

Figure 3.14 Circuit diagram for Y = (A + B · C) + (B′ + C)

3.8 UNIVERSAL GATES

Universal gates are those gates that can be used for implementing any gate such as AND, OR and NOT. Two examples of universal gates are the NAND and NOR gate.

3.8.1 NAND Universal Gate

Table 3.4 given below shows how a NOT, AND and OR gates can be replaced by a NAND gate. The truth table of a NAND gate is shown in Fig. 3.15.

Table 3.4   Replacing NOT, AND and OR gates with NAND gate

Gate	Symbol	Description
NOT gate		A NOT gate is made by joining in the inputs of a NAND gate.
AND gate		An AND gate can be implemented by following a NAND gate with a NOT gate to get a NOT NAND, that is, AND output.
OR gate		Three NAND gates are used to implement an OR gate.

Steps to Convert a Given Expression into a Circuit Diagram using only NAND Gates

Step 1: Read the expression carefully and draw its corresponding circuit diagram.
Step 2: Replace every AND, OR, and NOT gate with its equivalent NAND gate.
Step 3: Redraw the circuit.
Step 4: Identify and remove double inversions (i.e., back-to-back inverters, if any).
Step 5: Redraw the final circuit.

A	B	Output Y
0	0	1
0	1	1
1	0	1
1	1	0

Figure 3.15 Truth table for NAND gate

Example 3.5 $Y = A + (B \cdot C)$ has been represented using AND and OR gates. Represent it using NAND gates.

Solution

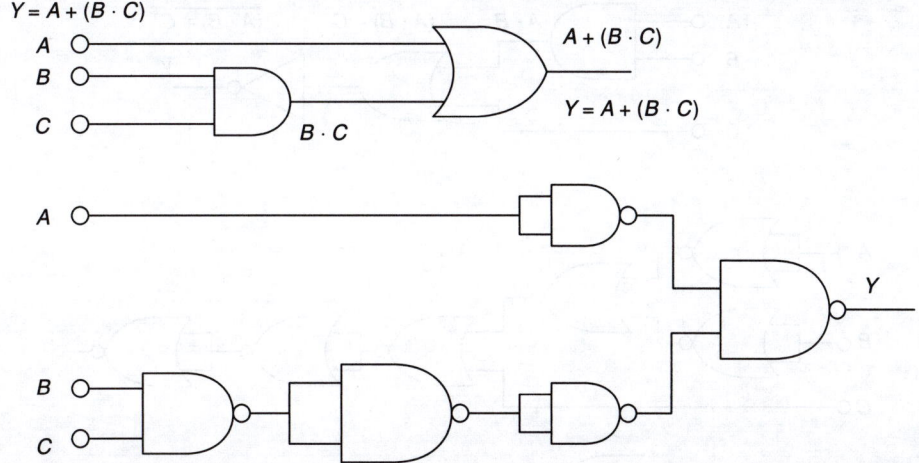

3.8.2 NOR Universal Gate

Table 3.5 given below shows how a NOR gate can replace other gates. The truth table of a NOR gate is shown in the Fig. 3.16.

Table 3.5 Replacing NOT, AND and OR gates with NOR gate

Gate	Symbol	Description
NOT gate	A — [NOR with joined inputs]	The NOT gate is implemented by joining the inputs of a NOR gate. This is because a NOR gate is equivalent to an OR gate leading to a NOT gate.
AND gate	A, D — [two NOR inverters feeding a NOR]	AND gate can be implemented by inverting the inputs to a NOR gate.
OR gate	A, B — [NOR followed by NOT]	The OR gate is nothing but a NOR gate followed by a NOT gate.

Steps to Convert a Given Expression into a Circuit Diagram using only NOR Gates

Step 1: Read the expression carefully and draw its corresponding circuit diagram.
Step 2: Replace every AND, OR, and NOT gate with its equivalent NOR gate.
Step 3: Redraw the circuit.
Step 4: Identify and remove double inversions (i.e., back-to-back inverters, if any).
Step 5: Redraw the final circuit.

A	B	Output Y
0	0	1
0	1	0
1	0	0
1	1	0

Figure 3.16 Truth table for NOR gate

Example 3.6
$Y = (A \cdot B) + C$ has been represented using AND, OR, and NOT gates. Represent it using the NOR universal gate.

$$y = \overline{(A \cdot B) + C}$$

[Circuit diagram: A, B into AND gate giving $A \cdot B$, then OR with C giving $(A \cdot B) + C$, then NOT gate giving $\overline{(A \cdot B) + C}$ = y]

Solution

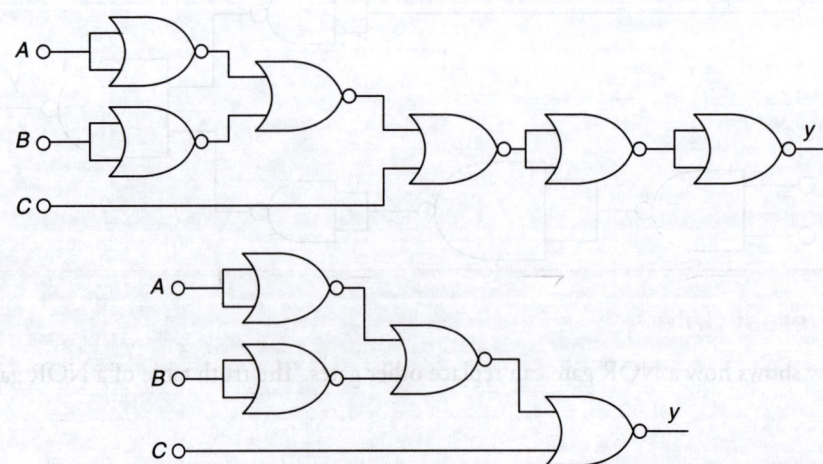

Boolean Algebra 59

Example 3.7 Represent the expression (A+B).(C+D) using only NAND gates.

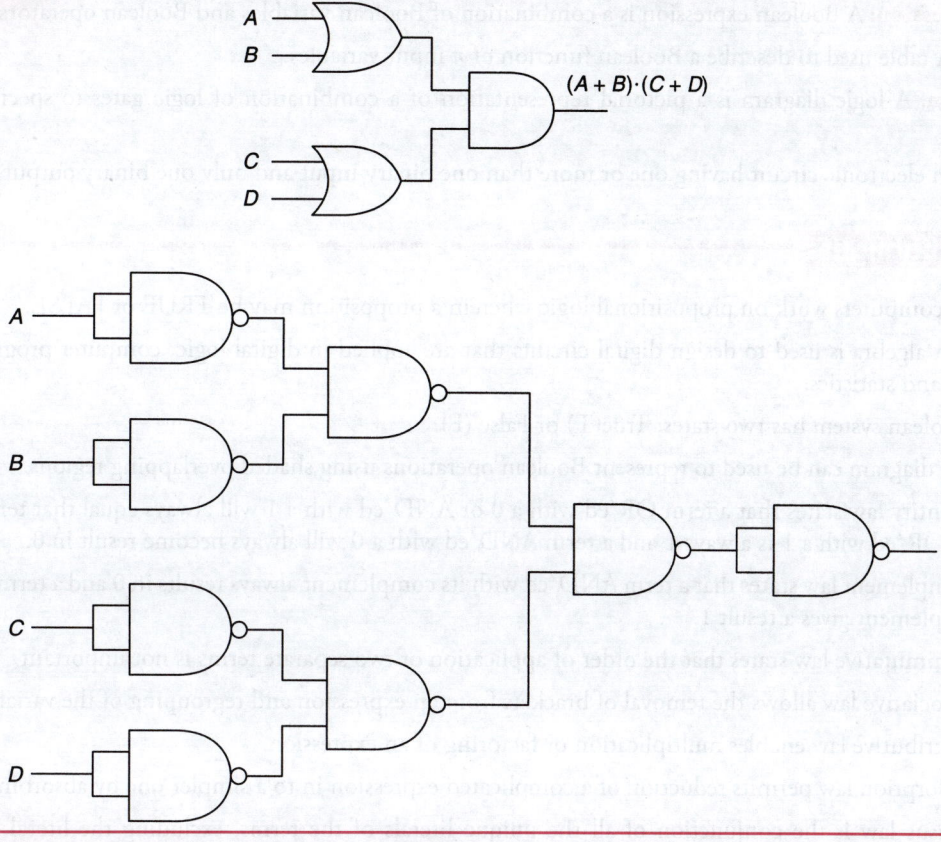

Example 3.8 Represent the expression (A+B).(C+D) using only NOR gates.

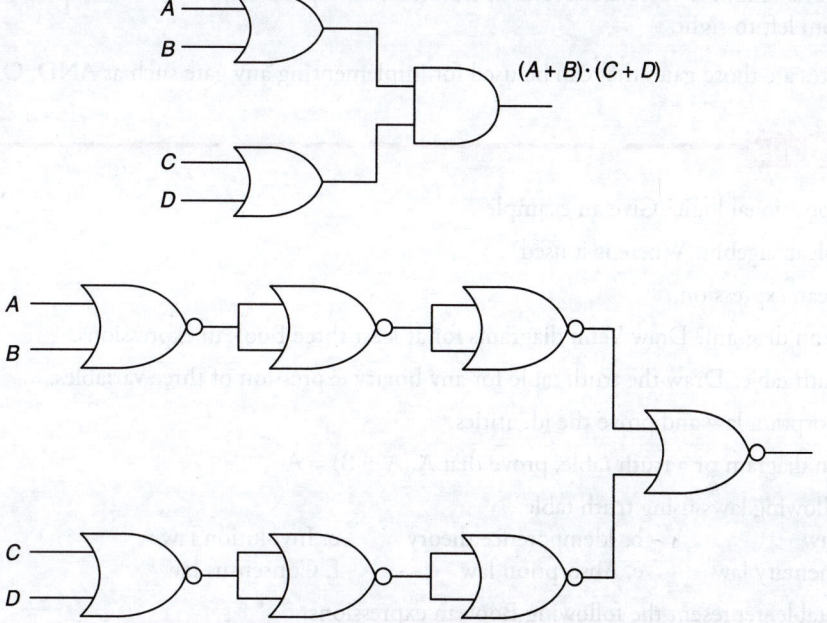

Key Terms

Boolean expression: A Boolean expression is a combination of Boolean variables and Boolean operators.

Truth table: A table used to describe a Boolean function of *n* input variables.

Logic diagram: A logic diagram is a pictorial representation of a combination of logic gates to specify a Boolean expression.

Logic gate: An electronic circuit having one or more than one binary input and only one binary output.

Chapter Highlights

- Binary computers work on propositional logic wherein a proposition may be TRUE or FALSE.
- Boolean algebra is used to design digital circuits that are applied in digital logic, computer programming, set theory, and statistics.
- The Boolean system has two states: True(T) or False (F).
- A Venn diagram can be used to represent Boolean operations using shaded overlapping regions.
- The identity law states that a term OR'ed with a 0 or AND'ed with a 1 will always equal that term. Similarly, a term OR'ed with a 1 is always 1 and a term AND'ed with a 0 will always become result in 0.
- The complement law states that a term AND'ed with its complement always results in 0 and a term OR'ed with its complement gives a result 1.
- The commutative law states that the order of application of two separate terms is not important.
- The associative law allows the removal of brackets from an expression and regrouping of the variables.
- The distributive law enables multiplication or factoring of an expression.
- The absorption law permits reduction of a complicated expression in to a simpler one by absorbing like terms.
- Consensus law is the conjunction of all the unique literals of the terms, excluding the literal which is not negated in one term but negated in the other.
- Boolean expressions have an order of precedence and parentheses can be used to group operands to change the order of evaluation. If there are several operators in an expression with the same precedence then, they are evaluated from left to right.
- Universal gates are those gates that can be used for implementing any gate such as AND, OR, and NOT.

Review Questions

1. What is propositional logic? Give an example.
2. What is Boolean algebra? Where is it used?
3. Define Boolean expression.
4. What is a Venn diagram? Draw Venn diagrams for at least three Boolean expressions.
5. What is a truth table? Draw the truth table for any binary expression of three variables.
6. Give the absorption law and prove the identities.
7. Using a Venn diagram or a truth table, prove that $A.(A + B) = A$
8. Prove the following laws using truth table.
   a. Identity law b. Idempotence theory c. Involution law
   d. Complementary law e. Absorption law f. Consensus law
9. Using truth table, represent the following Boolean expressions.
   a. $(X + Y)' = X'.Y'.$ b. $X'.Y' + X'.Y$
   c. $X.Y.Z' + X'.Y'.Z'$ d. $X'.Y.Z' + X.Y'$

e. $A(B' + C') + A.B'$
f. $A.B'(C + B.C') + C'$
g. $X[(Y' + Z) + Z']$
h. $A + B + A.B'$

9. Verify the following expressions using truth table.
   a. $X + XY = X$ b. $(A+B)' = A'.B'$

10. Give the dual expression for the following Boolean expressions.
    a. $A.A' = 0$
    b. $A + 0 = A$
    c. $(A + B) \cdot (A'+C') \cdot (B + C)$
    d. $A.(A'+B)$
    e. $(A+B) \cdot (A+B') \cdot (A'+B)$
    f. $(A \cdot 1)+(A+0+A')$
    g. $(X+Y+Z) \cdot (X+Y'+Z).(X'+Y+C')$
    h. $(A+B) \cdot (A'+C')(B+C)$

11. Draw the logic diagram for the following expressions.
    a. $X.Y + X.Z' + Y'.X'.Z$ b. $(A + B) \cdot (A' + C').(B + C)$ c. $X.Y + Y'.Z + Z'.X'$
    d. $P'.Q'.R'.S + P.Q.R'.S' + P.Q.R'.S + P.Q.R.S'$ e. $A.B + A'.B'$

12. Write a short note on De Morgan's Law.

13. What does duality principle state?

14. What do you mean by precedence of binary operators? Give an example.

15. What are universal gates? Represent any Boolean expression having at least three variables using a logic circuit with only NAND gates.

16. Using different laws in Boolean algebra, prove the following Boolean expressions.
    a. $A \cdot B + A' \cdot C + B \cdot C = A \cdot B + A' \cdot C$ b. $(A+B)(\bar{A}+C)(B+C) = (A+B)(\bar{A}+C)$

17. Identify the Boolean expression from the given circuit diagrams.

a.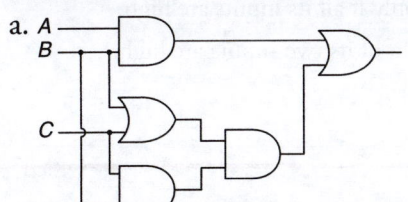

b.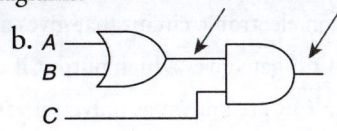

c.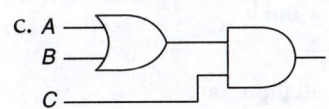

d.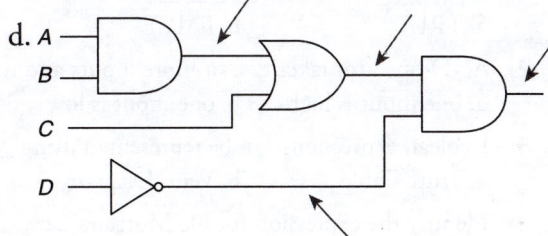

e.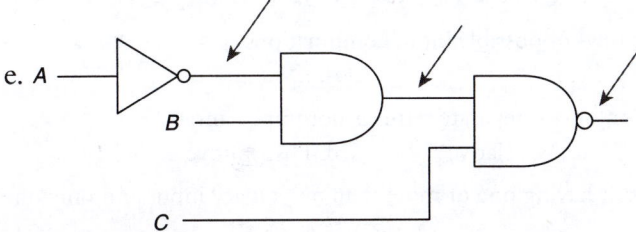

Fill in the Blanks

1. Computers work on _____ logic.
2. In Boolean logic, 1 means _____.
3. _____ is used to negate the value of the operand.

4. $x \cap (x \cup y) = x$ is _____ law.
5. De Morgan's law is given as _____.
6. $A + 0 =$ _____ and $A + A =$ ____.
7. The _____ law enables multiplication or factoring of an expression.
8. _____ is a pictorial representation of a combination of logic gates to specify a Boolean expression.
9. A number of logic gates are combined to form an _____.

State True or False

1. A Boolean system has only one state.
2. OR operator can take only two inputs.
3. The interior and exterior of a region of a particular variable corresponds to the values 1 (true) and 0 (false) respectively.
4. A truth table lists all possible values of input combinations of the function and the output that will be produced based on these input combinations.
5. $A + A' = 1$ and $A.A' = 0$, is given by Complement Law.
6. The distributive law allows the removal of brackets from an expression and regrouping of the variables.
7. We can obtain the Boolean expression by analyzing the circuit diagram or vice versa.
8. The OR gate is an electronic circuit that gives a high output (1) only if all its inputs are high.
9. The 'Exclusive-OR' gate gives a high output if either, but not both, of its two inputs are high.
10. EXOR and EXNOR are known as universal gates.

Multiple Choice Questions

1. A proposition may be _____.
   a. TRUE   b. FALSE   c. a or b   d. a and b
2. AND operator takes two or more inputs and returns a '1' only if _____.
   a. one input is high   b. one input is low   c. all inputs are high   d. all inputs are low
3. Boolean expressions can be represented using _____.
   a. Truth Table   b. Venn Diagram   c. Both of these.   d. None of these.
4. Identify the expression for De Morgan's Law.
   a. $(X')' = X$ b. $x \cap (x \cup y) = x$ c. $x' \cap y' = (x \cup y)'$ d. None of these.
5. A Boolean function of n variables has ____ rows of possible input combinations.
   a. 2^n b. $2*n$ c. n d. $n - 1$
6. Which law states that the order of application of two separate terms is not important?
   a. Identity   b. Commutative   c. Associative   d. Distributive
7. Which of the following is an electronic circuit having one or more than one binary input and only one binary output?
   a. Boolean expression   b. Logic gate   c. Logic circuit   d. Truth table
8. Which gate is an electronic circuit that gives a high output if one or more of its inputs are high?
   a. AND   b. OR   c. NOT   d. NOR
9. The outputs of which gate is high if any of the inputs are low?
   a. NAND   b. OR   c. NOT   d. NOR

Answers

Fill in the Blanks
1. propositional
2. True
3. Boolean NOT (negation)
4. absorption
5. $x' \cap y' = (x \cup y)'$
6. A, A
7. distributive
8. Logic diagram
9. IC (Integrated Circuit)

State True or False
1. False
2. False
3. True
4. True
5. True
6. False
7. True
8. False
9. True
10. False

Multiple Choice Questions
1. c
2. c
3. c
4. c
5. a
6. b
7. b
8. b
9. a

System Software and Computing Techniques

4

Chapter Objectives

In this chapter we focus on the relevance and categories of computer software. Some key topics covered in the chapter include:

- Operating system and its role in managing computer resources
- Evolution of operating system from batch processing to real time and embedded operating system
- Types of operating systems based on their interface
- Concept of booting and BIOS
- Key system software including compiler, assembler, loader, linker and interpreter
- Introduction to cloud computing and blockchain technology

While working on computers, you must have observed that after pressing the Power button on the CPU box, it takes some time for the desktop to appear on the screen. But have you ever wondered why it takes so long? What actually happens in the computer when we switch it on? The answer to this question is that during this time the computer is loading the operating system into RAM. Once the operating system comes in the primary memory, it does all other work to help users to work with the computer system.

4.1 OPERATING SYSTEM – THE MANAGER OF COMPUTER'S RESOURCES

The Operating System (OS) is the most important system software in our computer. Once it is loaded in the RAM, it performs the following functions:

- The operating system *manages all computer hardware devices* including the main memory and other storage devices.
- The operating system acts as an *intermediary between the application software and the computer hardware*. This means that users can use the hardware and other system software only through the operating system (Fig. 4.1).
- The operating system *manages application software* and other system software in the computer.
- *Makes computer easier to use.* A computer system comprises of one or more CPU, memory and I/O devices like disks, tapes, printers, terminals, etc. Writing programs to correctly and efficiently use the computer is an extremely challenging job and requires in-depth knowledge of functioning of these resources. So, to make computers easy to use and manage, operating system is added as a layer in between the application programs and computer hardware to shield the users and programmers from the complexities of the underlying hardware.
- *Share resources* with all applications that are currently being run by the user. The operating system controls and efficiently utilizes hardware components like CPU, memory and I/O devices. It also facilitates sharing of CPU time amongst different user applications. Usually, users run different applications simultaneously (like creating a word document, sending email and listening to music) and each application constantly competes for CPU's time, memory, and use of

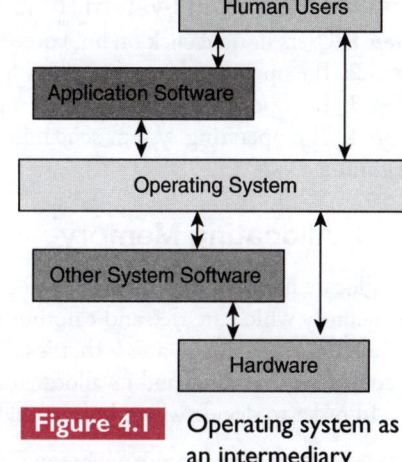

Figure 4.1 Operating system as an intermediary

input/output devices until they finish their execution. The operating system, therefore, ensures that each application gets the necessary resources it needs. For this, the operating system decides on when the CPU will execute which program, when all programs will be present in memory, when a given program will use the I/O device, etc.

- Every application running in the computer needs CPU, RAM and storage. In this scenario, the operating system keeps a *track of which user is using which resource and for how long*. It ensures that every user gets an equal chance to use the computer's resources (like files, memory and devices as shown in Fig. 4.2).
- The operating system manages and keeps a *track of the primary memory*. That is, what part of it is in use by whom, what part is not in use, etc. and reserves memory when a program requests it.
- The operating system allows users to *create and manage their files*. Users can arrange their files in folders and easily move, copy, delete and rename those files and folders.
- The operating system *monitors the performance* of the computer. It continuously checks how busy the CPU is, how fast data is being read from the hard drive, the speed of the Internet connection and so many other things.
- The operating system not only allows users to access the computer but also provides *protection* of one user's files from other users through one or more security mechanisms (like password protection).
- The operating system allows users to *create, copy, delete, move and rename a file*. The operating system also keeps a track of location, access time, modified time, and other details of files and directories (folders) saved on the secondary storage devices. Users can even restrict access of their files by other users.
- The operating system provides a *consistent application interface* that ensures that the applications developed by programmers on one computer will also run on other computers with same or different hardware configuration. The operating system can easily manage hardware from the thousands of vendors manufacturing computer equipment. For example, in Windows the steps to add a new printer will be the same irrespective of whether the printer was manufactured by HP, Cannon or of some other company.

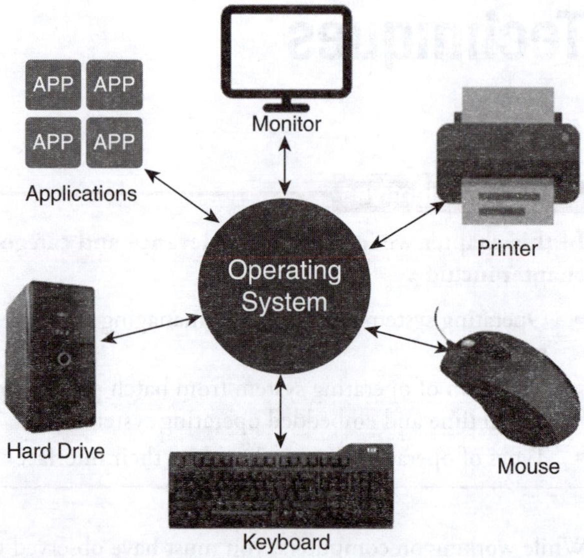

Figure 4.2 Operating system managing resources

How an Operating System Runs a Program

Step 1: Users double click on an icon or type an instruction to open a program or file.
Step 2: The operating system searches for that file or program on the secondary storage device.
Step 3: The operating system reserves a part of RAM and loads the file or program into it.
Step 4: The operating system schedules the process and instructs the CPU to start executing the program from the beginning.

4.1.1 Allocating Memory

To allocate memory to processes, the operating system keeps a list of chunks (also called partitions or blocks or holes) of memory which are free and can thus be allocated to the user's programs. When a process requires memory, the list of holes is scanned and a *hole* that is large enough for the process is allocated to it. Correspondingly, when a process is completely executed and its allocated memory is released, the released block of memory is added in the set of holes.

In order to decide which hole should be allocated to the process requesting for it, there are three ways:

First-fit According to this technique, the first hole that is big enough for the process is allocated to the requesting process.

Best-fit The smallest hole that is big enough to meet the memory requirements of the process is allocated.

Worst-fit In this technique, the process is allocated the largest hole available in the memory.

Example 4.1 Consider a scenario of memory of a computer system as given in figure where only one process P1 resides in the main memory. Now allocate memory for the following:

a. Process P2 of size 200k using first-fit technique.
b. Process P3 of size 30k using best-fit technique. Also tell which hole would have been allocated to it using first fit strategy.
c. Process P4 of size 100k using worst-fit technique. Also tell which hole would have been allocated to it using first-fit and best-fit strategies.

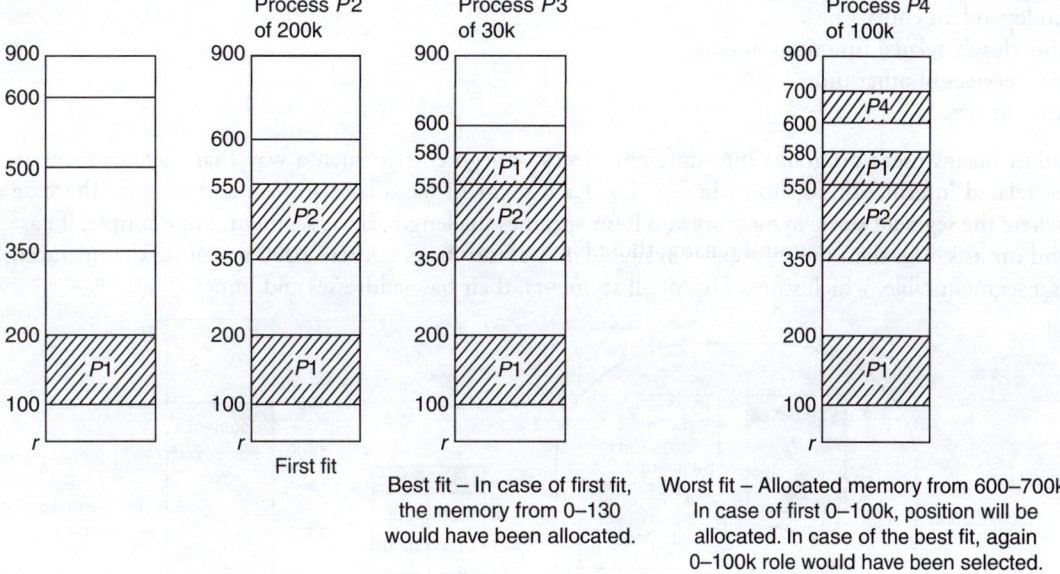

Best fit – In case of first fit, the memory from 0–130 would have been allocated.

Worst fit – Allocated memory from 600–700k, In case of first 0–100k, position will be allocated. In case of the best fit, again 0–100k role would have been selected.

d. Process P5 of size 500k using any technique.

Note that even though 500k memory space is available in the system, it still cannot be allocated to process P5 because the available memory is fragmented. This problem is called memory fragmentation and can be handled well by paging and segmentation techniques.

Paging In paging, the main memory is divided into fixed size blocks called *frames*. Similarly, the user's program is divided into fixed-size blocks called *pages*. Generally, the size of a page is equal to the size of a frame which usually varies from 1 KB to 8 KB. When a process has to be executed, its pages are loaded into the available memory frames. The operating system keeps track of all frames available in the memory. To execute a program consisting of n pages, the operating system needs n free frames in the memory.

Paging technique handles the problem of fragmentation by allowing a program's pages to be loaded anywhere in the memory (not necessarily in consecutive frames). However, for this technique to be successful, the operating system maintains a page table that acts as an index specifying where the pages of the program are actually stored in memory.

For example, in Fig. 4.3, we see that the program has four pages – Page 0, 1, 2 and 3. From the page table we see that Page 0 is actually stored in Frame 1, Page 1 is stored in Frame 4, so on and so forth.

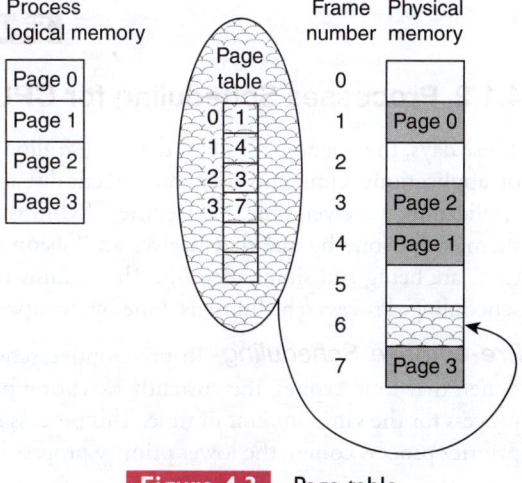

Figure 4.3 Page table

Segmentation While paging is a far better technique than best-fit, worst-fit and first-fit techniques, it suffers from internal fragmentation. Internal fragmentation means a certain amount of space is wasted within the memory frame. This occurs when the allocated memory or frame is slightly larger than requested memory. For example, if a page (frame) size is 4k, but the program needs only 2k, then the entire frame of 4k will be allocated to the program out of which 2k will be used and 2k amount of space will be wasted. Therefore, another important technique to manage memory is segmentation. *Segmentation is free from the problem of internal fragmentation.*

The other idea behind using segmentation is that programmers view an application as a collection of related program units where each unit:

- is an independent entity
- contains closely related functions or data
- may use services of other units
- may vary in size.

Segmentation breaks user's programs into different pieces or segments in such a way that each segment represents a group of related information as shown in Fig. 4.4. Each segment has a base address and a limit. The base address specifies where the segment starts in memory and limit specifies the length of the segment. For example, if base address is 1000 and limit is 400, then the segment is available in memory from address 1000 to 1400. The operating system maintains a segment table, which stores a list of all segments, their base addresses and limits.

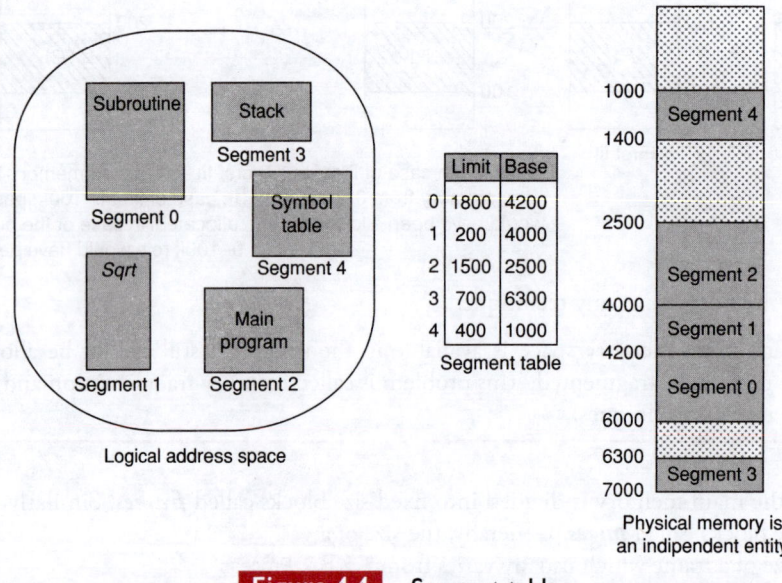

Figure 4.4 Segment table

4.1.2 Processes Scheduling for CPU

These days, the operating systems that we use allow users to run multiple programs or applications simultaneously. But practically, a single CPU can run only one application at a given time. Hence, the CPU must schedule processes and execute them so fast one by one that it gives an illusion to the user that all his applications are being run simultaneously. This is known as CPU scheduling or process scheduling. Process scheduling is done by the operating system. Generally, there are two types of process scheduling.

> Process means a program/application that is currently being executed by the CPU.

Pre-emptive Scheduling In pre-emptive scheduling, each process is given a small amount of time to execute. When that time expires, the currently executing process is temporarily suspended and the CPU is allotted to another process for the same amount of time. This process repeats until all the processes get executed. Moreover, when a higher priority process comes, the lower priority process is suspended and the higher priority process is executed first.

Non pre-emptive Scheduling In non-pre-emptive scheduling, the first process is completely executed; then the CPU executes the next process. This process is repeated until all the processes get executed. There is no use of deciding the CPU scheduling policy in this scenario as the execution of second job will strictly follow the first.

Non pre-emptive CPU Scheduling Techniques There a number of ways to decide which next process will be executed in case of pre-emptive scheduling. Some of them are discussed below.

First Come First Serve (FCFS) In this technique, *the process that enters first in memory will be executed first*. The scheduling policy is very simple to implement as it just takes the first process, execute it and then allots CPU to the next process in sequence. The main drawback of FCFS policy is poor performance and long waiting times for small processes.

For example, if the first process needs 23 ms to execute and the second process just needs 5 ms, the second process will have to wait for 23 ms for the complete execution of the first process.

Shortest Job first In this technique, the CPU time requirements of each process must be known in advance so that a queue can be maintained to store processes in increasing order of their CPU time requirements. Though this is the best approach to follow, it is very difficult to implement as the time required cannot always be known in advance. Hence, the technique stresses on executing the shortest job first. This technique may lead to starvation of long jobs that had entered very early in the system.

Round Robin In this technique, the CPU is allotted to *each process on FCFS basis for a specified time* (called time quantum). If the first process gets completely executed in this time quantum, it is removed from the ready queue. Otherwise, it is temporarily suspended and the CPU is given to the second process for the same time quantum. This technique is repeated until all the processes get completely executed.

Example 4.2 Consider three processes P1, P2 and P3 with CPU time requirements given as 20 ms, 10 ms and 5 ms. Show the scheduling process using FCFS, SJF and Round Robin policies. Take time quantum as 5 ms.

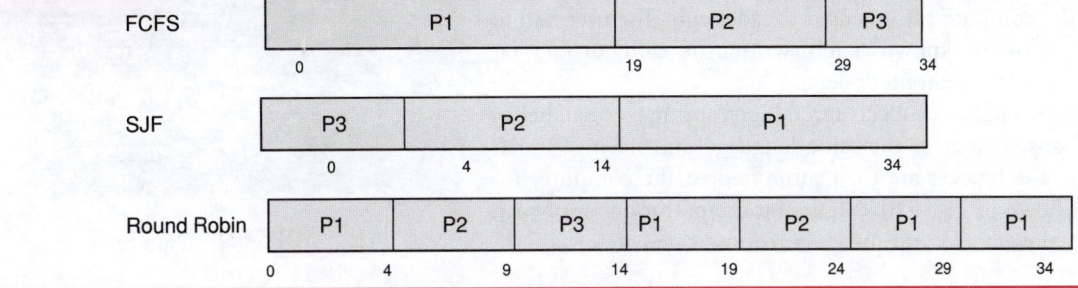

4.2 COMMONLY USED OPERATING SYSTEMS

Figure 4.5 gives a pie chart of some commonly used operating systems. These operating systems can be described as:

Microsoft Windows 10 It is a proprietary operating system created by Microsoft Company. Microsoft Windows is the most commonly used operating system since 1985. The latest version of Windows is Windows 10. Windows 10 can be used on multiple devices including desktop computers, tablets, and smartphones.

Apple Mac OS Apple Mac operating system is used only on Apple computers. It is a proprietary operating system created by Apple only for its own devices. Mac OS is popular among its users because of features like Siri (which is a natural-voice personal assistant) and FaceTime which is Apple's video-calling program.

Linux Operating System
Unlike many other operating systems, Linux is not developed by a particular company. Rather, it was initially created by Finnish programmer Linus Torvalds in 1991. After that, computer programmers from all over the world contributed to

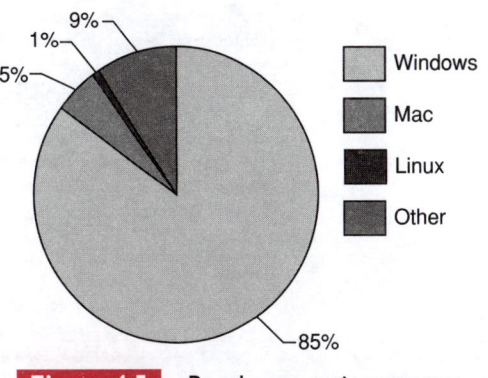

Figure 4.5 Popular operating systems

Many of the devices like Android phones, cameras, wearable watches, cars, refrigerators and more use Linux.

its further development. Thus, Linux is an open-source operating system and anybody can see and edit its source code (set of instructions).

Companies generally use Linux on their servers (computers on which all the data of the company is stored) because it is secure, and they can get excellent support from a large community of users.

Ubuntu Linux It is an open source operating system that is based on the Linux operating system. Ubuntu has become popular among millions of users worldwide. It is a GUI operating system that is used both on personal computers as well as server computers. Figure 4.6 shows some of the popularly used operating systems.

> Ubuntu is an African word that literally means "humanity to others." Ubuntu was first released in 2004.

Figure 4.6 Different operating systems

4.3 TYPES OF OPERATING SYSTEM

In this section, we will read about different types of operating systems that were available in the market. This will help you to realize how it has evolved and come a long way to make our work simpler and faster.

4.3.1 Batch Processing Systems

In this type of operating system, there is no direct interaction between the user and the computer. It was used decades ago. The user had to submit his work (better known as job) written on cards or tape (as shown in Fig. 4.7) to a computer operator.

The computer operator collects several jobs and makes batches of similar jobs (jobs written in the same language and having similar requirements). The batches are then submitted to the computer for execution (as shown in Fig. 4.8). No doubt, the performance of such systems is very slow as a lot of time is wasted to create batches.

Figure 4.7 Data tape

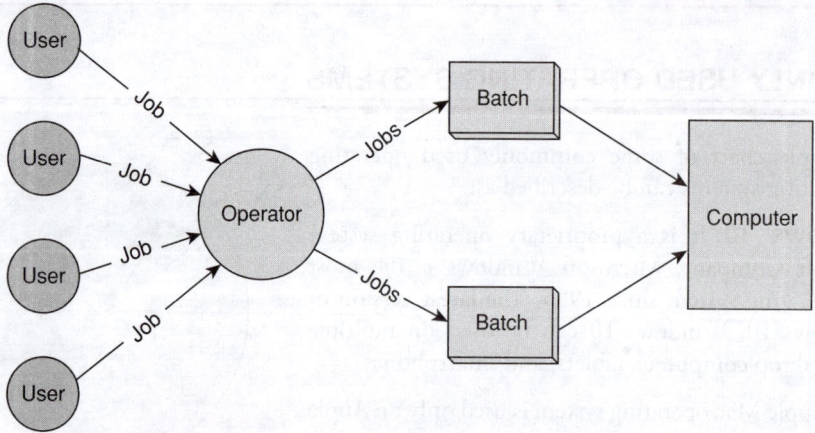

Figure 4.8 Batch processing operating system

4.3.2 Single-user, Single-task Operating System

As the name implies, these operating systems work on a single task at a time and only a single user can use it at a time. MS-DOS, Palm OS used on palm-held computers and mobile OS are examples of single user, single task operating system.

Example: MS-DOS.

4.3.3 Multi-programming Systems

When you have a mock test in class, what happens? The teacher asks a student a question. If he/she is not able to answer, she immediately asks it to another student. This saves the teacher's time. Had the teacher been asking every student individually, then one student will have to go to her, the teacher will ask questions then the student will go back and send another student. This will waste a lot of time as the teacher will be sitting idle for the time the other student takes to come.

Same is the case in a single processing system in which only one program resides in the main memory. However, in a multi-programming operating system as shown in Fig. 4.9, two or more programs can reside in the main memory at the same time. The moment one program is executed, the CPU immediately takes the next program for execution. So, the main focus in a multi-programming system is to maximize the CPU usage. For this, the operating system decides on which process will get memory when and how much.

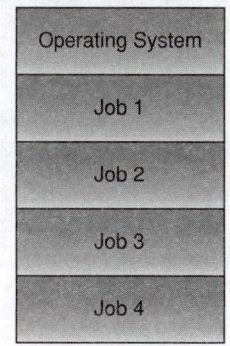

Figure 4.9 Multi-programming operating system

4.3.4 Time-sharing Systems or Multi-tasking Operating System

Multi-programming operating systems never use any cards because the process is entered on the spot by the user.

Time-sharing system goes one step ahead of multi-programming systems. In time-sharing systems, the main aim is to minimize the response time. And for this, multiple processes are executed at the same time by switching between them (refer Fig. 4.10). However, switches occur at a very fast pace so that users get an immediate response from the computer. For example, if there are five processes to be executed, the CPU will run each of them for less than one second. That is, it will place them in a queue. The first process is executed for say 0.001 seconds, then the second for 0.001 seconds, and so on. After the fifth process, it will return to the first process to execute it for another 0.001 seconds. This will be repeated until all the processes are completely executed.

Time sharing operating systems are also known as single-user, multi-tasking operating systems as only one user can use the computer but he can run a number of applications at the same time. All modern-day computers support time sharing system. For example, we can listen to music while typing a document in Word.

Example: Mac OS, MS Windows.

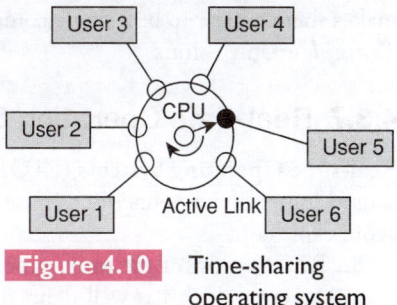

Figure 4.10 Time-sharing operating system

Response time is the time elapsed between submission of a request and the time the first response is produced.

4.3.5 Multiprocessor Systems

When you are given a big project and you are doing it all alone, then it may take you a month to complete it. But if your teacher asks for it to be completed by a group of three students, then the project work will be divided amongst three students. So, what is the advantage here? The project is completed in less time as you have more than one brain working on the project, right? Same is the case with computer systems.

In a multi-processor system (Fig. 4.11), several processors or CPUs are used. They all share a common memory. Multi-processor systems provide higher computing power and speed. This is because multiple processors work together under a single operating system.

Therefore, we can say that with multi-processor system, we get better performance by speeding up execution.

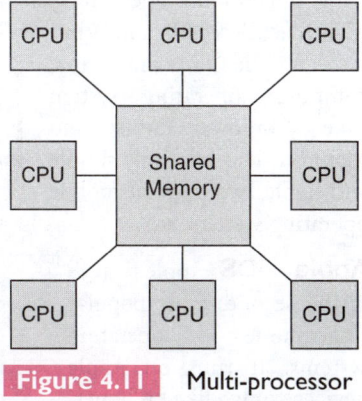

Figure 4.11 Multi-processor operating system

4.3.6 Distributed Operating Systems

The advancement in technology and decline in cost of computer systems have made it possible to design and develop distributed systems. A distributed system (Fig. 4.12) comprises of many computers that are connected by a network.

In this type of operating system, a user working on one computer can utilize the resources (including data or devices) of another computer on the same network. The main advantage of distributed system is that it enables fast processing and does not put the entire load of work on one machine.

> The main difference between distributed system and multi-processor system is that in multi-processor system there are multiple processors which share a common memory. But in a distributed system, there are multiple computer systems. No memory is shared.

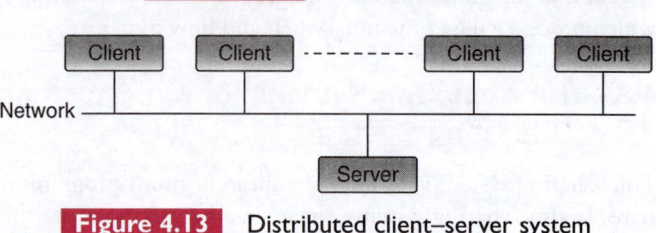

Figure 4.12 Distributed operating system

The most common example of a distributed system is the client–server system (as shown in Fig. 4.13), in which clients send requests to perform an action, and the server performs the action and returns the result to the client.

In a distributed operating system, all the computers work in co-operation with each other. Such an operating system manages all the computers and makes them appear to be a single computer system.
Examples: Unix, Linux.

Figure 4.13 Distributed client–server system

4.3.7 Real-time Operating System

Real-time Operating Systems (RTOS) are systems which demand very fast and quick response. For example, RTOS is used in petroleum refineries to measure temperature and provide alerts when the temperature gets too high so as to avoid explosion.

In RTOS, most of the time, processes remain in primary memory to provide immediate response. It is a time-bound system which has well-defined fixed time constraints. Processing must be complete within the defined constraints, or else the system will fail. RTOS are widely used in embedded systems, industrial robots, scientific research equipment and others.

4.3.8 Mobile Operating Sytem

A mobile operating system, also known as mobile OS, is an operating system that is specifically designed for mobile devices like smartphones, PDAs, tablet computers and other handheld devices. The mobile operating system provides a platform on which other applications (known as apps) can run.

Popular mobile operating systems are Android, Symbian, iOS, BlackBerry OS and Windows Mobile (refer Fig. 4.14).

A mobile OS is similar to a computer operating system (like Windows, Linux, and Mac) but it is relatively simple and light. Two popular mobile operating systems are

> Chromium is an operating system by Google which is used with Chromebooks.

Apple iOS Apple's iOS is the second most popular smartphone operating systems. It runs on Apple devices only like iPhones, iPad tablets and iPod Touch media players.

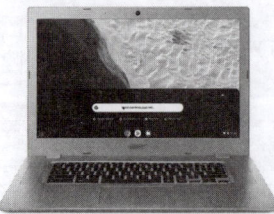

Google ChromeBook

Figure 4.14 Time-sharing operating system

Users can download various apps from Apple App Store. iOS apps are known for strong security that prevents access by unauthorized users. The user interface is very simple and efficient.

Google's Android OS

Android is the most popular operating system developed by Google and is used in smart phones and tablets. It is an open-source operating system based on Linux.

Android, like iOS, comes with an application and media store called the Play Store built by Google. Some phone manufacturers and other organizations also offer their own stores to install software and media.

Handheld operating systems are used in handheld devices like PDAs, tablets, smartphones. These systems have a comparatively small amount of memory, include slow processors, and have small display screens. Therefore, the operating system must manage memory and other resources efficiently. This includes returning all allocated memory back to the memory manager once the memory is no longer being used.

4.3.9 Embedded Operating System

Embedded operating system, as the name suggests, is embedded in a device. In an embedded system, the operating system is located in ROM. Generally, embedded systems do not have many resources. They are widely used in appliances like microwaves, washing machines, traffic control systems, cars, ATMs, airplane controls, point-of-sale (POS) terminals, digital cameras, GPS navigation systems, elevators, etc.

Google Android Operating System is used in phones and tablets while iOS Operating System is used in Apple iPhone and iPads.

4.4   TYPES OF OPERATING SYSTEM BASED ON USER INTERFACE

We now know that the operating system acts as an interface or intermediary between the user and the computer hardware. This means that the operating system provides an interface through which users can give commands to the computer. Therefore, based on the type of interface, operating systems can be classified into two groups.

4.4.1   Command Line Interface (CLI) or Character User Interface (CUI)

In this type of operating system, users type commands to give instructions to the computer. Although command line interface (as shown in Fig. 4.15) has been widely replaced by graphical user interface (GUI), advanced computer users still prefer CUI because of the following advantages:

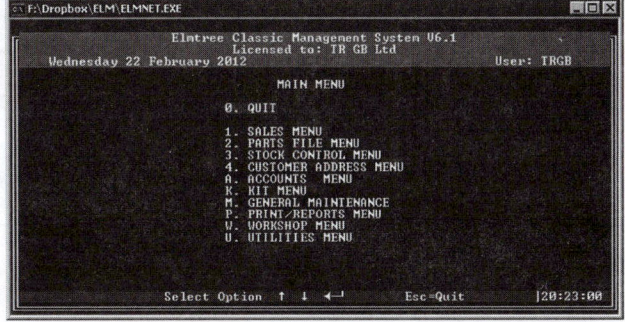

Figure 4.15   Command line user interface

- They provide a more concise and powerful means to control a program or operating system.
- CUI is very valuable for some type of operations. For example, if we have to rename 100 files in Windows, which is based on GUI, then it will take a long time. But with CUI, the same operation can be performed in just a few seconds.
- When sharing resources over the network, command line interface is widely used as some networking devices can be manipulated only by using a command line interface.
- A command line interface is stable. This means that once a user has learned executing commands, the procedure will never change (as compared to GUI). Even if new commands are introduced, the original ones will always remain the same.

However, a major drawback of command line interface is that users need to memorize commands to interact with the programs.

4.4.2 Graphical User Interface (GUI)

Modern operating systems are all based on GUI. In this type of operating system, users interact with the operating system by giving commands using mouse. That is, to give commands or instructions to the computer, users use the mouse to click icons, buttons, and menus, or whatever that is displayed on the screen. For example, to open the MS Word program you double click on its icon. To save a file, you click on the File Menu and then click on the Save option. To better understand the difference between CLI and GUI, refer Table 4.1.

Advantages of GUI
- With well-designed graphical user interfaces, users can get rid of the burden of learning complex commands to perform even small operations.
- The interface is intuitive. Thus, users take less time to learn and work with the system. For example, it is far simple to move a file from one directory to another by dragging its icon with the mouse than remembering and typing the complete command without any mistake to perform the same operation.
- Graphical user interface eases the task of transferring data from one application to another. However, the two applications must be running the same GUI. For example, we can easily incorporate a pie chart created in MS-Excel into a document created using MS-Word.
- GUI gives users an immediate visual feedback of the effect of user's action. For example, when a file is deleted, the icon of that file immediately disappears thereby notifying the user that the file has been removed from its current location.

Drawbacks of GUI
- A GUI requires more system resources than CLI. This is because a number of graphical elements like icons, menus, fonts, etc. have to be loaded. In addition to these elements, video drivers, mouse drivers, and other drivers must also be loaded which will use even more resources.
- Even today, most advanced tasks are performed using command line interface despite the fact that GUI also offers enough control over file system and operating system.
- Although it is easier for the users to work with GUI, it is much slower than using a command line.
- Though remote graphical access is possible with GUI, not all computers and network devices support manipulation using GUI.
- Each GUI system differs in design and structure from the other systems. Even different versions of the same GUI can have a lot of variations. For example, the GUI of Windows 7 is completely different from that of Windows 8.

Table 4.1 Difference between GUI and CUI

Command Line Interface (CLI)	Graphical User Interface (GUI)
The user must learn all the commands to use the computer.	The user does not need to learn any command.
The users must type full commands.	Users can even use shortcuts. For example to save a file, he can either click on menus or press Ctrl + S keys.
Since user has to learn lot of commands, it is difficult to work with	Since users have to just click and not learn, it is very easy to work with.
Only people having good knowledge of computer can work with CLI.	Even children and those who don't know much about computers can work with GUI.
Only keyboard is used as the input device.	Mouse and other pointing devices are also used as input devices.
Consumes less memory as there are no pictures, menus and icons.	Consumes more memory as there are lot of colors, pictures, menus and other items.
Examples: MS DOS	Examples: MS Windows, Linux, Ubuntu

4.5 DEVICE DRIVER

Device driver is a software that controls a particular type of hardware device attached to a computer. All devices such as printer, monitor, keyboard, scanner, optical device readers, mouse, etc. need a device driver to instruct a computer on how to communicate with the devices. Without a device driver, the computer will not be able to send and/or receive data correctly from hardware devices. Figure 4.16 illustrates the role of device drivers as an intermediary sitting between the operating system and the hardware devices.

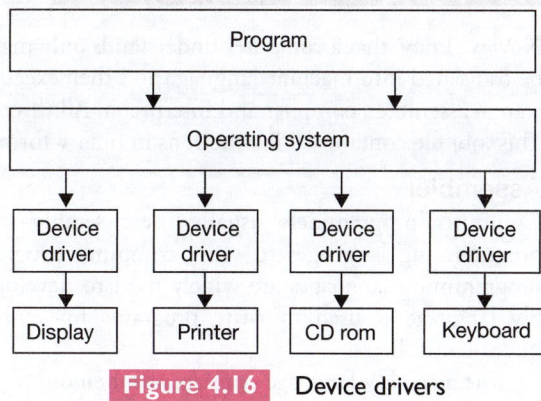

Figure 4.16 Device drivers

4.6 BOOTING THE COMPUTER

When a computer is started, the booting process takes place. In the booting process, POST (Power-On-Self-Test) is performed by BIOS. For this test, BIOS checks all the hardware and software that are attached or installed in the computer. Once POST is successful, all files that are stored in ROM and are necessary to start the computer are loaded in the memory. The operating system, device driver, antivirus software or any other software that must be loaded before the user starts operating computer are also loaded at this time.

There are two types of booting.

Warm Booting Warm booting takes place when the computer is started by pressing the power button on the CPU box.

Cold Booting Cold Booting is performed when the computer restarts. This means that the computer was initially running. Cold booting may occur due to several reasons like when the operating system has been updated, new software has been installed, voltage fluctuation, a virus attack, etc.

Table 4.2 compares the two types of booting.

Table 4.2 Difference between warm booting and cold booting

Cold Booting	Warm Booting
A computer is started from a shutdown or a powerless state.	A computer that was initially running is restarted without turning it off.
Initialized by pressing the power button on the CPU Box.	Initialized by the operating system.
Also known as dead start or hard booting.	Also known as soft booting.
Performs a complete reset of the computer.	Reset is not complete.
POST is performed.	POST is not performed.

4.7 WHAT IS BIOS?

BIOS or Basic Input/ Output System, is a ROM chip found on the motherboard. It allows users to access and set up the computer system at the most basic level.

As discussed earlier, it is the BIOS that performs the Power-On-Self-Test (POST). During this test, it identifies and initializes system devices like CPU, RAM, video display card, keyboard, mouse, hard disk, optical disc drive and any other hardware attached to the computer.

If all is well, then BIOS locates the MBR (Master Boot Record) on the hard disk and loads operating system files from there into the RAM (in case of Windows). From this point, the operating system takes control of the computer system.

4.8 PROGRAM TRANSLATORS

Now we know that a computer understands only machine language. Programs written using other languages must first be translated into machine language and then executed. To perform this translation work, we have three system software – assembler, compiler and interpreter. All three types of program translators generate an .obj file of the program. This .obj file contains all instructions in binary form.

Assembler

Computer programmers usually use assembly language or high-level programming languages to write computer programs. While high-level programming languages are widely used to develop software, the assembly language is used to write programs for embedded computers (or micro-controllers).

> A part of the assembly language program that adds two numbers and stores the result in SUM.
>
> IN AX, DX
> MOV A, DX
> IN AX, DX,
> ADD AX, A
> STA SUM, AX

The assembly language consists of mnemonics (or symbolic codes) for writing programs. These mnemonics are human-readable notation for the machine language instructions. To execute instructions written in assembly language, all mnemonics must be converted into machine language.

As the name suggests, an assembler converts an assembly language program into machine language program so that it can be executed by the computer (Fig. 4.17).

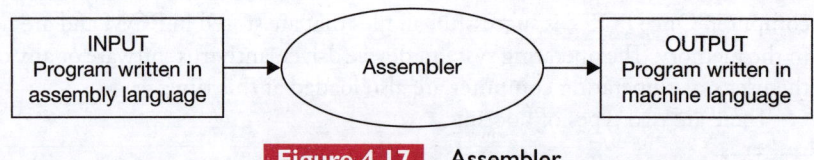

Figure 4.17 Assembler

Compiler

A compiler converts a high-level language program into machine language program so that it can be executed by the computer (Fig. 4.18). Every high-level language has its own compiler. For example, C language has a C compiler and C++ language has a C++ compiler. Therefore, C and C++ are known as compiled languages as they need a compiler to be translated into machine language.

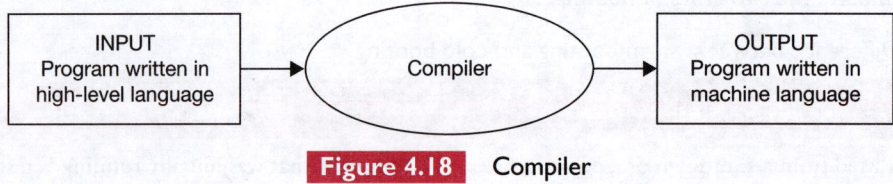

Figure 4.18 Compiler

Interpreter

An interpreter converts a high-level language program into machine language program so that it can be executed by the computer (Fig. 4.19). Every high-level language has its own compiler or interpreter. For example, Python language has a Python Interpreter and PHP has its own interpreter. Therefore, Python and PHP are known as interpreted languages as they need an interpreter to be translated into machine language.

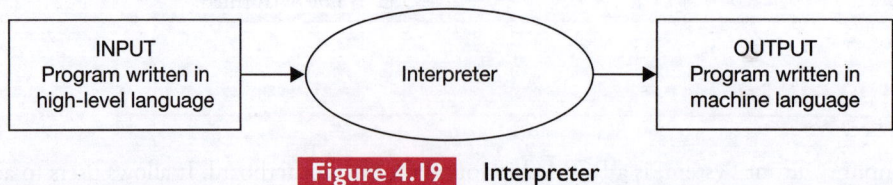

Figure 4.19 Interpreter

Difference between Compiler and Interpreter

You must be thinking that compiler and interpreter are same as they both do the same work. Although that is true, the difference lies in how they do the work of translation. Let us understand the difference between a compiler and interpreter by looking at Table 4.3.

Table 4.3 Difference between compiler and interpreter

Compiler	Interpreter
Translates the entire program into machine language in one go.	Translates one statement at a time into machine language.
Program translation is faster.	Program translation is slower.
Requires more memory.	Requires less memory.
Errors (if any) in the program are shown after the entire program is translated.	Errors (if any) in the program are shown after every statement is translated.
Once a program is compiled, the compiler is not required again. The program can be directly executed whenever required. Recompilation will be required only when changes are made to the program.	An interpreter is required every time the program has to be executed.
Example: C	Example: Python

4.9 LINKER AND LOADER

Linker is a part of the operating system that links our programs with libraries and packages that comes along with the language. For example, in some high-level programming languages like Python, users just write commands and include one or more packages in the program. The details of how the commands are to be executed are stored in the packages. So, to execute our program, the linker links our program with the specified packages.

> Translators convert source program into object program. Linker converts the object program into exe or executable program. The CPU runs the executable program.

Loader is a part of the operating system that loads the program from the hard disk into the main memory. A program can be executed by the CPU only if it is present in the main memory.

Putting it all together, we can understand the relationship between source, object and executable files using Fig. 4.20.

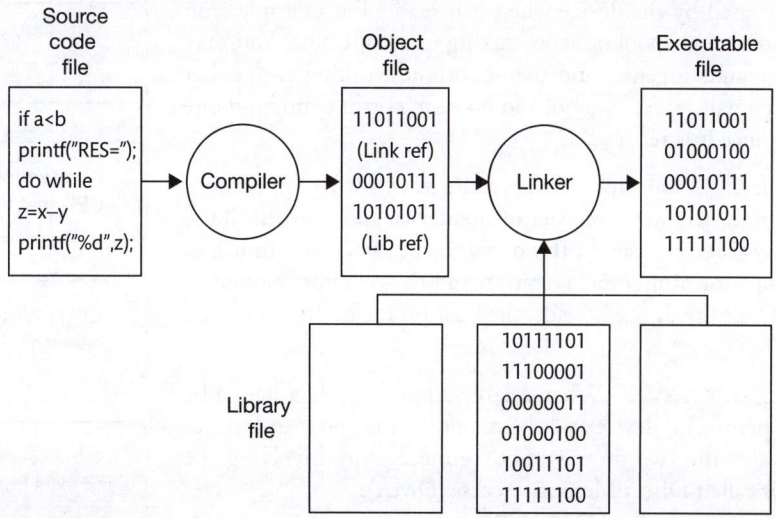

Figure 4.20 Relationship between source file, object file and executable file

4.10 DEVICE MANAGEMENT BY THE OPERATING SYSTEM

Different peripheral devices are connected to our computer, each having their own way of exchanging data. While some devices may send/receive data character by character, others may do it block by block. While some allow sequential access, others support random access of data. While some devices operate in a dedicated way (just connected to your computer), others may be shared among two or more computers. In such a scenario, it is the job of the operating system to manage and control the devices connected to the computer.

The device is plugged into computer on a port.

Figure 4.21 shows that the operating system communicates with the peripheral devices via the *device driver software* that comes along with each device. The device drivers hide the complexity of handling the devices.

Besides managing the peripheral devices, the operating system also provides various services related to Input/Output (I/O) like I/O scheduling, buffering, spooling, and error handling.

Figure 4.21 Operating system manages devices

Schedules I/O requests The operating system re-schedules or re-orders the I/O requests of processes to improve performance of the system.

Buffering Buffer is a small area of memory that stores the data while it is being transferred between two devices or between a device and an application. Since the speed of CPU is much higher than the speed of I/O devices, the I/O devices transfer data at a relatively slow speed. But the speed at which the data is processed is quite fast. In such a case, the operating system supports buffering to handle the speed mismatch by storing the data in a buffer. It sends the complete data to the CPU in one go. And until the entire data is available from the slow devices it keeps collecting it in the buffer.

Simultaneous Peripheral Operation On-line (Spooling) The operating system takes care of *spooling* to store the jobs for I/O devices in a spool. This spool can then be used by the device when it is ready. For example, you must have frequently observed spooling when taking out print outs. You may give several print commands together and then continue working with other applications. The printer will access its spool and take each print command one by and one to print it once it is ready.

Polling In polling, the CPU waits for a device to be ready for I/O operation. For this, it repeatedly reads the status register of the device and waits until the `busy_bit` in the status register is cleared. The `busy_bit`, when set, indicates that the device is busy performing some operation and thus cannot respond to any other command. Once the device is ready, the busy bit is cleared to indicate that it is finished.

Direct Memory Transfer (DMA) When a large amount of data has to be transferred between a peripheral device and the memory, it is better to transfer the data directly between the two units without unnecessarily involving the CPU. This approach is called Direct Memory Access (DMA).

Whenever there is a request for DMA, CPU relinquishes (or leaves) its control over the buses so that they can be used by devices and memory for data exchange.

Interrupt Handling An interrupt is a signal sent by peripheral devices to the CPU to notify it to suspend the current process and execute the appropriate part of the operating system. There are three types of interrupts:

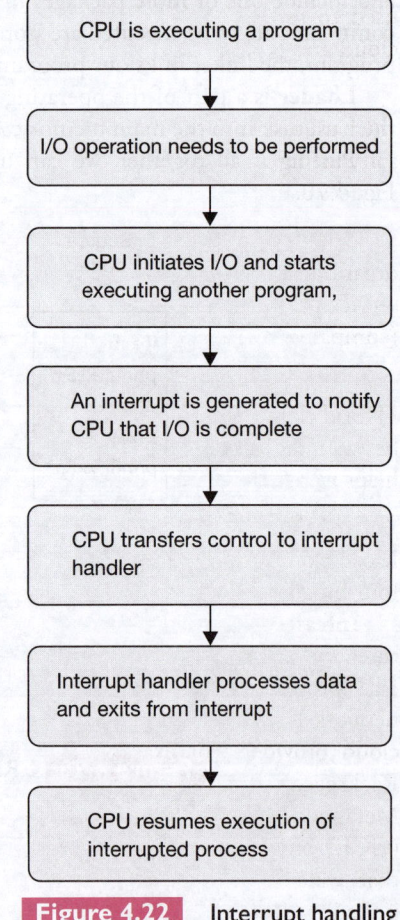

Figure 4.22 Interrupt handling

Hardware Interrupts are generated by hardware devices to signal the CPU that they need some attention from the operating system. These interrupts are generated when an I/O operation is completed, a key on the keyboard is pressed or when DMA is completed.

Software Interrupts are generated by programs in two cases – first, when the program has terminated and second, when the program requests some services from the operating system.

Traps are generated by the CPU itself to signal the operating system that an error has occurred and CPU needs its assistance to resolve the problem.

The process of interrupt handling is summarized in Fig. 4.22.

4.11 CLOUD COMPUTING

Cloud computing, in simple terms, means delivering computing services including servers, storage, databases, networking, software, analytics, and intelligence over the Internet ("the cloud"). However, users pay for only the cloud services they use. This helps them to lower operating costs of their business and run infrastructure more efficiently by scaling (or changing as sometimes business needs more services and at other times less) the needs of the business.

4.11.1 Types of Cloud Computing

There are different types of clouds (Fig. 4.23). Each cloud serves a specific purpose and is appropriate for a particular business. No one type of cloud computing is right for everyone. Therefore, before using cloud computing services, one must first determine the type of cloud that should be used to provide services. The different types of cloud are:

Public Cloud
- Multiple clients
- Hosted at providers location
- Shared infrastructure
- Access over Internet
- Low-cost

Private Cloud
- Single clients
- Hosted at providers / orgs location
- Access over Internet / Private Network
- High-security

Figure 4.23 Types of Clouds

Public cloud Public clouds are owned and operated by third-party cloud service providers. The cloud service provider usually delivers computing resources like servers and storage over the Internet. With a public cloud, all hardware, software and other supporting infrastructure is owned and managed by the cloud provider. Users can access these services using a web browser. Microsoft Azure is an example of a public cloud.

Private cloud A private cloud refers to cloud computing resources to be exclusively used by a single business or organization. Companies can either deploy a private cloud in their own company's head office or pay third-party service providers to host their private cloud. The cloud services of a private cloud are provided over a private network (company's own network) and not over a public network like the Internet.

Hybrid cloud
Hybrid clouds combine the characteristics of both public and private clouds. Now, data and applications can be shared between the two clouds. And due to this, a hybrid cloud gives business more flexibility, more deployment options and helps to better use existing infrastructure with greater security and control.

Types of Cloud Services

Most cloud computing services (Fig. 4.24) fall into four broad categories which are given below:

Infrastructure as a service (IaaS): The most basic category of cloud computing services is the IaaS. IaaS provides IT infrastructure like servers, storage, networks and operating systems as a service from a cloud provider. For example, DigitalOcean, Linode, Rackspace, Amazon Web Services (AWS), Cisco Metapod, Microsoft Azure, Google Compute Engine (GCE) provide scalable infrastructure for companies that want to host cloud-based applications without investing in their own servers.

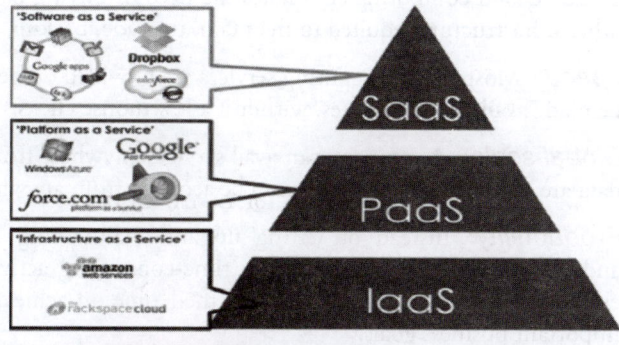

Figure 4.24 Types of cloud services

Platform as a service (PaaS): PaaS refers to cloud computing services that supply on-demand the platform or the environment for developing, testing, delivering and managing software applications. PaaS makes it easier for developers to quickly create applications, without having the need to set up or manage the underlying infrastructure of servers, storage, network and databases needed for development. Apache Stratos, Amazon Web Services Elastic Beanstalk, CloudBees, Cloud Foundry, Google App Engine, Heroku and IBM SmartCloud are popular examples of PaaS.

Software as a service (SaaS): Software as a service is a method for delivering software applications over the Internet. They are basically provided on demand and on a subscription basis. Cloud providers not only provide software applications but also provide the infrastructure required for the software. Software maintenance, upgrades and security are taken care of by the cloud provider. Users access the applications over the Internet, usually with a web browser on their phone, tablet or computer. Some very common examples of Saas include Google Workspace, Dropbox, Salesforce, Cisco WebEx, Concur and GoToMeeting.

> Cloud computing is a more efficient way of delivering computing resources.

4.11.2 Uses of Cloud Computing

Before the cloud computing era started, companies had to invest a lot to setup, maintain and upgrade the required hardware and software. However, today cloud computing is used by everybody having an **email account** or even a smart phone. Whenever we send or receive an email, **watch movies, listen to music, play games or store pictures and other files**, it is likely that we are cloud computing behind the scenes (Fig. 4.25).

Though cloud computing is only a few years old, it is now being used by organizations varying from tiny start-ups to global corporations. Few examples in which cloud computing is being extensively used include **creating new applications and testing** them, storage, back up and recover of data. For example, in smart phones you must have seen an app named cloud. When you save your files on the cloud using your phone, then even if you delete those files from your phone, they can still be recovered from the cloud.

Figure 4.25 Applications of cloud computing

Some cloud computing service providers (Fig. 4.26) are available free of cost for users. An example is Google Drive, which offers 15 GB of storage space to all users who have a Gmail account. Users can upload their important files, pictures and other documents on the Google Drive. Users just have to type the URL https://www.google.com/drive/ and enter their Gmail username and password. They can now upload their files and folders. Share them with others and do lots more.

Similarly, OneDrive from Microsoft offers 5GB storage space to all users having a Microsoft account.

Figure 4.26 Cloud computing service provider

4.11.3 Advantages

Cost: Cloud computing eliminates the need of buying hardware and software. Moreover, there is no IT team and other infrastructure required to maintain, upgrade, backup, and secure hardware or software.

Speed: Most cloud computing services are provided on demand, so even large amounts of computing resources can be made available in minutes, with just a few mouse clicks.

Global scale: A company can avail services anywhere from the best suitable geographic location. Applications and data are not tied to a device but can be accessed from anywhere.

Productivity: Instead of setting up and maintaining hardware and software and performing other time-consuming activities, the employees of the company can spend their time on achieving more important business goals.

> Gmail uses cloud to store and backup user's data, emails, pictures and other files. Netflix also uses cloud computing services to run its video streaming service.

Performance: The cloud computing service providers regularly upgrade to the latest, fastest and efficient computing hardware. This not only provides services at an extremely fast speed but is also beneficial for a business that can never invest money to buy the latest hardware for its use.

Reliability: Cloud computing takes data backup, keeps redundant copies of data at multiple locations within cloud provider's network and performs disaster recovery techniques so that even in case of failure of one or more computers, the business can remain operational.

Security: Cloud computing service providers use a broad set of technologies and controls to protect data, applications and infrastructure from potential threats.

Flexible and scalable: Cloud-based applications can be easily customized to increase or decrease power, storage, and usage of other hardware as users' needs change.

4.12 BLOCKCHAIN TECHNOLOGY

To understand blockchain technology let us take an analogy. You have worked with simple MS Word document and a Google Doc. Like MS Word document, Google Doc is also a word processing software. However, Google Doc allows users to share the document with other people. Users working on the same document need not copy it or transfer it to each other. They can simply share it. This sharing creates a decentralized distribution chain that gives everyone access to the document simultaneously. No user has to wait for other users to complete their piece of work in that document. Another big advantage here is that all changes made in the Google Doc are recorded in real-time, making changes completely transparent.

Same is the principle used in blockchain technology. A blockchain is a time-stamped series of immutable records of data that is managed by a network of computers (not by any single device). Each block is secured and linked to other blocks in a chain.

Information in a block is open so that it can be viewed by everyone. This makes blockchain technology transparent to users as everyone involved is accountable for their actions.

4.12.1 Key Terminology

Blockchain consists of a chain of **blocks** where each block stores data and a hash value. Moreover, every block has a pointer or a reference to the previous block in the chain.

The process of creating blocks is known as **mining**. Correspondingly, people mining blocks are called **miners**. Changing any data in a previously created block will require re-mining of not just that particular block (with the desired change), but also of all the blocks in the chain that were mined after that block. When a block is successfully mined, the change is accepted by all of the nodes on the network.

A **node** in blockchain technology is any electronic device that maintains copies of the blockchain and keeps the network functioning. Every node has its own copy of the blockchain. When a new block is mined, the network first gets it verified and approved from all the nodes thereby making the process of updating a blockchain transparent to every node. This also ensures that every node has the updated copy of blockchain, thus maintaining integrity and building trust among users.

In blockchain technology, **tokens** are created to represent any kind of digital asset (which may include music files, contracts, tickets, a patient's medical records, or any other document), track its ownership and execute its functionality according to a set of programming instructions.

Success Factors
Reasons for success of blockchain technology include:

- It is decentralized, meaning it is not owned by a single device
- The data is stored in encrypted form
- Every block is immutable, so no one can modify the data that is already stored within a blockchain
- The blockchain is transparent so anyone can view the data stored in a block.

4.12.2 Applications of Blockchain

Blockchain technology has infinite number of applications in almost every industry. Apart from bitcoins, it can be used in finance industry to track fraud, in the medical field to securely share patient medical records between healthcare professionals and track the usage of digital assets such as intellectual property to prevent their misuse.

Blockchain can be used for selling recorded **music** directly by artists, thereby cutting out commission paid by music companies and distributors like Apple or Spotify. Authors can even sell their E-books to avoid costs charged by Amazon and credit card processing companies.

In future, blockchain may even eliminate bank accounts and practically all services offered by banks.

Example of Blockchain Technology for Online Purchase

The word blockchain is made up of two words – block and chain. Here, block means any digital information stored in a chain where chain is usually a public database.

An online shopping website uses blocks to store information about transactions like the date, time, and price of your most recent purchase from the website. It also stores information about who is participating in the transaction. However, instead of using the user's actual name, a unique "digital signature" that works as a username is stored.

Every block also stores a unique cryptographic code called a "hash" that sets it apart from other blocks in the chain.

For example, if you have made a purchase and after paying for your order, you want to buy another product then a separate block will be created with another unique code.

When a purchase is done and a **block is created, the transaction is verified**. This verification is automatically done by a network of computers (Fig. 4.27). During this process, nodes confirm the details of the purchase, including the transaction's time, amount, and participants.

If the transaction is verified as accurate, then all its details like amount, user's digital signature, digital signature of shopping website are all **stored in the block.**

The block is then assigned a unique code for identification. This code is known as a **hash. Once hashed, the block is added to the blockchain.**

Any block in the blockchain, then becomes publicly available for anyone to view.

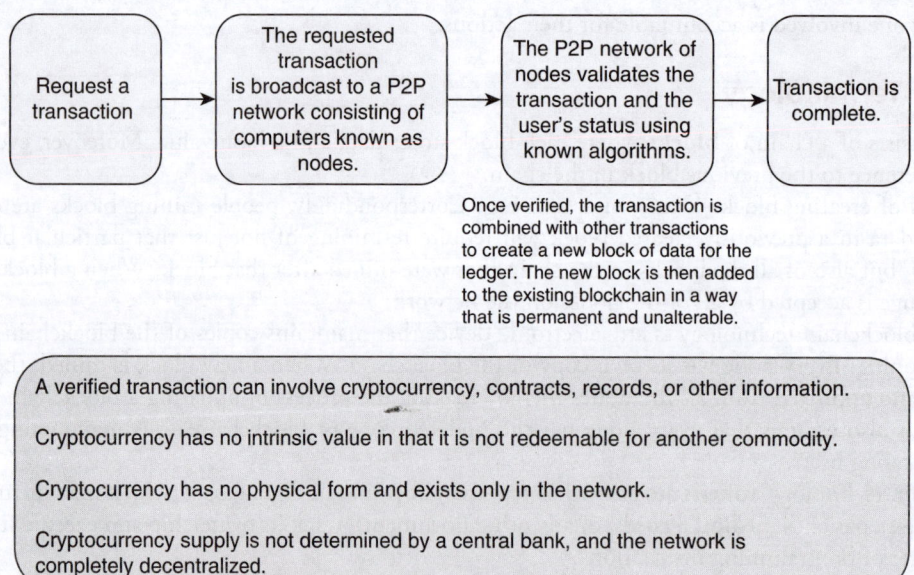

Figure 4.27 Process of adding blocks in a blockchain

4.12.3 Pillars of Blockchain

The three key pillars of blockchain technology that are applicable to any digital asset are: distributed, decentralized and transparent. Transparency ensures integrity of the document, which creates trust in the asset.

Blockchain is a new technology and many researchers are doing extensive research on it especially because it helps to reduce risk, stamps out fraud and maintains transparency in all transactions involving the digital asset. The three main properties of Blockchain Technology which have helped it gain widespread acclaim are as follows:

Decentralization

The traditional client–server models are centralized systems in which one entity controls all data transactions (Fig. 4.28). However, some issues with this system are:

- All data is stored in one place, so it is vulnerable to be attacked by hackers.
- If the software of the centralized system is being updated, the entire system halts.
- If the software of the centralized system shuts down due to some error, malicious software or an attack, the entire system halts.

In a decentralized system, the information is not stored by one device. Rather, every device in the network owns the information.

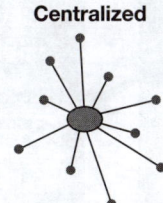

Centralized systems have a core authority that **dictates the truth** to the other participants in the network.

Decentralized systems have **no core authority** to dictate the truth to the other participants in the network.

Only **priveleged users** or institutions can access the history of transactions or confim new transactions

Every participant in the network can access the history of transactions or confirm new transactions.

Figure 4.28 Centralized vs. decentralized systems

Transparency

A user's identity is hidden via complex cryptography and represented only by their public address. For example, the message "Kiara sent 1 BTC" will be stored as "4TC5bhsFGkDwyz7voFXEmQwT2KbySt7CZO sent 1 BTC".

Here, the person's real identity is secure. However, anyone can see the transactions that were done by Kiara, not with her real name but with her public address. This level of transparency was never there in financial systems before.

Immutability

Immutability here means that once data is entered in a block, it cannot be changed or deleted.

4.12.4 Hashing in Blockchain

The term hashing means taking an input string of any length and giving an output of a fixed length. In blockchain technology, transactions are taken as input to a hashing algorithm (like SHA-256) which gives an output of a fixed length.

Input	Hash
Hi	3639EFCD08ABB273B1619E82E78C29A70F02C1051B1820E99FC395DCAA3326B8
Welcome to blockgeeks. Glad to have you here.	53A53FC9E2A03F9B6E66084BA701574C09CFSF01FB498C41731881BCDC68A7CB

In the hash generated, we can see that no matter how big or small the input is, the output will always have a fixed length of 256 bits.

The best part of the hash function is that even if a single change is made to the input, the hash changes drastically with no resemblance to its prior value. Consider, the two hash values given below. Though there is change in case of just one character, the hash code varies considerably.

Input	Hash
This is a test	C7BE1ED902FB8DD4D48997C6452FSD7E509FBCDBE2808B16BCF4EDCE4C07D14E
this is a test	2E99758548972A8E8822A047FA1017FF72F06F3FF6A016851F45C398732BCSOC

Now, if this was say the third block in the blockchain, then any chain in one block will also change the hash of the other blocks in the block chain as shown in Fig. 4.29.

With blockchain technology, each page in a ledger of transactions forms a block. That block has an impact on the next block or page through cryptographic hashing. In other words, when a block is completed, it creates a unique secure code, which ties into the next page or block, creating a chain of blocks, or blockchain.

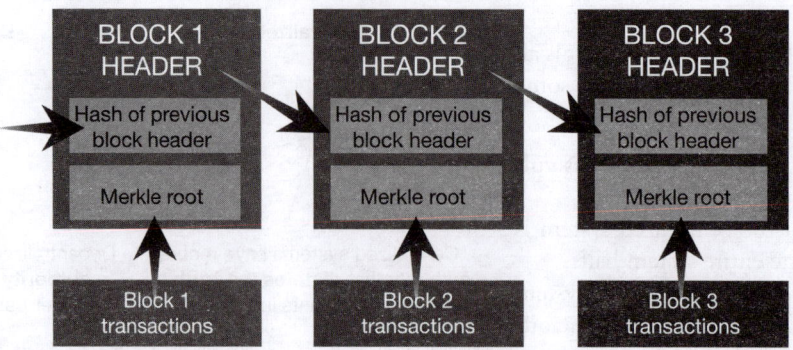

SIMPLIFIED BITCOIN BLOCKCHAIN

Figure 4.29 Connection between blocks in a blockchain

Key Terms

Process: A program or application that is currently being executed by the CPU.

Mobile operating system: An operating system that is specifically designed for mobile devices like smartphones, PDAs, tablet computers and other handheld devices.

BIOS or Basic Input/Output System: A ROM chip found on the motherboard that allows users to access and set up the computer system at the most basic level.

Assembler: System software that converts an assembly language program into machine language program so that it can be executed by the computer.

Device driver: A software that controls a particular type of hardware device that is attached to the computer.

Compiler: System software that converts a high-level language program into machine language program so that it can be executed by the computer. Compiler translates the entire program into machine language in one go.

Interpreter: System software that converts a high-level language program into machine language program so that it can be executed by the computer. It translates one statement at a time into machine language.

Linker: A part of the operating system that links our programs with libraries and packages which come along with the language.

Loader: A part of the operating system that loads the program from the hard disk into the main memory.

Buffer: A small area of memory that stores the data while it is being transferred between two devices or between a device and an application.

Interrupt: A signal sent by peripheral devices to the CPU to notify it to suspend the current process and execute the appropriate part of the operating system.

Cloud computing: Delivering computing services including servers, storage, databases, networking, software, analytics and intelligence over the Internet.

Blockchain: A blockchain is a time-stamped series of immutable records of data that is managed by a network of computers (not by any single device).

Mining: The process of creating blocks is known as **mining**. Correspondingly, people mining blocks are called **miners**.

Node: A **node** in blockchain technology is any electronic device that maintains copies of the blockchain and keeps the network functioning.

Hash: Every block stores a unique cryptographic code called a "hash" that sets it apart from other blocks in the chain.

Chapter Highlights

- The Operating System (OS) is the most important system software in our computer.
- The operating system acts as an intermediary between the application software and the computer hardware.
- The operating system monitors the performance of the computer. It continuously checks how busy the CPU is, how fast data is being read from the hard drive, the speed with which Internet is connected and so many other things.
- In paging, the main memory is divided into fixed-size blocks called frames. Similarly, the user's program is divided into fixed-size blocks called pages.
- Paging technique handles the problem of fragmentation by allowing a program's pages to be loaded anywhere in the memory (not necessarily in consecutive frames).
- While paging is a far better technique than best-fit, worst-fit and first-fit techniques, it suffers from internal fragmentation. Internal fragmentation means a certain amount of space is wasted within the memory frame. This occurs when the allocated memory or frame is slightly larger than the requested memory.
- Segmentation is free from the problem of internal fragmentation.
- Each segment has a base address and a limit. The base address specifies where the segment starts in memory and limit specifies the length of the segment.
- In pre-emptive scheduling, each process is given a small amount of time to execute. When that time expires, the currently executing process is temporarily suspended and the CPU is allotted to another process for the same amount of time.
- In non-pre-emptive scheduling, the first process is completely executed; then the CPU executes the next process.
- In CUI-based operating system, users type commands to give instructions to the computer.
- In GUI operating system, users give commands or instructions to the computer by clicking on icons, buttons, and menus.
- In the Booting process, POST (Power-On-Self-Test) is performed by BIOS. Once POST is successful, all files that are stored in ROM and are necessary to start the computer are loaded in the memory.
- When a large amount of data has to be transferred between a peripheral device and the memory, it is better to transfer the data directly between the two units without unnecessarily involving the CPU. This approach is called Direct Memory Access (DMA).

Review Questions

1. Give some important functions of the operating system.
2. How does an operating system run a program?
3. Discuss the three strategies used by an operating system to find a suitable hole for the program.
4. Explain the paging technique.
5. How does page table help the operating system to locate where the program is stored?
6. What is internal fragmentation problem? How can it be overcome?
7. Explain the segmentation technique.
8. Differentiate between pre-emptive and non-pre-emptive scheduling.
9. Discuss the different non-pre-emptive scheduling techniques.
10. What is a mobile operating system? Give examples.
11. Differentiate between CUI and GUI.
12. What happens during the booting process?
13. Differentiate between warm booting and cold booting.

14. Give the function of BIOS.
15. Differentiate between an interpreter and a compiler.
16. Explain the significance of buffering.
17. Differentiate between a hardware interrupt and software interrupt.
18. Explain the different types of clouds.
19. What are the different types of services provided by cloud computing?
20. How are blocks in a blockchain created?
21. Why are blocks immutable?
22. List some applications of blockchain technology.

Fill in the Blanks

1. _____ is the most important system software in our computer.
2. In paging, the main memory is divided into fixed size blocks called _____.
3. _____ acts as index specifying where the pages of the program are actually stored in memory.
4. Paging suffers from _____.
5. _____ maintains the segment table.
6. _____ is a program or application that is currently being executed by the CPU.
7. In _____ technique, CPU is allotted to each process on FCFS basis for a specified time.
8. The latest version of Windows is _____.
9. _____ is a mobile operating system developed by Google.
10. In the Booting process, _____ is performed by BIOS.
11. _____ Booting is performed when the computer restarts.
12. _____ is a ROM chip found on the motherboard that allows users to access and set up the computer system at the most basic level.
13. BIOS locates the _____ on the hard disk and loads operating system files from there into the RAM.
14. The _____ file contains all instructions in binary form.
15. _____ is a part of the operating system that loads the program from the hard disk into the main memory.
16. _____ is a signal sent by peripheral devices to the CPU to notify it to suspend the current process and execute the appropriate part of the operating system.
17. _____ means delivering computing services including servers, storage, databases, networking, software, analytics and intelligence over the Internet.
18. _____ is a time-stamped series of immutable records of data that is managed by a network of computers.
19. Every block has a _____ to the previous block in the chain.

State True or False

1. Operating system is added as a layer in between the application programs and computer hardware.
2. In the best-fit technique, the process is allocated the largest hole available in the memory.
3. In paging, size of a page is equal to the size of a frame.
4. In paging, a program's pages can be loaded anywhere in the memory.
5. Paging is in no way a better technique than best-fit, worst-fit and first-fit techniques.

6. External fragmentation means a certain amount of space is wasted within the memory frame.
7. CPU scheduling policy is not used in pre-emptive scheduling.
8. In round-robin technique, the CPU time requirements of each process must be known in advance.
9. Windows 10 can be used on desktop computers, tablets, and smartphones.
10. In CUI operating system, users give commands or instructions to the computer by clicking on icons, buttons, and menus.
11. Every device has a device driver that controls that device.
12. POST is performed by BIOS.
13. Warm booting takes place when the computer is started by pressing the power button on the CPU box.
14. In warm booting, POST is not performed.
15. Compiler translates one statement at a time into machine language.
16. A program can be executed by the CPU only if it is present in the main memory.
17. The speed of CPU is much slower than the speed of I/O devices.
18. Microsoft Azure is an example of a private cloud.
19. OneDrive is a cloud computing service which offers 15 GB of storage space to all users who have a Gmail account.
20. Data in a block is secured by encryption.
21. Changing any data in a previously created block will require re-mining of only that block.
22. Only key nodes store a copy of the blockchain.
23. A transaction is verified by users participating in the transaction.

Multiple Choice Questions

1. The operating system does not manage _____.
   a. Application software b. system software c. CPU d. None of these.
2. The technique in which the first hole that is big enough for the process is allocated to the requesting process is _____,
   a. Best-fit b. first-fit c. worst-fit d. All of these.
3. In paging, a user's program is divided into fixed size blocks called _____.
   a. pages b. blocks c. frames d. holes
4. To execute a program consisting of n pages, the operating system needs how many free frames in the memory?
   a. 1 b. n c. $n-1$ d. 0
5. Which of the following techniques suffer from external fragmentation?
   a. Paging b. Segmentation c. Best-fit d. Worst-fit
6. Each segment has a _____.
   a. base address b. limit c. ending address d. Only a and b.
7. In which technique, the process that enters first in memory will be executed first?
   a. FCFS b. Shortest Job First c. Round-robin d. None of these.
8. Which of the following is not a proprietary operating system?
   a. Linux b. Windows 10 c. Mac OS d. iOS
9. Which operating system is used on an iPad?
   a. Ubuntu b. Windows 10 c. iOS d. Android
10. Program translators (like assembler, compiler and interpreter) create a ____ file.
    a. .exe b. .obj c. .ps d. .docx

11. _____ produces the .exe file.
    a. Loader			b. Assembler		c. Linker		d. Loader
12. _____ is generated by the CPU itself to signal the operating system that an error has occurred.
    a. Hardware interrupt	b. Trap			c. Software interrupt	d. Interrupt
13. _____ clouds are owned and operated by third-party cloud service providers.
    a. Private			b. Public		c. Hybrid		d. All of these.
14. _____ provides servers, storage, networks and operating systems as a service from a cloud provider.
    a. IaaS			b. PaaS			c. SaaS			d. HaaS
15. In blockchain technology, _____ are created to represent any kind of digital asset
    a. blocks			b. tokens		c. hashes		d. digital signatures
16. Which of the following terms mean that no one can modify the data that is already stored within a blockchain?
    a. Decentralized		b. Encrypted		c. Transparent		d. Immutable

Answers

Fill in the Blanks
1. Operating System (OS)
2. frames
3. Page table
4. internal fragmentation
5. Operating system
6. Process
7. Round Robin
8. Windows 10
9. Android
10. POST (Power-On-Self-Test)
11. Cold
12. BIOS
13. MBR (Master Boot Record)
14. .obj
15. Loader
16. Interrupt
17. Cloud computing
18. Blockchain
19. pointer/ reference
20. Radio Frequency Transceiver

State True or False
1. True
2. False
3. True
4. True
5. False
6. False
7. False
8. False
9. True
10. False
11. True
12. True
13. False
14. True
15. False
16. True
17. False
18. False
19. False
20. True
21. False
22. False
23. False

Multiple Choice Questions
1. d	3. a	5. b	7. a	9. c	11. c	13. b	15. b
2. b	4. b	6. d	8. a	10. b	12. b	14. a	16. d

Algorithms and Pseudocodes

5

Chapter Objectives

This chapter elaborates on the following concepts:

- Algorithms – their features, advantages and limitations
- Flowcharts – their symbols, relevance, pros and cons
- Pseudocodes – Examples, advantages and disadvantages
- Decomposition technique to solve complex problems

Just imagine you have a younger sibling studying in class I and he/she has Art and Craft exam tomorrow. Your sibling is finding it very difficult to prepare for the exam, so your mother has asked you to teach him/her to make a yacht in origami. How will you do it?

You will think of simple steps and do one step at a time. Before going to the next step, you will make sure that the current step is completed, right? These steps can be given as shown in Fig. 5.1.

Now, imagine that your mother is not at home and your grandfather has asked you to make a cup of tea. What will you do? Just call your mother and ask her to tell how she makes tea for him, right? Your mother will instruct you step by step, and you will follow the same instructions to make tea.

Similarly, when writing programs for a computer, first instructions are written in the form of algorithms or graphically depicted using flowcharts.

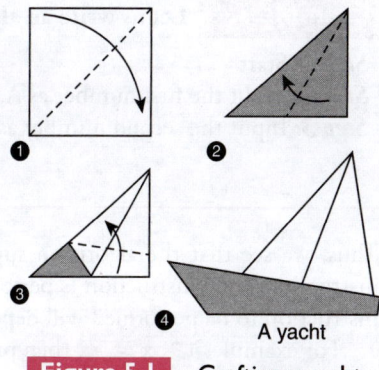

Figure 5.1 Crafting a yacht

Just as an architect designs a model of the building before starting its construction, a programmer works on an algorithm or flowchart before writing programs. Therefore, algorithms and flowcharts form the blueprint of the computer programs. Anyone can easily understand the solution of a problem or the logic of a program just by looking at its algorithm or flowchart.

5.1 ALGORITHM

An algorithm is a set of step-by-step instructions for solving a problem or completing a particular task. In the field of computers, algorithms are written to instruct the computer how to perform a task. However, every algorithm must give correct output in a finite (countable) number of steps. So, we can say that a good algorithm should have the following characteristics.

- It should be precise (small).
- It should not be ambiguous (confusing).
- The solution should be obtained by performing a limited number of steps.
- The algorithm should be clear, readable and easy to understand.

Example 5.1 Let us write an algorithm to add two numbers.

Step 1: Start
Step 2: Input the first number as A.
Step 3: Input the second number as B.
Step 4: Set SUM as A + B.
Step 5: Output SUM.
Step 6: End

Example 5.2   Let us write an algorithm to check if two numbers are equal.

Step 1: Input the first number as A.
Step 2: Input the second number as B.

Step 3: `IF A = B`
         `Then PRINT "EQUAL"`
      `ELSE`
         `PRINT "NOT EQUAL"`
Step 4: End

Example 5.3   Let us write an algorithm to find whether a number is even or odd.

Step 1: Start
Step 2: Input the number as A.
Step 3: Divide A by 2.
Step 4: Set remainder as R.

Step 5: `IF REMAINDER = 0, THEN`
         `Output EVEN`
      `ELSE,`
         `Output ODD`
Step 6: End

Example 5.4   Let us write an algorithm to find the larger of two numbers.

Step 1: Start
Step 2: Input the first number as A.
Step 3: Input the second number as B.

Step 4: `IF A > B, THEN`
         `Output A`
      `ELSE,`
         `Output B`
Step 5: End

Thus, we see that the algorithm supports *sequential* instructions and decision control instructions. In sequential instructions, one instruction is performed after the other in a specified sequence. In a *decision-control* flow, the next instruction to be performed will depend on the result of the decision.

For example, `IF x = y`, then print "EQUAL". Hence, the general form of IF construct can be given as:

    `IF` *condition* `then` *instruction_block*

A condition, in this context, is any statement that may evaluate either to a `true` value or a `false` value. In the above example, a variable x can either be equal to y or not equal to y. However, it cannot be both true as well as false. If the condition is true then the instruction block is executed. A decision statement can also be stated using IF-ELSE construct. Its general form is,

    `IF` *condition*
        `Then` *instruction_block 1*
    `ELSE` *instruction_block 2*

Here, if the condition is true then *instruction_block* 1 is executed else *instruction_block* 2 is executed.

Besides sequential and decision-control statements, we can also write **looping** instructions. Looping instructions are used to repeat one or more instructions(s) over and over again. The number of times an instruction is performed will depend on a condition.

Repetition is usually implemented using constructs like *while, do-while* and *for* loops. These loops execute one or more steps until some condition is true. If the condition is true, the instruction in the loop is performed; else, it is not.

Example 5.5   Display the first five natural numbers.

Step 1: Start
Step 2: `SET I = 1`
Step 3: Output I
Step 4: `SET I = I + 1`

Step 5: `IF I > 5, THEN`
         `Go to Step 6`
      `ELSE,`
         `Go to Step 3`
Step 6: End

In the above algorithm, did you notice that we are repeatedly performing steps 3, 4 and 5 until I becomes greater than 5. And each time we repeat the steps, the value of I is updated so that it comes close to the terminating condition and hence, complete in a finite number of steps.

5.2 SOME MORE ALGORITHMS

Let us write some more algorithms:

Example 5.6 Write an algorithm for interchanging/swapping two values.

Step 1: Input first number as A
Step 2: Input second number as B
Step 3: SET TEMP = A
Step 4: SET A = B
Step 5: SET B = TEMP
Step 6: PRINT A, B

Example 5.7 Write an algorithm to print the grade obtained by a student using the following rules.

Step 1: Enter the Marks obtained as M
Step 2: IF M>75
    then PRINT O
Step 3: IF M>=60 AND M<75
    then PRINT A
Step 4: IF M>=50 AND M<60
    then PRINT B
Step 5: IF M>=40 AND M<50
    then PRINT C
  ELSE
    PRINT D
Step 6: END

Marks	Grade
Above 75	O
60–75	A
50–60	B
40–50	C
Less than 40	D

Example 5.8 Write an algorithm to find sum of first N natural numbers.

Step 1: Input N
Step 2: SET I = 0, SUM = 0
Step 3: Repeat Step 3 and 4 while I <= N
Step 4:   SET SUM = SUM + I
        SET I = I + 1
Step 5: PRINT SUM
Step 6: END

5.3 FLOWCHART

A flowchart is a graphical or symbolic representation of a process. They are basically used to design and document complex processes to help viewers to visualize the logic of the process. Flowcharts help viewers gain a better understanding of the process and find flaws, bottlenecks, and other less obvious features within it.

When designing the flowchart, each step in the process is depicted by a different symbol. The symbols in the flowchart are linked together with arrows to show the flow of direction in the process. The symbols of a flowchart include:

Terminal: The oval symbol indicates the start and end of the solution. They are the first and last symbols in the flowchart.

Input/Output: A parallelogram is used to depict input/output instructions.

Processing: A rectangle represents arithmetic instructions like addition, subtraction, division and multiplication.

Decision: Diamond symbol represents a decision point. All decision-based instructions that check a condition and give result as yes/no and true/false are indicated by diamond in flowchart. Every decision box has two arrows coming out. One arrow will specify which instruction will be performed if the condition is True or answer is YES and the other will specify the instruction to be executed when the condition is False or the answer is NO.

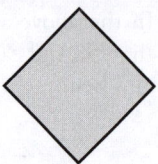

Connectors: Connectors are represented by a circle. Whenever flowchart becomes complex or it spreads over more than one page, then we can use connectors to avoid confusions and make the flowchart simple.

Flow lines: Flow lines indicate the exact sequence in which instructions are executed. Arrows shows the direction of flow of control. It specifies which instruction will be performed after a particular instruction.

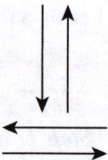

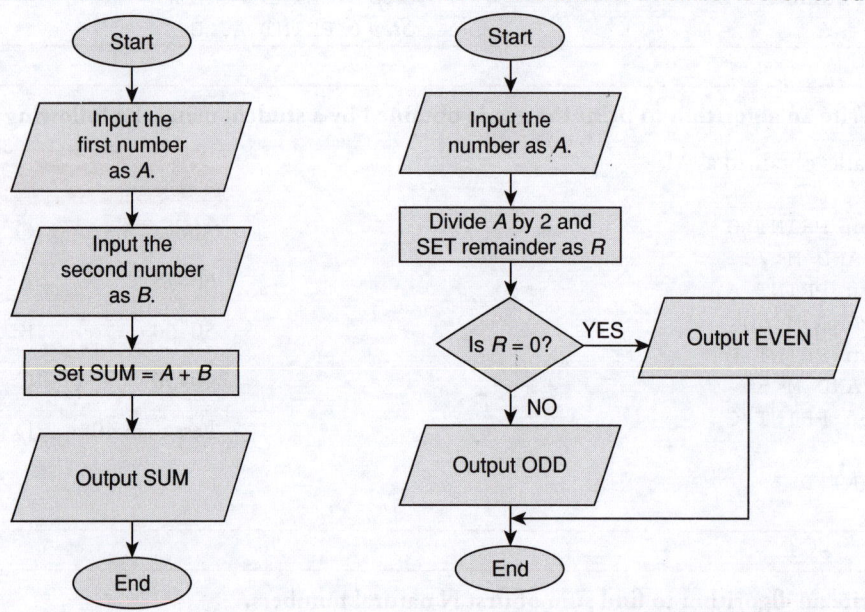

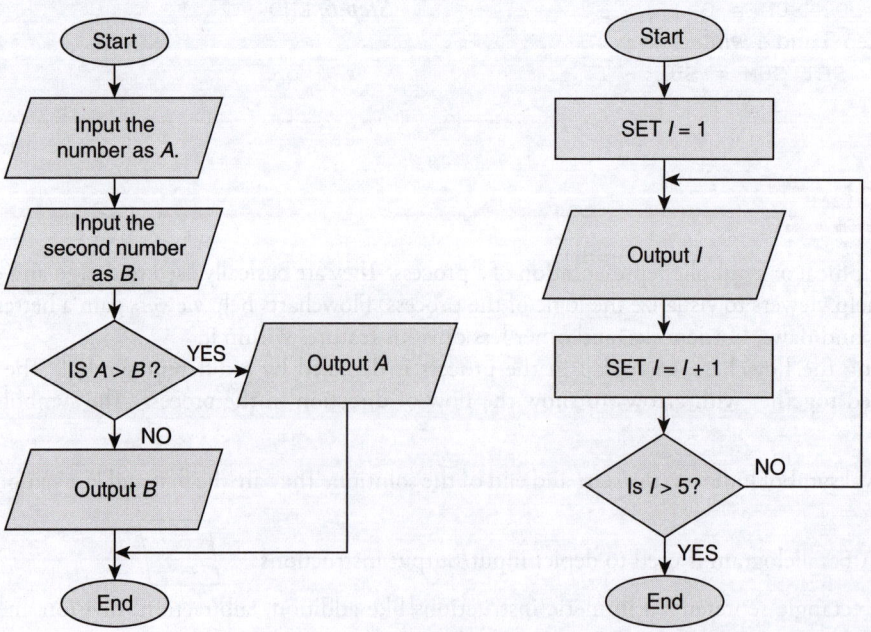

Flowchart to find the largest of three numbers

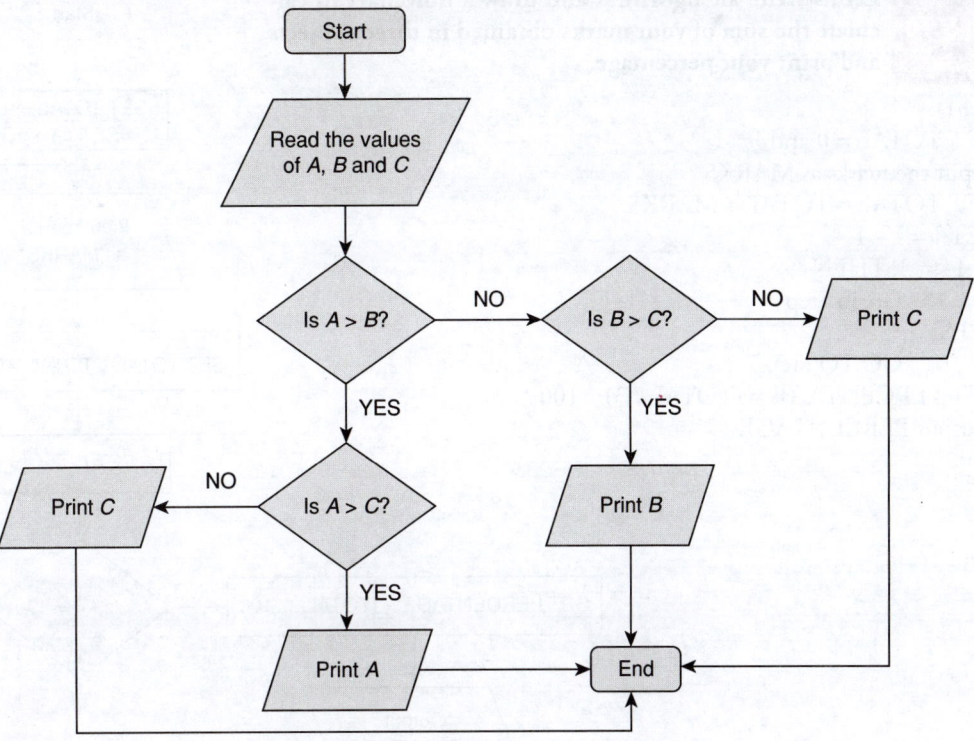

Example 5.9 **Draw a flowchart to calculate the salary of a daily wager.**

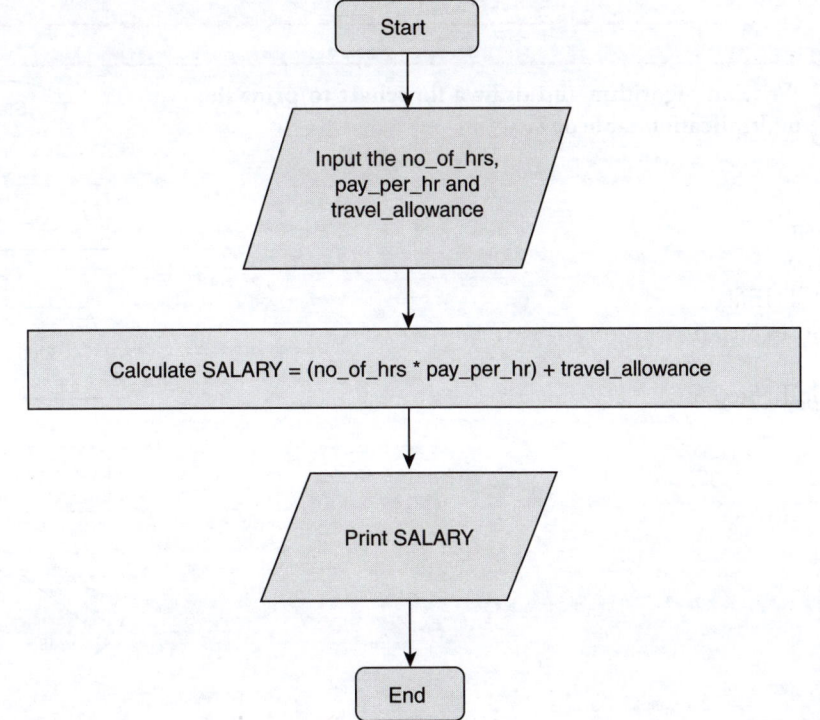

Example 5.10 Let us write an algorithm and draw a flowchart to calculate the sum of your marks obtained in three subjects and print your percentage.

Step 1: Start
Step 2: SET TOTAL = 0 and I = 1
Step 3: Input the marks as MARKS
Step 4: SET TOTAL = TOTAL + MARKS
Step 5: SET I = I + 1
Step 6: IF I <= 3, THEN
        Go To Step 3
   ELSE,
        GO TO Step 7
Step 7: SET PERCENTAGE = (TOTAL / 3) * 100
Step 8: Output PERCENTAGE
Step 9: End

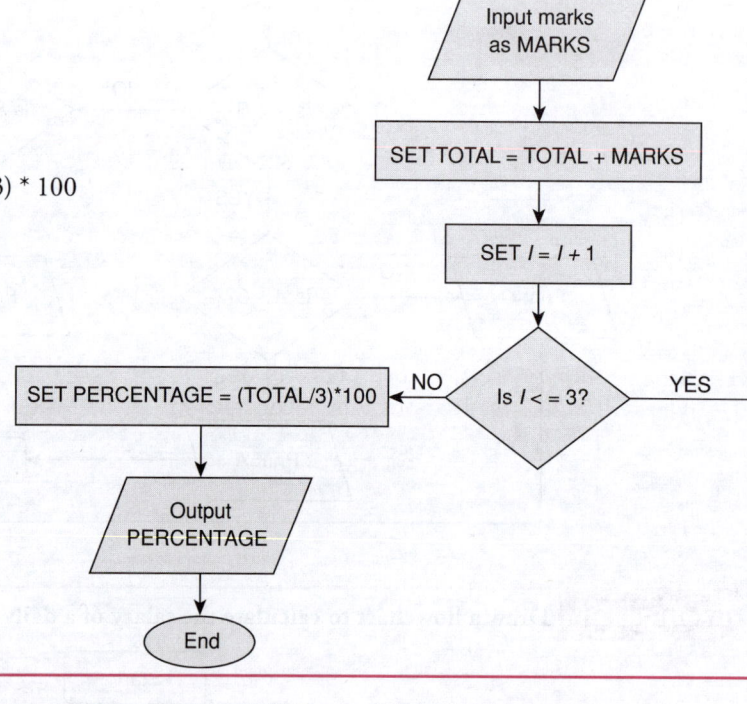

Example 5.11 Write an algorithm and draw a flowchart to print the multiplication table of 2.

Step 1: Start
Step 2: SET I = 0
Step 3: Output 2 * I
Step 4: SET I = I + 1
Step 5: IF I <= 10, THEN
        Go To Step 3
   ELSE,
        Go To Step 6
Step 6: End

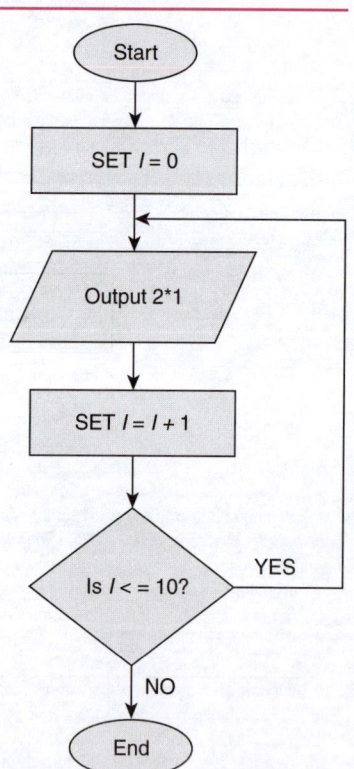

5.3.1 Significance of a Flowchart

- A flowchart is a *diagrammatic representation* that illustrates the sequence of steps that must be performed to solve a problem.
- They are usually drawn in the *early stages* of formulating computer solutions.
- Flowcharts facilitate *communication between programmers and users*. Once a flowchart is drawn, the programmers can make users understand the solution easily and clearly.
- Flowcharts are very important in the programming of a problem as they help the programmers to understand the *logic of complicated and lengthy problems*. Once the flowchart is drawn, it becomes easy for the programmers to write the program in any high-level programming language.

Hence, flowchart has become a necessity for better documentation of complex programs.

5.3.2 Advantages of Flowchart

- They are very good communication tools to explain the logic of a program.
- They help users to better understand the problem (or task) as well as the designed solution.
- They act as a guide or blueprint for the programmers to write programs based on the instructions specified.
- With flowcharts, there are lesser chances of errors in the program code.
- In case of any error, they help programmers to easily locate the point of error so that it can be rectified easily.
- Flowcharts help to analyse the problem in a more effective manner.
- Flowchart is also used for program documentation. They are even more helpful in case of complex programs.

5.3.3 Limitations of using Flowcharts

- Drawing flowcharts is a laborious and a time-consuming activity. Just imagine the effort required to draw a flowchart of a program that has 50,000 statements in it.
- The flowchart of a complex program can become complex and clumsy.
- At times, even a minor alteration in the solution may require complete re-drawing of the flowchart
- The essentials of what is done may get lost in the technical details of how it is done.
- There are no well-defined standards that limit the details that must be incorporated in a flowchart.

5.4 PSEUDOCODES

Pseudocode is a form of structured English that describes algorithms. It facilitates designers to focus on the logic of the algorithm without getting bogged down by the details of language syntax. An ideal pseudocode must be complete, describing the entire logic of the algorithm, so that it can be translated straightaway into a programming language.

Pseudocode is a compact and informal high-level description of an algorithm that uses the structural conventions of a programming language. It is basically meant for human reading rather than machine reading, so it omits the details that are not essential for humans.

Pseudocodes are an outline of a program that can easily be converted into programming statements. They consist of short English phrases that explain specific tasks within a program's algorithm. They should not include keywords in any specific computer language.

The sole purpose of pseudocode is to enhance human ability to understand the solution. They are commonly used in textbooks and scientific publications for documenting algorithms and for sketching out the program structure before the actual coding is done. This helps even non-programmers to understand the logic of the designed solution. There are no standards defined for writing a pseudocode because a pseudocode is not an executable program. Flowcharts can be considered as graphical alternatives to pseudocodes but they require more space on paper.

5.4.1 Keywords Used while Writing Pseudocodes

For looping and selection, the designer must include the keywords:

```
Do While ... EndDo; Do Until ... EndDo; Case ...EndCase; If ... EndIf; Call ...
with (parameters); Call; Return ...; Return; When, and so on.
```

Consider the following part of a pseudocode:

```
IF condition THEN
    sequence 1
ELSE
    sequence 2
ENDIF
```

Here, the ELSE keyword and sequence 2 are optional. If the condition is true, sequence 1 is performed; otherwise sequence 2 is performed. The following is an example of this construct:

```
IF age >= 18 THEN
    Display Eligible to vote
ELSE
    Display Not Eligible
ENDIF
```

The `WHILE` construct specifies a loop that tests a condition at the top. The loop is entered only if the condition is true. After each iteration, the condition will be tested and the loop will continue as long as the condition is true. The beginning and ending of the loop are indicated by the keywords `WHILE` and `ENDWHILE`. The general form is

```
WHILE condition
    sequence
ENDWHILE
```

An example of this construct is as follows:

```
WHILE i < 10
    Print i
    Increment i
ENDWHILE
```

A `CASE` construct indicates a multi-way branch based on conditions that are mutually exclusive. The pseudocode must include keywords such as `CASE`, `OF`, `OTHERS`, and `ENDCASE`. The general form is

```
CASE expression OF
condition 1 : sequence 1
condition 2 : sequence 2
...
condition n : sequence n
OTHERS:
default sequence
ENDCASE
```

Here, the keyword `OTHERS` is optional and specifies the default sequence. The following is an example of the CASE construct

```
CASE day OF
0 : print Sunday
1 : print Monday
2 : print Tuesday
3 : print Wednesday
4 : print Thursday
5 : print Friday
6 : print Saturday
ENDCASE
```

The REPEAT construct is similar to the WHILE loop, except that the test is performed at the end of the loop. The keywords used are REPEAT and UNTIL. The general form is

```
REPEAT
sequence
UNTIL condition
```

Here, sequence will be performed at least once as the test is performed after it is executed. After each iteration, the condition is evaluated, and the loop repeats if the condition is false.

The FOR loop is used for iterating a sequence for a specific number of times. The keywords used are FOR and ENDFOR. The general form is

```
FOR iteration bounds
sequence
ENDFOR
```

The following code illustrates a FOR loop:

```
FOR each student in the class
Add 10 as bonus marks
ENDFOR
```

Example 5.12 Write a pseudocode for calculating the price of a product after adding the sales tax to its original price.

Solution
```
1. Read the price of the product
2. Read the sales tax rate
3. Calculate sales tax = price of the item × sales tax rate
4. Calculate total price = price of the product + sales tax
5. Print total price
6. End
```
Variables: price of the product, sales tax rate, sales tax, total price

Example 5.13 Write a pseudocode to calculate the weekly wages of an employee. The pay depends on wages per hour and number of hours worked. Moreover, if the employee has worked for more than 30 hours, then he or she gets twice the wages per hour, for every extra hour that he or she has worked.

Solution
```
1. Read hours worked
2. Read wages per hour
3. Set overtime charges to 0
4. Set overtime hrs to 0
5. IF hours worked > 30 then
     a. Calculate overtime hrs = hours worked - 30
     b. Calculate overtime charges = overtime hrs × (2 × wages per hour)
     c. Set hours worked = hours worked - overtime hrs
ENDIF
6. Calculate salary = (hours worked × wages per hour) + overtime charges
7. Display salary
8. End
```
Variables: hours worked, wages per hour, overtime charges, overtime hrs, salary

Example 5.14   Write a pseudocode to read the marks of 10 students. If marks are greater than 50, the student passes, else the student fails. Count the number of students passing and failing.

Solution
```
1. Set pass to 0
2. Set fail to 0
3. Set no of students to 0
4. WHILE no of students < 10
     a. input the marks
     b. IF marks >= 50 then
           Set pass = pass + 1
        ELSE
           Set fail = fail + 1
        ENDIF
     ENDWHILE
5. End
```
Variables: `pass, fail, no of students, marks`

5.4.2 Advantages

- A pseudocode can be quickly and easily converted into a program that can be written in any programming language as its structure is similar to a programming language.
- Even non-programmers can easily understand pseudocodes.
- Pseudo code allows the programmers to focus on the steps required to solve a problem.
- They are independent of programming language. So once a pseudocode is in place, it can be used by programmer to code program in any language.
- Even a less experienced computer programmer can easily translate a pseudocode into a programming language
- Unlike flowcharts, pseudo code is compact. It does not tend to run over many pages. Its simple structure and readability make it easier to modify.
- A pseudocode expresses logic in plain natural language.

5.4.3 Disadvantages

- It is difficult to visualize the flow of the program, i.e., which branch leads to what?
- There are no accepted standards for writing a pseudocode. Everyone writing a pseudocode may follow a different style.
- Pseudocode can neither be compiled nor executed, so its correctness can be verified only when it is translated into a program.

5.4.4 Guiding Principles

When writing a pseudocode, one must remember the following points:

- The first statement in a pseudocode should be START (or BEGIN).
- The last statement in a pseudocode should be STOP (or END).
- Pseudocode should be concise. Do not give unnecessary details.
- To accept data from user, keywords that can be used are INPUT, READ, GET or OBTAIN.
- To print a message or display the result, use keywords like PRINT, DISPLAY, or WRITE.
- To make the pseudocode easily readable, capitalize the keywords.
- Statements should be written in simple English and should be independent of any programming language.
- Steps must be clear, unambiguous, finite, and must give the desired solution.
- Every line must have a single instruction.
- Each instruction should express just one action for the computer.
- A properly indented code that clearly highlights a particular control structure is preferred for better clarity.

5.5 DECOMPOSITION

Decomposition means *breaking down complex problems into smaller*, more manageable and simpler problems. We always teach young children to solve a problem in very easy steps. Similarly, whenever we have to solve a simple or a complex problem, we first write an algorithm or a pseudocode that gives *step-by-step simple* instructions for solving that problem.

In technical terms, we call this approach of solving problems **decomposition**. During decomposition, a large and complex problem is broken down or divided or decomposed into smaller problems. Algorithms that solve these smaller problems are then written.

Decomposition saves a lot of time and is also **less error-prone**. If there is a mistake, it would take longer to detect it in case the entire solution was scanned at once. But with decomposition, we know exactly the defaulting smaller solution and thus less time would be taken to repair it.

Another benefit to decomposition is that it facilitates **reusing of existing code**. That is, it allows programmers to easily reuse solution (or codes) written for a similar problem.

5.6 PROBLEM-SOLVING IN REAL LIFE

Decomposition is a useful problem-solving strategy. Every organization uses decomposition to carry out its daily tasks. For example, even a car manufacturing company first makes a list of the different parts it requires for making a car. It then decomposes the manufacturing process so that one factory can make the nuts and bolts, while another makes batteries and another makes the engine and so on.

5.6.1 Problem Decomposition

Real computational tasks are complicated. To accomplish them you need to think before you code. Steps for problem decomposition can be given as,

Step 1: Understand the problem.
Step 2: Write down the inputs and outputs.
Step 3: Use either top-down or bottom-up approach to solve the problem.
Step 4: Code one small piece at a time.
Step 5: After testing the code to ensure that it is working perfectly well, integrate it with other pieces of code that will together solve a part of the complex problem.

5.6.2 Top-down vs. Bottom-up Approach

A complex problem often divided into smaller problem units called **modules or functions**. The process of decomposing a problem into modules is called modularization. There are two main approaches to decompose a large and complex problem: top-down approach and bottom-up approach.

Top-down approach starts by dividing the complex problem into one or more modules. These modules can further be decomposed into one or more sub-modules, and this process of decomposition is iterated until the modules become too simple to solve independently.

Top-down design method is a form of stepwise refinement of the problem where we begin with the topmost module and incrementally add modules as required.

Bottom-up approach is just the reverse of top-down approach. In the bottom-up design, we start with designing the most basic or concrete modules and then proceed towards designing higher level modules. The higher-level modules are implemented by using the operations performed by lower-level modules. Thus, in this approach, sub-modules are grouped together to form a higher-level module. This process is repeated until the design of the complete algorithm is obtained.

Which of the two approaches is better is a difficult question to answer? So, the best way is a good blend of top-down and bottom-up approaches (Fig. 5.2).

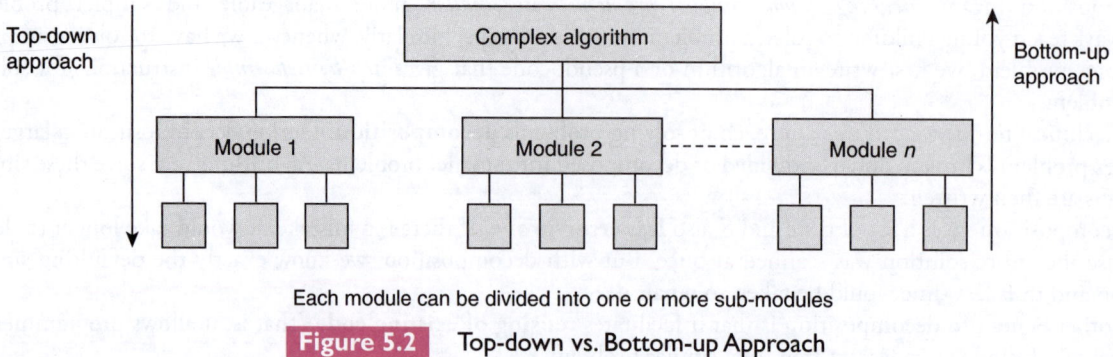

Figure 5.2 Top-down vs. Bottom-up Approach

Key Terms

Algorithm: An algorithm is a set of step-by-step instructions for solving a problem or completing a particular task.

Condition: A condition is any statement that may evaluate either to a true value or a false value.

Looping: Instructions used to repeat one or more instructions over and over again.

Flowchart: A flowchart is a graphical or symbolic representation of a process.

Pseudocode: A compact and informal high-level description of algorithms that helps designers to focus on the logic of the algorithm without getting bogged down by the details of language syntax.

Modularization: A complex problem often divided into smaller problem units called **modules or functions**. The process of decomposing a problem into modules is called modularization.

Chapter Highlights

- Like an architect designing a model of the building before starting its construction, a programmer works on algorithm or flowchart before writing programs.
- Algorithms and flowcharts form the blueprint of computer programs.
- Anyone can easily understand the solution or the logic of a program just by looking at its algorithm or flowchart.
- Every algorithm must give correct output in a finite (countable) number of steps.
- In sequential instructions, one instruction is performed after the other in the specified sequence.
- In a decision-control flow, the next instruction to be performed will depend on the result of the decision.
- Repetition is usually implemented using constructs like `while`, `do-while` and `for` loops.
- The symbols in the flowchart are linked together with arrows to show the flow of direction in the process.
- Decomposition means breaking down complex problems into smaller, more manageable and simpler problems.

Review Questions

1. Define algorithms.
2. Define flowcharts.
3. Explain the significance of writing algorithm and drawing flowchart.

4. Explain the symbols used in a flowchart.
5. What are the basic requirements that an algorithm must satisfy?
6. Write an algorithm and a pseudocode, also draw a flowchart for the following problems:
   a. To computer simple interest and compound interest.
   b. To convert distance from km to m and vice versa.
   c. To find smallest of three numbers entered by the user.
   d. To find the sum of the first 10 natural numbers.
   e. To determine if a number is divisible by 5 or not.
   f. To calculate parking charges, if

Type of vehicle	<=2 hours	>2 hours (for every additional hour)
Heavy vehicle	50	70
Four-wheeler	30	50
Two-wheeler	10	20

7. With the help of an example, explain the syntax of IF statement.
8. With the help of an example, explain the syntax of IF-ELSE statement.
9. How is repetition implemented in algorithms?
10. List some limitations of drawing a flowchart.
11. How does a pseudocode differ from an algorithm? Give the pros and cons of using a pseudocode.
12. Explain the iterative and conditional constructs used in a pseudocode.
13. Give some guiding principles of writing a pseudocode.
14. What is decomposition? How is it beneficial in developing complex programs?
15. Compare top-down with bottom-up approach of problem solving.

Fill in the Blanks

1. _____ and _____ form the blueprint of the computer programs.
2. In _____ instructions, one instruction is performed after the other in the specified sequence.
3. In a _____ flow, the next instruction to be performed will depend on the result of are represented the decision.
4. A _____, in programming context, is any statement that may evaluate either to a true value or a false value.
5. These loops execute one or more steps until some condition is _____.
6. _____ is a graphical or symbolic representation of a process.
7. A _____ is used to depict an input/output instructions.
8. _____ by a circle.
9. A _____ construct indicates a multi-way branch based on conditions that are mutually exclusive.
10. In _____ approach sub-modules are grouped together to form a higher-level module.

State True or False

1. A programmer works on an algorithm or flowchart after writing programs.
2. Anyone can easily understand the solution of a problem or the logic of a program just by looking at its algorithm or flowchart.
3. Every algorithm must give correct output in an infinite number of steps.
4. An algorithm should be precise.
5. The rectangle symbol indicates the start and end of the solution.
6. Every decision box has two arrows coming out.
7. Circles show the direction of flow of control.
8. Flowcharts are not a very good communication tools to explain the logic of a program.
9. With flowcharts, there are more chances of errors in the program code.
10. Pseudocode varies from one programming language to another.

Multiple Choice Questions

1. _____ is a set of step-by-step instructions for solving a problem or completing a particular task.
   a. Algorithm   b. Flowchart   c. Both of these.   d. None of these.

2. An algorithm should not be _____.
   a. precise   b. ambiguous   c. clear   d. readable

3. IF statements are used in _____ statements.
   a. sequential   b. decision control   c. repetition   d. loops

4. A condition, in programming context, is any statement that may evaluate to _____ value.
   a. true   b. false   c. a or b   d. a and b

5. _____ instructions are used to repeat one or more instructions(s) over and over again.
   a. Sequential   b. Decision control   c. Repetition   d. Loop

6. Repetition is usually implemented using _____ constructs.
   a. while   b. do-while   c. for loop   d. All of these.

7. The shape of the symbol representing arithmetic instructions is _____.
   a. oval   b. rectangle   c. parallelogram   d. diamond

8. Which of the following is not for iteration?
   a. IF...ELSE   b. WHILE...ENDWHILE
   c. FOR... END FOR   d. REPEAT... UNTIL

9. Pseudocode cannot be _____.
   a. compiled   b. executed   c. Both of these.   d. None of these.

10. Which of the following is the best approach for problem decomposition?
    a. Top-down   b. Bottom-up
    c. A combination of both   d. None of these.

Answers

Fill in the Blanks
1. Algorithms and flowcharts
2. sequential
3. decision-control
4. condition
5. true
6. Flowchart
7. parallelogram
8. Connectors
9. CASE
10. bottom-up

State True or False
1. False
2. True
3. False
4. True
5. False
6. True
7. False
8. False
9. False
10. False

Multiple Choice Questions
1. a
2. b
3. b
4. c
5. d
6. d
7. b
8. a
9. c
10. c

Basics of Computational Thinking

6

Chapter Objectives

The chapter aims to introduce Python as a programming language. To arouse interest in the language and enhance computational skills of the reader, we discuss the following topics.

- Understanding the relationship between computational thinking and programming skills
- Basic features, historical background, future scope, advantages, applications and limitations of Python
- Working with Python in interactive mode
- Writing Python scripts in IDLE
- Executing programs or rather scripts
- Introduction to Python character set, tokens, literals, numbers, strings and escape sequences
- Formatting numbers and understanding basic errors that may arise while working with floating-point values
- Strings, escape sequences and string operations
- Type conversion

Computational thinking is the process of breaking down a problem into a number of simple steps. It is a step that comes before programming. We all know that computer is a machine with no IQ. To make a computer solve any program, we have to give it instructions. Computers work on GIGO concept that is, Garbage-In–Garbage-Out principle. GIGO means that if we give incorrect data or instructions, then it will give wrong results. So, we must take utmost care to ensure that the data and instructions given as input to the computer are not only technically correct but also simple enough to understand.

6.1 COMPUTATIONAL SKILLS

Computational Thinking is a set of problem-solving methods that involve expressing problems and their solutions in ways that a computer could execute. It involves application of mental skills for designing computations that could be used to instruct computers to perform the tasks assigned by users. The benefits of learning and developing computational skills are:

- Computational thinking develops coding skills in students, which will help them to get better employment opportunities in future.
- Computational thinking enhances *critical thinking* and emotional competencies that result in long-term success.
- When students learn and practise computational thinking skills, it helps them to *excel* not only in the subjects of mathematics and computer science but also in social sciences, languages and arts.
- Moreover, a recent study concluded that computational thinking skills are highly correlated with and considered as a non-verbal measure of *intelligence*.
- A student with sound computational skills can easily articulate a problem and think *logically*.
- Students learn to *break down* the issues at hand and predict what may happen in the future.
- Students learn to analyse *cause and effect* of their actions or the actions of others.
- They learn to calculate the impact of the given situation. This helps them not only to improve their *performance* in studies and professional life but also to manage their relationships with those around them in a better way.

6.2 PROGRAMMING LANGUAGE PYTHON

Python is a powerful programming language with the right combination of performance and features that makes programming fun and easy. It is a high-level, interpreted, interactive, object-oriented and a reliable language that uses English-like words. It has a vast library of modules to support integration of complex solutions from pre-built components.

Python is an open-source project, supported by many individuals. It can be used on any operating system. Some features which make Python a complete programming language are given below.

- *Simple:* Python is a simple and a small language. Reading a program written in Python feels almost like reading English.
- *Easy to Learn:* A Python program is easy to read and understand. It uses a few keywords and a clearly defined syntax. This makes it easy for just anyone to pick up the language quickly.
- *Versatile:* Python supports development of a wide range of applications ranging from simple text processing to games.
- *Free and Open Source:* Python is an example of open-source software. Therefore, anyone can freely distribute it, read the source code, edit it and even use the code to write new (free) programs.
- *High-level Language:* When writing programs in Python, programmers do not have to worry about the hardware related details. They just need to concentrate on writing solutions for the current problem at hand.

> Python is being constantly improved by a community of users who have always strived hard to take it to the next level.

- *Interactive:* Programs in Python work in interactive mode. Users can give input and get the results accordingly. In this way, users feel as if they are directly communicating with the program.
- *Portable:* Python is a portable language. Hence, the programs behave the same on a wide variety of hardware platforms. The programs can work on any operating system without requiring any change.
- *Object-oriented:* Python supports object-oriented as well as procedure-oriented style of programming. While object-oriented technique encapsulates data and functionalities within objects, *procedure-oriented* technique, on the other hand, builds the program around procedures or functions which are nothing but reusable pieces of programs.
- *Interpreted:* We have already seen the difference between a compiler and an interpreter. Python program is processed at runtime by the interpreter.
- *Dynamic:* Python program executes dynamically. They can be copied and used for flexible development of applications. If there is any error, it is reported at run time to allow interactive program development.
- *Extensible:* Since Python is an open-source software, anyone can add modules to the Python interpreter. These modules enable programmers to add to or customize their tools to work more efficiently.
- *Embeddable:* Programmers can embed Python programs within their C, C++, COM, ActiveX, CORBA, and Java programs for added functionality.
- *Extensive Libraries:* Python has a huge library that allows programmers to perform a wide range of applications varying from text processing, maintaining databases to GUI programming.

Besides the above-stated features, Python has a big list of good features, such as

- *Easy maintenance:* Codes written in Python are easy to maintain.
- *Secure:* The Python language environment is secure from tampering.
- *Robust:* Python programmers cannot manipulate memory directly. Moreover, errors can be easily handled by the program code itself through exception handling procedures. For every syntactical mistake, a simple and easy-to-interpret message is displayed. All these things make the language robust.
- *Multi-threaded:* Python supports multi-threading, that is, executing more than one process (or copy) of a program simultaneously.
- *Garbage Collection:* Python performs garbage collection of all objects that are no longer used.

6.2.1 Limitations of Python

- *Parallel processing* can be done in Python but not as elegantly as done in some other languages (like JavaScript and Go Lang).
- Being an interpreted language, Python is *slow* as compared to C/C++. Python is not a very good choice for those developing a high-graphic 3d game that takes up a lot of CPU.
- As compared to other languages, Python is evolving continuously and there is little substantial *documentation* available for the language.
- As of now, there are fewer *users* of Python as compared to those using C, C++ or Java.

- It lacks true *multiprocessor support*.
- It has very limited *commercial support* point.
- Python is slower than C or C++ when it comes to computation heavy tasks and desktop applications.
- It is difficult to pack up a big Python application into a single executable file. This makes it difficult to distribute Python to *non-technical users*.

> BitTorrent, YouTube, Dropbox, Deluge, Cinema 4D and Bazaar are a few globally used applications based on Python.

6.2.2 History of Python

Python was developed by Guido van Rossum in the late '80s and early '90s at the National Research Institute for Mathematics and Computer Science in the Netherlands. It has been derived from many languages like ABC, Modula-3, C, C++, Algol-68, SmallTalk, Unix shell and other scripting languages. Since early 90's Python has been improved tremendously. Version 1.0 was released in 1991 which introduced several new functional programming tools and Version 2.0 brought list comprehensions. It was released in 2000 by the BeOpen Python Labs team. Python 2.7 which is still used today was supported until 2020. But there is no 2.8; instead, the support team will continue to support version 2.7 and concentrate on development of Python 3.

Currently, Python 3.7.x is already available. The newer versions have better features. These days, from data to web development, Python has emerged as a very powerful and popular language.

6.2.3 Applications of Python

Since its origin in 1989, Python has grown to become part of a plethora of web-based, desktop-based, graphic design, scientific and computational applications. Some of the key applications of Python include:

- Python is used to develop a wide range of applications including *image processing, text processing* and *web* at enterprise level using scientific and numeric data from network.
- 3D software like Maya includes Python which can be used for *automating* small user tasks.
- Python is a popular language for *web development.* For example, websites like Quora, Odoo and Google App engine have their codes written in Python. For web development, Python has frameworks such as Django, Pyramid, Flask and Bottle.
- *GUI-based Desktop Applications* can be easily developed in Python.
- Python is used to make *2D imaging software* such as Inkscape, GIMP, Paint Shop Pro and Scribus. It is also used to make *3D animation* packages, like Blender, 3ds Max, Cinema 4D, Houdini, Lightwave and Maya.
- Features like high speed, productivity and availability of tools, such as Scientific Python and Numeric Python, have made Python a preferred language to perform *computation and processing of scientific data*. 3D modeling software such as FreeCAD, and finite element method software like Abaqus, are coded in Python.

Moreover, SciPy is a collection of packages for mathematics, science, and engineering; Pandas is a data analysis and modelling library and IPython is a powerful interactive shell that supports ease of editing and recording a work session. In addition to this, IPython supports visualizations and parallel computing.

- Python has various modules, libraries and platforms that support development of *games*. While PySoy is a 3D game engine, PyGame, on the other hand, provides functionality and a library for game development. Games like Civilization-IV, Disney's Toontown Online, Vega Strike, etc. are coded using Python.
- Python is a suitable coding language for *customizing business applications*. For example, Reddit which was originally written in Common Lips, was rewritten in Python in 2005. A large part of YouTube code is also written in Python.
- Python is also used for *writing codes for operating system*. For example, Ubuntu's Ubiquity Installer, and Fedora's and Red Hat Enterprise Linux's Anaconda Installer are written in Python. Gentoo Linux uses Python for Portage – its package management system.
- Python is used to develop other *languages*. For example, Boo language uses an object model, syntax and indentation, similar to Python. Apple's Swift, CoffeeScript, Corba, and OCaml all have syntax similar to Python.
- Since Python is very easy to learn and an open-source language, it is widely used for *prototype development*.
- Python is used for *network programming* as it has easy-to-use socket interface, functions for email processing and support for FTP, IMAP and other Internet protocols.
- Python is a perfect language for teaching programming skills at the introductory as well as advanced level.

6.2.4 The Future of Python

Python has a huge user base that is constantly growing. It is a stable language that is going to stay for long. The strength of Python can be understood from the fact that this programming language is the most preferred language of companies, such as Nokia, Google, and YouTube, as well as NASA for its easy syntax. Python has a bright future ahead of it supported by a huge community of OS developers. The support for multiple programming paradigms including object-oriented Python programming, functional Python programming, and parallel programming models makes it an ideal choice for the programmers. Based on the data from Google Trends (Fig. 6.1), Python is amongst the top five most preferred languages in academics as well as industry.

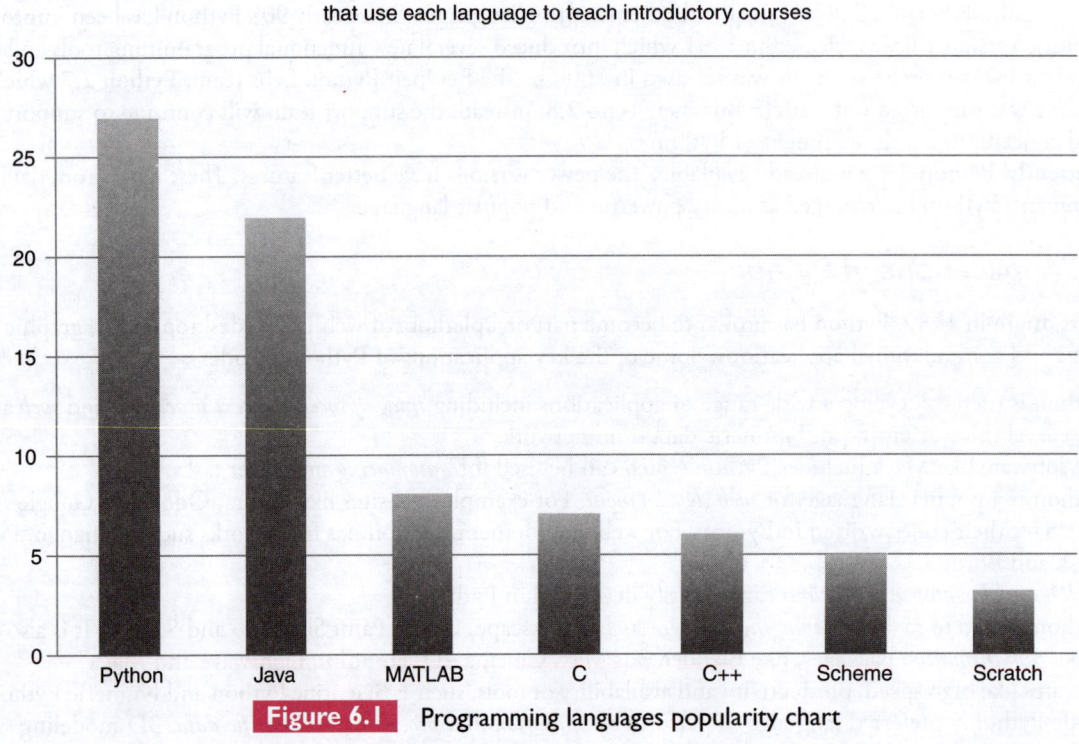

Figure 6.1 Programming languages popularity chart

Python is a high-speed dynamic language. Therefore, it works well in applications like photo development and has been embedded in programs such as GIMP and Paint Shop Pro. In fact, the YouTube architect, Cuong Do, has appreciated this language for the record speed with which it allows them to work. The best part is that more and more companies have started using Python for a broad range of applications ranging from social networks, through automation to science calculations.

6.3 WRITING AND EXECUTING THE FIRST PYTHON PROGRAM

Here onwards, we will be using Python, via the Python console. For that you need to first download Python from www.Python.org. The codes in this book have been developed on Python 3.7.3.

Once installed, the Python console can be accessed in several ways. We will discuss only two of them here. First, using the command line and running the Python interpreter directly. Second, using GUI software that comes installed with Python called IDLE (as shown in Fig. 6.2).

Basics of Computational Thinking

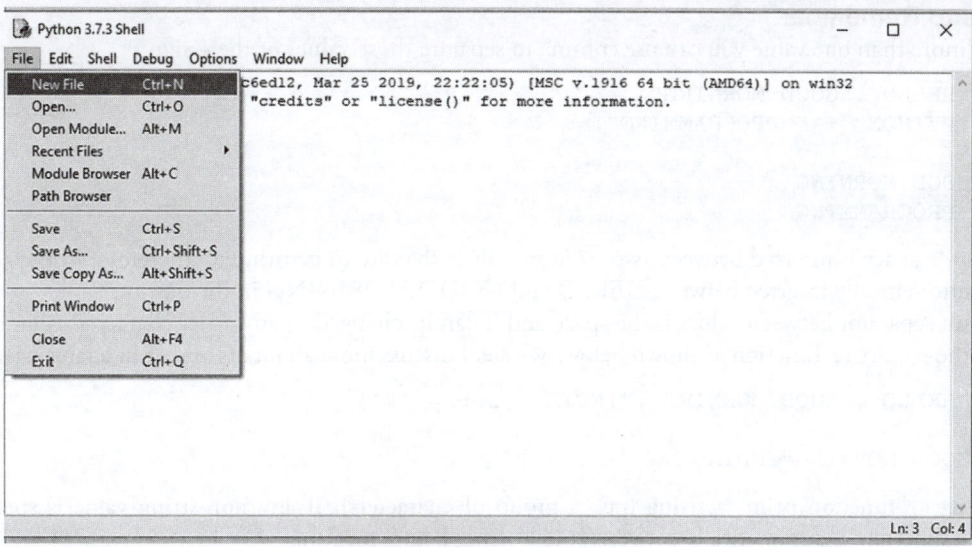

Figure 6.2 Python IDLE

6.4 INTERACTIVE PYTHON

The Python interactive console, also known as the Python interpreter or Python shell, provides programmers a quick way to execute commands without creating a Python file (with a .py extension). For the convenience of users, it provides support for everything including,

- all of Python's built-in functions
- pre-installed modules
- command history
- auto-completion feature.

The interactive console also enables programmers to paste code into programming files as and when required. It is a good alternative to execute commands when programmers want to quickly test some basic functionality of the Python language without having to write a whole script. To get the interactive interpreter, follow the steps given below.

Step 1: Click on Start button.
Step 2: Type Idle.
Step 3: Click on IDLE (Python GUI).

> The >>> symbol denotes the Python prompt.

The IDLE starts. You get a prompt of three right arrows. Type in your instructions at the prompt and press the enter key. **Let us print Hello World!!!** on the screen. For this, simply type the following line on the IDLE.
   Example: To print a message on the screen

```
>>> print("Hello World!!!")
Hello World!!!
```

More about the `print()` Function The `print()` function prints one or more literals (or values) followed by a newline. If you don't want to print on a new line then write end = ' ' after a comma as shown below.

```
# printing strings          #printing strings on the same line
print("Python")             print("Python", end= ' ')
print("Programming")        print("Programming")
OUTPUT                      OUTPUT
Python                      Python Programming
Programming
```

Key Points to Remember

- To print more than one value you can use comma to separate those values or the + sign.

  ```
  print("HELLO","GOOD MORNING")
  print("PYTHON" + " PROGRAMMING")
  OUTPUT
  HELLO GOOD MORNING
  PYTHON PROGRAMMING
  ```

- By default, a space is inserted between two or more values that are to be printed. Therefore, in the above code, a space is automatically inserted between HELLO and GOOD MORINING in the output.
- The default separator between values is the space and it can be changed to any other character using the sep argument in the `print()` function as shown below. We shall discuss more about argument in a later chapter.

  ```
  print("HELLO","GOOD MORNING","INDIA", sep = '#')
  OUTPUT
  HELLO#GOOD MORNING#INDIA
  ```

- The `print()` function prints a string (i.e., a group of characters). If any non-string value is specified in the `print()` function, it automatically converts it to a string before printing.

  ```
  print("Neha's Total Marks = ",98)
  OUTPUT
  Neha's Total Marks = 98
  ```

- The `print()` function automatically inserts a new line. So, in case we have multiple `print()` functions in the same program, then output of each `print()` function will be displayed on the next line or the new line.

  ```
  print("HELLO")
  print("GOOD MORNING")
  OUTPUT
  HELLO
  GOOD MORNING
  ```

6.5 WRITING PYTHON PROGRAMS USING THE IDLE EDITOR

In general, the standard way to save and run a Python program is as follows:

Step 1: Open an editor.
Step 2: Write the instructions
Step 3: Save it as a file with the file name having the extension .py.
Step 4: Run the interpreter with the command python program_name.py or use IDLE to run the programs.

To execute the program at the *command prompt*, simply change your working directory to C:\Python37 (or move to the directory where you have saved Python) then type python program_name.py.

If you want to execute the program in Python shell, then just press **F5** key (Fig. 6.3) or click on Run Menu and then select **Run Module**.

> To exit from the IDLE, click on File → Exit, or, press Ctrl + Q keys or type quit() at the command prompt.

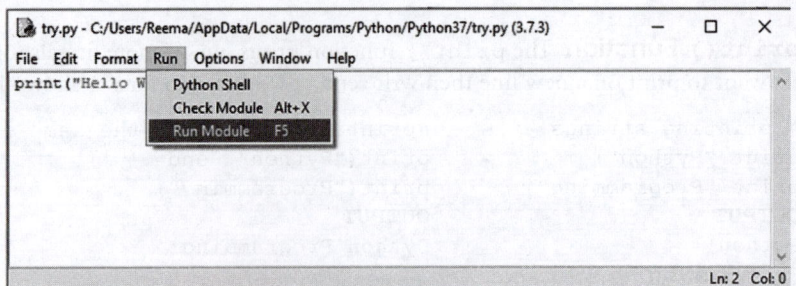

Figure 6.3 Executing Python code in IDLE

6.6 PYTHON CHARACTER SET

The character set of a language is a set of valid characters that the language can recognize. Such characters may be digits, alphabets, or any other symbol. Python supports Unicode encoding. The character set of Python includes:

- Lowercase English letters *a* through *z*.
- Uppercase English letters *A* through *Z*.
- Punctuation symbols like $,!, ?, etc.
- Whitespace characters which include a space (" "), tab, newline, etc.
- Non-printable characters like backspace ("\b") that cannot be printed but has a specific meaning.

6.7 PYTHON TOKENS

Tokens are the small units of a programming language (Fig. 6.4). Python supports the following types of tokens. In this chapter, we will read about literals in detail.

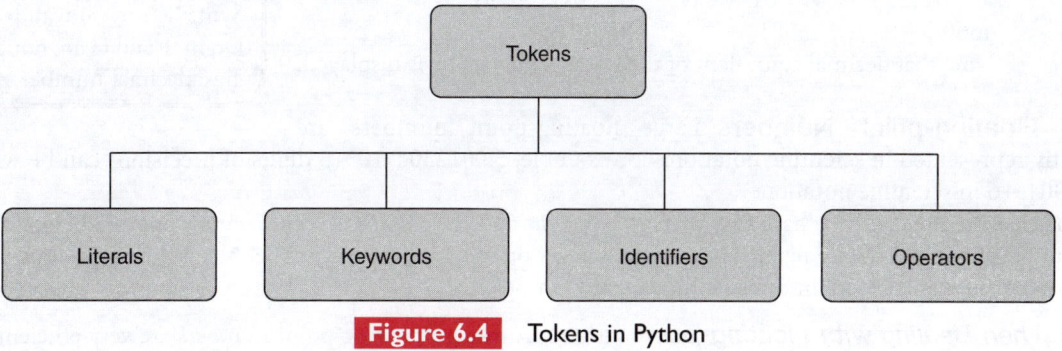

Figure 6.4 Tokens in Python

6.8 LITERAL CONSTANTS

The word "literal" has been derived from "literally". The value of a literal constant can be used directly in programs. For example, 7, 3.9, 'A', and "Hello" are examples of literal constants. The number 7 always represents itself and nothing else. Moreover, it is a constant because its value cannot be changed. Hence, it is known as *literal constant*. In this section, we will read about number and string constants in Python.

> **Programming Tip:** You can specify integers in octal as well as hexadecimal number system.

6.8.1 Numbers

Number, as the word suggests, refers to a numeric value. You can use four types of numbers in Python programs. These include integers, long integers, floating-point and complex numbers.

- Numbers like 5 or other whole numbers are referred to as *integers*. Integers can be positive or negative or even equal to zero. They do not have any decimal point.

  Bigger whole numbers are called *long integers*. For example, 535633629843L is a long integer. Note that a long integer must have 'l' or 'L' as the suffix.
- Numbers like are 3.23 and 91.5E-2 are termed as *floating-point numbers*. They are real numbers with a decimal point dividing the integer and fractional parts. The real part of the number can be either negative or positive or even equal to zero.
- Numbers of $a + bi$ form (like $-3 + 7i$) are *complex numbers*, where *a* is the real part and b is the imaginary part of the number. Both *a* and *b* are floating-point numbers and *i* represents square root of -1.

> The 'E' notation indicates powers of 10. In this case, 91.5E-2 means 91.5 * 10-2.

Remember that commas are never used in numeric literals or numeric values. Therefore, numbers like 3,567, 1,23.89 or –8,904 are not allowed in Python.

Types of Integer Literals There are three types of integer literals – decimal, octal and hexadecimal integer literal.

- **Decimal Integer Literal:** Any integer literal that does not start with a zero (0) is a decimal integer literal. Example, +17, –26, 1234, –89072.
- **Octal Integer Literal:** Any integer literal that starts with digit zero followed by letter o is treated as an octal integer literal in Python. Example, 0o12, 0o7654. Type the following statements in IDLE and see the output.

    >>> 0o12   >>> –0o12   >>> 0o7654
    10   –10   4012

    Note that decimal equivalent of the octal value is displayed

    >>> Oo1789
    SyntaxError: invalid syntax
    Digits 8 and 9 are not there in octal number system.

- **Hexadecimal Integer Literal:** Any integer literal that starts with digit zero followed by letter x is treated as a hexadecimal integer literal in Python. Example, 0x1234, 0xA7B6F. Type the following statements in IDLE and see the output.

    >>> 0x1234   >>> 0xABCD   >>> 0x7B9CF1
    4660   43981   8101105

    Note that decimal equivalent of the hexadecimal value is displayed.

    >>> OxTGlF
    SyntaxError: invalid token
    Digits T and G are not there in hexadecimal number system.

Large Floating-point Numbers Large floating-point numbers are efficiently represented in scientific notation. For example, $5.0012304*10^6$ (6 digits of precision) can be written as 5.0012304e+6 in scientific notation.

In a scientific notation, we have two parts – exponent and the mantissa. The mantissa appears before e and the exponent part follows e. While mantissa can be an integer or a floating-point number, the exponent is always an integer. Both mantissa and exponent can be either negative or positive.

Errors When Dealing with Floating-point Values Although floating-point numbers are very efficient at handling large numbers, there are some issues while dealing with them as they may produce following errors.

- **The Arithmetic Overflow Problem:** When two very large floating-point numbers are multiplied, it may result in an *arithmetic overflow*. Arithmetic overflow is a condition that occurs when a calculated result is too large. For example, just try to multiply 2.7e200 * 4.3e200. You will get result as inf, which means infinity. Infinity denotes that an arithmetic overflow has occurred.
- **The Arithmetic Underflow Problem:** Arithmetic underflow occurs when one floating-point number is divided by another. It is a condition that occurs when a calculated result is too small in magnitude to be represented. For example, just try to divide 3.0e-400/5.0e200. You will get the result as 0.0. The value 0.0 indicates that an arithmetic underflow has occurred.
- **Loss of Precision Problem:** When you divide 1 by 3, you know that the results is 0.33333333…, where 3 is repeated infinitely. Since any floating-point number has a limited precision and range, the result is just an *approximation* of the true value. Python automatically displays a rounded result to keep the number of digits displayed manageable. For most applications, this slight loss in accuracy is of no practical concern but in scientific computing and other applications in which precise calculations are required, it may be a big issue.

Built-in `Format()` Function: Any floating-point value may contain an arbitrary number of decimal places, so it is always recommended to use the built-in `format()` function to produce a string version of a number with specific number of decimal places. Observe the difference between the following outputs.

`# Without using format()`
`>>> float(16/(float(3)))`
`5.333333333333333`
	`# Using format()`
	`>>> format(float(16/(float(3))), '.2f')`
	`'5.33'`

Here, .2f in the `format()` function rounds the result to two decimal places of accuracy in the string produced. For very large (or very small) values, 'e' can be used as a *format specifier*. The `format()` function can also be used to format floating-point numbers in scientific notation. Look at the result of the expression given below.

```
>>> format(3**50,'.5e')
'7.17898e+23'
```

The result is formatted in scientific notation with five decimal places of precision. This feature is especially useful when displaying results in which only a certain number of decimal places is needed. Finally, the `format()` function can also be used to insert a comma in the number as shown below.

```
>>> format(123456.8901,',.2f')
'123,456.89'
```

Simple Operations on Numbers Python can carry out simple operations on numbers. To perform a calculation, simply enter numbers and the type of operations that need to be performed on them directly into the Python console, and it will print the answer, as shown below.

>>> 17 + 56	>>> 90 + 50 - 40	>>> 35 * 15	>>> 108 / 12	>>> -10 * 14
73	100	525	9.0	-140

Dividing a number by zero in Python generates an error and no output is produced, as shown below.

```
>>> 117 / 0
Traceback (most recent call last):
  File "<pyshell#7>", line 1, in <module>
    117 / 0
ZeroDivisionError: division by zero
```

When two numbers are divided, a floating-point number is always produced.

>>> 15 / 5	>>> 75 / 15.0	>>> 39.0 / 3	>>> 24.0 / 2.0
3.0	5.0	13.0	12.0

You can easily work with a floating-point number and an integer because Python automatically converts the integer to a float. This is known as **implicit conversion or type coercion**. An implicit conversion is performed by the compiler without the programmer's intervention.

Quotient and Remainder When diving two numbers, if you want to know the quotient and remainder, use the floor division (//) and modulo operator (%), respectively. These operators can be used with both floats and integers. Observe the following statements and their output. When we divide 78 by 5 we get a quotient of 15 and a remainder of 3.

>>> 18 // 4	>>> 18 % 4	>>> 324.0 // 6.0	>>> 234.567 % 6.5
4	2	54.0	0.5670000000000073

Exponentiation Besides +, -, *, /, Python also supports ** operator. The ** operator is used for exponentiation, i.e., raising one number to the power of another. Consider the statements given below and observe the output.

>>> 11 ** 3	>>> 5.25 ** 4
1331	759.69140625

6.8.2 Strings

A *string* is a group of characters. We have already printed a string in our first program in which we had printed "HELLO WORLD !!!". In Python, there are three ways in which a string can be used.

- **Using Single Quotes (')**: For example, a string can be written as 'HELLO'.
- **Using Double Quotes (")**: Strings in double quotes are exactly same as those in single quotes. Therefore, 'HELLO' is same as "HELLO".
- **Using Triple Quotes (''' ''')**: A multi-line string is specified using triple quotes. We can use as many single quotes and double quotes as required in a string within triple quotes. An example of a multi-line string can be given as,

> All spaces and tabs within a string are preserved in quotes (single quote as well as double).

```
>>> ''' HELLO WORLD !!!
'GOOD MORNING'
"WELCOME TO THE WORLD OF 'PYTHON PROGRAMMING' "
HAPPY LEARNING....'''
' HELLO WORLD !!!\n\'GOOD MORNING\'\n"WELCOME TO THE WORLD OF \'PYTHON PROGRAMMING\' "\nHAPPY LEARNING....'
```

Note that all the characters, spaces, tabs, new lines, and quotes (single as well as double) are preserved within triple quotes.

>>> `'Hello'` `'Hello'`	>>> `"HELLO"` `'HELLO'`	>>> `'''HELLO'''` `'HELLO'`

*Irrespective of the way in which a string is specified, all strings are **immutable**. This means that once you have created a string, you cannot change it.*

String Literal Concatenation
Python concatenates two string literals that are placed side by side. Consider the code below wherein Python has automatically concatenated three string literals.

```
>>> 'HELLO' 'WORLD'
'HELLOWORLD'
```

Unicode Strings
Unicode is a standard way of writing international text. That is, if you want to write some text in your native language like Hindi, then you need to have a Unicode-enabled text editor. Python allows you to specify Unicode text by prefixing the string with a u or U. For example,

> The 'U' prefix specifies that the file contains text written in a language other than English.

```
>>> u"Shubh Prabhat"
'Shubh Prabhat'
```

Escape Sequences
Some characters like comma (,), double quotes (") and back slash (\) cannot be directly included in a string. Such characters must be escaped by placing a backslash before them as given below.

```
>>> print('How's life?')
    SyntaxError: invalid syntax
>>> print('How\'s life?')
How's life?
```

The reason for the error was that Python gets confused as to where the string starts and ends. So, we need to clearly specify that this single quote does not indicate the end of the string. This indication can be given with the help of an *escape sequence* as specified in the second string – *a single quote preceded by a backslash*.

Similarly, to print double quotes in a string enclosed within double quotes, we must precede the double quotes with a backslash as given below.

```
>>> print("Sheena asked, "Will you come with me?"")
SyntaxError: invalid syntax
>>> print("Sheena asked,\"Will you come with me?\"")
Sheena asked, "Will you come with me?"
```

> **Remember:** When a string is printed, the quotes around it are not displayed.

Other useful escape sequences are:

Table 6.1 Some of the escape sequences used in Python

> An escape sequence is treated as a single character.

Escape Sequence	Purpose	Example	Output
\\	Prints Backslash	print("\\")	\
\'	Prints single-quote	print("\'")	'
\"	Prints double-quote	print("\"")	"
\a	Rings bell	print("\a")	Bell rings
\f	Prints form feed character	print("Hello\fWorld")	Hello World
\n	Prints newline character	print("Hello\nWorld")	Hello World
\t	Prints a tab	print("Hello\tWorld")	Hello World
\o	Prints octal value	print("\o56")	.
\x	Prints hex value	print("\x65")	e

Multi-line strings When specifying a string, if a single backslash (\) is added at the end of the line then it indicates that the string is continued in the next line, but no new line is added otherwise. For example,

```
>>> print("Hello World,\
Good Morning !!!")
Hello World,Good Morning !!!
```

Raw Strings If you want to specify that a string should not handle any escape sequences and want it to be displayed exactly as specified, then you need to specify that string as a *raw string*. A raw string is specified by prefixing r or R to the string.

> Raw strings are not processed in any special way, not even escape sequences.

```
>>> R"How\'s life at your end?"
"How\\'s life at your end?"
```

String Formatting We have already used the built-in `format()` function to format floating-point numbers. The same function can also be used to control the display of strings. The syntax of `format()` function is given as,

`format(value, format_specifier)`

where, `value` is the value or the string to be displayed, and `format_specifier` can contain a combination of formatting options.

Example: Commands to display 'PYTHON' left-justified, right-justified and centre-aligned in a field width of 30 characters.

>>> format('PYTHON','<30') 'PYTHON '	>>> format('PYTHON','>30') ' PYTHON'	>>> format('PYTHON','^30') ' PYTHON '

Here, the '<' symbol means to left justify. Similarly, to right justify the string use the '>' symbol and the '^' symbol to centrally align the string.

We have seen above that `format()` function uses blank spaces to fill the specified width. But you can also use the `format()` function to fill the width in the formatted string using any other character as shown below.

```
>>> print('PYTHON', format('-','-<10')'PROGRAMMING')
PYTHON----------PROGRAMMING
```

String Concatenation Like numbers, we can also add two strings in Python. The process of combining two strings is called *concatenation*. Two strings, whether created using single or double quotes, are concatenated in the same way.

`>>>'HI... and ....'+'BYE'`
`HI... and .... BYE`
	`>>>'''PYTHON'''+'''`
	`PROGRAMMING''')`
	`'PYTHONPROGRAMMING'`
		`>>>'''PYTHON'''+'''`
		`PROGRAMMING''')`
		`'PYTHONPROGRAMMING'`

Slice a String A substring of a string is called a **slice**. You can extract subsets of strings by using the slice operator ([ ] and [:]). You need to specify index or the range of index of characters to be extracted. The index of the first character is 0 and the index of the last character is *n*–1, where *n* is the number of characters in the string.

```
Index from        P    Y    T    H    O    N
the start         0    1    2    3    4    5    Index from
                 -6   -5   -4   -3   -2   -1    the end
```

The syntax of slice operation is s[start:end:stride], where start specifies the beginning index of the substring and end is the index of the last character of the string s. *Omitting either start or end index by default takes start or end of the string. Omitting both means the entire string.*

If you want *to extract characters starting from the end of the string, then you must specify the index as a negative number.* For example, the index of the last character is –1.

Specifying Stride while Slicing Strings: In the slice operation, you can specify a third argument as the *stride*. The stride specifies the number of characters to move forward after the first character is retrieved from the string. By default, the value of stride is 1, which means that every character between two index numbers is retrieved. If stride is 2, then every second character is accessed, if stride is 3 then every third character is accessed, and so on.

```
#Slice operation on string
>>> str = "Python Programming is Fun"
>>> str[0]                 #prints the first character
p
>>> str[4:10]              #prints characters from 4 to 9
on Pro
>>> str[5:]                #prints all characters staring from fifth character
n Programming is Fun
>>> str[-1]                #prints the last character
n
>>> str[:-1]               #prints all except the last character
Python Programming is Fu
>>> str[-7:]               #prints last seven cha racter
is Fun
>>> str[3:15:2]            #prints every 2nd character from 3rd - 15th character
'hnPorm'
```

Did you notice that when we use the slice operator, elements are accessed from left towards right? For any index n (positive or negative), s[:n] + s[n:] = s, this means that the slice operation always partitions the string into two parts in such a way that all characters are conserved.

Even the whitespace characters are skipped as they are also a part of the string. *If you omit the first two arguments and only specify the third one, then the entire string is used in steps.* We can even have a negative value in the stride. For example, if the value of stride is −1 then the string is printed in reverse order.

| #print every third character
str="Python programming is fun"
print(str[::3])
OUTPUT
Ph oai n | #print string in reverse
str="Python programming is fun"
print(str[::-1])
OUTPUT
nuf si gnimmargorp nohtyP | #print every third character in the
#reversed string
str="Python programming is fun"
print(str[::-2])
OUTPUT
nfs nmagr otP |

6.9 TYPE CONVERSION

In Python, it is just not possible to complete certain operations that involve different types of data. For example, it is not possible to perform "4" + 7 since one operand is an integer and the other is of string type.

Another situation in which type conversion is a must is when you want to accept a non-string value (integer or float) as an input. The input() function which accepts input(s) from the user takes it as a string. In case the user has to enter a numeric value then the string value must be explicitly type casted to numbers (integers or floats) so that calculations can be performed on them. In such situations, the user must perform conversions between data types.

```
>>>"7"+"4"     >>>int("7")+int("3")
'74'           10
```

```
x =input(" Enter the first number:")         x = int(input("Enter the first number: "))
y =input(" Enter the second number : ")      y = int(input("Enterthe second number : "))
print(x + y)                                  print(x + y)
OUTPUT                                        OUTPUT
Enter the first number: 7                     Enter the first number: 7
Enter the second number: 4                    Enter the second number : 4
74                                            11
```

Python provides several built-in functions to convert a value from one data type to another. These functions return a new object representing the converted value. Some of them are given in Table 6.2.

Table 6.2 Functions for type conversions

Function	Description	Example
int(x)	Converts x to an integer	int(3.5) gives 3
float(x)	Converts x to a floating-point number	float('123') gives 123.0
str(x)	Converts x to a string	str(123.45) gives '123.45'
tuple(x)	Converts list x to a tuple	tuple([1,2,3]) gives (1, 2, 3)
list(x)	Converts tuple x to a list	list((1,2,3)) gives [1, 2, 3]
set (x)	Converts x to a set	set([1,2,3]) gives {1, 2, 3}
ord(x)	Converts a single character to its integer value	ord('D') gives 68
oct(x)	Converts an integer to an octal string	oct(9} gives '0oll'
hex(x)	Converts an integer to a hexadecimal string	hex(1234} gives '0x4d2'
chr(x)	Converts an integer to a character	chr(70) gives 'F'
complex(x)	Converts to a complex number	complex(3,-8) gives (3-8j)

However, before using type conversions to convert a floating-point number into an integer number, remember that `int()` converts a float to an int by truncation (discarding the fractional part) and not by rounding to the nearest whole number. The `round()` works more appropriately by rounding a floating-point number to the nearest integer as shown below. The `round()` can even take a second, optional argument which is usually a number that indicates the number of places of precision to which the first argument should be rounded.

```
>>> int(3. 7)              >>> round(3.7)          >>> round(1234.56789012,2)
3                          4                       1234.57
```

Note that each argument passed to a function has a specific data type. If you pass an argument of the wrong data type to a function, it will generate an error. For example, you cannot find the square root of a string. If you don't know what type of arguments a function accepts, you should use the `help()` before using the function.

Key Terms

Statement: A statement in Python is an instruction given to the computer to perform any kind of action.

Computational thinking: The process of breaking down a problem into a number of simple steps.

Decomposition: Breaking down complex problems into smaller, more manageable and simpler problems.

Pattern recognition: Looking for patterns in puzzles and categorizing them.

Pattern generalization or abstraction: Identifying the details that are relevant to solving the problem at hand and ignoring the details that are not relevant to it.

Algorithm design: Laying out the steps and rules that must be followed to find a solution to the given problem at hand.

String: A string is a group of characters.

String concatenation: The process of combining two strings.

Slice: A substring of a string is called a slice.

Chapter Highlights

- GIGO stands for Garbage-in–Garbage-Out, meaning that if we give incorrect data or instructions, then a computer program will give wrong results.

- Python is a high-level, interpreted, interactive, object-oriented and reliable language.

- Once installed, the Python console can be accessed in several ways. We discuss only two of them here. First, using the command line and running the Python interpreter directly. Second, using a GUI software that comes installed with Python called IDLE.

- If you want to execute the program in Python shell, then press **F5** key or click on Run Menu and then select **Run Module**.

- The character set of a language is a set of valid characters that the language can recognize. Such characters may be digits, alphabets, or any other symbol.

- Tokens are the small units of the programming language. Python supports literals, keywords, identifiers and operators as tokens.

- Number, as the word suggests, refers to a numeric value. You can use four types of numbers in Python programs. These are integers, long integers, floating points and complex numbers.

- When two very large floating-point numbers are multiplied, it may result in an *arithmetic overflow*. Arithmetic overflow is a condition that occurs when a calculated result is too large.

- Arithmetic underflow occurs when one floating-point number is divided by another. It is a condition that occurs when a calculated result is too small in magnitude to be represented.

- Any floating-point value may contain an arbitrary number of decimal places, so it is always recommended to use the built-in `format()` function to produce a string version of a number with a specific number of decimal places. It can also be used to control the display of strings.

- A raw string does not handle any escape sequences. It is specified by prefixing r or R to the string.

Review Questions

1. What is computational thinking? List some advantages of computational thinking.
2. List the key skills in computational thinking.
3. Explain the features of Python.
4. Give some applications of Python.
5. What do you understand by the term Python character set?
6. Write a short note on literals in Python.
7. What problems can pop-up while dealing with floating-point numbers?
8. With the help of an example, explain the use of `format()` function.
9. What is a string in Python? Explain the different ways in which you can define a string.
10. Differentiate between implicit conversion and type conversion.
11. What is an escape sequence? Give examples. Why are they called so?
12. Write the commands to display the text "I love programming" in a width of 50 characters when the text is left-justified, right justified and centre aligned.
13. Write a command to print the string in reverse.
14. Justify the statement: "Python is a free and open source programming language".
15. Which of the following expressions would result in overflow or underflow error? Justify your answer.
    a. `1.23e+150*4.56e+100`
    b. `6.78e-100/4.67e+200`
16. Identify the expressions which will involve coercion and the ones which will involve explicit type conversion
    a. `5.0+2`
    b. `6.5*3.0`
    c. `7.0+float(8)`
    d. `6.2*5.0`
    e. `5.7+int(9.0)`
17. Find and correct the error (if any).
    a. `>>> print('It is Teacher's Daty today ')`
    b. `>>> print("Rohan knows "Hindi","English","Punjabi"")`

Fill in the Blanks

1. _____ is the process of breaking down a problem into a number of simple steps.
2. A _____, in Python, is an instruction given to the computer to perform any kind of action.
3. _____ means that if we give incorrect data or instructions, then it will give wrong results.
4. _____ means looking for patterns in the puzzles and categorizing them.
5. Python files are stored with a _____ extension.
6. The _____ function prints one or more literals (or values) followed by a newline.
7. To execute Python script file, _____ key is pressed.
8. _____ are the small units of the programming language.
9. Large floating-point numbers are efficiently represented in _____ notation.
10. _____ denotes that an arithmetic overflow has occurred.
11. _____ function is used to produce a string version of a number with specific number of decimal places.
12. The ____ prefix specifies that the file contains text written in language other than English.
13. A _____ is specified by prefixing r or R to the string.
14. The process of combining two strings is called _____.
15. The _____ specifies the number of characters to move forward after the first character is retrieved from the string.

State True or False

1. Computational thinking is a step that comes after programming.
2. Pattern recognition means Identifying the details that are relevant to solving the problem and ignoring the details that are not relevant in solving the problem at hand.
3. Python is an interpreted programming language.
4. Python is an open-source programming language.
5. Programmers can embed Python programs within their C, C++ codes.
6. Parallel processing can be done in Python.
7. Integers can be specified as octal and hexadecimal numbers also.
8. Arithmetic underflow is a condition that occurs when a calculated result is too large.
9. Strings are mutable in Python.
10. When specifying a string, if a single backslash (\) at the end of the line is added then it indicates that the string is continued in the next line, but no new line is added otherwise.

11. A Unicode string does not handle any escape sequences. It is specified by prefixing r or R to the string.
12. format() function can be used to control the display of strings.
13. The default value of stride is 0.
14. Whitespace characters are also counted as a character in the string.
15. Computational thinking means thinking like a computer or to give instructions to a computer.
16. Coding is not a part of computational thinking.
17. Computational thinking involves considering different options carefully before deciding upon the best one.
18. \r represents a newline.
19. An escape sequence is treated as a single character.

Multiple Choice Questions

1. _____ means breaking down complex problems into smaller, more manageable and simpler problems.
   a. Decomposition   b. Pattern recognition   c. Abstraction   d. Algorithm design

2. Laying out the steps and rules that must be followed to find solution to the given problem at hand.
   a. Decomposition   b. Pattern recognition   c. Abstraction   d. Algorithm design

3. Python is a/an _____ language.
   a. high-level   b. interpreted   c. object-oriented   d. All of these.

4. Python programs work on any of the operating system without requiring any change. This means that Python is _____.
   a. Interactive   b. simple   c. portable   d. dynamic

5. Which of the following is not a valid token in Python?
   a. Character set   b. literals   c. identifiers   d. keywords

6. Which of the following is not a valid literal constant in Python?
   a. 1.2   b. 5   c. H5   d. "H5"

7. Which of the following is not a valid number in Python?
   a. 50000000000L
   b. 5E10
   c. 5000000000.123455D
   d. 3 – 8i

8. The value _____ indicates that an arithmetic underflow has occurred.
   a. -inf   b. inf   c. 0.0   d. All of these.

9. Which of the following is known as the exponentiation operator?
   a. %   b. //   c. **   d. ^

10. By default, the format() function uses _____ character to fill the specified width.
    a. blank spaces   b. >   c. <   d. ^

11. A string can be sliced using which of the following operators?
    a. []   b. [:]   c. Both a and b.   d. None of these.

12. The index of the first character is ____ and the index of the last character is ____, where n is the number of characters in the string.
    a. 0, n
    b. 0, n – 1
    c. 1, n
    d. 1, n – 1

13. The index of the last character is _____.
    a. –1
    b. 0
    c. n – 1
    d. n

14. Which of the following statements is syntactically not correct?
    a. a = input ( )
    b. a = input ("enter a number")
    c. a = input (enter a number)
    d. a = INPUT ("enter a number")c

15. Which of the following statements is correct?
    a. a = 10 * 5
    b. 50 = 10 * 5
    c. 15 + 60 = y
    d. print 3 * 4

16. Identify the invalid string literal.
    a. 'PYTHON'
    b. «PYTHON»
    c. '"PYTHON"'
    d. «»PYTHON»»

17. Identify the valid floating-point value.
    a. 9
    b. 23/4
    c. 123,456.67
    d. 1.2

18. Which of the following is a valid long floating-point value?
    a. 1.2e
    b. 1.2e2.3
    c. 1.2e01
    d. 1,234e9

19. Which of the following is not a valid integer literal in Python?
    a. 0o123
    b. 0x123
    c. 0X123
    d. 0123

Give the Output

1. ```
   print("Hello")
   print("My Dear Students", end = ' ')
   print("Let us learn Python")
   print("Programming")
   ```

2. ```
   >>> format(10**25,'.2e')
   ```

3. ```
   >>> format(987654321.315978,',.3f')
   ```

4. ```
   >>> 'PYTHON'
   ```

5. ```
   >>> "PROGRAMMING IN PYTHON"
   ```

6. ```
   >>> ''' I ENJOY PROGRAMMING
   IN
   PYTHON'''
   ```

7. ```
   >>> 'PYTHON' "PROGRAMMING"
   ```

8. ```
   >>> print("Python Programming \
   is FUN !!!!")
   ```

9. ```
   >>> print(R'It is Teacher's Day today ')
   ```

10. ```
    >>> "I" + 'LOVE' + '''PROGRAMMING'''
    ```

11. ```
    str = "I Love Programming in Python"
    print(str[0])
    print(str[7])
    print(str[-5])
    print(str[7:10])
    print(str[::2])
    print(str[3:11:3])
    print(str[:-7])
    print(str[-6:])
    ```

12. ```
    >>> print(type(int('10')))
    ```

13. ```
    >>> str(print())+"abc"
    ```

14. ```
    >>> print(print("abc"))
    ```

15. ```
    >>> str(print("abc"))+"xyz"
    ```

16. ```
    >>> print(print("abc",end=" "))
    ```

17. `(10<20) and (20 < 10) or (5 < 30) and not (15 < 40)`

Answers

Fill in the Blanks
1. Computational thinking
2. Statement
3. GIGO
4. Pattern recognition
5. .py
6. `print()`
7. F5
8. Tokens
9. scientific
10. Infinity (inf)
11. `format()`
12. 'U'
13. raw string
14. String concatenation
15. stride

State True or False
1. False
2. False
3. False
4. True
5. True
6. True
7. True
8. False
9. True
10. True
11. False
12. True
13. False
14. True
15. False
16. True
17. True
18. False
19. True

Multiple Choice Questions
1. a
2. d
3. d
4. c
5. a
6. c
7. c
8. c
9. c
10. a
11. c
12. b
13. a
14. c
15. a
16. d
17. d
18. c
19. d

Give the Output
1. OUTPUT
   Hello
   My Dear Students Let us learn Python
   Programming
2. '1.00e+25'
3. '987,654,321.316'
4. 'PYTHON'
5. 'PROGRAMMING IN PYTHON'

6. 'I ENJOY PROGRAMMING\nIN\nPYTHON'
7. 'PYTHONPROGRAMMING'
8. Python Programming is FUN !!!!
9. It is Teacher's Day today
10. 'ILOVEPROGRAMMING'
11. OUTPUT
    I
    P
    y
    Pro
    ILv rgamn nPto
    o o
    I Love Programming in
    Python
12. <class 'int'>
13. 'Noneabc'
14. abc
    None
15. abc
    'Nonexyz'
16. abc None
17. False

Python – Building Blocks

Chapter Objectives

This chapter allows readers to understand the basic building blocks of Python. The topics listed below are discussed here in detail.

- Variables and identifiers
- Creating, initializing and assigning values to variables
- Multiple assignments that is unique to Python
- Relevance of comments in program code
- Data types, operators and expressions
- Indentation that may change the logic of the program altogether

We have already seen that a statement in Python is an instruction that performs an action. A statement may or may not display a value. For example, the statement, sum = 2 + 3, adds two values but does not display any value. But the statement, print(sum) displays the value that we obtain after adding 2 and 3.

In Python, no symbol is used to terminate a statement. Users just have to press the Enter key after typing the statement. Although we can type multiple statements in a single line using semi-colon (;) between the two statements, it is always better to type one statement in a single line for more clarity. So, avoid writing the two statements as,

> A line in Python can contain maximum 79 characters.

```
>>> sum = 2 + 3; print(sum)
5
```

In the last chapter, we started learning about tokens in Python. We have already covered literals. In this section, we will read about other tokens like keywords, identifiers and operators.

7.1 VARIABLES AND INDENTIFIERS

Using just literal constants, nothing much can be done in programs. For developing complex programs, we must store information to manipulate it as and when required. This is where *variables* can help.

Variable, in simple terms, means something that may change. We can store any piece of information in a variable and this information may change. For example, a variable today_temp may have value = 30 today but tomorrow it may be 29 or 31.

Thus, we see that in Python, variable represents a named location that has a value which can be processed as and when required (as for calculating values).

To be identified easily, each variable is given an appropriate name. Variable names are examples of **identifiers**. *Identifiers*, as the name suggests, are names given to identify something. This something can be a variable, function, class, module or other objects. For naming any identifier, there are some basic rules that you must follow. These rules are:

- The first character of an identifier must be an underscore ('_') or a letter (upper or lowercase).
- The rest of the identifier name can be underscores ('_'), letters (upper or lowercase), or digits (0–9).
- Identifier names are case-sensitive. For example, myvar and myVar are **not** the same.
- Punctuation characters such as @, $, and % are not allowed within identifiers.

> **Remember:** Python is a case-sensitive language.

Examples of valid identifier names are sum, __my_var, num1, r, var_20, First, etc.

Examples of invalid identifier names are 1num (starting with a digit), my-var (punctuation and special characters not allowed), %check (first character should be an alphabet or an underscore), Basic Sal (space not allowed), H#R&A (special characters not allowed), etc.

7.1.1 Creating Variables

To create a variable in Python, just assign a value to the identifier using the 'equal to' sign (also known as the assignment operator). For example, the following statements create variables with different values in Python.

```
num = 7
float_num = 12.34
ch = 'A'
str = "ABC"
print(num)
print(float_num)
print(ch)
print(str)
```

OUTPUT
```
7
12.34
A
ABC
```

When we create a variable, Python creates labels referring to those values as shown in Fig. 7.1.

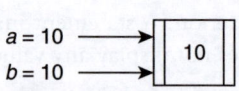
Here, both variables *a* and *b* have the same value. A label with value 10 is created and both variables point to the same label.

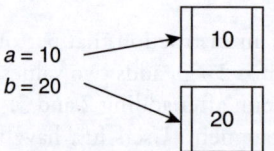
Here, the value of the variables are changed. Both variables *a* and *b* have differrent values. A label with label 20 is created and both variables point to their label.

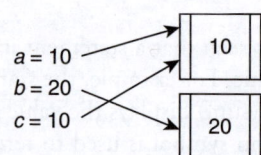
Here, both variables *a* and *b* have different values. A label with value 10 and another with label 20 is created and both variables point to their label. When the variable *c* is created with same value as that of *a*, it points to the label to which *a* is pointing.

Figure 7.1 Creating labels

Do you know that Python IDLE remembers variables and their values? Just type the following lines in the command console of IDLE and observe the output.

```
>>> x = 10
>>> y = 20
>>> str1 = "HELLO"
>>> print(str1)
HELLO
>>> print(x * y)
200
```

7.1.2 Data Types of Identifiers

In any programming language, data type is a classification that specifies which type of value a variable has. It also specifies the type of mathematical, relational or logical operations that can be applied to it without causing an error. For example, a string data type is used to hold textual data. An integer is a data type that can store whole numbers.

Python has various standard data types that are used to define the operations possible on them and the storage method for each of them. Based on the data type of a variable, the interpreter reserves memory for it and also determines the type of data that can be stored in the reserved memory.

The five standard data types supported by Python include numbers, string, list, tuple, and dictionary. We can even create our own data types in Python (like classes). In this chapter, we will learn about numbers and strings. Other data types will be explored in subsequent chapters.

> **Remember:** Python is a purely object-oriented language. It refers to everything as an object including numbers and strings.

7.1.3 Assigning or Initializing Values to Variables

In Python, programmers need not explicitly declare variables to reserve memory space. The declaration is done automatically when a value is assigned to the variable using the equal sign (=). The operand on the left side of equal sign is the name of the variable and the operand on its right side is the value to be stored in that variable.

Program to Display Data of Different Types using Variables and Literal Constants

```
age = 27
salary = 1234567
gender = 'M'
name = "Siva"

print("NAME:"+name)              # To convert integer to a string
print("AGE:"+str(age))
print("SALARY:"+str(salary))
print("GENDER:"+gender)          # To concatenate or to join two strings
```

OUTPUT

NAME : Siva
AGE : 27
SALARY : 1234567

To run this program, type the code in IDLE. Save it with a suitable name with an extension .py. Press F5 or click on *Run* and then on *Run Module*.

In the code, the program assigns literal constant 27 to the variable age using the assignment operator (=). Similarly, we have assigned literal constants to other variables and then printed their values.

In Python, you can reassign variables as many times as you want to change the value stored in them. You may even store value of one data type in a statement and then a value of another data in a subsequent statement. This is possible because Python variables do not have specific types; so you can assign an integer to a variable, and later assign a string to the same variable.

Program to Reassign Values to a Variable

```
age= 27 =1                       # age is an integer
print("AGE: ",age)

age= 'TWELVE'                    # age is a string
print("AGE: ",age)

age = 15.6                       # age is a floating point number
print("AGE: ",age)
```

OUTPUT

AGE: 27
AGE : TWELVE
AGE: 15.6

While re-assigning values to variables, be cautious about ensuring that the right type of value is used in operations. This is very much evident from the code given below.

```
a = 10
a = a*10
print (a)
a = "PYTHON"
a = a/10
print(a)
```

OUTPUT
100
Traceback (most recent call last) :
  File "C : \Python37\try .py" , line 5, in <module>
    a = a/10
TypeError: unsupported operand type(s) for /:
' str ' and ' int'
```

**The `type()` Function** The `type()` function having the syntax `type(object)` is used to determine the data type of the object. This function should be used to ensure that the right type of values is used in the expressions.

```
num = 10
print (type (num))
val = 3 . 4
print (type (val))
ch = ' a'
print (type (ch))
str = "abc"
print (type (str))
```

OUTPUT
<class 'int'>
<class 'float'>

<class 'str'>
<class 'str'>
```

lvalue and rvalue As the name suggests, expressions that come on the left side of the assignment operator are known as the lvalue. Correspondingly, expressions that come on the right side of the assignment operator are known as the rvalue.

This means that, lvalues are those objects to which values can be assigned. And rvalues are the literals. That is, they are expressions that evaluate a value and come on the right-hand side of the assignment operator.

Remember that

- literals or expressions that evaluate a value cannot come on the left-hand side of the assignment operator.
- variable names can come on the left-hand side of the assignment operator.

Valid lvalue and rvalue	Invalid lvalue and rvalue
a = 10	10 = a
B = 1*20	a*20 = b

7.2 MULTIPLE ASSIGNMENTS

Python allows programmers to assign a single value to more than one variable simultaneously. For example,

$$\text{sum = flag = a= b = 0}$$

In the above statement, all four integer variables are assigned a value 0. You can also assign different values to multiple variables simultaneously as shown below.

$$\text{sum, a, b, mesg = 0, 3, 5, "RESULT"}$$

Here, variable sum, *a*, and *b* are integers (numbers) and mesg is a string. sum is assigned a value 0, *a* is assigned 3, *b* is assigned 5 and mesg is assigned "RESULT".

Remember that *trying to reference a variable that has not been assigned any value causes an error*. This may happen if you have mistakenly used a variable without assigning it a value prior to its use or have deliberately deleted or removed a variable using the del statement and then tried to use it later in your code. The examples given below illustrate this concept.

Also remember that the right-hand side expression is evaluated before assignment is done and if there are multiple expressions in a statement separated by commas, then expressions on the RHS are evaluated from *left to right* and assigned in the same order.

```
x,y = 10,20
y,y = y+5, y-20  # last value of y persists
print("x = ",x, " y = ",y)
```

OUTPUT
x = 10 y = 0

Programs to assign and access variables

```
>>>name= "Kartik"
>>>age= 15
>>> print(name)
Kartik
>>> print(grade)
Traceback (most recent call last):
 File "<pyshell#8>", line 1, in <module>
   print(grade)
NameError: name 'grade' is not defined
```

Variable not declared prior to use

```
>>>name= "Kartik"
>>>age= 15
>>> grade = 'O'
>>> print(name)
Kartik
>>>del age
>>> print(age)
Traceback (most recent call last):
 File "<pyshell#14>", line 1, in <module>
   print( age)
NameError: name 'age' is not defined
```

Variable being used after it is deleted

7.2.1 Data Type Boolean

Boolean is another data type in Python. A variable of Boolean type can have one of the two values – *True* or *False*. Similar to other variables, the Boolean variables are also created while we assign a value to them or when we use a relational operator on them.

Remember: Boolean variables are also created by comparing values using the == operatot.

>>>Boolean_ var =True >>>Boolean_var True	>>> 30 ==50 False	>>>"HELLO" == 'HELLO' True
>>> 10 !=10 False	>>"Python3.7" != "Python3.4" True	>>>50>80 False
>>> 20 <=20 True	>>> 13 == 13.0 False	>>>13>=13.0 True

7.3 INPUT OPERATION

Real-world programs need to be interactive. By interactive, we mean that you need to take some sort of input or information from the user and work on that input to get the desired result.

To take input from the users, Python makes use of the `input()` *function*. The `input()` function prompts the user to provide some information on which the program can work and give the result. However, we must always remember that the *input function takes user's input as a string*. So, whether you input a number or a string, it is treated as a string only.

Program to Read Variables from the User

```
name= input("What's your name?")
age = input("Enter your age:")
print(name+ ",you are" +age+ " years old")
```

OUTPUT
What's your name? Goransh
Enter your age : 13
Goransh, you are 13 years old

To read integers or floating-point numbers using the `input()` **function**, you must use the `int()` and the `float()` function respectively. The `int()` function is used to convert a non-integer value to an integer. Similarly, the `float()` function is used to convert a non-floating-point value into a floating-point value. Hence, the output of the `input()` function which returns a string value can be passed to the `int()` or `float()` function to get a numeric value.

```
a = int (input ("Enter a number : "))
a = a + 10
print(a)
```

OUTPUT
Enter a number : 10
20

```
marks = float(input("Enter your total marks : "))
avg = marks/5.0
print (avg)
```

OUTPUT
Enter your total marks : 495
99.0

7.4 COMMENTS

Comments are added in a program to describe the statements in the program code. They make the program easily readable and understandable by the programmer as well as other users who are seeing the code. In Python, a hash sign (#) that is not inside a string literal begins a comment. *All characters following the # and up to the end of the line are part of the comment.*

Program to use Comments

```
#Program to find the cost of a dozen pens
price_1 = int(input("Enter the price of 1 pen : "))
price_12 = price_1 * 12  # dozen means 12
print("Price of a dozen pens= ", price_12)
```

OUTPUT
Enter the price of 1 pen : 10
Price of a dozen pens = 120

Some important points to remember about comments are:
- Comments are the non-executable statements in a program.
- The interpreter simply ignores the comments.
- When the program is run, comments are not displayed.
- Comments can be either typed in a new line or on the same line after a statement or expression.
- A program can have any number of comments.

7.4.1 Multi-line Comments

In Python, multi-line comments are also known as docstrings. They can be specified in two ways. First, by using three single quotes (or apostrophe). Second, by using three double quotes. They are used when explanation of the statements cannot be sufficiently given in one line. The code given below demonstrates the use of multi-line comments.

```
''' adding two
numbers'''
sum = 2 + 3
print(sum)
"""calculating average
of the two numbers
"""
avg = sum/2.0
print(avg)
```

OUTPUT
```
5
2.5
```

Did you notice that comments are not printed?

7.5 RESERVED WORDS

In every programming language there are certain words which have a pre-defined meaning. These words also known as reserved words or keywords that cannot be used for naming identifiers. Table 7.1 shows a list of Python keywords.

All the Python keywords contain lowercase letters only.

Table 7.1 Reserved words in Python

and	assert	break	class	continue	def	del	elif	else	except
exec	finally	for	from	global	if	import	in	is	lambda
not	or	pass	print	raise	return	try	while	with	yield

7.6 INDENTATION

Whitespace at the beginning of the line is called *indentation*. These whitespaces or indentations are very important in Python. In a Python program, the leading whitespace including spaces and tabs at the beginning of the logical line determines the indentation level of that logical line.

The level of indentation groups statements to form a block of statements. This means that statements in a block must have the same indentation level. Python checks the indentation level very strictly and gives an error if indentation is not correct.

In the code below, there is a tab at the beginning of the second line. The error indicated by Python tells us that there is an indentation error. Python does not allow you to arbitrarily start new blocks of statements.

```
a= 10
    a=a+1      #Indentation Error
print(a)
```

```
a = 10
a = a + 1
print(a)
```

OUTPUT
```
11
```

Remember: Use a single tab for each indentation level.

Like other programming languages, Python does not use curly braces ({...}). Therefore, to indicate blocks of code for class and function definitions or for flow control (discussed later in the book), it uses only indentation to form a block. *All statements inside a block should be at the same indentation level.*

7.7 OPERATORS AND EXPRESSIONS

Operators are the constructs that are used to manipulate the value of operands. Some basic operators include +, –, * and /. An expression in a programming language is any valid combination of tokens that represents a value. There are two types of expressions:

Simple expressions in which there are only values. For example, 29.

Complex expression in which one or more operators are used on operand(s) to generate a value. For example, in the expression sum = 2 + 4. Here, 2 and 4 are operands and + is the operator. 10 * 8 / 2 is another example of a complex expression.

> Operands are values on which operators are applied to generate a value.

However, expressions can also be classified as arithmetic expressions, logical expressions, string expressions and relational expressions, where

- Arithmetic expressions consist of numbers and arithmetic operators.
- Logical expressions have literals or variables and logical operators.
- Relational expressions have literals or variables and relational operators.
- String expressions have string operands and string operators (like, * and +).

Different operators supported by Python include:
a. Arithmetic operators b. Comparison (Relational) operators c. Assignment operators
d. Logical operators e. Unary operators f. Bitwise operators
g. Membership operators h. Identity operators

7.7.1 Arithmetic Operators

Some basic arithmetic operators are +, –, *, /, %, ** and //. You can apply these operators on numbers as well as on numeric variables to perform corresponding operations. For example, if $a = 10$ and $b = 20$, then the result of the operations can be shown as given in Table 7.2.

Table 7.2 Arithmetic operators

Operator	Description	Example	Output
+	Addition – Adds the operands	`>>> print(a + b)`	30
–	Subtraction – Subtracts operand on the right from the operand on the left of the operator	`>>> print(a - b)`	-10
*	Multiplication – Multiplies the operands	`>>> print(a * b)`	200
/	Division – Divides operand on the left side of the operator with the operand on its right. The division operator returns the quotient.	`>>> print(b / a)`	2.0
%	Modulus – Divides operand on the left side of the operator with the operand on its right. The modulus operator returns the remainder.	`>>> print(b % a)`	0

//	Floor Division – Divides the operands and returns the quotient. It also removes the digits after the decimal point. If one of the operands is negative, the result is floored (rounded away from zero towards negative infinity).	`>>> print(24//5)`
		`>>> print( 24.0//5.0)`
		`>>> print(-37//4)`
		`>>> print(-17.0//3)`
			4
			4.0
			-10
			-5.0

**	Exponent – Performs exponential calculation. That is, it raises operand on the right side to the operand on the left of the operator.	`>>> print(a**b)`	10^{20}

7.7.2 Comparison Operators

Comparison operators, also known as *relational operators*, are used to compare the values on its either side and determine the relation between them. For example, assuming $a = 10$ and $b = 20$, we can use the comparison operators on them as specified in Table 7.3.

Table 7.3 Comparison operator

Operator	Description	Example	Output
==	Returns true if the two values are exactly equal.	`>>> print(a == b)`	False
!=	Returns true if the two values are not equal.	`>>> print(a != b)`	True
>	Returns true if the value at the operand on the left side of the operator is greater than the value on its right side.	`>>> print(a > b)`	False
<	Returns true if the value at the operand on the right side of the operator is greater than the value on its left side.	`>>> print(a < b)`	True
>=	Returns true if the value at the operand on the left side of the operator is either greater than or equal to the value on its right side.	`>>> print (a >= b)`	False
<=	Returns true if the value at the operand on the right side of the operator is either greater than or equal to the value on its left side.	`>>> print (a <= b)`	True

7.7.3 Assignment and In-place or Shortcut Operators

Assignment operator, as the name suggests, assigns value to the operand. In-place operators, also known as *shortcut operators*, that include +=, -=, *=, /=, %=, //= and **= allow you to write codes like num = num + 10 more concisely, as num += 3. Different types of assignment and in-place operators are given in Table 7.4.

> Remember that <, > operators can also be used to compare strings lexicographically.

Example 7.1 Application of the += operator on strings

```
>>> str1 = "PYTHON"
>>> str2 = "PROGRAMMING"
>>> str1 += str2
>>> print(str1)
PYTHONPROGRAMMING
```

Table 7.4 Assignment and In-place Operator

Operator	Example
=	c = a, assigns value of a to c
+=	a += b is same as a = a + b
-=	a -= b is same as a = a - b
*=	a *= b is same as a = a * b
/=	a /= b is same as a = a / b
%=	a %= b is same as a = a % b
//=	a //= b is same as a = a // b
**=	a **= b is same as a = a ** b

7.7.4 Unary Operators

Unary operators act on single operands. Unary minus operator is strikingly different from the arithmetic operator that operates on two operands and subtracts the second operand from the first operand. When an operand is preceded by a unary minus sign, its value is negated.

For example, if a number is positive, it becomes negative when preceded with a unary minus operator. Similarly, if the number is negative, it becomes positive after applying the unary minus operator. Consider the given example.

> Remember that unlike other programming languages, Python does not support prefix and postfix increment or decrement operators.

```
>>>a = -5        >>>a = -5
>>>b = -a        >>>b = -a
>>>print(b)      >>>print(b)
OUTPUT           OUTPUT
5                -5
```

7.7.5 Bitwise Operators

As the name suggests, bitwise operators perform operations at bit level. These operators include bitwise AND, bitwise OR, bitwise XOR, and shift operators. Bitwise operators expect their operands to be integers and treat them as a sequence of bits.

Bitwise AND (&): When we use the bitwise AND operator, the bit in the first operand is ANDed with the corresponding bit in the second operand. The bitwise-AND operator compares each bit of its first operand with the corresponding bit of its second operand. If both bits are 1, the corresponding bit in the result is 1 and 0 otherwise.

Bitwise OR (|): When we use the bitwise OR operator, the bit in the first operand is ORed with the corresponding bit in the second operand. The bitwise-OR operator compares each bit of its first operand with the corresponding bit of its second operand. If one or both bits are 1, the corresponding bit in the result is 1 and 0 otherwise.

Bitwise XOR (^): When we use the bitwise XOR operator, the bit in the first operand is XORed with the corresponding bit in the second operand. That is, the bitwise-XOR operator compares each bit of its first operand with the corresponding bit of its second operand. If one of the bits is 1, the corresponding bit in the result is1 and 0 otherwise.

Bitwise NOT (~): The bitwise NOT, or complement, is a unary operation that performs logical negation on each bit of the operand. By performing negation of each bit, it actually produces the ones' complement of the given binary value. Bitwise NOT operator sets the bit to 1, if it was initially 0 and sets it to 0, if it was initially 1.

The truth tables of these Bitwise operators are summarized in Table 7.5.

Table 7.5 Truth tables for bitwise operators

A	B	A&B	A	B	A|B	A	B	A^B	A	!A
0	0	0	0	0	0	0	0	0	0	1
0	1	0	0	1	1	0	1	1	1	0
1	0	0	1	0	1	1	0	1		
1	1	1	1	1	1	1	1	0		

```
>>> x = 6              >>> x = 6              >>> x = 6              >>> x = 6
>>> y = 8              >>> y = 8              >>> y = 8              >>> print(~x)
>>> print(x&y)         >>> print(x|y)         >>> print(x^y)         -7

OUTPUT                 OUTPUT                 OUTPUT
0                      14                     14
```

You can check the result of bitwise operator by converting a number into binary using the **bin() function**. For example, >>> bin(15) will give '0b1111'. >>> bin(7) gives '0b111'. >>> 15 & 7 gives 7, as 1 1 1 1 & 0 1 1 1 gives 0 1 1 1.

```
1111
0111
0111
```

7.7.6 Shift Operators

Python supports two bitwise shift operators. They are shift left (<<) and shift right (>>). These operations are used to shift bits to the left or to the right. The syntax for a shift operation can be given as: **operand op num,**

where the bits in operand are shifted left or right depending on the operator (left if the operator is << and right if the operator is>>) by number of places denoted by num.

If we left shift 01011101, then after first left shift we will get, 10111010. After second left shift, we will get, 01110100.

If we right shift 01011101, then after first right shift we will get, 00101110, After second left shift, we will get, 00010111.

```
>>> x = 5              >>> x= 80
>>> y = 4              >>> y = 4
>>> x >> y             >>>x >> y
80                     5
```

When we apply a left shift, every bit in x is shifted to the left by one place. Therefore, the MSB (most significant bit) of x is lost and the LSB of x is set to 0.

If you observe carefully, you will notice that ***shifting once to the left multiplies the number by 2.*** On the contrary, when we apply a right shift, every bit in x is

> Remember that Bitwise operators cannot be applied to float or double variables.

shifted to the right by one place. Therefore, the LSB (least significant bit) of x is lost and the MSB of x is set to 0. *When we shift once to the right, it divides the number by 2.*

7.7.7 Logical Operators

Python supports three logical operators—logical AND, logical OR, and logical NOT. As in case of arithmetic expressions, the logical expressions are evaluated from left to right.

- *Logical AND:* Logical AND operator is used to simultaneously evaluate two conditions or expressions with relational operators. If expressions on both the sides (left and right side) of the logical operator are true, then the whole expression is true; else it is false. For example, (a > b) and (a > c), will return TRUE only if the value of a is greater than the values of b and c.
  The AND operator tests the second operand only if the first operand is true.

> Remember that the Truth table of logical and, or and not is exactly same as that of Bitwise AND, OR and NOT operators.

- *Logical OR:* Logical OR operator is used to simultaneously evaluate two conditions or expressions with relational operators. If one or both the expressions of the logical operator is true, then the whole expression is true. This means that the expression is false only if both the expressions are false. For example, (a > b) or (a != b) will return TRUE if a is either greater than b or less than b. It will return FALSE if a is equal to b.
- *Logical NOT:* The logical NOT operator takes a single expression and negates the value of the expression. Logical NOT produces a zero if the expression evaluates to a non-zero value and produces a 1 if the expression produces a zero. In other words, it just reverses the value of the expression. For example,

```
>>> a = 10                              >>> a = 0
>>> b = not a   a is non-zero (or       >>> b = not a   a is zero (or FALSE) so
>>> print(b)    TRUE) so b is FALSE     >>> print(b)    b is TRUE
False                                   True
```

It can be noted that the *logical expressions operate in a shortcut (or lazy) fashion and stop the evaluation when it knows the final outcome for sure.* For example, in a logical expression involving logical AND, if the first operand is false, then the second operand is not evaluated as it is certain that the result will be false. Similarly, for a *logical expression involving logical OR, if the first operand is true, then the second operand is not evaluated as it is certain that the result will be true.*

7.7.8 Membership Operators

Python supports two types of membership operators – **in** and **not in**. These operators, as the name suggests, test for membership in a sequence such as strings, lists, or tuples that will be discussed in later chapters and are listed below.

```
>>> str1="HELLO"                        >>> str1="HELLO"
>>> 'L' in str1                         >>> 'e' not in str1
True                                    True
>>> 'T' in str1                         >>> 'E' not in str1
False                                   False
```

- *in operator:* The operator returns True if a variable is found in the specified sequence and False otherwise.
- *not in operator:* The operator returns True if a variable is not found in the specified sequence and False otherwise.

```
>>> a = "r"
>>> str = "Good Morning"
>>> a in str
True
>>> 'R' in str
False
```

7.7.9 Identity Operators

Python supports two types of identity operators. These operators compare the memory locations of two objects and are given as follows.

> The `id()` function returns a unique id of the object. Every object in Python has its own unique id which is assigned to the object when it is cleared. This id is the object's memory address, and will be different for each time you run the program.

- **is Operator:** Returns True if operands or values on both sides of the operator point to the same object and False otherwise. For example, if *a is b* returns TRUE if id(a) is same as id(b).
- **is not Operator:** Returns True if operands or values on both sides of the operator do not point to the same object and False otherwise. For example, if *a is not b* returns TRUE if id(a) is not same as id(b).

We have learnt that Python creates labels when a variable is created. Two variables with the same value refer to the same label and thus have the same id. This concept can be understood by the following example.

```
>>> a = 10
>>> b = 10
>>> a is b
True
>>> a = 20
>>> b = 10
>>> a is b
False
```

When the is operator returns True, it also indicates that the equality operator will also return True. But this is not always applicable the other way. That is, two objects having the same value and returning True with equality operator may return False with the is operator. This generally happens in three cases.

- First, when input is taken from the user
- Second, with integer literals having several digits
- Third, with floating-point and complex numbers.

In all the cases, Python creates two different objects even if they have same value. This is illustrated below.

```
CASE 1:
>>> s1 = "HELLO"
>>> s2 = input("Enter a string:")
Enter a string : HELLO
>>> s1 == s2
True
>>> s1 is s2
False
```

```
CASE 2:
>>> s1="HELLO"
>>> n2 = 1234567
>>> n1 == n2
True
>>> n1 is n2
False
```

```
CASE 3:
>>> n1 = 1.23
>>> n2 = 1.23
>>> n1 == n2
True
>>> n1 is n2
False
```

7.7.10 Operators Precedence and Associativity

Table 7.6 lists all operators from highest precedence to lowest. When an expression has more than one operator, then it is the relative priorities of the operators with respect to each other that determine the order in which the expression will be evaluated.

Remember that,

Operators are associated from left to right. This means that operators with same precedence are evaluated in a left-to-right manner.

Parentheses can change the order in which an operator is applied. The operator in parenthesis is applied first even if there is a higher priority operator in the expression.

```
>>>5*6+3
33
>>>5+6*3
23
```

* has higher precedence than +. Hence, first the operands will be multiplied and then addition will be performed.

Table 7.6 Operator precedence chart

Operator	Description
()	Parenthesis (for grouping)
**	Exponentiation
~, +,-	Complement, unary plus and minus
*, /, %, //	Multiply, divide, modulo and floor division
+,-	Addition and subtraction
>>, <<	Right and left bitwise shift
&	Bitwise 'AND'
^,l	Bitwise exclusive 'OR' and regular 'OR'
<=, <, >, >=	Comparison operators
<>, ==, !=	Equality operators
=, %=, /=,l/=, -=, +=,*=, **=	Assignment operators
Is, is not	Identity operators
In, not in	Membership operators
Not, or, and	Logical operators

Let us try some more codes to see how operator precedence works in our expressions.

```
>>> (50 + 40) * 10 / 20
45.0
>>> 50+ (40 * 10) / 20
70.0
>>> 50*100/5//4
250.0
```

```
>>> ((50+ 40) * 20) / 10
180.0
>>> (False==False) or True
True
>>> (((50*100)/15)//4)
250.0
```

```
>>> (50+ 40) * (20 / 10)
180.0
>>> False==(False or True)
False
>>> 50*(100/(5//14))
5000.0
```

7.8 EXPRESSIONS IN PYTHON

In any programming language, an expression is any legal combination of symbols (like variables, constants and operators) that represents a value. Every language has its own set of rules that define whether an expression is valid or invalid in that language. *In Python, an expression must have at least one operand (variable or constant) and can have one or more operators. On evaluating an expression, we get a value.*

Operand is the value on which the operator is applied. These operators use constants and variables to form an expression. A * B + C – 5 is an example of an expression, where, +, *, – are operators; A, B and C are variables and 5 is a constant. Some valid expressions in Python are: x = a / b, y = a * b, z = a^ b, x = a > b, etc. When an expression has more than one operator, then the expression is evaluated using the operator precedence chart.

An example of an illegal expression can be a+ –b or <y++. When the program is compiled, the validity of all expressions is checked. If an illegal expression is encountered, an error message is displayed.

In Python, we can categorize expressions based on the data type of the result obtained on evaluating an expression. These types of expressions include,

- *Constant Expressions* that involve only constants. Example: 8 + 9 – 2
- *Integral Expressions* that produce an integer result. Example:
  a = 10, b = 5
  c = a * b
- *Floating-point Expressions* produce floating-point results. Example: a * b / 2
- *Relational Expressions* return either *true* or *false* value. Example: c = a > b
- *Logical Expressions* combine two or more relational expressions and return a value as *true* or *false*. Example: a > b and y! = 0.
- *Bitwise Expressions* manipulate data at bit level. Example: x = y & z.
- *Assignment Expressions* assign a value to a variable. Example: c = 10.

> Remember that deleted variables can be used again in the code if and only if you reassign them some value.

PROGRAMMER'S ZONE

1. **Write a program to enter a number and display its hex and octal equivalent and its square root.**
   ```
   num = int(input("Enter a number : "))
   print("Hexadecimal of " + str(num) + " : " + str(hex(num)))
   print("Octal of " + str(num) + " : " + str(oct(num)))
   print("Square root of " + str(num) + " : " + str(num**0.5))
   ```

   OUTPUT
   ```
   Enter a number : 17
   Hexadecimal of 17 : 0x11
   Octal of 17 : 0o21
   Square root of 17 : 4.123105625617661
   ```

2. **Write a program to read and print values of variables of different data types.**
   ```
   num = int(input("Enter Roll Number : "))
   fees = float(input("Enter Fees : "))
   ```

```
grade = input("Enter the grade : ")
name = input("Enter the name : ")
#Print the values of variables
print(ROLL NUMBER = ,num)
print(NAME = ,name)
print(FEES = ,fees)
print(GRADE = ,grade)
```

OUTPUT

```
Enter Roll Number : 1
Enter Fees : 99999
Enter the grade : A
Enter the name : Priya
ROLL NUMBER = 1
NAME = Priya
FEES = 99999.0
GRADE = A
```

3. **Write a program to calculate area of a triangle using Heron's formula.**
   (<u>Hint</u>: **Heron's formula is given as: area = sqrt(S*(S-a)*(S-b)*(S-c)))**

```
a = float(input("Enter the first side of the triangle : "))
b = float(input("Enter the second side of the triangle : "))
c = float(input("Enter the third side of the triangle : "))
print(a,b,c)
S = (a+b+c)/2
area = (S*(S-a)*(S-b)*(S-c))**0.5
print("Area = ",area)
```

OUTPUT

```
Enter the first side of the triangle : 6
Enter the second side of the triangle : 8
Enter the third side of the triangle : 10
6.0 8.0 10.0
Area = 24.0
```

4. **Write a program to calculate the distance between two points.**

```
x1 = (int(input("Enter the x coordinate of the first point : ")))
y1 = (int(input("Enter the y coordinate of the first point : ")))
x2 = (int(input("Enter the x coordinate of the second point : ")))
y2 = (int(input("Enter the y coordinate of the second point : ")))
distance = ((x2-x1)**2+(y2-y1)**2)**0.5
print("Distance = ", distance)
```

OUTPUT

```
Enter the x coordinate of the first point : 1
Enter the y coordinate of the first point : 1
Enter the x coordinate of the second point : 5
Enter the y coordinate of the second point : 5
Distance = 5.656854249492381
```

5. **Write a program to perform addition, subtraction, multiplication, division, integer division, and modulo division on two integer numbers.**

```
num1 = int(input("Enter two numbers : "))
num2 = int(input("Enter two numbers : "))
add_res = num1+num2
sub_res = num1-num2
mul_res = num1*num2
idiv_res = num1//num2
modiv_res = num1%num2
fdiv_res = float(num1)/num2
print(num1, " + ", num2," = ", add_res)
print(num1, " - ", num2, " = ", sub_res)
print(num1, " * ", num2, " = ", mul_res)
print(num1," / ",num2," = ",idiv_res," (Integer Division)")
print(num1," // ",num2," = ",fdiv_res," (Float Division)")
print(num1," % ", num2," = ",modiv_res," (Modulo Division)")
```

OUTPUT

```
Enter two numbers : 25
Enter two numbers : 4
25 + 4 = 29
25 - 4 = 21
25 * 4 = 100
25 / 4 = 6 (Integer Division)
25 // 4 = 6.25 (Float Division)
25 % 4 = 1 (Modulo Division)
```

6. **Write a program that demonstrates the use of relational operators.**

```
x = 30
y = 10
print(x, " < ", y, " = ", x<y)
print(x, " == ", y, " = ", x==y)
print(x, " != ", y," = ", x!=y)
print(x, " > ", y," = ", x>y)
print(x, " >= ", y," = ", x>=y)
print(x, " <= ", y," = ", x<=y)
```

OUTPUT

```
30 < 10 = False
30 == 10 = False
30 != 10 = True
30 > 10 = True
30 >= 10 = True
30 <= 10 = False
```

7. **Write a program to calculate the volume of a cylinder.**

```
radius = float(input("Enter the radius : "))
height = float(input("Enter the height : "))
volume = 3.14*radius*radius*height
print("VOLUME = %.2f"%volume)
```

OUTPUT
```
Enter the radius : 7
Enter the height : 14
VOLUME = 2154.04
```

8. **Write a program to print the digit at one's place of a number.**
   ```
   num = int(input("Enter any number : "))
   digit_at_ones_place = num%10
   print("The digit at ones place is : ",digit_at_ones_place)
   ```

   OUTPUT
   ```
   Enter any number : 12345
   The digit at ones place of 12345 is 5
   ```

9. **Write a program to swap two numbers without using a temporary variable.**
   ```
   n1 = int(input("Enter the first number : "))
   n2 = int(input("Enter the second number : "))
   n1, n2 = n2, n1
   print("The first number is = ",n1," and the second number = ",n2)
   ```

   OUTPUT
   ```
   Enter the first number : 6
   Enter the second number : 9
   The first number is = 9 and the second number = 6
   ```

10. **Write a program to calculate the average of two numbers. Print their deviation.**
    ```
    n1 = int(input("Enter the two numbers : "))
    n2 = int(input("Enter the two numbers : "))
    avg = (n1+n2)/2
    dev1 = n1-avg
    dev2 = n2-avg
    print("AVERAGE = ",avg)
    print("Deviation of first num =",dev1)
    print("Deviation of second num =",dev2)
    ```

    OUTPUT
    ```
    Enter the two numbers : 10
    Enter the two numbers : 20
    AVERAGE = 15.0
    Deviation of first num = -5.0
    Deviation of second num = 5.0
    ```

11. **Write a program to convert degrees Fahrenheit into degrees Celsius.**
    ```
    Fahrenheit = float(input("Enter the temperature in Fahrenheit : "))
    Celsius = (0.56)*(Fahrenheit-32)
    print("Temperature in degrees Celsius = %.2f"%Celsius)
    ```

    OUTPUT
    ```
    Enter the temperature in Fahrenheit : 100
    Temperature in degrees Celsius = 38.08
    ```

12. **Write a program to calculate the total amount of money in the piggybank, given the coins of Rs 10, Rs 5, Rs 2, and Re 1.**

    ```
    num_of_10_coins = int(input("Enter the number of 10Rs coins in the piggybank : "))
    num_of_5_coins = int(input("Enter the number of 5Rs coins in the piggybank : "))
    num_of_2_coins = int(input("Enter the number of 2Rs coins in the piggybank : "))
    num_of_1_coins = int(input("Enter the number of 1Re coins in the piggybank : "))
    total_amt = num_of_10_coins*10+num_of_5_coins*5+num_of_2_coins*2+num_of_1_coins
    print("Total amount in the piggybank =",total_amt)
    ```

    OUTPUT
    ```
    Enter the number of 10Rs coins in the piggybank : 5
    Enter the number of 5Rs coins in the piggybank : 20
    Enter the number of 2Rs coins in the piggybank : 30
    Enter the number of 1Re coins in the piggybank : 50
    Total amount in the piggybank = 260
    ```

13. **Write a program to calculate the bill amount for an item, given its quantity sold, value, discount, and tax.**

    ```
    qty = float(raw_input("Enter the quantity of item sold : "))
    val = float(raw_input("Enter the value of item : "))
    discount = float(raw_input("Enter the discount percentage : "))
    tax = float(raw_input("Enter the tax : "))
    amt = qty*val
    discount_amt = (amt*discount)/100
    sub_total = amt-discount_amt
    tax_amt = (sub_total*tax)/100
    total_amt = sub_total + tax_amt
    print "**********BILL************"
    print " Quantity sold : \t ",qty
    print "Price per item : \t",val
    print "\n \t \t ---------------"
    print "Amount : \t\t",amt
    print "Discount : \t\t-",discount_amt
    print " \t \t ------------------"
    print "Discounted Total : \t",sub_total
    print "Tax : \t\t\t + «",tax_amt
    print " \t \t ------------------"
    print "Total amount to be paid ",total_amt
    ```

    OUTPUT
    ```
    Enter the quantity of item sold : 10
    Enter the value of item : 100
    Enter the discount percentage : 15
    Enter the tax : 8
    **********BILL************
     Quantity sold :    10.0
    Price per item :    100.0
            ---------------
    Amount :    1000.0
    ```

```
Discount :              - 150.0
                        ------------------
Discounted Total :   850.0
Tax :              + 68.0
                   ------------------
Total amount to be paid 918.0
```

14. **Write a program to calculate a student's result based on two examinations, 1 sports event and 3 activities conducted. The weightage of activities = 30 per cent, sports = 20 per cent, and examination = 50 per cent.**

```
ACTIVITIES_WEIGHTAGE = 30.0
SPORTS_WEIHTAGE = 20.0
EXAMS_WEIGHTAGE = 50.0
EXAMS_TOTAL = 200.0
ACTIVITIES_TOTAL = 60.0
SPORTS_TOTAL = 50.0
exam_score1 = int(input("Enter the marks in first examination (out of 100) : "))
exam_score2 = int(input("Enter the marks in second examination(out of 100) : "))
sports_score = int(input("Enter the score obtained in sports activities (out of 50) : "))
activities_score1 = int(input("Enter the marks in first activity (out of 20) : "))
activities_score2 = int(input("Enter the marks in second activity (out of 20) : "))
activities_score3 = int(input("Enter the marks in third activity (out of 20) : "))
exam_total = exam_score1 + exam_score2
activities_total = activities_score1 + activities_score2 + activities_score3
exam_percent = float(exam_total * EXAMS_WEIGHTAGE / EXAMS_TOTAL)
sports_percent = float(sports_score * SPORTS_WEIHTAGE / SPORTS_TOTAL)
activities_percent  =   float(activities_total  *   ACTIVITIES_WEIGHTAGE  / ACTIVITIES_TOTAL)
total_percent = exam_percent + sports_percent + activities_percent
print("\n\n ********************* RESULT**************************")
print("\n Total percent in examination :", exam_percent)
print("\n Total percent in activities :",activities_percent)
print("\n Total percent in sports", sports_percent)
print("\n ----------------------------------------------------------")
print("\n Total percentage", total_percent)
```

OUTPUT

```
Enter the marks in first examination (out of 100) : 89
Enter the marks in second examination(out of 100) : 80
Enter the score obtained in sports activities (out of 50) : 35
Enter the marks in first activity (out of 20) : 17
Enter the marks in second activity (out of 20) : 19
Enter the marks in third activity (out of 20) : 16
 ********************* RESULT**************************
 Total percent in examination : 42.25
 Total percent in activities : 26.0
 Total percent in sports 14.0
 ----------------------------------------------------------
 Total percentage 82.25
```

Key Terms

Variable: Variable means something that may change. In Python programs, any piece of information can be stored in a variable and the information may change.

Identifiers: Names given to identify a variable, function, class, module or any other object.

Lvalue: Expressions that come on the left side of the assignment operator

Rvalue: Expressions that come on the right side of the assignment operator.

Docstring: In Python, multi-line comments are also known as docstring.

Keywords: Reserved words in a programming language that have a pre-defined meaning.

Operators: Constructs used to manipulate the value of operands.

Operands: Values on which the operator is applied.

Expression: An expression in a programming language is any valid combination of tokens that represents a value.

Unary operator: Operator applied on a single operand.

Chapter Highlights

- To create a variable in Python, just assign a value to the identifier using the equal to sign.
- When we create a variable, Python creates labels referring to those values.
- Variables can hold values of different types called data types.
- Based on the data type of a variable, the interpreter reserves memory for it and also determines the type of data that can be stored in the reserved memory.
- The five standard data types supported by Python include – numbers, string, list, tuple, and dictionary.
- In Python, you can reassign variables as many times as you want to change the value stored in them. You may even store the value of one data type in a statement and then the value of another data in a subsequent statement.
- The `type()` function is used to determine data type of an object.
- Python allows programmers to assign a single value to more than one variable simultaneously.
- Trying to reference a variable that has not been assigned any value causes an error. This may happen if you have mistakenly used a variable without assigning it a value prior to its use or have deliberately deleted or removed a variable using the del statement and then tried to use it later in your code.
- A variable of Boolean type can have one of the two values – True or False.
- Comments are added in a program to describe the statements in the program code. They make the program easily readable and understandable by the programmer as well as other users who are seeing the code.
- To take input from the users, Python makes use of the `input()` function.
- Whitespace at the beginning of the line is called indentation. These whitespaces at the beginning of the logical line determines the indentation level of that logical line.
- Comparison operators, also known as relational operators, are used to compare the values on its either side and determine the relation between them.
- Unary operators act on single operands. When an operand is preceded by a unary minus sign, its value is negated.
- Python supports two bitwise shift operators. They are shift left (<<) and shift right (>>). These operations are used to shift bits to the left or to the right. The syntax for a shift operation can be given as: operand op num
- Python supports two types of membership operators – in and not in. These operators test for membership in a sequence such as strings, lists or tuples.

Review Questions

1. What are identifiers? List some rules that must be kept in mind while naming an identifier.
2. With the help of a diagram explain what happens when a variable is created in Python.
3. With the help of an example explain how variables can be re-assigned values in Python.
4. Can we re-assign a value of another data type to a variable? If yes, why?
5. Differentiate between lvalue and rvalue.
6. What do you understand by the term multiple assignment?
7. What are Boolean variables? How are they created?
8. What are comments? How are they written in Python?
9. What is a docstring? How is it defined in a Python program?
10. Why is indentation necessary in Python?
11. Logical expressions operate in a shortcut (or lazy) fashion. Justify this statement.
12. Will the statement, print "Python # Programming" be executed? If yes, justify its output.
    Hint: The # is inside a string, so it is just considered as a character and not as comment.
13. Differentiate between = and ==.
    Hint: The = is used to assign value but the == is used to test if two things have the same value.
14. Which data type will you use to represent the following data values?
    a. Number of days in a week
    b. The circumference of a circle
    c. You school fees
    d. Distance between moon and the earth
    e. Your favorite book
    f. Whether or not you will take the entrance exam.
15. Which type of value will you use for storing the following information?
    a. Employee ID   b. Employee Name   c. Employee Salary   d. Phone Number
16. Which of the following are correct type conversions?
    a. int (8.2+6.3)
    b. str (5.6 * 6.7)
    c. float ("12"+"3.4")
    d. str (6/4)
17. Express the following floating-point numbers in scientific notation:
    a. 123.456789   b. 0.000123456   c. 1.234567
18. Evaluate the following arithmetic expressions using the rules of operator precedence in Python.
    a. 4+5*10   b. 6+7*2+5   c. 20//4*2   d. 5*6**3   e. 24//6//3
    f. 4**2**3   g. 100-(15*3)   h. 50%7   i. -(100/6)+5
19. Write the following values in the exponential notation.
    a. 1230.4567   b. 0.00000056009   c. 7000809.000000000003
20. Evaluate the following expressions:
    a. True and False
    b. (100<10) and (100>50)
    c. True or False
    d. (100<10) or (100>200)
    e. not(True) and False
    f. not (100<10) or (100>50)
    g. not(True and False)
    h. not (100<10 or 100>50)
    i. not True and False
    j. 100<10 and not 100>50
    k. not True and False or True
    l. not (100<10 or 50<200)
21. Which of the following results in True?
    a. >>>90 == 90 and 11==11
    b. >>>31==51 and 71==31
    c. >>>72!=12 and 25==25
    d. >>>54<51 and 61>86
    e. 15<20 or 20

22. Identify the correct arithmetic expression in Python:
    a. 10(13+76)　　　b. (15*16)(47+18)　c. 14*(33-52)　　d. 15***2

23. Give an appropriate Boolean expression for each of the following.
    a. Check if variable var is greater than or equal to 10, and less than 100.
    b. Check if variable var is less than 100 and greater than or equal to 10, or it is equal to 50.
    c. Check if either the name 'Kalam' or 'Azad' appears in a list of names assigned to variable names.
    d. Check if the name 'Abdul' appears and the name 'Maulana' does not appear in a list of names assigned to variable names.

23. Write the data types of the following:
    a. type(5+4)　b. (20*345)　c. type(987/45)　d. type(2345//12)　e. type(123%34)

24. Identify the data types of the following literals: 9, 29.4, 5j, 3+7i

25. Write the following expressions in Python:

    $$\frac{-b \pm \sqrt{b^2 - 4ac}}{2a} \qquad \sqrt{a^2 + b^2} \qquad \frac{\pi}{2}rh \qquad (a-b)^2 = a^2 - 2ab + b^2 \qquad d = a^{mn}/a^{-3} \qquad (e^m)^n = e^{mn}$$

26. Differentiate between a. bool('0') and bool('') b. bool(0k) and bool('0k')

Programming Exercises

1. Write a program to calculate the Body Mass Index (BMI) of a person. (BMI = kg/m^2, where kg is the person's weight and m is his/her height in metres).

2. Write a program to perform string concatenation.

3. Write a program to demonstrate printing a string within single quotes, double quotes and triple quote.

4. Write a program to print the ASCII value of a character.

5. Write a program to read a character in upper case and then print it in lower case.

6. Write a program to swap two numbers using a temporary variable.

7. Write a program to read the address of a user. Display the result by breaking it in multiple lines.

8. Write a program to calculate simple interest and compound interest.

9. Write a program that prompts users to enter two integers x and y. The program then calculates and displays x^y.

10. Write a program that prompts user to enter his first name and last name and then displays a message "Greetings!!! First name Last name".

11. Write a program to calculate salary of an employee given his basic pay (to be entered by the user), HRA = 10 per cent of basic pay, TA = five per cent of basic pay. Define HRA and TA as constants and use them to calculate the salary of the employee.

12. Write a program to prepare a grocery bill. Enter the name of the items purchased, quantity in which it is purchased and its price per unit. Then display the bill in the following format.
    ```
    *************** B I L L ****************
    Item Quantity            Price Amount
    *****************************************
    Total Amount to be paid
    *****************************************
    ```

13. Energy is calculated as, $e = mc^2$, where m is the mass of the object and c is its velocity. Write a program that accepts an object's mass (in kilograms) and velocity (in metres per second) and displays its energy.

14. Write a program that calculates the number of seconds in a day.
15. Write a program to read and display the details of a student. While printing use '-' to separate two values.
16. Write a program that prompts the user to enter the first name and the last name. Then display the following message.
    ```
    Hello firstname lastname
    Welcome to Python!
    ```

Fill in the Blanks

1. A line in Python can have maximum ____ characters.
2. ____ are used to store values.
3. Names given to identify a variable, function, class, module or any other object are generally known as _____.
4. >>>not 10 ==10 gives the answer _____.
5. >>>not 100>700 gives _____.
6. A variable in Python is assigned a value by using the _____ operator.
7. When we create a variable, Python creates _____ referring to those values.
8. Variables can hold values of different types called _____.
9. _____ are those objects to which values can be assigned.
10. To take input from the users, Python uses the _____ function.
11. The _____ function is used to convert a non-integer value to an integer.
12. In Python, multi-line comments are also known as _____.
13. The level of _____ groups statements to form a block of statements.
14. Value on which the operator is applied is called _____.
15. _____ operator is used to negate the value of the operand on which it is applied.
16. _____ expressions operate in a shortcut (or lazy) fashion and stop the evaluation when it knows the final outcome for sure.
17. If a is b returns TRUE, then _____.
18. _____ can change the order in which an operator is applied.
19. Literals of the form a + bi are called _____.
20. 123.45E-9 is equal to _____.
21. _____ converts an integer to a floating-point number.
22. The ___ operator returns the quotient after division.
23. To find x^y, you will use _____ operator.
24. _____ is a group of characters.
25. Variable names can contain only _____, _____ and _____.
26. >>>90 != 70 gives output _____.
27. 29%0 = _____.

28. int("10"+"20") will give _____.
29. _____ operator treats operand as a sequence of bits.
30. >>> print (format(12356.265901, '.3f')) will result in the value _____.

State True or False

1. In Python, a semi-colon is used to terminate every statement.
2. Python allows writing multiple statements in a single line.
3. The first character of an identifier must be a dollar sign ($).
4. Python is a case-sensitive language.
5. Based on the data type of a variable, the interpreter reserves memory.
6. While re-assigning values to a variable, the data type must not change.
7. Python variables do not have specific data types.
8. Comments are written to make the program easily readable and understandable.
9. Comments are the executable statements in a program.
10. When a program is run, comments are not displayed.
11. All keywords are written in uppercase characters.
12. Statements in a block must have the same indentation level.
13. Arithmetic operators are also known as relational operators.
14. Relational operators can be used to compare strings.
15. Python does not support prefix and postfix increment/decrement operators.
16. Bitwise OR operator produces the ones' complement of the given binary value.
17. Shifting once to the right multiplies the number by 2.
18. The is operator returns true if operands or values on both sides of the operator do not point to the same object and false otherwise.
19. INT = 2; print(INT) will give an error.
20. The id() function can be used to print the address of the variable.

Multiple Choice Questions

1. Which of the following is a valid identifier in Python?
   a. _AaBb   b. 1A_Bb   c. @AaBB   d. Aa-Bb
2. Which of the following can be the first character of a valid identifier in Python?
   a. #   b. @   c. _   d. -
3. Which of the following is known as the string concatenation symbol?
   a. +   b. *   c. ,   d.
4. Which function is used to is determine data type of an object?
   a. data()   b. type()   c. val()   d. str()

5. A variable can be removed by using the _____ statement.
   a. Remove b. erase c. del d. delete

6. Boolean variables are created using which of the following operator(s)?
   a. Equality b. assignment c. Both a and b. d. None of these.

7. The input function takes user's input as a/an _____.
   a. integer b. floating-point c. string d. None of these.

8. All characters following the _____ symbol and up to the end of the line are part of the comment.
   a. # b. _ c. % d. @

9. Which operator is used for integer division?
   a. / b. % c. // d. \

10. If both bits are 1, the corresponding bit in the result is 1 and 0 otherwise. This is a feature of which bitwise operator?
    a. AND b. NOT c. OR d. XOR

11. Which operator returns TRUE if a variable is found in the specified sequence and FALSE otherwise?
    a. is b. not is c. in d. not in

12. Identify valid assignment statements.
    a. x = y + 2 b. a = a++ c. x + y = 10 d. x + 10 = y

13. Which line of code produces an error?
    a. "one" + "2" b. 'one' + 2 c. 1 + 2 d. "1" + "two"

14. abc ="AABBCC"; print(abc*3)
    a. abcabcabc b. "abcabcabc" c. ABCABCABC d. AABBCCAABBCCAABBCC

15. Identify the correct variable creation statement.
    a. my_var =7 b. 123my_var =10 c. my var = 12 d. 10 = myvar

16. Bitwise operator can be applied on which data type?
    a. Integer b. Float c. String d. Complex number

17. Which operator is also known as string repetition operator?
    a. + b. * c. & d. ^

18. The following statement will produce __ lines of output.
    print('Python \n Programming \n is\n ---Fun')
    a. 1 b. 2 c. 3 d. 4

19. Identify the expression that may result in arithmetic overflow.
    a. a*b b. a**b c. a/b d. a+b

20. Which operations do not result in 9?
    a. 95 // 10 b. 130 % 11 c. 3 **3 d. 81 ** 0.5

Give the Output

1. ```
   x,y,z = 10,20,30
   y,z,x = x+5, y+7, z-3
   print("x = ",x, " y = ",y, "z = ",z)
   ```
   ```

2. ```
   x,y = 10,20
   y,z = x+5, y-20
   print("x = ",x, " y = ",y,» z = ",z)
   ```

3. ```
   >>> 350 + 230 - 170
   ```

4. ```
   >>> (51 + 9.7 - 4) * 100
   ```

5. ```
   >>> 110%(95//3)
   ```

6. ```
   >>> 'Python Programming is fun… '
   ```

7. ```
   >>>"Python Programming is fun…"
   ```

8. ```
   >>>'''Python… \n Programming?'''
   ```

9. ```
   >>> print("Python \n Programmiung")
   ```

10. ```
    >>> print("PYTHON !!!!"*3)
    ```

11. ```
    >>>x = 100 ; x *= 3 ; print(x)
    ```

12. ```
    >>> s1 = "HELLO"     ;     s1 += "WORLD"     ;     print(s1)
    ```

13. ```
    days = "Mon Tue Wed Thu Fri Sat Sun"
    months = "Jan\nFeb\nMar\nApr\nMay\nJun\nJul\nAug"
    print("Days are : "+ days)
    print("Months are: "+ months)
    print(""" There's a new dream today.
    I'll tell you some other day.
    Come on, let's enjoy. """)
    ```

14. ```
    # print ABCD
    Nothing
    ```

15. ```
    >>> num1 = "7"
    >>> num1 += "10"
    >>> num2 = int(num1) + 3
    >>> print (float(num2))
    ```

16. ```
    name = input("Enter a word :")
    print ('HELLO' + name)
    ```

17. ```
    >>> abs(100-200) * 3
    ```

18. ```
    >>>float("5678" * int(input("Enter a number:")))
    ```

19. ```
    >>> int = 2;  print(int)
    ```

20. ```
    a,b = 10,20
    b,a = a *5, b /2
    print("a = ",a, " and b = ", b)
    ```

21. ```
    a,b = 10,20
    a,b,a = a*10, b*5,a*20
    print("a = ",a, " and b = ", b)
    ```

22. ```
    x =10
    print(id(x))
    x = x + 10
    print(id(x))
    x = x - 10
    print(id(x))
    ```

23. `0 or 10`

24. `10 or 0`

25. `0 or 0`

26. `"abc" or ""`

27. `'' or ''`

28. `'k' or 'r'`

29. `10 ** 3 ** 2`

30. `7 -5 -12 > -5 *3 +8`

31. `len(str(7 -5 -12 > -5 *3 +8)) == len('true')`

32. `bool('0') and (10 < 20)`

33. `23%5 is 23%5`

34. `20 or len(20)`

35. `10 == 10.0`

36. `10 == int(10)`

37. `str(10)==str('10.0')`

38. `'R' == 'R'`

39. `70/(7-(2+4))or 4<5`

40. `5 < 9 or 60/(10-(6+4))`

41. `len("abcd") == 30/6 or 30/10`

42. `2 * (5 *(len("007")))`

43. `30 < 70 and 40 > 50`

44. `N = 1 + 1 + 1 == 0.3; print(N)`

45. ```
    a = True;    b = 0<5
    a==b   ;    a is b
    ```

46. ```
    print(bool(int('0')))
    print(bool(str(0)))
    print(bool(float('0.0')))
    print(bool(str(0.0)))
    ```

47. ```
    a,b,c = 12,13,16
    d = a + b *c/b
    print(d)
    ```

Find the Error

1. ```
   >>>10+'20'+30+'40'
   ```

2. ```
   >>>'10'*'20'
   >>>'PYTHON'*7.0
   ```

3. ```
   x = 10
   print(x)
   ```

4. ```
   x = 123.456
   print('%'+x)
   ```

5. ```
   x = 1; y = 2;
   print(x+y+z)
   ```

6. ```
   if = 5; print(if)
   ```

7. ```
   a = 10; b = 20; print(a;b)
   ```

8. ```
   x =10
   y = x * 30
   x = "PYTHON"
   z = x/10
   ```

9. ```
   name = int(input("Enter your name : "))
   print("HELLO", name)
   ```

10. ```
    print(len(bool(0)))
    ```

11. ```
    >>> print("HELLO"/2)
    ```

12. ```
    >>> print(type(int("HELLO")))
    ```

13. ```
    >>>n1 = 20
    >>>n2 = 30
    >>>del num1
    >>>n2 = 40
    >>>n1 = 50
    >>>print(num1 - num2)
    ```

14. ```
    n1 = 90
    n2 = n1 + 50
    n2 = int(str(n2) + "40")
    print(num2)
    ```

Answers

Fill in the Blanks
1. 79
2. Variables
3. identifiers
4. False
5. True
6. assignment
7. labels
8. data types
9. lvalues
10. input()

Python – Building Blocks 151

11. int()
12. docstring
13. indentation
14. operand
15. Unary minus
16. Logical
17. id(a) is same as id(b).
18. Parentheses
19. complex numbers
20. 0.00000012345

21. float()
22. / or //
23. **
24. String
25. underscore, upper case, lower case character
26. True
27. ZeroDivisionError
28. 1020
29. Bitwise
30. 12356.266

State True or False

1. False
2. True
3. False
4. True
5. True
6. False
7. False
8. True
9. False
10. True
11. False
12. True
13. False
14. True
15. True
16. False
17. False
18. False
19. False
20. True

Multiple Choice Questions

1. a
2. c
3. a
4. b
5. c
6. c
7. c
8. a
9. c
10. a
11. c
12. a
13. b
14. d
15. a
16. a
17. b
18. d
19. b
20. c

Give the Output

1. x = 27 y = 15 z = 27
2. x = 10 y = 15 z = 0
3. 410
4. 5670.0
5. 17
6. 'Python Programming is fun…'
7. 'Python Programming is fun…'
8. 'Python… \n Programming?'
9. Python
   Programmiung
10. PYTHON !!!!PYTHON !!!!PYTHON !!!!
11. 300
12. HELLOWORLD
13. Days are : Mon Tue Wed Thu Fri Sat Sun
    Months are: Jan
    Feb
    Mar
    Apr
    May
    Jun
    Jul
    Aug
    There's a new dream today.
    I'll tell you some other day.
    Come on, let's enjoy.
14. No output
15. 713.0
16. HELLO(input)
17. 300
18. 5678567856785678.0 (if input = 4)
19. 2
20. a = 10.0 and b = 50
21. a = 200 and b = 100
22. 140705644503984
    140705644504304
    140705644503984
23. 10
24. 10
25. 0
26. 'abc'
27. ''
28. 'k'
29. 1000000000
30. False
31. False
32. True
33. True
34. True
35. True
36. True
37. False
38. True
39. 70.0
40. True
41. 3.0
42. 30

43. False
44. False
45. True   True

46. False   True   False   True
47. 28.0

Find the Error

1. `TypeError: unsupported operand type(s) for +: 'int' and 'str'`
2. `TypeError:can't multiplay sequence by non-int of type 'str'`
   `TypeError: can't multiply sequence by non-int of type 'float'`
3. `Error! Tab at the start of the line`
4. `TypeError: cannot concatenate 'str' and 'float' objects`
5. `NameError: name 'z' is not defined`
6. `SyntaxError: invalid syntax`
7. `SyntaxError: invalid syntax`
8. `TypeError: unsupported operand type(s) for /: 'str' and 'int'`
9. `ValueError: invalid literal for int() with base 10: 'ABC'`
10. `TypeError: object of type 'bool' has no len()`
11. `TypeError: unsupported operand type(s) for /: 'str' and 'int'`
12. `ValueError: invalid literal for int() with base 10: 'HELLO'`
13. `NameError: name 'num1' is not defined`
14. `NameError: name 'num2' is not defined`

Decision Control Statements

8

Chapter Objectives

The chapter discusses a very crucial set of statements that may alter the sequence of program flow. These statements include conditional branching statements such as:

- The `if` statement
- The `if-else` statement
- The nested `if` statement
- The `if-elif-else` Statement

Until now, we have executed simple statements in Python. Such statements are executed sequentially from the first line of the program to the last. That is, the second statement is executed after the first; the third statement is executed after the second, and so on. This way of execution is known as **sequential control flow**.

However, in some cases we may want to either execute only a selected set of statements (i.e., selection control) or execute a set of statements repeatedly (i.e., iterative control). In such cases, decision control system comes into picture.

A *decision control statement* is a statement that determines the flow of control in a program. Flow of control means deciding on which instruction would next be executed. A decision control statement can skip either one or more instructions. The three fundamental methods of control flow in a programming language are *sequential, selection, and iterative control*.

Selection and iterative control are a part of decision control system. Thus, a decision control statement can alter (change) the flow of a sequence of instructions. And this type of conditional processing helps users to extend the usefulness of programs.

Programmers can make programs that determine which statements of the code should be executed and which should be ignored in certain circumstances. Figure 8.1 shows the categorization of decision control statements.

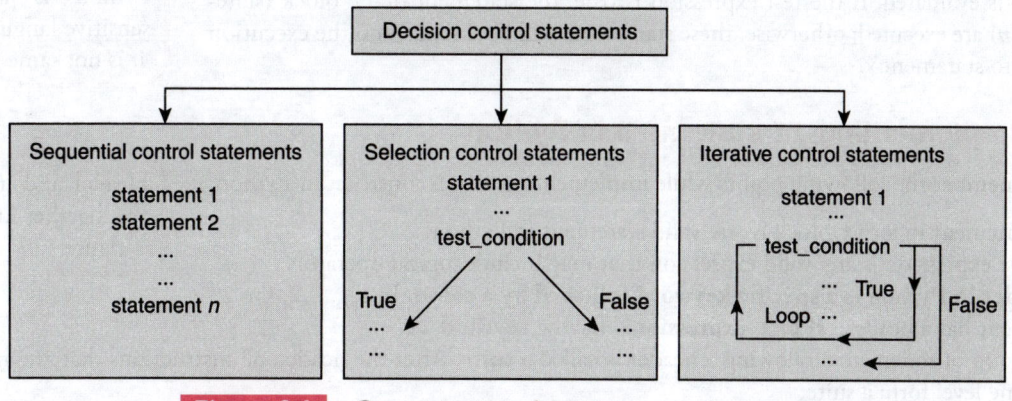

Figure 8.1 Categorization of decision control statements

8.1 SELECTION/CONDITIONAL BRANCHING STATEMENTS

The decision control statements usually jump from one part of the code to another depending on whether a particular condition is satisfied or not. That is, they execute statements selectively based on certain decisions. Such type of decision control statements is known as *selection control statements* or *conditional branching statements*. Python language supports different types of conditional branching statements which are as follows:

- `if` statement
- Nested `if` statement
- `if-else` statement
- `if-elif-else` statement

8.2 `if` STATEMENT

An `if` statement is the simplest form of decision control statement that is frequently used in decision making. An `if` statement is a selection control statement based on the value of a given Boolean expression. The general form of a simple `if` statement is shown in Fig. 8.2.

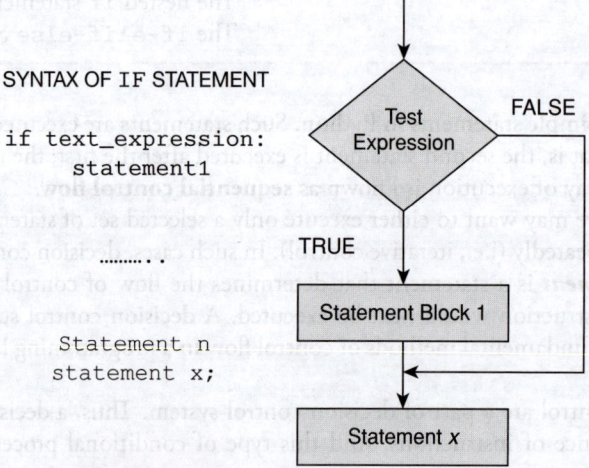

Figure 8.2 `if` statement construct

The `if` block may include 1 or more statements. According to the figure, first the test expression is evaluated. If the test expression is true, the statement of `if` block (statement 1 to *n*) are executed; otherwise, these statements will be skipped and the execution will jump to statement x.

> Python is a case sensitive language. So, if is not same as IF.

8.2.1 Implementing `if` statement in Python

Always remember the following points while implementing an `if` construct in Python.

- The statement in an `if` block is any valid statement in Python.
- The test expression is any valid expression that may include logical operators.
- **A header in Python is a specific keyword followed by a colon.** In Fig. 8.2, the `if` statement has a header, "**if text_expression:**" having keyword `if`.
- The group of statements following a header is called a **suite**. After the header, all instructions that are indented at the same level form a suite.
- While four spaces are commonly used for each level of indentation, any number of spaces may be used.

> Header and its suite are together known as a clause.

Example 8.1 Program to increment a number if it is positive.

```
x = 10    #Initialize the value of x
if(x>0):  #test the value of x
    x = x+1  #Increment the value of x if it is > 0
print(x)  #Print the value of x
```

> Remember to properly indent the statements that are dependent on the previous statements.

OUTPUT
x = 11

In the above code, we take a variable *x* and initialize it to 10. In the test expression, we check if the value of *x* is greater than 0 or not. If the test expression evaluates to true, then the value of *x* is incremented and is printed on the screen. Note that the print statement will be executed even if the test expression is false.

Python uses indentation to form a block of code. Other languages such as C and C++, use curly braces to accomplish this.

Example 8.2 Write a program to determine whether a person is eligible to vote.

```
age= int(input("Enter the age :"))
if(age>=18):
     print("You are eligible to vote")
```

OUTPUT
Enter the age : 35
You are eligible to vote

Example 8.3 Write a program to determine the character entered by the user.

```
char= input("Press any key : ")
if(char.isalpha()):
     print("The user has entered a character")
if( char.isdigit()):
     print("The user has entered a digit")
if(char.isspace()):
     print("The user entered a white space character" )
```

OUTPUT
Press any key : 7
The user has entered a digit

8.3 if-else STATEMENT

Although `if` statement plays a vital role in conditional branching, its usage is very limited. Its simplicity is also its drawback. In the `if` statement, the test expression is evaluated; if the result is true, the statement(s) followed by the expression is executed. But, if the expression is false, nothing useful happens. Using an `if-else` statement solves this problem. The general form of a simple `if-else` statement is shown in Fig. 8.3.

```
SYNTAX OF IF-ELSE STATEMENT

if test_expression:
       statement block 1

else:
       statement block 2


statement x;
```

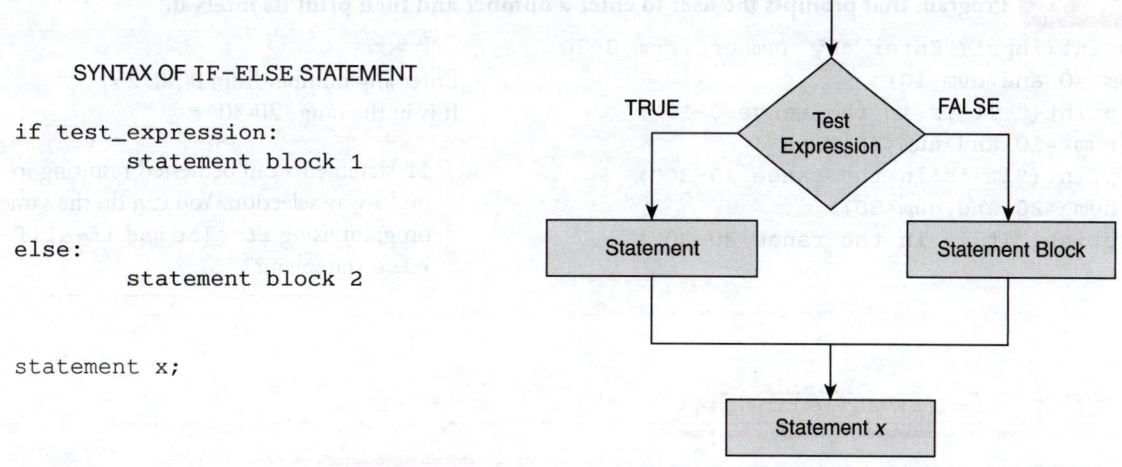

Figure 8.3 `if-else` statement construct

In the above syntax, we have written the statement block. A statement block may include one or more statements. According to the if–else construct, first the test expression is evaluated. If the expression is true, statement block 1 is executed and statement block 2 is skipped. Otherwise, if the expression is false, statement block 2 is executed and statement block 1 is ignored. In any case, after the statement block 1 or 2 gets executed the control will pass to statement *x*. Therefore, statement *x* is executed in every case.

Example 8.4	Write a program to determine whether a person is eligible to vote or not. If he is not eligible display how many years are left to be eligible.

```
age = int(input("Enterthe age : "))
if(age>=18):
    print("You are eligible to vote")
else:
    yrs = 18 - age
    print("You have to wait for " + str(yrs) +" years")
```

OUTPUT
Enter the age : 10
You have to wait for 8 years

Example 8.5	Write a program to find larger of two numbers.

```
a = int(input("Enter the value of a : "))
b = int(input("Enter the value of b : "))
if(a>b):
    large = a
else:
    large = b
print("Large= ",large)
```

OUTPUT
Enter the value of a: 50
Enter the value of b : 30
Large= 50

8.4 NESTED `if` STATEMENTS

A statement that contains other statements is called a *compound statement*. To perform more complex checks, `if` statements can be nested, that is, it can be placed one inside the other. In such a case, the inner `if` statement is the statement part of the outer one. Nested `if` statements are used to check if more than one condition is satisfied. Consider the code given below to understand this concept.

Example 8.6	Program that prompts the user to enter a number and then print its interval.

```
num = int(input("Enter any number from 0-30: "))
if(num>=0 and num<10):
    print(" It is in the range 0-10")
elif(num>=10 and num<20):
    print("lt is in the range 10-20")
elif(num>=20 and num<30):
    print("lt is in the range 20-30")
```

OUTPUT
Enter any number from 0-30: 25
It is in the range 20-30

> `if` statements can be nested resulting in multi-way selection. You can do the same program using `if-else` and `if-elif-else` statements.

8.5 `if-elif-else` STATEMENT

Python supports `if-elif-else` statements to test additional conditions apart from the initial test expression. The `if-elif-else` construct works in the same way as a usual `if-else` statement. If-elif-else construct is also known as **nested-if construct**. The `elif` (short for `else if`) statement is a shortcut to `if` and `else` statements. *A series of `if` and `elif` statements have a final else block, which is executed if none of the `if` or `elif` expressions is True.* Its syntax is given in Fig. 8.4.

Comparing Floating-point Numbers
Never test floating-point numbers for exact equality. This is because floating-point numbers are just approximations, so it is always better to test floating-point numbers for 'approximately equal' rather than testing for exactly equal. We can test for approximate equality by finding the difference between the two floating-point numbers (that are to be tested) and comparing their absolute value of the difference against a very small number, epsilon.

SYNTAX OF IF-ELIF-ELSE STATEMENT

```
if ( test expression 1)
      statement block 1
elif ( test expression 2)
      statement block 2
..........................

elif (test expression N)
      statement block N
else
      statement block x
statement y
```

Figure 8.4 if-elif-else syntax

Note that it is not necessary that every `if` statement should have an `else` block as Python supports simple `if` statements also. After the first test expression or the first `if` branch, the programmer can have as many `elif` branches as he wants depending on the expressions that have to be tested. The final `else` block is called if none of the `if` or `elif` expressions is True.

Remember that the `elif` and `else` part are optional.

Example 8.7   To test whether a number entered by the user is negative, positive or equal to zero.

```
num = int(input("Enter any number : "))
if(num==0):
    print("The value is equal to zero" )
elif(num>0):
    print("The number is positive")
else:
    print("The number is negative")
```

OUTPUT
Enter any number : -10
The number is negative

Example 8.8   Write a program to determine whether the character entered is a vowel or not.

```
ch = input("Enter any character : ")
if(ch=="A" or ch=="E" or ch=="I" or ch=="O" or ch=="U"):
    print ch,"is a vowel")
elif(ch=="a" or ch=="e" or ch=="i" or ch=="o" or ch=="u"):
    print(ch,"is a vowel")
else:
    print(ch, "is not a vowel")
```

OUTPUT
Enter any character: h
h is not a vowel

In the program to test whether a number is positive or negative, note that if the first test expression evaluates a true value, then the rest of the statements in the code will be ignored and after executing the `print` statement that displays "The value is equal to zero", the control will jump to `return 0` statement.

Python assumes any non-zero and non-null values as TRUE. Similarly, all values that are either zero or null are assumed as FALSE value.

Use the AND/OR operators to form a compound relation expression. In Python, the following expression is invalid.

if (60 ≤ marks ≤ 75) :

The correct way to write is,

if ((marks ≥ 60) and (marks ≤ 75) :

Keep the logical expressions simple and short. For this, you may use nested if statements.

PROGRAMMER'S ZONE

1. **Write a program to find whether the given number is even or odd.**
```
num = int(input("Enter any number : "))
if(num%2==0):
    print(num,"is even")
else:
    print(num,"is odd")
```

OUTPUT
```
Enter any number:125
125 is odd
```

2. **Write a program to enter any character. If the entered character is in lower case then convert it into upper case and if it is an upper case character then convert it into lower case.**
```
ch = input("Enter any character : ")
if(ch >= 'A' and ch <='Z'):
    ch = ch.lower()
    print("The entered character was in upper case. In lower case it is : " + ch)
else:
    ch = ch.upper()
    print("The entered character was in lower case. In upper case it is : " + ch)
```

OUTPUT
```
Enter any character: c
The entered character was in lower case. In upper case it is:C
```

3. **A company decides to give bonus to all its employees on Diwali. A 5% bonus on salary is given to the male workers and 10% bonus on salary to the female workers. Write a program to enter the salary of the employee and sex of the employee. If the salary of the employee is less than Rs 10,000 then the employee gets an extra 2% bonus on salary. Calculate the bonus that has to be given to the employee and display the salary that the employee will get.**
```
ch = input("Enter the sex of the employee (m or f) : ")
sal = int(input("Enter the salary of the employee : "))
if (ch=='m'):
    bonus = 0.05*sal
else :
    bonus = 0.10*sal
amt_to_be_paid = sal+bonus
print(" Salary = ",sal)
print(" Bonus = ",bonus)
print(" *******************************")
print("Amount to be paid : ",amt_to_be_paid)
```

OUTPUT
```
Enter the sex of the employee (m or f) : f
Enter the salary of the employee : 50000
Salary = 50000
Bonus = 5000.0
********************************
Amount to be paid : 55000.0
```

4. **Write a program to find whether a given year is a leap year or not.**
    ```
    year = int(input("Enter any year : "))
    if((year%4==0 and year %100!=0) or (year%400 == 0)):
        print("Leap Year")
    else:
        print("Not a Leap Year")
    ```

    OUTPUT
    ```
    Enter any year: 2000
    Leap Year
    ```

5. **Write a program to find the greater of two numbers.**
    ```
    x = int(input("Enter the first number : "))
    y = int(input("Enter the second number : "))
    if(x==y):
        print("The two numbers are equal")
    elif(x>y):
        print(x,"is greater than",y)
    else:
        print(x,"is less than",y)
    ```

    OUTPUT
    ```
    Enter the first number: 6
    Enter the second number: 3
    6 is greater than 3
    ```

6. **Write a program to find the greatest number from three numbers.**
    ```
    num1 = int(input("Enter the first number : "))
    num2 = int(input("Enter the second number : "))
    num3 = int(input("Enter the third number : "))
    if(num1>num2):
        if(num1>num3):
            print(num1,"is greater than",num2,"and",num3)
        else:
            print(num3,"is greater than",num1,"and",num2)
    elif(num2>num3):
        print(num2,"is greater than",num1,"and",num3)
    else:
        print("The three numbers are equal")
    ```

    OUTPUT
    ```
    Enter the first number: 13
    Enter the second number: 43
    Enter the third number: 25
    43 is greater than 13 and 25
    ```

7. **Write a program that prompts the user to enter a number between 1 and 7 and then displays the corresponding day of the week.**

```
num = int(input("Enter any number between 1 to 7 : "))
if(num==1): print("Sunday")
elif(num==2): print("Monday")
elif(num==3): print("Tuesday")
elif(num==4): print("Wednesday")
elif(num==5): print("Thursday")
elif(num==6): print("Friday")
elif(num==7): print("Saturday")
else :
print("Wrong input")
```

OUTPUT

```
Enter any number between 1 to 7: 5
Thursday
```

8. **Write a program to calculate tax, given the following conditions:**
   If income is less than 1,50,000 then no tax
   If taxable income is 1,50,001 - 300,000 then charge 10% tax
   If taxable income is 3,00,001 - 500,000 then charge 20% tax
   If taxable income is above 5,00,001 then charge 30% tax

```
MIN1 = 150001
MAX1 = 300000
RATE1 = 0.10
MIN2 = 300001
MAX2 = 500000
RATE2 = 0.20
MIN3 = 500001
RATE3 = 0.30
income = int(input("Enter the income : "))
taxable_income = income - 150000
if(taxable_income <= 0):
    print("No tax")
elif(taxable_income>=MIN1 and taxable_income<MAX1):
    tax = (taxable_income - MIN1) * RATE1
elif(taxable_income>=MIN2 and taxable_income<MAX2):
    tax = (taxable_income - MIN2) * RATE2
else:
    tax = (taxable_income-MIN3)*RATE3
print("TAX = ",tax)
```

OUTPUT

```
Enter the income: 2000000
TAX = 404999.7
```

9. **Write a program to take input from the user and then check whether it is a number or a character. If it is a character, determine whether it is in upper case or lower case.**

```
ch = input("Enter the character : ")
if(ch>="A" and ch<="Z"):
    print("Upper case character was entered")
```

```python
    elif(ch>='a' and ch<='z'):
        print("Lower case character was entered")
    elif(ch>='0' and ch<='9'):
        print "A number was entered"
```

OUTPUT
```
Enter any character: C
Upper case character was entered
```

10. **Write a program to enter the marks of a student in four subjects. Then calculate the total, aggregate and display the grade obtained by the student. If the student scores an aggregate greater than 75%, then the grade is Distinction. If aggregate is 60>= and <75, then the grade is First Division. If aggregate is 50>= and <60, then the grade is Second Division. If aggregate is 40>= and <50, then the grade is Third Division. Else, the grade is Fail.**

```python
marks1 = int(input("Enter the marks in Mathematics : "))
marks2 = int(input("Enter the marks in Science : "))
marks3 = int(input("Enter the marks in Social Science : "))
marks4 = int(input("Enter the marks in Computers : "))
total = marks1+marks2+marks3+marks4
avg = float(total)/4
print("Total = ",total,"\t Aggregate = ",avg)
if(avg>=75):
    print("Distinction")
elif(avg>=60 and avg<75):
    print("First Division")
elif(avg>=50 and avg<60):
    print("Second Division")
else:
    print("Fail")
```

OUTPUT
```
Enter the marks in Mathematics: 90
Enter the marks in Science: 91
Enter the marks in Social Science: 92
Enter the marks in Computers: 93
Total = 366    Aggregate = 91.5
Distinction
```

> While forming the conditional expression, try to use positive statements rather than using compound negative statements.

11. **Write a program to calculate the roots of a quadratic equation.**

```python
a = int(input("Enter the values of a : "))
b = int(input("Enter the values of b : "))
c = int(input("Enter the values of c : "))
D = (b*b)-(4*a*c)
deno = 2*a
if(D>0):
    print("REAL ROOTS")
    root1 = (-b + D**0.5)/deno
    root2 = (-b - D**0.5)/deno
    print("Root1 = ",root1,"\tRoot2 = ",root2)
    print "EQUAL ROOTS"
    root1 = -b/deno
    print("Root1 and Root2 = ",root1)
else:
    print("IMAGINARY ROOTS")
```

> Do not use floating-point numbers to check for equality in the test expression.

12. **Write a program that prompts the user to enter three angles. Check whether the angles are that of a triangle or not.**

```
ang1= int(input("Enter the first angle : "))
ang2= int(input("Enter the first angle : "))
ang3= int(input("Enter the first angle : "))
if (ang1 + ang2 + ang3) == 180:
    print("The angles are angles of a triangle")
else:
    print("The angles are not the angles of a triangle")
```

OUTPUT
```
Enter the first angle: 120
Enter the first angle: 40
Enter the first angle: 20
The angles are angles of a triangle
```

Key Terms

Sequential control flow: A programming style in which the statements in a program are executed one after the other.

Flow control: Flow control means control on which statement would be executed next.

Decision control flow: A type of flow control in which either a selected set of statements is executed or a particular set of statements is executed repeatedly.

Selection control statements: Decision control statements that allow the flow control to jump from one part of the code to another depending on whether a particular condition is satisfied or not. Since they execute statements selectively based on certain decisions, such type of decision control statements is known as selection control statements or *conditional branching statements*.

Clause: Combination of a header and its suite.

Suite: Group of statements following the header.

Nested (or compound) statement: A statement that contains other statements is called a compound statement.

Chapter Highlights

- A test expression is any valid expression that may include logical operators.
- After the header, all instructions that are indented at the same level form a suite.
- Python uses indentation to form a block of code.
- An `if-else` statement specifies what has to be done if the statement is true as well as when it is false.
- Nested `if` statements are used to check if more than one condition is satisfied.
- A series of `if` and `elif` statements have a final `else` block, which is executed if none of the `if` or `elif` expressions is True.

Review Questions

1. What is flow control?
2. Differentiate between sequential control flow and selection control flow.
3. Why do we need decision control statements?

4. With the help of a flowchart, explain the syntax of the following statements:
   a. `if`   b. `if-else`   c. `if-el-if`   d. nested `if`
5. What are conditional branching statements? How does Python support such statements?
6. How will you identify the suite of an `if` statement?
7. With the help of an example explain why `if-else` statement is better than a simple `if` statement.
8. What do you mean by a nested `if` statement? How is it implemented In Python?
9. Why should we not use floating-point numbers to test for exact equality?
10. Change the indentation to make the code syntactically correct.
    ```
    if condition1:
    statement1
    elif condition2:
    statement2
    elif condition3:
    statement3
    elif condition4:
    statement4
    ```
11. Under what conditions, Programming will be printed?
    ```
    if a < 10:
      print("Python")
    elif a < 20:
      print("Programming")
    else:
      print("is fun..")
    ```

Programming Exercises

1. Write a program to check whether a number is divisible by 10 or not. If the number is not divisible, then print how much should be added to it to make it completely divisible by 10.
2. Write a program to verify whether a candidate is eligible to appear for an exam or not. The minimum and maximum age of person appearing for the exam is 21 and 35 respectively.
3. Write a program that prompts the user to enter an angle and then prints its quadrant.
4. Write a program that prompts the user to enter a number between 1–12 and then display the corresponding month of the year.
5. Write a menu-driven program that prompts the user to enter the two sides of a rectangle. The user can then choose from a given set of options, if he/she needs to calculate perimeter, area or diagonal of the rectangle.
6. Write a program that prompts users to enter a character (A, B, C, D, E). Then using `if-elif-else` construct, display Outstanding, Very Good, Good, Average and Fail respectively.
7. Write a program that determines whether a student is eligible for PG course or not. To be eligible, the student must have obtained more than 80% in X and XII examination, and 70% plus marks in Graduation. If the student changes his stream (Science, Commerce, Arts), then deduct 5% from his Graduation score.
8. Write a program to read a floating-point number and an integer. If the value of the floating-point number is greater than 3.14 then multiply the value of the integer with 100.
9. Write a program that prompts the user to enter two integers. Divide the greater number with the smaller one and print the remainder and quotient thus obtained.
10. What output will be generated when the expression 5 or 100/0 is evaluated? What change can you do so that Python reports a Divide-by-Zero Error?

11. Write a program that accepts the current date and the date of birth of the user. Then calculate the age of the user and display it on the screen. Note that the date should be displayed in the format specified as dd/mm/yy.

12. Write a code to calculate the amount to be paid by a customer by considering the following points.
    If the amount_to_be_paid >=30000, then discount = 30%.
    If the amount_to_be_paid >=20000, then discount = 20%.
    If the amount_to_be_paid >=10000, then discount = 10%.
    Otherwise, discount = 5%

13. Write a program that prompts the user to enter his/ her age (15–18 years) and then display the perfect height and weight for that age.

Age	Weight (kg)	Height (cm)
15	56	170
16	60	173
17	64	175
18	66	176

14. Write a program that prompts the user to enter his/her body temperature. Check and display whether the user has normal body temperature, high fever or low fever.

15. Write a program that prompts the user to enter a number. Display the square root of the number. Remember that square root of negative numbers is not defined.

16. Write a program that prompts the user to enter the lengths of three sides. Check whether these are the sides of a triangle.
    Hint: Sides of a triangle follow the rule, a + b > c. Similarly, b + c > a and a + c > b.

17. Write a program that prompts the user to enter the angles of a triangle. Check whether the triangle is acute-, obtuse- or right-angled.

18. Write a program to check whether a number entered by the user is positive, negative or equal to zero.

19. Write a program that prompts users to enter status code 'S', 'M', 'D', or 'U' and returns the string 'Separated', 'Married', 'Divorced', or 'Unmarried', respectively. In case an inappropriate letter is passed, print an appropriate message.

20. An employee's total weekly pay is calculated by multiplying the hourly wage and number of regular hours plus any overtime pay, which in turn is calculated as total overtime hours multiplied by 1.5 times the hourly wage. Write a program that takes as inputs the hourly wage, total regular hours, and total overtime hours and prints an employee's total weekly pay.

21. Write a program to calculate electricity bill based on the following information.

Consumption Unit	Rate of Charge
0 – 150	Re 3 per unit
151 – 350	Rs 100 plus Rs 3.75 per unit exceeding 150 units
301 – 450	Rs 250 plus Rs 4 per unit exceeding 350 units
451 – 600	Rs 300 plus Rs 4.25 per unit exceeding 450 units
Above 600	Rs 400 plus Rs 5 per unit exceeding 600 units

Fill in the Blanks

1. _____ means control on which statement would be executed next.
2. _____ is the simplest form of decision control statements.
3. Header and its suite together form a _____.

4. Python uses _____ to form a block of code.
5. A _____ statement contains other statements.
6. A series of if and elif statements have a final _____ block.
7. _____ and _____ operators are used to form a compound relational expression.
8. _____ is a short form of else if statement. Ans
9. Python uses _____ to form a block of code.
10. A series of if elif statements have a final _____ block, which is executed if none of the if or elif expressions is True.
11. Python assumes any non-zero and non-null values as _____.
12. _____ begins with a keyword and ends with a colon.
13. ```
    x = 10
    y = 20
    __x>y__
    print print("In if")
    _____
            print ("In else")
    ```
14. Fill the blanks to print *Python* on the screen.
    ```
    x = 10
    y = 50
    if x>10 __ y<100:
    ___ ("Python")
    ```

State True or False

1. A sequential control program can skip one or more statements.
2. In selection control statements, all the statements are executed from the first one to the last.
3. A group of statements following the header is known as a clause.
4. After the header, all instructions that are indented at the same level form a suite.
5. It is mandatory to use four spaces to define each level of indentation. Ans
6. The final else block in an if-elif-else statement is executed when none of the if or elif expressions is True.
7. You can use floating point numbers for checking for equality in the test expression.
8. Indentation identifies a statement block.
9. Statements within a suite can be indented at different levels.
10. elif and else blocks are optional.

Multiple Choice Questions

1. Which part of if statement should be indented?
   a. The first statement   b. All the statements   c. Statements within the if block   d. None of these.
2. A programming style in which the statements in a program are executed one after the other.
   a. Sequential   b. Decision control   c. Iterative control   d. None of these.
3. A test expression must have a/an _____ operator.
   a. arithmetic   b. logical   c. unary   d. assignment
    ```

4. In an if statement, which of the following headers are optional?
   a. If　　　　　　b. elif　　　　　　c. else　　　　　　d. Both b and c.
5. A logical expression should not be _____
   a. simple　　　　b. long　　　　　　c. positive　　　　d. Both b and c.
6. Which of the following is placed after the if condition?
   a. ;　　　　　　　b. .　　　　　　　c. :　　　　　　　d. ,

Give the Output

1.  ```
    if(5.0 < 9.0):
        print("DONE")
    ```

2.  ```
    years = 99
    if(years == 100):
        print("Century")
    elif(years == 75):
        print("Platinum Jublee")
    elif(years == 50):
        print("Half Century")
    elif(years == 25):
        print("Silver Jublee")
    elif(years == 10):
        print("Decade")
    else:
        print("Long way to go….")
    ```

3.  ```
    years = 99
    if years > 30:
        print("30")
    if years < 50:
        print("50")
    if years == 7:
        print("70")
    ```

4.  ```
    num = int((10*6 + 10 - 20) > 0)
    if num == 50:
        print("You win...")
    else:
        print("Try Again")
    ```

5.  ```
    num = 3
    if (num ** 3) > (5%2 - 3 * 4 /2):
        if (num // 4) >= 2:
            print("You win")
        else:
            print("Try Again")
    ```

6.  ```
    num = 3
    if num == 2:
        print("Yes")
    elif num == 4:
        print("Yes")
    elif num == 8:
        print("Yes")
    else:
        print("Number is not an even number")
    ```

7. ```
   if(10 == 100) and (100 + 200 > 300):
       print("Win Win..")
   else:
       print("Oh No !!!")
   ```
8. ```
   if not True:
       print("WRONG")
   elif not((10+10 - 20 * 3) == 30):
       print("Really !")
   else:
       print("May Be")
   ```
9. ```
   if (10 << ((41 - 40 // 2 + 1)%2)) == 60:
       print("WoW")
   else:
       print("Gosh")
   ```
10. ```
    a = 5
    b = 70
    if not 10 + 10 == b or a == 40 and 70== 80:
        print("Yeah")
    elif a != b:
        print("Nope")
    ```
11. ```
    num = 10
    if num > 30:
        if num > 40:
            print("Python")
        else:
            print("Programming")
    elif num < 20:
        if(num!=0):
            print("is fun..")
    print("Isnt it !!!")
    ```
12. ```
    weather = 'foggy'
    if weather == 'sunny':
        print("Take your shades")
    elif weather == 'raining':
        print("Take your umbrella")
    else:
        print("Stay at home")
    ```

Answers

Fill in the Blanks

1. Flow control
2. If statement
3. clause
4. indentation
5. compound/nested
6. else
7. and, or
8. elif
9. indentation
10. else
11. True
12. Header
13. `if, :, else:`
14. `or, print`

State True or False

1. False
2. False
3. False
4. True
5. False
6. True
7. True
8. True
9. False
10. True

Multiple Choice Questions
1. b
2. a
3. b
4. d
5. b
6. c

Give the Output
1. Done
2. Long way to go….
3. 30
4. Try Again
5. Try Again
6. Number is not an even number
7. Oh No !!!
8. Really !
9. Gosh
10. Yeah
11. is fun..
    Isnt it !!!
12. Stay at home

Basic Loop Structures/Iterative Statements

Chapter Objectives

This chapter elucidates the concept of iterative statements in Python. Like decision control statements, the iterative statements may also change the flow of program control. Here, we shall learn about:

- while loop
- for loop
- The range() function
- Nested loops
- The technique to choose an appropriate loop for the given situation
- Path breaking statements like break, continue, pass and else

In the last chapter, we had read about decision-controlled statements and covered conditional branching statements including if, if-else and if-elif-else statements. In this chapter, we will study iterative statements through which Python supports basic loop structures. Iterative statements are used to repeat the execution of one or more statements. In Python, iterative statements are implemented through while loop and for loop.

9.1 while LOOP

The while loop provides a mechanism to repeat one or more statements while a particular condition is true. Figure 9.1 shows the syntax and general form of representation of a while loop.

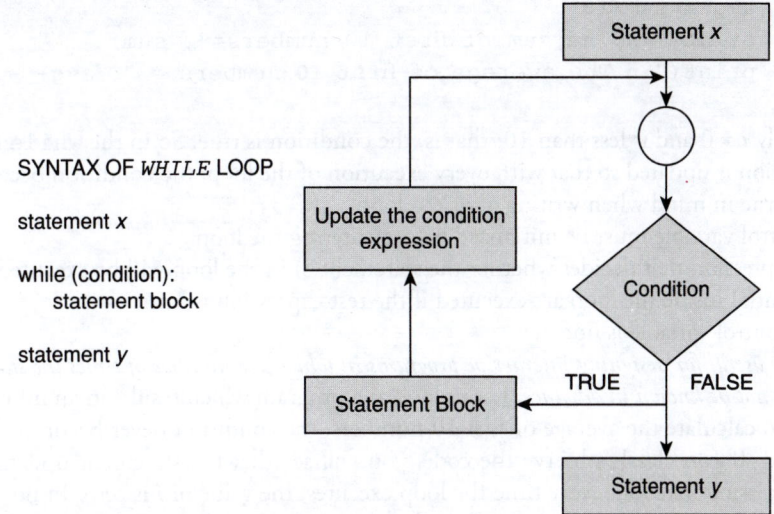

Figure 9.1 The while loop construct

Note that in the while loop, the condition is tested before any of the statements in the statement block is executed. If the condition is true, only then the statements will be executed; otherwise if the condition is false, the control will jump to statement *y*, which is the immediate statement outside the while loop block.

> Iterative statements are used to repeat the execution of a list of statements, depending on the value of an integer expression.

We must update the condition with every iteration of the loop. This is necessary because it is this condition which determines when the loop will end. If we do not update the condition, then it will never become false. This will result in an infinite loop which is never desirable.

A while loop is also referred to as a top-checking loop since control condition is placed as the first line of the code. If the control condition evaluates to False, then the statements enclosed in the loop are never executed. Look at the following example code.

Example 9.1 — To print the first 10 numbers using a while loop.

```
i = 0
while(i< =10):
       print(i,end=' ')
       i = i+1
```

OUTPUT
0 1 2 3 4 5 6 7 8 9 10

Example 9.2 — Write a program to calculate the sum and average of first 10 numbers.

```
i = 0
s = 0
while(i<=10):
   s = s+i
   i=i+1
avg = float(s)/10
print("The sum of first 10 numbers is : ",s)
print("The average of first 10 numbers is :",avg)
```

OUTPUT
The sum of first 10 numbers is : 55

```
i = 0
sum=0
avg= 0.0
while(i<=10):
    sum = sum + i
avg = sum/10
print("\n The sum of first 10 numbers=", sum)
print("\n The average of first 10 numbers = ", avg)
```

> The infinite loop is a loop which never stops running. Its condition always True.

In the program, initially $i = 0$ and is less than 10; that is, the condition is true. So in the while loop, the value of i is printed and the condition is updated so that with every execution of the loop, the condition becomes more approachable. This has to be borne in mind when writing a while loop,

First, the loop control variable must be initialized before entering the loop.

Second, the test expression that decides whether the statement(s) in the loop will be executed or not, is evaluated.

Third, the statement(s) inside the loop are executed if the test expression is True.

Fourth, the loop control variable is updated.

while loop is very useful for designing interactive programs in which the number of times the statements in loop has to be executed may or may not be known in advance. Let us look at a program which results in an infinite loop. Though the program is supposed to calculate the average of first 10 numbers, the condition never becomes false, and the desired output is *not* generated. If you clearly observe the code, you will see that the statement updating the value of loop control variable (i) is missing here. So, every time the loop executes, the value of i is zero. In no way, will the value of i become equal to or greater than 10. Hence, an infinite loop – a loop that never ends is entered.

Once you get stuck in an infinite loop, either press Ctrl + C keys on the keyboard or press the close button of the Python shell window.

9.2   for LOOP

Like the while loop, the for loop provides a mechanism to repeat a task until a particular condition is true. The for loop is usually known as a determinate or definite loop because the programmer knows exactly how many times the loop will repeat. The number of times the loop has to be executed can be determined mathematically by checking the logic of the loop.

The `for..in` statement is a looping statement used in Python to iterate over a sequence of objects, i.e., go through each item in a sequence. Here, by sequence we mean just an ordered collection of items. The flow of statements in a `for` loop can be given as in Fig. 9.2.

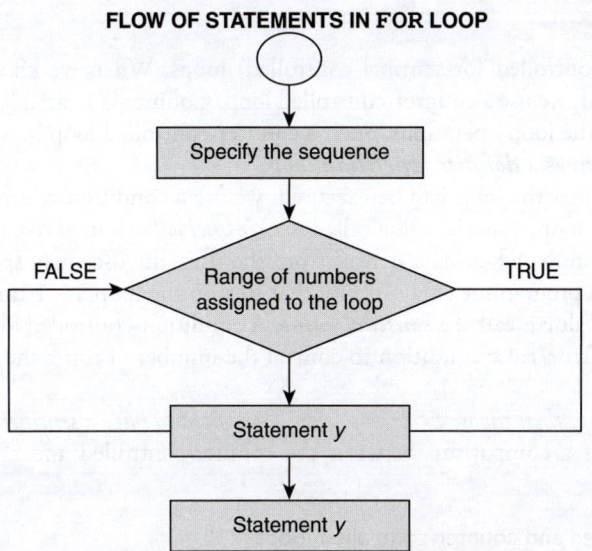

SYNTAX OF FOR LOOP
```
for loop_contol_var in sequence:
    statement block
```

Figure 9.2 `for` loop construct

When a `for` loop is used, a range of sequence is specified (only once). The items of the sequence are assigned to the loop control variable one after the other. The `for` loop is executed for each item in the sequence. With every iteration of the loop, a check is made to ensure if the loop control variable has been assigned all the values in the sequence. If all the values have not been assigned, the statement block of the loop is executed; else, the statements comprising the statement block of the `for` loop are skipped and the control jumps to the immediate statement following the `for` loop body. Note that every iteration of the loop must make the loop control variable closer to the end of the sequence.

Let us print all the characters in a string using the `for` loop. We know that a string is a sequence of characters. So, the `for` loop statement(s) will be executed for each character in the string.

```
for i in "PYTHON":
    print(i, end = ' ')
P Y T H O N
```

9.3 THE `range()` FUNCTION

The `range()` is a built-in function in Python that is used to iterate over a sequence of numbers. The syntax of `range()` is **range(beg, end, [step])**

The **range()** generates a sequence of numbers starting with **beg** (inclusive) and ending with one less than the number **end**. The **step** argument is optional (hence, written in brackets). By default, every number in the range is incremented by 1 but we can specify a different increment using step. It can be both negative and positive, but not zero.

> Step can be either positive or negative but cannot be zero.

Program to print first *n* numbers using the `range()` in a `for` loop.

```
for i in range(1, 5):
    print(i, end= ' ')
```
OUTPUT — Print numbers in the same line
1 2 3 4

```
for i in range(1, 10, 2):     (beg, end, step)
    print (i, end= ' ')
```
OUTPUT
1 3 7 9

The `range()` function has produced values 1, 2, 3 and 4. Did you notice that the statement(s) of the for loop is executed for each value of the loop control variable (which is *i*, here). Initially, *i* is 1, in the next iteration it is 2, and so on. The loop continues until all the values in the sequence are processed.

9.4 SELECTING AN APPROPRIATE LOOP

Loops can be either counter-controlled or condition-controlled (or sentinel-controlled) loops. When we know in advance the number of times the loop should be executed, we use a counter-controlled loop. Counter is a variable that must be initialized, tested, and updated for performing the loop operations. Such a counter-controlled loop in which the counter is assigned a constant or a value is also known as a ***definite repetition loop***.

When we do not know in advance the number of times the loop will be executed, we use a condition-controlled (or sentinel-controlled or indefinite loop) loop. In such a loop, a special value called the *sentinel value* is used to change the loop control expression from True to False. For example, when data is read from the user, the user may specify when they want the execution to stop. For example, the programmer may specify that to stop the loop a – 1 (or any other value) should be entered, they may enter –1. This value is called a ***sentinel value***. A condition-controlled loop is often useful for indefinite repetition loops as they use a True/False condition to control the number of times the loop is executed.

If your requirement is to have a *counter-controlled loop, then choose* `for` *loop; else, if you need to have a sentinel-controlled loop then go for a* `while` *loop.* Table 9.1 shows a comparison between the counter-controlled and condition-controlled loops.

Table 9.1 Comparison between condition-controlled and counter-controlled loops

Attribute	Counter-controlled Loop	Condition-controlled Loop
Number of execution	Used when number of times the loop has to be executed is known in advance.	Used when number of times the loop has to be executed is not known in advance.
Condition variable	In counter-controlled loops, we have a counter variable.	In condition-controlled loops, we use a sentinel variable.
Value and limitation of variable	The value of the counter variable and the condition for loop execution, both are strict.	The condition for loop execution is strict but the value of the sentinel variable may vary.

```
i = 0                    i = 0                         for i in range(11):
while(i<=10):            while(1):                         print(i, end = ' ')
    print(i, end=' ')        print(i, end = ' ')     Counter-controlled
    1+=1                     i+=1
Counter-controlled           if(i==11):
                                 break
                         Condition-controlled
```

9.5 NESTED LOOPS

Nested loop means that a loop is placed inside another loop. Although both `for` and `while` loop can be nested, we usually use nested `for` loops as they are easiest to control. In such a case, the inner `for` loop can be used to control the number of times a particular set of statements will be executed and the outer `for` loop can be used to control the number of times the inner loop is repeated. In Python, loops can be nested to any desired level.

Basic Loop Structures/Iterative Statements

| Example 9.3 | Write a program to print the following pattern. | Example 9.4 | Write a program to print the following pattern. |

Pass 1- 1 2 3 4 5
Pass 2- 1 2 3 4 5
Pass 3- 1 2 3 4 5
Pass 4- 1 2 3 4 5
Pass 5- 1 2 3 4 5

```
for i in range(1,6):
        print{"PASS",i,"- ",end='')
        for j in range{1,6):
                print(j, end=' ')
        print()
```

****
****
****
****
****

```
for i in range(5):
        print()
        for j in range{5):
                print "*",end='')
```

9.6   THE break STATEMENT

The break statement is used to terminate the execution of the nearest enclosing loop in which it appears. The break statement is widely used with for loop and while loop. When the compiler encounters a break statement, the control passes to the statement that follows the loop in which the break statement appears. Its syntax is quite simple, just type the keyword **break**.

Note that the code is meant to print first 10 numbers using a while loop, but it will actually print only numbers from 0 to 4. As soon as i becomes equal to 5, the break statement is executed and the control jumps to the statement following the while loop.

Hence, the **break** *statement is used to exit a loop from any point within its body, bypassing its normal termination expression.* When the break statement is encountered inside a loop, the loop is immediately terminated, and program control is passed to the next statement following the loop. Figure 9.3 shows the transfer of control when the break statement is encountered.

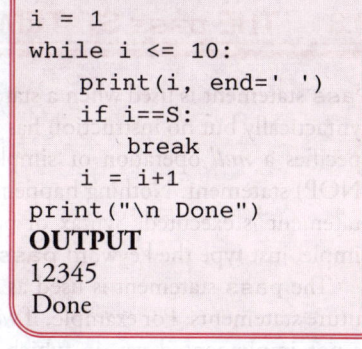

Program to demonstrate the break statement
```
i = 1
while i <= 10:
    print(i, end=' ')
    if i==S:
        break
    i = i+1
print("\n Done")
```
OUTPUT
12345
Done

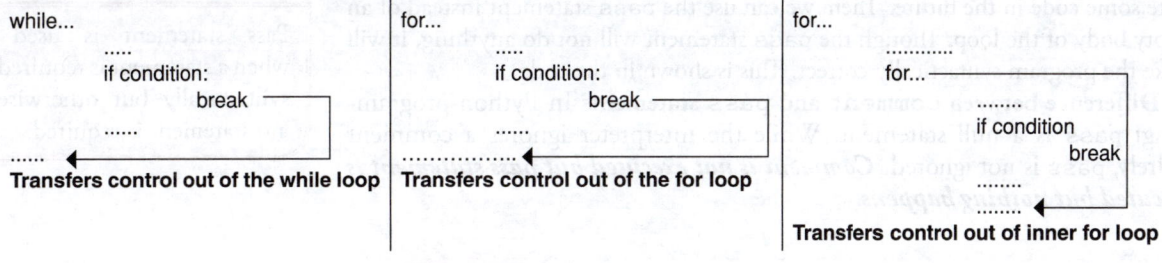

Figure 9.3   The break statement

9.7   THE continue STATEMENT

Like the break statement, the continue statement can only appear in the body of a loop. When the compiler encounters a continue statement then the rest of the statements in the loop are skipped and the control is unconditionally transferred to the loop-continuation portion of the nearest enclosing loop. Its syntax is quite simple, just type the keyword **continue**.

When the continue statement is encountered in the while and for loop, the control is transferred to the statement that tests the controlling expression. However, if placed with a for loop, the continue statement causes a branch to the code that updates the loop variable.

Program to demonstrate the continue statement
```
for i in range(1,11):
        if(i==S):
                continue
        print(i, end=' ')
print("\n Done")
```
OUTPUT
1 2 3 4 6 7 8 9 10
Done

Note that the code is meant to print numbers from 0 to 10. But as soon as *i* becomes equal to 5, the continue statement is encountered, so rest of the statement(s) in the `for` loop are skipped. In the output, there is no 5 (5 could not be printed as continue caused early increment of *i* and skipping of statement that printed the value of i on screen). Figure 9.4 illustrates the use of `continue` statement in loops.

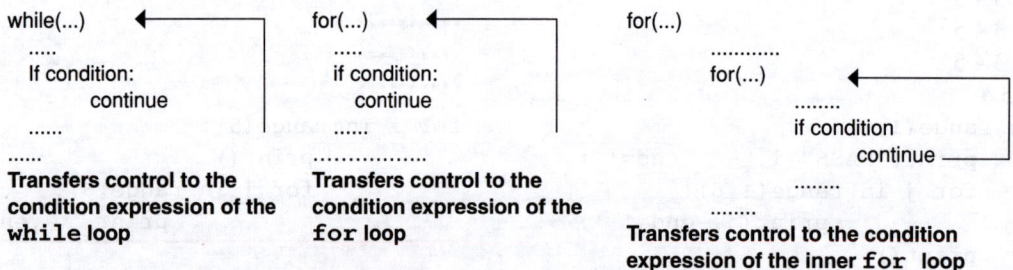

Figure 9.4 The `continue` statement

Hence, the `continue` statement is the opposite of the `break` statement. It forces the next iteration of the loop thereby skipping any statements that were a part of the loop. The `continue` statement is usually used to restart a statement sequence when an error occurs.

9.8 THE pass STATEMENT

Pass statement is used when a statement is required syntactically but no instruction has to be executed. It specifies a *null* operation or simply **No Operation** (NOP) statement. Nothing happens when the pass statement is executed. Syntax of pass statement is simple, just type the keyword **pass**.

The pass statement is used as a placeholder for future statements. For example, if we have a loop that is not implemented yet, in which we may wish to write some code in the future. Then, we can use the pass statement instead of an empty body of the loop. Though the pass statement will not do anything, it will make the program syntactically correct. This is shown in the code.

Difference between comment and pass statements In Python programming, pass is a null statement. While the interpreter ignores a comment entirely, pass is not ignored. *Comment is not executed but pass statement is executed but nothing happens.*

Program to demonstrate pass statement
```
for i in range(5):
    pass  #The statement is doing nothing
    print(i,end = ' ')
print("Done")
```
OUTPUT
0 1 2 3 4 Done

> Pass statement is used when a statement is required syntactically but otherwise no statement is required.

9.9 THE else STATEMENT USED WITH LOOPS

We have studied `if-else` block in the previous chapter. We can also have an `else` statement associated with loop statements. *If the `else` statement is used with a `for` loop, the `else` statement is executed when the loop has completed iterating. But when used with the `while` loop, the `else` statement is executed when the condition becomes false.*

```
for i in range(3):
    print(i, end=' ')
else:
    print("Done")
```
OUTPUT
0 1 2 Done

```
i = 10
while(i<0):
    print(i)
    i = i + 1
else:
    print(i, "is not negative so loop did not execute")
```
OUTPUT
i is not negative so loop did not execute

PROGRAMMER'S ZONE

1. **Write a program to print 10 horizontal hyphens(-).**
   ```
   i = 1
   while(i<=10):
       print("-",end=' ')
       i = i+1
   ```
   OUTPUT

   _____

2. **Write a program to calculate the sum of numbers from *m* to *n*.**
   ```
   m = int(input("Enter the value of m : "))
   n = int(input("Enter the value of n : "))
   s = 0
   while(m<=n):
           s = s+m
           m = m+1
   print("SUM = ",s)
   ```
   OUTPUT
   ```
   Enter the value of m : 3
   Enter the value of n : 9
   SUM =  42
   ```

3. **Write a program to read the numbers until −123 is encountered. Also count the negative, positive and zeroes entered by the user.**
   ```
   negatives = positives = zeroes = 0
   print("Enter -1 to exit...")
   while(1):
       num = int(input("Enter any number : "))
       if(num==-123):
          break
       if(num==0):
          zeroes = zeroes+1
       elif(num>0):
          positives = positives+1
       else:
          negatives = negatives+1
   print("Count of positive numbers entered : ",positives)
   print("Count of negative numbers entered : ",negatives)
   print("Count of zeroes entered : ",zeroes)
   ```
   OUTPUT
   ```
   Enter -1 to exit...
   Enter any number : 17
   Enter any number : 19
   Enter any number : 11
   Enter any number : 13
   Enter any number : -30
   Enter any number : -60
   Enter any number : -70
   ```

```
Enter any number : 40
Enter any number : 50
Enter any number : 0
Enter any number : -15
Count of positive numbers entered :  6
Count of negative numbers entered :  3
Count of zeroes entered :  1
```

4. **Write a program to read the numbers until –123 is encountered. Find the average of positive numbers and negative numbers entered by the user.**

```
neg_count = 0
neg_s = 0
pos_count = 0
pos_s = 0
print("Enter -1 to exit....")
num = int(input("Enter the number : "))
while(num!=-123):
    if(num<0):
        neg_count=neg_count+1
        neg_s=neg_s+num
    else:
        pos_count=pos_count+1
        pos_s=pos_s+num
    num = int(input("Enter the number : "))
neg_avg = float(neg_s)/neg_count
pos_avg = float(pos_s)/pos_count
print("The average of negative numbers is : ",neg_avg)
print("The average of positive numbers is : ",pos_avg)
```

> if statement is run once if condition is True, and never if it is False. A while statement is similar, except that it can be run more than once.

OUTPUT
```
Enter -1 to exit....
Enter the number : 1
Enter the number : 2
Enter the number : 3
Enter the number : -4
Enter the number : -5
Enter the number : -6
Enter the number : 8
Enter the number : -9
Enter the number : 10
Enter the number : -123
The average of negative numbers is :  -6.0
The average of positive numbers is :  4.8
```

5. **Write a program to calculate the average of numbers entered by the user.**

```
s = 0
count = 0
print "Enter -1 to stop...."
num = 0
while(num != -1):
    s = s+num
```

```
        num = int(input("Enter the marks : "))
        count = count+1
avg = float(s)/count
print "TOTAL MARKS : ",s,"\tAVERAGE MARKS : ",avg
```

OUTPUT
```
Enter -1 to stop....
Enter the marks : 90
Enter the marks : 98
Enter the marks : 97
Enter the marks : 89
Enter the marks : 79
Enter the marks : 96
Enter the marks : -1
TOTAL MARKS :   549    AVERAGE MARKS :    78.4285714286
```

6. **Write a program to find whether the given number is an Armstrong number or not.**
   Hint: An Armstrong number of three digits is an integer such that the sum of the cubes of its digits is equal to the number itself. For example, 371 is an Armstrong number since 3**3 + 7**3 + 1**3 = 371.
   ```
   n = int(input("Enter the number : "))
   s = 0
   num = n
   while(n>0):
           r = n%10
           s = s+(r**3)
           n = n/10
   if(s==num):
           print("The number is Armstrong")
   else:
           print("The number is not Armstrong")
   ```

   OUTPUT
   ```
   Enter the number : 373
   432 is not an Armstrong number
   ```

7. **Write a program to enter a decimal number. Calculate and display the binary equivalent of this number.**
   ```
   decimal_num = int(input("Enter the decimal number: "))
   binary_num = 0
   i = 0
   while(decimal_num!=0):
           remainder = decimal_num%2
           binary_num = binary_num+remainder*(10**i)
           decimal_num = decimal_num/2
           i = i+1
   print("The binary equivalent =",binary_num)
   ```

   OUTPUT
   ```
   Enter the decimal number : 8
   The binary equivalent = 1000
   ```

8. **Write a program to enter a binary number and convert it into decimal number.**
   ```
   binary_num = int(input("Enter the binary number : "))
   decimal_num = 0
   ```

```
i = 0
while(binary_num!=0):
        remainder = binary_num%10
        decimal_num = decimal_num+remainder*(2**i)
        binary_num = binary_num/10
        i = i+1
print("The decimal equivalent is",decimal_num)
```

OUTPUT
```
Enter the binary number : 1010
The decimal equivalent is 10
```

9. **Write a program to enter a number and then calculate the sum of its digits.**
```
sumOfDigits = 0
num = int(input("Enter the number : "))
while(num!=0):
        temp=num%10
        sumOfDigits = sumOfDigits+temp
        num=num/10
print("The sum of digits is :",sumOfDigits)
```

OUTPUT
```
Enter the number : 456
The sum of digits = 15
```

10. **Write a program to calculate the GCD of two numbers.**
```
num1 = int(input("Enter the two numbers : "))
num2 = int(input("Enter the two numbers : "))
if(num1>num2):
        dividend = num1
        divisor = num2
else:
        dividend = num2
        divisor = num1
while(divisor!=0):
        remainder = dividend%divisor
        dividend = divisor
        divisor = remainder
print("GCD of",num1,"and",num2,"is",dividend)
```

> To stop an infinite loop, press Ctrl + C keys or close the IDLE.

OUTPUT
```
Enter the first number : 40
Enter the second number : 10
GCD of 64 and 14 is = 10
```

11. **Write a program to print the reverse of a number.**
```
num = int(input("Enter the number : "))
print("The reversed number is :",)
while(num!=0):
        temp = num%10
        print(temp, end=' ')
        num = num/10
```

OUTPUT
```
Enter the number : 678
The reversed number is : 8 7 6
```

12. **Write a program using for loop to calculate the average of first *n* natural numbers.**
    ```
    n = int(input("Enter the value of n : "))
    avg = 0.0
    s = 0
    for i in range(1,n+1):
        s = s+i
    avg = s/i
    print("The sum of first",n,"natural numbers is",s)
    print("The average of first",n,"natural numbers is",avg)
    ```

    OUTPUT
    ```
    Enter the value of n : 10
    The sum of first n natural numbers = 55
    n The average of first n natural numbers = 5.500
    ```

13. **Write a program to print the multiplication table of *n*, where *n* is entered by the user.**
    ```
    n = int(input("Enter any number : "))
    print("Multiplication table of",n)
    print("*********************************")
    for i in range(1,11):
        print(n,"X",i,"=",n*i)
    ```

    OUTPUT
    ```
    Enter any number : 5
    Multiplication table of 5
    **********************
    5 X 0 = 0
    5 X 1 = 5
    …..
    5 X 20 = 100
    ```

14. **Write a program using for loop to print all the numbers from *m* to *n*, thereby classifying them as even or odd.**
    ```
    m = int(input("Enter the value of m : "))
    n = int(input("Enter the value of n : "))
    for i in range(m,n+1):
        if(i%2==0):
            print(i,"is even number")
        else:
            print(i,"is odd number")
    ```

    OUTPUT
    ```
    Enter the value of m : 10
    Enter the value of n : 15
    10 is even number
    11 is odd number
    12 is even number
    13 is odd number
    14 is even number
    15 is odd number
    ```

15. **Write a program using for loop to calculate the factorial of a number.**

```
num = int(input("Enter the number : "))
if(num==0):
      fact = 1
fact = 1
for i in range(1,num+1):
      fact = fact*i
print("Factorial of",num,"is",fact)
```

OUTPUT
```
Enter the number : 6
Factorial of is : 720
```

16. **Write a program to classify a given number as prime or composite.**

```
number = int(input('Enter number : '))
isComposite = 0
for i in range(2,(number-1)/2):
   if(number%i == 0):
      isComposite = 1
      break
if(isComposite == 1):
   print("Number is Composite")
else :
   print("Number is prime")
```

OUTPUT
```
Enter the number : 17
17 is a prime number
```

17. **Write a program using while loop to read the numbers until −1 is encountered. Also count the number of prime numbers and composite numbers entered by the user.**

```
total_prime = 0
total_composite = 0
while(1):
   num = int(input("Enter no. "))
   if(num == -1):
      break
   is_composite = 0
   for i in range(2,(num-1)/2):
      if(num%i == 0):
         is_composite = 1
         break
   if(is_composite):
      total_composite+=1
   else:
      total_prime+=1
print("total composite : ",total_composite)
print("total prime : ",total_prime)
```

OUTPUT
```
Enter no. 12
Enter no. 17
Enter no. 15
Enter no. 27
Enter no. 39
Enter no. 29
Enter no. 37
Enter no. -1
total composite :   4
total prime :   3
```

18. **Write a program that prints whether every number in a range is prime or composite.**
```
n = int(input("Enter the value of n : "))
i=2
print("1 is neither prime nor composite")
while i<n:
  flag = 0
  for j in range(2,i-1):
    if(i%j==0):
      flag=1
      print(i,"is a composite number")
      break
  if(flag==0):
    print(i,"is a prime number")
  i = i+1
```

OUTPUT
```
Enter the value of n : 10
1 is neither prime nor composite
2 is a prime number
3 is a prime number
4 is a composite number
5 is a prime number
6 is a composite number
7 is a prime number
8 is a composite number
9 is a composite number
```

19. **Write a program to calculate pow(*x,n*).**
```
num = int(input("Enter the number : "))
n = int(input("Till which power to calculate?"))
result = 1
for i in range(n):
        result = result*num
print(num,"raised to the power",n,"is",result)
```

OUTPUT
```
Enter the number : 3
Till which power to calculate : 5
3 raised to the power 5 is 243
```

20. **Write a program that displays all leap years from 2000–2050.**
    ```
    print("Leap Years from 2000-2050 are : ")
    for i in range(2000,2051):
            if(i%4==0):
                    print(i,end=' ')
    ```
    OUTPUT
    ```
    Leap Years from 2000-2050 are :
    2000 2004 2008 2012 2016 2020 2024 2028 2032 2036 2040 2044 2048
    ```

21. **Write a program to sum the series – $1 + 1/2 + \ldots + 1/n$.**
    ```
    n = int(input("Enter the number : "))
    s = 0.0
    for i in range(1,n+1):
            a = 1.0/i
            s = s+a
    print("The sum of 1,1/2......1/"+str(n)+" is "+str(s))
    ```
    OUTPUT
    ```
    Enter the number : 7
    The sum of 1,1/2......1/5 is  2.5928571428571425
    ```

22. **Write a program to sum the series – $1/1^2 + 1/2^2 + \ldots 1/n^2$.**
    ```
    n = int(input("Enter the number : "))
    s = 0.0
    for i in range(1,n+1):
            a = 1.0/(i**2)
            s = s+a
    print("The sum of series is",s)
    ```
    OUTPUT
    ```
    Enter the number : 7
    The sum of series is  1.511797052154195
    ```

23. **Write a program to sum the series – $1/2 + 2/3 + \ldots n/(n+1)$.**
    ```
    n = int(input("Enter the number : "))
    s = 0.0
    for i in range(1,n+1):
            a = float(i)/(i+1)
            s = s+a
    print("The sum of 1/2+2/3......n/(n+1) is",s)
    ```

    > Using break or continue statement outside a loop caused an error.

    OUTPUT
    ```
    Enter the number : 7
    The sum of 1/2+2/3......n/(n+1) is  5.2821428571428575
    ```

24. **Write a program to sum the series – $1/1 + 2^2/2 + 3^3/3 + \ldots n^2/n$.**
    ```
    n = int(input("Enter the value of n : "))
    s = 0.0
    for i in range(1,n+1):
            a = float(i**i)/i
            s = s+a
    print("The sum of the series is",s)
    ```

OUTPUT
```
Enter the value of n : 7
The sum of the series is  126126.0
```

25. **Write a program to calculate sum of cubes of numbers 1–n.**
```
n = int(input("Enter the value of n : "))
s = 0
for i in range(1,n+1):
    a = i**3
    s = s+a
print("The sum of cubes is",s)
```

OUTPUT
```
Enter the value of n : 4
The sum of cubes is 100
```

26. **Write a program to find the sum of squares of odd numbers.**
```
n = int(input("Enter the number : "))
s = 0
for i in range(1,n+1):
    if(i%2!=0):
        term = i**2
    else:
        term = 0
    s = s+term
print("The sum of squares of odd number less than",n,"is",s)
```

OUTPUT
```
Enter the number : 10
The sum of squares of even number less than 10 is 165
```

27. **Write a program to print the following pattern.**
```
*
**
***
****
*****
```
```
for i in range(1,6):
    print()
    for j in range(i):
        print("*", end=' ')
```

> The continue statement is used to stop the current iteration of the loop and continue with the next one.

28. **Write a program to print the following pattern.**
```
1
1 2
1 2 3
1 2 3 4
1 2 3 4 5
```
```
for i in range(1,6):
    print()
    for j in range(1,i+1):
        print(j, end=' ')
```

29. Write a program to print the following pattern.

```
    1
    2 2
    3 3 3
    4 4 4 4
    5 5 5 5 5
```

```
for i in range(1,6):
    print()
    for j in range(1,i+1):
        print(i, end=' ')
```

30. Write a program to print the following pattern.

```
    0
    1 2
    3 4 5
    6 7 8 9
```

```
count = 0
for i in range(1,5):
    print()        #prints a new line
    for j in range(1,i+1):
        print(count, end=' ')
        count = count+1
```

31. Write a program to print the following pattern.

```
    A
    AB
    ABC
    ABCD
    ABCDE
    ABCDEF
```

```
for i in range(1,7):
    ch = 'A'
    print()
    for j in range(1,i+1):
        print(ch, end=' ')
        ch = chr(ord(ch)+1)
```

32. Write a program to print the following pattern.

```
        1
       1 2
      1 2 3
     1 2 3 4
    1 2 3 4 5
```

```
N = 5
for i in range(1,N+1):
    for k in range(N,i,-1):
        print(" ", end=' ')
    for j in range(1,i+1):
        print(j, end=' ')
    print()
```

33. Write a program to print the following pattern.

```
            1
           1 2 1
          1 2 3 2 1
         1 2 3 4 3 2 1
        1 2 3 4 5 4 3 2 1
```

```
N = 5
for i in range (1 , N+1) :
    for k in range(N,i,-1) :
        print( " " , end=' ' )
    for j in range(1,i+1):
        print(j, end=' ')
    for 1 in range(i-1 , 0 ,-1) :
        print(1 , end= ' ' )
    print()
```

Basic Loop Structures/Iterative Statements 185

34. **Write a program to print the following pattern.**

```
            1              N = 5
          2 2              for i in range(1 , N+1) :
        3 3 3                  for k in range(N,i , -1):
      4 4 4 4                      print("", end=' ')
    5 5 5 5 5                  for j in range(1,i+1) :
                                   print(i , end=' ')
                               print()
```

35. **Write a program to calculate the square root of all positive numbers entered by the user.**

```
import math
while(1):
    num = int(input("Enter no. "))
    if(num == -111):
        break
    elif num < 0:
        print("Square root of negative numbers cannot
     be calculated")
        continue
    else:
        print("Square root of ", num, " = ", math.sqrt(num))
```

> When the compiler encounters a continue statement then the rest of the statements in the loop are skipped and the control is unconditionally transferred to the loop-continuation portion of the nearest enclosing loop.

OUTPUT
```
Enter no. 169
Square root of  169  =  13.0
Enter no. 64
Square root of  64  =  8.0
Enter no. 625
Square root of  625  =  25.0
Enter no. -16
Square root of negative numbers cannot be calculated
Enter no. -111
```

> break statement terminates the loop and transfers execution to the statement immediately following the loop.

Key Terms

Iterative statement: Statements that repeat the execution of a block of statements depending on the value of an integer expression.

Definite repetition loop: A counter-controlled loop in which the counter is assigned a constant or a value is also known as a definite repetition loop.

Nested loop: A loop that is placed inside another loop.

Chapter Highlights

- In Python, iterative statements are implemented through `while` loop and `for` loop.
- The `while` loop provides a mechanism to repeat one or more statements while a particular condition is true.
- The value of the loop control variable is updated with every iteration of the loop.
- The `for` loop provides a mechanism to repeat a task until a particular condition is true.
- The `for..in` statement is a looping statement used in Python to iterate over a sequence of objects.
- The `range()` is a built-in function in Python that is used to iterate over a sequence of numbers.
- Loops can be either counter-controlled or condition-controlled (or sentinel-controlled) loops.

- When we do not know in advance the number of times the loop will be executed, we use a condition-controlled loop.
- The `break` statement is used to terminate the execution of the nearest enclosing loop in which it appears.
- When the compiler encounters a `continue` statement then the rest of the statements in the loop are skipped and the control is unconditionally transferred to the loop-continuation portion of the nearest enclosing loop.
- `Pass` statement is used when a statement is required syntactically but no instruction has to be executed. It specifies a null operation or simply No Operation (NOP) statement.
- If the `else` statement is used with a `for` loop, the `else` statement is executed when the loop has completed iterating. But when it is used with the `while` loop, the `else` statement is executed when the condition becomes false.

Review Questions

1. With the help of a flowchart, explain the construct of a `while` loop.
2. Why is the value of the loop control variable updated with every iteration of the loop?
3. With the help of a flowchart, explain the construct of a `for` loop.
4. With the help of an example explain the use of `range()` function.
5. Differentiate between a condition-controlled and a counter-controlled loop.
6. With the help of an example, explain the use of `break` statement.
7. What happens when the pass statement executes?
8. Differentiate between the comment and the pass statements.
9. When is the else statement with loops executed?
10. What will happen if we replace the break statement in the code with a `continue` statement?
11. Fill in the blanks to complete the code:
    a. create a loop that increments the value of x by 3 and prints the odd values from 0–100.
    ```
    x = 0
    ___ x <= ___
       ___(x)
       x += 2
    ```
    b. to create a for loop that prints only the even values in the range 0–50:
    ```
    ____ i in range(_____):
       print(___)
    ```
12. Identify the definite and indefinite loop.
    ```
    n = input('Enter a number: ')     x = 0
    while n != -1:                    while x<10:
        n = input('Enter a number:  ')    print 10**num
                                      n = n+1
    ```
13. Correct the code to produce the desired output.
    ```
    for i in range(10,0):    i=10              i=10 ;  result = 1
       print(i)              while(i>0):       while(i>0):
                                print(i)          result = result + i**2
                                i-1               i = i+1
                                                  print(result)
    ```
14. The following for loops are written to print numbers from 1 to 10. Are these loops correct? Justify your answer.
    ```
    for i in range(10):    for i in range(10):    for i in range(10):
        print(i)               num = i+1              print(i)
                               print(num)             i = i+1
    ```

15. Write the following piece of code using for loop.
    ```
    i = 20
    while i>0:
        print(i)
        i = i-2
    ```

Programming Exercises

1. Write a program that converts a decimal number into its equivalent octal value.
2. Write a program that converts an octal number into its equivalent decimal value.
3. Write a function that accepts two positive numbers n and m where m<=n, and returns numbers between 1 and n that are divisible by m.
4. Write a program to convert time in hours into minutes and vice-versa.
5. Write a program to calculate conveyance charges to be paid by the users. Enter the type of car as a character (like s for sedan, p for prime, m for mini) and distance in km. Calculate charges as given below: sedan – 17 Rs per km, prime – 12 Rs per km, mini – 10 Rs per km.
6. Modify the above program to calculate the conveyance charges. Read the km when the user sits in the car and the time of his/her exit. Calculate the difference between the two readings and calculate the charges based on following rules.

Car Type	Rate up to First 5 km	Rate after First 5 km
Mini	10	10
Prime	20	12
Sedan	30	17

7. Write a program to sum the series $1^2/1 + 2^2/2 + 3^2/3 +.....+n^2/n$.
8. Write a program that prints cube of numbers in the range `(1,n)`.
9. Write a program that prompts user to enter the distance between his/her home and school. If the distance is in kilometers, display it in meters and vice versa.
10. Write a program that displays Python Programming as:
    a. python programming   b. PYTHON PROGRAMMING   c. pYTHON pROGRAMMING
11. Write a program that prompts users to enter numbers. Once the user enters `-1`, it displays the count, sum and average of even numbers and that of odd numbers.
12. Write a program to display the `sin(x)` value where x ranges from 0 to 360 in steps of 45.
13. Write a program that displays all the numbers from `1-100` that are not divisible by 7 as well as by 11.
14. Write a program that accepts any number and prints the number of digits in that number.
15. Write a program that prints numbers from 100 to 1 in steps of 4.
16. Write a program to generate the following pattern:
    ```
    * * * * *
    *       *
    *       *
    *       *
    * * * * *
    ```

17. Write a program to generate the following pattern:
    ```
    $ * * * *
    * $     *
    *   $   *
    *     $ *
    * * * * $
    ```

18. Write a program to generate the following pattern:
    ```
    $ * * * $
    * $   $ *
    *   $   *
    * $   $ *
    $ * * * $
    ```

19. Write a program that reads integers until the user wants to stop. When the user stops entering numbers, display the largest of all the numbers entered.

20. Write a program to generate the Fibonacci series.

21. Write a program to print first 20 even numbers in descending order.

22. Write a program to print the sum of the following series:
    a. $-x + x^2 - x^3 + x^4 + ...$
    b. $1 - x + x^2/2! - x^3/3! + ...$

23. Write a program to print the following pattern:

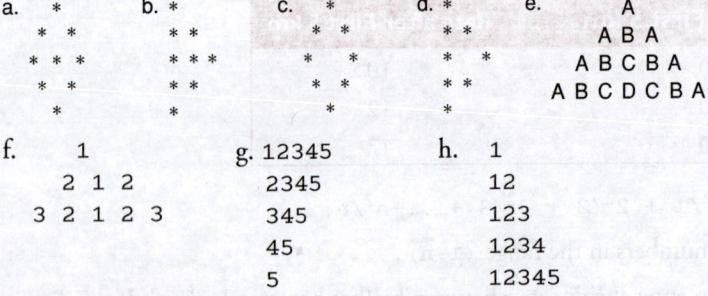

```
f.    1              g. 12345         h. 1
     2 1 2              2345             12
    3 2 1 2 3           345              123
                        45               1234
                        5                12345
```

Fill in the Blanks

1. _____ statements are used to repeatedly execute one or more statements in a block.
2. In Python, iterative statements are implemented through _____ and _____ loops.
3. An _____ loop will occur if the condition of `while` loop never becomes false.
4. The `for` loop provides a mechanism to repeat a task until a particular condition is _____.
5. The _____ function in Python is used to iterate over a sequence of numbers.
6. When we know in advance the number of times the loop should be executed, we use a _____ -controlled loop.
7. When we do not know in advance the number of times the loop will be executed, we use a _____ -controlled loop.
8. When _____ statement is encountered, the rest of the statements in the loop are skipped and the control is unconditionally transferred to the loop-continuation portion of the nearest enclosing loop.
9. The _____ statement specifies a null operation.
10. The _____ statement is executed when the for loop has completed iterating.

State True or False

1. The `while` loop repeats one or more statements while a particular condition is false.
2. Iterative statement repeats the execution of a block of statements depending on the value of an expression that evaluates to an integer value only.
3. In the `while` loop, the condition is tested after the statement block is executed at least once.
4. The value of the loop control variable is updated with every alternate iteration of the loop.
5. An infinite loop will occur if the condition of `while` loop is always false.
6. The `for` loop is executed for each item in the sequence.
7. Every iteration of the loop must make the loop control variable farther from the end of the sequence.
8. The step argument in the `range()` function is optional.
9. Sentinel value is used in counter-controlled loop.
10. Both `for` and `while` loop can be nested. Ans
11. The `break` and `continue` statements can only appear in the body of a loop.
12. In a `for` loop, the `continue` statement causes a branch to the code that updates the loop variable.
13. The `pass` statement is a non-executable statement that is ignored by the compiler.
14. The number of times the loop control variable is updated is equal to the number of times the loop iterates.
15. In a `while` loop, the loop control variable is initialized in the body of the loop.

Multiple Choice Questions

1. Which keys are not pressed to exit from the infinite loop?
   a. Alt + C b. Ctrl + C c. Alt + F4 d. Ctrl + Q
2. The step argument in the `range()` function cannot be _____.
   a. less than zero b. greater than zero c. zero d. none of these
3. `range(1,5)` will generate numbers _____.
   a. 0, 1, 2, 3, 4, 5 b. 0, 1, 2, 3, 4 c. 1, 2, 3, 4 d. 1, 2, 3, 4, 5
4. By default, every number in the range is incremented by ____.
   a. 0 b. 1 c. 2 d. 3
5. In a counter-controlled loop, the counter must be _____.
   a. initialized b. tested c. updated d. All of these.
6. A loop within another loop is also known as a _____ loop.
   a. sentinel-controlled b. condition-controlled
   c. counter-controlled d. nested
7. Which statement is used to terminate the execution of the nearest enclosing loop in which it appears?
   a. `break` b. `continue` c. `pass` d. `else`
8. In a `while` loop, if the body is executed n times, then the test expression is executed _____ times.
   a. n – 1 b. n c. n + 1 d. 2n
9. ```
   i = 1
   while i > 0:
       print("loop")
   ```
   The above loop is best example of _____ loop.
   a. nested b. infinite c. counter-controlled d. condition-controlled
   ```

10. How many numbers will be printed?
    ```
    i = 5
    while i>=0:
        print(i)
        i=i-1
    ```
    a. 5   b. 6   c. 4   d. 0

11. How many numbers will be printed?
    ```
    i = 10
    while True:
        print(i)
        i = i - 1
        if i<=7:
            break
    ```
    a. 1   b. 2   c. 3   d. 4

12. How many lines will be printed by this code?
    ```
    while False:
        print("Hello")
    ```
    a. Hello   b. 0   c. 10   d. Countless

Give the Output

1.  ```
    for i in range(1,20):
        if i%5==0:
            break
        else:
            print(i)
    ```

2.  ```
    for i in range(1,20):
        if i%5==0:
            continue
        else:
            print(i)
    ```

3.  ```
    while(4>5):
        print("DONE")
    else:
        print("NOT DONE")
    ```

4.  ```
    for i in range(1,5):
        for j in range(1,i):
            print('#',end = ' ')
        print()
    ```

5.  ```
    while(5*2 > 10):
        print("JUST DO IT")
    else:
        print("DONE")
    ```

6.  ```
    a = 10; b = 0
    while(a>b):
        print(a,b)
        a=a-1
        b=b+1
    ```

7. ```
   run = True
   a = 100
   while run == True:
       print(a)
       a = a - 10
       if a < 40:
           run = False
   ```

8. ```
   for i in range(100,50,-10):
       print(i)
   ```

9. ```
   for i in range(100,50,-10):
       print(i)
   ```

10. ```
    x = 10; y = 5
    for i in range(x-y*2):
        print("%")
    ```

11. ```
    for letter in "HELLO":
        pass
    ```

12. ```
    i=1
    while i<=6:
        print(i),
        i=i+1
    print("Done")
    ```

13. ```
    i=0
    while i<10:
        i = i + 1
        if(i == 5):
            print("\n Continue")
            continue
        if(i==7):
            print("\n Breaking")
            break
        print(i),
    print("\n Done")
    ```

14. ```
    for i in range(5):
            print("hello!", end= " ")
    ```

15. ```
    for i in range(10):
        if not i%2==0:
            print(i+1)
    ```

16. ```
    for i in range(10,0,-1):
        print(i, end = ' ')
    ```

17. ```
    for i in range(5,25,3):
        print(i, end = ' ')
    ```

18. ```
    for i in "PYTHON":
        print(i,'-',end='')
    ```

19. ```
    for i in range(10):
        pass
    print(i)
    ```
    ```

20.
```
while True:
    str = input("Enter a string (Bye to exit) : ")
    if str == "bye":
        break
    print(str)
else:
    print("Exiting......")
```

Find the Error

1.
```
while(i<10):
    print(i)
```

Answers

Fill in the Blanks
1. Flow control
2. while, for.
3. infinite
4. true
5. range()
6. counter
7. condition
8. continue
9. pass
10. else

State True or False
1. False
2. True
3. False
4. False
5. False
6. True
7. False
8. True
9. False
10. True
11. True
12. True
13. False
14. True
15. False

Multiple Choice Questions
1. a
2. c
3. c
4. b
5. d
6. d
7. a
8. c
9. b
10. b
11. c
12. b

Give the Output
1. 1,2,3,4
2. 1
3. NOT DONE
4. #
   ##
   ###
5. DONE
6. 10 0
7. 100 90 80 70 60 50 40
8. 100 90 80 70 60
9. No output
10. No output
11. No output on the screen.
12. 1 2 3 4 5 6 Done
13. 1 2 3 4
    Continue 6 Breaking Done
14. hello! hello! hello! hello! hello!
15. 2 4 6 8 10
16. 10 9 8 7 6 5 4 3 2 1
17. 5 8 11 14 17 20 23
18. P -Y -T -H -O -N -
19. 9
20. No output when bye is entered.

Find the Error
1. `NameError: name 'i' is not defined`

Functions and Modules

10

Chapter Objectives

This chapter helps the reader to think like computer professionals and engineers by breaking big complex problems into smaller and simpler ones. It illustrates how to create building blocks on which solution of real-world problems can be fabricated. The topics covered in this chapter include:

- Defining, calling and re-defining functions
- Working with built-in modules
- Creating own customized packages
- Using popular built-in functions
- Variable lifetime and scope
- Vital statements like `return` and `global`
- Function composition

In the previous chapters, we have used Python to write many useful programs. To further extend the usability of our programs, we must learn about the concept of functions. To understand functions, consider a scenario. If you are a project manager working on a very big project, then will you give the entire project to a single person or divide the project into *n* pieces and allocate each person an individual piece?

Of course, you will divide and allocate. Same is the case with programs. Instead of writing the entire code in one place, we must break the program into different functions or modules. Each module should then be coded individually. Whenever the functionality of these modules is required, it can just be called. In a program, you can call a function any number of times depending on the requirements.

10.1 FUNCTION

A function is a block of organized and reusable program code that performs a single, specific, and well-defined task. Consider Fig. 10.1, which explains how a function `func1()` is called to perform a well-defined task. As soon as `func1()` is called, the program control is passed to the first statement in the function. All the statements in the function are executed and then the program control is passed to the statement following the one that called the function.

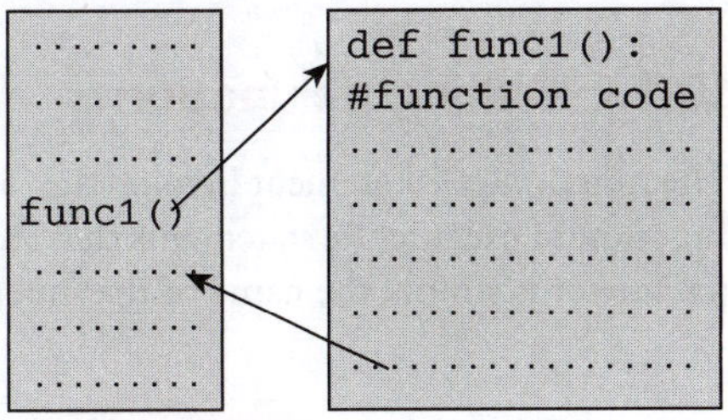

In Fig. 10.2, we see that `func1()` calls another function named `func2()`. Therefore, `func1()` is known as the **calling function** and `func2()` is known as the **called function**. The moment the compiler encounters a function call, instead of executing the next statement in the calling function, the control jumps to the statements that are a part of the called function. After the called function is executed, the control is returned to the calling program.

Figure 10.1 Calling a Function

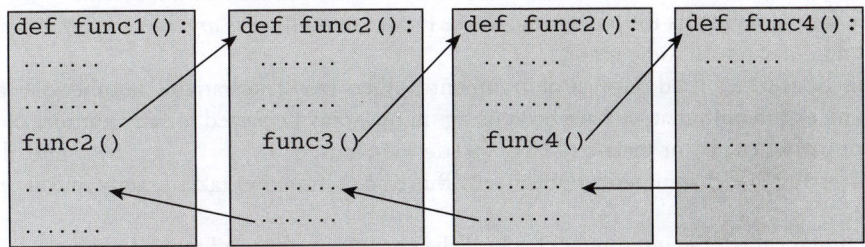

Figure 10.2 Calling a function from another function

There is no rule that the `func1()` can call only one function; it can call as many functions as it wants and as many times as it wants. For example, a function call placed within `for` loop or `while` loop may call the same function multiple times until the condition holds true.

10.1.1 Need for Functions

Functions are needed to facilitate ***each function to be written and tested separately***. This simplifies the process of getting the total program to work.

Moreover, if a big program has to be developed without the use of any function, then there will be countless lines in the code and maintaining that program will be quite messy.

In fact, ***all the libraries in Python*** contain a set of functions that the programmers can use in their programs. These functions have been pre-written and pre-tested, so the programmers use them without worrying about their code details. In this chapter, we will be using some libraries in our programs.

Functions or modules ***speed up program development*** as the programmer needs to concentrate only on the code that he/she has to write. Also, when a big program is broken into multiple functions and then written by different programmers, the workload gets divided and program development gets speeded up.

Besides Python libraries, programmers can themselves ***make their own functions*** and modules to be used in other programs as well.

Thus, *code reuse* is one of the most prominent reasons to use functions. Large programs usually follow the DRY principle, that is, **Don't Repeat Yourself** principle. In the absence DRY principle, the programmer has to re-write the same piece of code multiple times thereby not only increasing the size and complexity of the code but also making it more prone to errors. For example, you have been using the `print()` function so often. Just imagine if you had to yourself write the code to display output of a variable without using the `print()` function, then even a small 2–3 line code will have many more lines of complex instructions.

Once a function is written it can be called multiple times wherever its functionality is required (as shown in Fig. 10.3). This not only saves us from rewriting the same instructions but also reduces the complexity of programs. Even a beginner can easily write codes for solving his/her problems without getting bogged down by unnecessarily writing instructions which are pre-written to do a particular task.

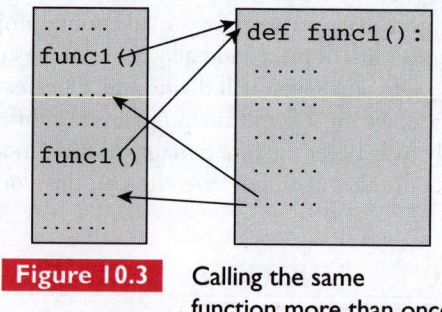

Figure 10.3 Calling the same function more than once

10.1.2 Calling a Function

The function call statement invokes the function. When a function is invoked, the program control jumps to the called function to execute the statements that are a part of that function. The syntax of calling a function that does not accept parameter is simply the name of the function followed by parentheses, which is given as,

`function_name()`

Function call statement has the following syntax when it accepts parameters.

`function_name(variable1, variable2, …)`

Also, remember certain points that must be remembered while calling a function.

- A function that is called or invoked to use its functionality is known as the *called function*.
- A function may take some inputs for processing. These inputs are known as *arguments/ parameters*.
- The called function may return some result.
- While some functions take a fixed number of arguments, others may take variable number of arguments. For example, the `print()` function that we have been using till now may be passed for any number of arguments, such as `print(a)` or `print(a,b)` or `print("The value of and b is : ", a, b)`. Here, the same function is being passed for 1, 2 and 3 arguments respectively. But `ord()` function takes exactly one argument and prints its ASCII value.
- When the function is called, the interpreter checks if the correct number and type of parameters are passed in the function call. It also checks the type of the returned value (if it returns a value).

10.2 MODULES

In the previous section, we have seen that functions help us to reuse a particular piece of code. Modules go a step ahead. They allow you to reuse one or more functions in your programs, even in the programs in which those functions have not been defined.

Simply put, *module is a file with a .py extension that has definitions of all functions and variables that you would like to use even in other programs.* The program in which you want to use functions or variables to be defined in a module will simply import that particular module (or .py file).

> Modules are pre-written pieces of code that are used to perform common tasks like generating random numbers, performing mathematical operations, etc.

The basic way to use a module is to add **import module_name** as the first line of your program and then write **module_name.var** to access functions and values with the name var in the module. Let us first use the standard library modules.

Program to print the PATH variable

```
import sys      ← Importing a module named sys
print("\n PYTHONPATH = \n", sys.path)
```
Using the path variable defined in sys module

OUTPUT
```
PYTHONPATH =
['C:\\Users\\Reema\\AppData\\Local\\Programs\\Python\\Python37\\Lib\\idlelib',
'C:\\Users\\Reema\\AppData\\Local\\Programs\\Python\\Python37\\python37.zip',
'C:\\Users\\Reema\\AppData\\Local\\Programs\\Python\\Python37\\DLLs',
'C:\\Users\\Reema\\AppData\\Local\\Programs\\Python\\Python37\\lib',
'C:\\Users\\Reema\\AppData\\Local\\Programs\\Python\\Python37',
'C:\\Users\\Reema\\AppData\\Local\\Programs\\Python\\Python37\\lib\\
site-packages']
```

In the above code, we *import* the sys module (short form of system) using the `import` statement to use its functionality related to the Python interpreter and its environment. When the import sys statement is executed, Python looks for the sys.py file in one of the directories listed in its sys.path variable. If the file is found, then the statements in the module are executed.

10.2.1 Module Loading and Execution

A module imported in a program must be located and loaded into memory before it can be used. Python first searches for the modules in the current working directory. If the module is not found there, it then looks for the module in the directories specified in the PYTHONPATH environment variable. If the module is still not found or if the PYTHONPATH variable is not defined, then a Python installation-specific path (like C:\Python37\Lib) is searched. If the module is not located even there, then an **ImportError** exception is generated.

Once a module is located, it is loaded in memory. A compiled version of the module with file extension **.pyc** is generated. Next time when the module is imported, this .pyc file is loaded rather than the .py file, to save the time of recompiling.

A new compiled version of a module is again produced whenever the compiled version is out of date (based on the dates when the .pyc file was created/modified). Even the programmer can force the Python shell to reload and recompile the .py file to generate a new .pyc file by using the **reload()** function.

10.2.2 The `from...import` Statement

A module may contain definition for many variables and functions. ***When you import a module, you can use any variable or function defined in that module.*** But if you want to use only selected variables or functions, then you can use the `from...import` statement. For example, in the given program you are using only the path variable in the sys module, so you could have better written **from sys import path**.

To import more than one item from a module, use a comma separated list. For example, to import the value of PI and sqrt() from the math module you can write

```
from math import pi, sqrt
```

If all the identifiers in the sys module are to be imported, you can use the from sys import * statement. However, you should avoid using the import * statement as it would consume a lot of memory.

You can also import a module with a different name using the **as** keyword. This is particularly more important when a module has either a long or confusing name.

For example,

```
from math import sqrt as square_root
      ……
print(square_root(81))
```

Python also allows you to pass **command line arguments** to your program, which will be required for execution. This can be done using the **sys** module. The **argv** variable in this module keeps a track of command line arguments passed to the .py script. To understand this, just open a new file, save it as main.py (or any other name) and write the following code in it.

```
import sys
print(sys.argv)
```

To execute this program code, go to Command Prompt (in Windows), write

```
C:\ Python37>python main.py Python programming is fun
```

In the above statement, did you notice that apart from program name, you passed some information to the program? The program may use this information in any way for processing it. Here, we have just accepted the command line arguments and printed them on the screen using sys.argv. You will get the output as,

```
['try.py', 'Python', 'programming', 'is', 'fun']
```

```
# Program to demonstrate sys.exit
import sys
print("Python Programming is Easy and Fun ... ")
sys.exit("Exiting Program ........")
```
OUTPUT
Python Programming is Easy and Fun ...

We can also use the **sys.exit([arg])** to exit from Python. Here, **arg** is an optional argument, which can either be an integer giving the exit status or another type of object.

If it is an integer, zero signifies successful termination and any nonzero value indicates an error or abnormal termination of the program. Generally, **sys.exit("Error Message")** is a quick way to exit a program when an error occurs.

10.2.3 Name of Module

Every module has a name. You can find the name of a module by using the __**name**__ attribute of the module.

```
#Program to print name of a module
print("Python Programming is Easy and Fun ... ")
print("Name of this module is:", _name_)
```
OUTPUT
Python Programming is Easy and Fun ...
Name of this module is : _main_

> #Program that uses the
> #from … import statement
> ```
> from math import pi
> print(" PI=",+ pi)
> ```
> **OUTPUT**
> 3.141592653589793

> This imports * statement imports all names except those beginning with an underscore(_).

Observe the output and always remember that for every standalone program written by the user the name of the module is __main__.

10.3 THE dir() FUNCTION

dir() is a built-in function that lists the identifiers defined in a module. These identifiers may include functions, classes and variables. If you mention the module name in the dir() function as given below, it will return the list of the names defined in that module.

dir(module_name)

If no name is specified, the dir() will return the list of names defined in the current module.

10.4 PACKAGES IN PYTHON

A package is a hierarchical file directory structure that **has modules and other packages within it.** Like modules, you can very easily create packages in Python.

Remember that ***every package in Python is a directory which must have a special file called __init__.py**. This file may not even have a single line of code. It is simply added to indicate that this directory is not an ordinary directory and contains a Python package. In your programs, you can **import a package** in the same way as you import any module.

For example, to create a package called MyPackage, create a directory (or folder) called MyPackage having all the modules and the __init__.py file. Now, to use a module named m1 in a program, you must first import it. This can be done in two ways.

```
import MyPackage.m1
or
from MyPackage import m1
```

The import statement first checks if the item is defined in the package. If it is unable to find it, an **ImportError** exception is raised.

> By convention, modules are named using lower case letters and optional underscore.

> Though you can write the import statement anywhere in the code before using the module, it is always recommended to write all import statements at the top of the program code.

10.5 PYTHON – MATH MODULE

Python has a standard library that has many important and useful built-in functions (like print(), ord(), int(), etc). Besides these built-in functions, the library also has various modules that have functionalities for specified actions.

```
#Program to print the value of PI and e
import math
print("PI = ", math.pi)
print(" Epsilon= ",math.e)
```
OUTPUT
PI= 3.141592653589793
Epsilon = 2. 718281828459045

Some of the most popular mathematical functions are defined in the math module. These include trigonometric functions, representation functions, logarithmic functions, angle conversion functions, etc. In addition, two mathematical constants – PI and Epsilon are also defined in this module. Let us print the two values. Remember that before using the math module, we must first import it by writing **import math**. Then, the specific function can be used by writing, **math.function_name**.

Functions like sin, cos, tan, etc. that need an angle accept the values in radians as an argument. In case you want to specify angle in degrees then the math.degree() function must be used. Table 10.1 lists some commonly used built-in function in the math module.

Table 10.1 Built-in functions in math module

Function	Description	Example

`ceil(x)`	Returns the smallest integer greater than or equal to x.	`import math`
		`print(math.ceil(1.2345))`
		OUTPUT
		2

`fabs(x)`	Returns the absolute value of x	`import math`
		`print(math.fabs(-5.6))`
		OUTPUT
		5.6

`factorial(x)`	Returns the factorial of x	`import math`
		`print(math.factorial(6))`
		OUTPUT
		720

`floor(x)`	Returns the largest integer less than or equal to x	`import math`
		`print(math.floor(-5.6))`
		OUTPUT
		-6

`fmod(x, y)`	Returns the remainder when x is divided by y	`import math`
		`print(math.fmod(-100,6))`
		OUTPUT
		-4.0

`modf(x)`	Returns the fractional and integer parts of x	`import math`
		`print(math.modf(-123.456))`
		OUTPUT
		(-0.45600000000000307, -123.0)

`trunc(x)`	Returns the truncated integer value of x	`import math`
		`print(math.trunc(-123.456))`
		OUTPUT
		-123

`exp(x)`	Returns e**x	`import math`
		`print(math.exp(10))`
		OUTPUT
		22026.465794806718

`log(x[, base])`	Returns the logarithm of x to the base (defaults to e)	`import math`
		`print(math.log(100,10))`
		OUTPUT
		2.0

`log2(x)`	Returns the base-2 logarithm of x	`import math`
		`print(math.log2(1024))`
		OUTPUT
		10.0

`log10(x)`	Returns the base-10 logarithm of x	`import math`
		`print(math.log10(1000))`
		OUTPUT
		3.0

`pow(x, y)`	Returns x raised to the power of y	`import math`
		`print(math.pow(10,4))`
		OUTPUT
		10000.0

(Continued)

Table 10.1 Continued

Function	Description	Example

`sqrt(x)`	Returns the square root of x	`import math`
		`print(math.sqrt(10000))`
		OUTPUT
		`100.0`

`cos(x)`	Returns the cosine of x	`import math`
		`print(math.cos(90))`
		OUTPUT
		`-0.4480736161291701`

`hypot(x, y)`	Returns the Euclidean norm, sqrt(x*x + y*y)	`import math`
		`print(math.hypot(6,8))`
		OUTPUT
		`10.0`

`sin(x)`	Returns the sine of x	`import math`
		`print(math.sin(90))`
		OUTPUT
		`0.8939966636005579`

`tan(x)`	Returns the tangent of x	`import math`
		`print(math.tan(90))`
		OUTPUT
		`-1.995200412208242`

`degrees(x)`	Converts angle x from radians to degrees	`import math`
		`print(math.radians(90))`
		OUTPUT
		`1.5707963267948966`

`radians(x)`	Converts angle x from degrees to radians	`import math`
		`print(math.degrees(1.5707963267948966))`
		OUTPUT
		`90.0`

`uniform (a,b)`	It returns a floating-point number x, such that a <= x < b	`>>>random.uniform (5,10)` `5.52615217015`
`randrange([start,] stop [,step])`	It returns a random item from the given range	`>>>random.randrange(100,1000,3)` `150`

10.6 BUILT-IN FUNCTIONS

Built-in functions are the functions that are built into Python and can be accessed in programs. These functions are always available and for use, and the programmer does not have to import any module to use them. In Python, a small set of basic functions are available as built-in functions; the rest of the functions are available as a part of some other module. This was purposely done to keep the core language precise. Some of the frequently used built-in functions are given in Table 10.2.

Apart from these functions, we also have functions like `bool ( )`, `chr ( )`, `float ( )`, `int ( )`, `long ()`, `str ( )`, `type ( )`, `id ( )`, `tuple ( )`, etc. that we have already used until now.

Table 10.2 Built-in functions

Function	Purpose	Example
`abs(x)`	Returns distance between x and zero, where x is a numeric expression.	`>>>abs(-90)` `90`
`max()`	Returns the largest of its arguments	`>>> max(10,30,20)` `30`
`min()`	Returns the smallest of its arguments	`>>> min(10,30,-20)` `-20`
`divmod(x,y)`	Returns both quotient and remainder obtained when x is divided by y	`>>> divmod(S2, 7)` `(7, 3)`
`len(x)`	Returns length or the number of items in a sequence (like string).	`>>> len("PYTHON")` `6`
`round( x [, n])`	Returns float x rounded to n digits from the decimal point, where x and n are numeric expressions. If n is not provided then x is rounded with no digits after decimal.	`>>> round(12.3456, 2)` `12.35`

10.7 COMPOSITION

Composition is the art of combining simple function(s) to build more complicated ones, i.e., the result of one function is used as the input to another. For example, if there are two functions fn1 and fn2, such that

$$a= fn2\ (x)$$
$$b= fn1\ (a)$$

then call to the two functions can be combined as

$$b= fn1\ (fn2\ (x))$$

Similarly, we can have a statement composed of more than two functions. In such a case, the result of one function is passed as argument to the next and the result of the last function is the final result. For example, **math.exp (math.log (a+1))**.

Composition is used to package the code into modules so that they may be used in many different unrelated places. Also, composition makes the modules easy to maintain.

10.8 FUNCTION DECLARATION AND DEFINITION

Any function can be compared to a black box (that is used for an entity having unknown implementation) that takes in input, processes it and then spits out the result. However, we may also have a function that does not take any inputs at all, or that does not return anything at all. While using functions we use the terminology given below.

- A function *f* that uses another function *g* is known as the *calling function* and *g* is known as the *called function*.
- The inputs that the function takes are known as *arguments/ parameters*.
- When a called function returns some result back to the calling function, it is said to *return* that result.
- The calling function may or may not pass *parameters* to the called function. If the called function accepts *arguments*, the calling function will pass *parameters*, else it does not.
- *Function declaration* is a declaration statement that identifies a function with its name, a list of arguments that it accepts and the type of data it returns.
- *Function definition* consists of a function header that identifies the function, followed by the body of the function containing the executable code for that function

> Besides using built-in functions, users can also write their own functions. Such functions are called user-defined functions.

10.9 FUNCTION DEFINITION

There are two basic types of functions, built-in functions and user-defined ones. The built-in functions are available as a part of the Python language. For example, `dir()`, `len()` or `abs()`. The user-defined functions, on the other hand, are functions created by users in their programs using the `def` keyword.

As a Python programmer, you can write any number of functions in your program. However, to define a function, you must keep the following points in mind.

- Function blocks starts with the keyword **def.**
- The keyword is followed by the function name and parentheses (( )). The function name is used to uniquely identify the function.
- After the parentheses, a colon (:) is placed.
- Parameters or arguments that the function accepts are placed within parentheses. Through these parameters, values are passed to the function. They are optional. In case no values are to be passed, nothing is placed within the parentheses.
- The first statement of a function can be an optional statement – the documentation string of the function or *docstring* describes what the function does. We will discuss this later in the book.
- The code block within the function is properly indented to form the block code.
- A function may have a **return[expression]** statement. That is, the return statement is optional. If it exits, it passes back an expression to the caller. A return statement with no arguments is the same as return None.
- You can assign the function name to a variable. Doing this will allow you to call the same function using the name of that variable.

> Function naming follows the same rules as writing identifiers in Python.

Example 10.1 Program that subtracts one number from another using function.

```
def diff(x,y):         # function to subtract two numbers
    return x-y
a = 20
b = 10
operation = diff       # function name assigned to a variable
print(operation(a,b))  # function called using variable name
```

> The words before parentheses specify the function name, and the parentheses are function arguments.

OUTPUT
```
10
```

When a function is defined, space is allocated for that function in the memory. A function definition comprises of two parts:

- Function header
- Function body

> The indented statements form body of the function.

The syntax of a function definition can be given as:

```
def function_name(variable1, variable2,..)
    documentation string
    statement block
    return [expression]
```

Function Header
Function Body

> The parameter list in the function definition as well as the function declaration must match with each other.

In the given code, the name of the function is func. It takes no arguments, and prints "Hello World" four times. The function is first defined before being called. The statements in the function are executed only when the function is called.

Example 10.2 To write a function that displays a string repeatedly.

```
def func():
    for i in range (4):
        print ("Hello world")
func()    # function call
```

OUTPUT
```
Hello world
Hello world
Hello world
Hello world
```

> Before calling a function, you must define it just as you assign variables before using them.

Key points to remember

- Function name and the number and type of arguments in the function call must be same as that given in the function definition.
- If, by mistake, the parameters passed to a function are more than that it is specified to accept, then an error would be returned.

Example 10.3 Program to demonstrate the mismatch between function parameters and arguments.

```
def func(i, j):
    print("Hello World", i, j)
func(5)
```

OUTPUT
```
TypeError: func() takes exactly 2 arguments (1 given)
```

> It is a logic error if the arguments in the function call are placed in a wrong order.

- If, by mistake, the parameters passed to a function are less than that the function is specified to accept, then an error would be returned.

Example 10.4 Program to demonstrate the mismatch between function parameters and arguments.

```
def func(i):
    print("Hello World", i)
func(5, 5)
```

OUTPUT
```
TypeError: func() takes exactly 1 argument (2 given)
```

> You can call a function from another function or directly from the Python prompt.

- Names of variables in function call and header of function definition may vary.

Example 10.5 Program to demonstrate mismatch of name of function parameters and arguments.

```
def func(i):          # function definition header accepts a
variable with name i
print("Hello World", i)
j = 10
func(j)    # Function is called using variable j
```

OUTPUT
```
Hello World 10
```

- If the data type of the argument passed does not match with that expected in function, then an error is generated.

Example 10.6 Program to demonstrate mismatch between data types of function parameters and arguments.

```
def func(i):
  print("Hello World" + i)
func(5)
```

OUTPUT
```
TypeError: cannot concatenate 'str' and 'int' objects
```

- Arguments may be passed in the form of expressions to the called function. In such a case, arguments are first evaluated and converted to the type of formal parameter and then the body of the function gets executed.

Example 10.7 Program to demonstrate that the arguments may be passed in the form of expressions to the called function.

```
def func(i):
    print("Hello World", i)
func(5+2*3)
```

OUTPUT
```
Hello World 11
```

- The parameter list must be separated with commas.
- If the function returns a value then it may be assigned to some variable in the calling program. For example,

```
variable_name = function_name(variable1, variable2, …);
```

Example 10.8 Program to add two integers using functions.

```
def total(a, b):    #function accepting parameters
    result = a+b
    print("Sum of", a, "and", b, "=", result)
a = int(input("Enter the first number :"))
b = int(input("Enter the second number :"))
total(a,b) #function call with two arguments
```

OUTPUT
```
Enter the first number : 10
Enter the second number : 20
Sum of 10 and 20 = 30
```

Let us now try a program using function. In the `total()` we have declared a variable result just like any other variable. Variables declared within a function are called local variables. We will read more about it in the next section.

10.10 VARIABLE SCOPE AND LIFETIME

In Python, you cannot just access any variable from any part of your program. Some of the variables may not even exist for the entire duration of the program. The part of the program in which you can access a variable and the parts of the program in which a variable exists depend on how the variable has been declared. Therefore, it is essential to understand these two things:

Scope of the variable: Part of the program in which a variable is accessible is called its *scope*.

Lifetime of the variable: Duration for which the variable exists is called its *lifetime*.

10.10.1 Local and Global Variables

Global variables are those variables which are defined in the main body of the program file. They are visible throughout the program file. As a good programming habit, you must try to avoid the use of global variables because they may get altered by mistake and then result in erroneous output. But this does not mean that you should not use them at all. As a golden rule, use only those variables or objects that are meant to be used globally, like functions and classes, which are put in the global section of the program (i.e., above any other function or line of code).

> Trying to access local variable outside the function produces an error.

Correspondingly, a variable which is defined within a function is *local* to that function. A local variable can be accessed from the point of its definition until the end of the function in which it is defined. It exists as long as the function is executing. Function parameters behave like local variables in the function. Moreover, whenever we use the

> Variables can only be used after the point of their declaration.

assignment operator (=) inside a function, a new local variable is created (provided a variable with the same name is not defined in the local scope).

Example 10.9 Program to understand the difference between local and global variables.

```
num1 = 10      # global variable
print("Global variable num1 =", num1)
def func(num2):     # num 2 is function parameter
    print("In Function - Local Variable num2 =",num2)
    num3 = 30    #num3 is a local variable
   print("In Function - Local Variable num3 =",num3)
func(20)     #20 is passed as an argument to the function
print("num1 again =", num1) #global variable is being accessed
#Error- local variable can't be used outside the function in which it is defined

print("num3 outside function =", num 3)
```

OUTPUT
```
Global Variable num1 = 10
In Function - Local Variable num2 = 20
In Function - Local Variable num3 = 30
num1 again = 10
num3 outside function =
Traceback (most recent call last):
  File "C:\Python27\Try.py", line 12, in <module>
    print ("num3 outside function =", num 3)
NameError: name 'num3' is not defined
```

Table 10.3 lists the differences between global and local variables.

Table 10.3 Comparison between global and local variables

Global Variables	Local Variables
1. They are defined in the main body of the program file.	1. They are defined within a function and are local to that function.
2. They can be accessed throughout the program file.	2. They can be accessed from the point of its definition until the end of the block in which it is defined.
3. Global variables are accessible to all functions in the program.	3. They are not related in any way to other variables with the same names used outside the function.

10.10.2 Resolution of names

As discussed in the previous section, *scope* defines the visibility of a name within a block. If a local variable is defined in a block, its scope is that particular block. If it is defined in a function, then its scope is all blocks within that function.

When a variable name is used in a code block, it is resolved using the nearest enclosing scope. If no variable of that name is found, then a **NameError** is raised. In the code given above, str is a global string because it has been defined before calling the function.

You cannot define a local variable with the same name as that of a global variable. If you want to do that, you must use the global statement. The code given below illustrates this concept.

> Try to avoid the use of global variables and global statement.

Example 10.10

Program that demonstrates using a variable defined in global namespace.
```
def func():
    print(str)
str = "Hello World!!!"
func()
```
OUTPUT
```
Hello World!!!
```

Example 10.11 Program that demonstrates using a local variable with the same name as that of global variable.

```
def f():
    print(str) #global
    str = "Hello World!" #local
    print(str)
str = "Welcome to Python Programming!"
f()
```

OUTPUT
```
UnboundLocalError: local variable 'str' referenced before assignment
```

```
def f():
    global str
    print(str)
    str = "Hello World!"
    print(str)
str = "Welcome to Python Pro-
gramming!"
f()
```

OUTPUT
```
Welcome to Python Programming!
Hello World!
```

10.11 THE return STATEMENT

In all our functions written above, nowhere have we used the return statement. But you will be surprised to know that every function has an implicit return statement as the last instruction in the function body. This implicit return statement returns nothing to its caller, so it is said to return NONE where NONE means nothing. But you can change this default behaviour by explicitly using the return statement to return some value back to the caller. The syntax of return statement is,

> A function may or may not return a value. A return statement with no arguments is the same as return None.

return [expression]

The expression is written in brackets because it is optional. If the expression is present, it is evaluated and the resultant value is returned to the calling function. However, if no expression is specified then the function will return **None**.

The return statement is used for two things.

- Return a value to the caller
- To end and exit a function and go back to its caller

It should be noted that in the output None is returned from the function. The return value may or may not be assigned to another variable in the caller.

Example 10.12 Program to write a function without a return statement and print its return value. As mentioned earlier, such a function should return None.

```
def display(str):
  print(str)
#assigning return value to another variable
x = display("Hello World")
print(x)
#print return value without assigning it to
another variable
print (display("Hello Again"))
```

OUTPUT
```
Hello World
None
Hello Again
None
```

Example 10.13 To write another function, which returns an integer to the caller.

```
def cube(x):
  return (x*x*x)
num = 10
result = cube(num)
print('Cube of ', num, ' = ', result)
```

OUTPUT
```
Cube of 10 = 1000
```

Key points to remember
- The return statement must appear within the function.
- Once you return a value from a function, it immediately exits that function. Therefore, any code written after the return statement is never executed. The program given below illustrates this concept.

Example 10.14   *Program to demonstrate flow of control after the return statement.*

```
def display():
    print("In Function")
    print("About to execute return statement")
    return
    print("This line will never be displayed")
display()
print("Back to the caller")
```

OUTPUT
```
In Function
About to execute return statement
Back to the caller
```

10.12 THE random MODULE IN PYTHON

The random module in Python generates numbers randomly and it has some very useful functions. In this section, we will study few functions defined in the random module.

> The return statement cannot be used outside of a function definition.

random(): The random() function returns the next random floating-point number in the range [0.0, 1.0). Look at the code given below that generates a random floating-point number. Note that you may get another number as the system just generates any value every time you run this code.

```
import random
print(random.random())
```

OUTPUT
```
0.3793508665239418
```

randint(a,b): The randint() function is used to generate a random integer number in the range specified by the arguments a and b. The random integer generated is such that it is less than or equal to b and greater than or equal to a.
```
import random

print(random.randint(1,100))
```

OUTPUT
```
15
```

random.randrange(start, stop [, step]): The randrange() function is used to generate a random integer number within a given range. The range is specified using the start and stop arguments. The step argument is optional, and its default value is 1.

```
import random
print(random.randrange(70,100,10))
```

OUTPUT
```
90
```

random.choice(seq): Use the random.choice() method to pick a random element from the sequence. Here, the sequence can be a list or string. This method returns a single item from the sequence.

```
import random
print(random.choice("HELLO WORLD"))
```
OUTPUT
```
L
```

random.sample(population, k): The `random.sample()` function is used to pick multiple random elements from a population. The function returns a list of *k* unique elements chosen from the population. The population can be a list, set or any sequence in Python.

```
import random
print(random.sample("PYTHONPROGRAMMING",3))
```
OUTPUT
```
['M', 'N', 'O']
```

random.choices(population, weights=None, *, cum_weights=None, k=1): The `random.choices()` function is used to choose more than one element from the sequence randomly with replacement.
```
import random
```

```
print(random.choices("PYTHONPROGRAMMINGISFUN",k=5))
```
OUTPUT
```
['I', 'I', 'M', 'R', 'T']
```

random.shuffle(x[, random]): The `random.shuffle()` function is used to shuffle or randomize a list or any other sequence in Python.

```
import random
list = [1,2,3,4,5,6,7,8,9,10]
random.shuffle(list)
print(list)
```
OUTPUT
```
[8, 10, 2, 6, 3, 5, 1, 9, 4, 7]
```

```
import statistics
list = [1,2,3,4,9,5,6,8,8,9,8,9,7,6,5,4,3,2,1]
mean = statistics.mean(list)
print("MEAN = ",mean)
med = statistics.median(list)
print("MEDIAN = ",med)
mode = statistics.mode(list)
print("MODE = ",mode)
sd = statistics.stdev(list)
print("STANDARD DEVIATION = ",sd)
sd = statistics.variance(list)
print("VARIENCE = ",var)
Output
MEAN = 5.2105263157894735
MEDIAN = 5
MODE = 9
STANDARD DEVIATION = 2.7402138474623765
VARIENCE = 7.508771929824561
```

random.uniform(start, end): The `random.uniform()` is used to generate a floating-point number within a given range. The range is specified using the `start` and end arguments.

```
import random
print(random.uniform(70.0, 89.9))
```

OUTPUT
75.98148226789161

The Statistics Module: Since Python is extensively used for data analysis, it has a statistics package that has functions for calculating the mean, median, mode, standard deviation, and variance of data.

PROGRAMMER'S ZONE

1. **Write a program that prints the absolute value and cube of a number.**
   ```
   import math
   a = -100
   print("a = ", a)
   a = abs(a)
   print("abs(a) = ", a)
   print("Cube of ",a, " = ", math.pow(a,3))
   ```

   OUTPUT
   ```
   a = -100
   abs(a) = 100
   Cube of 100 = 1000000.0
   ```

2. **Write a program to generate 10 random numbers between 1 and 100.**
   ```
   import random
   for i in range(10):
       value = random.randint(1,100)
       print(value)
   ```

   > *imports all objects from a module.

   OUTPUT
   66 68 14 7 76 8 70 43 60 70

3. **Write a program to display the date and time using the Time module.**
   ```
   import time
   localtime = time.asctime( time.localtime(time.time()) )
   print("Local current time :", localtime)
   ```

   OUTPUT
   Local current time : Mon Dec 16 21:34:27 2019

4. **Write a program that prints the calendar of a particular month.**
   ```
   import calendar
   print(calendar.month(2017, 1))
   ```

   OUTPUT
   ```
   October 2020
   Mo Tu We Th Fr Sa Su
    1  2  3  4
    5  6  7  8  9 10 11
   12 13 14 15 16 17 18
   19 20 21 22 23 24 25
   26 27 28 29 30 31
   ```

5. Write a program that uses the getpass module to prompt the user for a password, without echoing what they type to the console.

```
import getpass
password = getpass.getpass(prompt='Enter the password : ')
if password == 'cu2moro':
 print('Welcome to the world of Python Programming. ')
else:
 print('Incorrect password... Sorry, you cannot read our book.')
```

OUTPUT
```
Enter the password : cu2moro
Welcome to the world of Python Programming.
```

Key Terms

Function: A block of organized and reusable program code that performs a single, specific, and well-defined task.

Called function: A function that is called or invoked to use its functionality is known as the called function.

Arguments/parameters: A function may take some inputs for processing. These inputs are known as arguments/parameters.

Module: A file with a .py extension that has definitions of all functions and variables that you would like to use even in other programs.

Package: A hierarchical file directory structure that has modules and other packages within it.

Composition: Art of combining simple function(s) to build more complicated ones, i.e., the result of one function is used as the input to another.

Function declaration: A declaration statement that identifies a function with its name, a list of arguments that it accepts and the type of data it returns.

User-defined function: Besides using built-in functions, users can also write their own functions. Such functions are called user defined functions.

Scope of the variable: Part of the program in which a variable is accessible is called its scope.

Lifetime of the variable: Duration for which the variable exists is called its lifetime.

Global variables: Variables defined in the main body of the program file that are visible throughout the program file.

Local variable: Variable that can be accessed from the point of its definition until the end of the function in which it is defined.

Chapter Highlights

- When a function is called, the program control is passed to the first statement in the function.
- Once the execution of the program is complete, the control passes to the next statement after the function call.
- Understanding, coding and testing multiple separate functions are far easier than doing the same for one huge function.
- Large programs usually follow the DRY principle, that is, Don't Repeat Yourself principle. Once a function is written it can be called multiple times, wherever its functionality is required.
- A bad repetitive code abides by the WET principle, i.e., Write Everything Twice, or We Enjoy Typing.
- A function f that uses another function g, is known as the calling function and g is known as the called function.
- When a called function returns some result back to the calling function, it is said to return that result.
- To use the functions or variables defined in a module, you must first import that particular module (or .py file).
- Once a module is located, it is loaded in memory. A compiled version of the module with file extension .pyc is generated. The next time when the module is imported, this .pyc file is loaded, rather than the .py file, to save the time of recompiling.

- Built-in functions are the function(s) that are built into Python and can be accessed in programs. These functions are always available and for use, and the programmer does not have to import any module to use them.
- Function definition consists of a function header that identifies the function, followed by the body of the function containing the executable code for that function
- The documentation string of the function or docstring describes what the function does.
- A function may have a return[expression] statement. That is, the return statement is optional. If it exits, it passes back an expression to the caller. A return statement with no arguments is the same as return None.

Review Questions

1. Define function.
2. What happens when a function is called?
3. Differentiate between the called and the calling function.
4. Why should we use function in our programs?
5. Can a function call another function? Justify your answer with the help of an example.
6. Explain the syntax of function call statement.
7. What is a module? How can you use it?
8. Explain the utility of the `reload()` function.
9. Why do we use the as keyword while importing a module?
10. Differentiate between import and form..import statements.
11. What are command line arguments? How are they used in Python?
12. What do you understand by the term arguments? How do we pass them to a function?
13. Arguments may be passed in the form of expressions to the called function. Justify this statement with the help of an example.
14. What are modules? How do you use them in your programs?
15. Why do we use `dir()` function? What will happen if no name is specified in the `dir()` function?
16. What is a package? How is it different from a module?
17. What are built-in functions? Give some examples.
18. What do you understand by the term composition?
19. With the help of an example explain how a function can be defined in Python?
20. Explain the significance of return statement.
21. Differentiate between local and global variables.
22. Write the mathematical expressions corresponding to the following expressions in Python.
    a. `math.sqrt(a*a + b*b + c*c)`
    b. `5 + y*math.exp(3*y) - 7*y`
    c. `a + b /math.pow(x+y),3)`
    d. `1 + (math.cos(x) / math.tan(x))`
    e. `math.fabs(math.exp(3) - 2*x)`

Programming Exercises

1. Write a program that prints the time taken to execute a program in Python.
2. Write a function that returns the absolute value of a number.
3. Write a program that plays a game IN–OUT. Generate a random number, if that number is divisible by 5 or 10, then print IN. If that number is divisible by both, print OUT and exit the program.

4. Write a program that prompts user to enter a number. Continuously generate a random number until the number generated by the system does not match with that of the user.
5. Write a function that accepts three integers, and returns True if they are sorted, otherwise it returns False.
6. Write a function `is_prime()` that returns a 1 if the argument passed to it is a prime a number and a 0 otherwise.
7. Write a menu-driven program to add, subtract, multiply, and divide two integers using functions.
8. Write a program using function that calculates the hypotenuse of a right-angled triangle.
9. Write a function that accepts a number *n* as input and returns the average of numbers from 1 to *n*.
10. Write a program using function to calculate *x* to the power of *y*, where *y* can be either negative or positive.
11. Write a program using function to calculate compound interest given the principal, rate of interest, and number of years
12. Write a function that accepts three integers and returns True if any of the integers is 0; otherwise it returns False.
13. Write a function that accepts two positive numbers *n* and *m* where *m<=n*, and returns numbers between 1 and *n* that are divisible by *m*.
14. Write a function that displays "Hello name", for any given name passed to it.
15. Write a program to print the prime factors of a number.
    Write a program that prompts user to enter 10 numbers. Find the smallest and the second smallest number entered by the user

Fill in the Blanks

1. Once the execution of the program is complete, the control passes to the _____ statement after the function call.
2. The function _____ statement invokes the function.
3. In range(0, 100, 5) name of the function is _____ and it has _____ arguments.
4. _____ error is caused by importing an unknown module.
5. The _____ is used to uniquely identify the function.
6. After the called function is executed, the control is returned to the_____.
7. You can find the name of a module by using the _____ attribute of the module.
8. _____ is a built-in function that lists the identifiers defined in a module.
9. Every package in Python is a directory, which must have a special file called_____.
10. Packages have an attribute _____, which is initialized with a list having the name of the directory holding the __init__.py file.
11. To import the sqrt and cos function from the math module, write _____.
12. Trying to import a module that is not available results in _____.
13. Python's preinstalled modules forms the _____.
14. The _____ command is used to force the reloading of a given module.
15. When a function is called, the interpreter checks the _____ and _____ of parameters that are passed in the function call.
16. To use the functions or variables defined in a module, you must first _____ that particular module.
17. The import * statement imports all names except _____. .
18. We can find the name of a module by using the _____ attribute of the module.

19. _____ describes what the function does.
20. _____ *of the variable* specifies the part of the program in which a variable is accessible.
21. The _____ function returns the next random floating-point number in the range [0.0, 1.0).
22. The _____ function is used to pick multiple random elements from a population.
23. The _____ module has functions for calculating the mean, median, mode, standard deviation, and variance of data.

State True or False

1. When a function is called, the program control is passed to the last statement in the function.
2. Every function can be written more or less independently of the others.
3. When a function call is encountered, the control jumps to the calling function.
4. A function can call only one function.
5. Code reuse is one of the most prominent reasons to use functions.
6. Large programs usually follow the WET principle.
7. We can have a function that does not take any inputs at all.
8. The calling function may or may not pass *parameters* to the called function.
9. The return statement is optional.
10. Every function takes a fixed number of arguments.
11. Arguments may be passed in the form of expressions to the called function.
12. A function cannot be used on the left side of an assignment statement.
13. It is mandatory to place all import statements at the beginning of a module.
14. With the "import *moduleName*" statement, any item from the imported module must be prefixed with the module name.
15. All Python Standard Library modules must be imported before any programmer-defined modules.
16. If a particular module is imported more than once in a Python program, the interpreter will load the module only once.
17. A function can be called from anywhere within a program.
18. A statement can call more than one function.
19. Function calls may contain arguments that are function calls.
20. The **argc** variable in the **sys** module keeps a track of command line arguments passed to the .py script.
21. All import statements must be written at the top of the program code.
22. Duration for which the variable exists is called its *lifetime*.
23. We should use more of global variables than local variables.
24. You cannot define a local variable with the same name as that of global variable.
25. A function must return a value.

Multiple Choice Questions

1. DRY principle makes the code _____ .
   a. reusable   b. loop forever   c. bad and repetitive   d. complex.
2. A function can call _____ number of other functions.
   a. 0   b. 1   c. $n-1$ d. n

3. Which of the following is not correct about a function?
   a. It is pre-written   b. It is pre-tested   c. It slows down development   d. it simplifies coding

4. What is the output of this code?
   ```
   import random as r
   print(random.randomint(1, 10))
   ```
   a. An error occurs   b. 1   c. 10   d. any random value

5. How would you refer to the sqrt function if it was imported like this?
   ```
   from math import sqrt as square_root
   ```
   a. math. square_root   b. math.sqrt   c. sqrt   d. square_root

6. If the number of arguments in a function definition and function call does not match then which type of error is returned?
   a. NameError   b. ImortError   c. TypeError   d. NumberError

7. If no variable of the given input name is found, then a _____ is raised.
   a. NameError   b. ImortError   c. TypeError   d. NumberError

8. Modules are files saved with _____ extension.
   a. .py   b. mod   c. mdl   d. imp

9. The import * statement imports all names in the module except those beginning with _____.
   a. %   b. $ c. _   d. !

10. How would you refer to the randint function if it were imported by writing
    ```
    from random import randint as r_int?
    ```
    a. random.rnd_int   b. r_int   c. randint.r_int   d. randint

11. Identify the correct way of calling a function named display() that prints Hello on screen.
    a. print(display)   b. displayHello   c. result = display()   d. displayHello()

12. Which function returns the smallest integer greater than or equal to *x*?
    a. ceil()   b. fabs()   c. factorial()   d. floor()

13. Which function is used to generate a random integer number in the range specified by the arguments a and b?
    a. random()   b. randint()   c. randrange()   d. choice()

14. Which function is used to pick a random element from a sequence?
    a. random()   b. randint()   c. randrange()   d. choice()

Give the Output

1. ```
   from random import randint as r
   for i in range(10):
       value = r(1,100)
       print(value)
   ```

2. ```
   import math
   print(math.fmod(-12345,9))
   ```

3. ```
   num = 10
   def show():
       var = 20
       print("In Function var is - ",
       num)
   show()
   print("Outside function, var is - ",
       num)
   ```

4. ```
   def f():
       s = "Hello World!"
       print(s)
   s = "Welcome to Python Programming"
   f()
   print(s)
   ```

5. ```
   def f():
       global var
       print(var)
       var = 10
       print(var)
   var = 100
   f()
   ```
   ```

6. ```
   def display (str):
       print(str+"!")
   display ("Hello World")
   ```

7. ```
   def sqr(x):
       print(x*x)
   sqr(10)
   ```

8. ```
   def mul_twice(x,y):
       print(x*y)
       print(x*y)
   mul_twice(5, 10)
   ```

9. ```
   def func():
       global x
       print("x =", x)
       x = 100
       print('x is now = ', x)
   x = 10
   func()
   print('x =', x)
   ```

10. ```
    def func1():
        var = 3
        func2(var)
    def func2(var):
        print(var)
    func1()
    ```

11. ```
    def func(x):
        print 'x = ', x
        x = 100
        print('In Function, x after
            modification = ', x)
    x = 50
    func(x)
    print('Outside Function, x = ', x)
    ```

12. ```
    def display( str ):
       print(str)
       return;
    display("Hello World !!")
    display("Welcome    to    Python
        Programming")
    ```

13. ```
    def sum( num1, num2 ):
        total = num1 + num2
        print("Inside function, Total
    = ", total)
        return total;
    total = sum( 10, 20 )
    print("Outside the function, Total =
        ", total)
    ```

14. ```
    def min(x,y):
        if x<y:
            return x
        else:
            return y
    print(min(4, 7))
    ```

15. ```
    def add(x, y):
        sum = x + y
        return sum
        print("This won't be printed")
    print(add(10,20))
    ```

16. ```
    def func():
        """Do nothing.
        Nothing doing.
        """
        pass
    print(func.__doc__)
    ```

17. ```
    def C_to_F(c):
            return c * 9/5 + 32
    print C_to_F(37)
    def display(name, deptt, sal):
        print("Name: ", name)
        print("Department: ", deptt)
        print("Salary: ", sal)
    display(sal = 100000, name="Tavisha",
        deptt = "IT")
    display(deptt = "HR", name="Dev", sal
        = 50000)
    ```

18. ```
    def display(mesg):
        return mesg + "!"
    print_str = display
    str = print_str("Hello")
    print(str)
    ```

19. ```
    from random import randint as r
    for i in range(10):
        value = r(1,100)
        print(value)
    ```

20. ```
    def is_even(x):
        if x==0:
            return True
        else:
            return is_odd(x-1)
    def is_odd(x):
        return not is_even(x)
    print(is_even(22))
    ```
    ```

21. ```
    def display(x):
        for i in range(x):
            print(i)
            return
    display(5)
    ```

Find the Error

1. ```
   import math as m
   print(math.sqrt(25))
   ```

2. ```
   def func():
       print("Hello World")
   ```

3. ```
   var1 = "Good"
   def show():
       var2 = "Morning"
       print(var1)
       print(var2)
   show()
   print(var1)
   print(var2)
   ```

4. ```
   def f():
       print var
       var = 10
       print(var)
   var = 100
   f()
   ```

5. ```
   def f():
       var = 100
       print(var)
   f()
   print(var)
   ```

6. ```
   def func(var):
       var+=1
       var *= 2
       print(var)
   func(9)
   print(var)
   ```

7. ```
   def func1():
       var = 3
       func2()
   def func2():
       print(var)
   func1()
   ```

8. ```
   def display(x,y):
       print (x+y)
   display(10)
   ```

9. ```
   def func(a, b):
       print(a)
       print(b)
   func(b=10, 20)
   ```

10. ```
    def func1():
        print("func1()")
    func1()
    func2()
    def func2():
        print("func2()")
    ```

11. ```
    def sum_to(x):
        return x+sum_to(x-1)
    print(sum_to(5))
    ```

Answers

Fill in the Blanks

1. next
2. call
3. range, 3
4. ImportError
5. function name
6. calling program
7. __name__
8. dir()
9. __init__.py
10. __path__
11. from math import sqrt, cos
12. ImportError
13. Standard Library
14. reload()
15. number, type
16. import
17. those beginning with ___
18. __name__
19. docstring
20. *scope*
21. random()
22. randomsample()
23. statistics

State True or False

1. False
2. True
3. True
4. False
5. True
6. False
7. True
8. True
9. True
10. False
11. True
12. False
13. False
14. True
15. True
16. True
17. True
18. True
19. True
20. False
21. False
22. False
23. False
24. True
25. False

Multiple Choice Questions

1. a
2. d
3. c
4. a
5. a
6. c
7. a
8. a
9. c
10. c
11. c
12. a
13. b
14. d

Give the Output

1. 47 8 22 86 14 31 81 24 54 49
2. −6.0
3. In Function var is − 10
   Outside function, var is − 10
4. Hello World!
   Welcome to Python Programming
5. 100   10
6. Hello World!
7. 100
8. 50 50
9. x = 10
   x is now = 100
   x = 100
10. 3
11. x = 50
    In Function, x after modification = 100
    Outside Function, x = 50
12. Hello World !!
    Welcome to Python Programming
13. Inside function, Total = 30
    Outside the function, Total = 30
14. 4
15. This won't be printed
    30
16. Do nothing.
    Nothing doing.
17. 98.6
    Name: Tavisha
    Department: IT
    Salary: 100000
    Name: Dev
    Department: HR
    Salary: 50000
18. Hello!
19. 78 88 85 65 94 15 73 91 51 97
20. True
21. 0

Find the Error

1. NameError: name 'math' is not defined
2. No output as function is not called
3. NameError: name 'var2' is not defined
4. brackets in print function missing
5. NameError: name 'var' is not defined
6. NameError: name 'var' is not defined
7. NameError: name 'var' is not defined
8. TypeError: display() missing 1 required positional argument: 'y'
9. Keyword argument should be present as the last parameter in the function call statement
10. NameError: name 'func2' is not defined
11. Base condition is missing. RecursionError: maximum recursion depth exceeded

Strings

11

Chapter Objectives

The chapter discusses strings in detail to help the users understand key concepts such as:
- String indexing, traversal, comparing, appending, concatenation and multiplication
- Slicing a string
- Determining its length
- Formatting strings using formatting operators and `format()` function
- Built-in string methods, functions and operators

The Python string data type is a sequence made up of one or more individual characters, where a character could be a letter, digit, whitespace, or any other symbol enclosed within single, double or even triple quotes. Python has a built-in string class named "str" that has many useful features. We can create a variable of string type in many ways. For example,

```
lang = "Python"    gender = 'F'    choice = lang    message = str("How are you")
```

We have already seen that escape sequences works with each type of string literals. A multiple-line text within quotes must have a backslash \ at the end of each line to escape the new line.

11.1 STRING INDEXING

Individual characters in a string are accessed using the subscript ([ ]) operator. The expression in brackets is called an **index**. The index specifies the character to be accessed from the given set of characters in the string.

The index of the first character is 0 and that of the last character is *n* – 1 where *n* is the number of characters in the string. *If you try to exceed the bounds (below 0 or above n – 1), then an error is raised.*

11.2 FINDING THE NUMBER OF CHARACTERS IN A STRING

Python determines the length of a string by counting the number of characters in it. For example, len("abcd") is 4 since there are four characters. Though this calculation is simple, some points must be considered while counting.

a. An escape sequence is counted as a single character.
b. In a multi-line string created with triple quotes, the **EOL** (End-Of-Line) character at the end of the line is also counted. Usually, the EOL is the carriage return character when the Enter key is pressed.
c. In a multi-line string, backslash character at the end of the line is not counted.

>>>len("\n") 1	>>>len("HELLO\tWORLD") 13	>>>len("Neeru\'s Pen") 11	>>>len("Neeru's Pen") 11
>>>str1 = '''A B C D'''	>>>len(str1) 7	>>>str2 = '''A\ B\ C\ D'''	

11.3 TRAVERSING A STRING

A string is a sequence type (sequence of characters). It can be traversed in two ways: first, by accessing each character in the string and second, by accessing the element at each index. The `len()` function returns the length of the string, i.e., the number of characters in the string. We can then use this function for loop in which the loop control variable varies from 0 to n – 1, where n is the number of characters in the string.

Whichever method you use, always remember that if you try to access a character *with index less than 0 and/or greater than n-1 then an IndexError:* string index out of range error will be generated.

Example 11.1

```
# traversing string
lang = "PYTHON"
for i in lang:
    print(i,end = ' ') # print each character
```

OUTPUT
P Y T H O N

```
# traversing string using index
lang = "PYTHON"
for i in range(len(lang)):
    print(lang[i],end = ' ')
```

OUTPUT
P Y T H O N

In the first code, the `for` loop executes for every character in str. The loop starts with the first character and automatically ends when the last character is accessed. In the second code, the string is traversed using the index of each character (rather than the character itself). We can also iterate through the string using the `while` loop.

Example 11.2

```
# traversing string using while loop
lang = "PYTHON"
index = 0
l = len(lang)
while index < l:
  ch = lang[index]
  print(ch,end = '')
  index +=1
```

OUTPUT
PYTHON

```
# access string out of index
lang = "PYTHON"
l = len(lang)
print(lang[l+1]) # not a part of string
```

OUTPUT
```
Traceback (most recent call last):
  File "C:\Users\Python37\try.py", line 3, in
<module>
    print(lang[l+1])
IndexError: string index out of range
```

In the above program, the `while` loop traverses the string and displays each character. The loop condition is index < len(lang); so the moment index becomes equal to the length of the string, the condition evaluates to false, and the body of the loop is not executed. As we said earlier, the index of the last character is len(message) – 1.

Key points to remember
- Even the whitespace characters, exclamation mark and any other symbols (like ?, <,>,*, @, #, $, %, etc.) that form a part of the string would be assigned their own index number.
- Index can either be an integer or an expression that evaluates to an integer.
- A character cannot be used for string indexing.

Example 11.3

```
# indexing string in different ways
msg = "PYTHON PROGRAMMING IS FUN"
i = 2
print(msg[i]) #index is an integer
print(msg[i*3+2]) #index is an expression that evaluates to an integer
print(msg['N']) #character as an index
```

OUTPUT
```
T
R
Traceback (most recent call last):
  File "C:\Users\Python37\try.py", line 5, in <module>
    print(msg['N']) #character as an index
TypeError: string indices must be integers
```

11.4 CONCATENATING, APPENDING AND MULTIPLYING STRINGS

The word **concatenate** means to join together. Python allows you to concatenate two strings using the + operator as shown below.

Example 11.4

```
# String Concatenation
str1 = "Python"
str2 = "Programming"
str3 = str1 + str2 # string concatenation
print("The concatenated string is:", str3)
```

OUTPUT
```
The concatenated string is:
PythonProgramming
```

```
# Appending and concatenating strings
str1 = "Good morning,"
name = Input("\n Enter your name :")
str1 += name   #appending strings
str2 = str1+". Welcome to Python Programming."
print(str2)
```

OUTPUT
```
Enter your name : Priya
Good morning, Priya. Welcome to Python Programming.
```

Append means to add something at the end. In Python, one string can be added at the end of another string using the += operator.

We can **multiply** a string using the * operator. When a string is multiplied with an integer number *n*, then the string is repeated *n* number of times. The order of string and integer is not important. Therefore, 5*"HI" is same as "HI"*5.

However, remember that you cannot multiply two strings. Also, you cannot multiply a string with a floating-point number.

Example 11.5

```
# multiplying string
str = "I WILL DO IT "
print(str*3) #multiplying string
```

OUTPUT
```
I WILL DO IT I WILL DO IT I WILL DO IT
```

```
# multiplying string
str = "PYTHON" * '3'
print(str)
```

OUTPUT
```
Traceback (most recent call last):
  File "C:\Users\Python37\try.py", line 2, in <module>
    str = "PYTHON" * '3'
TypeError: can't multiply sequence by non-int of type 'str'
```

```
# multiplying string
str = "HELLO" * 3.0
print(str)
```

OUTPUT
```
Traceback (most recent call last):
  File "C:\Users\Python37\try.py", line 2, in <module>
    str = "HELLO" * 3.0
TypeError: can't multiply sequence by non-int of type 'float'
```

11.5 THE `str()` FUNCTION

The `str()` function is used to convert values of any other type into string type. This helps the programmer to concatenate a string with any other data, which is otherwise not allowed.

Example 11.6

```
# concatenating string and a number
roll_no = 9
name = "Aditi"
print(name + " is roll number" + roll_no)
```

OUTPUT
```
Traceback (most recent call last):
  File "C:\Users\
TypeError: can only concatenate
str(not"int") to str
```

```
# concatenating string and a number
roll_no = 9
name = "Aditi"
print(name + " is roll number" + str(roll_no))
```

OUTPUT
```
Aditi is roll number 9
```

11.6 STRINGS ARE IMMUTABLE

Python strings are immutable. This means that once a string is created, it cannot be changed. If you try to modify an existing string variable, a new string is created.

Every object in Python is stored in memory. You can find out whether two variables are referring to the same object or not by using the `id()`. The `id()` returns the memory address of the given object. Since both `str1` and `str2` point to the same memory location, they both actually point to the same object.

In Python, two objects that have the same value have the same id. The moment the value of one object is changed, a new object is created with a different id.

From the output, it is clear that when values of `str1` and `str2` were same, their IDs were same as they were pointing to the same object. When we changed the value of `str2` and later of `str3`, the ids of the object changed.

Now can you guess the output of the following code?

```
str = "PYTHON"
str[3] = 'A'
print(str)
```

The code will result in an error – "TypeError: 'str' object does not support item assignment" simply because the strings are immutable. It does now allow any changes. If you want to make any kind of changes you must create a new string as shown below.

Always remember that we cannot delete or remove characters from a string. But can delete the entire string using the keyword `del`.

Example 11.7

```
# Checking object's ID
str1 = "Python"
str2 = "Python"
str3 = "Programming"
# ID of str1 and str2 will be same
print("ID OF STR1 = ",id(str1))
print("ID OF STR2 = ",id(str2))
print("ID OF STR3 = ",id(str3))
# changing the value of str2
str2 = "Programming"
# ID of str2 and str3 will be same
print("\n\n ID OF STR1 = ",id(str1))
print("ID OF STR2 = ",id(str2))
print("ID OF STR3 = ",id(str3))
# changing the value of str3
str2 = "Programming is fun"
# All IDs will be different
print("\n\n ID OF STR1 = ",id(str1))
print("ID OF STR2 = ",id(str2))
print("ID OF STR3 = ",id(str3))
```

OUTPUT
```
ID OF STR1 = 3091055531600
ID OF STR2 = 3091055531600
ID OF STR3 = 3091069698480

ID OF STR1 = 3091055531600
ID OF STR2 = 3091069698480
ID OF STR3 = 3091069698480

ID OF STR1 = 3091055531600
ID OF STR2 = 3091070019384
ID OF STR3 = 3091069698480
```

11.7 STRING FORMATTING OPERATOR

This string formatting operator (%) takes a format string on the left (that has %d, %s, etc.) and the corresponding values in a tuple (will be discussed in a subsequent chapter) on the right. The format operator, % allows users to construct strings, replacing parts of the strings with the data stored in variables. The syntax for the string formatting operation is:

> "<FORMAT>" % (<VALUES>)

> A tuple is made of values separated by commas inside parentheses.

The statement begins with a *format* string consisting of a sequence of characters and *conversion specifications*. Conversion specifications start with a % operator and can appear anywhere within the string. Following the format string is a % sign and then a set of values, one per conversion specification, separated by commas and enclosed in parentheses. If there is a single value, then parentheses are optional.

In the output we can see that %s has been replaced by a string and %d has been replaced by an integer value. You can either supply these values directly or by using variables. Table 11.1 lists other string formatting characters.

Example 11.8

```
# Formatting strings
roll_no = 23
name = "Aarish"
print("ROLL NO. =%d Name =%s"%(roll_no, name))
print("ROLL NO. =%d Name =%s"%(39, "Anika"))
```

OUTPUT
```
ROLL NO. = 23 Name = Aarish
ROLL NO. = 39 Name = Anika
```

Note that the number and type of values in the tuple should match the number and type of format sequences or conversion specifications in the string, otherwise an error is returned.

Example 11.9

```
# number of arguments don't match
>>>'%d %f %s'%(15, 92.75)
Traceback (most recent call last):
  File "<pyshell#0>", line 1, in <module>
    '%d %f %s'%(15, 92.75)
TypeError: not enough arguments for format string
```

```
# type of argument don't match
>>>'%d%f%s'%(92, "Myra", "Sood")
Traceback (most recent call last):
  File "<pyshell#1>", line 1, in <module>
    '%d% f% s'%(92, "Myra", "Sood")
TypeError: must be real number, not str
```

Table 11.1 Formatting symbols

Format Symbol	Purpose
%c	Character
%d or %i	Signed decimal integer
%s	String
%u	Unsigned decimal integer
%o	Octal integer
%x or %X	Hexadecimal integer (x for lower case characters a-f and X for upper case characters A-F)
%e or %E	Exponential notation
%f	Floating-point number
%g or %G	Short numbers in floating-point or exponential notation

Example 11.10

```
# String Formatting for printing the power of a number
i = 1
print("%-4s%-5s%-6s%-8s%-13s"%('i', 'i**2', 'i**3', 'i**4', 'i**5',))
while(i<=5):
   print("%-4d%-5d%-6d%-8d%-13d"%)(i, i**2, i**3, i**4, i**5)
   i+=1
```

OUTPUT

```
i    i**2 i**3  i**4    i**5
1    1    1     1       1
2    4    8     16      32
3    9    27    81      243
4    16   64    256     1024
5    25   125   625     3125
```

In Example 11.10, we have set the width of each column independently using the string formatting feature of Python. The - after each % in the conversion string indicates left justification. The numerical values specify the minimum length. Therefore, %-15d means it is a left justified number that is at least 15 characters wide.

11.8 THE format() FUNCTION

The `format()` function is also used for formatting strings. Format strings have curly braces {} as placeholders or replacement fields which get replaced. We can even use positional arguments or keyword arguments to specify the order of fields that have to be replaced. Consider the code given below and carefully observe the sequence of fields in the output. Then, compare the sequence as given in the arguments of `format()` function.

Example 11.11

```
# format() function with strings
str1 = "{}, {} {}".format('Python','is','Easy')
print("\n The default sequence of arguments is : " + str1)
str2 = "{1}, {0} {2}".format('Python','is','Easy')
print("\n The positional sequence of arguments (1, 0 and 2) is : " + str2)
str3 = "{c}, {b} Very {a}".format(a='Python',b='Is',c='Easy')
print("\n The keyword sequence of arguments is : " + str3)
```

OUTPUT

```
The default sequence of arguments is : Python, is Easy
The positional sequence of arguments (1, 0 and 2) is : Is Python Easy?
The keyword sequence of arguments is : Easy, Is Very Python
```

11.9 BUILT-IN STRING METHODS AND FUNCTIONS

Strings are an example of Python **objects**. An object is an entity that contains both data (the actual string itself) as well as functions to manipulate that data. These functions are available to any **instance** (variable) of the object.

Python supports many built-in methods to manipulate strings. A method is just like a function. The only difference between a function and a method is that method is invoked or called on an object. For example, if the variable `str` is a string, then you can call the `upper()` method as `str.upper()` to convert all the characters of `str` in upper case. Table 11.2 discusses some of the most commonly used string methods.

Table 11.2 Commonly used string functions and methods

Function	Usage	Example

`capitalize()`	This function is used to capitalize the first letter of the string.	`str = "python"`
		`print(str.capitalize())`
		OUTPUT
		`Python`

`center(width, fillchar)`	Returns a string with the original string centered to a total of width columns and filled with fillchar in columns that do not have characters	`str = "python"`
		`print(str.center(15, '*'))`
		OUTPUT
		`*****python****`

`count(str, beg, end)`	Counts the number of times `str` occurs in a string. You can specify beg and end as 0 to len of string to search the entire length of the string, or with any other value to just search a part of the string.	`str = "se"`
		`message = "He sells sea shells on the sea shore"`
		`print(message.count(str,0,len(message)))`
		OUTPUT
		`3`

`endswith(suffix, beg, end)`	Checks if string ends with suffix; returns True if so and False, otherwise. You can either set beg = 0 and end to length of the message to search the entire string or use any other value to search a part of it.	`message = "He sells sea shells on the sea shore"`
		`print(message.endswith("ore", 0,len(message)))`
		OUTPUT
		`True`

`startswith(prefix, beg, end)`	Checks if string starts with prefix; returns True if so and False otherwise. You can either set beg = 0 and end to length of the message to search entire string or use any other value to search a part of it.	`message = "He sells sea shells on the sea shore"`
		`print(message.startswith("sea", 0,len(message)))`
		OUTPUT
		`False`

`find(str, beg, end)`	Checks if `str` is present in string. If found, it returns the position at which `str` occurs in string; otherwise, it returns -1. You can either set beg = 0 and end to the length of the message to search the entire string or use any other value to search a part of it.	`message = "He sells sea shells on the sea shore"`
		`print(message.find("sea",0,len(message)))`
		OUTPUT
		`9`

`index(str, beg, end)`	Same as find but raises an exception if `str` is not found.	`message = "He sells sea shells on the sea shore"`
		`print(message.index("in", 0, len(message)))`
		ValueError: substring not found

`rfind(str, beg, end)`	Same as find but starts searching from the end. So it will return index of the last occurrence of `str` in the main string.	`message = "He sells sea shells on the sea shore"`
		`print(message.rfind("sea", 0, len(message)))`
		OUTPUT
		`27`

(Continued)

Table 11.2 Continued

Function	Usage	Example

`rindex(str, beg, end)`	Same as `rindex` but starts searching from the end and raises an exception if `str` is not found	`message = "He sells sea shells on the sea shore"`
		`print(message.rindex("gg", 0, len(message)))`
		OUTPUT
		`ValueError: substring not found`

`isalnum()`	Returns True if string has at least 1 character and every character is either a number or an alphabet and False otherwise.	`message = "JamesBond007"`
		`print(message.isalnum())`
		OUTPUT
		`True`

`isalpha()`	Returns True if string has at least 1 character and every character is an alphabet and False otherwise.	`message = «JamesBond007»`
		`print(message.isalpha())`
		OUTPUT
		`False`

`isdigit()`	Returns True if string contains only digits and False otherwise.	`message = "108"`
		`print(message.isdigit())`
		OUTPUT
		`True`

`islower()`	Returns True if string has at least 1 character and every character is a lowercase alphabet and False otherwise.	`message = "Python"`
		`print(message.islower())`
		OUTPUT
		`False`

`isspace()`	Returns True if string contains only whitespace characters and False otherwise.	`message = " "`
		`print(message.isspace())`
		OUTPUT
		`True`

`isupper()`	Returns True if string has at least 1 character and every character is an uppercase alphabet and False otherwise.	`message = "PYTHON"`
		`print(message.isupper())`
		OUTPUT
		`True`

`len(string)`	Returns the length of the string.	`str = "PYTHON"`
		`print(len(str))`
		OUTPUT
		`6`

`ljust(width[, fillchar])`	Returns a string left-justified to a total of width columns. Columns without characters are padded with the character specified in the `fillchar` argument	`str = " PYTHON"`
		`print(str.ljust(10, '*'))`
		OUTPUT
		`PYTHON****`
		`23351823`

`rjust(width[, fillchar])`	Returns a string right-justified to a total of width columns. Columns without characters are padded with the character specified in the `fillchar` argument	`str = "PYTHON"`
		`print(str.rjust(10, '&'))` **OUTPUT**
		`&&&&PYTHON`

`zfill (width)`	Returns a string left-padded with zeros to a total of width characters. It is used with numbers and also retains its sign (+ or -).	`str = "5678"`
		`print(str.zfill(10))`
		OUTPUT
		`0000005678`

(Continued)

Table 11.2 Continued

Function	Usage	Example

`lower()`	Converts all characters in the string into lowercase.	`str = "PYTHON"`
		`print(str.lower())`
		OUTPUT
		`python`

`upper()`	Converts all characters in the string into uppercase.	`str = "python"`
		`print(str.upper())`
		OUTPUT
		`PYTHON`

`lstrip()`	Removes all leading whitespace in the string.	`str = " PYTHON"`
		`print(str.lstrip())`
		OUTPUT
		`PYTHON`

`rstrip()`	Removes all trailing whitespace in the string.	`str = "PYTHON  "`
		`print(str.lstrip())`
		OUTPUT
		`PYTHON`

`strip()`	Removes all leading and trailing whitespace in the string.
	The `strip()` function, when used with a string argument, will strip (from both ends) any combination of the specified characters in the string
		`str = "   PYTHON    "`
		`print(str.strip())`
		`str = "abcPYabcTHONabc"`
		`print(str.strip("abc"))`
		OUTPUT
		`PYTHON`
		`PYabcTHON`

`max(str)`	Returns the highest alphabetical character (having highest ASCII value) from the string str.	`str = "PyThoN pRoGrAmMiNg"`
		`print(max(str))`
		OUTPUT
		`y`

`min(str)`	Returns the lowest alphabetical character (lowest ASCII value) from the string str.	`str = "PyThoNpRoGrAmMiNg"`
		`print(min(str))`
		OUTPUT
		`A`

`replace(old, new [, max])`	Replaces all or max (if given) occurrences of old in string with new	`str = "She sells sea shells on the sea shore"`
		`print(str.replace («se», «SE»))`
		OUTPUT
		`She SElls SEa shells on the SEa shore`

`title()`	Returns string in title case	`str = "she sells sea shells on the sea shore"`
		`print(str.title())`
		OUTPUT
		`She Sells Sea Shells On The Sea Shore`

`swapcase()`	Toggles the case of every character (upper case character becomes lower case and vice-versa)	`str = "PyThoNpRoGrAmMiNg"`
		`print(str.swapcase())` **OUTPUT**
		`pYtHOnPrOgRaMmInG`

(*Continued*)

Table 11.2 Continued

Function	Usage	Example

`split(delim)`	Returns a list of substrings separated by the specified delimiter. If no delimiter is specified, then by default, it splits strings at all whitespace characters	`str = "She, sells, sea shells, on the, sea shore"`
		`print(str.split(','))`
		OUTPUT
		`['She', ' sells', ' sea shells', ' on the', ' sea shore']`

`join(list)`	It is the opposite of split. The function joins a list of strings using the delimiter with which the function is invoked.	`str = ['Power','of','the','Universe','HE-MAN']`
		`print('#'.join(str))`
		OUTPUT
		`Power#of#the#Universe#HE-MAN`

`str.splitlines()`	Returns a list of the lines in the string. This method uses the newline characters like \r, \n to split lines.	`print('Python is \n\n a very \r simple language\r\n'.splitlines())`
		OUTPUT
		`['Python is ', '', ' a very ', ' simple language']`

11.10 COMPARING STRINGS

In Python, strings can be compared using relational operators like >, <, <=, <=, ==, !=. The comparison is done lexicographically, i.e., using ASCII value of the characters. The ASCII values of A–Z are 65-90, ASCII codes for a–z are 97–122 and for 0–9 the code is 48-57. This means that bread is greater than Bread because the ASCII value of 'b' is 98 and 'B' is 66.

```
>>> "PYTHON"==        >>>"PYTHON"          >>> "SMILE"<         >>>"GIVE"!= "EXPECT"
"python"              >= "python"          "laughter"           True
False                 False                True
```

Did you notice that String values are ordered using lexicographical (dictionary) ordering? For this, the comparison is done internally.

11.11 ord() AND chr() FUNCTIONS

```
ch = 'P'              ch = 'y'             print(ch r(79))      print(chr(117))
print(ord(ch))        print(ord(ch))       OUTPUT               OUTPUT
OUTPUT                OUTPUT               O                    u
80                    121
```

`ord()` function returns the ASCII code of the character and `chr()` function returns a character represented by an ASCII number.

11.12 in AND not in OPERATORS

`in` and `not in` operators can be used with strings to determine whether a character or a string is present in another string. Therefore, the `in` and `not in` operators are also known as membership operators.

Example 11.12

```
# using in operator
str1 = "Python programming is fun"
str2 ="is"
if str2 in str1:
  print("Found")
else:
  print("Not Found")
```

OUTPUT
Found

```
# using not in operator
str1 = "Arav is a very naughty boy"
str2 = "good"
if str2 not in str1:
  print("Arav is not a good boy.")
else:
  print("Arav is a very good boy.")
```

OUTPUT
Arav is not a good boy.

You can also use the `in` and `not in` operators to check whether a character is present in a word. Also remember that a string is a substring of itself.

```
>>> 'y' in "PYTHON"     >>> 'N' in "PYTHON"     >>> 'PYTHON' in 'PYTHON'     >>> 'V' in 'V'
False                   True                    True                         True
```

PROGRAMMER'S ZONE

1. Write a program that takes the username of an email address as input. Validate the information using isX function. The username must have both alphabets and digits.

   ```
   username = input("\n Enter the user name : ")
   if username.isalpha() == True:
       print("The user name must have at least one digit.")
   elif username.isdigit() == True:
       print("The user name must have at least one alphabet.")
   elif username.isalnum() == True:
       print("Correct username... You may proceed")
   ```

   OUTPUT
   Enter the user name : abc123
   Correct username... You may proceed

2. Write a program that encrypts a message by adding a key value to every character. (Caesar Cipher)
   Hint: *Say, if key = 3, then add 3 to every character*
   ```
   message = "PythonProgramming"
   index = 0
   while index < len(message):
       letter = message[index]
       print(chr(ord(letter) + 3),end=" ")
       index += 1
   ```
   OUTPUT
   S | w k r q S u r j u d p p l q j

   > Python does not have any separate data type for characters. They are represented as a single character string.

3. Write a program that uses `split()` to split a multiline string.
   ```
   info = '''Dear Students,
   This to inform you that,
   the department is organizing a Hackathon
   on 31st of this month.
   ```

```
Interested students may give their names to the undersigned.
Best Wishes,
Reema Thareja'''
print(info.split('\n'))
```

OUTPUT

['Dear Students,', 'This to inform you that, ', 'the department is organizing a Hackathon', 'on 31st of this month. ', 'Interested students may give their names to the undersigned. ', 'Best Wishes,', 'Reema Thareja']

4. Write a program to generate an abecedarian series.

   Hint: *Abecedarian refers to a series or list in which the elements appear in alphabetical order*
   ```
   str1 = "ABCDEFGH"
   str2 = "at"
   for letter in str1:
       print((letter + str2), end=" ")
   ```

   > The empty parentheses means that this method takes no argument.

   OUTPUT

   Aat Bat Cat Dat Eat Fat Gat Hat

5. Write a program that accepts a string from the user and re-displays the same string after removing the vowels from it.
   ```
   str = input("\n Enter a string : ")
   new_str = ""
   for i in str:
       if i not in "aeiouAEIOU":
           new_str += i
   print("The string without vowels is : ", new_str)
   ```

   OUTPUT
   ```
   Enter a string : Python Programming
   The string without vowels is : Pythn Prgrmmng
   ```

6. Write a program that finds whether a given character is present in a string or not. In case the character is present, it prints the index at which it is present. Do not use built-in find functions to search the character.
   ```
   str = input("Enter a string : ")
   ch = input("Enter the character to be searched : ")
   index = 0
   found = 0
   while(index < len(str)):
       if str[index] == ch:
           found = 1
           print(ch, "found in string at index : ", index)
           break
       index += 1
   if(found == 0):
       print (ch, " is not present in the string")
   ```

   > Calling a method is also known as method invocation.

   OUTPUT
   ```
   Enter a string : Python Programming
   Enter the character to be searched : a
   a found in string at index : 12
   ```

7. **Write a program that emulates the r_find function.**
    ```
    str = input("Enter a string : ")
    ch = input("Enter the character to be searched : ")
    index = len(str)-1
    found = 0
    while(index >= 0):
        if str[index] == ch:
            found = 1
            print(ch, "found in string at index : ", index)
            break
        index -= 1
    if(found == 0):
        print (ch, " is not present in the string")
    ```
    > The start and end parameters in find() and rfind() are optional.

    OUTPUT
    ```
    Enter the character to be searched : a
    a found in string at index :12
    ```

8. **Write a program that counts the occurrences of a character in a string. Do not use built-in count function.**
    ```
    str = input("\n Enter a string : ")
    ch = input("\n Enter the character to be searched : ")
    count = 0
    for i in str:
        if i == ch:
            count += 1
    print("In ", str, ch, " occurs ", count, " times")
    ```

    OUTPUT
    ```
    Enter a string : Python Programming
    Enter the character to be searched : n
    In Python Programming n occurs 2 times
    ```

9. **Modify the above program so that it starts counting from the specified location.**
    ```
    str = input("\n Enter a string : ")
    ch = input("\n Enter the character to be searched : ")
    loc = int(input("\n From which position do you want to start counting : "))
    count = 0
    index = loc
    while index < len(str):
        if str[index] == ch:
            count += 1
        index += 1
    print("In the string:, ch, " occurs ", count, " times from position", loc, " to end")
    ```
    > Python uses negative numbers to access the characters at the end of the string. Negative index numbers count back from the end of the string.

    OUTPUT
    ```
    Enter a string : she sells sea shells on the sea shore
    Enter the character to be searched : s
    From which position do you want to start counting : 5
    In the string soccurs6times from position 5to end
    ```

10. **Write a program to reverse a string.**
    ```
    str = input("\n Enter a string : ")
    new_str = ''
    i = len(str)-1
    while i>=0:
        new_str += str[i]
        i -= 1
    print("\n The reversed string is : ", new_str)
    ```
    OUTPUT
    ```
    Enter a string : PYTHON
    The reversed string is :NOHTYP
    ```

11. **Write a program to parse an email id to print from which email server it was sent and when.**
    ```
    info = 'From shreya.kumar@gmail.com Sun Apr 19 20:29:16 2020'
    start = info.find('@') + 1      # Extract characters after @ symbol
    end = info.find(".com") + 4     # Extract till m, find returns index of .
    mailserver = info[start:end]    # Extract characters
    start = end                     # Ignore whitespace
    end = len(info) # Extract till last character
    date_time = info[start:end]
    print("The email has been sent through " , mailserver,
    end = ' ')
    print("on " + date_time)
    ```

    > When using negative index numbers, start with the lower number first as it occurs earlier in the string.

    OUTPUT
    ```
    The email has been sent throughgmail.com onSun Apr 19 20:29:16 2020
    ```

12. **Write a program to convert every alternate character in a string to uppercase.**
    ```
    str = "helloworldofpython"
    length = len(str)
    new_str = ""
    for i in range(length):
        if(i%2 != 0):
            new_str += str[i].upper()
        else:
            new_str += str[i]
    print(new_str)
    ```
    OUTPUT
    ```
    hElLoWoRlDoFpYtHoN
    ```

Key Terms

Traversing a string: Accessing each character in the string, one at a time.

Dot notation: Use of the dot operator (.) to access functions inside a module.

Index: A variable or value used to access a member of an ordered set.

Slice: A part of a string obtained by specifying a range of indices.

Whitespace: Characters that move the cursor without printing visible characters.

Method: A function that is called on an object using dot notation.

Sequence: An ordered set of values in which each value is identified by an integer index.

Empty string: A string that has no characters and has a length = 0.

Format operator: % operator that takes a format string and a tuple to generate a string that includes values of the tuple formatted as specified by the format string.

Format sequence: Sequence of characters in a format string, like %d, which specifies how a value should be formatted.

Format string: String used with the % or format operator that contains format sequences.

Invocation: A statement that calls a method.

Immutable: The property of a sequence whose items cannot be assigned.

Chapter Highlights

- The Python string data type is a sequence made up of one or more individual characters, where a character could be a letter, digit, whitespace, or any other symbol.
- The `in` operator checks if one character or string is contained in another string.
- The whitespace characters, exclamation mark and any other symbol (like ?, <,>,*, @, #, $, %, etc) that forms a part of the string would be assigned its own index number.
- Concatenate means to join together and append means to add something at the end.
- A raw string literal which is prefixed by an 'r' passes all the characters as it.
- Python strings are immutable, which means that once the strings are created they cannot be changed.
- The number and type of values in the tuple should match the number and type of format sequences or conversion specifications in the string; otherwise an error is returned.
- Strings are examples of Python objects.
- `in` and `not in` operators can be used with strings to determine whether a string is present in another string. Therefore, the `in` and `not in` operators are also known as membership operators.
- The string module consists of a number of useful constants, classes and functions. These functions are used to manipulate strings.

Review Questions

1. With the help of an example, explain how we can create string variables in Python.
2. With the help of an example, explain how we can concatenate a string and a floating-point data.
3. Python strings are immutable. Comment on this statement.
4. Write a short note on format operator.
5. What will happen when the `strip()` is used with a string argument?
6. Explain the use of `format()` with the help of an example.
7. What is slice operation? Explain with an example.
8. With the help of an example, explain the significance of membership operators.
9. Differentiate between the following.
    a. a method and a function
    b. `find()` and `index()`
    c. `find()` and `rfind()`
    d. `captalize()` and `upper()`

10. Name the function to do the following operations:
    a. Returns a string with the original string centered to a total of width columns
    b. Checks if string ends with suffix; returns True if so and False otherwise
    c. Returns True if string has at least 1 character and every character is either a number or an alphabet and False otherwise
    d. Returns True if string has at least 1 character and every character is a lower case alphabet and False otherwise
    e. Removes all trailing whitespace in string
    f. Returns the highest alphabetical character (having highest ASCII value) from the string str.
    g. Toggles the case of every character
    h. Returns a list of substrings separated by the specified delimiter.
    i. The function joins a list of strings using the delimiter with which the function is invoked.

11. Returns a list of the lines in the string.

12. If str = 'Welcome to the world of Python Programming', answer the following:
    a. Write an instruction to print the tenth character of the string.
    b. Write an instruction that prints the index of the first occurrence of the letter 'o' in the string.

Programming Exercises

1. Modify the `find_ch` function so that it starts finding the character from the specified position in the string.

2. Write a program to calculate the length of a string.

3. Write a program to count the number of vowels and consonants present in a user-inputted string.

4. Write a program to count the number of lower case and uppercase characters present in a user-inputted string.

5. Write a program to count the number of digits, spaces and alphabets present in a user-inputted string.

6. Write a Python program to get a string made of the first 2 and the last 2 chars from a given a string. If the string length is less than 2, return instead the empty string.

7. Write a Python program to get a string from a given string where all occurrences of its first char have been changed to '$', except the first char itself.

8. Write a Python program to get a single string from two given strings, separated by a space and swap the first two characters of each string.

9. Program to copy a string.

10. Write a Python program to add `'ing'` at the end of a given string (length should be at least 3). If the given string is already ends with `'ing'` then add `'ly'` instead. If the string length of the given string is less than 3, leave it unchanged.

11. Write a program to find the first appearance of the substring 'not' and 'poor' from a given string, if 'bad' follows the 'poor', replace the whole 'not'...'poor' substring with 'good'. Return the resulting string.

12. Write a function that takes a list of words and returns the length of the longest one.

13. Write a program to remove the *n*th index character from a non-empty string.

14. Write a program to change a given string to a new string where the first and last chars have been exchanged.

15. Write a program to remove the characters which have odd index values of a given string.

16. Write a program to count the occurrences of each word in a given sentence.

17. Write a program that accepts a comma-separated sequence of words as input and prints the unique words in sorted form (alphanumerically).

18. Write a function to insert a string in the middle of a string.

19. Write a function to get a string made of 4 copies of the last two characters of a specified string (length must be at least 2).
20. Write a function to get a string made of its first three characters of a specified string. If the length of the string is less than 3 then return the original string.
21. Write a function to get the first half of a specified string of even length.
22. Write a function to reverses a string if its length is a multiple of 4.
23. Write a function to convert a given string to all uppercase if it contains at least 2 uppercase characters in the first 4 characters.
24. Write a program to sort a string lexicographically.
25. Write a program to remove newline characters from text.
26. Write a program to check whether a string starts with specified characters.
27. Write a program to remove existing indentation from all of the lines in a given text.
28. Write a program to add a prefix text to all of the lines in a string.
29. Write a program to set the indentation of the first line.
30. Write a program to print floating numbers up to 2 decimal places.
31. Write a program to print floating numbers up to 2 decimal places with sign.
32. Write a program to print floating numbers with no decimal places.
33. Write a program to print integers with zeros on the left of specified width.
34. Write a program to print integers with '*' on the right of specified width.
35. Write a program to display a number with comma separator.
36. Write a program to format a number with percentage.
37. Write a program to display a number in left-, right- and centre-aligned format of width 10.
38. Write a program to reverse words in a string.
39. Write a program to strip a set of characters from a string.
40. Write a program to create a mirror of the given string. For example, `"abc"` = `"abccba"`.
41. Write a program that removes all the occurrences of a specified character from a given string.
42. Write a program to check whether a string is palindrome or not.
43. Write a program to remove all the occurrences of a given word from the string.
44. Write a program to concatenate two strings in a third string. Do not use + operator.
45. Write a program to append a string to another string. Do not use += operator
46. Write a program to swap two strings.
47. Write a program to insert a string in another string.
48. Write a program to delete a string from another string.
49. Write a program to replace a string with another string. Do not use the `replace()`.
50. Write a program that removes leading and trailing spaces from a string.
51. Write a program to read a name and then display it in abbreviated form, for example, Janak Raj Thareja should be displayed as JRT.

52. Write a program to read a name and then display it in abbreviated form, for example, Janak Raj Thareja should be displayed as J.R. Thareja.
53. Write a program to count the number of characters, words, and lines in the given text.
54. Write a program to count the number of digits, upper case characters, lower case characters, and special characters in a given string.
55. Write a program to extract the first *n* characters of a string.
56. Write a program to copy n characters of a string from the *m*th position in another string. Do not use the slice operation.
57. Write a program to delete the last character of a string.
58. Write a program to delete the first character of a string.
59. Write a program to encrypt a string using substitution cipher.
60. Write a program that encrypts a string using multiplicative cipher. Generate the key randomly.
61. Write the command to print "hello world" as "Hello world".
62. Write the command to print "hello world" as "Hello World".
63. Write the command to print "hEllo WoRlD" as "HeLlO wOrLd".
64. Write the command to print "hello world" as "Hello Friends".
65. Write a program that prompts the user to enter a 10-digit mobile number. Display the number by putting a '-' after area code and next three digits. (like 123-456-7890).
66. Write a program that prompts the user to enter five words. If the length of any word is less than 8 or if the word does not contain any digit then prompt the user to enter that word again.

Fill in the Blanks

1. String is a sequence made up of one or more _____.
2. A multiple-line text within quotes must have a _____ at the end of each line.
3. Individual characters in a string are accessed using the _____ operator.
4. _____ error is generated when index out of bounds is accessed.
5. _____ means to join together.
6. The _____ function is used to convert values of any other type into string type.
7. The _____ returns the memory address of that object.
8. Conversion specifications start with a _____ operator.
9. A method is invoked or called on an _____.
10. _____ function checks if a string ends with suffix.
11. _____ function toggles the case of every character.
12. The _____ returns a list of the lines in the string.
13. Omitting both ends in the slice operation means selecting the _____.
14. If we access the string from the first character then we use a _____ based index but when doing it backward the index starts with _____.
15. _____ function returns the ASCII code of the character.

16. _____ and _____ operators are known as membership operators.
17. _____ function is used to know the details of a particular item.
18. _____ function displays the methods in a module.

State True or False

1. Character in a string could be a letter, digit, whitespace, or any other symbol.
2. Python treats strings as contiguous series of characters delimited by single or double quotes but not triple quotes.
3. Python has a built-in string class as well as a string module that has many methods.
4. Index can either be an integer or an expression that evaluates to a floating point number.
5. In a string, all whitespace characters are also assigned an index value.
6. Raw strings do not process escape sequences.
7. 'r' is used as a prefix for Unicode strings.
8. We cannot delete or remove characters from a string.
9. The % operator takes a format string on the right and the corresponding values in a tuple on the left.
10. Conversion specifications start with a % operator and can appear anywhere within the string.
11. The number and type of values in the tuple should match the number and type of format sequences or conversion specifications in the string.
12. The - after each % in the conversion string indicates right justification.
13. You can access a string using negative indexes.
14. `odr()` function returns character represented by a ASCII number.
15. A string is a substring of itself.
16. Strings are compared based on ASCII values of their characters.

Multiple Choice Questions

1. The index of the first character in the string is _____.
   a. 0 b. 1 c. n-1 d. n
2. The index of the last character in the string is _____.
   a. 0 b. 1 c. n-1 d. n
3. Which error is generated when the index is not an integer?
   a. IndexError b. NameError c. TypeError d. BoundError
4. Which of the following word best means to add something at the end?
   a. Concatenate b. Append c. Join d. Add
5. In Python a string is appended to another string by using which operator?
   a. + b. * c. [] d. +=
6. Which operator is used to repeat a string n number of times?
   a. + b. * c. [] d. +=
7. The `print` statement prints one or more literals or values followed by a/an _____.
   a. Newline b. Tab c. Whitespace d. Exclamation

8. Which error is generated when a character in a string variable is modified?
   a. IndexError b. NameError c. TypeError d. BoundError

9. You can delete the entire string by using which keyword?
   a. del b. erase c. remove d. delete

10. Which operator takes a format string on the left and the corresponding values in a tuple on the right?
    a. + b. * c. [] d. %

11. Which character is used for hexadecimal integers in the format string?
    a. u b. x c. d d. s

12. When using find(), if str is not present in the string then what is returned?
    a. 0 b. –1 c. n–1 d. ValueError

13. If "   Cool   " becomes "COOL", which two functions must have been applied?
    a. strip() and upper()
    b. strip() and lower()
    c. strip() and capitalize()
    d. lstrip() and rstrip()

14. In the split(), if no delimiter is specified then by default it splits strings on which characters?
    a. Whitespace b. comma c. newline d. colon

15. The splitlines(), splits lines in strings on which characters?
    a. Whitespace b. comma c. newline d. colon

16. By default, the value of stride is ____.
    a. 0 b. -1 c. 1 d. n-1

17. To print the original string in reverse order, you can set the stride as ____.
    a. 0 b. -1 c. 1 d. n-1

18. Identify the correct result from the following.
    a. ord('10') = 50 b. chr(72) = 'H' c. chr(55) = 9 d. ord('z') = 123

19. Which of these patterns would not match the string "Good Morning" when used with match()?
    a. Good b. Morning c. Go d. Good Morn

Give the Output

1. ```
   s = "Welcome"
   print s[1:3]
   ```

2. ```
   s = "Welcome"
   print s[ : 6]
   ```

3. ```
   s = "Welcome"
   print s[4 : ]
   ```

4. ```
   s = "Welcome"
   print s[1:-1]
   ```

5. ```
   str = "Welcome"
   print "come" in str
   ```

6. ```
   str = "Welcome"
   print "come" not in str
   ```

7. ```
   "free" == "freedom"
   ```

8. ```
   print("12" + "34")
   ```

9. "man" != "men"

10. >>> 3*"PYTHON"

11. str = "Welcome to Python"
    print(str.isalnum())

12. "Hello".isalpha()

13. "14-10-2106".isdigit()

14. print "hello".islower()

15. "\t".isspace()

16. str = "Hello"
    print str.startswith("he")

17. str = "Hello, welcome to the world of Python"
    print str.find("o")

18. str = "Hello, welcome to the world of Python"
    print str.find("if")

19. str = "Hello, welcome to the world of Python"
    print str.rfind("of")

20. str = "Hello, welcome to the world of Python"
    print str.count("o")

21. "us" not in "success"

22. "mi" in "ours"

23. for i in 'Python':
        print 2 * i,

24. string.find("abcdabcdabcd", "cd", 3)

25. string.find("abcdabcdabcdabcdabcd", "cd", 7, 13)

26. a = 10
    b = 20
    print "3**4 = %d and %d * %d = %f" % (3**4, a, b, a * b)

27. print "%d %f %s" % (7, 15, 28)
    print "%-.2f" % 369
    print "%-10.2f%-10.2f" % (91, 23.456)
    print "%5.2f %5.2f $%5.2f" % (9, 1.2, 55.78)

28. str1 = 'Welcome!'
    str2 = 'to Python'
    str3 = str1[:2] + str2[len(str2) - 2:]
    print str3

29. print("She sells sea shells on the sea shore.".find("sea", 3, -6))

30. len("She sells sea shells on the sea shore.")

31. ```
    str = "Welcome to the world of Python"
    print(str[:10].find("t"))
    ```

32. ```
    str = "Welcome to the world of Python"
    start = 3
    end = 10
    print(str[start:end])
    ```

33. ```
    str = "Hello"
    print str.startswith('h')
    print str.lower().startswith('h')
    ```

34. ```
    'In %d years I have saved %g %s.' % (3, 4.5, 'lakh rupees')
    ```

35. ```
    ', '.join(['Sun', 'Stars', 'Planets'])
    ```

36. ```
    ' '.join(['Welcome', 'to', 'the', 'world', 'of', 'Python!'])
    ```

37. ```
    'Hello'.join(['Welcome', 'to', 'the', 'world', 'of', 'Python!'])
    ```

38. ```
    "Good morning students".split()
    ```

39. ```
    'WelcomeHellotoHellotheHelloworldHelloofHelloPython!'.split('Hello')
    ```

40. ```
    >>> s = 'abcdefghijkl'
    >>> print(s[-100:-5],s[-100:5])
    ```

41. ```
    s1 = "HELLO"
    s2 = s1 + s1[-1]
    print(s2)
    print(s1[:-1])
    print(s1[-1:])
    ```

42. ```
    str = "xyz"
    while(len(str)<=4):
        if(str[-1] == 'z'):
            str = str[0:3]+'c'
        elif 'a' in str:
            str = str[0] + 'bb'
        elif 'x' not in str:
            str = '1'+str[1:]+'z'
        else:
            str = str+'*'
    print(str)
    ```

43. ```
    str = "helloworldofpython"
    print(str[10],str[11:30])
    ```

44. ```
    str1 = '''PYTHON
    PRO'''
    str2 = '''PYTHON\
    PRO'''
    print(len(str1)>len(str2))
    ```

45. ```
    str1= 'PYTHON'; str1[-4]
    ```
    ```

Find the Error

1. ```
   str = "Hello world"
   str[6] = 'W'
   print(str)
   ```

2. `"%s %s %s %s" % ('Welcome', 'to', 'Python')`

3. `"%s %s %s" % ('East', 'West', 'North', 'South')`

4. `"%d %f %f" % (10, 20, 'Hello')`

5. ```
   str = 'abcdefgh'
   str[5] = 'a'
   print(str)
   str = 'Python'
   print(str)
   ```

6. ```
   str = "Hello World"
   del str[2]
   print(str)
   ```

7. `print("Hello World" + 10)`

8. `print("Hello" * "World")`

Answers

Fill in the Blanks

1. characters
2. backslash (\)
3. subscript ([ ])
4. IndexError
5. concatenate
6. str()
7. id()
8. %
9. object
10. endswith()
11. swapcase()
12. splitlines()
13. entire string
14. zero, –1
15. ord()
16. in and not in
17. type()
18. dir()

State True or False

1. True
2. False
3. True
4. False
5. True
6. True
7. False
8. True
9. False
10. True
11. True
12. False
13. True
14. False
15. True
16. True

Multiple Choice Questions

1. a
2. c
3. c
4. b
5. d
6. b
7. a
8. c
9. a
10. d
11. b
12. b
13. a
14. a
15. c
16. c
17. b
18. b
19. b

Give the Output

1. el
2. Welcom
3. ome
4. elcom
5. True
6. False
7. False
8. 1234
9. True
10. 'PYTHONPYTHONPYTHON'
11. False
12. True
13. False
14. True
15. True
16. False
17. 4
18. –1
19. 28
20. 6
   ```

21. True
22. False
23. PP yy tt hh oo nn
24. 6
25. 10
26. 3**4 = 81 and 10 * 20 = 200.000000
27. 7 15.000000 28
    369.00
    91.00   23.46
    9.001.20 $55.78
28. Weon
29. 10
30. 38
31. 8
32. come to
33. False
    True

34. 'In 3 years I have saved 4.5 lakh rupees.'
35. 'Sun, Stars, Planets'
36. 'Welcome to the world of Python!'
37. 'WelcomeHellotoHellotheHelloworldHelloofHelloPython!'
38. ['Good', 'morning', 'students']
39. ['Welcome', 'to', 'the', 'world', 'of', 'Python!']
40. abcdefg abcde
41. HELLOO
    HELL
    O
42. xvzc*
43. o fpython
44. True
45. 'T'

Find the Error

1. TypeError: 'str' object does not support item assignment
2. TypeError: not enough arguments for format string
3. TypeError: not all arguments converted during string formatting
4. TypeError: float argument required, not str
5. TypeError: 'str' object does not support item assignment
6. TypeError: 'str' object doesn't support item deletion
7. TypeError: can only concatenate str (not "int") to str
8. TypeError: can't multiply sequence by non-int of type 'str'

Lists

12

Chapter Objectives

This chapter introduces list as an important and very powerful data structure in Python. The reader will get to learn the following things in this chapter:

- Creating lists
- Accessing and updating its values
- Relational operations
- Nested lists
- The `eval()` function
- Creating deep copies and shallow copies of a given list
- Difference between list cloning and list aliasing
- List operations and methods

List is a versatile data type available in Python, in which elements are written as a list of comma-separated values (items) between square brackets. Lists in Python are mutable as we can change the value of their elements. This is in striking contrast with strings, which are immutable.

The key feature of list is that it can have elements that belong to different data types. The syntax of defining a list can be given as, **List_variable = [val1, val2, …]**

```
list_A = [1,2,3,4,5]           list_B = ['A', 1, 'C', 2, 'E']
print(list_A)                  print(list_B)
[1, 2, 3, 4, 5]                ['A', 1, 'C', 2, 'E']
list_C = ["HELLO","WORLD")     list_D = [1, 'a ', 'HELLO')
print(list_ C)                 print( list_ D)
['HELLO', 'WORLD']             [1, 'a ', 'HELLO']
```

We can even create an empty list by writing **list_variable = []**. An empty list is equivalent to False when used with logical operators.

```
>>> list = []
>>> list == True
        False
```

12.1 ACCESSING VALUES IN LISTS

Like strings, lists can also be sliced and concatenated. To access values in a list, square brackets are used to slice along with the index or indices to get the value stored at that index. As discussed earlier, the syntax for the slice operation is,
seq = List[start:stop:step]

For example,
  seq = List[::2] *# gets every other element, starting with index 0*
  seq = List[10::3] *# gets every third element, starting with index 10*
  seq = List[-3] *# gets the third element from the end*
  seq = List_A[-3] *# 3rd element from the end*
  seq = List[3:] *# get all elements starting from the third index at the beginning*

```
num_list = [2,4,6,8,10,12,14,16,18,20]
print("num_list is:", num_list)
print("First element in the list is",
num_list[0])
print("num_list[2:5] = ", num_list[4:7])
print("num_list[::2] = ", num_list[::3])
print("num_list[1::3] = ", num_list[1::2])
```

OUTPUT
```
num_list is : [2, 4, 6, 8, 10, 12,
14, 16, 18, 20]
First element in the list is 2
num_list[2:5] = [10, 12, 14]
num_list[::2] = [2, 8, 14, 20]
num_list[1::3] = [4, 8, 12, 16, 20]
```

If the start and end values of the slice operation are beyond the size of the list, then all the elements within the specified range are returned. For example, consider the example given in which the start and end values are out of range of the size of the list.

Note that the valid index range of the list is 0–4. The values –9 and 9 are beyond the size of the list, so the entire list is returned. But in the second case, when start = –3 and end = 9, –3 lies in the valid range which is the third element from the end, hence the result.

```
I = [1,2,3,4,5]        I = [1, 2,3,4,5]
print(l[-9:9])         print(I[-3:9])
OUTPUT                 OUTPUT
[1, 2, 3, 4, 5]        [3, 4, 5]
```

12.2 THE eval() FUNCTION

```
>>> eval("10     >>> eval("20    >>> eval("30 - 5   >>> eval(" 'HELLO'
== 10")         <= 10")          * 4 + 20")          * 3")
True            False            30                  'HELLOHELLOHELLO'
```

The eval() function is used to evaluate and return the result of an expression as a string.

We can use the eval() function to read value(s) of any type. However, its use is discouraged as we may get unforeseen problems as a result of using this function.

12.3 UPDATING VALUES IN LISTS

Example 12.1

Let us write a program that uses the eval () function to accept a list of numbers and print the sum of the elements.
```
list= eval(input("Enter values : "))
print (list)
sum(list)
print("SUM = " , sum(list))
```

OUTPUT
```
Enter values : [1,2,3,4,5,6,7,8,9,10]
[1 , 2 , 3 , 4 , 5 , 6 , 7 , 8 , 9 , 10]
SUM = 55
```

Once created, one or more elements of a list can be easily updated by giving the slice on the left-hand side of the assignment operator. You can also append new values in the list and remove existing value(s) from the list using the append() method and del statement respectively.

Example 12.2

Using the eval () function to accept input of different types.
```
a = eval(input("Enter an integer : "))
print (type (a))
b = eval(input("Enter a float : "))
print (type (b))
c = eval(input( "Enter a tuple : "))
print (type (c))
d = eval(input("Enter a list : "))
print (type (d))
```

OUTPUT
```
Enter an integer : 1
<class 'int'>
Enter a float : 2.3
<class 'float'>
Enter a tuple : (4,5, 6)
<class 'tuple ' >
Enter a list : [7, 8, 9]
<class 'list'>
```

Example 12.3

```
num_list = [2,4,6,8,10,12,14,16,18,20]
print("List is : ", num_list)
num_list[5] = 100
print("List after udpation is : ", num_list)
num_list.append(200)
print("List after appending a value is ", num_list)
del num_list[3]
print("List after deleting a value is ", num_list)
```

OUTPUT
```
List is : [2, 4, 6, 8, 10, 12, 14, 16, 18, 20]
List after udpation is : [2, 4, 6, 8, 10, 100, 14, 16, 18, 20]
List after appending a value is [2, 4, 6, 8, 10, 100, 14, 16, 18, 20, 200]
List after deleting a value is [2, 4, 6, 10, 100, 14, 16, 18, 20, 200
```

If you know exactly which element(s) to delete, use the del statement; otherwise, use the remove() method to delete the unknown elements.

Example 12.4

```
num_list = [2,4,6,8,10,12,14,16,18,20] del
num_list[3:6] #deletes numbers at index 3,4,5
print(num_list)
del num_list[:] #deletes all the numbers from
the list
print(num_list) # an empty list is printed
```

OUTPUT
```
[2, 4, 6, 14, 16, 18, 20]
[]
```

```
del(num_list)
print(num_list)   # the list no
longer exists
```

OUTPUT
```
Traceback (most recent call last):
  File "C:\Users\Reema\Python\
Python37\try.py",
line 5, in <module>
  print(num_list) #the list no
loger exists
NameError: name 'num_list' is not
defined
```

Note that when we write del num_list, the entire variable is deleted. If you make any attempt to use this variable after the del statement, then an error will be generated.

12.4 RELATIONAL OPERATIONS ON LISTS

We can compare two list objects using relational operators like ==, >, <, >=, <=, !=, etc. Python compares elements of a list in lexicographical order. Each element of the list is compared with the corresponding element in the other list. However, to use operators like >=, <=, >, < the two values must be of compatible type; otherwise an error will be generated.

Example 12.5

```
l1 = [1,2,3]
l2 = [1,2,3]
l3 = [1,[2,3]]
print(l1==l2)
print(l1==l3)
```

OUTPUT
```
True
False
```

```
l1 = [1,2,3]
l2 = [1,3,3]
print(l1>=l2)
print(l1<=l2)
```

OUTPUT
```
False
True
```

```
l1 = [1,2,3,4]
l2 = [1,3,3]
print(l1>=l2)
```

OUTPUT
```
True
```

```
l1 = [1,2,3,4]
l2 = ['a','b','c']
l3 = [1.0,2.0,3.0]
print(l1>=l3)
print(l2>=l3)
```

OUTPUT
```
True
Traceback (most recent call last):
  File "C:\Python37\try.py",line 5, in <module>
print(l2>=l3) Type Error: '>=' not supported between instances of 'str' and 'float'
```

12.5 NESTED LISTS

Nested list means a list within another list. We have already said that a list has elements of different data types. So besides other elements, a list can also have another list as its element. For example, `list1 = [1,2,'a',[5.0,6,"ABCD"], "BYE"]`. Here, `list1` is a list that has another list at index 3.

To *insert items from another list* at a particular location, we can use the slice operation. This would create a nested list, i.e., a list within another list.

Remember that you can specify an element in the nested list by using a set of indices. For example, assuming that the inner list starts at index 3 in the main list, to print the second element of the nested (or the inner) list, we will write `print list[3][1]`. The first index specifies the starting location of the nested list in the main list and the second index specifies the index of the element within the nested list. The code given below clarifies this concept.

Example 12.6

```
# Creating a Nested List
listl = [1,2,'a',[5.0,6,"ABCD"],"BYE"]
i=0
while i<(le n(listl)):
  print{"Listl[",i,"] = ",listl[i])
  i+=1
```

OUTPUT
```
Listl[0] = 1
Listl[1] = 2
Listl[2] = a
Listl[3] = [5.0, 6, 'ABCD']
Listl[4 ] = BYE
```

```
#Inserting a list within another list-
creating a nested list
num_list = [2,4,12,14]
print{"Original List : ", num_list)
num_list[2] = [6,8,10]
print("After inserting another list, the
updated list is : ", num_list)
print("Second element of nested list is :
",num_list[2][1))
```

OUTPUT
```
Original List : [2, 4, 12, 14]
After inserting another list, the updated
list is : [2, 4, [6, 8, 10], 14]
Second element of nested list is : 8
```

12.6 LIST ALIASING AND CLONING

When one list is assigned to another list using the assignment operator (=), then a new copy of the list is not made. Instead, assignment operation makes the two variables point to the same list in memory. This is also known as *aliasing*.

Cloning lists: If you want to modify a list and also keep a copy of the original list, then you should create a separate copy of the list (not just the reference). This process is called *cloning*. The slice operation is used to clone a list.

Example 12.7

```
list1 = [1,2,3,4,5,6,7,8,9,10]
print("List1 = " , list1)
list2 = list1 #list aliasing
print("List2 = " , list2)
list3 = list1[2:5] #list cloning
print("List3 = ", list3)
```

OUTPUT
```
List1 = [1, 2, 3, 4, 5, 6, 7, 8, 9, 10]
List2 = [1, 2, 3, 4, 5, 6, 7, 8, 9, 10]
List3 = [3, 4, 5]
```

12.7 DELETING ELEMENTS

We can delete one or more elements from the list by using the `del` statement. The syntax to remove a single element from the list is `del list_variable[index]`. And to remove more than one element from the list, we use the syntax, `del[start:stop]`. Finally, to remove the entire list, we need to write `del list_variable`.

Example 12.8

```
I =[1,2,3,4,5,6,7,8,9,10)
print(I)
#deleting third element
del I[2]
print(I)
#deleting fourth, fifth, sixth and seventh elements from the list
delI[2:6]
print(I)
#deleting the entire list
print("Deleting List ........ ")
del I
print(I)
```

OUTPUT
```
[1, 2, 3, 4, 5, 6, 7, 8, 9, 10)
[1, 2, 4, 5, 6, 7, 8, 9, 10)
[1, 2, 8, 9, 10)
Deleting List ....... .
Traceback (most recent call last): File "C:\Python37\try.py", line 12, in <module> print(I)
NameError: name 'I' is not defined
```

12.8 DEEP COPIES AND SHALLOW COPIES IN PYTHON

When copying lists or any other object in Python, we can make a deep copy of the original object or a shallow copy. *A deep copy makes a new and separate copy* of an *entire* object or list with its own unique memory address. Therefore, any changes made in the new copy of the object/list will not be reflected in the original one.

A deep copy creates a new list or object by recursively copying the elements from the original object to the new one. So, both the objects are completely independent of each other. This is similar to the concept of passing by value in languages like C++, Java and C#.

A shallow copy also makes a separate new object or list. However, in this case, instead of copying the elements to the new object, *it simply copies the references to their memory addresses*. Hence, changes made in the original object, would also be reflected in the copied object, and vice versa. Therefore, both the copies are dependent on each other. This is similar to the concept of passing by reference in programming languages like C++, C#, and Java.

Talking in terms of lists, ***the `assignment` operator is used to create a shallow copy of the list and the `list()` creates a deep copy*** as illustrated below.

Example 12.9

```
#Creating a shallow copy of a list
l1 = [1,2,3,4,5]
l2 = l1
print("L1 = ", l1)
print("l2 = ", l2)
l1[2] = 10
print("L1 = ", l1)
print("L2 = ", l2)
OUTPUT
L1 = [1, 2, 3, 4, 5]
L2 = [1, 2, 3, 4, 5]
L1 = [1, 2, 10, 4, 5]
L2 = [1, 2, 10, 4, 5]
```

```
# Creating a deep copy of a list
l1 = [1,2,3,4,5]
l2 = list(l1)
print("L1 = ", l1)
print("L2 = ", l2)
l1[2] = 10
print("L1 = ", l1)
print("L2 = ", l2)
OUTPUT
L1 = [1, 2, 3, 4, 5]
L2 = [1, 2, 3, 4, 5]
L1 = [1, 2, 10, 4, 5]
L2 = [1, 2, 3, 4, 5]
```

12.9 BASIC LIST OPERATIONS

Lists behave in a similar way as strings when operators like + (concatenation) and * (repetition) are used. Common operations on lists are discussed in Table 12.1.

Table 12.1 Operations on lists

Operation	Description	Example	Output
`len`	Returns length of list	`len([1,2,3,4,5,6,7,8,9,10])`	10
`concatenation`	Joins two lists	`[1,2,3,4,5] + [6,7,8,9,10]`	`[1, 2, 3, 4, 5, 6, 7, 8, 9, 10]`
`repetition`	Repeat elements in the list	`"Love", "Python"*2`	`['Love', 'Python', 'Love', 'Python']`
`in`	Checks if the value is present in the list	`'a' in ['a','e','i','o','u']`	True
`not in`	Checks if the value is not present in the list	`9 not in [0,2,4,6,8]`	True
`max`	Returns maximum value in the list	`>>> num_list = [1,0,3,7,4,2,4,9]` `>>> print(max(num_list))`	9
`min`	Returns minimum value in the list	`>>> num_list = [1,0,3,7,4,2,4,9]` `>>> print(min(num_list))`	0
`sum`	Adds the values in the list that has numbers	`num_list = [1,2,3,4,5,6,7,8,9,10]` `print("SUM = ", sum(num_list))`	SUM = 55
`all`	Return True if all elements of the list are true (or if the list is empty)	`>>> num_list = [8,9,0,10]` `>>> print(all(num_list))`	False

(Continued)

Table 12.1 Continued

Operation	Description	Example	Output
any	Return True if any element of the list is true. If the list is empty, returns False	``>>> num_list = [,0,1,2,4,9]`` ``>>> print(any(num_list))``	True
List	Convert tuple, string or to a list	``>>> list1 = list("PYTHON")`` ``>>> print(list1)``	['P', 'Y', 'T', 'H', 'O', 'N']

Sorted	Return a new sorted list. The original list is not sorted.	``>>> list1 = [1,0,3,7,4,2,9]``
		``>>> list2 = sorted(list1)``
		``>>> print(list2)``
			[0,1,2,3,4,7,9]

12.10 LIST METHODS

Python has various methods to help programmers work efficiently with lists. Some of these methods are summarized in Table 12.2.

Table 12.2 List methods

Method	Description	Syntax	Example	Output
append()	Appends an element to the list. In insert(), if the index is 0, then element is inserted as the first element and if we write, list.insert(len(list), obj), then it inserts obj as the last element in the list. That is, if index = len(list), then insert() method behaves exactly the same as append() method.	list.append(obj)	num_list = [1,2,3,4] num_list.append(5) print(num_list)	[1,2,3,4,5]
count()	Counts the number of times an element appears in the list	list.count(obj)	num_list = [1,2,3,4,3,2,4,6] print(num_list.count(4))	1
index()	Returns the lowest index of obj in the list. Gives a ValueError if obj is not present in the list	list.index(obj)	num_list = [1,2,3,4,3,2,4,6] print(num_list.index(3))	2
insert()	Inserts obj at the specified index in the list.	list.insert(index, obj)	num_list = [1,2,3,4,5] num_list.insert(3, 0) print(num_list)	[1,2,3,0,4,5]

(*Continued*)

Table 12.2 Continued

Method	Description	Syntax	Example	Output

pop()	Removes the element at the specified index from the list. Index is an optional parameter. If no index is specified then it removes the last object (or element) from the list.	`list.pop([index])`	`num_list = [1,2,3,4,5]`
			`print(num_list.pop())`
			`print(num_list)`
				5
				[1, 2, 3, 4]

remove()	Removes or deletes obj from the list. ValueError is generated if obj is not present in the list. If multiple copies of obj exist in the list, then the first value is deleted.	`list.remove(obj)`	`num_list = [0,1,2,3,4,5]`
			`num_list.remove(0)`
			`print(num_list)`
				[1, 2, 3,4,5]

reverse()	Reverses the elements in the list.	`list.reverse()`	`num_list = [1,2,3,4]`
			`num_list.reverse()`
			`print num_list`
				[4,3,2,1]

sort()	Sorts the elements in the list	`list.sort()`	`num_list = [3,5,0,4,1]`
			`num_list.sort()`
			`print(num_list)`
				[0,1,3,4,5]

extend()	Adds the elements in a list to the end of another list. Using + or += on a list is similar to using `extend()`.	`list1.extend(list2)`	`num_list1 = [1,2,3]`
			`num_list2 = [4,5,6]`
			`num_list1.extend(num_list2)`
			`print(num_list1)`
				[1, 2, 3, 4, 5, 6]

You may be confused between a method and a function. Observe the above two tables. Clearly, a **function** is a piece of code that is directly called by a name. It may or may not accept parameters and may or may not return data. All data that is to be used by a function is explicitly passed (or made global). Example, `len(list1)`.

However, a **method** is a piece of code that is called by name of the object followed by a dot operator and name of the method. Example, `list1.sort()`.

Key points to remember

- The `sort()` method uses ASCII values to sort the values in the list. Since lower case characters' ASCII value starts from 97 and upper case character's starts from 65, upper case characters appear before lower case characters when sorting is done.
- Items in a list can be deleted by assigning an empty list to a slice of elements as shown in the codes below.
- The `range()` function can be used to print index as shown in the code given below.

Example 12.10

```
list1 = ['1', 'a', "Abc", '2', '8', "def"]
list1.sort()
print(list1)
```

OUTPUT
```
['1', '2 ', 'Abc', 'B', 'a', 'def')
```

```
list= ['P',' r','o','g','r',' a','m','m','i','n','g']
list[3:6] = []
print(list)
```

OUTPUT
```
('P', 'r', 'o', 'm', 'm', 'i', 'n', 'g']
```

```
list = [ 'B','Y','E']
for i in range(len(list)):
    print("index: ", i)
```

OUTPUT
```
index : 0
index : 1
index : 2
```

- If you give an index out of range of the legal indices, then an **IndexError** will be generated. For a list, the legal indices include index from 0 to length of the list – 1. Consider the example, given below.

Example 12.11

```
list = [1,'a',3.4,"PYTHON"]
print(len(list))
# error because length is 4 and we are accessing an index out of range
print(list[4])
```

OUTPUT
```
4
Traceback (most recent call last):
  File "C:\Python37\try.py", line 4, in <module>
    print(list[4])
IndexError: list index out of range
```

- The + operator can also be used to join two lists. However, if you try to join a number or string or any other data with a list using the + operator, **TypeError** will be generated.

Example 12.12

```
l1 = [1,2,3,4,5]
l2 = l1 + 6
print(l2)
```

OUTPUT
```
Traceback (most recent call last):
  File "C:\Python37\try.py", line 2, in <module>
    l2 = l1 + 6
TypeError: can only concatenate list (not "int") to list
```

#Correct Way
```
l1 = [1,2,3,4,5]
l2 = l1 + [6]
print(l2)
```

OUTPUT
```
[1, 2, 3, 4, 5, 6]
```

- Like strings, lists can also be repeated using the * operator.
- While the append() method adds a single element to a list, the extend() method is used to add multiple elements from one list to another list.

Example 12.13

```
# Repeating a list
l1 = ['B','Y','E']
l2 = l1 * 3
print(l2)
```

OUTPUT
```
['B','Y','E','B','Y','E','B','Y','E']
```

#Difference between append() and extend()
```
l1 = [1,2,3,4,5]
l1.append(6)
l1.extend([7,8])
print(l1)
```

OUTPUT
```
[1, 2, 3, 4, 5, 6, 7, 8]
```

In the insert() method, if we specify a negative index that is not in the set of valid indices, the element is added at the beginning of the list (Example 12.14).

If the pop() method is called on an empty list, then an IndexError will be generated (Example 12.15).

Example 12.14

```
l1 = [1,2,3,4,5]
l1.insert(-10,123)
print(l1)
```

OUTPUT
```
[123, 1, 2, 3, 4, 5]
```

Example 12.15

```
l1 = []
l1.pop()
```

OUTPUT
```
Traceback (most recent call last):
File "C:\ Python37\try.py", line 2, in <module>    l1.pop()
IndexError: pop from empty list
```

PROGRAMMER'S ZONE

1. Write a program that creates a list of numbers from 1-20 that are either divisible by 2 or divisible by 4 without using the filter function.

   ```
   div_2_4 = []
   for i in range(2, 22):
       if(i%2 == 0 or i%4 == 0):
           div_2_4.append(i)
   print(div_2_4)
   ```

   > The sort() method uses ASCII values to sort the values in the list.

   OUTPUT
   ```
   [2, 4, 6, 8, 10, 12, 14, 16, 18, 20]
   ```

2. Write a program that defines a list of countries that are a member of BRICS. Check whether a country is a member of BRICS or not.

   ```
   country = ["Brazil", "India", "China", "Russia", "Sri Lanka"]
   is_member = input("Enter the name of country : ")
   if is_member in country:
       print(is_member, "has also joined BRICS")
   else:
       print(is_member, " is not a member of BRICS")
   ```

   > An error is generated if you try to delete an element from the list or insert an element that is not present in the list.

   OUTPUT
   ```
   Enter the name of country : Pakistan
   Pakistan is not a member of BRICS
   ```

3. Write a program to create a list of numbers in the range 1 to 10. Then delete all the even numbers from the list and print the final list.

   ```
   num_list = []
   for i in range(1, 11):
       num_list.append(i)
   print("Original List : ", num_list)
   for index, i in enumerate(num_list):
       if(i%2==0):
           del num_list[index]
   print("List after deleting even numbers : ",num_list)
   ```

   OUTPUT
   ```
   Original List :  [1, 2, 3, 4, 5, 6, 7, 8, 9, 10]
   List after deleting even numbers :  [1, 3, 5, 7, 9]
   ```

4. Write a program to print the index at which a particular value exists. If the value exists at multiple locations in the list, then print all the indices. Also count the number of times that value is repeated in the list.

   ```
   num_list = [1,2,3,4,5,6,5,4,3,2,1]
   num = int(input("Enter the value to be searched : "))
   i=0
   count = 0
   while i<len(num_list):
       if num == num_list[i]:
           print(num, " found at location", i)
           count += 1
       i += 1
   print(num, " appears ", count, " times in the list")
   ```

   > It is safer to avoid aliasing when you are working with mutable objects.

Lists 251

OUTPUT
```
Enter the value to be searched : 4
4 found at location 3
4 found at location 7
4 appears 2 times in the list
list_words = []
```

> When using slice operation, an IndexError is generated in the index if the index is outside the list.

5. **Write a program that creates a list of words by combining the words in two individual lists.**
```
list_words = []
for x in ["Hello ", "World "]:
    for y in ["Python", "Programming"]:
        word = x + y
        list_words.append(word)
print("List combining the words in two individual lists is : ", list_words)
```

OUTPUT
```
List combining the words in two individual lists is : ['Hello Python', 'Hello Programming', 'World Python', 'World Programming']
```

6. **Write a program that forms a list of the first character of every word in another list.**
```
list1 = ["Hello", "Welcome", "To", "The", "World", "Of", "Python"]
letters = []
for word in list1:
    letters.append(word[0])
print(letters)
```

OUTPUT
```
['H', 'W', 'T', 'T', 'W', 'O', 'P']
```

7. **Write a program to remove all duplicates from a list.**
```
num_list = [1,2,3,4,5,6,7,6,5,4]
print("Original List : ", num_list)
i=0
while i<len(num_list):
    num = num_list[i]
    for j in range(i+1, len(num_list)):
        val = num_list[j]
        if val == num:
            num_list.pop(j)
    i = i + 1
print("List after removing duplicates : ",num_list)
```

> The index must be an integer. If you specify a non-integer number as the index, then TypeError will be generated.

OUTPUT
```
Original List : [1, 2, 3, 4, 5, 6, 7, 6, 5, 4]
List after removing duplicates : [1, 2, 3, 4, 5, 6, 7]
```

8. **Write a program that counts the number of times each word is repeated in a list.**
```
words =["abc","def","ghi","lmn","lmn","def","pqr","rst","abc","lmn","def","xyz"]
length = len(words)
dups = []
uniq = []
```

```
i = 0
for word in words:
    count = words.count(word)
    print(word,count, end = ' ')
    words.remove(word)
```

OUTPUT
```
abc 2    ghi 1    lmn 3    pqr 1    abc 1    def 3
```

9. **Write a program to create a list of numbers in the specified range in particular steps. Reverse the list and print its values.**
```
num_list = []
m = int(input("Enter the starting of the range : "))
n = int(input("Enter the ending of the range : "))
o = int(input("Enter the steps in the range : "))
for i in range(m,n, o):
    num_list.append(i)
print("Original List :", num_list)
num_list.reverse()
print("Reversed List : ", num_list)
```

OUTPUT
```
Enter the starting of the range : 2
Enter the ending of the range : 30
Enter the steps in the range : 3
Original List : [2, 5, 8, 11, 14, 17, 20, 23, 26, 29]
Reversed List : [29, 26, 23, 20, 17, 14, 11, 8, 5, 2]
```

> append() and insert() methods are list methods. They cannot be called on other values such as string or integers.

10. **Write a program that passes a list to a function that scales each element in the list by a factor of 10. Print the list values at different stages to show that changes made to one list is automatically reflected in the other list.**
```
def change(list1):
    for i in range(len(list1)):
        list1[i] = list1[i] * 10
    print("After change in function, List is : ", list1)
num_list = [1,2,3,4,5,6]
print("Original List is : ", num_list)
change(num_list)
print("List after change is : ", num_list)
```

OUTPUT
```
Original List is :  [1, 2, 3, 4, 5, 6]
After change in function, List is :  [10, 20, 30, 40, 50, 60]
List after change is :  [10, 20, 30, 40, 50, 60]
```

11. **Write a program to create a series of Fibonnacci numbers.**
```
fib = [0,1]
sum = 0
a = 0
b = 1
for i in range(1,11):
```

```
        sum = a + b
        fib.append(sum)
        a = b
        b = sum
    print(fib)
```

OUTPUT

```
[0, 1, 1, 2, 3, 5, 8, 13, 21, 34, 55, 89]
```

12. **Write a program to add two matrices (using nested lists).**

```
    X = [[2,5,4],
        [1 ,3,9],
        [7 ,6, 2]]
    Y = [[1,8,5],
        [7,3,6],
        [4,0,9]]
    result = [[0,0,0],
            [0,0,0],
            [0,0,0]]
    for i in range(len(X)):
        for j in range(len(X[0])):
            result[i][j] = X[i][j] + Y[i][j]
    for r in result:
      print(r)
```

OUTPUT

```
[3, 13, 9]
[8, 6, 15]
[11, 6, 11]
```

13. **Program to find median of a list of numbers.**

```
    List = []
    n = int(input("Enter the number of elements to be inserted in the list : "))
    for i in range(n):
       print("Enter number ", i + 1, " : ")
       num = int(input())
       List.append(num)
    print("Sorted List is......")
    List = sorted(List)
    print(List)
    i = len(List) - 1
    if n%2 != 0:
        print("MEDIAN = ", List[i//2])
    else:
        print("MEDIAN = ", (List[i//2] + List[i+1//2])/2)
```

OUTPUT

```
Enter the number of elements to be inserted in the list : 6
Enter number 1 : 2
Enter number 2 : 9
Enter number 3 : 1
Enter number 4 : 7
```

```
Enter number 5 : 4
Enter number 6 : 8
Sorted List is......
[1, 2, 4, 7, 8, 9]
MEDIAN = 6.5
```

14. **Program to generate the Fibonacci sequence and store it in a list. Then find the sum of the even-valued terms.**

    ```
    a = 0
    b = 1
    n = int(input("Enter the number of terms : "))
    i=2
    List = [a,b]
    while i<n:
        s = a + b
        List.append(s)
        a = b
        b = s
        i += 1
    print(List)
    i=0
    sum = 0
    while i<n:
        sum += List[i]
        i += 2
    print("SUM = ", sum)
    ```

    > An alias is a second name for a piece of data. In Python, aliasing happens whenever one variable's value is assigned to another variable using the assignment operator[=].

    OUTPUT
    ```
    Enter the number of terms : 10
    [0, 1, 1, 2, 3, 5, 8, 13, 21, 34]
    SUM = 33
    ```

15. **Write a program that prompts the user to enter a list. Re-write the elements in another list in such a way that all even numbers are copied at the beginning and all odd numbers are copied at the end of the new list.**

    ```
    list = eval(input("ENter the list elements : "))
    length = len(list)
    new_list = []
    beg = 0
    end = length -1
    for i in list:
        if(i%2==0):
            new_list.insert(beg, i)
            beg +=1
        else:
            new_list.insert(end, i)
            end -= 1
    print(new_list)
    ```

    OUTPUT
    ```
    [2, 4, 6, 8, 10, 12, 1, 11, 3, 5, 9, 7]
    ```

16. **Write a program that prints the largest and the second largest value in a list of numbers.**
    ```
    list = eval(input("ENter the list elements : "))
    length = len(list)
    largest = sec_largest = list[0]
    for i in range(1,length-1):
        if(list[i]>largest):
            sec_largest = largest
            largest = list[i]
    print("LARGEST = ", largest,»SECOND LARGEST = ",sec_largest)
    ```

    OUTPUT
    ```
    ENter the list elements : [9,4,0,2,11,7,6,5]
    LARGEST = 11 SECOND LARGEST = 9
    ```

17. **Write a program that splits a string when a vowel is found. Also find the maximum length of the substring.**
    ```
    str = "HelloWorldPythonProgrammingisfun"
    l= []
    j=0
    k=0
    length = len(str)
    for i in range(length):
        if str[i] not in 'aeiou':
            j+=1
        else:
            l.append(str[k:j])     # appending consonant sub string
            k = j+1                # starting index of next consonant substring
            j = i +1               # starting index of next consonant substring
    print(l)
    length = len(l)                # finding len of list
    maxlen = 0
    for i in range(length):
        lenx = len(l[i])           # length of an element in list
        if(lenx>maxlen):
            maxlen = lenx
            maxsub = l[i]
    print(maxlen,maxsub)
    ```

    OUTPUT
    ```
    ['H', 'll', 'W', 'rldPyth', 'nPr', 'gr', 'mm', 'ng', 'sf']
    7 rldPyth
    ```

Key Terms

Immutable data: Data which cannot be modified. Assigning values to elements or slices of immutable data results in a runtime error.

Mutable data value: Data which can be modified.

List: A mutable data structure that can have elements that belong to different data types.

Nested list: Nested list means a list within another list.

List aliasing: When one list is assigned to another list using the assignment operator (=), then a new copy of the list is not made. Instead, assignment makes the two variables point to the one list in memory. This is also known as aliasing.

List cloning: The process of creating a separate copy of the list (not just the reference) is known as list cloning. The slice operation is used to clone a list.

Chapter Highlights

- List is a versatile data type available in Python, in which elements are written as a list of comma-separated values (items) between square brackets.
- Like strings, lists can also be sliced and concatenated.
- Once created, one or more elements of a list can be easily updated by giving the slice on the left-hand side of the assignment operator.
- We can append new values in the list and remove existing value(s) from the list using the `append()` method and `del` statement respectively.
- To insert items from another list at a particular location, we can use the `slice` operation. This would create a nested list, that is, a list within another list.
- Lists behave in a similar way as strings when operators like + (concatenation) and * (repetition) are used.

Review Questions

1. What is a list?
2. How can we define a list in Python?
3. With the help of an example demonstrate how lists can be sliced to access its values?
4. Explain the syntax of the slice operation.
5. What is the role of `del` statement in list variables?
6. Differentiate between shallow copy and deep copy of an object in Python.
7. Differentiate between the use of `del` statement and `remove()` function.
8. What is a nested list? How can we make one in Python?
9. Differentiate between list cloning and list aliasing.
10. Differentiate between `pop()` and `remove()` methods of list objects.
11. Explain the purpose of the following functions:
    a. `sorted()`　　b. `list()`　　c. `any()`　　d. `sum()`　　e. `min()`
12. Name the function or the operator that can be used for the following tasks:
    a. Return length of list
    b. Repeat elements in the list
    c. Join two lists
    d. Check if the value is present in the list
    e. Return maximum value in the list.
13. Name the methods that can be used in the following situations:
    a. Append an element to the list
    b. Count the number of times an element appears in the list
    c. Return the lowest index of obj in the list.
14. Explain the purpose of the following methods in Python:
    a. `insert()`　　b. `reverse()`　　c. `extend()`

15. Given a list, l = [1,2,3,4,5], write instructions for the following tasks,
    a. Set the third element to 100
    b. Insert 200 at the second index
    c. Append 300 to the list
    d. Remove the fourth element from the list
    e. Sort the list
    f. Reverse the list.

16. Given a list L = [1,2,3,4,[5,6,7,8],9,10], write expressions that will print the values:
    a. [5,6,7,8]   b. [6,7]   c. [2,3,4]   d. [1,3,[5,6,7,8], 10]

Programming Exercises

1. Write a program that creates a list of numbers in the series 2^n-1. Display only the even indexed values in this list.

2. Write a program that prints the elements along with their indices from the start and end of the list.

3. Write a program that reads two lists. Make another list of all those elements in the first list that are also present in the second list.

4. Write a program that creates a list ['a','bb','ccc','dddd',....]

5. Write a program that forms a list of numbers in the series
    a. 2/9, −5/13, 8/17, …
    b. $x, -x^2/2!, x^3/3!, -x^4/4!, x^5/5!,…$

6. Make a list of five random numbers. Write instructions to sum the elements and find the mean of the elements.

7. Write a program that adds the corresponding elements of two lists.

8. Make a list of the first ten letters of the alphabet, then using the slice operation do the following operations
    a. Print the first three letters from the list
    b. Print any three letters from the middle
    c. Print the letters from any particular index to the end of the list.

9. Write a program that prints the maximum value of the second half of the list.

10. Write a program that finds the sum of all the numbers using a `while` loop.

11. Write a program that finds the sum of all even numbers in a list.

12. Write a program that reverses a list using a loop.

13. Write a program to find whether a particular element is present in the list using a loop.

14. Write a program that prompts the user to enter an alphabet. Print all the words in the list that starts with that alphabet.

15. Write a program that prompts a number from user and adds it in a list. If the value entered by user is greater than 100, then add "EXCESS" in the list

16. Write a program that counts the number of times a value appears in the list. Use a loop to do the same.

17. Write a program to insert a value in a list at the specified location using while loop.

18. Write a program that creates a list of numbers from 1–50 that is either divisible by 3 or divisible by 6.

19. Write a program to create a list of numbers in the range 1 to 20. Then delete all the numbers from the list that are divisible by 3.

20. Write a program to randomly select an item from a list.

21. Write a program to print the string "HELLOWORLD" as

    ```
    H     E
     L   L
      O W
       O R
        LD
    ```

Fill in the Blanks

1. _____ defines a particular way of storing and organizing data in a computer.
2. When using slice operation, _____ is generated if the index is outside the list.
3. [10,20] < [20,10] will return _____.
4. `insert()`, `remove()` and `sort()` returns _____.
5. The `sort()` method uses _____ values to sort the values in the list.
6. _____ is used to print both index as well as an item in the list.
7. Fill in the blanks to create a list and print its second element.

   `List = ___10, 20, 30, 40]`

   `print(list[___])`

8. Fill in the blanks to create a list, reassign its third element and print the list.

   `List = [1,2,3,4,5__`

   `List[__] = 30`

   `print(__)`

9. Fill in the blanks to print "Hello" if the list contains 'H':
   `Letters = ['W', 'G', 'H']`
   `__ 'H'__ Letters:`
   `print("_____")`

10. Fill in the blanks to add 'G' to the end of the list and print the list's length.
    `Letters.____('G')`
    `print(__ ___)`

11. Fill in the blanks to print the letters in the list.
    `Letters = ['H', 'E', 'L', 'L','O']`
    `___ i __Letters__`
    `print(i)`

12. Fill in the blank to print the first two elements of the list:
    `List = [1,2,3,4,5,6]`
    `print(list[0_])`

13. The range of index values for a list of 10 elements will be _____.

State True or False

1. The index value starts from zero.
2. List is an immutable data structure.
3. Once created, one or more elements of a list can be easily updated.

4. It is possible to edit, add and delete elements from a list.
5. Slice operation can be used to insert items from another list or sequence at a particular location.
6. The slice operation is used to clone a list.
7. We cannot insert a list into another list.
8. When a list is assigned to another using the assignment operator, then a new copy of list is made.
9. Items in a list can be deleted by assigning an empty list to a slice of elements.
10. If you specify a non-integer number as the index, then IndexError will be generated.
11. Python sorts the original list with the help of sorted() function.

Multiple Choice Questions

1. If List = [1,2,3,4,5], then List[5] will result in _____.
   a. 4   b. 3   c. 2   d. Error

2. If List = [1,2,3,4,5] and we write List[3] = List[1], then what will be List[3]?
   a. 1   b. 3   c. 2   d. 4

3. type(x) will print _____.
   a. <class 'list'>   b. <class 'tuple'>
   c. <class 'int'>   d. Error

4. If List = [1,2,3,4,5,6,7,8,9,10], then print List[8:4:-1] will give _____.
   a. [2,3,4,5]   b. [9,8,7,6]   c. [6,7,8,9]   d. [5,4,3,2]

5. If List = min([sum([10,20]),max(abs(-30),4)]), then List = _____
   a. 10   b. 20   c. 30   d. 4

6. Which slice operation will reverse the list?
   a. Lists[-1::] b. numbers[::-1] c. numbers[:-1:] d. List[9:8:1]

7. If List = (12,8,7,5), then print(max(min(List[:2]),abs(-6))) will print _____.
   a. 12   b. 8   c. 7   d. 5

8. Which operator is used for list aliasing?
   a. =   b. +   c. *   d. &

9. Which operation is used for list cloning?
   a. assignment b. slice   c. comparison d. repetition

Give the Output

1. ```
   colors = ['red', 'blue', 'green']
   print(colors[2])
   print(len(colors))
   ```

2. ```
   list = ['abc', 'def', 'ghi', 'jkl']
   print(list[1:-1])
   list[0:2] = 'xyz'
   print(list)
   ```

3. ```
   list = ['abc', 'def', 'ghi', 'jkl', [1,2,3,4,5]]
   print(list[4][2])
   ```
   ```

4. ```
   list = ['p','r','o','g','r','a','m','m','i','n','g']
   print(list[2:5])
   print(list[:-5])
   print(list[5:])
   print(list[:])
   ```

5. ```
   even = [2,4,6]
   print(even + [10, 12, 14])
   print(even*2)
   even.insert(1,0)
   print(even)
   del even[2]
   print(even)
   ```

6. ```
   list = ['p','r','o','g','r','a','m']
   list.remove('p')
   print(list)
   print(list.pop(1))
   print(list)
   print(list.pop())
   print(list)
   ```

7. ```
   list = [9,4,3,8,0,2,3,6]
   print(list.index(3))
   print(list.count(8))
   list.sort()
   print(list)
   list.reverse()
   print(list)
   print(0 in list)
   ```

8. ```
   list = [(1, 2), [3, 4], '56', 78, 9.0]
   print(list[0], type(list[0]))
   print(list[2:3], type(list[0:1]))
   print(list[2], type(list[2]))
   ```

9. ```
   list =[ [1,2]*3 ] *4
   print(list)
   ```

10. ```
    list = [10, 20, 30, 40, 50, 60, 70, 80, 90]
    print(list[-4:-1])
    print(list[-1:-4])
    print(list[-5:])
    print(list[-6:-2:2])
    print(list[::-1])
    ```

11. ```
    list = [[10, 20, [30, 40, [50, 60]]]]
    print(list[0])
    print(list[0][2])
    print(list[0][2][2])
    print(list[0][0])
    print(list[0][2][1])
    print(list[0][2][2][0])
    ```

12. ```
    List = [100, 90, 80, 70, 60, 50]
    List[2] = List[1] - 20
    if 30 in List:
        print(List[3])
    else:
        print(List[4])
    ```

13. ```
    List = list(range(2, 20, 3))
    print(List[5])
    ```

14. ```
    def add_two(x):
        return x+2
    List = [10,20,30,40,50]
    result = list(map(add_two,List))
    print(result)
    ```

15. ```
    str = "abcdefghijklmno"
    for i in range(0, len(str), 2):
        print(str[i], end = ' ')
    ```

16. ```
    >>> eval("10 ** 2")
    ```

17. ```
    eval("'hello' + 'py'")
    ```

18. ```
    l1 = [1,2,3]
    l2 = ['a','b','c']
    l3 = [1.2,3.4,5.6]
    l4 = l1 + l2 + l3
    print(l4)
    ```

19. ```
    print([1,2,8,9] < [1,2,8,9,10])
    ```

20. ```
    l = [1,2,3,4,5,6,7,8,9,10]
    print(l[-1])
    print(l[l[0]])
    print(l[l[-8]])
    print(l[l[l[0]+1]]+2)
    ```

21. ```
    msg = ["PYTHON","is","a",["simple","iterpreted","OOP"],"language"]
    print(msg[2:4])
    print(msg[2:4][1][2])
    print(msg[2:4][1][2][1])
    print("im" in msg[2:4][1][2][1])
    print(msg[2:4][1][1][3:])
    print(msg[1]+msg[4])
    ```

22. ```
    >>> [1,2,3] +[1,2,3] == [1,2,3]*2
    ```

23. ```
    l = [1,2,3]
    l * 3 == [l,l,l]
    ```

24. ```
    msg = ["PYTHON","is","a",["simple","interpreted","OOP"],"language"]
    print(msg[::2])
    print('n' in msg[4])
    print(msg[2] in msg[4])
    ```
    ```

25. ```
    l = [1,2,3]
    print((l + [4,5,6])[3])
    ```

26. [1,2] == [1,2]

27. [1,2] is [1,2]

28. ```
    L = [1,2,3,4,5,6,7,8,9,10,11,12,13,14]
    print(L[::-1])
    print(L[-1:-2:-3])
    ```

29. ```
    for i in [1,2,3]:
        for j in [4,5,6]:
            print(i,j, end = "  ")
    ```

30. ```
    count = 0
    for i in range(5):
        for j in range(10):
            count = count + 1
    print(count)
    ```

31. ```
    list = [55, 66, 77, 88, 99]
    print("random.choice to select a random element from a list - ", random.choice(list))
    ```

32. ```
    import random
    city_list = ['New York', 'Los Angeles', 'Chicago', 'Houston', 'Philadelphia']
    print("Select random element from list - ", random.choice(city_list))
    ```

Find the Error

1. ```
   list = ['abc', 'def', 'ghi', 'jkl']
   print list[2.0]
   ```

2. ```
   even = [2,4,6]
   del even
   print(even)
   ```

3. ```
   list = [(1, 2), [3, 4], '56', 78, 9.0]
   list.remove('abc')
   ```

4. ```
   msg = "Hello"
   msg.append("World")
   print(msg)
   ```

5. [1,2,3] + 2

6. ```
   L = [1,2,3,4]
   L.remove(7)
   ```

7. [1,2,3] * 3.0
   ```

Answers

Fill in the Blanks
1. Data structure
2. IndexError
3. True
4. None
5. ASCII
6. enumerate() function
7. [, 1
8.], 2, List
9. if, in, Hello
10. append, len, (, Letters,)
11. for, in, :
12. :2
13. 0–10

State True or False
1. True
2. False
3. True
4. True
5. True
6. False
7. False
8. False
9. True
10. False
11. True

Multiple Choice Questions
1. b
2. c
3. d
4. b
5. c
6. b
7. b
8. a
9. b

Give the Output
1. green, 3
2. ['def', 'ghi']
   ['xyz', 'ghi', 'jkl']
3. 3
4. ['o', 'g', 'r']
   ['p', 'r', 'o', 'g', 'r', 'a']
   ['a', 'm', 'm', 'i', 'n', 'g']
   ['p', 'r', 'o', 'g', 'r', 'a', 'm', 'm', 'i', 'n', 'g']
5. [2, 4, 6, 10, 12, 14]
   [2, 4, 6, 2, 4, 6]
   [2, 0, 4, 6]
   [2, 0, 6]
6. ['r', 'o', 'g', 'r', 'a', 'm']
   o
   ['r', 'g', 'r', 'a', 'm']
   m
   ['r', 'g', 'r', 'a']
7. 2
   1
   [0, 2, 3, 3, 4, 6, 8, 9]
   [9, 8, 6, 4, 3, 3, 2, 0]
   True
8. ((1, 2), <type 'tuple'>)
   (['56'], <type 'list'>)
   ('56', <type 'str'>)
9. [[1, 2, 1, 2, 1, 2], [1, 2, 1, 2, 1, 2], [1, 2, 1, 2, 1, 2], [1, 2, 1, 2, 1, 2]]
10. [60, 70, 80]
    []
    [50, 60, 70, 80, 90]
    [40, 60]
    [90, 80, 70, 60, 50, 40, 30, 20, 10]
11. [10, 20, [30, 40, [50, 60]]]
    [30, 40, [50, 60]]
    [50, 60]
    10
    40
    50
12. 60
13. 17
14. [12, 22, 32, 42, 52]
15. a c e g i k m o
16. 100
17. 'hellopy'
18. [1, 2, 3, 'a', 'b', 'c', 1.2, 3.4, 5.6]
19. True
20. 10   2   4   6
21. ['a', ['simple', 'iterpreted', 'OOP']]
    OOP   O   False   rpreted   islanguage
22. True
23. False
24. ['PYTHON', 'a', 'language']
    True
    True
25. ['PYTHON', 'a', 'language']   True   True
26. True
27. False
28. [14, 13, 12, 11, 10, 9, 8, 7, 6, 5, 4, 3, 2, 1]
    [14]
29. 1 4   1 5   1 6   2 4   2 5   2 6   3 4   3 5   3 6
30. 50
31. random.choice to select a random element from a list - 55
32. Select random element from list - Chicago

Find the Error

1. `TypeError: list indices must be integers, not float`
2. `NameError: name 'even' is not defined`
3. `ValueError: list.remove(x): x not in list`
4. `AttributeError: 'str' object has no attribute 'append'`
5. `TypeError: can only concatenate list (not "int") to list`
6. `ValueError: list.remove(x): x not in list`
7. `TypeError: can't multiply sequence by non-int of type 'float'`

13

Tuple

Chapter Objectives

The chapter analyzes another important data structure in Python – that is, tuple. The chapter explains where and how tuples can be used to manipulate data. The topics discussed in this chapter include:

- Creating and accessing values of a tuple
- Updating and deleting values
- Indexing, assigning, joining and unpacking tuple objects
- Using tuples to return multiple values from a function
- The count() and zip() methods
- Comparing tuples and lists
- Nested tuples

In the last chapter, we studied lists. In this chapter we will look into another data type in Python – the tuple. A tuple is very similar to lists but differs in two things.

- First, a tuple is an immutable object. This means that while you can change the value of one or more elements in a list, you cannot change the values in a tuple.
- Second, tuples use parentheses to define its elements whereas lists use square brackets.

13.1 CREATING A TUPLE

Creating a tuple is very simple and almost similar to creating a list. You need to just put the different comma-separated values within a parenthesis.

| ```
#Creates an empty tuple
Tup1 = ()
print(Tup1)
OUTPUT
()
``` | ```
#Creates tuple with a
single element
Tup1 = (5,)
print(Tup1)
OUTPUT
5
``` | ```
#Tuple of integers
Tup1 = (1,2,3,4,5)
print(Tup1)
OUTPUT
(1, 2, 3, 4, 5)
``` |
|---|---|---|
| ```
#Creates a tuple of
#mixed values
Tup5 = (1,"abc"
,2.3,'d')
print(Tup5)
OUTPUT
(1, 'abc', 2.3, 'd')
``` | ```
#A tuple of characters
Tup1 = ('a','b','c','d')
print(Tup1)
OUTPUT
('a', 'b', 'c', 'd')
``` | ```
# Creates a tuple of strings
Tup1 = ("abc",''def'',''ghi")
print(Tup1)
OUTPUT
('abc', 'def', 'ghi')
``` |
| ```
#Tuple of floating-point
#numbers
Tup1 = (1.2,2.3,3.4,4.5)
print(Tup1)
OUTPUT
(1.2, 2.3, 3.4, 4.5)
``` | | |
```

Key points to remember

- Any set of comma-separated values written without an identifying symbol like brackets or parentheses, etc., is treated as a tuple by default.
- If you want to create a tuple with a single element, you must add a comma after the element. In the absence of a comma, Python treats the element as an ordinary data type.
- We can use the `eval()` function to input a tuple. But while specifying the input elements, enclose them within parentheses as shown in the code.

```
print('A', "bed", 5, 6.7)
OUTPUT
A bcd 5 6.7
```

```
a,b,c = 10, 20,30
print(a,b,c)
OUTPUT
10 20 30
```

```
# comma after first element
Tup = (15,)
print type(Tup)
OUTPUT
<type 'tuple'>
```

```
#comma missing
Tup = (10)
print type(Tup)
OUTPUT
<type 'int'>
```

```
#eval() Function to read Tuple
Tup = eval(input("Enter values of the tuple :"))
print(Tup)
print(type(Tup))
OUTPUT
Enter values of the tuple: (1,2,'a','bcd',7.8)
(1, 2, 'a', 'bcd', 7.8)
<class 'tuple'>
```

- We can also use the `tuple()` function to create a tuple with the specified sequence.

```
#Using the tuple() Function
tup = tuple("abc")
print(tup)
tup = tuple ([1, 2,3])
print(tup)
OUTPUT
('a' , ' b ', 'c ")
(1, 2 , 3)
```

13.2 UTILITY OF TUPLES

In real-world applications, tuples are extremely useful for representing *records* or structures as we call in other programming languages. These structures store related information about a subject together. The information belongs to different data types. For example, a tuple that stores information about a student will have roll_no, name, course, total_marks, avg, etc. If you carefully observe these individual elements, you will see that they belong to different data types. For example, roll_no can be an integer or an alphanumeric value, name and course will be a string, total_marks and avg can be floating-point numbers.

> **Example 13.1**
>
> ```
> Program to illustrates divmod() function
> quo, rem = divmod(157,4)
> print("Quotient = ",quo)
> print("Remainder = ",rem)
> ```
> **OUTPUT**
> Quotient= 39
> Remainder= 1

Some built-in functions return a tuple. For example, the `divmod()` function returns two values – quotient as well as the remainder after performing the divide operation.

Example 13.2

```
Tup1 = (1,20,3,40,5,60,7,80,9,100,11,120)
print("Tup[4:8] = ", Tup1[4:8])
print("Tup[:5] = ", Tup1[:5])
print("Tup[3:] = ", Tup1[3:])
print("Tup[:] = ", Tup1[:])
print("Tup[:-4] =", Tup1[:-4])
print("Tup[-1:5] =", Tup1[-1:5])
print("Tup[::-2] =", Tup1[::-2])
```

OUTPUT

```
Tup[4:8] = (5, 60, 7, 80)
Tup[:5] = (1, 20, 3, 40, 5)
Tup[3:] = (40, 5, 60, 7, 80, 9, 100, 11, 120)
Tup[:] = (1, 20, 3, 40, 5, 60, 7, 80, 9, 100, 11, 120)
Tup[:-4] = (1, 20, 3, 40, 5, 60, 7, 80)
Tup[-1:5] = ()
Tup[::-2] = (120, 100, 80, 60, 40, 20)
```

13.3 ACCESSING VALUES IN A TUPLE

Again, like other sequences (like strings and lists), indices in a tuple start at 0. Slice operation, concatenation and other operations possible with other sequences can also be applied on tuples.

In the slice operation, we can also use negative indices, strides and even expressions.

When accessing a tuple, if the index is out of the range of legal indices of the tuple, then Python raises an IndexError.

The start and stop parameters of the slice operation specify the boundaries of elements to be accessed. All elements falling within the boundary are returned.

Example 13.3

```
#Slice operation on a tuple
tup = (1,'a',2,'bcd',3.4,5,'e',6.7,'efg')
print(tup[3])
print(tup[10 - 4 *2 + 5])
print(tup[-5])
print(tup[3:6])
print(tup[2:7:2])
print(tup[-10:10])
```

OUTPUT

```
bcd
6.7
3.4
('bcd', 3.4, 5)
(2, 3.4, 'e')
(1, 'a', 2, 'bcd', 3.4, 5, 'e', 6.7, 'efg')
```

13.4 UPDATING TUPLE

We have already said that **tuple is immutable**. So, you cannot change the value(s) in the tuple. You can only extract values from a tuple to form another tuple.

Example 13.4

```
#Updating tuple
tup = (1,'a ',2,'bcd',3.4,5,'e')
tup[3] = 'Not Possible'
print(tup)
```

OUTPUT

```
Traceback (most recent call last):
  File "C:\Python37\try.py",line 2, in <module>
    tup(3) = 'Not Possible'
TypeError: 'tuple' object does not support item assignment
```

Example 13.5

```
tup = (1,2,3)
print(tup[10])
```

OUTPUT

```
Traceback (most recent call last):
  File "C:\Python37\try.py",line 2, in <module>
print(tup[10])
IndexError: tuple index out of range
```

```
tup = (1,2,3)
print(tup[ -10: 10])
```

OUTPUT

(1, 2, 3)

13.5 DELETING ELEMENTS IN TUPLE

Since tuple is an immutable data structure, you cannot delete value(s) from it. Of course, you can create a new tuple that has all elements in your tuple except the ones you do not want (those you wanted to be deleted). However, the entire tuple can be deleted by using the `del` statement.

Example 13.6

```
Tup1 = (1,2,3,4,5)
Tup2 = (6,7,8,9,10)
Tup3 = Tup1 + Tup2
print(Tup3)
```

OUTPUT

(1, 2, 3, 4, 5, 6, 7, 8, 9, 10)

```
Tup1 = (1,2,3,4,5)
del Tup1[3] #delete an element
print(Tup1)
```

OUTPUT

```
Traceback (most recent call last):
  File "C:\Users\Python37\try.py", line 2, in <module>
    del Tup1[3]
Type Error: 'tuple' object doesn't support item deletion
```

```
Tup1 = (1,2,3,4,5)
#delete tuple
delTup1
print(Tupl)
```

OUTPUT

```
Traceback (most recent call last):
  File "C:\Users\Python37\try.py", line 4, in <module>
    print(Tupl)
NameError: name 'Tupl' is not defined
```

13.6 JOINING TUPLES

Like lists, two or more tuples can be joined using the + operator. The + operator requires that both the operands must be of tuple types. Numbers or any other type values cannot be added to a tuple. To add a single element to a tuple, we must use comma after the value.

Example 13.7

```
#Joining Tuples
tup1 = (1,2,3)
tup2 = (4,5,6)
tup3 = tup1 + tup2
print(tup3)
```

OUTPUT

(1, 2, 3, 4, 5, 6)

```
#Joining tuples with a
#non-number value
tup1 = (1,2,3)
tup2 = tup1 + 'a'
print(tup2)
```

OUTPUT

```
Traceback (most recent call last):
  Fi le "C:\Python37\try.py", line 2, in <module>
    tup2 = tup1 +'a'
TypeError: can only concatenate tuple (not "str") to tuple
```

```
#Joining single
#value to a tuple
tup1 = (1,2,3)
tup2 = tup1 + (4,)
print(tup2)
```

OUTPUT

(1, 2, 3, 4)

13.7 UNPACKING TUPLES

Creating a tuple from a set of values is called packing. Correspondingly, creating individual values from a tuple is known as unpacking. The syntax of unpacking can be given as,

```
var1, var2, var3, ...., varn = tuple_variable
```

While unpacking a tuple, remember that the number of elements in the tuple must match with the number of variables on the left side of the assignment operator.

Tuple packing and unpacking are very useful to change the values in a tuple. We know that tuples are immutable objects in Python, so their values cannot be changed. In case we need to change values, there are three ways – unpacking and packing the tuple is just one of them.

Example 13.8

```
# Unpacking tuple
tup = (1,'a',2.0,'bcd',3)
(a,b,c,d,e) = tup
print("a = ",a, end = '')
print("b = ",b, end = '')
print("c = ",c, end = '')
print("d = ",d, end = '')
print("e = ",e, end = '')
```

OUTPUT
```
a = 1 b = a c = 2.0 d = bcd e = 3
```

```
# Packing tuple
a=1; b='a'; c=2.0; d='bcd'
tup = (a,b,c,d)
print("tup = " ,tup)
```

OUTPUT
```
tup = (1, 'a', 2.0, 'bcd')
```

The first way is to create a new tuple with modified values.

The second way is to first unpack the tuples into variables. Modify the value of the variables and then pack those variables to form a tuple.

The third way is to convert a tuple into a list using the `list()` function. Modify the list values and then use the `tuple()` function to convert the list into a tuple.

13.8 BASIC TUPLE OPERATIONS

Like strings and lists, you can also perform operations such as concatenation, repetition, etc. on tuples. The only difference is that a new tuple should be created when a change is required in an existing tuple. Table 13.1 summarizes some operations on tuples.

Table 13.1 Operations on tuples

Operation	Expression	Output
Length	`len((1,2,3,4,5,6))`	6
Concatenation	`(1,2,3) + (4,5,6)`	(1, 2, 3, 4, 5, 6)
Repetition	`('Python..')*3`	Python.. Python.. Python..'
Membership	`5 in (1,2,3,4,5,6,7,8,9)`	True
Iteration	`for i in (1,2,3,4,5,6,7,8,9,10):` `    print(i,end=' ')`	1,2,3,4,5,6,7,8,9,10

Comparison (Use >, <, ==)	`Tup1 = (1,2,3,4,5)`
	`Tup2 = (1,2,3,4,5)`
	`print(Tup1>Tup2)`
		False

(Continued)

Table 13.1	Continued	
Operation	Expression	Output
Maximum	`max(1,9,3,6,4,0)`	9
Minimum	`min(1,9,3,6,4,0)`	0
Convert to Tuple (converts a sequence into a tuple)	`tuple("PYTHON")` `tuple([1,2,3,4,5])`	('P', 'Y', 'T', 'H', 'O', 'N') (1, 2, 3, 4, 5)

While using the **max()** and **min()** functions, remember that the values in the tuple must be of the same type. If the values are not of the same type, then **TypeError** will be returned.

Example 13.9

```
# Finding largest and smallest
value
tup = (23,75,12,90,82)
print("Largest Value= ",max(tup))
print("Smallest Value = ",min(tup))
```

OUTPUT
Largest Value = 90
Smallest Value = 12

```
#Finding largest and smallest value in a tuple
tup = (23,'a',12.56,90,'bcd')
print("Largest Value= ",max(tup))
print("Smallest Value = ",min(tup))
```

OUTPUT
Traceback (most recent call last):
  File "C:\Python37\try.py", line 3, in <module>
    print("largest Value = ",max(tup))
TypeError: '>'not supported between instances of 'str' and 'int'

13.9 TUPLE ASSIGNMENT

Tuple assignment is a very powerful feature in Python. It allows a tuple of variables on the left side of the assignment operator to be assigned values from a tuple given on the right side of the assignment operator. Each value is assigned to its respective variable.

In case an expression is specified on the right side of the assignment operator, that expression is first evaluated and then assignment is done. This feature makes tuple assignment quite versatile. The codes given below show the different ways of tuple assignment.

Example 13.10

```
#An unnamed tuple of values assigned to values of
#another unnamed tuple
(val1, val2, val3) = (10,20,30)
print(val1, val2, val3)
Tupl = (10, 20, 30)
(val1, val2, val3) = Tupl #tuple assigned to
another tuple
print(val1, val2, val3)
```

OUTPUT
10 20 30
10 20 30

```
#Expressions are evaluated
before assignment
(val1, val2, val3, val4)= (1+2,
4/3 - 5 , 6%7, 8 ** 2)
print(val1, val2, val3, val4)
```

OUTPUT
3 -3.666666666666667 6 64

Note that *when assigning values to a tuple, you must make sure that the number of values on both the sides of the assignment operator must be same.* Otherwise, an error will be generated as shown in Example 13.11.

Example 13.11

```
(val1, val2, val3, val4) = (1+2, 6%7, 8 ** 2)
print(val1, val2, val3, val4)
Traceback (most recent call last):
  File "C:\Users\Python37\try.py", line 1, in <module>
    (val1, val2, val3, val4) = (1+2, 6%7, 8 ** 2)
ValueError: not enough values to unpack (expected 4, got 3)
```

13.10 ACCESSING USING INDEX

Like other sequences, we can access an individual element of a tuple by using its index. Correspondingly, we can also get the index of an element by specifying the element in the index method. The index() method is used to get the index of an element in the tuple. If the element being searched is not present in the list, then error is generated. The syntax of index() is given as, **list.index(obj)** where, obj is the object whose index has to looked.

Example 13.12

```
Tup = (11, 67, 642,'AB',
"Good Morning", 4.5)
print(Tup.index('AB'))
```
OUTPUT
3

```
Tup = (11, 67, 642,'AB', "Good Morning", 4.5)
print(Tup.index(5.4))
Traceback (most recent call last):
  File "C:\Users\Python37\try.py", line 2, in <module>
    print(Tup.index(5.4))
ValueError: tuple.index(x): x not in tuple
```

13.11 TUPLES FOR RETURNING MULTIPLE VALUES

We have learnt that a function can return only a single value. But at times, we need to return more than one value from a function. In such situations, it is preferable to group together multiple values and return them together.

Example 13.13

```
#Program to return the highest as well as the lowest score
def max_min_score(vals):
    x = max(vals)
    y = min(vals)
    return (x,y)
score = (99, 98, 90, 97, 89, 86, 93, 82}
(max_ score, min_score) = max_min_score(score)
print(" Highest Score = ", max_ score)
print(" Lowest Score = ", min_score)
```
OUTPUT
Highest Score = 99
Lowest Score = 82

13.12 NESTED TUPLES

In Python, users can easily define a tuple inside another tuple. Such a tuple is called a nested tuple. Consider the nested table in the code given in Example 13.14 that stores and prints the details of employees.

Example 13.14

```
#Nested Tuple
Emps = (("Arav", "Back Office", 35000), ("Chaitanya", "Technical Assistant",
50000), ("Dhruvika", "Programmer", 100000))
for i in Emps:
  print(i)
```

OUTPUT

```
('Arav', 'Back Office', 35000)
('Chaitanya', 'Technical Assistant', 50000)
('Dhruvika', 'Programmer', 100000)
```

You can even specify a list within a tuple. The code given below prints the name of the topper and her marks in 4 subjects. These marks are specified as a list in the tuple Topper.

Example 13.15

```
# List within a nested tuple
Toppers = (("Janvi",[94, 95, 96, 97]),("Khushi",[99, 95, 90, 93]), ("Myra",[91,
95, 93, 94]))
print("SecondTopper is:", Toppers[1])
```

OUTPUT

```
Second Topper is: ('Khushi', [99, 95, 90, 93])
```

13.13 THE count() METHOD

The count() method returns the number of elements with a specific value in a tuple.

Example 13.16

```
#count() method on tuple
tup = (10,7,8,10,9, 7,3,8,5,8,1,8)
print(tup.count(8))
tup = ("abc","def","abc","efg")
print(tup.count("abc"))
```

OUTPUT

```
4
2
```

13.14 THE zip() FUNCTION

Zip is a built-in function that takes two or more sequences and "zips" them into a list of tuples. The tuple thus formed has one element from each sequence. The code given below illustrates this concept.

Example 13.17

```
#Count number of y using count()
tup = "xyyyyzyyyzxzzedbgsyyy"
print(" Number of y = ", tup.count('y'))
```

OUTPUT

```
Number of y = 10
```

```
# zip() method
Tup = (2,4,6,8,10)
List1 = ('A','E','I','O','U]
print(list((zip(Tup, List1))))
```

OUTPUT

```
[(2, 'A'), (4, 'E'), (6, 'I'), (8, 'O'),
(10, 'U')]
```

From the output, we see that the **result of `zip()` function is a list of tuples** where each tuple contains a character from the list and an integer from the tuple. The example, we had seen had an equal number of values in the list and tuple but **if the two sequences have different lengths then the result have the length of the shorter one** as illustrated in the code given below. We can even print the elements in a tuple using the for statement as shown below.

Example 13.18

```
#zip() method with unequal parameters
Tup = (2,4,6)
listl = ['A','E','I','O','U']
print(list((zip(Tup, Listl))))
```

OUTPUT
[(2, 'A'), (4, 'E'), (6, 'I')]

```
#printing tuple with for loop
Tup = (2,4,6)
list1 = ['A','E','I','O','U']
Tup = list((zip(Tup, Listl)))
fori, char in Tup:
   print(i, char)
```

OUTPUT
2A
4E
6I

Key points to remember

- Tuples can be converted into lists, and vice-versa using the built-in `tuple()` function that takes a list and returns a tuple with the same elements. Similarly, the `list()` function takes a tuple and returns a list.
- You cannot divide or subtract tuples. If you try to do so you will get a TypeError with "unsupported operand type."
- Since tuples are immutable, they do not support methods like `sort` and `reverse`, as these methods modify the existing sequence.

Example 13.19

```
# list from tuple and
vice versa
Tup = {2,4,6}
List1 = list(Tup)
print("LIST = ", Listl)
Listl = Listl +
[8,10,12]
Tup1 = tuple(List1)
print("TUPLE = ", Tup1)
```

OUTPUT
LIST = [2, 4, 6]
TUPLE= (2, 4, 6, 8, 10, 12)

```
#subtracting two tuples
Tup1 = (2,4,6)
Tup2 = (1,3,5)
Tup3 = Tup1 - Tup2
print(Tup3)
```

OUTPUT
Traceback (most recent call last):
  File " C:\Users\Python37\try.py", line 3, in <module>
    Tup3 = Tup1 - Tup2
TypeError: unsupported operand type(s) for -: 'tuple' and 'tuple'

```
# reverse method on tuple
Tup1 = (2,1,4,8,6)
Tup1.reverse()
print(Tup1)
```

OUTPUT
Traceback (most recent call last):
  File "C:\Users\try.py", line 2, in <module>
    Tup1.reverse()
AttributeError: 'tuple' object has no attribute 'reverse'

- However, Python has a built-in function `sorted()`, which takes any sequence as a parameter and returns a new list with the same elements but in a different order. For example, the code given below illustrates this concept.
- You can use string formatting feature to print values in the Tuple. This is shown in the code given below.

Example 13.20

```
#Program to sort a tuple of values
Tup = {5,1,0,2,8,3,9}
print(sorted(Tup))
```

OUTPUT
[0, 1, 2, 3, 5, 8, 9]

```
#Program to illustrate string formatting with tuple
Tup ={"Mira", 12, 94.534}
print("%s studying in class %d scored %.2f aggregate" %{Tup[0], Tup[1], Tup[2]})
```

OUTPUT
Mira studying in class 12 scored 94.53 aggregate

13.15 ADVANTAGES OF TUPLE OVER LIST

Although tuples are similar to lists, there are some advantages of implementing a tuple over a list. Some of these advantages are listed below.

- Since tuple are immutable, iterating through tuple is faster than iterating over a list. This means that tuple performs better than a list.
- Tuples can be used as key for a dictionary but lists cannot be used as keys. We will learn about dictionaries in the next chapter.
- Tuples are best suited for storing data that is write-protected (you can read the data but cannot write to it).
- Tuples can be used in place of lists where the number of values is known and small.
- If you are passing a tuple as an argument to a function, then the potential for unexpected behavior due to aliasing gets reduced.
- Multiple values from a function can be returned using a tuple.

PROGRAMMER'S ZONE

1. **Write a program to swap two values using tuple assignment.**
    ```
    val1 = 5
    val2 = 7
    print("val1 = ",val1, " val2 = ",val2)
    (val1,val2) = (val2,val1)
    print("val1 = ",val1, " val2 = ",val2)
    ```

    OUTPUT
    ```
    val1 = 5 val2 = 7
    val1 = 7 val2 = 5
    ```

    > If a negative value is used for the step, the slice is done backwards.

2. **Write a program using a function that returns the area and perimeter of a rectangle whose length and breadth are passed as argument.**
    ```
    def cal_a_p(l,b):
        return (l*b, 2*(l+b))
    l = float(input("Enter the length of the rectangle : "))
    b = float(input("Enter the breadth of the rectangle : "))
    (area, perimeter) = cal_a_p(l,b)
    print("Area of the rectangle = ", area)
    print("Perimeter of the rectangle = ", perimeter)
    ```

    OUTPUT
    ```
    Enter the length of the rectangle : 7
    Enter the breadth of the rectangle : 5
    Area of the rectangle =  35.0
    Perimeter of the rectangle =  24.0
    ```

    > Tuples are faster than lists, but they cannot be changed.

    > You cannot add elements to a tuple. Methods like append or extend do not work with tuple.

3. **Write a program that has a nested list to store toppers' details. Edit and reprint the details.**
    ```
    Toppers = (("Mayank", "BCA",94.0), ("Chainika", "BTech", 90.0), ("Dhruv", "BSc", 89))
    for i in Toppers:
        print(i)
    choice = input("Do you want to edit the details : ")
    ```

    > Slicing can be done on tuples.

```
if choice == 'y':
    name = input("Enter the name of the students whose details are to be edited : ")
    new_name = input("Enter the correct name : ")
    new_course = input("Enter the correct course : ")
    new_aggr = input("Enter the correct aggregate : ")
    i = 0
    new_Toppers = ()
    while i<len(Toppers):
        if Toppers[i][0] == name:
            new_Toppers += (new_name, new_course, new_aggr)
        else:
            new_Toppers += Toppers[i]
        i+=1
for i in new_Toppers:
    print(i,end = ' ')
```

> If the index specified in the Tuple slice is too big, then an IndexError exception is raised.

OUTPUT
```
('Mayank', 'BCA', 94.0)
('Chainika', 'BTech', 90.0)
('Dhruv', 'BSc', 89)
Do you want to edit the details : y
Enter the name of the students whose details are to be edited : chainika
Enter the correct name : Priyanshu
Enter the correct course : BTech
Enter the correct aggregate : 95
Mayank BCA 94.0 Chainika BTech 90.0 Dhruv BSc 89
```

4. **Write a program that scans an email address and forms a tuple of user name and domain.**
```
addr = 'learn_python@gmail.com'
user_name, domain_name = addr.split('@')
print("User Name : ", user_name)
print("Domain Name : ", domain_name)
```

> You can't delete elements from a tuple. Methods like remove or pop do not work with tuple.

OUTPUT
```
User Name : learn_python
Domain Name : gmail.com
```

5. **Write a program that has numbers (both positive as well as negative). Make a new tuple that has only odd values from this list.**
```
Tup = (-12,11,22,-19,13,44,-18,15,26)
newTup = ()
for i in Tup:
    if i%2 == 0:
        newTup += (i,)
print(newTup)
```

> Unlike lists, tuples do not support remove(), pop(), append(), sort(), reverse(), and insert() methods.

OUTPUT
```
(-12, 22, 44, -18, 26)
```

6. Write a program that has two sequences. The first program stores some questions and the second stores the corresponding answers. Use the zip() function to form a valid question-answer series.

```
Ques = ["National Bird", "Prime Minister", " number of bones"]
Ans = ["Peacock", "Narendra Modi", 206]
for q,a in zip(Ques, Ans):
    print("Our", q, " is : ", end=" ")
    print( a)
```

> Reassigning a value in a tuple causes a TypeError.

OUTPUT

```
Our National Bird is : Peacock
Our Prime Minister is : Narendra Modi
Our number of bones is : 206
```

Key Terms

Tuple: An immutable data structure that stores related items together.

Packing a tuple: Creating a tuple from a set of values is called packing.

Unpacking a tuple: Creating individual values from a tuple is known as unpacking.

Nested tuple: Tuple inside another tuple.

Chapter Highlights

- A tuple is an immutable object. This means that while you can change the value of one or more elements in a list, you cannot change the values in a tuple.
- Tuples use parentheses to define their elements whereas lists use square brackets.
- Any set of comma-separated values written without an identifying symbol like brackets or parentheses, etc., is treated as a tuple by default.
- We can use the `eval()` function to input a tuple.
- The `tuple()` function is used to create a tuple with the specified sequence.
- When accessing a tuple, if the index is out of the range of legal indices of the tuple, then Python raises an IndexError.
- Since tuple is an immutable data structure, you cannot delete value(s) from it.
- Two or more tuples can be joined using the + operator. The + operator requires that both the operands must be of tuple types.
- `Zip` is a built-in function that takes two or more sequences and "zips" them into a list of tuples.
- Python has a built-in function `sorted()`, which takes any sequence as a parameter and returns a new list with the same elements but in a different order.

Review Questions

1. With the help of an example, explain the significance of + and * operators when used with tuples.
2. Can we change the value of one or more elements in a tuple? Justify your answer.
3. How is a tuple different from a list?

4. Can we add or delete values from a tuple?
5. What are nested tuples?
6. Explain different ways of defining a tuple?
7. How will you join two tuples?
8. With the help of an example differentiate between packing and unpacking a tuple.
9. Why do we use the `index()` function?
10. Demonstrate the use of membership operators on a tuple.
11. Explain the use of `zip()` function.
12. Differentiate between `sort()` and `sorted()`.
13. List some advantages of using tuple over lists.

Programming Exercises

1. Write a program that creates a list ['a', 'b', 'c'], then create a tuple from that list. Now, do the opposite. That is, create the tuple ('a', 'b', 'c'), and then create a list from it.
2. Create a tuple that has just one element, which in turn may have three elements 'a', 'b', and 'c'. Print the length of this tuple.
3. Write a program that has a predefined list. Create a copy of this list in such a way that only those values that are in valid_tuple are added in the new list.
4. Create a nested tuple that has marks of at least 5 students obtained in three subjects. Now, perform the following operations on it.
   a. Display the marks of the fourth student.
   b. Display the marks obtained by the second student in the first subject.
   c. Display the total marks obtained by each student.
   d. Find the average (or mean) marks obtained by each student.
   e. Using the average marks obtained by each student, calculate the average marks obtained by all the students (finding the mean of means).
   f. For each student display the maximum and minimum marks obtained.
5. Write a program that concatenates the first tuple at the end of the second tuple.
6. Write a program that creates the following tuples.
   i. Squares of first 10 natural numbers
   ii. Cube of first 10 odd numbers
   iii. First 10 multiples of 7
   iv. –5, –3, –1, 1, 3
7. Write a program that creates a tuple of at least 10 pair of values. Count the number of pairs having both values odd.
8. Write a program that has two tuples. Check if the first tuple is a super-set of the second tuple.

Fill in the Blanks

1. _____ use parentheses to define its elements.
2. _____ function takes two or more sequences and "zips" them into a list of tuples.

3. To add a single element in the set, use the _____ method and to add multiple elements in the set, use the _____ method.
4. The _____ function to create a tuple with the specified sequence.
5. The entire tuple can be deleted by using the _____ statement.
6. If tup = ("abc", "def", "ghi", "jkl"), tup[–1] will print _____.
7. print(len((((('a',1,'bcd',3.0),'e',4.5),'fgh',(99,1.0)))) will give output ___.
8. We can access an individual element of a tuple by using its _____.
9. _____ are used to return more than one value from a function.
10. The _____ method returns the number of elements with a specific value in a tuple.

State True or False

1. You cannot perform operations like concatenation, repetition, etc., on tuples.
2. It is possible to specify a list within a tuple.
3. If a sequence is specified without parenthesis, it is to be treated as a list by default.
4. Lists are faster than tuples.
5. A tuple can be sliced.
6. Once created, one or more elements of a tuple can be easily updated.
7. It is possible to edit, add and delete elements in a tuple.
8. Tuples can store information that belongs to different data types.
9. Numbers or any other type values cannot be added to a tuple.
10. `max()` and `min()` functions can be used on a tuple iff the values in it are of different data types.
11. In the `zip()` function, if the two sequences have different lengths, then the result has the length of the longer one.
12. Tuples cannot be divided or subtracted.

Multiple Choice Questions

1. If tup = ("abc", "def", "ghi", "jkl"), then tup("def") will return _____.
   a. 1   b. 2   c. 0   d. Error
2. print((0, 10, 20) < (0, 30, 40)) will print _____.
   a. True   b. False   c. Equal   d. Error
3. Which data structure allows you to return multiple values from a function?
   a. List   b. Tuple   c. Dictionary   d. Set
4. Which of the following will not create a tuple?
   a. T = ()   b. t = (10)   c. t = ([1,2],)   d. t = ((1,2),3)
5. Which of the following functions can be used to input a tuple?
   a. `input()`   b. `eval()`   c. `tuple()`   d. `raw_input()`
6. Which function returns a tuple of two values?
   a. `divmod()`   b. `input()`   c. `eval()`   d. `tuple()`

7. Indices in a tuple start at _____.
   a. -1   b. 0   c. 1   d. 10

8. Which error is returned when index is out of the range of legal indices of the tuple?
   a. ValueError   b. TypeError   c. IndexError   e. SliceError

9. Which error is returned when we try to modify the value of an element in a tuple?
   a. ValueError   b. TypeError   c. IndexError   e. NameError

10. The result of zip() function is a list of _____.
    a. tuples   b. lists   c. values   d. strings

11. Which error is returned if we divide two tuples?
    a. ValueError b. TypeError   c. IndexError   e. NameError

12. Identify the function or method which is not supported on tuples?
    a. sorted()   b. reverse()   c. count()   d. index()

13. Identify the function or method which is supported on tuples?
    a. append()   b. extend()   c. sort()   d. list()

Give the Output

1. ```
   tup1 = (1,2,3)
   tup2 = (1.0,2.0,3.0)
   print(tup1 == tup2)
   ```

2. ```
   Tup = ("abc", "def")
   (key, value) = Tup
   print(key, value)
   ```

3. ```
   Tup = (1,2,3)
   Add_Tup = Tup + Tup
   print(Add_Tup)
   Mul_Tup = Tup * 3
   print(Mul_Tup)
   ```

4. ```
   msg = "HelloWorld"
   pairs = []
   for i in range(1, len(msg), 2):
       first = msg[i - 1]
       second = msg[i]
       pairs.append((first, second))
   for item in pairs:
       print(item)
   ```

5. ```
   Tup  = (1, 'abc')
   List = [1, 'abc']
   print(Tup == List)
   print(Tup == tuple(List))
   print(list(Tup) == List)
   print((1, 2) + (3, 4))
   ```
   ```

6. ```
   list = ['Good', 'Morning']
   y, x = list
   print(x, y)
   ```

7. ```
   A = ('Chinu', 30, 'Female')
   B = ('Varun', 32, 'Male')
   for i in [A, B]:
       print('%s is a %d year old %s' %i)
   ```

8. ```
   Tup = ('Good',)
   for i in range(4):
       Tup = (Tup,)
   print(Tup)
   ```

9. ```
   Tup1='a','bcd',12.34
   Tup2=Tup1,(5,6,7,8)
   print(Tup2)
   ```

10. ```
    Tup = (1, 2, [3, 4])
    Tup[2][0] = 5
    print(Tup)
    ```

11. ```
    Tup = ("Good Morning")
    print(Tup.index('M'), end = ' ')
    print(Tup.index('n', 5))
    print(Tup.index('r',4,8))
    ```

12. ```
    t = (1,2,3,'a')
    l = list(t)
    l
    ```

13. ```
    tup = (1,2,3,4,5,6,7,8,9)
    print(tup[3:5]*3)
    ```

14. ```
    tup = (10,7,8,9,6,3,4,5,0,1,2)
    print(tup[0])
    print(tup[tup[3]])
    print(tup[-4])
    print(tup[tup[-2]])
    print(tup[tup[tup[7]]-4])
    print(tup[10*2-15+3])
    ```

15. ```
    t = (1,2,3)
    a,b,c = (x,y,z) = t
    print(a,b,c)
    print(x,y,z)
    ```

16. ```
    t =('a')
    print(type(t))
    t =('a',)
    print(type(t))
    ```
    ```

17. ```
    t = (1,2,3)
    tup = ('GO',) + t
    print(tup)
    ```

18. ```
    t1 = (1,2,3)
    t2 = (4,5)
    print(t1 + t2)
    ```

19. ```
    t1 = (1,2,3)
    t2 = t1 * (3)
    print(t2)
    ```

20. ```
    t1 = (1,2,3)
    t2 = ('1','2')
    print(t1 + t2)
    ```

21. ```
    t = (78,98,80,76,53,54,78,98,87,74)
    print(t[3:])
    print(t[:6])
    print(t[-4:])
    print(t[-4:4])
    print(t[:])
    ```

22. ```
    t =("Python","Programming","is","fun")
    (a,b,c,d) = t
    print(t[0][0] + t[1][1]+t[1])
    ```

23. ```
    t1 = 'a','b'
    t2 = ("a","b")
    print(t1==t2)
    ```

24. ```
    t = ('a',('b',('c',('d',))))
    print(len(t))
    print(t[1][0])
    print('c' in t)
    ```

25. ```
    t = (1,2,(3,4),5,(6,(7,8),9))
    print(len(t))
    print(t[3]+10)
    print(t[t[1]])
    print(t[t[1]][1]*10)
    ```

26. ```
    t = ((1,2),)*7
    print(t)
    print(len(t[3:8]))
    ```

27. ```
    tup = ("abc","def")
    x,y = tup
    print x, y
    ```
    ```

Find the Error

1. ```
   tup = ("abc", "def", "ghi", "jkl")
   tup.append("mno")
   ```

2. ```
   Tup1 = (9,8,7,6,5)
   Tup2 = (1,2,3,4,5)
   print(Tup1 - Tup2)
   ```

3. ```
   tup.remove("abc")
   ```

4. ```
   Tup = ('abc', 'def', 'ghi','jkl')
   Tup[2] = 'xyz'
   ```

5. ```
   x, y = 10, 20, 30
   ```

6. ```
   x = {1, 2, 3, 4, 5}
   x.add([6,7,8])
   print(x)
   ```

7. ```
   tup1 = (1,2,3)
   tup2 = tup1 + (2)
   print(tup2)
   ```

8. ```
   tup = (23,12.56,90,[34,56])
   print("Largest Value = ",max(tup))
   ```

9. ```
   (a,b,c,d) = (10,20,30)
   ```

10. ```
    t = (1,2,3,4,5)
    print(t[10])
    ```

11. ```
    t1 = (1,2,3)
    t2 = (1,2)
    print(t2-t1)
    ```

12. ```
    t1 = (1,2,3)
    t2 =  t1 *(4,)
    print(t2)
    ```

13. ```
    t = (1,)*3
    t[0] = 2
    print(t)
    ```

14. ```
    Tup = (1,2,3,4.0,"abc")
    print(min(Tup))
    ```

15. ```
    students = ("Bhavya", "Era", "Falguni","Huma")
    index = students.index("Falguni")
    print("Falguni is present at location : ", index)
    index = students.index("Isha")
    print("Isha is present at location : ", index)
    ```
    ```

Answers

Fill in the Blanks
1. Tuples
2. `zip()`
3. `add()`, `update()`
4. `tuple()`
5. `del`
6. `jkl`
7. 3
8. index
9. Tuples
10. `count()`

State True or False
1. False
2. True
3. False
4. False
5. True
6. False
7. False
8. True
9. True
10. False
11. True
12. True

Multiple Choice Questions
1. a
2. a
3. b
4. b
5. b
6. a
7. b
8. c
9. b
10. a
11. b
12. b
13. d

Give the Output
1. True
2. abc def
3. (1, 2, 3, 1, 2, 3)
   (1, 2, 3, 1, 2, 3, 1, 2, 3)
4. ('H', 'e')
   ('l', 'l')
   ('o', 'W')
   ('o', 'r')
   ('l', 'd')
5. False
   True
   True
   (1, 2, 3, 4)
6. Morning Good
7. Chinu is a 30 year old Female
   Varun is a 32 year old Male
8. (('Good',),)
   ((('Good',),),)
   (((('Good',),),),)
   ((((('Good',),),),),)
9. (('a', 'bcd', 12.34), (5, 6, 7, 8))
10. (1, 2, [5, 4])
11. 5, 8, 7
12. [1, 2, 3, 'a']
13. (4, 5, 4, 5, 4, 5)
14. 10   1   5   7   2   0
15. 1 2 3
    1 2 3
16. <class 'str'>   <class 'tuple'>
17. ('GO', 1, 2, 3)
18. (1, 2, 3, 4, 5
19. (1, 2, 3, 1, 2, 3, 1, 2, 3)
20. (1, 2, 3, '1', '2')
21. (76, 53, 54, 78, 98, 87, 74)
    (78, 98, 80, 76, 53, 54)
    (78, 98, 87, 74)
    ()
    (78, 98, 80, 76, 53, 54, 78, 98, 87, 74)
    ['programming', 'is']
    False
    ('but', 'fun')
    False
22. PrProgramming
23. True
24. 2   b   False
25. 5   15   (3, 4)   40
26. ((1, 2), (1, 2), (1, 2), (1, 2), (1, 2), (1, 2), (1, 2))   4
27. abc def

Find the Error
1. `AttributeError: 'tuple' object has no attribute 'append'`
2. `TypeError: unsupported operand type(s) for -: 'tuple' and 'tuple'`
3. `NameError: name 'tup' is not defined`
4. `TypeError: 'tuple' object does not support item assignment`
5. `ValueError: too many values to unpack (expected 2)`
6. `TypeError: unhashable type: 'list'`

7. `TypeError: can only concatenate tuple (not "int") to tuple`
8. `TypeError: '>' not supported between instances of 'list' and 'int'`
9. `ValueError: not enough values to unpack (expected 4, got 3)`
10. `IndexError: tuple index out of range`
11. `TypeError: unsupported operand type(s) for -: 'tuple' and 'tuple'`
12. `TypeError: can't multiply sequence by non-int of type 'tuple'`
13. `TypeError: 'tuple' object does not support item assignment`
14. `ValueError:`
15. `Falguni is present at location : 2`
    ```
    Traceback (most recent call last):
      File "C:\Users\Reema\AppData\Local\Programs\Python\Python38-32\try1.py",
        line 4, in <module>
      index = students.index("Isha")
    ValueError: tuple.index(x): x not in tuple
    ```

Dictionaries

14

Chapter Objectives

This chapter introduces dictionary data structure for mapping identifiers to their respective values. To this end, we shall discuss the following topics:

- Creating dictionaries
- Accessing and traversing values
- Adding, deleting and modifying items
- `pop()` and `copy()` method
- Nested dictionaries
- Built-in functions and methods
- Comparison of list with dictionary

Dictionary is a data structure in which we store values as a **pair of key and value.** Each key is separated from its value by a colon (:) and consecutive items are separated by commas. The entire set of items in a dictionary is enclosed in curly braces ({}). The syntax for defining a dictionary is

```
dictionary_name = {key_1: value_1, key_2: value_2, key_3: value_3}
```

If there are many keys and values in dictionaries, then we can also write just one key-value pair on a line to make the code easier to read and understand. This is shown below.

```
dictionary_name = {key_1: value_1,
                   key_2: value_2,
                   key_3: value_3,
                   }
```

While keys in the *dictionary must be unique and be of any immutable data type (like strings, numbers, or tuples), there is no stringent requirement for uniqueness and type of values.* That is, value of a key can be of any type. Remember that dictionaries are not sequences, rather they are **mappings**. Mappings are collections of objects in which the objects are stored by key instead of by relative position.

> Using a mutable object as a dictionary key causes a TypeError.

Dictionary is like an associative array (also known as a hash) in which any key of the dictionary can be associated or mapped to a value.

14.1 CREATING A DICTIONARY

The syntax to create an empty dictionary can be given as **dictionary_variable** = [], and the syntax to create a dictionary with key-value pair is: `dictionary_variable = {key1 : val1, key2 : val2, …}`. In this syntax, we can specify key-value pairs separated by a colon in curly brackets as shown below.

```
#To create an empty dictionary
Dict = {}
print Dict
OUTPUT
{}
```

```
#Create a dictionary with key-value pairs
Dict = {'EMP NO' : '123', 'Name' : 'Aaditya',
'Department': 'SALES'}
print(Dict)
OUTPUT
{'EMP NO': '123', 'Name': 'Aaditya',
'Department': 'SALES'}
```

14.1.1 Creating a Dictionary Using `dict()` Method

To create a dictionary with one or more key-value pairs, you can also use the `dict()` function. The `dict()` creates a dictionary directly from a sequence of key-value pairs. For example, the line of code given below creates a dictionary using a list of key-value pairs.

Example 14.1

```
#Creating a dictionary using dict() function
Dict = dict([('EMP _NO', '123'),('Name', Aaditya),('Department', 'SALES')])
print(Dict)
```

OUTPUT
```
{'EMP NO': '123', 'Name': 'Aaditya', 'Department': 'SALES'}
```

We can enclose the keys and values in a separate tuple and then use them as argument in the `zip()` function. The output of the `zip()` function can then be passed as an argument to the `dict()` function so that the dictionary can be created using the two tuples.

Note that in the program, the `zip()` function clubs the first value from the `heads` tuple with the first value in the `vals` tuple, then the second value from both the tuples are clubbed, and finally the third value is clubbed.

Example 14.2

```
#Creating dictionary using keys and values that
#are stored as tuples
heads = ('Roll No','Name','Marks')
vals = ('101','Mishti',99)
Student = dict(zip(heads,vals))
print(Student)
```

OUTPUT
```
{'Roll No': '101', 'Name': 'Mishti', 'Marks': 99}
```

14.2 ACCESSING VALUES IN A DICTIONARY

To access values in a dictionary, square brackets are used along with the key. Note that if you try to access an item with a key that is not specified in the dictionary, a KeyError is generated.

Example 14.3

```
#Accessing dictionary values
Dict= {'EMP NO' : '123', 'Name' :
'Aaditya', 'Department' : 'SALES'}
print("Dict[EMP NO) = ", Dict['EMP_NO'])
print("Dict[Name) = ", Dict['Name'])
print("Dict[Department] =",
Dict['Department'])
```

OUTPUT
```
Dict[EMP_NO] = 123
Dict[Name] = Aaditya
Dict[Department] = SALES
```

```
# Accessing key which is not present in
dictionary
Dict= {'EMP NO' : '123', 'Name' :
'Aaditya'}
print("Dict[EMP_NO] =", Dict['EMP_NO'])
print("Dict[Name] = ", Dict['Name'])
print("Dict[Department] =",
Dict['Department'])
```

OUTPUT
```
Dict[EMP NO)= 123
Dict[ Name]= Aaditya
Traceback (most recent call last):
  File "C:\Users\Python37\try.py",
line 4, in <module>
    print("Dict[Department] =",
Dict['Department'])
KeyError: 'Department'
```

14.3 ADDING AN ITEM IN A DICTIONARY

To add a new entry or a key-value pair in a dictionary just specify the key-value pair as you had done for the existing pairs. The syntax to add an item in a dictionary is **dictionary_variable[key] = val.**

14.4 MODIFYING AN ITEM IN A DICTIONARY

Example 14.4

```
# adding and modifying values in a dictionary
Dict= {'EMP _NO' : '123', 'Name' : 'Aaditya'}
print("Original dictionary", Dict)
Dict['Department']= 'Sales' #new key-value pair added
Dict['Name']= 'Aadi' #existing value modified
print("Updated Dictionary",Dict)
```
OUTPUT
```
Original dictionary {'EMP_NO': '123', 'Name': 'Aaditya'}
Updated Dictionary {'EMP_NO': '123', 'Name': 'Aadi', 'Department': 'Sales'}
```

To modify an entry, just overwrite the existing value with the new value.

14.5 DELETING ITEMS

One or more items in a dictionary can be deleted using the **del** keyword. To delete or remove all the items in just one statement, use the `clear()` function. Note that the `clear()` method does not delete the dictionary, it just deletes all the elements inside the dictionary. To remove an entire dictionary from the memory, we can again use the `del` statement **as del Dict_name.** The syntax to use the `del` statement can be given as, **del dictionary_variable[key].**

```
#deleting entries and the entire dictionary
Dict= {'EMP _NO': '123', 'Name': 'Aaditya','Department': 'Sales'}
print("Original Dictionary", Dict)
del Dict['EMP _ NO'] #a particular key-value pair deleted
print("After deleteing EMP _NO", Dict)
Dict.clear() #all entries deleted
print("After deleteing all entries ", Dict)
del Dict #delete dictionary
print("Printing Dictionary after deleting it", Dict)
```
OUTPUT
```
Original Dictionary {'EMP NO': '123', 'Name': 'Aaditya', 'Department': 'Sales'}
After deleteing EMP _NO {'Name': 'Aaditya', 'Department': 'Sales'}
After deleteing all entries {}
Traceback (most recent call last):
  File "C:\Users\Python37\try.py", line 8, in <module>
    print("Printing Dictionary after deleting it", Dict)
NameError: name 'Dict' is not defined
```

14.5.1 The `pop()` Method

The `pop()` method can be used to delete a particular key from the dictionary. The syntax of the `pop()` method is, **dict.pop(key [, default])**

The `pop()` method removes an item from the dictionary and returns its value. *If the specified key is not present in the dictionary, then the default value is returned.* Since default value is optional, if you do not specify the default value and the key is also not present in the dictionary, then a KeyError is generated.

Another method, **popitem()**, randomly pops and returns an item from the dictionary. The use of these methods is illustrated in the program given below.

```
#Program to randomly pop an element from a dictionary
Dict= {'EMP _NO' : '123', 'Name': 'Aaditya','Department': 'Sales'}
print("Original Dictionary", Dict)
print("Name is : ", Dict.pop('Name')) #returns Name
print("Dictionary after popping Name is : ", Dict)
print("Salary is : " , Dict.pop('Salary', -1)) #returns default value
print("Randomly popping any item : ",Dict.popitem())
print("Dictionary after random popping is:", Dict)
print("Designation is:", Dict.pop('Designation')) #generates error
print("Dictionary after popping Designation is : ", Dict)
OUTPUT
Original Dictionary {'EMP _ NO': '123', 'Name': 'Aaditya', 'Department': 'Sales'}
Name is : Aaditya
Dictionary after popping Name is : {'EMP _ NO': '123', 'Department': 'Sales'}
Salary is : -1
Randomly popping any item : ('Department', 'Sales')
Dictionary after random popping is : {'EMP _NO': '123'}
Traceback (most recent call last):
  File "C:\Users\Python37\try.py", line 9, in <module>
    print("Designation is :", Dict.pop('Designation')) #generates error
KeyError: 'Designation'
```

Key points to remember

- Keys must have unique values. *Keys should not be duplicated in a dictionary*. If you try to add a duplicate key then the last assignment is retained.

Example 14.5

```
#Dictionary with duplicate keys
Dict = {'EMP_NO' : '123', 'Name' : 'Aaditya','Department' : 'Sales',
'EMP_NO' : '456'}
print(Dict)
```

OUTPUT
{'EMP_NO': '456, 'Name ': 'Aaditya', 'Department': 'Sales'}

- In a dictionary, *keys should be strictly of a type that is immutable*. This means that a key can be of strings, number or tuple type but it cannot be a list which is mutable. In case you try to make your key a mutable type, then a **TypeError** will be generated.
- The keys() method of dictionary returns a list of all the keys used in the dictionary, in an arbitrary order. Use the sorted() function to sort the keys.

Example 14.6

```
# Program to use tuple as keys
Dict = {(1,2),([3,4])}
print{Dict}
```

OUTPUT
```
Traceback (most recent call last):
  File "C:\Users\Python37\try.py",
line 5, in <module>
    Dict = {{1,2),([3,4])}
TypeError: unhashable type: 'list'
```

```
# Dictionary with sorted keys
Dict= {'EMP_NO' : '123', 'Name' :
'Aaditya','Department': 'Sales','EMP_NO':
'456'}
print(sorted{Dict.keys()))
```

OUTPUT
['Department', 'EMP_NO', 'Name']

Example 14.7

```
# Program to check single key in a dictionary
Dict = {'EMP_NO' : '123', 'Name' : 'Aaditya', 'Department' : 'Sales',
'EMP_NO' : '456'}
if 'Department' in Dict
  print(Dict['Department'])
```

OUTPUT
```
Sales
```

- The **in keyword** can be used to check whether a single key is in the dictionary.

  The key-value pairs can be specified as a list or as a tuple. To create a dictionary out of this list or tuple, it must be passed as an argument to the `dict()` function.

Example 14.8

```
# Dictionary using a tuple of lists having key-value pairs
Student = dict((['RoiiNp', '101 '),('Name', 'Krish'],['Marks ',90]))
print( Student)
```

OUTPUT
```
{'Roll Np': '101', 'Name ': 'Krish', 'Marks': 90}
```

In the given program, we have used a tuple having a list of keys and values as its elements. In the same way, we could have also used nested tuples.

14.6 TRAVERSING A DICTIONARY

Looping over a Dictionary can be done to access only values, only keys or both using the `for` loop. We can use the `items()` method that returns a list of tuples (key-value pair). The `keys()` method returns a list of keys in the dictionary. The `values()` method returns a list of values in dictionary.

Example 14.9

```
#Program to access items in a dictionary
Dict: = {'EMP _ NO' : '123', 'Name' : ' Aaditya'.'Department' : 'Sales',
'EMP_NO' : '456'}
print:("KEYS : " ,end = ' ')
for key in Dict:
  print:(key, end ='') #accessing only keys
print("\nVALUES : ", end = ' ')
for val in Dict:.values():
  print(val, end = ' ') # accessing only values
print("\nDICTIONARY : ", end = ' ')
for key, val in Dict.items():
  print:(key, val, "\t", end = ' ') # accessing keys and values
```

OUTPUT
```
KEYS : EMP_NO Name Department
VALUES : 456 Aaditya Sales
DICTIONARY : EMP_NO 456    Name Aaditya    Department Sales
```

14.7 NESTED DICTIONARIES

Like any other sequence, we can also have nested dictionary in Python. A nested dictionary has a dictionary defined inside another dictionary.

Example 14.10

```
#Program to illustrate nested dictionary
Employees= {'Aman' : {'EMP _NO':90, 'Sal':89, 'Desig': 'Analyst'},
    'Sadhvi' : {'EMP NO':91, 'Sal':87, 'Desig': 'Programmer'},
    'Kiyan' : {'EMP NO':92, 'Sal':92, 'Desig': 'Testing Professional'}}
for key, val in Employees.items():
  print(key, val)
```

OUTPUT
```
Aman {'EMP _NO': 90, 'Sal': 89, 'Desig': 'Analyst'}
Sadhvi {'EMP NO': 91, 'Sal': 87, 'Desig': 'Programmer'}
Kiyan {'EMP _ NO': 92, 'Sal': 92, 'Desig': 'Testing Professional'}
```

14.8 THE copy() METHOD

The copy() method of dictionary returns a shallow copy of the dictionary, i.e., the dictionary returned will not have a duplicate copy of the original dictionary but will have the same reference. This means that both the copies of dictionaries will point to the same object (or address) in the computer's memory.

Example 14.11

```
# Program using copy() method
Emp = {'EMP _ NO' :90, 'Sal ' :89, 'Desig': 'Analyst'}
print("Original Emp : " ,Emp)
Emp_ Copy = Emp.copy()
print("Copied Emp : " , Emp_ Copy)
Emp_Copy('Sal' ] = 99
print("Emp after modification : ", Emp)
print("Copy of Emp after modification : " , Emp_Copy)
```

OUTPUT
```
Original Emp : {'EMP _ NO': 90, 'Sal' : 89, 'Des ig': 'Analyst'}
Copied Emp : { 'EMP _ NO' : 90, 'Sal': 89, 'Desig': 'Analyst'}
Emp after modification : {'EMP _ NO': 90, 'Sal ' : 89, 'Desig': 'Analyst'}
Copy of Emp after modification : {'EMP _ NO' : 90, 'Sal' : 99, Desig': 'Analyst' }
```

14.9 BUILT-IN DICTIONVARY FUNCTIONS AND METHODS

Table 14.1 discusses some methods and functions that can be used on dictionaries in Python.

Table 14.1 Methods and functions of dictionaries

Operation	Description	Example	Output
len(Dict)	Returns the length of dictionary. That is, the number of items (key-value pairs)	Emp = {'EMP_NO':90, 'Sal':89, 'Desig': 'Analyst'} print(len(Emp))	3

(Continued)

Table 14.1 Continued

Operation	Description	Example	Output
`str(Dict)`	Returns a string representation of the dictionary	`Emp = {'EMP_NO':90, 'Sal':89, 'Desig': 'Analyst'}` `print(str(Emp))`	{'EMP_NO': 90, 'Sal': 89, 'Desig': 'Analyst'}
`Dict.get(key)`	Returns the value for the key passed as argument. If the key is not present in the dictionary, it will return the default value. If no default value is specified, then it will return None	`Emp = {'EMP_NO':90, 'Sal':89, 'Desig': 'Analyst'}` `print(Emp.get('Desig'))`	Analyst

`Dict.setdefault(key, value)`	Sets a default value for a key that is not present in the dictionary	`Emp = {'EMP_NO':90, 'Desig': 'Analyst'}`
		`Emp.setdefault('Sal',0)`
		`print("Emp gets a salary = ", Emp.get('Sal'))`
			Emp gets a salary = 0

`Dict1.update(Dict2)`	Adds the key-value pairs of Dict2 to the key-value pairs of Dict1	`Emp1 = {'EMP_NO':90, 'Desig': 'Analyst'}`
		`Emp2 = {'Name' : 'Krish', 'Sal' : 89}`
		`Emp1.update(Emp2)`
		`print(Emp1)`
			{'EMP_NO': 90, 'Desig': 'Analyst', 'Name': 'Krish', 'Sal': 89}

`in and not in`	Checks whether a given key is present in the dictionary or not.	`Emp = {'EMP_NO':90, 'Sal':89, 'Desig': 'Analyst'}`
		`print('Name' in Emp)`
		`print('Name' not in Emp)`
			False
			True

14.10 DIFFERENCE BETWEEN A LIST AND A DICTIONARY

Given below are the main differences between a list and a dictionary.

- First, a list is an ordered set of items. But a dictionary is a data structure that is used for matching one item (key) with another (value).
- Second, in lists, you can use indexing to access a particular item. But the index should be a number. In dictionaries, you can use any type (immutable) of value as an index. For example, when we write `Dict['Name']`, where `Name` acts as an index but it is not a number but a string.
- Third, lists are used to look up a value whereas a dictionary is used to take one value and lookup another value. For this reason, dictionary is also known as a *lookup table*.
  In fact, the main advantage of a dictionary is that you don't need to search for a value one by one in the entire set of values; you can find a value instantly.
- Fourth, the key-value pair may not be displayed in the order in which it was specified while defining the dictionary. This is because Python uses complex algorithms (called hashing) to provide fast access to the items stored in the dictionary. This also makes the dictionary preferable to use over a list of tuples.

PROGRAMER'S ZONE

1. **Write a program that has a dictionary of metropolitan cities and their codes. Add another city in the pre-defined dictionary; print all the items in the dictionary and try to print the code for a state that does not exist. Set a default value prior to printing.**

```
Codes = {'Delhi' : '011', 'Mumbai' : '022', 'Chennai' : '044'}
Codes['Kolkatta'] = '033'    # add another state
Codes.setdefault('','Sorry, no idea')
print("Code for Kolkata is : ", Codes['Kolkata'])
print("-" * 5, "CODES", "-" * 5)
for i in Codes.items():
    print(i)
print("Code for Mumbai : ", Codes.get('Mumbai'))
```

OUTPUT

```
(Code for Kolkata is : 033
----- CODES -----
('Delhi', '011')
('Mumbai', '022')
('Chennai', '044')
('Kolkata', '033')
('', 'Sorry, no idea')
Code for Mumbai : 022
```

> Dictionary keys are case sensitive. Two keys with same name but in different case are not the same in Python.

2. **Write a program that has two dictionaries. The first dictionary has subject names and codes. The second dictionary has subject codes and their average marks. Print the average marks of all the subjects.**

```
subjects = {'Computer Science' : 'CS', 'Political Science' : 'Pol', 'Philosophy' :
'Phil', 'Commerce' : 'Com'}
avg_marks = {'CS' : 96, 'Pol' : 78, 'Phil' : 84, 'Com' : 95}
for i in subjects:
    print("Average Marks in ", i, "(", subjects[i], ") = ", avg_marks[subjects[i]])
```

OUTPUT

```
Average Marks in Commerce ( Com ) = 95
Average Marks in Philosophy ( Phil ) = 84
Average Marks in Computer Science ( CS ) 5 = 96
Average Marks in Political Science ( Pol ) = 78
```

3. **Write a program that creates a dictionary of squares and cubes of numbers entered by the user.**

```
print("Enter -1 to exit....")
Squares = {}
while True:
    r = int(input("Enter number : "))
    if r == -1:
        break
    else:
        Dict = {r:[r*r , r*r*r]}
        Squares.update(Dict)
print(Squares)
```

> In Python "None" is a special value like null or nil, which means no value.

OUTPUT
```
Enter -1 to exit....
Enter number : 3
Enter number : 5
Enter number : 2
Enter number : 7
Enter number : -1
{3: [9, 27], 5: [25, 125], 2: [4, 8], 7: [49, 343]}
```

4. Write a program that has a set of words in the English language and their corresponding words in Hindi. Define another dictionary that has a list of words in Hindi and their corresponding words in Hindi. Take all words from the English language and display their meanings in both the languages.

```
E_H = {'Friend' : 'Mitr', 'Teacher' : 'Shikshak', 'Book' : 'Pustak', 'Queen' :
'Rani'}
H_U = {'Mitr' : 'Dost', 'Shikshak' : 'Adhyapak', 'Pustak' : 'Kitab', 'Rani' :
'Begum'}
for i in E_H:
    print(i, "in Hindi means", E_H[i], "and in Urdu means", H_U[E_H[i]])
```

OUTPUT
```
Book in Hindi means Pustak and in Urdu means Kitab
Teacher in Hindi means Shikshak and in Urdu means Adhyapak
Friend in Hindi means Mitr and in Urdu means Dost
Queen in Hindi means Rani and in Urdu means Begum
```

5. Write a program that calculates fib(n) using a dictionary.

```
Dict = {0: 0, 1: 1}
def fib(n):
    if n not in Dict:
        val = fib(n-1) + fib(n-2)
        Dict[n] = val
    return Dict[n]
n = int(input("Enter the value of n : "))
print("Fib(", n, ") = ", fib(n))
```

> A KeyError occurs on an invalid access of a key, like when a key that is used is not present in dictionary.

OUTPUT
```
Enter the value of n : 10
Fib( 10 ) =  55
```

6. Write a program that prompts the user to enter a message. Now count and print the number of occurrences of each character.

```
def count(message):
    letter_counts = {}
    for letter in message:
        letter_counts[letter] = letter_counts.get(letter, 0) + 1
    print(letter_counts)
message = input("Enter a message : ")
count(message)
```

OUTPUT
```
Enter a message : Python Programming is Fun
{'P': 2, 'y': 1, 't': 1, 'h': 1, 'o': 2, 'n': 3, ' ': 3, 'r': 2, 'g': 2, 'a':
1, 'm': 2, 'i': 2, 's': 1, 'F': 1, 'u': 1}
```

7. **Write a program to store a sparse matrix as a dictionary.**
```
matrix = [[0,1,0,0,2],
          [0,0,3,0,],
          [4,0,0,5,0]]
Dict = {}
print ("Sparse Matrix")
for i in range(len(matrix)):
    print("\n")
    for j in range(len(matrix[i])):
        print(matrix[i][j], end = ' ')
        if matrix[i][j]!=0:
            Dict[(i,j)] = matrix[i][j]
print("\n Sparse Matrix can be efficiently represented as Dictionary : ")
print(Dict)
```

OUTPUT
```
Sparse Matrix
0 1 0 0 2
0 0 3 0
4 0 0 5 0

 Sparse Matrix can be efficiently represented as Dictionary :
{(0, 1): 1, (0, 4): 2, (1, 2): 3, (2, 0): 4, (2, 3): 5}
```

> Collision means two or more keys pointing to the same location.

8. **Write a program that inverts a dictionary. That is, it makes key of one dictionary the value of another and vice-versa.**
```
Emp = {'EMP_NO':90, 'Sal':89, 'Desig': 'Analyst'}
inverted = {}
for key, val in Emp.items():
    inverted[val] = key
print("Original Dictionary : ", Emp)
print("Inverted Dictionary : ", inverted)
```

OUTPUT
```
Original Dictionary : {'EMP_NO': 90, 'Sal': 89, 'Desig': 'Analyst'}
Inverted Dictionary : {90: 'EMP_NO', 89: 'Sal', 'Analyst': 'Desig'}
```

9. **Write a program that has a dictionary of names of students and a list of their marks in 4 subjects. Create another dictionary from this dictionary that has name of the students and their total marks.**
```
Marks = {'Amish' : [87,90,91, 85], 'Anand' : [85,90,91,89], 'Siya' : [80,79,
81,75]}
Tot_Marks = Marks.copy()
for key, val in Marks.items():
    tot = sum(val)
    Tot_Marks[key] = tot
print(Tot_Marks)
```

OUTPUT
```
{'Amish': 353, 'Anand': 355, 'Siya': 315}
```

10. **Find the employee getting the highest salary.**
    ```
    Emp = {'Amish': 35, 'Anand': 55, 'Siya': 65}
    max = 0
    New_Emp = ''
    for key, val in Emp.items():
        if val>max:
            max = val
            New_Emp = key
    print("Employee with maximum salary is : ", New_Emp, "with salary = ", max)
    ```
    OUTPUT
    ```
    Employee with maximum salary is : Siya with salary = 65
    ```

11. **Write a program that prompts the user to enter a filename. Open the file and print the frequency of each word in it.**
    ```
    text = input('Enter the message: ')
    counts = dict()
    for line in text:
        words = line.split()
        for word in words:
            if word not in counts:
                counts[word] = 1
            else:
                counts[word] += 1
    print(counts)
    ```

    > Trying to index a key that isn't part of the dictionary returns a KeyError.

    OUTPUT
    ```
    Enter the file name: File1.txt
    {'a': 1, 'and': 1, '#': 1, 'language': 1, 'Python': 1, 'of': 1, 'is': 1,
    'Welcome': 1, 'Programming': 1, 'to': 1, 'interesting': 1, 'very': 1, 'world':
    1, 'the': 1, 'Reading': 1, 'Hello': 1, 'simple': 1, 'Happy': 1}
    ```

12. **Write a program to count the number of characters in the string and store them in a dictionary data structure.**
    ```
    str = "Python is a wonderful programming language"
    len = len(str)
    Dict = {str:len}
    print(Dict)
    ```
    OUTPUT
    ```
    {'Python is a wonderful programming language': 42}
    ```

13. **Write a program combine_lists that combines these lists into a dictionary.**
    ```
    keys = ['EName', 'Degignation', 'Salary']
    values = ["Om", 'Vice President', 1000000]
    details = zip(keys, values)
    Dict = dict(details)
    print(Dict)
    ```

    > In the get() method, if we specify the key as argument which does not even exist in dictionary, then NameError will be returned.

    OUTPUT
    ```
    {'EName': 'Om', 'Degignation': 'Vice President', 'Salary': 1000000}
    ```

14. Write a program that finds whether a particular value is present in the dictionary or not. Do not use `values()` method.

```
Dict = {"Amna":4,"Brij":2,"Chaitanya":5,"Divyanka":3}
v = int(input("Enter the value to be searched : "))
flag = 0
for i in Dict:
    if(Dict[i] == v):
        print(i)
        flag = 1
if(flag == 0):
    print("Value not present")
```

OUTPUT

```
Enter the value to be searched : 5
Chaitanya
```

15. Write a program that has a dictionary of states and their codes. Add another state in the pre-defined dictionary; print all the items in the dictionary and try to print the code for a state that does not exist. Set a default value prior to printing.

```
states = {'Delhi' : '011', 'Mumbai' : '022', 'Chennai' : '044', 'Rajasthan' : 'RJ'}
states['Tamil Nadu'] = 'TN'    # add another state
states.setdefault('Karnataka','Sorry, no idea')
print("Code for Rajasthan is : ", states['Rajasthan'])
print("-" * 5, "CODES", "-" * 5)
for i in states.items():
    print(i)
print("Code for Karnataka : ", states.get('Karnataka'))
```

Key Terms

Dictionary: A collection of key-value pairs that map the keys to values. While keys can be of any immutable type, there is no such restriction on its associated value which can be of any type.

Key: Data that is *mapped to* a value in a dictionary. Keys are unique data items that are used to look up values in a dictionary.

Key-value pair: A pair of items in a dictionary. Key is used to lookup for a value stored in the dictionary.

Hash function: A function used to compute the location for a key.

Lookup: A dictionary operation that takes a key and finds the corresponding value.

Nested dictionary: A dictionary inside another dictionary.

Mappings: A collection of objects where objects are stored by key instead of by relative position.

Chapter Highlights

- While keys in the dictionary must be unique and be of any immutable data type (like strings, numbers or tuples), there is no stringent requirement for uniqueness and type of values.
- Dictionaries are not sequences, rather they are mappings.
- To create a dictionary with one or more key-value pairs, the `dict()` function is used.

- To access values in a dictionary, square brackets are used along with the key to obtain its value.
- If an item with a key that is not specified in the dictionary is accessed, a KeyError is generated.
- One or more items in a dictionary can be deleted using the `del` keyword.
- The `clear()` method does not delete the dictionary, it just deletes all the elements inside the dictionary.
- The `pop()` method removes an item from the dictionary and returns its value. If the specified key is not present in the dictionary, then the default value is returned.
- Keys must have unique values. Keys should not be duplicated in a dictionary.
- The `keys()` method of dictionary returns a list of all the keys used in the dictionary in an arbitrary order. Use the `sorted()` function to sort the keys.
- The key-value pairs can be specified as a list or as a tuple.
- The `copy()` method of dictionary returns a shallow copy of the dictionary, i.e., the dictionary returned will not be a duplicate copy of the original dictionary but will have the same reference.

Review Questions

1. What is a dictionary?
2. How is a dictionary different from a list?
3. Discuss at least two ways in which you can create a dictionary.
4. Can lists be used as keys? Justify your answer.
5. How is the `zip()` function used to create a dictionary?
6. How will you add key-value pairs in a dictionary?
7. How will you modify key-value pairs in a dictionary?
8. Differentiate between the `del` statement and `clear()` method.
9. When will we use the `pop()` method?
10. List some restrictions which you will keep in mind when creating a dictionary.
11. Draw a comparison between a list and a dictionary.

Programming Exercises

1. Create a dictionary of products purchased and their MRPs. Calculate the bill and display to the customer.
2. Find `fib(n)` using dictionaries.
3. Write a program that prompts the user to enter a string and returns in alphabetical order, a letter and its frequency of occurrence in the string. (Ignore Case)
4. Write a program to implement sparse matrix using a dictionary.
5. Write a program that has a dictionary of your friends' names (as keys) and their birthdays. Print the items in the dictionary in a sorted order. Prompt the user to enter a name and check if it is present in the dictionary. If the name does not exist, then ask the user to enter DOB. Add the details in the dictionary.
6. Write a program that displays a menu and its price. Take the order from the customer. Check if the ordered product is in the menu. In case it is not there, the customer should be asked to reorder and if it is present then product should be added in the bill.
7. Write a program that prints the maximum and minimum value in a dictionary.

8. Write a program to get a dictionary from an object's fields.
9. Write a program to remove duplicates from a dictionary.
10. Write a program to check if a dictionary has some key-value pairs stored in it.
11. Using dictionary comprehension, create a dictionary of numbers and their squares in the range (10).
12. Write a program that displays information about an employee. Use nested dictionary to do the task.
13. Write a program that prints keys with same values in the dictionary.
14. Write a program that prints keys with different values in the dictionary.
15. Write a program that accepts two dictionaries. Print all the keys that are present in both the dictionaries.
16. Create a dictionary which has name of the student as key and his total marks as value. Now, perform the following operations on this dictionary.
    a. Display the marks obtained by a particular student.
    b. Display the names of all the students who scored 90 and above.
    c. Display all key-value pairs sorted by keys.
    d. Display all key-value pairs sorted by marks.
    e. Create a list of all students.
    f. Create another list having marks obtained by the students.
17. Create a dictionary storing names of months as keys and the number of days as values.
18. Create a dictionary using nested tuple.

Fill in the Blanks

1. Fill in the blanks to print "Hi", if the key 90 is present in the dictionary named "Dict".
   if ___ ___ ___
   print("Hi")

2. Fill in the blanks to create a list, dictionary, and tuple.
   List=__"abc", "def"__
   Dict=__1:"abc", 2:"def"__
   Tup=__"abc","def"__

3. _____ is a collection of objects that stores objects by key instead of by relative position.
4. The _____ function can be used to create a dictionary with one or more key-value pairs.
5. One or more items in a dictionary can be deleted using the _____ keyword.
6. The _____ method of dictionary returns a list of all the keys used in the dictionary in an arbitrary order.
7. The _____ method of dictionary returns a shallow copy of the dictionary.
8. The _____ function returns a string representation of the dictionary.
9. The _____ function returns the value for the key passed as argument.
10. Dictionary is also known as a _____ table.

State True or False

1. Keys in the dictionary must be of any mutable data type.
2. Tuples can be used as key for a dictionary but lists cannot be used as keys.

3. Values in a dictionary must be unique.
4. Slicing and concatenation operations are not possible on dictionaries.
5. Dictionary keys are case insensitive.
6. Dictionaries are sequences.
7. To remove an entire dictionary from the memory, we can use the `clear()` method.
8. `pop()` method randomly pops and returns an item from the dictionary.
9. Keys of a dictionary can be sorted using the `sorted()`.
10. The key-value pairs can be specified as a list or as a tuple.

Multiple Choice Questions

1. If Dict = {1:2, 3:4, 4:11, 5:6, 7:8}, then print(Dict[Dict[3]]) will print _____ .
   a. 2 b. 8 c. 11 d. 6

2. Which data structure does not allow duplicate values?
   a. List b. Tuple c. Dictionary d. Set

3. Which data structure does not support indexing?
   a. List b. Tuple c. Dictionary d. Set

4. Using a mutable object as dictionary will result in which error?
   a. TypeError b. KeyError c. NameError d. IndexError

5. Which error is returned if an item with a key, which is not specified in the dictionary, is accessed?
   a. TypeError b. KeyError c. NameError d. IndexError

6. _____ method can be used to delete a particular key from the dictionary.
   a. `clear()` b. `del` c. `pop()` d. `delete()`

7. Which error will the `pop()` method generate if the default value is not specified and the key is also not present in the dictionary?
   a. TypeError b. KeyError c. NameError d. IndexError

8. A _____ cannot be used as a key in the dictionary.
   a. strings b. number c. tuple d. list

9. Which error will be generated if the key of the dictionary is a list?
   a. TypeError b. KeyError c. NameError d. IndexError

Give the Output

1. ```
   Dict = {"India":"New Delhi", "Nepal":"Kathmandu", "USA":"Washington DC"}
   del Dict["Nepal"]
   for key,val in Dict.items():
       print(key,val)
   ```

2. ```
   Dict = {"India":"New Delhi", "Nepal":"Kathmandu", "USA":"Washington DC"}
   print(Dict.get("Russia"))
   print(Dict.get("Pakistan", "No Idea"))
   ```

3. ```
   Studs = {'Mitanshi', 'Harshita', 'Pritika'}
   Toppers = {}.fromkeys(Studs, 0)
   ```
   ```

```
   print(Toppers)
   Toppers['Mitanshi'] = 97
   Toppers['Harshita'] = 92
   Toppers['Pritika'] = 89
   Toppers.setdefault('Nisha', -1)
   print(Toppers)
```

4. ```
   Toppers = {}
   Toppers['Mitanshi'] = 97
   Toppers['Harshita'] = 92
   Toppers['Pritika'] = 89
   print('Harshita got ' + str(Toppers.get('Harshita')) + ' marks.')
   ```

5. ```
   rec = {'Name': {'First': 'Chaitanya', 'Last': 'Raj'},
                  'Marks': [80, 76, 84],
                  'Course': 'BTech'}
   print(rec['Name'])
   print(rec['Name']['Last'])
   print(rec['Marks'])
   rec['Marks'].append(72)
   print(rec)
   ```

6. ```
   Dict = {"Amna":4,"Brij":2,"Chaitanya":5,"Divyanka":3}
   s = 0
   for v in Dict.values():
       s = s + v
   print(s)
   ```

7. ```
   Dict = {"Amna":4,"Brij":2,"Chaitanya":5,"Divyanka":3}
   n = ''
   for i in Dict:
       if n < i:
           n = i
   print(n)
   ```

8. ```
   Dict = {"Amna":4,"Brij":2,"Chaitanya":5,"Divyanka":3}
   n = 'Chaitanya'
   v = 10
   if n in Dict:
       Dict[n] = v
   print(Dict)
   ```

9. ```
   Dict = {'a':1, 'b':2, ('c','d'):3}
   print(Dict)
   ```

10. ```
    Dict = {'a':1, 'b':2, 'c':3,'d':4}
    v = Dict['c']
    if v in Dict:
        print("FOUND")
    ```
    ```

```
        else:
            print("NOT FOUND")
```

11.
```
Dict = {'a':1, 'b':2, 'c':3,'d':4}
k = ''
for i in Dict:
  if i > k:
      k = i
      v = Dict[i]
print(k,v)
List = list(Dict.items())
List.sort()
print(List)
```

12.
```
Dict = {'a':1, 'b':2, 'c':3,'d':4, 'e':[5,6,7,8]}
print(Dict)
```

13.
```
Dict = {10:"TEN","HUNDRED":100,(1,2):("ONE","TWO")}
print(Dict)
```

14.
```
List = [10,10,10,20,30,30,20,40,40,40]
counts= {}
L= []
for i in List:
    if i not in L:
        L.append(i)
        counts[i] = 1
    else:
        counts[i] += counts[i]
print(counts)
```

15.
```
List = [10,10,10,20,30,30,20,40,40,40]
counts = {}
for i in List:
    if i in counts:
        counts[i] += 1
    else:
        counts[i] = 1
print(counts)
```

16.
```
Dict = {}
Dict[1] = 1
Dict['1'] = 2
Dict[1] += 1
sum = 0
for i in Dict:
    sum += Dict[i]
print(sum)
```

Find the Error

1. ```
   Dict = {"India":"New Delhi", "Nepal":"Kathmandu"}
   print(Dict["USA"])
   ```
2. ```
   Dict = {}
   print(Dict[0])
   ```
3. ```
   Dict = {'a':1, 'b':2, ['c','d']:[3,4]}
   print(Dict)
   ```
4. ```
   msg = "How are you doing?"
   counts = {}
   for c in msg:
       counts[c] = counts[c] + 1
   print(counts)
   ```
5. ```
   Dict = {}
   Dict[(1,2,3)] = 10
   Dict[[3,2,1]] = 20
   print(DIct)
   ```
6. ```
   Dict = {'a':1,'b':2,'c':3,'d':4}
   print(Dict['a','b'])
   ```

Answers

Fill in the Blanks
1. 90, in, Dict
2. [], {}, ()
3. Mappings
4. dict()
5. del
6. keys()
7. copy()
8. str()
9. get()
10. lookup

State True or False
1. False
2. True
3. False
4. True
5. False
6. False
7. False
8. False
9. True
10. True

Multiple Choice Questions
1. c
2. b
3. d
4. a
5. b
6. c
7. b
8. d
9. a

Give the Output
1. India New Delhi
2. None
   No Idea
3. {'Pritika': 0, 'Harshita': 0, 'Mitanshi': 0}
   {'Pritika': 89, 'Harshita': 92, 'Nisha': –1, 'Mitanshi': 97}
4. Harshita got 92 marks.

5. {'Last': 'Raj', 'First': 'Chaitanya'}
   Raj
   [80, 76, 84]
   {'Course': 'BTech', 'Name': {'Last': 'Raj', 'First': 'Chaitanya'}, 'Marks': [80, 76, 84, 72]}
6. 14
7. Divyanka
8. {'Amna': 4, 'Brij': 2, 'Chaitanya': 10, 'Divyanka': 3}
9. {'a': 1, 'b': 2, ('c', 'd'): 3}
10. NOT FOUND
11. d 4
    [('a', 1), ('b', 2), ('c', 3), ('d', 4)]
12. {'a': 1, 'b': 2, 'c': 3, 'd': 4, 'e': [5, 6, 7, 8]}
13. {10: 'TEN', 'HUNDRED': 100, (1, 2): ('ONE', 'TWO')}
14. {10: 4, 20: 2, 30: 2, 40: 4}
15. {10: 3, 20: 2, 30: 2, 40: 3}
16. 4

Find the Error
1. KeyError: 'USA'
2. KeyError
3. TypeError: unhashable type: 'list'
4. KeyError: 'H'
5. TypeError: unhashable type: 'list'
6. KeyError: ('a', 'b')

Sorting

15

Chapter Objectives

This chapter focuses on arranging data items in a specific order. We shall discuss two main sorting techniques in this chapter, namely,

- Bubble sort
- Insertion sort

We also present applications, illustrative examples, algorithms and program code for these techniques.

The term sorting means arranging the elements of the array so that they are placed in some relevant order which may either be ascending or descending. That is, if A is a list of numbers, then the elements of A are arranged in sorted order (ascending order) in such a way that, $A[0] < A[1] < A[2] < \ldots < A[N]$. For example, if the list A is initialized as,

$$A = [31, 45, 10, 7, 3, -4, 29]$$

Then the sorted array in ascending order can be given as, $A = [-4, 3, 7, 10, 29, 31, 45]$.

Similarly, the sorted array in descending order can be given as, $A = [45, 31, 29, 10, 7, 3, -4]$.

A sorting algorithm is defined as an algorithm that puts the elements of a list in a certain order (that can either be numerical order, lexicographical order or any user-defined order). Efficient sorting algorithms are widely used to optimize the use of other algorithms like search and merge algorithms, which require sorted lists to work correctly.

15.1 BUBBLE SORT

Bubble sort is a very simple method that sorts the array elements by repeatedly moving the largest element to the highest index position of the array (in case of arranging elements in ascending order). In bubble sorting, consecutive adjacent pairs of elements in the array are compared with each other. If the element at lower index is greater than the element at the higher index, the two elements are interchanged so that the smaller element is placed before the bigger one. This process is continued till the list of unsorted elements is exhausted.

This procedure of sorting is called bubble sort because the smaller elements "bubble" to the top of the list. Note that at the end of the first pass, largest element in the list will be placed at its proper position (i.e., at the end of the list).

Note that if the elements are to be sorted in descending order, then with each pass the smallest element is moved to the lowest index of the array.

15.1.1 Bubble Sort Example

To discuss bubble sort, let us consider an array that has the following elements:

$$A = [31, 45, 10, 7, 3, -4, 29]$$

Pass 1:
(a) Compare 31 and 45. Since 31 < 45, then no swapping is done
(b) Compare 45 and 10. Since 45 > 10, swapping is done
31, **10, 45**, 7, 3, −4, 29
(c) Compare 45 and 7. Since 45 > 7, swapping is done
31, 10, **7, 45**, 3, −4, 29
(d) Compare, 45 and 3. Since, 45 > 3, swapping is done
31, 10, 7, **3, 45**, −4, 29
(e) Compare 45 and −4. Since 45 > −4, swapping is done
31, 10, 7, 3, **−4, 45**, 29
(f) Compare 45 and 29. Since 45 > 29, swapping is done
31, 10, 7, 3, −4, **29, 45**

Observe that after the end of the first pass, the largest element is placed at the highest index of the array. All the other elements are still unsorted.

Pass 2:
(a) Compare 31 and 10. Since 31 > 10, swapping is done
10, 31, 7, 3, −4, 29, 45
(b) Compare 31 and 7. Since 31 > 7, swapping is done
10, **7, 31**, 3, −4, 29, 45
(c) Compare 31 and 3. Since 31 > 3, swapping is done
10, 7, **3, 31**, −4, 29, 45
(d) Compare 31 and −4. Since 31 > −4, swapping is done
10, 7, 3, **−4, 31**, 29, 45
(e) Compare 31 and 29. Since 31 > 29, swapping is done
10, 7, 3, −4, **29, 31**, 45

Observe that after the end of the second pass, the second largest element is placed at the second highest index of the array. All the other elements are still unsorted.

Pass 3:
(a) Compare 10 and 7. Since 10 > 7, swapping is done
7, 10, 3, −4, 29, 31, 45
(b) Compare 10 and 3. Since 10 > 3, swapping is done
7, **3, 10**, −4, 29, 31, 45
(c) Compare 10 and −4. Since 10 > −4, swapping is done
7, 3, **−4, 10**, 29, 31, 45
(d) Compare 10 and 29. Since 10 < 29, no swapping is done
7, 3, **−4, 10**, 29, 31, 45

Observe that after the end of the third pass, the third largest element is placed at the third highest index of the array. All the other elements are still unsorted.

Pass 4:
(a) Compare 7 and 3. Since 7 > 3, swapping is done
3, 7, −4, 10, 29, 31, 45
(b) Compare 7 and −4. Since 7 > −4, swapping is done
3, **−4, 7**, 10, 29, 31, 45
(c) Compare 7 and 10. Since 7 < 10, no swapping is done
3, **−4, 7**, 10, 29, 31, 45

Observe that after the end of the fourth pass, the fourth largest element is placed at the fourth highest index of the array. All the other elements are still unsorted.

Pass 5:
(a) Compare 3 and –4. Since 3 > –4, swapping is done
   –4, 3, 7, 10, 29, 31, 45
(b) Compare 3 and 7. Since 3 > 7, no swapping is done
   –4, **3,** 7, 10, 29, 31, 45

Observe that after the end of the fifth pass, the fifth largest element is placed at the fifth highest index of the array. All the other elements are still unsorted.

Pass 6:
(a) Compare –4 and 3. Since -4 < 3, no swapping is done
   –4, 3, 7, 10, 29, 31, 45

Observe that after the end of the sixth pass, the sixth largest element is placed at the sixth largest index of the array. In our case, this completes the sorting of the given set of numbers. The entire list is sorted now.

15.1.2 Algorithm for Bubble Sort

If we see the basic methodology of the working of bubble sort, we can generalize the working as follows:

(1) In Pass 1, A[0] and A[1] are compared, then A[1] is compared with A[2], A[2] is compared with A[3], and so on. Finally, A[$n-2$] is compared with A[$n-1$]. Pass 1 involves $n-1$ comparisons and places the biggest element at the highest index of the array.

(2) In Pass 2, A[0] and A[1] are compared, then A[1] is compared with A[2], A[2] is compared with A[3], and so on. Finally, A[$n-3$] is compared with A[$n-2$]. Pass 2 involves $n-2$ comparisons and places the second biggest element at the second highest index of the array.

(3) In Pass 3, A[0] and A[1] are compared, then A[1] is compared with A[2], A[2] is compared with A[3], so on and so forth. Finally, A[$n-4$] is compared with A[$n-3$]. Pass 3 involves $n-3$ comparisons and places the third biggest element at the second highest index of the array.

....

....

($n-1$) In Pass $n-1$, A[0] and A[1] are compared so that A[1] < A[2]. After this step, all the elements of the array are arranged in ascending order.

Example 15.1

```
BUBBLE_SORT(A, N)
Step 1: Repeat steps 2 For I = 0 to I < N-1
Step 2:         Repeat For J = 0 to J < N - I
Step 3:                 If A[J] > A[J + 1], then
                            SWAP A[J] and A[J+1]
                [End of Inner Loop]
        [End of Outer Loop]
Step 4: EXIT
```

The above steps show the algorithm for bubble sort. In this algorithm, the outer loop is for the total number of passes which is $n-1$. The inner loop will be executed for every pass. However, the frequency of the inner loop will decrease with every pass because after every pass one element will be in its correct position. So, for every pass, the inner loop will be executed $N-I$ times, where N is the number of elements in the array and I is the count of the pass.

Example 15.2

```
# Program to show insert sort.
def sort(A):
  n = len(A)
  for i in range(n):
    for j in range(n-i-1):
      if(A[j]>A[j+1]):
      A[j],A[j+1] = A[j+1],A[j]
  return(A)
A = [23,12,56,43,78,90,3]
print("\n Original List: ",A)
A= sort(A)
print("\n Sorted List: ",A)
```

OUTPUT
```
Original List : [23, 12, 56, 43, 78, 90, 3]
Sorted List : [3, 12, 23, 43, 56, 78, 90]
```

15.1.3 Complexity of Bubble Sort

Before discussing the complexity of algorithms, let us get introduced to the Big-O notation. The Big-O notation, where O stands for 'order of', is concerned with what happens for very large values of n. Here, n is the number of elements to be sorted. For example, if a sorting algorithm performs n^2 operations to sort n elements, then that algorithm would be described as an $O(n^2)$ algorithm.

When expressing complexity using the Big-O notation, constant multipliers are ignored. So, an $O(4n)$ algorithm is equivalent to $O(n)$, which is how it should be written.

Thus, the complexity of any sorting algorithm depends upon the number of comparisons that are made. In bubble sort, we have seen that there are, in total, $n-1$ passes. In the first pass, $n-1$ comparisons are made to place the highest element in its correct position. Then in Pass 2, there are $n-2$ comparisons, and the second highest element is placed in its position. Therefore, to compute the complexity of the bubble sort, we need to calculate the total number of comparisons made. For this purpose, the number $f(n)$ of comparisons made can be given as,

$$f(n) = (n-1) + (n-2) + (n-3) + \ldots + 3 + 2 + 1 = n(n-1)/2 = n^2/2 + O(n) = O(n^2)$$

Therefore, the complexity of a bubble sort algorithm is $O(n^2)$; this means that to execute, bubble sort requires time that is proportional to n^2, where n is the total number of elements in the array. Therefore, to summarize, we can write time complexities as,

- Best case O describes an upper bound for all combinations of input. It is possibly lower than the worst case. For example, when sorting an array, the best case is when the array is already correctly sorted.
- Worst case O describes a lower bound for worst-case input combinations. It is possibly greater than the best case. For example, when sorting an array, the worst case is when the array is sorted in reverse order.
- If we simply write O, it means the same as worst-case O.

Worst-case Complexity The time required to sort values in the worst case is $O(n^2)$. The worst case occurs when the values to be sorted are already sorted but in reverse order. This means that if you have to sort a set of values that are already arranged in descending order, in ascending order and vice-versa. In such a case, each element has to be compared with each of the other elements. This means that for every nth element, $n-1$ number of comparisons are made. Therefore, the total number of comparisons = $n \times (n-1)$ which is approximately equal to n^2 for large values of n

Best-case Complexity Bubble sort performs fastest when the values are already sorted in the specified order. In such a case, only the outer loop will execute for *n* values but the inner loop will not perform any swap operation resulting in a linear complexity of $O(n)$.

Average-case Complexity Average case means when the values are not sorted at all. They are in jumbled order. In such a case, it will take $O(n^2)$ time to sort the values either in ascending or in descending order.

15.1.4 Applications of Bubble Sort

Bubble sort is a perfect sorting algorithm when the complexity of the code does not matter and a short code is required for ease of understanding. It is a very simple algorithm that is used to sort an unsorted list of elements, preferably in ascending order. You must have seen your teachers arranging all students in a queue in increasing order of their heights using this algorithm.

Bubble sort has been proved to be the fastest sorting algorithm under certain circumstances. It was once a popularly used sorting technique mainly because it was one of the first sorting algorithms that was rigorously analysed.

Bubble sort was extensively used in days when tape drives were used to store data. In such a drive, no random access to data is allowed. Only two records can be accessed at any given time. So, bubble sort was the best viable option.

Though, today it makes little sense to use bubble sort when faster algorithms are available. However, bubble sort is still preferred by some when either a small amount of data has to be sorted or the data is nearly sorted.

15.2 INSERTION SORT

Insertion sort is a very simple sorting algorithm in which the sorted array (or list) is built, one element at a time. We all are familiar with this technique of sorting as we usually use it for ordering a deck of cards while playing bridge.

The main idea behind insertion sort is that it inserts each item into its proper place in the final list. To save memory, most implementations of the insertion sort algorithm work by moving the current data element past the already sorted values and repeatedly interchanging it with the preceding value until it is in its correct place.

Although insertion sort is less efficient when compared with other more advanced algorithms such as quick sort, heap sort and merge sort, we will still read about its technique to gain an understanding of the subject.

15.2.1 The Insertion Sort Technique

Insertion sort works as follows:

- The array of values to be sorted is divided into two sets, one that stores sorted values and the other that contains unsorted values.
- The sorting algorithm will proceed until there are no elements in the unsorted set.
- Suppose there are *n* elements in the array. Initially the element with index 0 (assuming LB, Lower Bound = 0) is in the sorted set, the remaining elements are in the unsorted set
- The first element of the unsorted partition has array index 1 (if LB = 0)
- During each iteration of the algorithm, the first element in the unsorted set is picked up and inserted into the correct position in the sorted set.

15.2.2 Example of Insertion Sort

Consider an array of integers given below. Sort the values in the array using insertion sort.

| 39 | 9 | 45 | 63 | 18 | 81 | 108 | 54 | 72 | 36 |

Pass 1:

| 39 | 9 | 45 | 63 | 18 | 81 | 108 | 54 | 72 | 36 |

Pass 2:

| 9 | 39 | 45 | 63 | 18 | 81 | 108 | 54 | 72 | 36 |

Pass 3:

| 9 | 39 | 45 | 63 | 18 | 81 | 108 | 54 | 72 | 36 |

Pass 4:

| 9 | 39 | 45 | 63 | 18 | 81 | 108 | 54 | 72 | 36 |

Pass 5:

| 9 | 18 | 39 | 45 | 63 | 81 | 108 | 54 | 72 | 36 |

Pass 6:

| 9 | 18 | 39 | 45 | 63 | 81 | 108 | 54 | 72 | 36 |

Pass 7:

| 9 | 18 | 39 | 45 | 63 | 81 | 108 | 54 | 72 | 36 |

Pass 8:

| 9 | 18 | 39 | 45 | 54 | 63 | 81 | 108 | 72 | 36 |

Pass 9:

| 9 | 18 | 39 | 45 | 54 | 63 | 72 | 81 | 108 | 36 |

Pass 10:

| 9 | 18 | 36 | 39 | 45 | 54 | 63 | 72 | 81 | 108 |

Note that in Pass 1, A[0] is the only element in the sorted set.
In Pass 2, A[1] will be placed either before or after A[0], so that the array A is sorted
In Pass 3, A[2] will be placed either before A[0], in-between A[0] and A[1] or after A[1], so that the array is sorted.
In Pass 4, A[3] will be placed in its proper place so that the array A is sorted.

In Pass n, A[$n-1$] will be placed in its proper place so that the array A is sorted.

Therefore, we conclude that to insert the element A[K] in the sorted list A[0], A[1], ... A[$K-1$], we need to compare A[K] with A[$K-1$], then with A[$K-2$], then with A[$K-3$] and so on until we meet an element A[J] such that A[J] <= A[K].

In order to insert A[K] in its correct position, we need to move each element A[$K-1$], A[$K-2$], ..., A[J] by one position and then A[K] is inserted at the ($J+1$)th location. The algorithm for insertion sort is given in below.

15.2.3 Algorithm for Insertion Sort

Based on the above discussion, the algorithm for insertion sort can be given as shown in Example 15.3.

Example 15.3

```
Insertion sort (ARR, N) where ARR is an array of N elements
Step 1: Repeat Steps 2 to 5 for K = 1 to N-1
Step 2:     SET TEMP = ARR[K]
Step 3:     SET J = K - 1
Step 4:     Repeat while TEMP <= ARR[J]
                    SET ARR[J + 1] = ARR[J]
                    SET J = J - 1
            [END OF INNER LOOP]
Step 5:     SET ARR[J + 1] = TEMP
     [END OF LOOP]
Step 6: EXIT
```

In the algorithm, Step 1 executes a for loop which will be repeated for each element in the array. In Step 2, we store the value of the *K*th element in TEMP. In Step 3, we set the *J*th index in array. In Step 4, a for loop is executed; that will create space for the new element from the unsorted list to be stored in the list of sorted elements. Finally, in Step 5, the element is stored at the *J*th location.

15.2.4 Advantages of Insertion Sort

The following are the advantages of the sorting algorithm:

- Easy to implement
- Efficient to use on small sets of data
- Efficient implementation on data sets that are already substantially sorted
- Performs better than algorithms like selection sort and bubble sort. Insertion sort algorithm is much simpler than the shell sort, with only a small trade-off in efficiency. While, the insertion sort is over twice as fast as the bubble sort, it is almost 40% faster than the selection sort.
- Requires less memory space (only O(1) of additional memory space)
- Is said to be online as it can sort a list as and when it receives new elements

Example 15.4

```
# Program to show insert sort.
def insertionSort(A):
  for index in range(1,len(A)):
    val = A[index]
    pos =index
    while pos>0 and A[pos-1]>val:
      A[pos]=A[pos-1]
      pos = pos-1
    A[pos]=val
  return(A)
A = [15,11,16,19,12,17,13]
A = insertionSort(A)
print("Sorted List: ",A)
```

OUTPUT
```
Sorted List: [11,12,13, 15, 16, 17, 19]
```

15.2.5 Applications

The insertion sort performs well when the number of values to be sorted is small and the cost of comparisons exceeds the cost of swaps. Insertion sort is not only used as a stand-alone sorting algorithm but also as a part of other sorting algorithms (like binary merge sort) to sort groups of smaller number of values.

15.2.6 Complexity of Insertion Sort Algorithm

For an insertion sort, the best case occurs when the array is already sorted. In this case the running time of the algorithm is linear (i.e., $O(n)$). This is because, during each iteration, the first element from unsorted set is compared only with the last element of the sorted set of the array.

Similarly, the worst case of the insertion sort algorithm occurs when the array is sorted in reverse order. In the worst case, the first element of the unsorted set has to be compared with almost every element in the sorted set. Furthermore, every iteration of the inner loop will have to shift the elements of the sorted set of the array before inserting the next element. Therefore, in the worst case, insertion sort has a quadratic running time (i.e., $O(n^2)$). The time complexities can be summarized as given below.

Worst-case Complexity Worst case occurs the values are already sorted in descending order. In such a scenario, to insert the last element, we need at most $n-1$ comparisons and at most n-1 swaps. To insert the second to last element, we need at most $n-2$ comparisons and at most $n-2$ swaps, so on and so forth.

The number of operations needed to perform insertion sort is therefore, $2 \times (1+2+ .. +n-2+n-1)$ which is approximately equal to $n(n-1)$ or $O(n^2)$ complexity.

Average-case Complexity The average case complexity of insertion sort algorithm is same as worst case complexity. This case occurs when values are present in the list in a jumbled order.

Best-case Complexity The best case occurs when the values are already sorted and thus no swapping is done. In such a case, the complexity will be $O(n)$ because n comparisons will be made. But the inner loop that performs shifting will not be executed thereby saving n operations in each execution of the inner loop.

Key Terms

Bubble sort: A sorting algorithm which sorts by comparing each adjacent pair of values in a *list* in turn, swapping the values if necessary, and repeating the pass through the list until no swaps are done. The execution time of the bubble sort is $O(n^2)$.

Insertion sort: A sorting algorithm that sorts by repeatedly taking the next value and inserting it into the final sorted list. The execution time of the insertion sort is $O(n^2)$.

Sort: The process of arranging values in a predetermined order. There are dozens of algorithms, the choice of which depends on factors such as the number of values relative to working memory, the cost of comparing keys vs. the cost of moving items, etc.

Chapter Highlights

- A sorting algorithm is defined as an algorithm that puts elements of a list in a certain order (that can either be numerical order, lexicographical order or any user-defined order).

- Bubble sort is a very simple method that sorts the array elements by repeatedly moving the largest element to the highest index position of the array (in case of arranging elements in ascending order).

- In bubble sort algorithm, if the elements are to be sorted in descending order, then with each pass the smallest element is moved to the lowest index of the array.

- The complexity of any sorting algorithm depends upon the number of comparisons that are made.

- Worst case in a bubble sort occurs when the values to be sorted are already sorted, but in reverse order.
- Bubble sort performs fastest when the values are already sorted in the specified order.
- Bubble sort is a perfect sorting algorithm when the complexity of the code does not matter and a short code is required for ease of understanding.
- Insertion sort algorithm works by moving the current data element past the already sorted values and repeatedly interchanging it with the preceding value until the current data is in its correct place.
- The insertion sort performs well when the number of values to be sorted is small and the cost of comparisons exceeds the cost of swaps.
- Insertion sort is also used as a part of other sorting algorithms (like binary merge sort) to sort groups of smaller number of values.
- For an insertion sort, the best case occurs when the array is already sorted. In this case the running time of the algorithm is linear (i.e., $O(n)$).

Review Questions

1. Define sorting.
2. Give the importance of sorting.
3. What are the different types of sorting techniques? Which sorting technique has least worst-case complexity?
4. Why is bubble sort algorithm called so?
5. Discuss the time complexity of bubble sort algorithm in all three cases – best, average and worst case.
6. Discuss the time complexity of insertion sort algorithm in all three cases- best, average and worst case.
7. Explain the difference between bubble sort and insertion sort. Which algorithm will you prefer to use and in which condition?
8. List some advantages of using Insertion Sort technique.
9. Consider the list of values given below. Demonstrate how bubble sort and insertion sort will be applied on this list to sort the values in ascending order.
   a. 81, 27, 36, 54, 18   b. B, Z, A, S, L, O, P, K
10. Consider the list of values given below. Demonstrate how bubble sort and insertion sort will be applied on this list to sort the values in descending order.
    a. 81, 27, 36, 54, 18   b. B, Z, A, S, L, O, P, K.
11. Give the advantages of insertion sort.
12. A certain sorting technique was applied to the following data set: 48, 52, 20, 34, 87, 90
    After two passes, the rearrangement of the data set is given as below. Identify the sorting algorithm used.
    87, 90, 34, 52, 48, 20   87, 90, 34, 52, 48, 20
    87, 34, 52, 48, 20, 90   20, 87, 90, 34, 52, 48

Programming Exercises

1. Write a program to implement bubble sort. Given the numbers 7, 1, 4, 12, 67, 33 and 45, how many swaps will be performed to sort these numbers using bubble sort?

2. Write an algorithm for bubble sort.

3. Write an algorithm for insertion sort.

4. Write a program to implement bubble sort. Also analyze the strength and weakness of the bubble sort algorithm.

5. Write a program to implement insertion sort. Also analyze the complexity of the insertion sort algorithm.

6. Write a program to sort integer values in descending order using bubble sort.

7. Modify bubble sort and insertion sort programs so that the program, besides displaying the sorted array, also displays the number of data moves needed to sort the array.
   Hint: Data move means movement of data element from one position in the array to another

8. Write a program to sort an array of integers in descending order using insertion sort.

9. Create a nested tuple of 10 students. Each tuple should have Roll No., Name and Marks of a student. Sort the tuple values in descending order of marks.

10. Create a nested list of 10 employees. Each list should store EName, EDept and EDesig of a particular employee. Sort the list in ascending order of department.

11. Write a program that sorts a list of random numbers in descending order of the digit at one's place.

12. Write a program that has a dictionary, listing the names of the students and their marks. Sort the key value pairs in ascending order of names.

Fill in the Blanks

1. Sorting means _____.

2. In _____ sorting, consecutive adjacent pairs of elements in the array are compared with each other.

3. $O(n^2)$ is the running time complexity of _____ algorithm.

4. In the worst case, insertion sort has a _____ running time.

5. The time required to sort values in the worst case is _____.

6. In bubble sort, worst case occurs when _____.

7. Best-case complexity of bubble sort is ____.

8. Average-case complexity of insertion sort is ____.

State True or False

1. Bubble sort can arrange values only in ascending order.
2. Insertion sort algorithm works by moving the current data element past the already sorted values.
3. For an insertion sort, the worst case occurs when values are already sorted.
4. The average-case complexity of insertion sort algorithm is the same as worst-case complexity.
5. For an insertion sort, the best case occurs when the array is already sorted.
6. The average case of insertion sort has a quadratic running time.
7. Bubble sort performs worst when the values are already sorted in the specified order.
8. In bubble sorting, after the end of the second pass, the second largest element is placed at the second index of the array.
9. The complexity of any sorting algorithm depends upon the number of comparisons that are made.

Multiple Choice Questions

1. A card game player arranges his cards as he picks them one by one. To which sorting technique you can compare this example?
   a. Bubble Sort b. Insertion Sort c. Both of these. d. None of these.

2. In which sorting, consecutive adjacent pairs of elements in the array are compared with each other.
   a. Bubble Sort b. Insertion Sort c. Both of these. d. None of these.

3. If there are 20 numbers to sort and you are supposed to choose an algorithm that will perform lesser number of operations, then you will choose which algorithm?
   a. Bubble Sort b. Insertion Sort c. Both of these. d. None of these.

4. To sort a list of 30 random numbers, which algorithm will you prefer to use?
   a. Bubble sort b. Insertion sort c. None of these. d. Any of these.

5. Complexity of bubble sort is $O(n)$ in _____ case(s).
   a. Best b. Worst c. Average d. None of these.

6. Complexity of insertion sort is _____ in best case.
   a. $O(\log(n))$ b. $O(n)$ c. $O(n^2)$ d. None of these.

7. Bubble sort is a perfect sorting algorithm when _____.
   a. complexity of the code does not matter b. a short code is required
   c. a small number of values have to be sorted d. All of these.

Answers

Fill in the Blanks
1. arranging the elements in a specific order
2. bubble
3. worst case bubble sort and insertion sort
4. $O(n^2)$
5. $O(n^2)$
6. the values to be sorted are already sorted, but in reverse order
7. $O(n)$
8. $O(n^2)$

State True or False

1. False
2. True
3. False
4. True
5. True
6. True
7. False
8. False
9. True

Multiple Choice Questions

1. b
2. b
3. b
4. b
5. a
6. b
7. d

Society, Law and Ethics - I

16

Chapter Objectives

In this chapter, we discuss very sensitive issues relating to security in the cyber world. A netizen must always practice ethical behavior and be aware of IT laws that impose heavy penalty and imprisonment on anyone breaking those laws. Topics covered in this chapter include:

- The role of Internet in our lives
- Netiquette that one must possess while working on the Internet
- Ethics that help us to understand what is considered as acceptable behavior and what is not
- Issues that affect cyber security including plagiarism, hacking, cyber bullying, phishing, spamming, spoofing, eavesdropping
- Digital footprints
- Malware including virus, worms, Trojan horse, adware, spyware, keyloggers and ransomware
- System and data protection through passwords, firewalls and antivirus software

These days, the Internet is extensively being used for exchanging data or messages. Some data may be personal and thus confidential in nature. For example, when we do online banking or buy any product from a website, we send our password and credit card number through the Internet. Any person with malicious intentions can intercept (illegally access) our data and misuse it. However, the most common threats to Internet security comes either from the use of malware or through frauds such as phishing. In this chapter, we will therefore read about safely browsing the web, protecting one's identity, appropriate usage of social networks and protection from malware.

16.1 THE INTERNET – OCEAN OF INFORMATION AND OPPORTUNITIES

The Internet is a great invention that has opened the world to people by stripping away geographical barriers and sharing information instantly. The number of people using Internet is on constant rise. The graph given in Fig. 16.1, clearly shows that the number of Internet users in India has increased manifold in the last few years and will grow even more in the coming years. To understand the reason behind this sharp increase, we will need to know the advantages of the Internet.

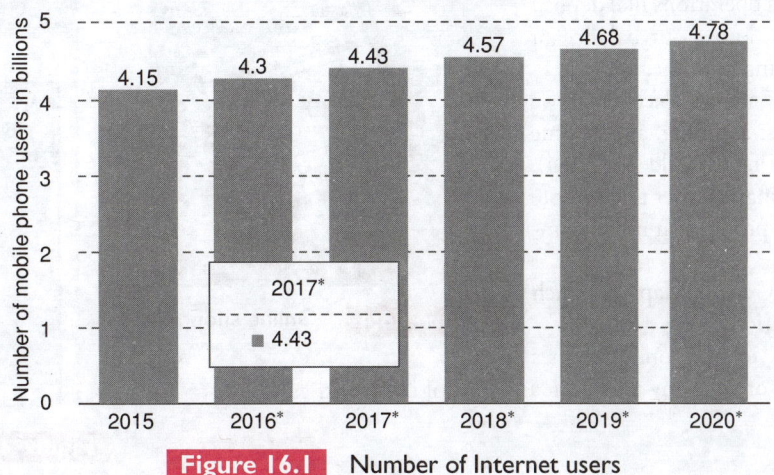

Figure 16.1 Number of Internet users

16.1.1 Advantages

- Internet is an ocean of information. We can find information on almost every subject and at every level (from material for kindergarten children to research papers on cutting-edge topics) on the Internet. There are many powerful search engines which help us to easily find out relevant information from the Internet (Fig. 16.2).
- Anybody can conduct an extensive research on a particular topic by sitting at home. There are numerous articles and research works published by people all over the world.
- There are message boards and group discussion websites where people can discuss ideas on any topic. We can participate in those discussions and know about the opinions of other participants on any given subject.

Figure 16.2 Search engines

- People can use blogging websites to share their knowledge and experiences on a particular topic with other people having a similar interest in that topic.
- The Internet offers free email service that allow users to send their emails instantly to people located anywhere in the world.
- We can watch breaking news and live sports or other live events on the Internet. So even at places where we cannot carry our TV set, Internet on computer or smartphone can help.
- We can watch movies and listen songs on the Internet. We can even download them for free.
- Using Skype or other programs with video calling features, we can hold a video conference with anyone in the world (Fig. 16.3).
- We can make friends over the Internet and can get connected with our friends and relatives living in any part of the world. Internet is an easy, cheap and fast way to connect with people worldwide.
- Matrimonial sites like shaadi.com, jeevansati.com, etc., have helped people to find a suitable match for themselves.
- Jobs site like MonsterIndia has helped people to gain employment.

Figure 16.3 Video conferencing

- Many universities are offering online courses on the Internet. Anyone from any part of the world can enroll in these courses, attend online lectures, submit online assignments and take online tests to get themselves evaluated to get the completion certificate. Imagine yourself doing a course from the prestigious Stanford University in US or from IITs in India while sitting at home.
- Websites like MakeMyTrip help us to plan an entire trip using the Internet. We can see pictures of many places; decide a destination, book tickets, book hotels, cabs and everything using the Internet.
- With Internet banking, we can perform all sorts of banking operations like deposit or transfer money, know our balance or pay bills while sitting at home.
- Internet offers 24*7 marketplace where we can shop for almost anything, at any time and from anywhere in the world (Fig. 16.4).
- Companies are using Internet to promote (or advertise) their products at much competitive rates.
- People are using Google Maps to reach their travel destinations. (Fig. 16.5)
- Internet allows us to play online games either individually or with any person in any part of the world.

Figure 16.4 Online shopping

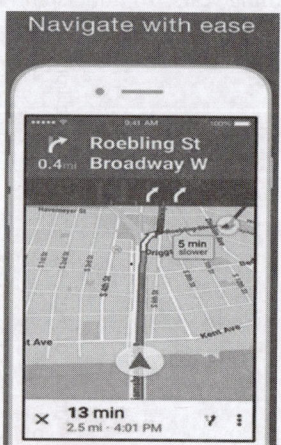

Figure 16.5 Google Maps

- Companies are providing technical support for their products online. They are also using Internet to get their customers' feedback. This helps them to directly get in touch with their customers and improve their products.
- Images from safety camera installed in banks and other places are transferred to the control room using Internet.
- Before buying any product or booking a hotel, we can read the reviews written by other users. This help us to make an informed decision (Fig. 16.6).
- Internet allows even a common man to sell his products (even a second-hand product).
- Students who also work as bloggers are earning income by writing blogs. Blogging websites give a platform to those students who are interested in media and want to be writers in the future. Blogging hones their professional skills for future use.

Figure 16.6 Checking reviews

The Internet has revolutionized our lives and made it very convenient. But, it has an ugly side also. The following are some disadvantages of the Internet.

- Though there is lot of information on the Internet, there is no guarantee that the information is 100% accurate. This is because anybody from anywhere can post information. Do you know that even you can post information on Wikipedia? Find out how.
- On social networking sites (refer Fig. 16.7), we find many people who are on the lookout for making friendship with innocent people to take full advantage of their innocence. Many people get addicted to the Internet. They become less active interactive with their friends and loved ones in the real world and therefore losing them.

Figure 16.7 Social networking sites

- Pornographic websites are easily viewed by children. Children also gain access to content that is not appropriate at their age.
- People who are fond of net surfing spend hours together going from one website to another. This adds to their sedentary lifestyles and thus make them prone to problems like obesity, hypertension, constant pain in neck and shoulders, strain on eyes, etc.
- Students copy information from the Internet to complete their work. This reduces their ability to think and be creative. They may even unknowingly use copyrighted material and thus land themselves in trouble.
- Some people offer easy loans, enticing business offers, free holiday packages, etc., to fool innocent people and extract money from them.
- Some malicious users create viruses and other malware to intentionally harm computers or steal information about other people.
- There are many online games that contain violence, which has a negative influence on children. Children who play lot of online games often become violent on small provocation.
- Many people deliberately connect with children to extract personal information from them. They use this information to arrange a theft or even kidnap the children.

16.2 NETIQUETTE

Netiquette, Network Etiquette, or Internet Etiquette is a set of rules that should be followed when a person is working on the Internet. These rules define a set of dos and don'ts to be followed while working on the Internet.

Netiquette has been defined to make the Internet experience pleasant and enjoyable for everyone. Some of these rules include:

- Do not reply to any unknown messages or messages that make us uncomfortable.
- Do not exchange any personal information on Internet without your parent's permission.
- Always discuss your Internet activities with your parents.

- Avoid using Internet in the absence of your teachers or parents.
- Never share your passwords with anyone.
- Treat others as you would like to be treated. Do not write something that would hurt other's feelings (refer Fig. 16.8).
- Do not write in capital letters as it is treated as shouting.
- Do not use too many emoticons.
- Do not send fake emails.
- Do not talk to a stranger. Never arrange for a meeting with a person whom you met on the Internet.
- For doing homework, do not just copy the contents from the Internet. That is cheating. Just take hints and write your own answers.
- Do not write messages in someone else's name.
- Do not write very long messages.
- Start your message with a greeting.
- Never use rude, abusive or bad words in your message.
- Do not forward unnecessary emails especially those which states forward to 10 people to change your luck in 24 hours, etc.

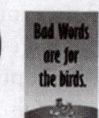

Figure 16.8 Net etiquette

Use nickname and not your real name for chatting. Also do not agree to meet someone you met online.

16.3 ETHICS IN COMPUTING

Ethics is a set of moral values that govern the behavior of a person (Fig. 16.9). Ethics in computing refers to a set of moral values that regulate the use of computers. Let us take two examples to understand the term computer ethics.

- It may be easy for an individual to duplicate copyrighted electronic content but computer ethics states that it is wrong to do so without the author's approval.
- It may be possible to access someone's personal information on a computer but computer ethics states that one should not do so. We must always respect others' privacy.

Figure 16.9 Ethics deals with judging whether an act is good or bad. Some of the rules of ethics have been converted to laws

16.4 ISSUES IN CYBER SAFETY

So now we understand that any activity that may directly or indirectly, intentionally or un-intentionally harm any person or computer is considered to be unethical. Given below are a few unethical practices that every Internet user must refrain from doing. Some of the unethical activities have been legally bonded, so the person caught involved in it can be severely punished as per the cyber laws of his/her country. For example, copying and using someone else's copyright material without taking permissions from the owner of the copyright is not only unethical but also a punishable offence. In this section, we will learn about some unethical practices on the Internet and preventive measures that one must take to stay safe.

16.4.1 Plagiarism

Plagiarism means copying someone else's work and publishing it as one's own. The work may be a simple text, image, or even an idea. Often, we may have to write some definitions or text or use an image that has to be taken as it is. While doing so, we must publish the work with an appropriate reference or citation, or else it will be considered plagiarism. Even if the original content has been modified by rewording the text, it is still considered plagiarism if no credit is given to the original source (Fig. 16.10).

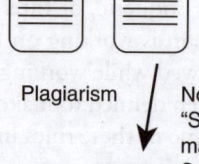

Plagiarism

No credit given "Stealing of published material"
Small modifications made

Figure 16.10 Plagiarism

On the World Wide Web, a lot of information is present on almost every topic in a digital format. While this makes it easier to access information, it also opens the door to easily plagiarize other people's work. Since it is very easy to copy-paste digital information, plagiarism has become a serious problem.

Preventive measures: There are strict laws including the international copyright law to protect digital content against plagiarism. The international copyright law states that every individual's published work is automatically protected by copyright. One cannot copy another person's work without his or her approval. Anyone found doing this will be heavily penalized.

Using pirated software is equivalent of stealing. Similarly, using text or image on a website without giving credit to the original creator is another form of stealing.

Why do students plagiarize?
- Lack of interest
- Laziness
- Lack of preparation
- Lack of understanding
- Competition
- Cultural differences
- Pressure / fear
- Excessive demands
- No consequences

If you are taking some information then always give reference of the book or source and/or a link to the website from where the information has been taken. If a large amount of content has to be taken then you should contact the author and ask for permission.

16.4.2 Hacking

Hacking means the act of identifying weakness in a computer system or even a network. Once the weakness is identified, it is exploited to gain access to that computer. For example, if someone has set a very weak password then a hacker (people who hack) can break the password to access the system.

Hacking is very serious problem today as computers have become a must-have device for all of us and a stand-alone computer without being connected to any network or the Internet is just not enough in today's era. We need to be connected for more information, for better ways to do routine tasks, to socialize and to run a successful business. But this exposes our computers to hackers. *Hackers hack computer systems to commit fraudulent acts such as privacy invasion, stealing corporate/personal data, etc.*

Hacking can either be ethical or unethical. Ethical hacking is done when someone deliberately accesses the computer but not to break its security and steal data. It is done only to identify any weakness in the system so that they can be overcome. Ethical hackers are usually experts in computer technology with a sound knowledge of computer hardware and software.

Unethical hacking, on the other hand, is done by hackers who gain unauthorized access to the computer system and also get access to secured accounts. These hackers always have wrong intentions and they gain access usually by cracking passwords and other security codes. Therefore, unethical hackers are also known as crackers.

Preventive Measures
- Create complex passwords. Password should consist of a combination of numbers, upper- and lower-case letters, and special characters that are difficult to guess (Fig. 16.11).
- Create a different password for every account. This ensures that even if the hacker has broken your password of one account, at least the others are safe.
- Never tell your passwords to anyone. Not even to your close friend. Do not even write it down on the last page of your notebook or at places which can be easily accessed by others.
- Change your passwords often. You must at least change it once in every 4–5 months.
- Do not repeat your password. Always set a new one. Websites like Gmail never allows you to choose a previous password.
- After checking your emails and using your other accounts, do not forget to log out.
- Install antivirus software and firewalls (discussed later in this chapter).

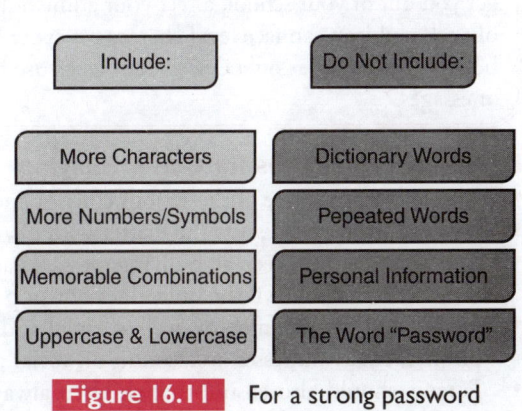

Figure 16.11 For a strong password

16.4.3 Disrespecting Values and Traditions

Never upload animations, pictures or other material that can hurt others' religious, cultural and social beliefs or promote any kind of discrimination (like social, economic, racial, etc.) amongst people.

Preventive measure: Block the people sending such messages and never get yourself involved in such discussions.

> Every individual is equal before law. Portraying people of a particular religion, region, background, skin color as superior to other is not just unethical but also illegal. There is always a thin line between freedom of speech and decency of speech. Do not cross it.

16.4.4 Spreading Rumor and Cyber Bullying

Cyber bullying or Internet bullying is a form of teen violence that has already caused lasting harm to young people. Some teens use Internet to bully or harass another person (classmates or neighborhood friends). As a result, the victim goes into depression or develops anxiety problems. In many cases victims have even committed suicide (Fig. 16.12).

In cyber bullying, teens have been found involved in the following activities. We have laid special emphasis on this point so that students can understand the sensitivity of the matter and avoid such practices.

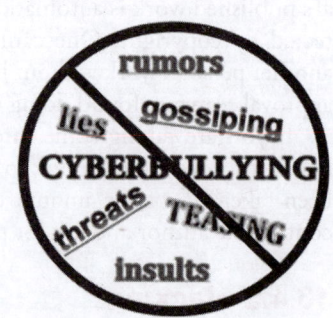

Figure 16.12 Cyber bullying and its effects

- Sending threatening messages through smart phones or emails
- Spreading rumors through social networking websites or through group messages.
- Stealing someone's email id and password and using it to send threatening or damaging messages to a third person.
- Taking pictures of someone and spreading it through the Internet.
- Sexting, or circulating sexually suggestive pictures or messages about a person.

> **SERIOUS NOTE:** Teens often think that cyber bullying is only for fun. But remember that such activities can get you out of your school, affect your admission in college and in getting a job in a reputed organization. Parents of such children can face legal charges for cyber bullying. If cyber bullying involved sexting, then the offender can be registered as a sex offender. Even if teens use fake email ids, there are many ways to find out who had sent these messages.

Preventive Measures for Cyber Bullying

- Make children aware of the serious consequences of cyber bullying.
- The victim should discuss the matter with his/her parents and teachers.
- The victim should keep all bullying messages as a proof that can be shown to the teachers, parents of the bully and may be to the police if the bully does not stop sending such messages. Never delete them.
- Block the bully's number as well as email address. Parents should ensure that teens do not use personal mobile phones, email addresses or accounts on social networking websites.
- Parents should also ensure that children always use the computer in the living room and not in their personal rooms so they can keep a check on what the children are doing.

16.4.5 Phishing

Phishing is the act of sending an email or messages to a user falsely claiming to be a legitimate authority. Phishing is done to scam the user to get his or her personal information (this is an example of identity theft).

Phishing emails usually ask the user to visit a website (that is actually bogus) to update his/her personal information like password, credit card number, social security number, or bank account numbers (refer Fig. 16.13). All this information is already available with the legitimate website. The bogus website captures the details entered by the user and uses it to commit a crime.

The bogus website is created in such a way that it looks exactly like the original website. This is done so that user does not suspect the website before entering the information.

Figure 16.13 Phishing attack

Preventive Measures
- If you get an email from a company with which you are not associated with, do not give any personal information.
- Bogus website will have spelling and grammar errors. Always check for such errors as they indicate a phishing attack.
- If a bank website is asking for your account number, then it would have at least specified the other details correctly. But a bogus website does not display any such information, it only asks for your details.
- Bogus websites will give you very short deadlines to fill the information (like within 24 hours) but a genuine one will give you ample time. So, beware.
- The bogus website will have a different URL that can be easily identified. So, if a website is asking for personal information, do not forget to check its URL.
- If you have got an email asking for your personal information. Do not fill it at once. Rather, contact the company directly through their e-mail address or phone.

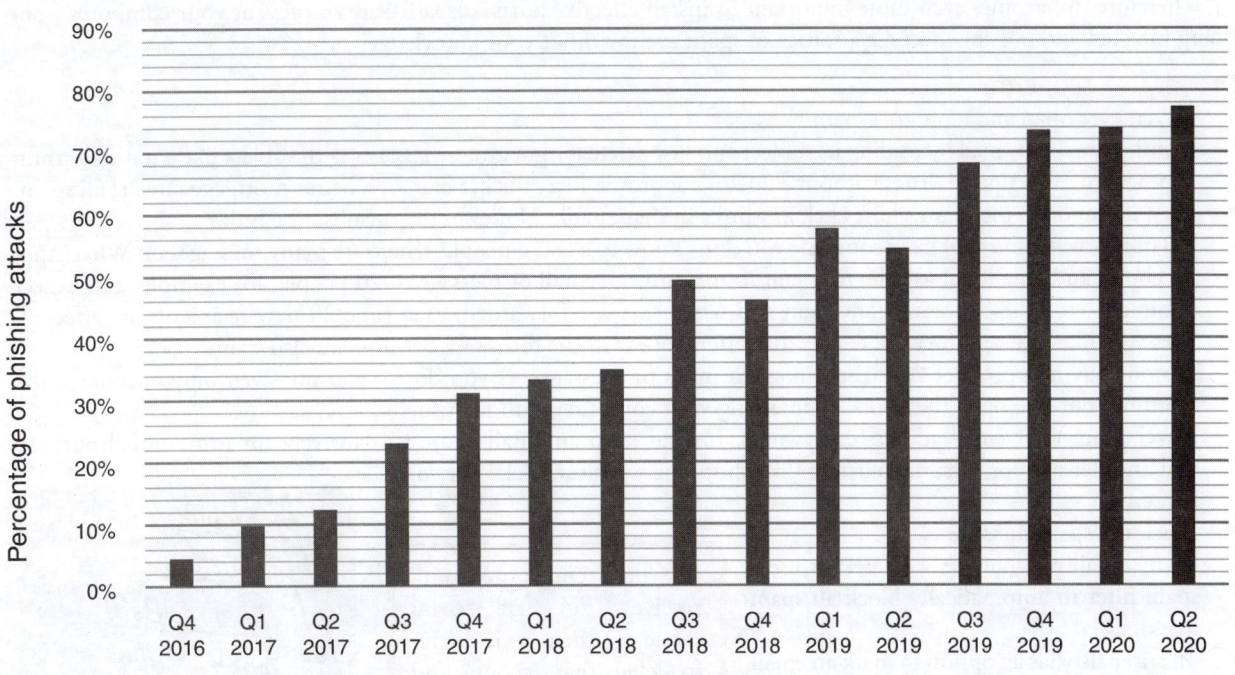

Source: APWG

- A phishing email always states that the user's account or password or credit card number is expiring, the user's account is being hacked and that the account information needs to be changed. It may say that the user's credit card number has been duplicated and he or she needs to log in to confirm recent orders or transactions. Remember this and do not become a prey.
- Never respond to emails coming from an unknown person, especially from a foreign country.
- Never respond to emails that threatens to harm unless a huge amount of money is paid.
- A legitimate email asking for your details will always have your name but a fraudulent email will have generic greetings "Dear Customer".

16.4.6 Spamming

Spamming means sending unwanted emails in bulk (to a large number of recipients). Spam is considered to be an electronic junk mail which is usually sent for advertising products (Fig. 16.14). Most spam emails often advertise dubious (not trustworthy) products, get-rich-quick schemes, enticing business opportunities, winning of a lottery or get-easy-loan schemes.

Though spam email is a very cost-effective medium to commercially advertise a product, for the receiver it is a waste of time. Spammers get email addresses which are publicly available on the Internet and use those addresses to send mails to the masses.

In many countries, spamming is considered to be an illegal activity and a person found guilty of spamming has to appear before the court. Therefore, very often spammers either hide or forge the origin of their messages to circumvent laws and anti-spammer lists used by anti-spam software.

Figure 16.14 Spamming

These days, spam is sent from computers that are infected by **computer viruses**. Virus-makers and spammers have together come up with an idea to use the infected computers as spam-sending "drones" or "zombies". We know that virus spreads rapidly and generates massive amounts of spam, that too when sent from legitimate addresses. Now, even if someone is to be punished, it will be the owner of the infected computer system who is himself a victim.

There was a time 95% of email messages sent worldwide were recognized as spam.

Therefore, it becomes even more important to install effective **antivirus software** to prevent your computer from being infected and possibly become a source of spam even without your knowledge.

Preventive Measure
- Never, ever open and reply to a spam message.
- Identify the spam email by reading its subject and just delete it right away. Messages with subject like a more youthful appearance, prescription drugs without a doctor's approval, love, thicker hair, or a better mortgage rate are all spam.
- Even if you open the spam, don't click *any* links in that email. Not even the unsubscribe link.
- Do not forward an email from someone you don't know to a list of people. There are many messages on WhatsApp, Facebook and email that ask the recipient to forward the email or message to 20 people, for example, and expect a miracle, etc. These messages are spam and when they are forwarded, each time 20 new recipients are affected. Messages like sign-and-forward emails that often appear in the form of a petition are also spam.
- Do not buy any product advertised in spam mails or messages. If you do so, you not even only encourage the spammer but also open the doors for infecting your computer with malware.
- Never share your email address everywhere. Instead keep an email address exclusively for professional purpose and another one for personal purpose (like shopping websites, social networking, etc.).
- Block the spam messages.
- Many email programs as well as ISPs use a spam filter to automatically block all spam messages.
- The user also has an option to mark an email as Spam, so that next time it comes from the same sender, it is automatically sent to the 'Spam' or 'Junk' folder (Fig. 16.15).

If your email account receives lot of spam messages then it is better to delete that account and create a new one with a different id.

Figure 16.15 Spam folder

16.4.7 Spoofing

The word *spoof* means to hoax, trick, or deceive. Correspondingly, spoofing means tricking or deceiving computer systems or other computer users. This is either done by hiding one's identity or faking the identity of another user on the Internet.

Spoofing can be done in several ways. In the first variant, ***email spoofing***, messages are either sent using a bogus e-mail address or faking the e-mail address of another user. However, since most of the email servers today have security features, it is extremely difficult for unauthorized users to send spoofed emails.

In the second variant of spoofing, which is also known as ***IP spoofing***, the IP address of a certain computer is masked so that it becomes difficult for other systems to determine the sender (real sender) of the data. For example if I send you a letter, in the From address, I may write your friend's address instead of mine. If I do this, you will think that you got the letter from your friend. It will be very difficult for you to know that it was me not your friend who had sent that letter.

In its third variant, the cyber criminals ***fake an identity*** (like an online username). For example, when posting on a web discussion forum, a user may pretend to be a representative of a company, when actually he/she has no association with it. Moreover, in online chat rooms, users may fake their age, gender, and location.

Prevention

The only way to prevent spoofing is to make sure that you know who you are communicating with. This is especially important when you are giving out private information over the Internet.

IP spoofing attacks usually take place when trust relationships use IP addresses (rather than user logins) to verify machines' identities to access systems. Cyber criminals use spoofing attacks to impersonate machines with access permissions.

- Avoid trust relationships
- Use spoofing detection software
- Use cryptographic network protocols such as Secure Shell (SSH) and HTTPs which encrypt data before it is sent and authenticate data as it is received.

16.4.8 Eavesdropping

Eavesdrop, in general terms, mean the practice of actually standing under the eaves of a house and listening to conversations inside. In computers, eavesdropping means unauthorized real-time interception of a private communication, such as a phone call, email, instant message, videoconference or fax transmission.

Voice over IP (VoIP) Internet calling systems that don't use encryption make it relatively easy for an intruder to intercept calls. These calls can be recorded without being observed by the callers.

Even systems that use encryption are vulnerable to such attacks. In August 2009, a Trojan known as Peskyspy was found, which was specifically designed to access Skype call audio before it was encrypted.

> Encryption means changing the actual information in such a way that it appears to be some random data. For example, HELLO can be sent as KHOOR. Did you notice that here, 3 is added to every character making it difficult to understand what information was originally sent?

The activities of eavesdropping do not disrupt the normal operation of the systems being eavesdropped on. Obviously, when we are overhearing someone else's private conversation, we will never want to disturb the conversation so that we can get maximum information. While eavesdropping, both parties of the communication – the sender and receiver are completely unaware that their communication is being intercepted and data is being stolen.

Devices with microphones including laptops and cell phones can be hacked to remotely activate their microphones and send data to the attacker.

An eavesdropping attack, which is also known as a sniffing or snooping attack, is difficult to detect because it does not cause network transmissions to appear to be operating abnormally.

> Eavesdropping on a conventional telephone line is known as wiretapping.

Prevention

- Do a full network scan to know what devices are connected to a network and what software is installed on those devices

- Use firewalls
- Use the latest version of operating system and update it regularly
- Update antivirus software
- Avoid using public networks, especially for sensitive transactions (like banking applications). Public Wi-Fi networks are an easy target for eavesdropping attacks. Anyone with easily available password can join the network and use free software to monitor network activity and steal login id, password and other confidential data that users transmit over the network.

In addition to the above ways, 24 × 7 control over access by outsiders to the computers must be protected. Continuous supervision of people doing repairs or maintenance work in the company must be done to ensure that they do not make alterations. Thorough inspection must be done of all new furnishings, decorations or equipment brought recently must be done by a qualified person.

16.4.9 Digital Footprint

Digital footprints mean footprints or traces that a user leaves when he/she is online. Whenever a user fills a registration form, sends an e-mail, uploads pictures/ videos or any other file, searches for some information, he leaves traces of personal information about himself/herself on the Internet. Therefore, a digital footprint is the data generated as a result of actions and communications online that can be traced back to the user. There are two types of digital footprints – Active and Passive (Fig. 16.16).

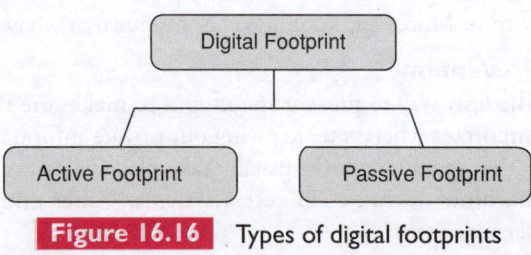

Figure 16.16 Types of digital footprints

- **Active footprints** are those footprints that a user leaves intentionally. For example, we leave active footprints whenever we post or like a comment on Facebook, tweet on Twitter, upload a file, send an email, chat and make phone calls (voice or video) over the Internet.
- **Passive footprints** are left by a user unintentionally. For example, whenever we visit a website, search information or shop online, we leave behind information about ourselves. The websites keep a track of how many times we have visited a website and for what kind of information.

A digital footprint is relatively permanent and once the data is in public or even semi-public domain (like on Facebook), the user has very little control over how it will be used by others. Therefore, we should be very particular about our online activities.

> While shopping online, websites record your movement from one webpage to another. They do this to keep a note of the products you are looking for. This information helps them to do targeted advertisement (show advertisements of those products in which you are interested).

16.4.10 Social Networking Sites and Specific Usage Rules

Everyone who uses the Internet has a digital footprint. Though you don't have to worry about it, you must keep a check on what data you are leaving behind. For example, never post any content that may lead you to trouble. Even if you delete your posts, tweets or emails, remember that it is still present on the Internet.

Moreover, digital footprints are of big interest to hackers who are looking to steal your identity. Remember that these days, digital footprints are also used by employers, schools, other institutions or individuals to whom your clear identity and reputation matters (Fig. 16.17).

To keep a check on what information about you is available online, just enter your name in different search engines and see what all information is displayed.

If you are on Facebook or on any other social networking site then you can control who can see your posts by making changes in the Privacy Settings. For example, Facebook allows you to limit posts merely to people in your Friends List.

Your parents, teachers, employers, future colleges, and police can find your posts.

Figure 16.17 Anybody can follow digital footprints

However, remember that even after changing your privacy settings, the posts are still available on the Internet. There have been many complaints by Facebook users that "friends-locked" photographs can be seen as public images on Google Image Search. Therefore, keep the following points in mind while surfing the Internet.

Build a positive image online (Fig. 16.18). Post only those things that contribute to the image of you that you want your parents, teachers, friends, relatives and employers (in future) to see.

Skip the negative tweets and un-tag yourself from posts or pictures on social networking websites that are either rude or controversial.

You can start blogging to showcase your work or a hobby about which you are really passionate.

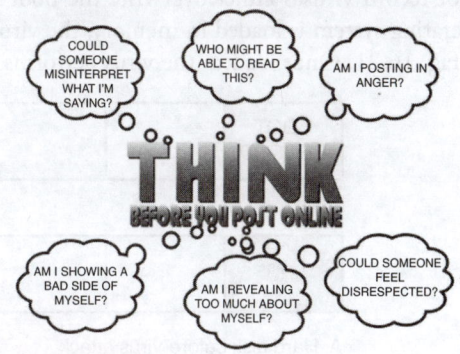

Figure 16.18 Using social networking sites

16.5 MALWARE

Malware or malicious software means software designed with wrong intentions. A malware is specifically written to gain access to a computer either to harm it by disturbing its operations or gather sensitive information from it. Moreover, a malware is usually embedded or hidden within legitimate software that is either useful or attractive.

No doubt, malware is a big threat to computer security. When we say malware, it includes all the terms like computer virus, spyware, worms, Trojan horse, etc (Fig. 16.19).

16.5.1 VIRUS (Vital Information Resources Under Seige)

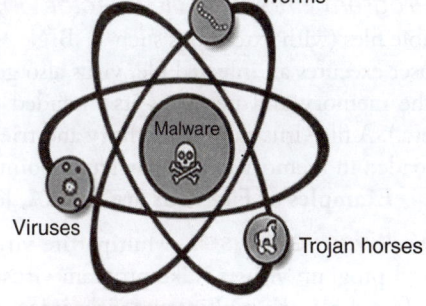

Figure 16.19 Types of malware

A computer virus is a small program that gets loaded in the computer without the user's knowledge and replicates (repeats) itself. Virus is harmful for the computer as by copying itself repeatedly in computer's memory, it quickly uses all available memory and finally halts the system. A virus can even corrupt or delete files from the computer and may spread itself to other computers by using the user's email.

Therefore, computer viruses are always undesirable as they slow down the computer's performance, cause erratic behavior, loss of data, and frequent crashes.

Features of virus: A virus replicates itself. It is always embedded in a legitimate file. Moreover, a virus gets activated by an external action as for example, when a user downloads and opens a file that contains virus.

Sources of virus: Sources of computer virus include the following:
- Files that are either attached in email messages or sent while chatting
- Embedded in funny images, greeting cards and in audio / video files as shown in Fig. 16.20.
- Some files downloaded from the Internet may contain virus

Examples of virus are: W32.Sfc!mod, ABAP.Rivpas.A, Accept.3773, ILOVEYOU, Code Red, Melissa, Stuxnet.

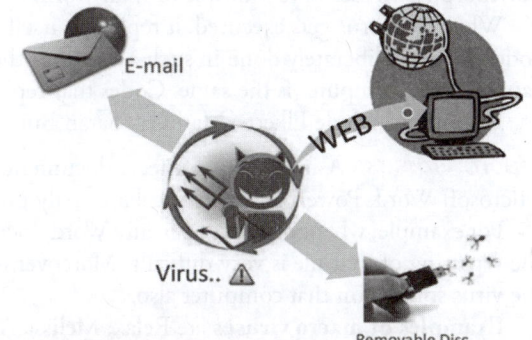

Figure 16.20 Virus attack can be done through emails, pen drives, or through the Internet.

Types of Virus We can broadly classify computer viruses under different categories:

Boot viruses: In the days when floppy disks were used to transfer data, these viruses were used to infect the disks. However, as floppy disks are no longer used, the boot virus infects only the master boot records of the hard disk.

> The master boot record on the hard disk is the first sector on the hard disk.

The boot record stores code that loads the operating system in the memory when the computer is turned on. Boot record viruses either overwrite the boot record or move it to a different location in the hard disk. When the operating system is loaded in memory, the virus also somehow gets loaded along with the operating system as shown in Fig. 16.21. Once loaded, the virus performs malicious activities without getting noticed.

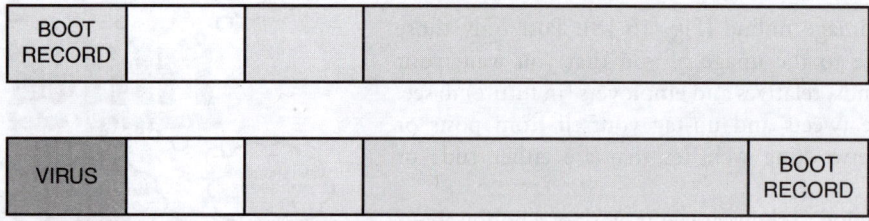

A. Hard disk before virus attack
B. Hard disk infected with boot record or the boot sector virus. The virus has relocated the boot record.

Figure 16.21 Boot virus attack

Examples of boot viruses include Polyboot.B, AntiEXE, Disk Killer, and Stoned.

Program viruses or file infector viruses: These are the most common type of viruses. They infect only executable files (with extensions such as .BIN, .COM, .EXE, .SYS) of applications, music files, videos, games, etc. When the user executes an infected file, virus also gets executed along with the file. On being executed, the virus gets loaded in the memory and performs its intended task (like overwriting or deleting files, etc.). A file virus stays in memory and tries to infect all programs and files that are loaded in memory at that particular point of time.

> It is easier to identify and remove a program virus than a boot virus.

Examples of File virus are Snow.A, Jerusalem, and Cascade.

Multipartite viruses: Multipartite viruses are a combination of boot viruses and program viruses. Like program viruses, they infect an executable file. When the user unknowingly executes the infected file, the multipartite virus infects the master boot records in the hard disk just like the boot record virus. Examples of multipartite virus include Emperor, Anthrax, Tequilla, and One_Half.

Stealth viruses: These viruses are very difficult to detect as they make use of different techniques to avoid detection. Some stealth virus may be coded in such a way that if the user has instructed the computer to read one file, then stealth virus may result in reading of another file.
Examples: Frodo, Joshi, Whale.

Polymorphic viruses: The word poly means many and polymorphic means 'many forms'. So, as the name implies, polymorphic viruses have multiple or many forms.

When this virus gets executed, it replicates itself. However, while replicating, the virus makes small changes in the code. This is deliberately done in such a way that the code is slightly different but the malicious intentions and harm caused to the computer is the same. Codes that replicate in this way are difficult to be detected by antivirus.
Examples include Elkern, Marburg, Satan Bug, and Tuareg.

Macro viruses: A macro virus infects documents that contain macros (a special type of program). Programs like Microsoft Word, PowerPoint and Excel are easily prone to this type of virus as they support macros.

For example, whenever users open any Word document, the uninfected document also gets infected. Once infected, the repairing of that file is very difficult. Moreover, when a macro virus-infected file is opened on another computer, the virus spreads on that computer also.
Examples of macro viruses are Relax, Melissa.A, Bablas, O97M/Y2K, and WM.NiceDay.

Resident viruses: A resident virus, as the name suggests, resides in the computer's memory (RAM) and performs all its intended tasks (like corrupting other opened files and programs). A resident virus can run independently even without the originally infected file.
Examples include Randex, CMJ, Meve, and Mr Klunky.

> Autoexec.bat is a batch file stored in the root directory of the hard disk. It is used to perform some vital operations when the computer is booted.

Direct-action viruses: These viruses replicate and perform their intended action only when the infected file is being executed. At other times, the virus becomes dormant (in sleep mode). Direct-action viruses get activated (or come in action) when a specific condition is met. It then infects all the files in its directory and some other files (in the directories specified in the AUTOEXEC.BAT file PATH). Example is the Vienna virus.

Overwrite viruses: The overwrite virus deletes the data stored in the infected file so that it is no longer usable. There is no way to recover the deleted contents; so the only option that the user has is to delete the entire file.

Examples are Way, Trj.Reboot, and Trivial.88.D.

Directory virus: As the name suggests, directory virus affects the directories. The virus changes the file path (or file location). When the user opens a file whose location has been changed, the virus gets executed.

Network virus: As the name implies, network viruses rapidly spread through a network. They replicate through files shared on the network.

Examples are Nimda and SQL Slammer.

FAT virus: File allocation table (FAT) is a table maintained by the operating system, which stores information about location, size, and other details of files stored on the hard disk. The FAT virus attacks the file allocation table.

Once the FAT is infected, it becomes impossible for the computer to locate files. Moreover, the virus spreads to other files when the FAT tries to access them. A file infected by the FAT virus becomes inaccessible to the users.

Virus Symptoms and Harm Caused by Virus As discussed earlier, viruses operate in different ways. While some viruses are active only when the application to which it is attached is running, others will be running as long as the computer is on. Although virus executes without getting noticed by the user, the user can still get some symptoms that will indicate that his/her computer has been infected. Some of these symptoms are:

- Your computer is running slower than normal.
- Computer applications are not working correctly.
- Some important files cannot be accessed.
- You are unable to take a print.
- Unusual error messages are being flashed on the screen.
- Dialog boxes and menus are not being displayed properly.
- Files have double (two) extensions on attachments (Fig. 16.22).
- The antivirus program (discussed in next section) is suddenly disabled or not working.
- You are not able to install any antivirus program in your computer.
- You get some new and unusual icons the computer's desktop.
- Strange music or sounds can be heard from the speakers
- A program that you were using has disappeared from the computer without you deleting it.
- Unwanted programs start running automatically.
- The home page of your web browser gets changed.
- Advertisements are being displayed even when you are not browsing the Internet.
- Hardware devices are not responding.

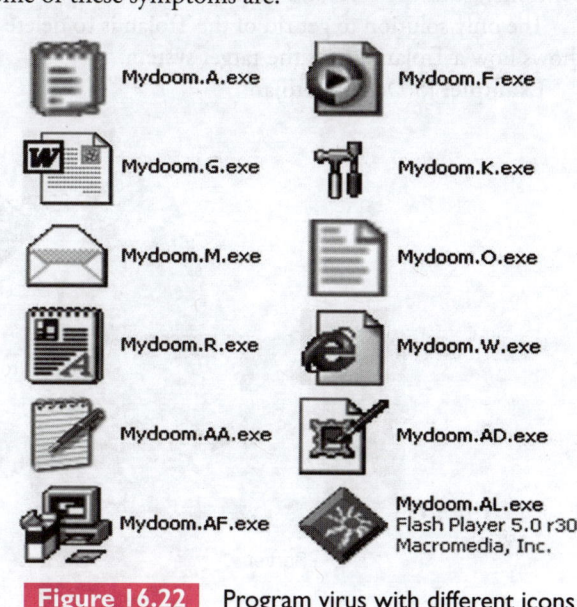

Figure 16.22 Program virus with different icons

16.5.2 Worms

Worms are malicious programs that take control over the computers on which they get installed and steal confidential data from it.

Like viruses, worms also replicate themselves and spread to other computers through a network (Fig. 16.23). Once a worm gets installed, it uses the email program of the user to send a copy of itself to everyone whose email address is present in the user's address book.

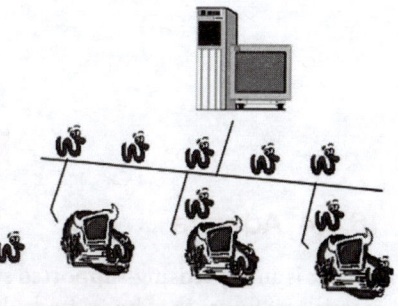

Figure 16.23 Worms spreading though Internet

However, unlike viruses, most worms do not interfere with the normal use of a computer. They do not harm any file stored on the computer. Moreover, they exist as separate entities and do not attach themselves to other files or programs.

Due to replication, worms take a lot of space in the hard disk, take more time of the CPU (to replicate and spread the infection to other computers), and take more time on the Internet connection. This, in turn, slows down the computer. The user may not be able to access the Internet properly at a good speed and ultimately the computer may even stop responding (hang).

Examples of worm are: W32.SillyFDC.BBY, Packed.Generic.236, W32.Troresba.

> A computer virus is more dangerous than a worm as it makes changes or deletes your files while worms only replicates itself with out making changes to your files/data.

16.5.3 Trojan Horse

A Trojan horse is a **non-replicating** malicious program that pretends to be harmless so that users may easily download it on their computer. It is usually **embedded within a harmless program.**

When the program containing a Trojan horse is executed, the Trojan also gets executed along with it. This may result in slow response from the computer, display of annoying messages on the computer screen, theft of data (email addresses, passwords and other confidential information like credit card number) and loss of data (by deleting files). Some Trojans may even give unauthorized access of the victim's computer to its controller, ruin the FAT, and install a virus.

> The name Trojan Horse came from the wooden horse used by the Greek Army to conquer the City of Troy and save the beautiful Helen.

The only solution to get rid of the Trojan is to delete the infected file or program from the computer. Figure 16.24 shows how a Trojan infects the target system.

Example: JS.Debeski.Trojan

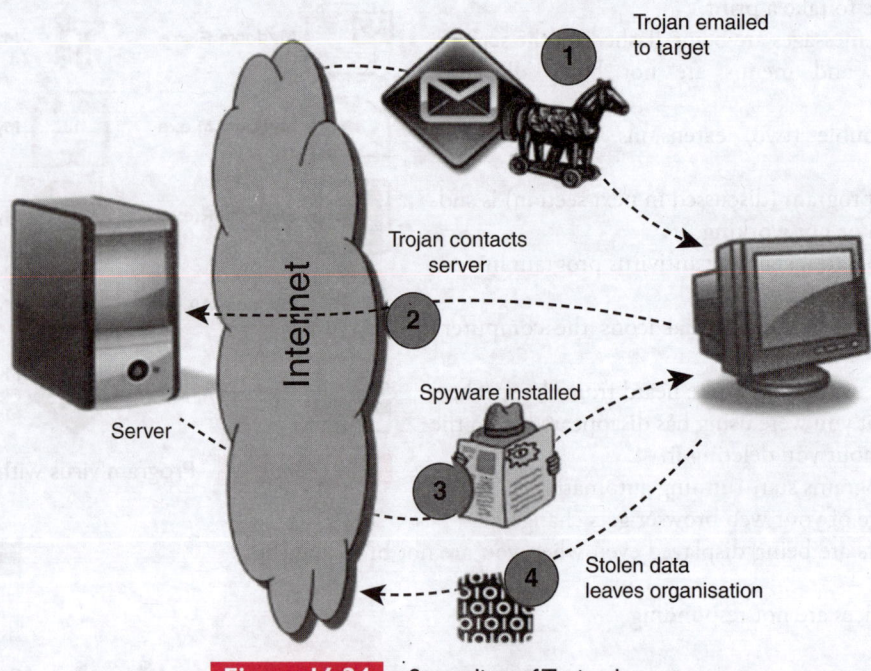

Figure 16.24 Spreading of Trojan horse

16.5.4 Adware

Adware is an **advertising-supported software**. It is usually embedded within a software, especially software that can be freely downloaded from the Internet. When users download a software that has adware inside it, the adware gets installed in the user's computer. Adware can also be spread through email attachments and shared files on the network. Moreover, some adware can automatically get downloaded while browsing any website.

> Most antivirus software can detect and remove Trojan horses.

Once an adware is installed, advertising banners and pop-ups are displayed while the user is working on the Internet. Adware comes under the category of malware because most of the times, the ads that they display are unwanted and are displayed without the user's permission. Adware displays so many unwanted advertisements that it starts annoying the user and distracts them from doing their work.

> Adwares are used by companies for marketing purpose.

16.5.5 Spyware

Spyware is a malicious program that monitors the user's activity on his or her computer and reports it to another person with malicious intentions. Spyware sends all this information without the user's permission. Usually, spyware is used for the following.

> Spyware is a big threat to a user's privacy and security while working on the Internet.

- Monitoring the user's Internet browsing patterns to collect information about his Login-ids, passwords, bank, or credit card information
- Installing adware, virus, Trojan horse or any other malicious programs
- Redirecting web browsers to untrusted sites

Spyware, like other malicious programs, is embedded in a software that can be freely downloaded from the Internet. Once installed, it is very difficult to remove them from the computer.

> Unlike spyware, adware does not transfer the user's personal information to another location. Both, however, slow down the computer and display unwanted advertisements to annoy the user.

16.5.6 Keyloggers

Keylogger is a malicious software that, once installed in your computer, records everything that you type on your computer. This is especially installed to get your log-in names, passwords, and other sensitive information. After recording what we are typing, the keylogger sends this information to its controller.

16.5.7 Ransomware

You must have heard the name of ransomware. We often get news on TV and messages on WhatsApp to be aware of a new ransomware and do not click this or that. But have you ever tried to know what is ransomware?

Ransomware is a malicious program which, when installed, displays a screen that warns you that you have been locked out of your computer and you need to pay some money (or ransom) to use your device. Such messages are not real notices. They clearly indicate malware infection because even if you pay to unlock the system, the system will either not unlock you or will lock you out again.

16.5.8 Sweeper Attacks

Sweeper attack is another type of malicious program used by unscrupulous people to delete all the data from the computer system.

Some interesting facts about malware are given in Fig. 16.25.

Look at the graphs given below. What do you interpret?

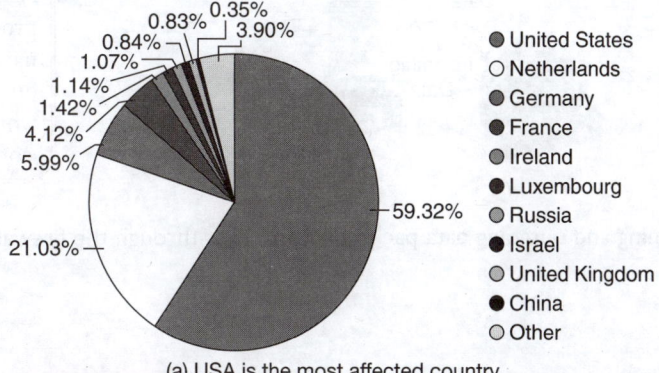

(a) USA is the most affected country

Figure 16.25 Statistics about malware and cyber attacks

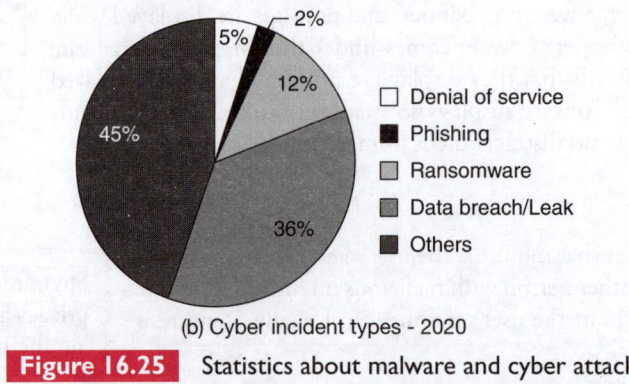

(b) Cyber incident types - 2020

Figure 16.25 Statistics about malware and cyber attacks

Source: (a) https://securelist.com/it-threat-evolution-q1-2020-statistics/96959/ (b) https://www.govtech.com/policy/2020-marks-a-record-breaking-year-for-cyber-attacks-against-schools.html

16.6 SAFELY ACCESSING WEBSITES AND COMMUNICATING DATA

The best way to protect from malware is to deploy a firewall and implement an antivirus software. Both the techniques are explained below.

16.6.1 Firewall

Firewall is either a hardware or a software that is installed between the network of an organization and the rest of Internet. We have already seen that a computer connected to the Internet is open to several types of attacks. In organizations, a lot of confidential data is stored on the computers. No company would like their sensitive information to be disclosed to an unauthorized person or deleted or overwritten by a malicious program. Therefore, sound protection of computers in an organization is of prime importance. In Fig. 16.26, we see that the main purpose of a firewall is to separate a secure area from a less secure area and to control communication between the two.

We can use a software firewall in our home computer to prevent unwanted access of the computer over a network connection. For example, you can set the firewall to limit Internet access to e-mail only, so that no other types of information can pass between your computer and the Internet.

> In our home computers, we usually use software firewall (or personal firewalls.)

In many schools, you cannot open Facebook, YouTube or download a song or movie. This is because the firewall is configured to reject any data going to or coming from these websites. Firewalls have become so important today that every operating system including Windows, Mac, Linux, etc. offer built-in support for maintaining and testing firewalls on the computer and the firewall is turned on by default.

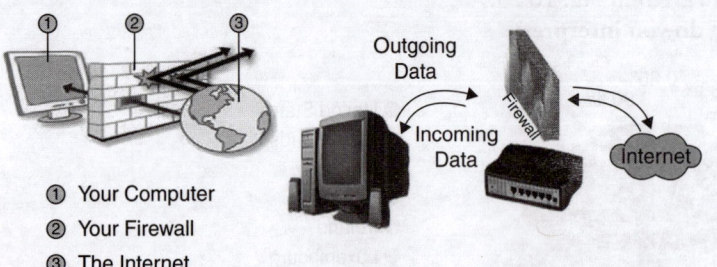

① Your Computer
② Your Firewall
③ The Internet

> A firewall is a software program or piece of hardware that helps screen out hackers, viruses, and worms that try to reach your computer over the Internet.

Figure 16.26 All incoming and outgoing data packets have to pass through the firewall

Types of Firewalls
The different types of firewalls are explained in this section.

Packet filtering This technique examines each data packet that either enters or leaves the network. Based on the result of examination, it accepts or rejects the packet depending on user-defined rules.

Although packet filtering is a fast, efficient and effective technique, it is difficult to configure and is susceptible to spoofing. Moreover, packet filter firewalls cannot tell whether a packet is part of an existing data exchange or a new one. This is because each packet is treated in isolation. Thus, packet filtering can allow or reject data packets based on the IP address of the sender and receiver machines.

Stateful firewalls Stateful firewall overcomes the drawback of packet filters by recording all connections passing through it. This gives enough information to determine whether a packet is the start of a new connection, an existing connection, or not a part of any connection. When the state of the packet is known, the firewall can speed up packet processing by allowing a packet of an existing connection without further analysis and evaluating only those packets (based on rules) that are coming through a new connection. Stateful firewall analyses data packets irrespective of IP address, they just check the state of the data packets.

Application-layer firewalls or Proxy firewalls With increasing attacks against web servers, a firewall is required to protect servers and the applications running on them. For this, application firewalls that inspect and filter packets are implemented to block specific content (such as malware or certain websites) and report when applications are misused.

However, practically speaking, most firewalls use more than one technique to implement security mechanisms. Proxy firewalls block or allow traffic based on specific rule sets. These rules can be based on the following features.

- *IP addresses* Block data coming from or going to a certain IP address or a range of IP addresses
- *Domain names* Allow or disallow data from certain specific domain names or domain name extensions such as .edu, .com, .gov, .net, .mil, etc.
- *Protocols* Allow or disallow data that uses protocols such as IP, SMTP, FTP, UDP, ICMP, and Telnet. Every protocol supports a different type of service
- *Keywords* Allow or disallow data flow that contains certain keywords or phrases. This is done to block offensive or unwanted data from flowing in.

Cloud Firewalls When cloud computing technology is used to deliver a firewall service, it is called a cloud firewall, or firewall-as-a-service (FaaS). Cloud firewalls usually have proxy firewalls installed but it is not mandatory that only a proxy firewall will be used to provide firewall service through cloud.

The main advantage of using cloud-based firewalls is that they are very easy to scale when demand for such a firewall grows in an organization. I such a case, additional capacity has to be added to the cloud server to filter larger traffic loads.

Which Firewall is Best to Use?
The particular firewall that will be used depends on the capabilities of the network, compliance requirements for the industry, and the resources available to manage these firewalls.

Basically, the question "which firewall is best to use?" should actually be framed as "why should we use only one firewall?" A single protection layer, no matter how robust it is, will not be enough to protect an organization's hardware and software. To provide better protection, multiple layers of firewalls should be used. For example, in an organization, there can be a hardware firewall or a cloud firewall at the perimeter of the network (point at which Internet is connected with internal computers and software firewalls installed and used on every individual computer.

Having additional firewalls helps to make the network more difficult to crack. Every additional layer provides extra protection to the computers making it more time-consuming and riskier for the attackers to reach all of your most sensitive information.

16.6.2 Antivirus – Definition and Examples

An antivirus is a software that prevents, detects, and removes malicious programs (like virus, worms, Trojan horses, spyware, and adware) that are harmful to the computer systems.

There are different types of antivirus software available in the market. They may implement different strategies but all of them perform the same task. The two main techniques that are used by antivirus programs are:

Signature-based approach: In this technique, the antivirus software has a file known as virus dictionary that contains a list of known viruses. When the user runs the antivirus program, it searches for matches in the virus dictionary. If a match is found, it means that the antivirus program has detected a virus in the computer. At this moment, the antivirus may take any one of the following actions:

> Antivirus software must be updated regularly, so that the virus dictionary can incorporate the definition of the recently identified viruses.

- Delete the file.
- Quarantine the file so that it is inaccessible to other programs. This will prevent the virus from spreading.
- Remove the virus from the file.

> Quarantine is like a sealed glass jar that does not allow anything to enter or escape it. The user can just look inside to see if it is a virus or not.

When does signature or dictionary-based antivirus software work?

Antivirus programs based on this technique examine a file when it is created, opened, closed, or attached with an email. Besides this, users can also run this program to do a complete hard disk scan to check for the presence of any kind of virus in the computer system.

Suspicious behavior or heuristic-based approach: In this technique, the antivirus monitors the behavior of all programs. The moment an attempt is made to modify an executable program, it is flagged as suspicious behavior. The user is then notified about it and the antivirus program asks for user's permission to allow or disallow the write operation.

Unlike the signature-based technique, the suspicious behavior approach protects the computer from new viruses that are not present in the virus dictionary.

However, the drawback of this approach is that it may give a large number of warning messages. The users get bogged down by so many messages and start ignoring them. They just click 'Accept' for every change made to an executable program thereby limiting the utility of antivirus software. The heuristic-based technique is thus not used widely.

> Antivirus programs may slow down your computer system. But this slow-down is very negligible.

Most antivirus programs therefore use a hybrid approach which combines signature-based and heuristic-based techniques.

Examples of commonly used antivirus programs include Bitdefender, Avast, AVG Antivirus, Norton Antivirus, McAfee, Avira (Fig. 16.27).

Although free antivirus programs are good, those which cost a little money are even better. However, if you don't want to spend money in buying the right antivirus program for your computer, we would suggest to at least download a free one as something is always better than nothing. Amongst free antivirus programs, you can use Avira, Avast, Panda Cloud and others.

> Avoid using web-based antivirus scans as most of them contains malicious software.

Figure 16.27   Popular antivirus software

16.6.3 Cyber Safety

Though it is very difficult to keep one's computer fully protected from malware, especially virus infection, it is not impossible. Some of the measures that could be taken to ensure the safety of your computer against malicious software are given below.

Install Antivirus Software: The importance of antivirus software has already been discussed in the previous section. You must have it installed in your computer.

Keep your Antivirus Software Up-to-date: Having antivirus software is just not enough. New viruses are added on the Internet every day; so you must regularly update the antivirus software. Updating the antivirus will add new viruses detected in the virus dictionary. Once the new viruses are added in the dictionary, the antivirus software will easily detect their presence in the computer. This would ensure protection against the newly added viruses.

> Free antivirus software is better than nothing, but it does not provide full protection.

Schedule Regular Scan-runs with your Antivirus Software: Installing an antivirus program and updating it frequently is just a part of the solution. To get its full benefit, we must run a full scan of the computer with this software. Make it a habit to run a scan weekly, if not daily. This will help your antivirus to catch any newly injected virus in your computer.

Regularly update the Operating System: Irrespective of the operating system you are using, you must always keep it up-to-date. Companies developing operating systems are continuously adding features to protect their operating systems from any kind of infection. So, updating the operating system will add another layer of security in the computer system (Fig. 16.28).

Figure 16.28 Regularly update and scan the computer to check for any malware attack

Password-protect your Antivirus: You must set a password for your antivirus program. This will ensure that no other person or program can change its settings (like disable it). Many viruses change the settings of the antivirus program so that they are not detected and reported to the user.

Secure Your Network: Many people use a Wi-Fi connection to connect to other computers (or devices like smartphones and tablets) and form a small network. People with wrong intentions may use this Wi-Fi connection to transfer files that have malicious software hidden in them. Therefore, always set a password to connect to the wireless connection. Also make sure that you always set a strong password so that it is difficult to be guessed by others.

Think Before You Click: Do not visit websites that allow you to download pirated software (that is a duplicate copy of original software, available free of cost). There are high chances of virus being present in pirated software.

Moreover, you must always download files or programs from a trusted website. If you are not sure whether a website is trusted or not, enter its name in a search engine (like Google) and read the reviews written by other users. Download from the website only if you are satisfied with the reviews and not otherwise.

> If you have to download a software, always download it from the website of its developer company.

Some more tips you must remember while clicking on a link
- Before downloading software, **read all security warnings**, license agreements, and privacy statements associated with it.
- If you think a particular website is not safe then never click "Agree" or "OK" to close that window. Instead, click the Close button in the corner of the window or press **Alt + F4** on the keyboard to close the window.
- Most of the **free music and video download websites** will ask you to first download a software. Never ever download them. They have virus and other malicious software embedded in them. Refer Fig. 16.29 here. The information is too good to be believed.
- **Browse Safely:** While surfing the Internet, you must have seen some pop-ups and banners inviting you to click on them. Do not click on such links.

Figure 16.29 Such messages are symptoms of malware attack

Open emails with caution Do not open an email attachment sent by someone who you do not know or trust. Some emails may even ask you to click on a link to download a particular file. Do not click if you are not sure of the sender. Even if the attachment and link has come from a known sender, scan it using before opening or clicking on it.

> A good antivirus software will automatically scan any attachment that you receive through email.

Don't Use Open Wi-Fi Do not use free and open (with no password) Wi-Fi connection at public places like restaurants, bus stops, hotels, railway stations, airports, etc. This is because as anyone can connect to and gain access to your computer or phone either to steal your personal data or transfer unwanted files with malicious software.

Do not allow anyone to insert their pen drives into your computer
Pen drives and other portable storage devices (like CDs, DVDs) may contain virus. A virus-infected storage device can easily inject virus in your computer as well. So do not allow any unknown person to use your computer and insert a pen drive.

> After inserting a pen drive into your computer, first scan with an antivirus software before using it.

Key Terms

Netiquette, Network Etiquette, or Internet Etiquette: A set of rules that should be followed when a person is working on the Internet.

Ethics: A set of moral values that govern the behavior of a person. Ethics in computing refers to a set of moral values that regulate the use of computers.

Plagiarism: Copying someone else's work and publishing it as your own.

Hacking: The act of identifying weakness in a computer system or even a network.

Hackers: People who hack computer systems to commit fraudulent acts such as fraud, privacy invasion, stealing corporate/personal data, etc.

Ethical hacking: Hacking done to deliberately access the computer but not to break its security and steal data. It is done only to identify any weakness in the system so that they can be overcome.

Crackers: Unethical hackers who have wrong intentions and gain access, usually by cracking passwords and other security codes.

Sexting: Circulating sexually suggestive pictures or messages about a person.

Phishing: The act of sending an email or messages to a user falsely claiming to be a legitimate authority.

Spamming: Sending unwanted emails in bulk (to a large number of recipients).

Antivirus software: Software that prevents a computer from being infected and possibly become a source of spam without the user's knowledge.

Spoofing: The act of tricking or deceiving computer systems or other computer users.

Digital footprints: Footprints or traces that a user leaves when he/she is online.

Malware: Also known as malicious software, it is any software that is designed with wrong intentions.

Worms: Malicious programs that take control over the computers on which they get installed and steal confidential data from it.

Trojan horse: A non-replicating malicious program that pretends to be harmless so that users can easily download it on their computer.

Spyware: A malicious program that monitors users' activity on their computer and reports it to another person with malicious intentions.

Keylogger: A malicious software that, once installed in your computer, records everything that you type on your keyboard.

Firewall: A hardware or a software that is installed between the network of an organization and the rest of Internet.

Eavesdrop: The practice of unauthorized real-time interception of a private communication such as a phone call, email, instant message, videoconference or fax transmission.

Chapter Highlights

- Internet is an ocean of information.
- There are strict laws including the international copyright law to protect digital content against plagiarism.
- Password should consist of a combination of numbers, upper- and lower-case letters and special characters that are difficult to guess.
- Cyber bullying or Internet bullying is a form of violence that is used to bully or harass another person.
- In *email spoofing*, messages are either sent using a bogus e-mail address or faking the e-mail address of another user.
- *In IP spoofing*, the IP address of a certain computer is masked so that it becomes difficult for other systems to determine the sender (real sender) of the data.
- Right to privacy has recently been declared as a fundamental right of every Indian citizen. The right to privacy is seen as protection against the invasion of one's privacy by the government, companies and other individuals.
- A digital footprint is relatively permanent and once the data is in public or even semi-public domain (like on Facebook), the user has very little control over how it will be used by others. Therefore, we should be very careful about our online activities.
- A computer virus is a small program that gets loaded in the computer without the user's knowledge and replicates (repeats) itself.
- File allocation table (FAT) is a table maintained by the operating system that stores information about location, size, and other details of files stored on the hard disk. The FAT virus attacks the file allocation table.
- Adware is an advertising-supported software. It is usually embedded within a software, especially software that can be freely downloaded from the Internet.
- Ransomware is a malicious program which, when installed, displays a screen that warns you that you have been locked out of your computer and you need to pay some money (or ransom) to use your device.
- When cloud computing technology is used to deliver a firewall service, it is called a cloud firewall, or firewall-as-a-service (FaaS).

Review Questions

1. Why is security over the Internet a matter of great concern?
2. List some reasons for using the Internet.
3. How are children affected by using Internet?
4. What do you understand by the term 'Netiquette'? List some network etiquette that one must keep in mind while browsing the Internet.
5. What does the term 'ethics' imply when working with computers?
6. What is plagiarism? How can we protect our work from being plagiarized?
7. Define hacking. Is it possible to be protected from such an unethical activity? Justify your answer.
8. Hacking can either be ethical or unethical. Comment.
9. How will you choose an ideal password?
10. What is cyber bullying?
11. How will you identify a bogus website?
12. How does spamming effect users?
13. Why is it necessary to install an antivirus software in the computer?
14. What is spoofing? Discuss its variant.
15. What does Right to Privacy state?

16. What are digital footprints?
17. Differentiate between active and passive digital footprints.
18. Why is virus categorized as a malware?
19. When can you conclude that your system has been infected with a virus?
20. Give one difference between (a) a virus and a worm (b) a virus and a Trojan Horse.
21. What is adware? How is it different from a spyware?
22. Write a short note on how a firewall works.
23. Define antivirus. Also explain the technique by which they perform their intended task.
24. List few ways using which you can safeguard yourself while working on the Internet.

Fill in the Blanks

1. People can use _____ websites to share their knowledge and experiences on a particular topic.
2. Websites like _____ can be used to plan a trip.
3. _____ is a set of rules that should be followed when a person is working on the Internet.
4. _____ is a set of moral values that govern the behavior of a person.
5. _____ means copying someone else's work and publishing it as your own.
6. There are strict laws like _____ to protect digital content against plagiarism.
7. _____ is the act of sending an email or messages to a user falsely claiming to be a legitimate authority.
8. Phishing is done to _____ the user.
9. _____ is considered to be an electronic junk mail, which is usually sent for advertising products.
10. A _____ is used to automatically block all spam messages.
11. In _____, messages are either sent using a bogus e-mail address or faking the e-mail address of another user.
12. _____ includes the right to be left alone and freedom from undue interference.
13. _____ is the first sector on the hard disk.
14. _____ viruses are a combination of boot viruses and program viruses.
15. A _____ virus resides in the computer's memory (RAM) and perform all its intended tasks (like corrupting other opened files and programs).
16. Unlike viruses, most _____ do not interfere with the normal use of a computer.
17. When cloud computing technology is used to deliver a firewall service, it is called a _____, or _____.
18. Antivirus software based on _____ approach has a file known as virus dictionary that contains a list of known viruses.
19. _____ means unauthorized real-time interception of a private communication, such as a phone call, email, instant message, videoconference or fax transmission.

State True or False

1. Skype can be used for text as well as video conferencing.
2. Any activity that may directly or indirectly, intentionally or un-intentionally harm any person or computer is considered to be ethical.

Society, Law and Ethics - I

3. Plagiarism is the act of identifying weakness in a computer system or even a network.
4. Ethical hackers are those who have wrong intentions and gain access usually by cracking passwords and other security codes.
5. Password should consist of a combination of numbers, upper- and lower-case letters, and special characters that is difficult to guess.
6. We must use the same password for every account.
7. To avoid forgetting passwords, we must write it on paper.
8. We must not upload animations, pictures or other material that can hurt other's religious, cultural and social beliefs or promote any kind of discrimination.
9. In phishing, a bogus website is created to extract confidential information from the user.
10. Most spam emails often advertise dubious (not trustworthy) products.
11. In email spoofing, the IP address of a certain computer is masked so that it becomes difficult for other systems to determine the sender (real sender) of the data.
12. Active footprints are left by a user unintentionally.
13. Digital footprints are permanent in nature.
14. A malware is usually embedded or hidden within legitimate software that is either useful or attractive.
15. Multipartite viruses make use of different techniques to avoid their detection.
16. Antivirus software can be used to protect computers from Trojan horse attack.
17. Signature-based antivirus protects the computer from new viruses that are not present in the virus dictionary.
18. Firewalls and antivirus software can protect computers from eavesdropping attacks.

Tick the Right Answer

		Do	Don't
1.	Reply to any unknown messages or the messages that makes us uncomfortable.	○	○
2.	Exchange any personal information on Internet without your parent's permission.	○	○
3.	Discuss your Internet activities with your parents.	○	○
4.	Use Internet in the absence of your teachers or parents.	○	○
5.	Treat others as you would like to be treated.	○	○
6.	Write in capital letters as it is treated as shouting.	○	○
7.	Use too many emoticons.	○	○
8.	Send fake emails.	○	○
9.	Talk to a stranger.	○	○
10.	Copy the contents from the Internet.	○	○
11.	Write very long messages.	○	○
12.	Start your message with greetings.	○	○
13.	Forward unnecessary emails especially those which states forward to 10 people to change your luck in 24 hours, etc.	○	○

Multiple Choice Questions

1. MonsterIndia is an example of _____.
   a. matrimonial website   b. job portal
   c. blogging website   d. online message forum

2. Which of the following is not a preventive measure to protect our work from plagiarism?
   a. Copyright law   b. Give reference   c. Author's permission   d. none of these

3. We cannot protect our _____ from being plagiarized?
   a. text   b. idea   c. image   d. None of these.

4. _____ means sending unwanted emails in bulk (to a large number of recipients).
   a. Spamming   b. Spoofing   c. Phishing   d. Hacking

5. _____ means tricking or deceiving computer systems or other computer users.
   a. Spamming   b. Spoofing   c. Phishing   d. Hacking

6. To prevent spoofing, we must not use _____.
   a. HTTPs   b. SSH   c. HTTP   d. trust relationships

7. We do not leave an active digital footprint when we _____ over the Internet.
   a. comment on Facebook   b. tweet on Twitter
   c. Search information   d. send an email

8. _____ is a software that is designed with wrong intentions.
   a. Antivirus   b. Malware   c. Firewall   d. Virus

9. _____ virus infect only executable files.
   a. Boot   b. Program   c. Multipartite   d. Polymorphic

Answers

Fill in the Blanks

1. blogging
2. MakeMyTrip
3. Netiquette
4. Ethics
5. Plagiarism
6. International Copyright Law
7. Phishing
8. scam
9. Spam
10. spam filter
11. email spoofing
12. Privacy
13. Master Boot Record
14. Multipartite
15. resident
16. worms
17. cloud firewall, firewall-as-a-service (FaaS)
18. signature-based
19. Eavesdropping

State True or False

1. True
2. False
3. False
4. False
5. True
6. False
7. False
8. True
9. True
10. True
11. False
12. False
13. True
14. True
15. False
16. True
17. False
18. True

Multiple Choice Questions

1. b
2. d
3. d
4. a
5. b
6. c
7. c
8. b
9. b

Society, Law and Ethics - II

17

Chapter Objectives

The chapter continues the discussion of the previous chapter and elaborates on security schemes with emphasis on:

- Individual right to privacy
- Intellectual property rights including copyright, trademark, patent, design rights and trade secrets
- Digital rights management
- Software licensing
- Open-source Software
- Internet frauds and scams
- IT Act 2000
- Child pornography
- Cyber forensics
- Impact of technology on society
- e-Waste management
- Identity theft and protection through unique IDs and biometrics
- Gender issues while teaching and using computers
- Disability issues while working with technology

Technology affects the way we communicate, learn, and think. It plays an important role in society today. However, technology has both positive and negative impacts on our daily lives. In this chapter, we will examine how technology has influenced our society, laws and ethics with the help of some real-world case studies.

17.1 INDIVIDUAL RIGHT TO PRIVACY

Right to privacy has recently been declared as a fundamental right of every Indian citizen. The right to privacy is seen as protection against the invasion of one's privacy by the government, companies and other individuals. Now that it has been declared as a fundamental right, India will soon have strict laws for data protection as other countries (like US and UK) have.

The right of privacy rests on the concept that every human being has some intrinsic value and that everyone should respect these values. Nobody is allowed to intrude on another person's privacy or to attack his or her honour and reputation. Therefore, everyone has the right to lawfully protect themselves from such interference or attacks.

The privacy of individuals also includes the right to determine how information concerning the individual is communicated to others and how that information is controlled.

17.1.1 Elements of Right to Privacy

The right to privacy includes the following points. Remember that you should not interfere with anyone's privacy either intentionally or unintentionally as such an attack will be tried in courts. Also, if someone intrudes on your privacy, never hesitate to fight for yourself as it is your fundamental right now.

- Privacy includes the right to be left alone and freedom from undue interference.
- The right to privacy also includes rules governing the collection and handling of personal data like credit information and medical records
- Every individual has the right to control personal matters which includes the right to limit communication and interference to his/her domestic and work space.
- Control of the disclosure of personal information
- Protection of the individual's independence, dignity and anonymity (identity).

> Many a time, privacy conflicts with freedom of speech, national security, police powers, ethical values and freedom of information.

17.2 INTELLECTUAL PROPERTY RIGHTS (IPR)

Intellectual Property Rights (or IPR) are rights that are applicable to creative work, which can be treated as an asset or physical property. They can be categorized into four main areas – copyright, trademarks, design rights and patents. Each of these are applicable in various situations and with their own set of technical rules. To protect your idea(s) effectively when launching a new product or doing any other important business activity, you may have to utilize one or more of the IPR types.

17.2.1 Copyright

Copyright applies to creative work such as those seen in literature, art, music and drama as well as in films, sound recordings, drawings, paintings, photography, typographical arrangements or any work that is recorded in some way. These rights protect the author's work by prohibiting unauthorised actions. The author is empowered to take legal action against instances of infringement or plagiarism.

Therefore, while obtaining permission to use creative works, we are talking about copyright law. To use someone else's work, we must take the author's permission.

Figure 17.1 Trademarks of popular companies

17.2.2 Trademarks

A trademark can be a name, word, slogan, design, symbol or any other item that is used to identify a product or organisation. Trademarks which are unique for a product or company as shown in Fig. 17.1 are to be registered with an appointed government body. The process of registering trademarks may take up to two years in India. However, once registered, a trade mark is valid for ten years and can be renewed thereafter indefinitely for further ten-year periods

Once registered, trademarks are identified by the abbreviation 'TM', or the '®' symbol. In most countries, the national patent office also administers trademarks. You must have observed that all big brands have a trademark.

> Unlike copyrighted works, trademarks have different degrees of protection depending on factors including the consumer awareness of the trademark, the type of service and product it identifies, and the geographic area in which the trademark is used.

17.2.3 Design Rights

Designs must also be protected by both copyright and design rights. They may also be registered like patents. Once registered, designs are valid for a maximum of ten years and renewable for a further period of five years. Figure 17.2 shows some designs that have been infringed by others.

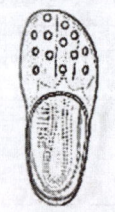   

Crocs D'517,789   Infringing   Apple D'604,305   Infringing

Figure 17.2 Trademarks of popular companies

17.2.4 Patents

Patents are applied to industrial processes and inventions. They also provide protection against unauthorised implementation of the invention. In general terms, patents are grants made by national governments that give the creator of an invention an exclusive right to use, sell or manufacture the invention. All patents must be registered. The process of registering, however, may take 2 to 3 years to complete.

In India, the regulatory authority for patents is the Patent Registrar under the office of the Controller General of Patents, Designs and Trade Marks, which is part of India's Ministry of Commerce and Industry. Once registered, patents are valid for 20 years from the date of filing an application (subject to an annual renewal fee).

India's patent law operates under the 'first to file' principle which states that if two people apply for a patent on a similar invention, then the first one to file the application is awarded the patent.

> Internet piracy of films, music, games and software is an issue in India, as is unauthorised copying of physical books.

17.2.5 Right of Publicity

A patchwork of state laws known as the right of publicity protects the image and name of a person against unauthorized use for commercial purposes. For example, no company can use a celebrity's or even a common man's name and picture to advertise its product.

17.2.6 Trade Secrets

The Trade Secret laws provide protection against sensitive business information. For example, a marketing plan or launch of a new product must be kept confidential as it gives the business an advantage over its competitors. Figure 17.3 shows some important features of trade secrets.

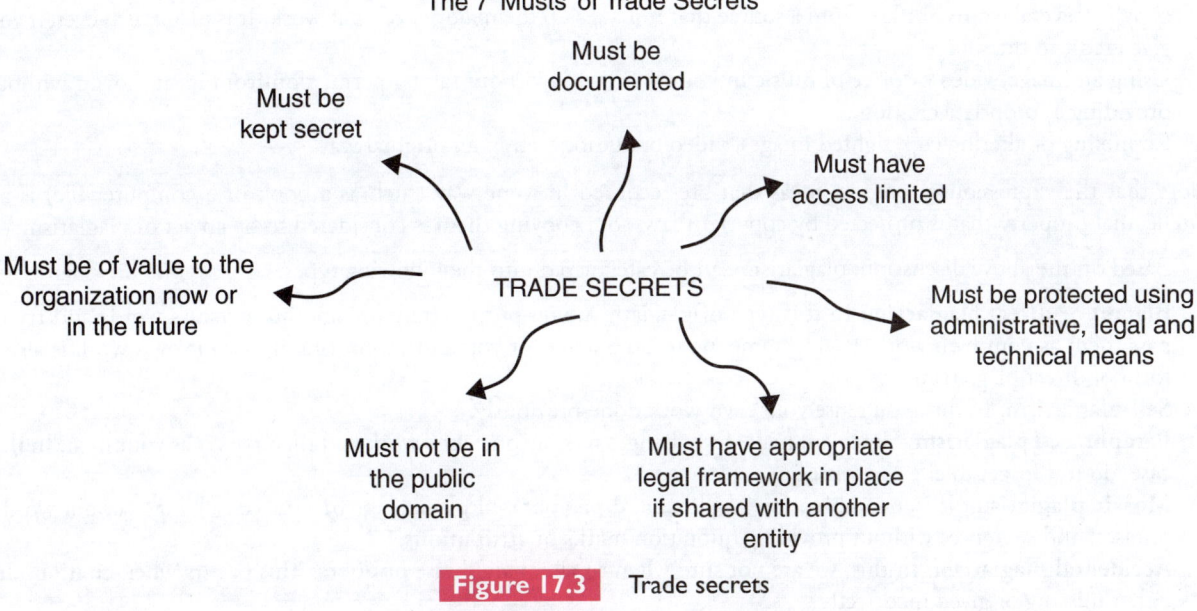

Figure 17.3 Trade secrets

Table 17.1 given below summarizes these techniques.

Table 17.1 Features of patents, trademarks, copyrights and trade secrets

		Protects	Infringement	Registration Process	Term	Comparative Costs
Patent	Utility Patent	Functional aspects	Make, use, offer, patent aspects sale, import	Yes	20 years upon filing	Expensive
	Design Patent	Ornamental features	Make, use, offer, sale, import	Yes	15 years upon filing	Moderate
Trademarks		Brands	Used in commerce	Optional	Potentially indefinite, limited by use	Inexpensive
Copyrights		Works of authorship	Copying, etc.	Optional	Life Plus 70 years	Inexpensive
Trade Secrets		Information	Misappropriation	No	Potentially indefinite, limited by secrecy	Depends

17.3 PLAGIARISM

Plagiarism is an act of fraud that involves both stealing someone else's work (as shown in Fig. 17.4) and lying about it afterward. The term also includes the following activities:

- to steal and pass off someone else's work as one's own
- copying words or ideas from someone else without giving credit
- to commit literary theft
- to present an idea or a product as new and original when it derived from an existing source
- giving incorrect information about the source of a quotation
- changing words but copying the sentence structure of a source without giving credit
- copying several words or ideas from a source that it makes up the majority of your work. It is plagiarism even if you give credit to the source.
- Using an image, video or piece of music in your own work without taking permission from its author or without providing appropriate citation
- Re-mixing or altering copyrighted images, video or audio, even in an original way.

Figure 17.4 Plagiarism (copying content)

Note that the expression of original ideas that are recorded in some way (such as a book or a computer file) is an intellectual property that is protected by copyright laws. So, copying them is considered to be an act of plagiarism.

Based on the above discussion, plagiarism can be categorized into the following types.

- **Blatant or direct plagiarism:** In this type of plagiarism, you purposefully use another person's words and try to pass them as your own work. Paying someone to do a work for you and submitting it as your own work is also a form of direct plagiarism
- **Self-plagiarism**: In this, you reuse your own work done previously.
- **Paraphrased plagiarism:** Here, you make few changes to someone else's work and then pass it as your own. In this case, do not forget to cite the source.
- **Mosaic plagiarism:** It is a combination of direct and paraphrased plagiarism. In this, you change certain words, phrases, and sentences without providing quotation marks or attributions.
- **Accidental plagiarism:** In this, we are not sure when to cite, paraphrase or quote. This occurs when citations are either missing or given incorrectly

We can avoid plagiarism by correctly citing the sources. Simply acknowledging the source from which the content is borrowed so that the reader gets the necessary information to go through the source is enough to prevent plagiarism.

We must take plagiarism very seriously because it entails serious consequences which may include:

- Imprisonment
- Heavy fines
- Destroyed student/professional reputation
- Legal repercussions
- Monetary repercussions
- It may also result in a failing grade, a suspension, or an expulsion.

> Plagiarism by students must be suppressed because this prevents them from exploiting their capabilities to do a better work.

Therefore, before submitting your work, you must check it to ensure that it is not plagiarised even accidentally. This can be done by using a good Plagiarism Checker tool. Some of these online tools are available for free and other sophisticated ones are available at a cost. These tools help us to detect plagiarized and paraphrased content using highly advanced AI technology. If the content is copied, the tool will highlight those words or lines or paragraphs and also tell you the source from which the content has been copied.

Many school and university students plagiarize by
- Copying answers for assignments from websites
- Copying answers from their friends
- Copying someone else's work (from books or any other source) without giving them credit.
- Giving incorrect information about the source of a quotation which prevents the users from getting a true copy of the source
- Copying the structure of the sentence but changing a few words, not giving the credit to the source and presenting it as your own work.
- Copying a major part from a source irrespective of whether you are giving it credit or not.
- Self-plagiarising the content. Many a time, students plagiarise their own work to get two or more grades or awards for the same piece of work created by them.
- Summarizing or rewording someone else's ideas without providing a citation.

Some guidelines to escape plagiarism
- Write your answers yourself in your own style.
- Do not copy long paragraphs. When copying a definition or any information that cannot be and should not be changed, use quotation marks to illustrate that it is a direct quote.

17.4 DIGITAL RIGHTS MANAGEMENT (DRM)

The distribution of digital content over the Internet has made traditional copyright law obsolete in practice. When a book is copied and distributed, the publisher can sue the culprit but how can the publisher control who is copying books when they are available online?

Every time an e-book, song, video or any other digital content is downloaded from the Internet without permission, the content creator loses money. Creating any content incurs a cost. And when users download it without paying the fees for using it, a loss is incurred by its creator. So, a mechanism is required to regain control of distribution by making it technologically impossible for consumers to make digital copies of the e-content.

DRM (refer Fig.17.5) is the use of technology and systems to protect copyrights for digital media. It encompasses techniques that limit copying and use of copyrighted works and proprietary software.

DRM is a powerful tool that enables publishers and/or authors to control what paying users can do with their works. It can prevent users from accessing or using certain assets, thereby protecting the copyrighted works from unauthorized use. Today, DRM is playing a significant role in data security. With DRM, authors can exercise more control on their digital content.

With increasing demand for peer-to-peer file exchange services such as torrent sites, online piracy has become an important issue. DRM does not catch those involved in piracy. Instead, it makes it impossible to steal or share the content in the first place.

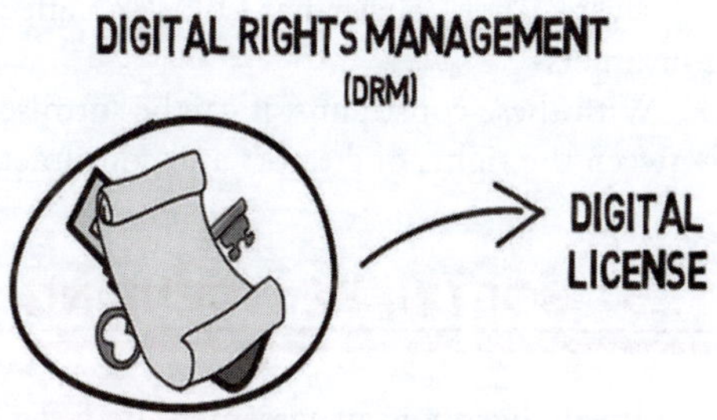

Figure 17.5 Digital rights management with digital license

17.4.1 How Digital Rights Management Works

DRM encompasses codes that prohibit copying, or codes that limit the time or number of devices on which a certain product can be accessed.

Publishers, authors, and other content creators use an application that **encrypts** data, e-book, software, or any other digital copyrighted material. Only those having appropriate decryption keys can access the material. DRM also use tools to limit or restrict what users are able to do with their materials. For example, DRM protects content creators by restricting or preventing users from,

- editing or saving their content.
- sharing or forwarding their product or content.
- printing their content. (or printing only a limited number of times)
- creating screenshots of their content.

> DRM software provides users features like differentiated pricing, special offers or limited usage without causing delays.

DRM also does the following things to protect the content creator's work:

- Sets an expiry date on the product or content. After this date, the user will no longer be able to access it.
- Limiting the number of uses by a user. For example, a document may be revoked after the user has opened it 20 times or if the user has listened to a song 10 times.
- Allowing only certain IP addresses, locations, or devices to access the contents. That is, if the content is available to US residents, then it cannot be accessed by people in other countries.
- Watermarking artworks and documents to provide ownership and identity details.
- Editing and saving.
- Revoking document when terms and conditions of DRM are violated.
- Enabling authors to retain ownership of their works. In the absence of DRM, people could easily copy someone else's work but DRM prevents anybody from copying and altering others' content.
- Disallowing audience to read or see any DRM protected content that is not meant for the user's age group. For example, a child will not be allowed to view an action movie meant for adults.

DRM also allows publishers and authors to access a list of people and number of times the content or software has been used by them. For example, the creator can see when and by whom his/her e-book or any other digital content was downloaded, printed and accessed. With every download the author gets paid an amount for his content. So, in this case, DRM helps authors to ensure that only paying users are able to access the digital content.

> DRM is used by companies to protect confidential information, share documents securely with third parties, and track document use to identify leaks.

17.4.2 Challenges of Digital Rights Management

- Users cannot access the digital content or product on any device or use it in whatever way they wish.
- DRM technology is not a perfect solution. Some users hack or use unethical means to figure out the decryption keys to get unauthorized access to the content.
- There are also some free tools available online that removes DRM codes to provide access to unauthorized users.

Some consumer rights groups like the Electronic Frontier Foundation, feel that the limitations imposed by DRM are too severe. They believe that DRM can affect innovation, hide product flaws and can thus cause inconvenience to the consumers.

With these constraints, it can be surmised that while advancing into the digital age, a balance must be maintained between the rights of creators and consumers.

17.5 SOFTWARE LICENSING

A software license is an agreement between the consumer and the creator of a software program that allows the consumer to do certain things that would otherwise be a violation of copyright laws. It provides legally binding guidelines for the use and distribution of software.

A software license gives an individual or an organization, the permission to use the software. However, in most situations, it is illegal to purchase one copy of software and then use it on multiple computers. In such a situation, the companies can purchase site licenses rather buying tens, hundreds, or thousands of individually licensed copies of a program.

The software license gives vital information regarding

- where and how and how often the software can be installed
- whether the consumer can copy, modify or redistribute the software
- whether the consumer can access the underlying source code of the software.

Many-a-time, the license agreement also mentions the price of the software and the licensing fees (if any).

Before using a software, we must carefully read the license to know how long the license lasts. A perpetual license does not expire. This means that once the software is purchased, it can be used any number of times. However, a term license expires after a specified period of time (often one year) and must be periodically renewed.

17.5.1 Types of Software Licenses

Based on the number of users, there are three types of software licences. They are:

- **Single-user license:** The software is licensed for a single user and can be installed on a single computer.
- **Multi-user license**: This license allows users to install the software on multiple (fixed) computers so that it can be used by multiple users. For example, a five-user multi-user license allows the software to be used by up to five people.
- **Site license:** Software can be installed on an unlimited number of computers, as long as they are at the location of the site license. Site licenses are usually for schools and businesses.

Based on whether the software is free, open source, proprietary or freeware.

While free software is available free of cost, users have to pay to get proprietary licenses to use a proprietary software. Free licenses provide a licensee with rights similar to the original owner. That is, the licensee of a free software may copy, modify and distribute creative work, provided a free license is obtained. However, with proprietary software, the original copyright owner maintains ownership. The copyright owner is just renting or leasing copyrighted materials to licensees.

Table 17.2 Comparing Free Software, Open-source Software, Freeware and Public-domain software

	Free software	Open-source software	Freeware	Public-domain software
Definition	"FREE" is a matter of liberty, not price	"OPEN" doesn't just mean access to the source code	"FREE" refers to price, while freedom of the use is restricted by creator	"PUBLIC DOMAIN" belongs to the public as a whole
Ground philosophy	Social movement	Development methodology	Marketing goals	Copyright disclamation
Ground rules	Four Freedoms https://www.gnu.org/philosophy/free-sw.html	Open Software initiative https://opensource.org/osd		Creative Common Organization https://creativecommons.org
Free of charge	Not necessary	Not necessary	✓ YES	✓ YES
Covered by copyright law	✓ YES	✓ YES	✓ YES	✗ NO
Examples	Linux, ubuntu	MySQL, Apache	Skype, Adobe Acrobat	SQLite

Therefore, as compared to proprietary software, free or open-source software has fewer restrictions. A free software license or an open-source license enables users to use the software without seeking anyone's permission. The users can also copy and redistribute the software to others for future development or use. Look at the Table 17.2 that compares such software licenses.

Conclusion: Software licensing describes the legal rights for authorized use of digital material. Infringing software license agreement incurs criminal charges related to licensed intellectual property (IP) and copyrighted material.

17.5.2 GPL or General Public License

Also referred as GNU GPL, it is the most commonly used free software license. This license allows the licensee to freely use, modify and redistribute the software. Basic guidelines supported by GPL states that the licensee can do the following things:

- Download and run the software
- Modify the software
- Redistribute free copies of the software
- Distribute modified versions of the software.

17.5.3 Apache Software License (ASL)

ASL is a license used with free and open-source software (FOSS) written by the Apache Software Foundation (ASF). ASL allows users to freely download and use the software either in whole or in part, for commercial, personal or organization's use. Users do not have to worry of paying for license.

The code of the software protected by ASL is openly distributed. ASL allows its users to freely analyse, modify and redistribute the code. Apache encourages its users to voluntarily improve the design of the software.

However, Apache requires the distributed software to have a copy of its license in such a way that it is easy to be found by others. Moreover, modified code or software is no longer treated as Apache's software. Rather, it would be attributed to the developer who modified the software, even though it still retains ASL.

Modified software cannot be used in any commercial property or trademarks that may use or imply that the ASF endorses the distribution. It also does not allow the use of any trademarks or logos showing that the modified software is owned by the ASF. Rather, it should clearly indicate who modified the software and in what way.

Users modifying the software should not send their code changes back to the ASF. They can only send a feedback. Figure 17.6 summarizes some of the key features of the Apache Software License.

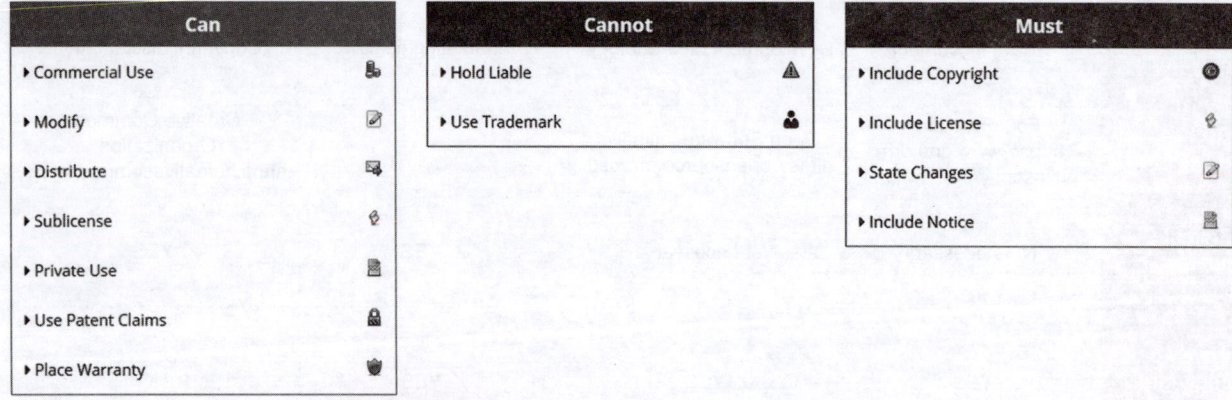

Figure 17.6 Summary of Apache Software License

17.6 OPEN SOURCE

The term "open source" refers to something that allows users to modify and share because its design is publicly accessible. In context of computer software, an open-source software can be openly exchanged, collaboratively developed and modified for further improvement. Anyone can inspect, modify, and enhance the source code of the software. Here, source code comprises of all the instructions or lines of code that make the software do its intended task. Computer users usually don't see this part. However, programmers who are interested in the source code, can use it to study the basic working of the software, improve it in some way and even fix parts that don't always work correctly.

17.6.1 Difference between Open-source Software and Other Types of Software

As discussed in the previous section, proprietary software has source code that is accessible only to the organization that created it. The organization maintains exclusive control over it and can inspect or modify it (if required). To use proprietary software, computer users must comply with a license and agree to certain terms and conditions expressed by the organization that created it. Microsoft Office and Adobe Photoshop are examples of proprietary software.

Source code of open-source software is available to users to view. Users can copy it, learn from it, alter it, or share it. LibreOffice, Gambas, GIMP, Firefox, Chrome, OpenOffice, Linux, and Android are some popular examples of open-source software.

Like proprietary software, users of open-source software must also accept the terms of a license. Open-source licenses affect the way people can use, study, modify and distribute software. Some open-source licenses, also known as "copyleft" licenses in contrast to copyright licences, say that anyone who releases a modified open-source program must also release the source code for that program alongside it. Some open-source licenses also state that anyone who alters and shares a program with others must also share that program's source code without charging a licensing fee for it.

17.6.2 Benefits of Open-source Software

People prefer to use open-source software to proprietary software because of the following reasons.

Control: Computer programmers have more control over open-source software as they can examine the code to understand its logic and make changes to it as and when required.

Training: Open-source software helps programmers to improve their programming skills. They can access the code, study it and make better software on their own. Programmers can also share their software with others, inviting comment and critique as they develop their skills. When other more experienced programmers see their code, they can identify errors in them (if any) and also correct them.

Security: Open-source software is more secure and stable than proprietary software. This is because anyone can view, update and upgrade the code to improve it and correct errors in it.

Stability: Open-source software is more stable than proprietary software. This is because in long-term projects, computer users are sure that the code has been distributed and many programmers are openly working on the code to maintain it and update it. They can easily rely on open-source software for critical tasks as they are sure it will not fall into disrepair if their original creators stop working on them.

Community: Open-source software often inspires a community of users and developers to be formed around it. These users and developers collectively produce, test, use and promote the software.

Transparency: Computer programmers and users can clearly see what kinds of data are moving where and what changes have been done in the code. This is not possible in proprietary software.

Reliability: Proprietary software can be updated only by the organization that created it. But open-source software is not confined to an individual organization, it spans countless programmers and is constantly updated through active open-source communities. Open standards and peer review ensure that open-source code is appropriately tested quite often.

Flexibility: Open-source software can be customized for a particular application.

Lower cost: Although open-source software is free, users have to pay a fee for technical support, security and managing interoperability.

No vendor lock-in: Open-source software can be used in anyway the user may wish. Restrictions for using the software are minimal or none.

17.7 CREATIVE COMMON LICENSE

Creative Commons is a non-profit organization that maintains a large library of creative works that can be shared and used by individuals and businesses, free of cost. The creator can claim free licenses through Creative Commons to share his/her work with the public.

Any user can use the Creative Commons licensed work such as artwork, photos, educational papers, scientific research or music for free as long as they follow the rules for attributing the creators. Thus, Creative Commons is seen as an alternative to copyright. Anybody can use the content by properly giving the credit to the creator.

It is a win–win situation for the user and the creator. No doubt, the user stands benefitted, but what about the creator? The creator can present his/her content in front of a large audience and this could help him/her to grow as a brand. Creators get the satisfaction that their work is now more viewed, liked, used and shared by the masses.

Guidelines are provided on the official Creative Commons website for Creative Commons licensed content state that it is essential to include written credit of the author's name, the title of the work, a link to the source and a link to the license.

Creative Commons offers a number of licenses to choose from. They include:

Attribution (CC BY): In this license, users can share, remix, edit and distribute work. The content can be shared commercially by giving proper credits to the author.

Attribution-ShareAlike (CC BY-SA): It is similar to the standard attribution license. The difference is that while Attribution (CC BY) allows users to place a standard copyright license with any work created by them, this is not possible with Creative Commons Attribution-ShareAlike.

Attribution-NoDerivs (CC BY-ND): With this license, users can reuse licensed work, even commercially as long as they give credit to the original author. However, a user cannot share adapted versions of the work.

Attribution-NonCommercial (CC BY-NC): In this, the users can remix, edit, and adapt licensed work, but they cannot use it commercially. However, users may create a remixed or edited work and get it copyrighted by its new owners.

Attribution-NonCommercial-ShareAlike (CC BY-NC-SA): With this license, licensed work can be edited, remixed, and built upon, but it cannot be offered commercially. Even the newly edited work cannot be copyrighted. In that sense, it is similar to Attribution-NonCommercial-ShareAlike license.

Attribution-NonCommercial-NoDerivs (CC BY-NC-ND): This is the most restrictive type of Creative Commons license. It just allows others to use the creator's work. So, others can download and share the creator's work by giving due credit to the author but they cannot change the work in anyway and cannot use it commercially.

As a user, you can easily find Creative Commons content online. There are different tools available for finding such content. For example, Creative Commons Search engine tool will search their entire database for Creative Commons images. Users can also filter searches for file type, sources, and even by license type. That is, to find content that can be modified and redistributed, the user has to filter for the BY and BY-SA licenses. Figure 17.7 summarises the features of Creative Commons licenses (Source: https://www.wur.nl/en/article/What-are-Creative-Commons-licenses.htm).

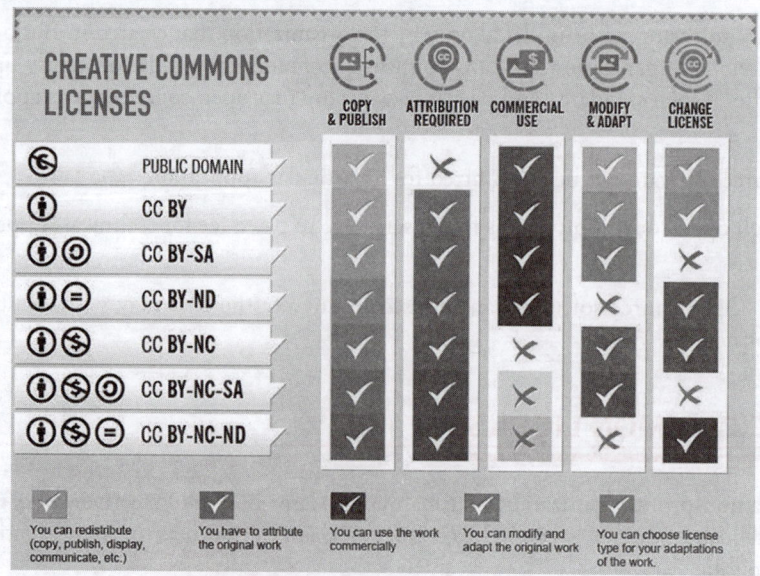

Figure 17.7 Creative Commons License

Similarly, **Google Images** has powerful advanced tools to quickly filter by usage rights. Just open Google Images, search for a phrase, and then click the Tools button. Click the Usage rights drop-down box to choose from a number of options. Google will then automatically filter images that are labelled with Creative Commons licenses, similar licenses, or are in the public domain. Just like when choosing content with the right Creative Commons license.

Even **Flickr** is a powerful image hosting service, most renowned for great photography. **Freesound** allows users to find free audio (including sound effects, songs, and atmospheric sounds) under Creative Commons. It rates the content and displays the download count, making it easy to find good-quality sounds for all sorts of content.

17.8 PRIVACY

Before reading about privacy, let us first understand what personal information is. Personal information means recorded information or opinions, whether true or not, that helps someone to identify whose information or opinion it is. For example, it can be a name, address, sex, age, financial details, marital status, education, criminal record, employment history, etc.

Privacy is a fundamental right. It is essential to autonomy and the protection of human dignity. Privacy is an important issue as it protects us and society against arbitrary and unjustified use of power. Strict privacy laws protect us from others who may wish to exert control on us. We can protect what can be known about us and done to us. We can limit who has access to our communications and information.

Undue interference from various sources may compel us to compromise on who we are and how we want to interact with the world around us. Privacy laws help to counter this and serves as the foundation upon which many other human rights are built. It helps to create barriers and manage boundaries to protect ourselves from unwarranted interference in our lives.

Privacy laws gives us a space to be ourselves without judgement and allows us to think freely without discrimination. When we talk of ensuring privacy, we must consider the following issues:

- the ethics of modern life
- the rules governing the conduct of commerce; and
- the restraints placed on use of information.

Today, with advancements in technology, our capabilities to protect privacy are greater than ever before, but the capabilities for surveillance have also improved manifold.

These days, it has become very easy to uniquely identify individuals amidst mass data sets and streams. It is now possible for companies and governments to monitor every conversation we conduct, each commercial transaction we make and every location we visit. These capabilities may adversely impact individuals, groups and even society as it may call for action against them.

The biggest challenge to privacy is that the right to privacy can be compromised without the individual being aware about it. Moreover, we are not even informed about the monitoring we are placed under, and not given the opportunity to question these activities.

In many countries, secret surveillance and lack of accountability has resulted in a risk to democratic life. Therefore, it is very important in the modern world to develop laws and technologies to strengthen the ability to freely enjoy this right.

17.8.1 Key Information Privacy Principles

Information privacy principles state that when an organisation collects personal information, it should:

- Collect only the information that is needed and not intrude unreasonably. People should know what information about them is collected and for what purpose.
- Information collected must be used and disclosed only for the purpose for which it has been collected or for any other related purpose those people would reasonably expect.
- Before collecting clearly state the purpose for which the information is being collected.
- Let people see their information and allow them to correct, if required.
- If possible, provide the option of not identifying people, especially when information about some controversial issue is collected.

- Ensure the protection of people's private information when it is transmitted anywhere outside the organisation.
- Do not collect confidential or highly personal information about people like their ethnic background, political views, etc.

If an organisation is found guilty of not following Information Privacy Principles, then it might have to make an apology, change a procedure, correct or delete personal information or even have to pay compensation.

17.9 COMPUTER FRAUD

Since computers and the Internet are used for a wide variety of tasks today and life without them has become indispensable, frauds related to computers have been increasing at a faster rate than ever before.

Computer fraud occurs when a person makes use of the internet and a computing device to obtain something of value to another individual. This can be information, but some take money or bank and personal information for later use. For example, hacking is a common form of computer fraud in which a hacker uses technological tools to remotely access a protected computer or system (Fig. 17.8). Another common form of computer fraud includes the interception of an electronic transmission unintended for the interceptor, such as passwords, credit card information, or other types of identity theft. Other types of computer fraud include:

Figure 17.8 Cyber safety at risk

- Emails requesting money
- Messages seeking personal information such as account numbers, Social Security numbers, and passwords
- Using someone else's computer to access personal information to perform fraudulent activity
- Installing spyware or malware on someone else's computer
- Violating copyright laws by copying someone else's information and using it in one's own name
- Illegally using someone's computer to change information, such as grades, work reports, etc.
- Denial-of-service attack in which the attacker prevents other innocent users from accessing a network
- Crimes intended to transmit or provide false or misleading information. Sending spam emails or participating in online auction fraud are examples of this type of computer fraud crime. The goal is often to convince people to part with money by misleading them.
- Crimes intended to obtain unlawful use of a computer or a computer system. Botnet crimes are an example of this type of computer fraud.
- Providing misleading information to obtain unlawful access. For example, unlawfully obtaining funds or information by pretending to be someone else.
- Emails promoting *too-good-to-be-true* investment opportunities or goods for sale
- Spreading false news for influencing people's opinions on current events.

While most of the computer fraud is done for gaining money, some also do it for bringing bad name to an organization by revealing their confidential data and spoiling their credibility.

Although there is no way to protect confidential data, organizations must take some steps to minimize the probability of such fraudulent activities. A few precautions are listed below:

- Be alert to the scams that are circulated over the internet.
- Individual users and organizations should not publish personal details or other important data on their websites or forums.
- The organization/firms should not broadcast much of their business details on the internet.
- Organizations must follow security policies, and procedures.
- People working from homes should ensure that any message seeking the organization's confidential data is valid and coming from the correct source (by checking digital signatures in it).

17.10 ILLEGAL DOWNLOADING

Illegal downloading is also known as downloading without paying. Whenever a content like book, movie, song or software is prepared, a cost is involved. Everyone involved in the process of preparing it wants to have monetary gains from the sale of that product. Therefore, the product is protected by copyright law so that it cannot be copied, reproduced or resold without their permission.

Downloading copyrighted content is a punishable crime. Correspondingly, distributing tsuch content, electronically or non-electronically, without the express permission of the copyright holder is also illegal.

17.11 INTERNET FRAUDS AND SCAMS

The downside of using Internet services (especially through those listed in Fig. 17.9) include stealing personal information, conduct of fraudulent transactions and the transmittal of the proceeds of fraud to financial institutions. Such frauds can occur in chat rooms, email, message boards, or on websites. Some common internet frauds are discussed below.

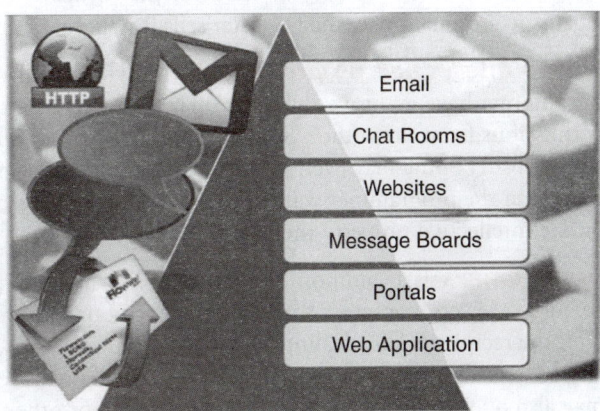

Figure 17.9 Tools used for Internet frauds

Purchase fraud occurs when a person purchases a product or service online and pays for it through fraud, for example, using a stolen or a fake credit card. As a result, merchants do not get paid for the transaction and lose money as a result.

Online auction fraud occurs when a fraudster starts an online auction of high-priced items on a website. He then accepts payment from the auction winner, but either does not deliver the product or delivers a product that is less valuable than the one offered. This is the most common fraud on the Internet.

Online retail fraud is similar to the auction fraud in which, after receiving the payment, either the product is not delivered or an inferior product is delivered.

Work-from-home scam occurs when business opportunities are advertised on the Internet and users are asked to pay nominal to substantial sums of money to get themselves registered. The fraudster collects thousands of dollars but never delivers the promised material or adequate information to the subscribers. Instead, he or she sends advice to the subscribers on how to place ads similar to the one through which the subscriber got recruited. In another scenario, the scammer accepts services from the victims (like writing directories, data entry, reading books, etc) but then refuse to reimburse them by rejecting their work, considering it sub-standard.

Phishing is a fraudulent activity in which a person or a business pretends to be trustworthy when actually it is not. It is basically done to acquire sensitive information like passwords, account numbers and credit card details. Phishing is usually done through official electronic notifications or messages, such as e-mails or instant messages.

For example, a phisher will ask a potential victim to enter his password by displaying messages like "verify your account", "confirm billing information" "enter your credit card number". Once the victim gives his details, the attacker could access the victim's information and use it for criminal purposes, such as spamming or transferring money in his account or shopping online with the victim's credit card number.

While sending fraudulent messages or emails, the fraudsters copy the code and graphics from legitimate websites to give victims the look and feel of a legitimate mail from the trusted website so that victims can comfortably provide them their private and confidential information. Scammers may also provide links to their websites that appear to be legitimate.

Pharming occurs when a hacker exploits vulnerability in the Domain Name System (DNS) to redirect website traffic from a legitimate website to his fraudulent website. This process of making the victim's computer to communicate with the wrong server is called domain hijacking.

The fraudster constructs a fake web site that looks similar to the legitimate site and asks for the user's personal information like his bank password, PIN number, bank account number, credit card number, etc to steal his information and misuse it. This combination of domain hijacking with a phishing website constitutes pharming.

Stock market fraud includes attempts to manipulate securities prices on the market for the personal profit of the scammer. The scammer usually follows any of the two methods to do this fraud. First is the pump-and-dump scheme in which false information is spread to cause a dramatic increase in price of thinly traded stocks in chat rooms, forums, internet boards, or email (as spam). This is called the "pump". The moment prices reach the desired level, scammers sell their stocks (called "dump") to innocent victims thereby making a substantial profit. Later when the prices again fall to their usual prices, the victims realize that it was all a fraud.

In the second technique, called short-selling or scalping, the scammer spreads false information that causes a dramatic decrease in prices. Once the stock price falls to the desired level, the scammer buys them in bulk and then reverses the false information or waits for the company to disapprove the information in the media. Once the stock regains its original price, the fraudster sells it making high profits.

Online intellectual property theft: Individuals all over the world who share their notes and information on the Internet have exclusive rights on their material. But many people or students just copy and use it without taking permissions from the author. Some people also copy others' text, images and multimedia data and put them on their own website. Some may even go a step ahead and copy someone else's program code or material and distribute it for free when the programmer wanted to sell it. This process of copying and using someone else's online material is called online intellectual property theft.

Spam emails is a common form of fraud in which the fraudster sends bulk emails to millions of email addresses to corrupt receivers' computers, steal their identity or fool them to pay for fraudulent products or services. These emails offer the recipients false dealings such as low-interest loans, winning lottery, fancy business proposals, free credit report checks, relationships with local singles, etc. Spam emails require recipients to open the email and click on a link which may also open up the computer to a virus, worm or other types of bugs that may corrupt the computer.

17.12 INFORMATION TECHNOLOGY ACT 2000

High-speed Internet connectivity has no doubt brought about a communication revolution. However, on the flipside, it has led to an increase in online crimes. A rise in these offences necessitated effective laws for protection online. Keeping this in mind, the Indian Parliament passed the Information Technology Act 2000 (No. 21 of 2000). This was conceptualized on the United Nations Commissions on International Trade Law (UNCITRAL) model.

The Government of India enacted the Information Technology (IT) Act with the objective to deliver and facilitate lawful electronic, digital, and online transactions, and mitigate cybercrimes. It defines the offences, along with the penalties for each category of offence, in detail.

The IT Act of India provides legal recognition for transactions involving exchange of electronic data and other means of electronic communication, commonly referred to as electronic commerce (or e-commerce). E-commerce involves alternatives to paper-based methods of communication and storage of information.

17.12.1 Salient Features of IT Act

Some of the key features of the IT Act are listed here:

1. Digital signatures have been replaced with electronic signatures.
2. A detailed note on offences, penalties, and breaches is given.
3. It talks about the justice dispensation systems for cybercrimes.
4. It provides details for the constitution of the Cyber Regulations Advisory Committee.
5. The Act is based on The Indian Penal Code 1860, The Indian Evidence Act 1872, The Bankers' Books Evidence Act 1891, The Reserve Bank of India Act 1934, etc.
6. It adds a provision to Section 81, which states that *nothing contained in the Act shall restrict any person from exercising any right conferred under the Copyright Act 1957.*

Some important sections of the Act are given in Table 17.3.

Table 17.3 Cybercrimes and punishments

Sections	Particulars	Punishment for the Offence
Section 43	Damage to computer system etc.	Compensation to the person affected.
Section 66	Computer related offence	Imprisonment for term of 3 years or fine for 5 lakh rupees or both.
Section 67	Publication or transmission of obscene material in e-form	Fine of 5 lakh rupees, and imprisonment of 3 years and double conviction on second offence.
Section 68	Not complying with directions of controller	Fine up to 1 lakh or imprisonment of 2 years or both.
Section 70	Protected system	Imprisonment up to 10 years and shall also be liable for a fine.
Section 72	Breaking confidentiality of the information of computer	Imprisonment for term of 2 years or fine for 1 lakh rupees or both.
Section 73	Publishing of false digital signatures	Imprisonment for term of 2 years or fine for 1 lakh rupees or both.
Section 74	Publishing of digital signature for fraudulent purpose	Imprisonment for term of 2 years or fine for 1 lakh rupees or both.

17.13 CHILD PORNOGRAPHY

Child pornography is defined as "any visual depiction of sexually explicit conduct involving a child which includes photograph, video, digital or computer-generated image indistinguishable from an actual child and an image created, adapted or modified but appear to depict a child".

In simple terms, Child Sexual Abuse Material or CSAM, legally known as child pornography, refers to any content that depicts sexually explicit activities involving a child. CSAM is often circulated for personal consumption. More recently, live-streaming sexual abuse has been reported in large numbers. In such instances, some people pay to watch the live abuse of a child through video conferencing software. This type of abuse is far more difficult to detect because of its real-time nature and the lack of digital evidence left behind following the crime.

CSAM is a global issue and the United States remains one of the largest producers and consumers of child abuse content in the world. Researchers have listed the risk factors that may increase the potential of children of any age group and background to be exposed to sexual abuse.

Child sexual abuse images and videos found online have both boys and girls who are in the age group 0-18 years. The severity of this abuse can be understood from the fact that the Canadian Centre for Child Protection found that in 78.30% of the images and videos, children under 12 years were depicted and 63.40% of those children were under 8 years of age. Also, they found that 80.42% of the children were girls, while 19.58% were boys.

CSAM causes trauma that carries into adulthood. Most of the times, CSAM victims are abused by their known people whom they trust. These offenders have close access to the children they are abusing. This closeness helps them to normalize sexual contact and maintain secrecy.

17.14 CYBER FORENSICS

Also known as computer forensics or digital forensics, it is the application of investigation and analysis techniques to gather and preserve evidence from one or more computing devices in a way that is suitable for presentation in a court of law. Cyber forensics performs a structured investigation and maintains a documented chain of evidences to know exactly what happened and who was responsible for it.

Forensic investigators follow a standard set of procedures: before starting their investigation, the first physically isolate the device to ensure no one can tamper with it. They make a digital copy of the device's storage media. Thereafter, investigation is done on the digital copy.

These days, there are many techniques and proprietary software for forensic applications that can be used to examine the data, search hidden folders and unallocated disk space to obtain any deleted, encrypted, or damaged files. Any evidence thus collected on the digital copy is carefully documented in a "finding report" and verified with the original in preparation for legal proceedings.

Cybercrimes include a wide range of activities varying from email scams to downloading copyrighted works for distribution, homicide, forgery and pornography, to name a few. Cyber forensics experts use a digital audit trail for investigating these crimes.

Earlier, like any other physical evidence, courts of law used to consider evidence collected from computer systems as legit. However, a few years back, digital evidence lost its credibility in the courts because cyber criminals had learnt to corrupt, destroy, or alter computer data. But a little later, cybercrime experts equipped themselves with techniques, tools and processes to extract the required information from computers without affecting the data in the process.

Apart from investigating cybercrimes, cyber forensics is also used in incident response and internal employee investigations.

Computer forensics deals with identifying, preserving, analyzing, and recovering data from computers and other digital media (including computer system, mobile device, cloud service) that can serve as evidence in civil proceedings. For example, in the high-profile case of Michael Jackson, his doctor, Dr Conrad Murray, was found guilty in 2011 for the involuntary manslaughter of the pop singer. His conviction was possible only because the investigating team could find digital evidence on his computer.

17.15 TECHNOLOGY AND SOCIETY

The meaning of "technology" implies the application of science or knowledge, the creation of a tool, or the use of a tool to solve a problem. People have always relied on technology, from the first tools used to build fire or store water to the wheel or the steam engine.

The digitization of information and communication has led to the exponential globalization of economy and society, significantly impacting cultures world-wide.

Technology has changed how the society communicates, learns, and thinks. We are living in the era in which life without technological advances has become just indispensable. Technology has improved the living standards of many people in the last few decades. Without technology, people would still be living within the geographical confines of their societies.

However, technology has both negative as well positive impacts on the society. Let us discuss both of them in this section.

17.15.1 Positive Impacts

Education: Technology has made learning more interesting, interactive and collaborative as shown in Fig. 17.10. It improves engagement of learners and also provides them better access to resources. With the advent of the Internet, an ocean of information is available 24 × 7. Students can complete their assignments easily and faster than ever before.

Students can also attend online classes, participate in online quizzes and take online exams while sitting at home. An education system assisted by technology expands the boundaries of traditional classrooms and encourages self-paced learning.

Students, researchers and teachers can collaborate with other students, researchers and teachers across the world and share their knowledge.

Figure 17.10 Technology of education

Communication: Technology has changed the way people communicate with one another worldwide. Examples of technological advancements that have made life easier include things like the Internet, phones, tablets, TV, Play Stations, movie and video games. Technology also introduced new ways of electronic communication including emails, social networking and video conferencing, to name a few. Even companies are using internet to provide better customer support services. Military personnel can conduct lethal drone strikes from across the globe.

Health Industry: Technological advancements within the health industry have helped in improving health of individuals. Many innovate apps enable people to check and record their weight, calories intake, heart rate and other parameters at any time of the day. With complex and advanced technology available in the surgery room, the probability of successful treatment and has increased manifold.

Economic globalization: Advancements in computing technology, instant communication, information transfer and transportation have made it possible for industrialized societies to outsource intense-labour jobs like manufacturing and telecommunications to countries where such services are much cheaper. This has improved their profit margins.

These technological advancements have also helped online businesses like Amazon and eBay flourish. These businesses effectively outsource the majority of their "labor" and "retail space" to the Internet and automated mechanization systems. The companies benefit from low overhead and high profits. Consumers benefit from low prices. As a result, brick-and-mortar stores tend to lose business (or go out of business) and their employees lose their jobs.

Improvements in Agriculture: Technologies of modern agriculture have allowed farmers to increase food production using lesser input and within a shorter period of time.

Small- and medium-sized farmers can better manage activities like sowing, ploughing and watering as shown in Fig. 17.11. Technology has also allowed researchers to develop genetic crops, which usually grows at a high pace. Genetically modified crops are also resistant to most of the diseases and pets.

Improvement in Transportation: Today's society is being greatly benefited from the new inventions in the field of transportation. Researchers have been able to design better engines that can be used in vehicles and identify roads that need to be re-constructed or where roads, flyovers, tunnels are needed for avoiding traffic congestion.

Figure 17.11 Technology in agriculture
Source: https://www.thehitavada.com/Encyc/2020/8/30/Importance-Of-Technology-In-Indian-Agriculture.html

17.15.2 Negative Impacts

Technology is not harmful to the individual or to the society by itself; it is the people themselves who are misusing the technology and blaming the technology for the harmful effects.

- Communicating through mobile phones and other technology has affected personal relationships. Now, most people have less face-to-face contact.
- People are so engrossed in social networking sites and other apps that they have less personal time. They don't even have enough time for themselves.
- Students' concentration in studies has been adversely affected. They are distracted by entertainment apps and are not as keen to focus on learning and educational apps.
- There is also loss of privacy because anyone can easily find information about any other person.
- The poor application of technology has resulted in the creation of more pollution to the environment, causing serious threat to the lives and property of the people of the society.
- Economic globalization has resulted in workers losing their jobs to outsourcing.
- Some of these technological advancements have increased stress levels and isolation within the society (Fig. 17.12).
- Some of the technological advancements have adversely affected certain industrial sectors like the print media. These advancements have either caused several businesses to shut down forever or shift their scope of business because there is a lack of demand for their type of goods and services. For example, many people prefer to read e-newspaper than buying

Figure 17.12 Technology side-effects

a printed paper. Music lovers no longer buy music CDs, they simply download it and save it to a folder on their computer. Also, people can now download or purchase movies online; this has adversely affected the sale of DVDs.
- Many fun games like football, basketball or tennis can now be played online. So, many people avoid going outside and play such games with their friends.
- Less-than-adequate interaction with people has resulted in depression among many youngsters as little or no proximity with friends and relatives takes a toll on their emotional well-being.

17.16 E-WASTE MANAGEMENT

Electronic equipment has become an integral part of our lives. Semiconductors and sensors used in wearable devices, computers, TVs and mobile phones, all produce e-waste (Fig. 17.13).

Moreover, the life span of these devices has become shorter. With cheaper technology and rapid advancements, people throw away their gadgets as soon as their batteries die and buy new ones. Even companies intentionally motivate this behaviour by making their products obsolete every 2-3 years (by updating the design or software and discontinuing support for older models) so that they continue to profit from steady sales.

In 2016, the world's population generated 49 million tons of e-waste which is approximately equal to about 4,500 Eiffel Towers. It is estimated that by the end of 2021, more than 60 million tons of e-waste will be produced.

Electronic waste or e-waste typically includes discarded computer monitors, motherboards, mobile phones and chargers, CDs, headphones, TVs, ACs and refrigerators. Apart from precious metals like gold, cobalt, silver, copper, platinum, palladium, lithium, e-waste also contains heavy toxic metals like lead, mercury, cadmium and beryllium, polluting PVC plastic and hazardous chemicals such as brominated flame retardants, which can harm human health and the environment.

Figure 17.13 Electronic waste
Source: https://www.pixelache.ac/events/talking-trash-lab-lecture

With ever-increasing demand for electronic equipment, manufacturers are beginning to face shortages of the raw materials needed to make their products, so reclaiming and reusing the materials from discarded products and waste makes economic and environmental sense. A recent study (https://www.sciencedaily.com/releases/2018/04/180404093956.htm) in China stated that mining copper, gold and aluminium from the ore costs 13 times more than recovering the metals through mining of e-waste.

Global E-Waste Monitor 2017 reported that India generates about 2 million tonnes (MT) of e-waste annually. India ranks fifth among e-waste producing countries, after the US, China, Japan and Germany.

In 2016–17, India treated only 0.036 MT of its e-waste. Moreover, about 95% of India's e-waste is recycled in the informal sector. Globally, only 20% global e-waste is recycled. A report by UN indicates that due to poor extraction techniques, the total recovery rate of cobalt from e-waste is only 30 per cent. Cobalt is a metal which is in great demand for laptop, smart phone and electric car batteries.

The report also states that one recycler in China produces more cobalt by recycling than by mining in one year. Recycled metals are also two to ten times more energy-efficient than metals obtained from their ores.

The UN report also suggests that reducing the amount of e-waste and improving the lifespan of electronic gadgets are essential for building a more circular economy. In such an economy, waste is reduced; resources are conserved and are fed back into the supply chain for developing new products.

Inspired by the report, the organizing committee of Tokyo Olympics that was supposed to be held in 2020 had ordered to make medals with 50,000 tonnes of e-waste. For this, nearly 8 tonnes of gold, silver and bronze were extracted by November 2018 to make 5,000 medals.

In India, laws to manage e-waste are already in place since 2011. It allows only authorised dismantlers and recyclers to collect e waste. These laws were strengthened in 2016 and over 21 products have been included under the purview of the rule. It also ensures the take-back of the end-of-life products.

A new arrangement called Producer Responsibility Organisation (PRO) has further strengthened the guidelines by making it mandatory for producers to manage 20% per cent of the waste generated by their sales. The law also states that the responsibility of producers is not confined to waste collection, but extends to ensure that the waste reaches the authorised recycler/dismantler.

Even after upgrading the laws, massive amounts of e-waste are being generated by the informal sector at huge health and environmental cost, polluting ground water and soil.

> Electronic devices are made of a complex mix of materials that include gold, silver, copper, platinum, palladium, lithium, cobalt and other valuable elements. These precious materials can be reclaimed through recycling.

E-waste is growing at a compound annual growth rate (CAGR) of about 30 per cent in the country. A record 53.6 million metric tonnes (Mt) of electronic waste was generated worldwide in 2019, up 21 per cent in just five years. (Source: UN's Global E-waste Monitor 2020). It is also estimated that by 2030 this number will reach 74 Mt!

Though India has more than 178 registered e-waste recyclers, many of them are not recycling waste at all.

The Ministry of Electronics and Information Technology (MeitY) started an e-waste awareness programme under Digital India, along with industry associations in 2015, to create awareness about the hazards of e-waste recycling by the unorganised sector, and to educate them about alternative ways of disposing it.

> With COVID-19 keeping people indoors, the usage of electronic devices has only gone up. Without proper intervention, it is likely to be over 100 million tonnes by 2050.

The programme's main focus is to adopt best practices for environment friendly e-waste recycling practices. This would help to generate jobs as well as viable business prospects for locals.

17.16.1 Development of Waste Recycling Technologies

The MeitY has also developed affordable technologies to recycle valuable materials and plastics in an environmentally friendly way. Some of these technologies can recycle up to 1000 kg/ day (~35 MT e-waste). This could then be made suitable for creating an eco-park in the country. Even a majority (76 per cent) of the waste plastics can be converted into suitable materials that can be used in all ways as original plastics are used. The technology has already been transferred for commercialisation.

Professor Veena Sahajwalla, Professor of Materials Science, UNSW Australia, suggests setting up of micro-factories in India that can transform e-waste into reusable material that can be converted into ceramics and plastic filaments for 3D printing. And metals like gold, silver, copper and palladium found in the e-waste can be separated for re-sale in conditions that are totally safe.

There is an immense potential for e-waste recycling in the country. But before that, there is a need for skill development and introduction of technology that adopts adequate safety measures in the country's informal sector.

Since India is highly deficient in precious mineral resources, there is a need for a well-designed, robust and regulated e-waste recovery regime which could generate jobs as well as wealth.

17.16.2 Formal vs. Informal Recycling

Recycling e-waste is practiced both formally and informally. Formal e-waste recycling involves disassembling the electronics, separating and categorizing the contents by material and cleaning them. Items are then separated for further sorting. However, the companies involved must adhere to **health and safety rules**. They must also use **pollution-control** techniques to minimize environmental hazards of handling e-waste. All this makes formal recycling **expensive** (refer Fig. 17.14). As a result, many companies and countries illegally export their e-waste to developing countries where recycling is cheap. For example, US is the second largest producer of e-waste after China, but it recycles only 40% of the e-waste and exports the rest to developing countries (in Asia) where informal recycling is typically cheap, unlicensed and unregulated.

Figure 17.14 Formal e-waste collection center

At these informal recycling workshops as shown in Fig. 17.15, workers including women and children recover valuable materials by burning devices to melt away non-valuable materials. For example, they melt toxic material like mercury and acids to recover gold. They also dismantle devices by hand to reclaim other materials of value. These people do not wear protective equipment and are unaware that they are handling dangerous materials. Inhaling toxic chemicals and direct contact with hazardous e-waste materials increases lead levels in blood, leads to spontaneous abortions, stillbirths, premature births, reduced birth weights, mutations, lung malfunction, congenital malformations, abnormal thyroid function, and neurobehavioral disturbances. Moreover, e-waste toxins contaminate water, air and soil. In addition to the health and environmental hazards, informal recycling also poses security risks. While formal recyclers usually wipe all data from the devices, informal recycling does not. Criminals search e-waste for credit card numbers and other financial information.

Figure 17.15 Informal recycling workshop
Source: https://www.flickr.com/photos/basel-action-network/9260624105/

Looking into these hazards, people in developing countries prefer to earn by dismantling, refurbishing, repairing and reselling used electronic devices. In China (also known as the e-waste capital of the world), 75 percent of households are involved in the recycling business. Informal recycling is practiced in India, Nigeria, Ghana and the Philippines.

17.16.3 Alternative Solutions of Disposal

With flooding e-waste material around the world, recycling alone is not enough. Therefore, some alternate solutions are being researched and practiced around the world. Some possible solutions are given below:

Design better electronic products that are safer, more durable, repairable and recyclable. Use of toxic materials should be minimized. Moreover, chemical engineers at Stanford University are working to develop the first fully biodegradable electronic circuit using natural dyes that dissolve in acid at a pH 100 times weaker than vinegar.

Companies should also manufacture phones that enable consumers to upgrade parts of their phones instead of having to entirely replace them. Google, LG and Motorola all released modular models, but they were not well received in the market as it looks clumsy and is costlier than the conventional models. However, people are now becoming aware of the e-waste problem and companies have begun to design modular phones that have market appeal.

We must repair and reuse the devices we have.

Extended Producer Responsibility *instructs* companies manufacturing electronic products to take the responsibility for the management and disposal of their products at the end of their lives. This will help to turn waste materials into a resource for producing new products. In USA, manufacturers provide consumers with free and convenient e-waste recycling.

A more convenient form of recycling through EcoATM is extensively used in US. EcoATM (refer Fig. 17.16) provides a convenient and safe way to recycle and sell e-waste at kiosks. The EcoATM evaluates the old phones, TVs and other devices, based on the model and condition and pays the right amount to the customer. Sold items are then either reused or responsibly recycled.

In China, the largest internet company, Baidu, and the United Nations Development Programme have developed a smartphone app that allows users to enter the item they want to recycle, its picture, size and the pick-up date along with their name and address. Within 24 hours, the item is picked up for recycling.

Giving informal recyclers financial incentives to divert e-waste to formal collection or recycling centres. For example, informal recyclers could be paid more to deliver e-waste to a formal collection centre than they would get for dismantling it by hand themselves.

Figure 17.16 EcoATM

Like developed countries, developing countries must also devise sophisticated disposal schemes and high-cost systems that are equipped to handle hazardous waste in the safest possible way.

In developing countries, the regulations that guide the disposition of e-waste is mostly fragmented and lack monitoring. These regulations should be made stringent and monitored effectively.

17.17 IDENTITY THEFT

Identity theft is a crime in which the criminal obtains and uses someone else's personal or financial information for making financial transactions or communicating false information.

In simple terms, identity theft is when someone steals another person's personal information and uses it without his/her permission. In such cases, the victim is left with damage to his/her credit, finances, reputation, and livelihood in many cases. Information for identity theft can be collected by:

- sifting through trash bins looking for bank account and credit card statements
- accessing corporate databases to steal lists of customer information.

Once the criminals get the personal and financial details of one or more persons, they can use it for the following types of identity thefts.

Criminal identity theft: It is used by a criminal to misrepresent himself as another person during arrest to avoid an arrest or conviction record. In this case, criminals present a fake ID or state-issued documents containing stolen credentials. If this theft is successful, the victim is charged instead of the criminal.

Medical identity theft: In this case, someone impersonates another person to obtain free medical care.

Loan fraud: In this theft, someone else's personal information is used to obtain a loan.

Government documents or benefits fraud: This means using someone else's personal information to obtain benefits from the government.

Financial identity theft: In this theft, someone uses another person's identity or information to obtain credit, goods, services or benefits. This is the most common form of identity theft.

Child identity theft: This theft happens when someone uses a child's identity for personal gains like using a child's information to buy a residence, find employment, obtain loans or avoiding arrest on outstanding warrants. Most of the times, the victim is a family member, child of a friend or someone else close to the criminal.

Social ID Theft: Stealing one's name, photos and other personal information to create a fake account with malicious intentions.

Senior identity theft: In this theft, the victim is any person above the age of 60. Since senior citizens always get some special privileges and concessions, the thieves can use their personal information to benefit from the advantages they avail.

Synthetic identity theft: In this, the criminal combines real (usually stolen) and fake information to create a new identity. This new identity is then used to open fraudulent accounts and make fraudulent purchases. Criminals can even steal money from any credit card company using this synthesized identity.

Identity thieves extensively use computer technology to obtain other people's personal information for identity fraud. For example, they search the hard drives of stolen or discarded computers, hack into computers or computer networks, access public records available online, install malware to infect computers, and use deceptive emails or text messages.

17.17.1 Avoiding Identity Thefts

We cannot protect ourselves from identity theft completely. But a little intelligence and awareness of how information related to him/her can be misused can help individuals to safeguard their information to a certain extent.

When someone gains access to an organization's data without authorization, it is a case of data breach. This is usually done to access full names, credit card numbers and other credentials of people. Some possible sources of identity theft include:

Unsecure Browsing: Do not browse unsecure sites and never share any information on an unsecure website or a website that has been compromised by hackers. Modern web browsers give an alert if you try to access a risky website.

Dark Web Marketplaces: The dark web is that part of the internet where one's personal information is available after being stolen. Hackers may use it for themselves or may sell it to others who have potentially nefarious intentions.

The dark web is a hidden network of websites is not accessible by normal browsers. People need special software to visit the dark web and mask their identities and activities, making it a haven for fraudsters. Personal information is available for sale on the dark web and it can be purchased by just anybody.

Malware Activity: Fraudsters install malware on a person's computer to steal his/her data or spy on his/her computer activity without being noticed.

Credit Card Theft: The simplest form of identity theft is credit card theft in which the credit card information of the victim is stolen to make unauthorized purchases. Credit card information is usually stolen through a data breach, physical theft, credit card skimmers and through online retail accounts where card information is stored.

Mail Theft: Personal information can be stolen through mails. Bank and credit card statements or any other document sent or received through the postal system can be intercepted and used to access personal data. Do not just throw away old mails. Shred (or tear) them before throwing in trash bins.

Phishing and Spam Attacks: Fraudsters use email and text messages and other forms of electronic communication to steal sensitive information. They send messages that look as if they are coming from a reputable source and ask for personal and confidential information from the receiver.

For example, a bogus email that pretends to be coming from the victim's bank asks the user to click on a given link that will take him to the bank's website. The user is supposed to login on the bank's website by entering the username and password. However, the fraudster directs the victim to a duplicate website of his bank to see the username and password that victim uses to access his online banking service.

Wi-Fi Hacking: Using public Wi-Fi at airports, department stores or coffee shops, fraudsters can access all messages passed through the connection. When a user types his/her password, bank account or credit card number or other personal information, the fraudster can easily intercept it and use it for personal gains.

Mobile Phone Theft: Our smartphones can provide vital information to identity thieves. We usually use apps that allow us to log in automatically without a password or fingerprint. If someone steals and unlocks our phone, then they can find any information found stored in the apps, emails, text messages, notes and more.

Card Skimming: Identify thieves often use a skimming device that can be placed over a card reader on an ATM or a fuel pump without being recognized by anyone. When the victim swipes a debit or credit card at a compromised machine, the skimmer reads the information from the card's magnetic stripe and either stores it or transmits it. This information can then be used to make purchases.

17.17.2 Steps to Protect One's Data

These days, people have accounts with various organizations and multiple websites; it is almost impossible to protect one's information completely from a data breach problem. However, certain steps can be taken to minimize these risks.

- Keep an eye on your credit reports regularly.
- Keep long and strong passwords to keep yourself safe and secure. Your password must consist of letters both in uppercase and lowercase, digits and symbols.
- Make sure that you never respond to unsolicited messages that seek your personal data such as name, birthdate and Aadhaar number.
- Update the antivirus and the operating system software of your devices regularly.
- To protect yourself from credit card fraud, set up a fraud alert that instructs potential creditors to contact you before granting credit in your name.

- Tear the receipts, copies of credit applications, insurance forms, physician statements, bank statements and other things that may reveal your personal information before discarding them.
- Delete all your data before discarding old computer hard drives.
- Change your passwords every 2–3 months for all your online accounts.
- Enable the security features on your mobile devices.
- Immediately contact the sender if your financial statements are late.
- Install firewalls and antivirus software on your computer.

17.17.3 Spotting Identity Theft and Dealing with It

Identity theft can be identified when one or more of the given situations are detected.

- Your existing bank or credit card accounts show purchases that you never made.
- A tax return filed with your information when you yourself have not filed it or when you find that your tax refund is stolen by someone.
- You are not receiving important mails such as bills or checks.
- Despite having an excellent credit rating, your credit transaction is denied.
- Money is withdrawn from your bank account without your knowledge.
- You receive unauthorized authentication messages via text or email for known or unknown accounts.
- You get an email from a website or an organization that says your account has been recently accessed. Was it you?
- You receive a bill claiming an amount for a health care service that you did not avail.

If you identify any such theft of your personal information, then you must immediately lock your phone and mobile devices with a secure password or set up a biometric screening. Make sure that your passwords are not stored in plain text anywhere on your device(s).

If you think that your credit card or debit card was stolen, then immediately contact the card issuer and your bank to lock your account.

You must also report the identity theft to the nearest local police station. This is very important as the fraud department at your bank, credit card issuers or other places where you have accounts will require you to provide a FIR.

17.18 UNIQUE ID AND BIOMETRICS

There are more than 7 billion human beings on Earth. Having billions of unique ID and password is next to impossible. In such a situation, biometrics can help in a big way.

Biometrics means any feature of humans that makes their identification easy and accurate. The most common example of a biometric recognition system that we use in our daily lives is our smartphone's fingerprint and facial recognition technology. With further improvement in technology, biometric systems will replace passwords. Biometric identifiers not only act as a mechanism for access control, they are also used to catch hold of criminals.

Biometric controls also include physiological traits like earlobe geometry, retina and iris patterns, voice waves, DNA and signatures; or behavioural characteristics like the unique way in which a person solves a security-authentication puzzle. To be useful, biometric data must be unique, permanent and collectible.

No matter which biometric methodology is used, the identification verification process is the same. A record of a person's unique characteristic is captured and stored in a database. At a later point in time, when identification verification is required, a new record is captured and compared with the previous records present in the database. If the data in the new record matches with one in the database record, the person's identity is confirmed.

With the advent of computer vision, researchers and industry experts are working for developing easier and more robust biometrics.

17.18.1 Processing Biometric Data

We can use biometric data for identification in the following ways.

- **Face recognition**. In this technique, the unique patterns of a person's face are measured by comparing and analysing facial contours.

- **Iris recognition:** The unique pattern of a person's iris, which is the colourful area of the eye surrounding the pupil, is identified.
- **Fingerprint scanner.** In this technique, the unique pattern of ridges and valleys on a finger is captured.
- **Voice recognition.** The unique sound waves in our voice as we speak to a device are used to verify our identity.
- **Hand geometry.** The length, thickness, width, and surface area of a person's hand is measured and stored. This is typically used in security applications.
- **Behavior characteristics.** Our behavioral aspects like the way we interact with a computer, press the keys, our handwriting, the way we walk, how we hold a computer mouse and perform other movements can be analysed to authenticate our identity.

Applications of Biometry We use biometric identifiers when we ask Siri, Alexa or Cortona for a weather update, or when we log in for online banking operations using our fingerprint (Fig. 17.17).

Police and crime branch collect DNA and fingerprints at crime scenes or may use video surveillance to analyse a suspect's gait or voice. Facial recognition technology is also used by them to pick out individuals from large crowds with considerable reliability.

Hand geometry is being used in industries to provide physical access to buildings. Signature comparison, however, is not a very reliable technique and so it is usually combined with extra layer of verification to verify an identity.

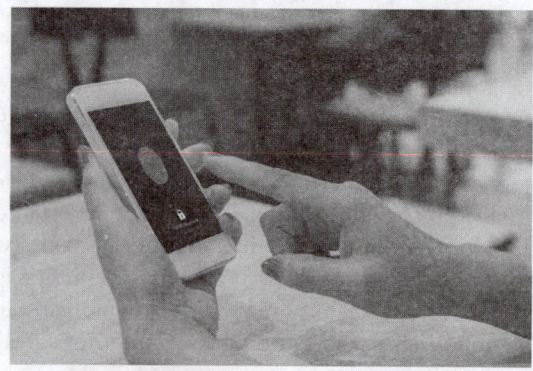

Figure 17.17 Using biometrics

The Unique ID Authority of India initiated the Aadhaar program in 2009. It is an example of a multi-step authentication process that incorporates iris scans, fingerprints from all 10 fingers and facial recognition. This information is linked to the Aadhaar card that is issued to every Indian citizen and made mandatory for accessing social services in India.

In China, facial recognition is used for routine purchases every day. New York, Chicago, and Moscow are linking CCTV cameras in their cities to facial recognition databases to help local police fight crime. Carnegie Mellon University is developing a camera that can scan the irises of people in crowds from a distance of 10 meters.

Dubai airport uses facial recognition to identify travellers when they pass through a tunnel in a virtual aquarium.

17.18.2 How Biometrics Work

A biometric system consists of three different components:

Sensor The sensors are used to record information. They are also used to read it when biometric information needs to be recognized.

Computer The computer or any computing device is used to storing and compare the information.

Software The software is used as an interface between the computer hardware and the sensors.

Advantage of Biometrics Biometric authentication and biometric identification is an exceptionally secure way to log in to devices and various services. It also helps to avoid remembering dozens of account passwords.

17.18.3 Downsides of Biometrics

There are serious privacy concerns with the use of biometrics. These include,

- Any collection of data could be hacked.
- When we use our biometric data at multiple locations, not all of them may be strongly secured.
- Biometric data is more vulnerable than any other kind of data. One can change passwords but not biometric features. Once your biometric data is compromised, it may no longer be in your control.
- Some pieces of biometric data may be duplicated. For example, a criminal can take a high-resolution picture of your ear from afar or copy your fingerprints from a glass you leave at a cafe. This information can then be used to hack into devices or accounts belonging to you.
- Laws governing biometrics are not the same everywhere.

Though the risks are real, biometric technology will always offer very compelling solutions for security. Biometric systems are convenient to use and difficult to duplicate.

17.18.4 How to Protect Your Biometric Data

There are a few measures that can be taken to protect our biometric data. Though nothing can protect it completely from being misused, something is always better than nothing.
- Give your biometric information only in limited places which you think will be highly secured.
- Use the latest software and regularly update them.
- Do not use facial recognition and fingerprint for every app that you use.

Biometrics authenticators like Microsoft's 'Windows Hello' or Apple's 'FaceID' are emerging as strong authentication tools as they are using infra-red scanning and live video detection to confirm the identity of a person.

17.19 GENDER ISSUES WHILE TEACHING AND USING COMPUTERS

Gender gap in computing has become a global concern due to the emergence of the Information Technology. The field of IT has become male dominant. *With lesser number of women pursuing education in computer science and working in this field, the gender gap has widened further.* Concerns of gender diversity and growing importance of computing and technology in society has motivated public policy debates addressing gender equality issues.

Do you know that in the early days of computers and computing, women were well-represented in this field? They often worked as "human computers," making complicated calculations. However, they were always paid less than their male counterparts. Due to the lack of labour resources during the Second World War, women were actively recruited into computer jobs that would have been otherwise done by men. Early programmers on machines such as ENIAC were mostly women (refer Fig. 17.18). In those days, programming was treated as a low skill clerical job and was thus given to women. Creation of hardware was considered to be a difficult task and was therefore offered to men.

Women were also asked to perform punch-card operations which were done *in noisy rooms, involving heavy manual labour, no opportunity for growth, less pay, tight schedules, unfavourable work environments, demand for high accuracy and male-dominated behaviours.* This resulted in many women leaving their jobs. Slowly women started losing interest in computer education.

Figure 17.18 Women in computing
Source: https://www.pinterest.com/pin/403212972882759850/

However, today the scenario is changing. Parents have understood that a job in the computing industry provides a safe working environment to women. They have also realized that IT is a flourishing sector with many job opportunities. So, they encourage their girl child to pursue a career in computing.

Unlike in many developed countries, in India, a growing number of women are studying and taking careers in technical fields. The percentage of women engineers graduating from IITs and other reputed engineering colleges are constantly increasing. Even in countries like Saudi Arabia, Bulgaria and Romania, more and more women are pursuing coding and technology. But despite all this, women still remain underrepresented in IT and related fields.

Although teenage girls are now using computers and the Internet at rates similar to their male peers, they are five times less likely to join a career in IT.

17.19.1 Reasons for Gender Gap

- In 1980s when use of computer started gaining popularity, it was marketed as a *tool for boys* and men.
- Boys having computers started playing with it as a toy. *Fidgeting with computers* aroused boys' interest and stepped up their readiness for joining computer science courses.
- Very *few girls joined computer science* courses as compared to boys.
- *Lack of a degree* in computer science made it difficult for girls to get a job in the IT field.
- In many cultures, especially the Indian culture, many women did not think of pursuing further studies because of the *societal expectation* that women should be married and raise children.
- Many women could not join a computer science course because it is *expensive*. Parents usually do not prefer to invest more money on their girl's education. They either keep their money for educating their sons or for their girl's marriage.
- Girls doing computer science course at undergraduate and postgraduate levels felt that boys do not cooperate with them. Rather, they *compete* with them.
- Many companies do not prefer to hire women as they feel that women will leave their jobs when they get *married or have children*. And even if they don't quit their jobs, they will not be able to do their jobs with full dedication once they get married.
- Apart from academics, we learn more by peer networks through conferences, seminars and other events. Men have always been more involved in such *extra events* than women.
- Many companies *deny promotions* to women stating that their performance suffer because they have always been overburdened with family and office responsibilities. Instead of promotions women often receive a small salary hike.
- Women in technical roles often feel that the skills and feedback they bring to their jobs are *not valued*.
- Women also *lack the support* needed to promote their skills. They lack role models, networks and mentors that could help them to nurture talent and explore opportunities for career advancement.
- It is believed that women coming from a *higher socioeconomic status* have higher probability of taking up computer science courses and not quitting job for family issues. This makes computing companies hire women from well-to-do families and prestigious schools, which leaves fewer opportunities for women from the lower strata of society.

> Do you know that in the aptitude tests conducted by companies to recruit people, women perform better than men?

17.19.2 Advantages of Gender Diversity

- A gender-diverse team is more likely to create products that satisfy end-user requirements. In a team with few or no women, the technical decisions are usually based on men's experiences, opinions and judgement, resulting in a male-slanted bias.
- Gender-diverse teams are more productive, more creative, more innovative and more able to stay on schedule and within budget, compared to homogenous teams.

17.18.3 Results of Gender Gap

- Lack of participation of females in computing excludes them from the "new economy", which calls for sophisticated computer skills in exchange for high salary positions.
- A team with a smaller number of or no women misses a huge potential to consolidate their products and meet user expectations.

17.19.4 Steps to Promote Women

While boys usually see computers as a tool to play with, girls, on the other hand, see it as a tool useful primarily for what it can do. We need to understand both these mind-sets to form an efficient team. Therefore, to promote women in IT, we must take certain steps as given below.

- Focusing on *recruiting* as well as retaining women studying computer science.
- Introduction of *role models* to motivate more and more women to come forward in this field
- Using *advertisement* campaigns showing women working and excelling in computing
- *Reservation* of quotas for women in computer science courses as well as jobs.
- *Media* must promote girls to take up technical courses
- Promoting girl's *computer education* right from school level.
- Initiating programs like all-girl computer camps and girls' *after-school computer clubs* to develop the interest of girls in computer science at a young age. These groups can educate girls about the benefits and job opportunities within IT.
- IT Companies and government should give *special awards* to females for their computing and IT aptitude, leadership skills, academics, and their contributions to working towards filling the gender gap in IT. This will motivate women to come forward and excel in the field of computing.
- *Inspirational stories* of successful women in IT industry must be discussed in class and printed by media. Small videos showing their interview and special message for girls should also be telecast on TV channels.
- Tech giants like IBM, Google, Amazon, TCS, etc. should reach out to girl students in schools and colleges, prepare them for mock interviews to arouse their confidence and also give them *summer internship* opportunities.

17.20 DISABILITY ISSUES WHILE TEACHING AND USING COMPUTERS

Prior to the advent of computers, accessibility of resources was always a serious issue for all, especially for those with a disability. Differently abled students have also struggled as they are often *isolated in different classes or restricted to certain subjects* because schools had accessibility or instructional issues while handling these children. As a result, such students have always got *inadequate and unequal educational* opportunities.

Many users have learning disabilities due to which they process information differently and struggle while reading online or using certain kinds of software. Those with dyslexia and other vision impairments face several issues with accessibility. The colour scheme of a webpage can also be a big issue for the visually disabled.

17.20.1 Types of Disabilities

The most common disabilities that we encounter are:

Physical: Students with physical disabilities may use braces, cane, wheelchair or prosthetic limbs. They may also be dealing with muscular dystrophy, Lou Gehrig's disease, multiple sclerosis, or other conditions that pose challenges.

Sensory: Sensory disabilities include visual impairment and blindness, deafness and hard-of-hearing conditions. These disabilities impair students from utilizing traditional classroom materials and tools.

Cognitive: Students with cognitive disabilities face difficulties in memorizing, expressing themselves and processing information. This makes it difficult for them to perform their academic tasks in the same way as other students may perform.

Psychiatric: These disabilities include a wide range of problems. They include social phobias and other personality disorders that make it difficult for them to perform their academic as well as personal work consistently.

Health-related: Students suffering from chronic conditions like diabetes or epilepsy, cancer or any other disease may not be able to attend their classes regularly. Students may also not be able to walk or run to travel quickly from building to building for different classes on a college campus like other students do.

17.20.2 Using Computers and Technology to Address Disability Issues

Rapid development and application of computer-based technology has opened the world of opportunities for disabled students, bringing an end to their isolation. Now, disabled students can access material, communicate their ideas, showcase their work and participate in educational experiences like never before. Implementation of technologies in special education has simplified communication and improved the academic skills of students with disabilities (refer Fig. 17.19).

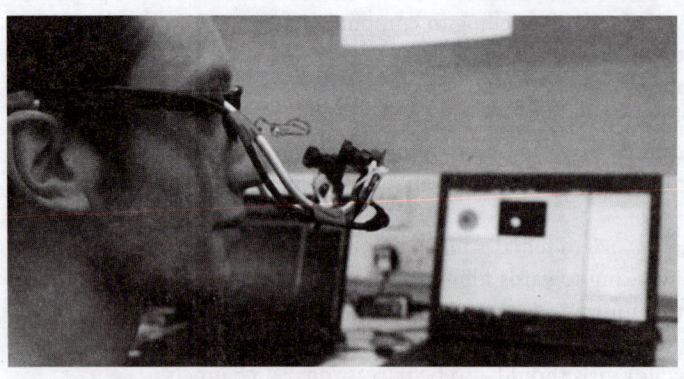
(a)

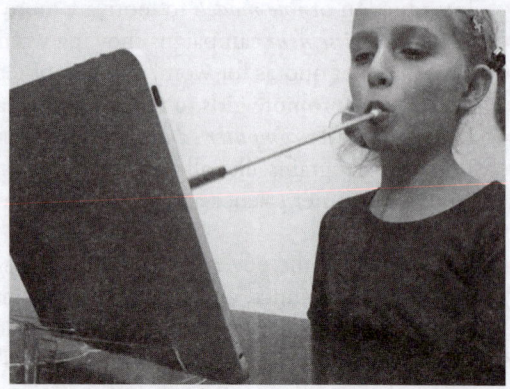
(b)

Figure 17.19 Promoting disabled people in computing

Source: (a) https://www.cultofmac.com/147506/dutch-inventor-creates-specialized-accessories-for-ipad-users-with-disabilities/ (b) https://usabilitygeek.com/gt3d-eye-tracker-makes-life-easier-for-physically-impaired-users/

Online courses provide greater accessibility for many students for whom it was difficult to attend regular college. Now, disabled students can be exposed to the same opportunities as the other students. This also helps them to avoid peer-groups that mock at their disabilities and make a serious dent to their self-confidence. Students can choose the pace of learning they are most comfortable with. This reduces their anxiety level, which plays a significant role in their education.

Adaptive keyboards, eye-tracking devices, voice recognition software and other computer adaptations can help those with motor disabilities (partial or total loss of function of a body part, usually a limb or limbs which may result in muscle weakness, poor stamina, lack of muscle control, or total paralysis) use technology fluently.

Braille reading and writing software are available today. Software that can read the content of webpages aloud and that written using braille keyboards are commonly used by the blind as well as visually impaired students.

Speech-recognition software: Blind, visually impaired students or those with physical limitations that prevent them from typing on a keyboard, use text-to-speech devices to write their assignments. When students speak into a microphone, the software translates their words into typed documents.

Text-to-speech software: This software helps visually impaired students to listen to the text that appears on a computer screen. It can read anything on the screen allowing students to participate in online activities, use email and text, and have immediate access to course materials.

Visual aids: Screen magnification software that enlarges portions of the screen where the reader directs the mouse, and screen reader software that translates screen text to Braille are examples of widely used visual aids.

Audio aids: Audio aids are used to amplify sound while alert devices use flashing lights or icons on the computer screen to signal users. This helps students with hearing difficulties to communicate over the phone with their own voice.

> Do you know that Stephen Hawking suffered from several disabilities and had almost no ability to move or speak on his own? He used speech-generating technology in which computer software translates what he types on a keyboard (he could type with small physical movements of two fingers) into a synthesized voice. Besides this, the computer software includes autocorrect feature. With this feature, he typed only a few letters; the rest were recognised and typed by the software.

Physical aids: Students with physical mobility issues use physical aids like audio books to hear what is written in the book and voice recognition software to help them type easily.

Augmentative communication systems help students with speech problems to overcome the communication barrier. They make extensive use of picture charts, books, and specialized software that predicts words for more effective communication.

Switches can be used by those students who are unable to use any keyboard or pointing device (Fig. 17.20). They can provide input by activating a particular switch. This input provides a signal to open a particular software or run a particular command.

These switches come in a variety of shapes and sizes and can be operated by any controlled movement of the body. They work best with cause-and-effect software and programs that require simple choices but can also be used to fully control a computer.

Figure 17.20 Switches to help disabled people provide input to computers

Thus, we can conclude that with modern technology, teachers can adapt the teaching and learning process to suit the needs of every individual student with minimum effort. They can choose a particular technique from the dozens of available learning tactics for best possible outcome.

Key Terms

Intellectual Property Rights (or IPR): Rights that are applicable to creative work, which can be treated as an asset or physical property.

Trademark: A name, word, slogan, design, symbol or any other item that is used to identify a product or organisation

Plagiarism: Act of fraud that involves both stealing someone else's work and lying about it afterward.

Personal information: Recorded information or opinions, whether true or not, that helps someone to identify whose information or opinion it is.

Phishing: A fraudulent activity in which a person or a business pretends to be trustworthy when actually it is not. It is basically done to acquire sensitive information like passwords, account numbers and credit card details.

Online intellectual property theft: The process of copying and using someone else's online material.

Spamming: A fraud in which the fraudster sends bulk emails to millions of email addresses to corrupt the receivers' computers, steal their identity or fool them by making them pay for fraudulent products or services.

Child pornography: Any visual depiction of sexually explicit conduct involving a child which includes photograph, video, digital or computer-generated image indistinguishable from an actual child and an image created, adapted or modified but appear to depict a child.

Computer forensics: Also known as digital forensics, it is the application of investigation and analysis techniques to gather and preserve evidence from one or more computing devices in a way that is suitable for presentation in a court of law.

Identity theft: A crime in which the criminal obtains and uses someone else's personal or financial information for making financial transactions or communicating false information.

Biometrics: Any feature of humans that make their identification easy and accurate.

Internet addiction: A behavioural addiction in which a person depends heavily on Internet and more specifically smartphones, computers, social networking sites, etc. to cope with stress in life.

Chapter Highlights

- Copyright applies to creative work such as those seen in literature, art, music and drama as well as in films, sound recordings, drawings, paintings, photography, typographical arrangements or any work that is recorded in some way.

- DRM is the use of technology and systems to protect copyrights for digital media. It encompasses techniques that limit copying and use of copyrighted works and proprietary software
- A software license is an agreement between the consumer and the creator of a software program that allows the consumer to do certain things that would otherwise be a violation of copyright laws.
- The term "open source" refers to something that allows users to modify and share because its design is publicly accessible.
- Computer fraud occurs when a person makes use of the Internet and a computing device to obtain something of value to another individual. It can be information, but can also be money or bank and personal information that someone may steal for later use.
- Downloading copyrighted content is a punishable crime. Correspondingly, distributing that content, electronically or non-electronically, without the express permission of the copyright holder is also illegal.
- Pharming occurs when a hacker exploits vulnerability in the Domain Name System (DNS) to redirect website traffic from a legitimate website to his fraudulent website.
- The IT Act of India provides legal recognition for transactions involving exchange of electronic data and other means of electronic communication, commonly referred to as electronic commerce (or e-commerce).
- Technology means the application of science or knowledge, the creation of a tool, or the use of a tool to solve a problem.
- Electronic waste or e-waste typically includes discarded computer monitors, motherboards, mobile phones and chargers, CDs, headphones, TVs, ACs and refrigerators.

Review Questions

1. Explain the different ways in which we can protect IPR.
2. Most of us have knowingly or unknowingly have plagiarized our assignments. List possible ways in which this could have been done. How can we prevent it?
3. Explain the relevance of DRM in today's era.
4. Differentiate between single-user license and site license.
5. List any five terms and conditions laid down by ASL.
6. Draw a comparison between open-source software and proprietary software.
7. As an informed netizen, what will you ensure before providing your personal information to a website?
8. Write a short note on the different types of frauds over the internet.
9. What happens in a stock market fraud?
10. Give the significance of IT Act 2000. Also state any two sections covered under the Act and state the punishment fixed under this Act.
11. What do you understand by the term "computer forensics"? How is it helpful?
12. Write an essay on the positive impacts of technology.
13. Technology has adversely affected our lives. Comment.
14. Why is e-waste a big concern for the entire world?
15. Differentiate between formal and informal recycling of electronic waste.
16. Why do people steal others' identity?
17. Why should we not use public Wi-Fi connection for financial transactions?
18. How can identity theft be done?
19. What is card skimming?
20. Why are women behind men in the field of teaching and using computers? How should they be motivated to come forward?

21. How is technology helping educators in teaching the disabled for teaching and how does it help the differently abled in using computers?

Fill in the Blanks

1. IPR can be categorized into _____, _____, _____ and _____.
2. A _____ can be a name, word, slogan, design, symbol or any other item that is used to identify a product or organisation.
3. No company can use a celebrity's or even a common man's name and picture to advertise their product. This ensures the right of _____.
4. In _____ plagiarism, you reuse your own work done previously.
5. _____ is an agreement between the consumer and the creator of software that states what the user can do and cannot do.
6. _____ is a non-profit organization that maintains a large library of creative works that can be shared and used free of cost.
7. In CC NC-SA, CC stands for _____, SA stands for _____, NC stands for _____. Moreover, N stands for _____.
8. _____ laws help us to protect ourselves from unwarranted interference in our lives.
9. In _____ attack, the attacker prevents other innocent users' access to a network.
10. Downloading and distributing _____ content is a punishable offence.
11. _____ occurs when a criminal purchases a product or service online and pays for it through fraud.
12. _____ performs a structured investigation and maintains a documented chain of evidences to know exactly what happened and who was responsible for it.
13. _____ is the application of science or knowledge, the creation of a tool, or the use of a tool to solve a problem.
14. E-waste has precious metals like _____ and _____.
15. _____ and _____ are toxic materials found in disposed electronic gadgets.
16. Retina and iris patterns are examples of _____.

State True or False

1. Patent applies to items including literary, artistic, musical and dramatic work.
2. Copyrights are applied to industrial processes and inventions.
3. Giving incorrect information about the source of a quotation is a case of plagiarism.
4. We must use a good Plagiarism Checker tool.
5. DRM encrypts the user's contents.
6. Code of proprietary software is publicly available.
7. Like proprietary software, users of open-source software must also accept the terms of a license.
8. Search engine tools have techniques to show music, images or files that are available under Creative Commons license.
9. Installing spyware or malware on someone else's computer is not a computer fraud.
10. In online purchase fraud, after receiving the payment, either the product is not delivered or an inferior product is delivered.
11. Phishing can be combined with pharming to create a more vulnerable attack.

12. We should open and respond to spam emails.
13. Communicating through mobile phones and other technology has affected personal relationships.

Multiple Choice Questions

1. _____ laws provide protection against sensitive business information.
    a. Copyright   b. Patent   c. Trade Secret   d. Patent
2. Which type of software license is used in schools?
    a. Single-user   b. Multi-user   c. Site   d. all of these
3. GNU and GPL are examples of _____ license.
    a. open-source   b. proprietary   c. DRM   d. All of these
4. Open-source license does not allow users to
    a. modify the software   b. redistribute free copies of the software
    c. Distribute modified versions of the software   d. None of these.
5. Identify the open-source software from the following:
    a. Microsoft Office b. Adobe Photoshop c. Mozilla Firefox   d. Mac iOS
6. _____ is a fraudulent activity in which a person pretends to be trustworthy to acquire sensitive information.
    a. Phishing   b. Pharming   c. Retail fraud   d. Spamming
7. Which fraudulent activity results in domain hijacking?
    a. Phishing   b. Pharming   c. Retail fraud   d. Spamming

Answers

Fill in the Blanks
1. copyright, trademarks, design rights and patents
2. trademark
3. publicity
4. Self-
5. Software license
6. Creative Commons
7. Creative Common, Non- Commercial, Share-Alike, Non-Derivative
8. Privacy
9. Denial-of-Service
10. copyrighted
11. Purchase fraud
12. Cyber forensics
13. Technology
14. gold, silver
15. Lead, mercury
16. biometric controls

State True or False
1. False
2. False
3. True
4. True
5. True
6. False
7. True
8. True
9. False
10. True
11. True
12. False
13. True

Multiple Choice Questions
1. c
2. c
3. a
4. d
5. c
6. a
7. b